Theatre in Your Life

Third Edition

Robert Barton
University of Oregon

Annie McGregor
The Pennsylvania State University

CENGAGE
Learning·

Australia • Brazil • Japan • Korea • Mexico • Singapore • Spain • United Kingdom • United States

***Theatre in Your Life*, Third Edition**
Robert Barton, Annie McGregor

Product Director: Monica Eckman

Product Manager: Kelli Strieby

Associate Content Developer: Erin Bosco

Media Developer: Janine Tangney

Marketing Manager: Jillian Borden

Content Project Manager: Dan Saabye

Art Director: Linda May

Manufacturing Planner: Doug Bertke

Rights Acquisition Specialist: Thomas
    McDonough

Production Service: Cenveo Publisher
    Services

Text and Cover Designer: Rokusek Design

Cover Image: Photo by Michael J. Lutch,
    courtesy of the A.R.T.

Compositor: Cenveo Publisher Services

Library of Congress Control Number: 2013940453

ISBN-13: 978-1-285-46348-3

ISBN-10: 1-285-46348-X

Cengage Learning
200 First Stamford Place, 4th Floor
Stamford, CT 06902
USA

Cengage Learning is a leading provider of customized learning solutions with office locations around the globe, including Singapore, the United Kingdom, Australia, Mexico, Brazil and Japan. Locate your local office at **international.cengage.com/region**.

Cengage Learning products are represented in Canada by Nelson Education, Ltd.

For your course and learning solutions, visit **www.cengage.com**.

Purchase any of our products at your local college store or at our preferred online store **www.cengagebrain.com**.

Instructors: Please visit **login.cengage.com** and log in to access instructor-specific resources.

Printed in China
2 3 4 5 6 7 17 16 15 14

To my sister, Pamela Barton Glaysher,
who greatly enriches my life.

−RB

To Mom, John, Tom, Jim, and Jen
…for loving me anyway.

−AM

Brief Contents

Contents

part II | Who Does Theatre?   66

chapter 3 | **Storytellers and Stories**   68

chapter 6   **The Production Team**   180

chapter **8**

Middle Stages 262

chapter 10   **Varieties of Stylization**   328

Preface

T*heatre in Your Life* is intended to be a guide

- for becoming an informed audience member so that theatre can enrich your entire life;
- for recognizing theatre in your everyday decisions;
- for noting how you are influenced by "staged" events and owning the ways that you stage parts of your life;
- for finding ways to get involved and discovering your own place in theatre;
- for recognizing theatre as a global and historical phenomenon; and, perhaps most important,
- for having fun through as many ways of discovering and doing theatre as possible.

The book is intended for an Introduction to Theatre class, in which most students are likely to be non-theatre majors seeking general humanities credit. Some students may be majors required to take the course as a prerequisite to more advanced work. Like all intro courses, students expect to learn how to experience and enjoy the subject more deeply should they decide to become further involved. For most, this means that they may become regular theatergoers. For theatre majors, this course can be a filter to help them choose where they wish to specialize within the theatrical spectrum. The course can also serve as an opportunity for all theatre majors in a department to start with the same foundations in terminology, organizational structure, and general understanding of the art.

Probably no course in theatre varies as much from school to school. It can focus on play production, dramatic literature, or theatre history. Because one term is insufficient to cover it all, the primary teaching issue becomes making the right choices for a particular student population. Even in large departments, the class can be small (as when offered in summer school or a night class) or huge. The teacher may work alone or have a team of assistants. The class may be limited to only large group sessions or subdivided into smaller lab meetings. A text needs to serve a variety of circumstances and goals without limiting an instructor's choices. It will undoubtedly be one or more, but rarely all, of the following:

- an introduction to dramatic literature—or how to read a play;
- an abbreviated introduction to theatre history that traces its development through the ages—or how theatre became what it is today;
- an introduction to play production, with units on acting, directing, design—or how to mount a play;

- a guide to being an informed audience member with regular play attendance—or how to view and evaluate a production;
- an examination of theatre as an influence on our lives, and how theatrical events, public demonstrations, street theatre, performance art, and staged political rallies all can shift tides of public opinion—or how to sense theatre in various contexts;
- a multicultural introduction to traditions, literature, and performance modes from a global perspective—or how to use theatre to understand culture.

Theatre in Your Life, although intended for a broad range of introductory courses, would be less effective in those focused exclusively on dramatic literature or on theatre history. We provide information on how to read a play, but we place considerably greater emphasis on how to see one and perform one. We cover high points in theatre history but do not attempt a comprehensive chronology; instead, we emphasize the most powerful historical influences. We focus strongly on the theatrical event.

Today's students are more likely to demand proof of theatre's relevant connections to their own lives than did their predecessors. They are less likely to be charmed by elitist or escapist theatre because they have so many other diversions in their lives. They are likely to crave connections between traditional theatre and other live performances and media experiences. They will be less interested in focusing exclusively on the Western theatre perspective and more interested in the full multicultural experience that theatre can afford, with a particular craving to have their own heritages honored and addressed. Each of these tendencies will only increase in the next few years, and we intend to address them.

Theatre in Your Life is intended to awaken readers to the constant presence of theatre in daily decision making and the forces around us that influence these decisions, making readers aware of how vital and constant a part of their lives theatre is. The book aims to excite students about the possibility of a deeper involvement in the theatre process as a source of potential personal enrichment. We define theatre as an event where an observer experiences a performance and responds. Live theatre is the most extraordinary, precious, and incomparable event within this spectrum, and we urge our readers to embrace it, but we do not limit discussion to just that. We explore the full range of the readers' experiences as audience, including those involving electronics.

Major Features

Several features distinguish *Theatre in Your Life:*

- **A conversational, accessible voice:** We like readers to feel as if they are being spoken to directly in a friendly, unpretentious fashion, with immediately accessible examples and humor. One of the co-authors has an established reputation for reader-friendly texts. The other is an award-winning professor, specializing in intro to theatre classes for over 20 years.

- **Theatre in everyday existence and how to get involved:** We believe that from christenings to graduation ceremonies to funerals, our lives are shaped by staged events as well as by spontaneous theatre. We also believe in the importance of being informed citizens, aware when politicians and others are influencing our opinion through performance rather than conviction and substance. Also, most students in intro-to-any-subject classes are asking if this subject might become their major source of greater involvement. We provide questions in each chapter to help readers determine whether a job making theatre might be one they wish to pursue further. Throughout the text, these elements are highlighted in **Theatre in Your Life** boxes.

- **Media/film as pathway to live theatre:** Although nothing surpasses the astonishing communal experience of great live theatre, it is not the audience/performance mode that dominates the lives of our students. We believe that their entire entertainment world should be used to illuminate and enhance their appreciation of theatre. Throughout the text, **Theatre in Media** boxes compare various aspects of live theatre with film and other media.

- **History that does not replicate a theatre history class:** We believe that the history portions of an introductory text should explain how today's theatre came to be and how to find connections between cultures and genres. Therefore, only those periods with powerful influence on the evolution of *today's* theatre are included. Whenever possible, we attempt to compare and contrast historical developments in the West with those in Asia and in Africa.

- **Cultural inclusiveness:** Our text includes current information on cultures beyond Western culture, the one that has dominated traditional theatre literature. We seek out underrepresented contingencies for alternative shared experiences and voices. Although we cannot cover every culture, we aim to provide at least one other perspective in each topic. Instead of isolating non-Western theatre to a single section of the text, we include it throughout. We balance classic Western plays and contemporary alternatives as equally valuable resources. We also draw on popular culture as a frequent point of reference.

Using the Text

Each chapter in the book stands alone and can be assigned in any order. Please feel free to choose any sequence of readings and omit those that do not work into your present curriculum. You can assign any chapter out of sequence and exclude any chapter without losing the sense of the text.

Designed to be flexible and conform to each instructor's style of teaching, we have not assumed that either chapters or dramatic interludes will be read in any particular order. For example, in Pennsylvania State University's "Art of the Theatre" course, we study the first two chapters ("Anticipation" and "Origins") during the first two weeks of the semester, presenting examples of monologues, scenes, and the origin stories in class performances by the

Acting Company. Then we spend several weeks on Chapter 3, "Storytellers and Stories," using *"Master Harold" . . . and the boys* (from *Life Themes: An Anthology of Plays for the Theatre*) as an example of "well-made" play structure and *M. Butterfly* (ditto) as an example of episodic structure. We then cover Chapter 7, "Early Stages," followed by a study of *Antigone*. We come back to Chapters 4 through 6 when the inclusion of those practitioners becomes appropriate for our method of teaching. We sincerely hope and strongly recommend that you will mix and match the chapters in whatever way works best for your syllabus and style of teaching.

New to This Edition

1. Companion Anthology

An adjunct volume, *Life Themes: An Anthology of Plays for the Theatre*, now available to those wishing to include scripts for the plays featured in Dramatic Interludes, edited and designed for live performance, along with extensive information on the plays themselves at a cost to students that is significantly lower than other anthologies.

2. Shakespeare's Impact

Expanded material on William Shakespeare, establishing his impact on the development of drama, theatre, our language, and the way we define our humanity.

3. Updated Classics

A Contemporary Classics look at the continued and expanding fascination with classic plays as they are being reinterpreted and adapted to connect with new audiences.

4. Non-Lit Theatre

New coverage of non-literary theatre with purely visceral theatrical intentions.

5. Extended Theatre in Media

Examination of recent media performance elements including theatre apps, three-dimensional, streaming, theatre blogs, and significant media milestones.

6. Additional Coverage

Discussions of theatre positions and practice, including:

Puppets and Puppetry

The Sound Designer

The Prop Master

The Projection Designer

Dramatic Interludes

At the end of the even-numbered chapters in the text are six Dramatic Interludes on the themes of Love, War, Generations, Rebellion, Dreams, and Values. Each interlude discusses and includes excerpts from two scripts, one a traditional or classic Western drama and the other a contemporary play by an underrepresented contingency. These include plays by African American, Asian American, and Hispanic playwrights. Four women writers are represented. At the end of each interlude, a feature called **EXPANSIONS** applies the ideas presented in the previous two chapters to the two featured plays.

Life Themes

Scripts to the twelve plays featured in the Dramatic Interludes are included in our new companion anthology, *Life Themes: An Anthology of Plays for the Theatre.* Each play has an extensive introduction focusing on the life and work of the playwright, the play's production history, and the major cultural influences on the creation and impact of the script, as well as its continued contemporary relevance. Information is also provided on additional works by each playwright and suggestions for further reading. Five of the plays are presented in editions/adaptations that are particularly accessible to students who have not read a large number of plays. *King Lear, Much Ado About Nothing*, and *Arms and the Man* are editions/adaptations prepared by Robert. *The Three Sisters* has been translated and adapted by Robert, and *Antigone* by Annie. Each of these five scripts is an acting edition prepared for actual performance. All are slightly shorter than the originals with occasional word or phrase substitutions designed to make them readily comprehensible to contemporary students.

Additional Supplementary Material

- **Theatregoer's Guide.** A brief manual providing everything you need to know about attending the theatre—from different types of theatre to tips for watching plays.
- **Theatre CourseMate.** *Theatre in Your Life* includes Theatre CourseMate, a complement to your textbook. Theatre CourseMate includes:
  - a MindTap Reader
  - interactive teaching and learning tools including:
    - Quizzes
    - Flashcards
    - Theatre Workshop
    - Audio presentations of Dramatic Interludes
    - and more
  - Engagement Tracker, a first-of-its-kind tool that monitors student engagement in the course

- **Online Instructor's Manual.** Save time, streamline your course preparation, and get the most from the text. This indispensable manual offers easy-to-use chapter outlines and advice on how to get students engaged and excited about theatre. Instructors can access this free resource by contacting their local sales representative.
- **Instructor Companion Website.** This password-protected instructor site provides access to the Online Instructor's Manual, as well as chapter-specific PowerPoint lecture slides for your class.

Go to www.login.cengage.com to access these resources.

Acknowledgments

For this edition, we would particularly like to thank Rob Schneider for his invaluable and savvy suggestions for updating all of our media coverage.

For using early versions of *Theatre in Your Life* and providing their feedback, we thank the former students of Annie McGregor's THEA 100 class for their patience and their feedback during the development of this text. We also thank Patrice McClain and Questor Hannah, the glossary queen and king, for their painstaking work. Annie also thanks her colleagues, the undergraduate and graduate students of the PSU School of Theatre, and Dan Carter, Director of the School of Theatre, for their kindness and support during the creation of this textbook.

Annie would like to particularly acknowledge the work of the graduate MFA acting company, graduating class of 2011, for the excellence of their performances in the creation of the new Internet course affiliated with this text.

We would like to thank the following colleagues for their work assisting us with the third edition: Glen Gourley, Francis Marion University; Roy Hudson, Troy University; Kent McFann, Saddleback College; Paris Peet, Shippensburg University of Pennsylvania; Jim Rambo, McLennan Community College; and Jane Sullivan, Jefferson College.

Helping with feedback for the second edition were Jim Bartruff, Emporia State University; Robyn Berg, Volunteer State Community College; Bartlett Blair, Wright State University—Main Campus; Vivian J. Dorsett, Prairie View A&M University; David A. Hermosillo, University of Dayton; Walter Johnson, Cumberland County College; Dr. Dawn Larsen, Francis Marion University; Darby Lofstrand, Northern Arizona University; Steven Nabors, Meridian Community College; Anastasia Pharr, Tarrant County College—Northwest; and Jennifer Toohey, Palm Beach Community College.

We would also like to thank those who helped us along in the development of the first edition: Michael Barbour, LeMoyne College; Claudia A. Beach, Henderson State University; Emily Becher, James Madison University; B. J. Bray, University of Arkansas at Little Rock; Leigh A. Clemons, Louisiana State University; H. Thorne Compton, University of South Carolina; Chris Cragin Day, Baylor University; J. Kevin Doolen, SUNY Albany; Kevin Dreyer, University of Notre Dame; Jeffrey Paul Entwistle, University of Wisconsin,

Green Bay; Anne Fliotsos, Purdue University; Kelly Carolyn Gordon, University of North Carolina, Greensboro; David A. Griffith, University of Toledo; Christine Z. Havko, University of South Carolina, Spartanburg; Charles L. Hayes, Radford University; Julie Holston, South Mountain Community College; Alicia Kae Koger, University of Oklahoma; Dr. Dawn Larsen, Volunteer State College; Merrill J. Lessley, University of Colorado, Boulder; Scott W. Malia, Northeastern University; Cheryl McFarren, Arapahoe Community College; Cynthia Miller, Pima County Community College; Frances Anne Pici, Georgia State University; P. Gibson Ralph, SUNY Brockport; Cara Rawlings, University of Miami; Michelle Rebollo, St. Louis City College; Richard A. Reiss, Kent State University; Carrie Sandahl, Florida State University; Tamara Segalla, Bridgewater State College; Joan Siegrist, West Virginia University; Jenn Stephenson, Queen's University at Kingston; Michael Sullivan, Fontbonne University; Steven Taft, University of Northern Iowa; Kristina Tollefson, University of Central Florida; Andrew Vorder Bruegge, St. Cloud University; and Samuel Zachary, Northern Kentucky University.

About the Authors

Robert Barton is a professor emeritus in acting at the University of Oregon and has also taught for the American Heritage Association in London. He has acted in most of the plays of Shakespeare and directed half of them. He is a prolific author, whose works include the books *Acting: Onstage and Off* (soon to be issued in its seventh edition), *Style for Actors*, *Voice: Onstage and Off* (with Rocco Dal Vera), both recently published in updated editions, and the new text *Acting Reframes: Using NLP to Make Better Decisions In and Out of the Theatre*. He most recently served as editor and adaptor of the twenty-first century edition of the classic text *The Craft of Comedy*. Robert is recipient of the Theatre Association's Best Book Award and has been honored as Outstanding Acting Coach by the American College Theatre Festival. He has numerous articles in scholarly journals, and his column, "Many Right Ways," appears in each edition of *Voice & Speech Review*.

Annie McGregor teaches script analysis and history/literature/criticism at The Pennsylvania State University School of Theatre, where she is currently Head of the BA Theatre program. She has received the Atherton Award for Teaching Excellence and the College of Arts and Architecture Award for Teaching Excellence. She is a sometime actor, with her most recent and most favorite role being Jean in *After Mrs. Rochester,* at the University of Oregon in its West Coast premiere. She is a regular dramaturg; her most recent projects include *Mother Courage and Her Children* and *Pentecost*. She is increasingly intrigued by the world of online teaching, after the successful launch and continued success of her "Art of the Theatre" web course. She also continues to direct projects, with her latest offerings being *The Odyssey* and *Arabian Nights*, both by her favorite playwright, Mary Zimmerman.

part I

What Is Theatre?

Muriel Miguel, a founding member of the Spiderwoman Theatre Company, performs her one-woman show *Red Mother*.

In Chapter 1, we will define theatre; identify what it gives us; explore its variations, including films and the personal theatre in our lives; identify how it can vary; and determine who makes it happen. We will ask some questions to help you determine whether or not you want to get more involved. We will provide information on going to the theatre, protocol for behavior, and some initial questions to help you get more out of a performance than you might otherwise.

In Chapter 2, we will offer examples of the very earliest plays ever performed, explore major ideas about how theatre originated, connect ritual to theatre, and explain the conditions of make-believe we all agree to as audience members.

In Dramatic Interlude 1, which follows these two chapters, we will look at two plays through the universal issue of Love, though in very different ways: *Much Ado About Nothing* by William Shakespeare and *M. Butterfly* by David Henry Hwang. The interlude summarizes the plays, reviews the ideas explored, and provides sample scenes from each.

In Expansion 1, we apply the concepts laid out in the first two chapters to the two featured plays and provide guidelines for writing about these and other plays in performance.

chapter 1
ANTICIPATION

Bobby Yip/Reuters/Corbis

A Chinese opera "Dan," or female-role performer, emerging from a curtain during a ritual (held every 60 years to chase away "ghosts" and maintain peaceful life) at Sheung Shui Heung in the rural New Territories, near Hong Kong.

In 2013, Tom Hanks made his Broadway debut in Nora Ephron's play *Lucky Guy,* about the corruption and greed of the 1980s.

Walter McBride/Corbis

Lesson Objectives:

Upon completion of this chapter, you will be able to:

1. Identify the four basic elements of any theatre event.
2. Experience the functions of theatre when you see an event.
3. Recognize the varieties of theatre experience that may be available in your own hometown and around the world.
4. Identify the life themes that make all human stories universal.
5. Navigate your way to theatre events and read signals about appropriate audience behavior from those sharing the event.
6. Know one way to approach a verbal or written response to a theatre production.

Introduction

You walk into a theatre full of anticipation. Even if the "theatre" is a chair in front of your television and you have just rented a DVD or streamed a new movie, you hope to be transported for the next few hours. You hope that the chair is magic, so that you can sit and watch, yet go on a journey—fueled by energy and navigated by imagination—into galactic possibilities. You hope that the show will take you away.

WENDY WASSERSTEIN
PLAYWRIGHT

There is nothing as human as sharing a laugh with strangers in the dark. We share these worlds and we're acknowledging that we're all made of the same stuff. Unlike reading a book or watching a television show, theatre is communal. Walking into a theatre, I always feel a profound anticipation of things to come.

For live theatre, your anticipation may be even greater. This is kind of a special occasion. You may have reserved tickets and gotten dressed up. Most of all, what you and the other audience members are seeing tonight will be different from any other performance of the show. Things could go wrong. They could go spectacularly right. There is danger and expectation. Great live theatre combines the fun of watching a film with the thrill of being at an athletic event or concert. You get to sit right there with the storytellers and be told a story.

You are breathing the same air as the actors. You are highly aware of each other's presence. For the duration of the performance, you have a special relationship with the actors and other audience members.

And you have power. The show is not complete without your response, without interaction between actors and audience. Whether you laugh really hard, remain stonily silent, or shift in your chair and cough, you affect the performance. You can change the actors, how hard they push or how relaxed they are. You make this show different than it would have been without you. In turn, the actors affect you. A performance might start strong and then lose its way. But then perhaps the actors adjust to the energy in the room and regain their connection with the audience. Each group brings energy to the event. Each charges and stimulates the other.

The physical presence of another human being creates variables. You may rehearse an important encounter with someone in your life, even scripting exactly what you intend to say and hoping for a specific response.

PETER BROOK
DIRECTOR

The theatre has one special characteristic. It is always possible to start again. In life this is a myth; we ourselves can never go back on anything. New leaves never turn, clocks never go back, we can never have a second chance. In the theatre, the slate is wiped clean all the time.

But he or she will almost always do or say something that makes it different from the way you planned it, perhaps giving you that look that always unhinges you or an answer that you never even considered.

Filmed performances, unlike theatre, are unchanging, but our response to them can change over time. If you watch the same film at various stages in your life, it may seem different with each viewing because you have changed over the years. The performances are the same, locked in celluloid permanence. But you aren't. And live theatre isn't, either.

This chapter will introduce you to the art of theatre, help you examine various theatre experiences you have already had, and prepare you for seeing a live performance. It will familiarize you with those who do theatre and with what theatre does for us, as well as offer some ideas about how it might become even more a part of your life.

What Is Theatre?

We can strip our definition of **theatre** down to its most basic elements: **actor, audience, space,** and **story.**

Do we need to be in a "real" theatre to do theatre? A big, formal building with an actual stage and a bank of seats? No—theatre is done in warehouses, in basements, on street corners, in churches, and in parks. It's done in garages, cafeterias, gyms, and playgrounds. Do we need a script? Not always—some theatre is based on improvisation and spontaneous suggestion.

What is needed (according to Shakespeare) is "a board and a passion." We need a place to perform and the overwhelming impulse to do so, combined with eagerness on the part of others to watch, listen, and participate—a passionate engagement on the part of those who present and those who observe. For an event to be called *live theatre,* we must have these four elements:

- **Actor:** Performers take on personas other than those of their normal daily existence. They become others, taking the best of childhood "dress up and let's pretend" into full role-playing. Even in a one-person autobiographical show, the actor assumes the role of narrator and also assumes

Philip Gould/Documentary Value/Corbis

FIGURE 1.1 Theatre can happen anywhere. Here, a young boy interacts with a street theatre performer in Jackson Park, in the French Quarter of New Orleans.

characters and selves from earlier times in his own life. There will always be some degree of transformation. Sometimes there is an astonishing transformation—to the degree that the actor is unrecognizable.

- **Audience:** Audience consists of those who agree to witness the enactment, to take the time to experience it with the actors. Most will make an effort to become engaged, to actually lose themselves by being swept up in what is presented. Whether audience members have paid a lot and anticipated this event for months or have just had their attention grabbed by a free performance while out walking, there is now a willingness to suspend the distractions of life's details and embark on an imaginative journey.

- **Space:** A space is a place transformed for a performance. If it is a large opera house, empty seats will be filled and lights will be dimmed around those seats and come up on a stage. Actors and scenery move around that stage, altering it over and over again. At the other extreme, if the space is a street corner, the audience members may form a circle around the actors, or they may agree to stand near the curb while the actors perform against a storefront. In any case, a place will be altered temporarily to reflect the redefined relationships between those who give and those who receive the performance.

- **Story:** A story is a tale told about the life of someone, real or imaginary, who has experienced or dreamed something worthy of attention. The story may have a fully developed beginning, middle, and end, or it may be incomplete and fragmentary. In some performances, such as a musical revue, there is no discernible plot. There are, however, songs that tell small stories or lay out fragments of stories, allowing the audience to fill in the details from their own lives. In each of these instances, at the very least, the singer says, "This is who I am, this is what is going on with me, let me tell you how I feel." Here, we get bits and pieces of a larger story. In abstract nonlinear theatre, we get snippets of lives, much like walking down a street, catching bits of conversation and glimpses of people in windows, on porches, or in alleys. We then tend to fill in the gaps according to our own experience and perceptions. In other performances, we get complete details, but there is always an invitation to enter the life of another.

How do these four elements separate theatre from other public events? If an actor, an audience, a space, and a story are needed, what's the difference between theatre and a sporting event? Well, no one knows how a game will end. In sports, a planned outcome is unethical, sometimes criminal. Although theatre is not always scripted, it is also rarely completely spontaneous. Even improv troupes, groups of actors (usually comic) who appear to invent their performance before our eyes, have rehearsed and planned for certain desired outcomes and have set ways to check in with each other to move the "discovered" story forward. Their performances are seldom, if ever, completely random. And while some athletes assume a public persona, it is rarely sustained or complex enough to be called acting.

PHILIP SEYMOUR HOFFMAN

ACTOR

Sports are like theatre. You do the same play, but it's different every night. There is discipline and creativity. When I used to be a wrestler, I would be on top and think, "Okay, if I hit his arm there I can get around here," and you see yourself do it. Same as acting. You have a goal and go after it. With sports, the margin for a different ending is greater.

Stephen Chernin/Stringer/Getty Images News/Getty Images

FIGURE 1.2 Political activism and theatrical elements are often combined for an attention-getting message. Here, performers at an environmental rally in New York dramatize their concerns about global warming by performing in costume.

Sometimes a nontheatrical event becomes theatre. Imagine you are at an outdoor political rally where people have come to share their feelings about a war. Strongly opposing opinions are presented with speeches, chants, demonstrations, and debates. Then imagine that someone gets up and says:

> This is the character Hector from the play *Tiger at the Gates* by Jean Giraudoux. Hector was the general of the Trojan army and lived over 3,000 years ago. At the moment of this speech, his country has just fought one war and is about to embark on another, the legendary and bloody Trojan War. Hector has just been asked to speak honoring those who have already died.

This commands attention. It is different from what the audience has heard up to now. In the silence, the speaker's voice carries throughout the space:

> You want me to give a speech honoring the dead of war? I don't think so. The speech would be a hypocritical defense of those of us who are still alive, a plea for acquittal. I am not so sure of my innocence. Besides, I have given that speech already. I gave it to them when they were still with me in their last minutes of life, in the aftermath of battle, while they could still give me what was left of their sight and hearing. Want to know what I said to them? There was one completely disemboweled, already turning up the whites of his eyes and I lied, "You're doing better. Going to get you home soon!" and another with his skull split in two and I said, "You look pretty funny with that broken nose, you know that?" And my aide, barely more than a boy, no really just a boy, with his left arm hanging useless and his last blood flowing out of him and I said, "Phew. It's a good thing for you it's the left arm you've splintered." And he smiled. So, what did I do? I gave them one final swig of life; it was all they asked for; they died drinking it. Now I would just ask them to forgive us, those of us who still

have our eyes, feel warmth, and can see the sun. And that's all there is to say. Let there be no more war. [English text by Robert Barton]

Because the speaker has become an actor by assuming the character of another, and because the outcome of Hector's story is known rather than random, the tale of his final encounter with his dying men becomes a moment of theatre in the midst of a political gathering. The actor has become someone else, whose story is one of the oldest in Greek mythology. It is no longer just someone expressing an opinion. It is art based on the idea of the unchanging nature of war over the vast expanse of time. It is far more powerful than if he had gotten up and said something like, "You know, people have been dying senselessly for thousands of years. It's time to stop." It does not matter how many people present know that Hector eventually died a horrific death in the very war he was trying to stop. There is enough of his story here to bring his ideas alive and to bring theatre to the debate.

What Does Theatre Give?

What will theatre do for us? What does it offer? In the previous instance, the invasion of a moment of theatre gives those present a chance to move beyond the particulars of the debate and into a more universal place. But what do we reap from regular attendance at the theatre, from making a habit of going to plays? What do those of us who do hope to receive? What, for us, is theatre's *function?*

1. **Theatre diverts us** and takes us out of our daily grind. Being told stories is good; having them acted out can be sublime. It can delight, distract, transport, and entertain us. Many plays and productions strive for little more than this, and many audiences find it fully satisfying and more than enough, though theatre can be much more.

2. **Theatre gives us an "emotional workout."** Many theatergoers report laughing and crying more at a performance than they did for weeks before, experiencing big, intense, and therapeutic emotional releases. Plays tend to take place on the most important days in characters' lives—when enormous changes take place and powerful feelings are present. These feeling are contagious. The same way that some go to the gym to work out physical muscles, some go to the theatre to work out emotional ones. Theatre can save us from our tendencies to be indifferent or disengaged or to become emotionally unplugged.

3. **Theatre can illuminate some aspect of the human condition,** tackling either important social and political issues or taking on the major questions about the meaning of life. The great plays can provide us with profound insights into the very act of being alive. Theatre can spur us to take action and bring about change, just as it can lead us to acceptance and peace in our lives. When we can sit and observe others struggling with our major issues and finding resolution, we can go empathically on the same journey and find inspiration.

4. **Theatre is a way for the community to come together and share essential experiences.** C. S. Lewis wrote, "We read to know we are not alone." It could be said that we go to plays to *prove* that we are not alone. In our increasingly technological world, we have become isolated—strangers in our own neighborhoods and communities. We are also a more mobile society, some of us changing location so often that we lose touch with our original community—our tribe of origin—and have difficulty accepting and being accepted by our new tribe. Theatre is a live and immediate communal experience. It provides us with the chance to share laughter, ideas, feelings, and wisdom. By sharing, we grow stronger as individuals, and we all can become more fully invested members of the tribe. Sometimes sacred, sometimes profane, live theatre is always about our shared humanity.

5. **Theatre gives us indelible memories.** Because we were there on a certain night, really *there* in the midst of the magic, we tend to remember, rehash, and relive our great moments in the theatre like no others. If you are new to theatre, you may have some concert memories of this kind. It did not matter how many CDs you had of a favorite band or how many times you saw them onscreen. Chances are, if you got to experience them in a space you actually shared, you will never forget it. If some of the songs were about deep, personal journeys, you probably felt something close to what happens when the story envelops us in the theatre.

> **AUTHOR'S INSIGHT**
>
> **ROBERT:** The last time I was in London, I saw two of the greatest living actors in the world, Judi Dench and Vanessa Redgrave, on stage. Though I had seen both on film many times, their live performances are now forever part of my mental landscape, more than their screen work. Why? I was physically present while they demonstrated their phenomenal power, presence, and command. I was there.

The Range of Theatre

All cultures have theatre in some form. People tell their stories and act out their issues. It is powerful to act out a concern, but it can be equally powerful to observe this enactment. Watching someone walk through your experiences clarifies and crystallizes them. At any given moment, all the following theatre groups may be simultaneously telling tales, raising questions, and, in some instances, offering answers:

- *The Bread and Puppet Theater* may be offering biting political satire in an open field, mesmerizing audiences with the use of gigantic and strikingly expressive puppets.
- *The Spiderwoman Theater* may be reviving its classic *Women in Violence* at an international festival, using broad comic devices to make serious points.
- *The New Globe Theatre,* the replica of the theatre used by Shakespeare in the Elizabethan era, may be staging a performance of one of his plays, featuring an all-male cast and rushes on the stage floor in authentic historical recreation.
- *The National Theatre of the Deaf* may be touring one of their adaptations of a classic children's book with both sign language and spoken

Joan Marcus

FIGURE 1.3 Danny Glover as Sam and Michael Boatman as Willie in Athol Fugard's *"Master Harold"...and the boys*, directed by Lonny Price at the Royale Theatre on Broadway.

sequences for deaf and nondeaf audiences. The Little Theatre of the Deaf is the children's wing of the National Theatre of the Deaf, formed in 1968 to reach out to young audiences and their families.

- ***The Beijing Opera*** may be warming up for one of its gymnastic extravaganzas, demanding Olympic-caliber athletic skills and astonishing precision from its cast.

- ***The Ridiculous Theatrical Company*** may be holding auditions for one of their gay literary satires, inspired by the legendary Charles Ludlam.

- ***The Access Theater Company*** may be rehearsing an original dance piece partnering disabled with nondisabled performers.

- ***The Intertribal Theatre Project*** may be presenting its *Coyote Tails* shows and workshops to military personnel on a base as part of their diversity training program.

- ***The San Francisco Mime Troupe*** may be setting up in a downtown park right in your city, where they will present broad farcical characters and get huge laughs while seriously attacking big government policies regarding personal privacy.

- ***The National Theatre,*** a modern and magnificent theatre in Havana, Cuba, may be presenting a "politically correct" professional production. Meanwhile, a struggling amateur production of a new play goes on in the empty, derelict shell of an old pre-Castro professional theatre, *and* a polished extravaganza is staged in the new Tropicana complex in Santiago de Cuba, where only foreigners are allowed to see the show.

- **Ogun's Mysteries,** a tale passed down orally through the generations, may be in preparation outside Dakar, Senegal, and in numerous other locations. The entire community is involved in this annual performance of the story of reunification with God. It is both a much-anticipated social entertainment and a deeply felt spiritual experience.

U Aung/Xinhua Press/Corbis

FIGURE 1.4 Dancers who are hearing impaired perform in Yangon, Burma, in 2011.

Robbie Jack/Tierra/Corbis

FIGURE 1.5 National Beijing Opera Company performance of *The Legend of White Snake* at Sadler's Wells Theatre in London.

AUTHOR'S INSIGHT

ANNIE: I was recently allowed to watch a modern troupe of performers training in classical Indian dance drama. We had a narrator who told the story as it was performed by young girls ranging from age 5 to 15. While it was at first all very exotic and unfamiliar, in a short time our eyes began to "see" the story being told. I recommend it to anyone.

- **The Silken Phoenix**—a musical theatre work celebrating three of Asia's greatest women poets from past centuries—may be touring the world, questioning the stereotype of passive Asian women and showing that accomplishment is possible even in a repressive society.

These are just samplings of theatre occurring globally and simultaneously. All these theatres impact lives.

CLOSE-UP

Tribute to Mako—Godfather of Asian American Theatre

Some actors never become household names but have a profound impact on live theatre, media, and the personal lives of others. Mako, the Japan-born actor whose birth name was Makoto Iwamatsu, was such a force during his forty-year career, ending with his death in 2006.

Back when most roles offered to Asian-heritage actors were caricatures or stereotypes, Mako took just such a part and used it to open the doors of Hollywood and Broadway to others. In the film *The Sand Pebbles,* he played the Chinese character Po-han, who spoke pidgin English, called white sailors "master," and treated them as such. But through the power of his acting, he transformed Po-han, compelled the audience to empathize and identify with his "coolie," and won an Oscar nomination for Best Supporting Actor. He proceeded to push actively for more and better roles for Asian Americans.

FIGURE 1.6　Japanese actor Mako in Stephen Sondheim's *Pacific Overtures,* presented by the East West Players, 1979.

According to George Takei, who played Sulu in *Star Trek,* "Most actors played such parts and did what they were told to do: giggle here, shuffle over there, bow, and go out. He was one of the early truly trained actors who was able to take stock roles, roles seen many times before, and make an individual—a live and vibrant character."

One of his most important contributions was founding the East West Players, the first Asian American theatre company in the United States. "What many people say is, 'If it wasn't for Mako, there wouldn't have been Asian American theatre,' " says Tim Dang, current artistic director of the company. "He is revered as sort of the godfather of Asian American theatre."

Mako was a familiar face in film, television, and live theatre. TV roles included appearances on *I Spy,* *M*A*S*H,* and *Walker, Texas Ranger.* He played a Japanese admiral in the film *Pearl Harbor,* a Singaporean in *Seven Years in Tibet,* and Akiro the Wizard in *Conan the Barbarian* and *Conan the Destroyer.* On Broadway, his multiple roles as reciter, shogun, emperor, and an American businessman in Stephen Sondheim's musical *Pacific Overtures* earned him a Tony Award nomination for Best Actor in a Musical.

As artistic director of East West Players, Mako trained generations of actors and playwrights and staged classics such as Shakespeare's *Twelfth Night* and Anton Chekhov's *Three Sisters.* He once devoted an entire season to plays pertaining to the internment of Japanese Americans during World War II to coincide with the start of a national discussion on internment reparations. Asian American theatre artists benefited from his training, his mentoring, and most of all from his example.

Who Makes Theatre Happen?

It takes a village to put on a show. Often, in the final stages of production, we have spent so much time together and so little with others in our lives that we begin to feel as if we have been together forever. Then the show closes and snaps us out of it. Mounting a theatre production is like a game with teams and elaborate rules; and like any team effort, players with complementary, collaborative skills are necessary for the play to be successful.

We will try to deal with nearly all the theatre artists in the course of this book, all of whom are the storytellers. Some are involved in preproduction work long before opening, others become involved as the play moves into rehearsal and production, and still others are involved in postproduction after the show closes. All are necessary to make the specific event happen in its own miraculous way. Look at Table 1.1. It may surprise you to learn that any production can easily involve a hundred people, and some twice that many. The chart omits important assistants who swell the number even more. If you have stayed at the end of a film to read all the credits, you know that, with technicians, this number can multiply several times in the world of film. While live-theatre jobs may be filled by separate individuals, many small theatre productions have only a handful of participants doing the ultimate multitasking. Sometimes the village is very small, with some extraordinarily hearty and versatile villagers.

There are a few grunt jobs in Table 1.1, involving labor without much demand for creativity. For the vast majority of these staff members, however, their job requires a tremendous amount of **imagination,** as well as the drive to realize fanciful visions in concrete ways. Play productions involve imagination driven by **impulse.** Webster defines the word *imagine* as "to form a mental image of something not actually present to the senses." As are the body and the emotions, the imagination is like a muscle; it needs exercise to stay healthy and strong. It requires engagement and the willingness to meet the object, event, or idea halfway, to participate in the experience. Children have an abundance of it, which, sadly, sometimes goes unnourished.

The imaginative impulse, traceable to the beginning of recorded human history, is a powerful source of joy or release. We use it to let our minds soar above unfortunate circumstances such as an unpleasant family event or a dead-end work situation. Imagination does not necessarily mean action, but for the artists of the theatre, it is all about making imaginative leaps and

FIGURE 1.7   The production team for a play involves many people. Here, director James Lapine rehearses the cast of *Amour* at the Music Box Theatre on Broadway.

Mark Peterson/Corbis News/CORBIS

KENNETH LONERGAN
PLAYWRIGHT, SCREENWRITER
We live in our imaginations. And the imaginative connection you get between a play or movie and its respective audience is as close as most of us ever get to each other.

Table 1.1	The Production Team

PREPRODUCTION	REHEARSAL/PRODUCTION	POSTPRODUCTION
PLAYWRIGHT (author)	ACTOR (performer)	CRITIC (writes journal reviews)
COMPOSER (creator of music)	GRAPHIC DESIGNER (creates images, layouts used in ads)	STRIKE CREW (dismantle and/or store physical production elements: props, costumes, set pieces, lights, etc.)
LYRICIST (author of song lyrics in a musical)	DRESSER (assists actors with preparation)	ALL OF THE ABOVE (memories)
LIBRETTIST/BOOK AUTHOR (author of dialogue in a musical)	MAKEUP DESIGNER (designs actors' makeup)	AUDIENCE (us)
PRODUCER (makes financial and business decisions)	MAKEUP ARTIST (assists actors in makeup application)	CRITIC (writes newspaper or broadcast review of the production)
MANAGING DIRECTOR (oversees day-to-day business)	HAIR/WIG ARTIST (designs/assists actors' hair/wigs)	
ARTISTIC DIRECTOR (oversees creative staff)	TECHNICAL DIRECTOR (oversees the construction of scenery and placement of light/sound equipment)	
GOVERNING BOARD (oversees everything and everyone)	SHOP FOREMAN (oversees craft persons in one of several areas)	
DIRECTOR (artistic guide)	SHOPPER (purchases cloth, clothing, and properties)	
CASTING DIRECTOR (assists in actor selection)	PATTERN DRAFTER (transfers costume design drawings into working patterns)	
MUSIC DIRECTOR (guides the music performers)	CUTTER (cuts patterns and fabrics for costumes)	
FIGHT DIRECTOR (creates and coaches stage fight choreography)	DRAPER (sews and fits mock-ups and costumes)	
CHOREOGRAPHER (designs dance and movement-based sequences)	PROP ARTISAN/MASTER (coordinates all items carried by actors)	
VOICE SPECIALIST (trains actors in use of voice, accents, and line interpretation)	SET DECORATOR (coordinates the detailing of the scenic environment)	
MOVEMENT SPECIALIST (designs and trains actors in physically demanding use of the body)	MASTER CARPENTER (oversees construction of all built units)	
DRAMATURG (research and text specialist)	MASTER ELECTRICIAN (hangs, focuses, maintains lights)	
DESIGNERS	SOUND ENGINEER (records sound effects and underscoring)	
SCENERY/SCENOGRAPHER (designs visual environments)	CREW HEAD (teaches and supervises crew members)	
COSTUME (designs clothing, wigs, masks, etc.)	CONSTRUCTION CREW (builds needed units)	
LIGHTING (designs lighting and often special effects)	RUNNING CREW/BOARD OPERATOR (makes changes to scenery, costumes, lights, etc., during the production)	
SOUND (designs auditory environment)	AUDIENCE (us)	
FX (devises special effects)	CRITIC (writes newspaper or broadcast review of the production)	
STAGE MANAGER (guides production communications before and after opening night)		
PUBLICIST ("sells" the production and/or theatre season)		

pushing forward to actualization. From the playwright trying to figure out how best to create a story that can be told in a few hours, to all those who figure out how to tell it, all the way to the marketing team who tries to connect the play imaginatively with its intended audience, there is constant envisioning and creative execution. In subsequent chapters, we will try to take you inside each of these artists' various journeys of imagination and impulse.

Having identified the personnel, let's now turn our attention to what theatre is likely to be about.

ANATOLE FRANCE
WRITER, CRITIC
To know is nothing: to imagine is everything.

JOHN KEATS
POET
I am certain of nothing but of the holiness of the Heart's affections and the truth of Imagination—what the imagination seizes as Beauty must be Truth—whether it existed before or not.

The Content of Theatre

One of the best things about theatre is its ability to show us both the surface differences and the essential sameness of human experience. It gives us windows into the lives and traditions of unfamiliar others (thereby reducing our fear of the unknown) and builds bridges into those same lives (as we see how much we all have in common).

Life Themes

Sometimes surface differences between us are so strange or exotic that it seems that we have little in common. But theatre always makes us aware that whatever we are experiencing in life, others are as well. Playwrights choose certain topics over and over, within which they explore human experience. We will address six of the most common, along with some film and play titles that you might recognize. Don't be surprised if you would put a particular film in a different category; it's all about the experience you had. (In our list, we include both films that are much honored and those that are much maligned, since art does not have to be great to deal with universal themes.)

1. **Love:** It makes the world go 'round, and it's never easy. (Films: *Hope Springs*; *Crazy, Stupid, Love*; *Moonrise Kingdom*; *The Perks of Being a Wallflower;* plays: *Much Ado About Nothing* and *M. Butterfly.*)

2. **War:** It invigorates hope. It destroys life. (Films: *Argo, War Horse, Zero Dark Thirty, Battleship,* plays: *Arms and the Man* and *9 Parts of Desire.*)

3. **Generations:** Parents want their children safe and secure. Children want an exciting new world. Or sometimes it's vice versa. (Films: *The Descendants, Beasts of the Southern Wild, Extremely Loud and Incredibly Close,* plays: *King Lear* and *Roosters.*)

4. **Rebellion:** The status quo isn't working. Social, cultural, or political upheaval may make things better. Or not. (Films: *The Hunger Games, The Help, Savages,* plays: *Antigone* and *"Master Harold"…and the boys*).

5. **Dreams:** All of us have ambitions, fantasies and hopes. They may barely resemble the lives for which we settle. (Films: *Midnight in Paris, The Tree*

FIGURE 1.8   A pair of tragic and comic masks is an ancient, universal symbol of the theatre. This Roman mosaic can be seen at the Musei Capitolini in Rome, Italy.

of Life, The Muppets, plays: *The Three Sisters* and *Bitter Cane.*)

6. **Values:** What if your most powerful beliefs about what is true are the exact opposite of those with whom you must coexist? (Films: *The Iron Lady, Moneyball, Wanderlust,* plays: *He and She* and *The Piano Lesson.*)

We will explore each of these life themes by examining the two play scripts in Dramatic Interludes, after each set of two chapters of this book. In each set of featured plays, the first is a Western European classic and a source of many of our theatrical traditions. The second is a contemporary play by or about underrepresented peoples: women, persons of color, and challenged or disenfranchised voices. Each pair of scripts will give us an effective taste of the best of the old and the new, the long-honored and the long-overdue.

Opposites

The universal symbol for the theatre is a set of two masks: one **tragic** and one **comic.** We can take any of the six life themes just described and decide to laugh or cry about them, and many artists challenge us to do both. In tragedy, death is nearly inevitable, but in comedy, life is. Characters in both can gain self-knowledge, but in tragedy, it often comes just too late to transform what is left of life, while in comedy, it is never too late to change perceptions and alter the future. The overwhelming presence of death or life tends to dominate.

The main character in a comedy is likely to make and be around friends (or at least amusing companions), while the tragic journey is a lonely one. Often, we in the audience seem to be the only true friend and confidant of the tragic hero. Comedy has a healthy, robust feeling to it, as if the actors have really big appetites and cannot wait to devour an enormous banquet right after the show. There's no such stomach for food in tragedy—too much anguish deep in the gut, too many heavy burdens. These contrasting interior landscapes affect the kind of light in the actors' eyes, the energy in their bodies, and the overall relationships that occur between characters and between actors and audience.

There are two other opposing, but coexisting, components of theatre. While we are audiences, we choose to believe that we are watching real people experiencing real life. This is called **suspension of disbelief.** We take our tendency to disbelieve and temporarily suspend it. At the same time, a part of us never forgets that we are watching a show and that messages are being conveyed to us. This is called **aesthetic distance.** These two concepts intermingle in intriguing ways. One allows us to forget ourselves and project ourselves into the lives of the characters on stage, while the other allows us to step back and gain insight into our own behavior—all at the same time.

Getting to the Theatre

Now, while you are studying the art form of theatre, is the perfect time to experience it firsthand. Here are some tips for finding information and obtaining tickets:

1. **Listings:** Your local newspaper probably has an Arts and Leisure section once a week, where information about play performances appears. Mid-sized and large cities also often have a free, widely distributed *Weekly Guide* with theatre listings. Most theatres have online listings, and all theatre departments have a central bulletin board with information about local productions.

2. **Free admission:** Most nonprofessional theatres need ushers and almost always give them free admission to the show. You sign up in advance to work a performance. You need to be there about 45 minutes before the show to be trained, but it is an easy and enjoyable job. It is fun to be part of the preperformance energy and to interact with people with whom you will be sharing the show. Also, if your school paper does not have a regular play reviewer and you are interested, you could offer to write a review for a production, in which case you are almost invariably given a complimentary press seat. This could be the beginning—in a few years, you could be the next Roger Ebert.

3. **Full-price tickets:** The cost to attend a show can vary widely. Tickets for students at a college theatre production average about $10, while some Broadway shows have ticket prices of $130 or more, often $500 for premium seating. Some sites falsely claim to offer discounted tickets, so go to the box office site for the play you wish to see to determine actual cost.

4. **Cheap tickets:** Many productions have preview performances for several days before they actually open. The show may not be quite as polished as it will be, but these tickets are less expensive. Most theatres have a student discount, which is often not advertised, so always ask about it. Some theatres also schedule special student performances, usually weeknights or matinees.

JANET SUZMAN
ACTOR

The regenerative twinkle of life and love gleams in the eye of comedy; the questioning mark of doom crouches on the forehead of tragedy.

* * * * *

When four comic actors were asked to complete the sentence "Comedy is to Tragedy as ____ is to ____," they answered:

ROBIN WILLIAMS: *"Clowns to Birthdays"*

KEVIN KLINE: *"Cream to Milk"*

JOHN CLEESE: *"Life to Death"*

JACK BLACK: *"'Bleep' to 'Bleep'" (two slang terms for male and female genitalia)*

RICHARD ZOGLIN
CRITIC

Is Broadway just for the 1%? Increasingly, it is looking that way. The chief culprit is the premium-seat phenomenon; those blocks of prime seats that every show now sets aside for well-heeled, or very desperate, theatergoers.

Richard Bain

FIGURE 1.9   Theatergoers outside the entrance to Stratford Festival's Studio Theatre.

Chances are that some funding for the theatre is included with your student fees, so you should receive a standard discount with your student ID.

5. **Rush tickets:** Rush tickets are bought the day of the performance, often an hour before curtain, when seats may be discounted to fill the house. Some touring shows (such as *Rent*) have a built-in clause requiring rush tickets for students at significantly reduced prices. In large theatres, tickets in the upper balcony are less expensive, and some venues also sell standing room, which allows you to lean on a platform at the back of the auditorium. Almost all theatres have group rates starting at 10 people, so if you can organize nine of your friends, it may be worth it. If you are attending as a class, your teacher may purchase clusters of tickets at group rates. Sometimes these are already built into the course fee.

6. **Ticket booths:** Located in large cities (in both London and New York, for example, the discount ticket booth is called TKTS), these booths offer reduced (30% to 50% off full price) tickets for professional productions available for that day's performance. Even a highly successful show may release discounted tickets if that day's performance looks as if it will fall short of a sellout. For a Broadway show, there are numerous alternatives to those $500 seats. The Broadway Box website (http://www.broadwaybox .com) collects discount codes found on posters, mail fliers, and other websites. The Frugal TheaterGoers Guide to Discount Tickets (http://home.roadrunner .com/~frugaltheatergoe) contains dozens of links to discount sites. The Theatre Development Fund (http://www.tdf.org) offers a buying service for students, teachers, and seniors for greatly reduced prices. However, many sites claiming to sell discount tickets actually have inflated prices, so it is always a good idea to go right to the site of the play itself for what may actually be the best price.

7. **Reservations:** Getting advance theatre reservations may well be your best plan if you do not need a super-cheap, same-day-only seat. If you want security, you

Ramin Talaie/Corbis News/Corbis

FIGURE 1.10   TKTS booths in New York City offer discounted theatre tickets day of show. TKTS are also a fixture in London.

will probably be happiest if you reserve by phone, online, or at the box office in advance because this allows you to choose exactly the seats you want (except for general-admission shows). Most audience members prefer to be in the middle of the house on an aisle. But if the show is a lavish spectacle or splashy musical, you can sit far back and still get the full effect.

Theatre Protocol

Appropriate behavior at a play will vary widely from place to place and culture to culture, as well as by the nature of the production. At some theatre events, an audience sitting quietly in the dark with their hands in their laps signals to the performers that they are failing to reach them. In another, the same behavior is considered to be the only appropriate response. Let your sensitivity to others guide your general behavior. You are not alone. Rude, distracting behaviors are not acceptable. You can subscribe to temporary membership in the tribe by paying attention to its protocol.

Certain rules are fairly universal. They may seem obvious. Theoretically, no one needs to be told about simple courtesies, but unfortunately, this is not always true.

1. *Turn off any electronic devices* that make noise so that all can have an event without interruption. Under no circumstances is it OK to text during a performance. You may not be making any noise, but your obvious discourtesy and lit phone screen are annoying and distracting to those around you.

2. *No productions can be recorded* on video, camera, or any other image-capturing system unless with the explicit written permission of the production. In most cases, attempts to do so would not only be rude, but illegal.

3. *Respecting the work is important.* Attention must be paid. If your personal mood or lack of interest prevents you from engaging in the work, let others around you enjoy their experience by not drawing attention to yourself by eating, talking, or texting.

4. If you have been required to report on the play as a class assignment, *try not to take notes during the performance.* It is distracting to the actors, the audience around you, and yourself. Sit back and experience the event. Trust that you will remember things until intermission or the final curtain.

5. If you are someone who does not retain impressions and you feel you *must* jot down notes or you will lose your insights forever, *do so briefly, discreetly, and quietly.* Never show up with a full-size notebook or clipboard. A few notecards or a small pad that fits in your pocket is all you need. Better yet, just take notes on the program, possibly checking names of those you wish to praise or putting question marks next to those who made decisions with which you disagree. In any case, these should be nothing more than brief reminders to help you fill in details later, and never to the extent that writing takes you out of the performance.

OSCAR WILDE
PLAYWRIGHT

The stage is not merely the meeting place of all the arts, but it is also the return of art to life.

Responding to Theatre

A fully realized response to theatre requires time and study. In the final chapter of this book, we provide guidelines for writing an informed critical review based on some exposure to the full spectrum of the world of the theatre. Like anything else, the more you know about the theatre, the more you can appreciate its nuances. A few of us, touched by genius in a particular area, can see, hear, and understand a great work in that field at first glance. For the rest of us, it takes time and study, just as it does to understand the power of a great abstract painter, an elegant mathematical formula, or the magnificent scale of molecular biology.

Nevertheless, you may well be asked to attend and respond to a show early in the term, so it is valuable to have a useful framework for doing so, one that allows an honest first impression without in-depth knowledge. If you are to be involved in extensive written analysis early in the term, we suggest that you skip to Chapter 12 and review that material. However, it is placed at the end of the book in the hope that after a full exposure to theatre, you will feel ready to provide *informed*, detailed criticism. Here, we will provide twelve questions that can enhance a response at the *beginning* of your exposure to live theatre. This list does not require expertise—just an honest willingness to assess your own experience.

1. How do you think your mood may have influenced your response to the performance?

2. What, if anything, seemed particularly noteworthy about the space in which the piece was performed?

3. What was the story? What happened? How did people change?

4. Was there a central conflict? Did someone win? How did you feel about his or her victory?

5. How did the time in which the play was set influence your response?

6. How did the setting or use of space work?

7. Were there significant ideas shared or lessons to be learned?

8. Which of your five senses were most and least stimulated by the event?

9. What did you think were the major strengths of this production?

10. What seemed to you to be its major weaknesses?

11. Did you have any prior experience with this play or this kind of play? If so, how do you think it influenced your response?

12. How, if at all, did this production make you interested or eager to attend more theatre?

(A more detailed list is available in Appendix A, and a response form can be found in Appendix B.)

Organizing Your Thoughts

Your response can be deeper and clearer by having guidelines around which to organize your thoughts.

1. **How will your familiarity with the material affect your response?** Have you seen this play or film before? Having the exact experience as the first time is impossible. Or have you, for example, studied a play by Shakespeare as literature and are so familiar with the text that you already have strong expectations? Or is the material completely new to you, so the freshness of your response will be unique to this production? You'll not see the same play in the same way ever again. You get only one first kiss in life.

2. Your response to a theatre event will more often be "mixed" than all good or all bad. We often "liked but didn't love" or "didn't enjoy but found interesting." **Rating an event on a scale of 1 to 10 can be a useful initial step in examining your experience.** Don't be surprised to find that you seldom give theatre a 1 or a 10.

3. Having established a production's place on your scale of 1 to 10, explain why you feel that way. **You should be able to discern and articulate the conditions of both the event and you.** We are all willing to critique other people's work, but sometimes we forget to critique ourselves:

   YOU—What mood or state of being did you bring into the theatre space? Were you focused or distracted? Eager or resigned? Physically well? Did you have dinner and a couple of drinks right before, or were you dying of hunger and couldn't wait to get out of there and have dinner? Did the event happen to intersect with things going on in your personal life in either a positive or negative way?

   THE ENVIRONMENT—What factors in the space contributed to your experience? Was it too hot or cold? Were the seats comfortable or cramped, or did you have to stand? Did you have an obstructed view? Did the people sitting near you share your experience, or did they irritate and distract you?

> **AUTHOR'S INSIGHT**
>
> **ANNIE:** Be aware of overdoing "environment" in your report. A few years ago, I read a review that discussed nothing but the uncomfortable seats in the theatre. Oh, and the writer's sore butt. Noteworthy, I'm sure, but it was as if no production had taken place at all.

The Production

Having critiqued factors beyond the production's control, you can confidently move on to the show itself. The first set of questions, "The Story," can be applied to the specific show that you are critiquing. The second set, "The World of the Play," can apply not just to the production, but to the culture of origin of the text or event. **Application 1**, at the end of **Dramatic Interlude 1: Love** following Chapter 2, will show how these questions can be answered for a classic play by Shakespeare and a popular contemporary play.

FIGURE 1.11 How would you critique a play set in an unconventional world, like this production of Edward Albee's *Seascape*, where an elderly couple, Nancy (Frances Sternhagen) and Charlie (George Grizzard) encounter Leslie (Frederick Weller) and Sarah (Elizabeth Marvel)—a *lizard* couple? Directed by Mark Lamos, at the Booth Theatre in New York. Set design by Michael Yeargan and costume design by Catherine Zuber.

Joan Marcus

The Story

1. **What happened?** Sometimes this is clear, sometimes not. In our personal theatre, we often get a befuddled feeling after an encounter, asking ourselves, "What just happened?" In live theatre, some stories are downright formulaic, while others are challenging.

2. **What was the central conflict?** Which characters took what side in the conflict? Who played on each team? What prize was at stake? Who won, who lost, who gave up, who changed sides?

3. **What was the primary emotional mood?** Tragic? Silly? Intellectual? Hectic? Sly? This is not about the emotions of the characters, but the overall emotional mood of the event (that is, the playwright's mood). Was there an overall mood, or did the production shift and alter unexpectedly?

The World of the Play

1. **Time:** When in history is the play written or evolved, set, and performed? How far does this production move away from the time period in which the piece was originally set? How familiar or unfamiliar are you with the time period?

2. **Space:** How is the space defined and viewed? What kind of space did the production use?

3. **Values:** What beliefs seem most widely shared by characters in this play? Which truths, ideals, and traditions are deemed to be self-evident?

4. **Structure:** What is the social and familial structure? How strictly enforced are the standards of behavior? What is the hierarchy of authority?

5. **Pleasure:** What is considered beautiful and desirable by these characters? What is the collective attitude toward sexuality and sensuality? What's hot and what's not?

6. **Senses:** Which, if any, of the five senses are most frequently and effectively stimulated? What is the quality of light, sound, and patterns that constitute the play's sensory world?

You will not be able to answer all the questions. But just considering them helps you enter the world of the play more openly, without the tendency to impose your own world on it. What things are so familiar that you wouldn't have noticed them ordinarily? Where do your personal and social norms bump up against those in the play? Is the world offering a "homecoming" or an adventure in an exotic alternative world? Let the event tell you what is important. "Loved it!" or "It sucked!" are legitimate immediate responses, but when sharing your response with others, something more thoughtful is needed. Exploring *why* you loved, hated, or felt ambivalent is interesting and illuminating.

Three Kinds of Theatre

In this book, we will examine the theatrical experience from three perspectives: *live theatre,* or performances with actors physically present; *media* or *screen theatre,* where electronics take the place of living human beings; and *personal theatre,* where we will ask you to consider theatrical elements in your own life. We will present these as featured boxes: **Theatre in Media,** which will examine our electronic theatrical experiences; and a two-part **Theatre in Your Life** feature, which will explore how your offstage or everyday existence involves theatrical elements and ways to consider your possible participation in the actual production of plays.

In a book about theatre, why will we spend time discussing filmed performances? Because many of our formative theatrical experiences have been with TV and film. Media are a crucial part of our private histories and personal mythologies. Many of our ideas about drama and life were formed in front of a screen. Most of us will spend many more hours of our lives there than in a theatre, particularly as home media centers and screening rooms become more common and the cost of attending live theatre continues to rise.

TONY KUSHNER

PLAYWRIGHT

Movies plunge you more into a story. In the theatre, you're always aware of everybody coughing and making noises and that can affect a performance. Movies don't care if you're coughing or having a coronary; the movie will keep playing.

ROBERT TOWNSEND

POPULAR CULTURE EXPERT, FILMMAKER

For many young people, life has been documented almost as if it were their own personal movie. Dad had a camera aimed right at them when they exited the womb. Then every time they took a first step or blew out the candles on their birthday cake, somebody was videotaping it. This is very different from those who just have their memories and a few photos.

LEONARDO DICAPRIO

ACTOR

I used what would later be my emotional range as an actor to fake the greatest illnesses or family tragedies to prevent me from exploring algebra.

DEREK LUKE

ACTOR

I lived in tough neighborhoods and the older boys picked on me, so I had to learn how to street-fight. That's when I became an actor. I studied the cool guys with their hard faces, hard walk, and hard talk.

JULIA STILES

ACTOR

Even when I was just a kid, I could walk around the city by myself and no one would mess with me. I learned to act tough and use my killer look.

THEATRE IN MEDIA

Film Audiences

Are you a movie baby? Has your entire life been a theatrical event, in the sense that the camera has been your audience and someone in your family was always filming? Did you know that others would watch your "performances" at a later time? Did you watch your favorite DVDs hundreds of times, memorizing every line and frame? If so, your digital adventures have formed who you are and how you will respond to any theatre event. And your experiences as both audience and actor have been very different from those of other generations.

Because cinematic experiences have been such a deep, rich part of our heritage, and because we all have such a powerful memory bank of screen references, we will use these resources throughout the book to enrich your future live theatre and media experiences.

Our experiences are also often not as simple as whether they are live or on film. We often experience a blended event, where both canned and live elements are present. During interactive performances of *The Rocky Horror Picture Show, The Sound of Music,* and *Grease* the constancy of the film projected is challenged and enhanced by the variety of live performances and audience participation in front of it. Also, more and more plays and performance art presentations incorporate prerecorded media into the overall experience, whether as part of the scenic design or actual dramatic interludes.

When we experience a film, it can result in a "half-and-half" theatre event—one-half (actors and story) unvarying and one-half (space and audience) live and variable. Imagine seeing a film for the first time:

- In a classroom with other students engaged and informed on the subject, all eagerly taking notes and looking forward to a lively discussion afterward.
- At the cineplex on opening night, after waiting in a long line, in a packed house, surrounded by hysterical fans of the leading actor or this series of films.
- In your own living room, surrounded by rowdy, imbibing friends, often loudly dissing and shouting back at the characters in the film and at each other.
- In the private screening room of your most hypercritical acquaintance, who will stop the film frequently to offer devastating critiques of the work of everyone involved.
- At your parents' home, after you just bought them this film in the hope that they will love it as much as you do (but you're not so sure about that).
- In a bunker near Mosul, Iraq, with soldiers from two different cultures and some recently rescued civilians, with the sound of explosives going off in the distance (and some here do not understand the language of the film, but all are grateful for the diversion).
- In a village in Uganda, where some of the film was shot, with a sheet serving as the projection screen and villagers seeing themselves for the first time, some delighted, others disturbed, some having to be cautioned by the tribal elders to quiet and calm themselves for the duration of the showing.

Think about your actual first exposure to one of your favorite films. Then think of all the other ways that that might have happened. Variations in space and audience can alter—in a live, interactive sense—your perceptions of the film and even how much of it you actually see and hear.

Yannick Tylle/Corbis

FIGURE 1.12   Invisible Children presents its "Kony 2012" movie where it was shot, in Gulu, Uganda.

THEATRE IN YOUR LIFE

Acting Our Lives

Unless you have actually acted in a play or worked on a production in some other capacity, you may have experienced theatre only as an audience member. But what about your personal theatre? Many of us do not stop to notice that whether a camera is present or not, we are starring in an ongoing event called My Life, while playing supporting roles and walk-ons in the lives of others.

We are all actors. Children act to try on roles; adults act to adjust to circumstances. In some professions, such as law and politics, much of the time spent on the job involves performance. But all of us give everyday performances, changing our behavior when we realize someone (even an audience of one) is watching. We may act more kindly than we would have otherwise. We may show off for someone we want to impress. Sometimes we behave so we don't get hassled or so we are allowed to join in with other people. Sometimes we act as if we are more graceful, compelling, or powerful than we really feel.

As we learn about live theatre, we can apply ideas to our ongoing personal theatre and gain awareness and even control of the elements (actor, audience, space, and story) of our own lives. If we learn from our mistakes, if we rehearse in our lives what we learn in the theatre, we can begin to discover how, in the words of Sam, the heroic black South African man in Athol Fugard's play "*Master Harold*"... *and the boys*, to "live life like champions, instead of always being just a bunch of beginners at it." We can learn to act our lives better.

(For a more detailed examination of this concept, see Robert's book *Acting: Onstage and Off*, now in its sixth edition.)

GETTING INVOLVED

Do you want to become engaged in theatrical productions? If so, how should you go about it? It will probably take at least the rest of this book to answer these questions, but now is a good time to start asking them. You will be introduced to a large number of ways to take part in the theatrical process. At the very least, you will become a more informed and insightful audience member so that going to a play will be a richer, juicier, and more complete experience. You will learn to see more, hear more, and even feel more as an audience member. If you to decide to audition for a play, sign up to work on a production crew, take an additional theatre class, write a play, or become involved in some other way, what will you take away? Those who have spent time in the theatre, even for only brief sojourns, often report that they felt they were in very good and lively company, that they got back in touch with what they most valued about the child in themselves, that they experienced enormous tolerance and respect for individuality and eccentricity, that they felt a genuine sense of community and play, and that they laughed a lot. Welcome to the world of the theatre.

SUMMARY

Your anticipation of a theatre experience tends to rise in proportion to the commitment that you have made to having it. Although most of our formative experiences as audience members were with media, the interaction of live actor and audience is often the source of our most indelible memories. Even our film experiences can have live elements sometimes. We all also have elements of theatre in our everyday lives, where we decide how to act just to survive. Every culture has had theatre for as far back as recorded time and probably long before that. There are numerous participants on the producing team of a play, but the essential ingredients are at least one actor and an audience sharing a space and telling a story. Some themes are so universal that they are chosen for plays over and over.

You will probably be going to a live theatre event in the near future. There are ways to attend the theatre at a reasonable cost. You can take your cues from the audience around you, but remember, certain behaviors are never appropriate. You may be asked to respond to a particular production, either formally or informally. Familiarity of the material, your mood, the environment, and other factors affect your response to the production. Guidelines to think about when forming a response to a production are time, space, values, structure, pleasure, and the senses. Theatre in your life can involve both an increased awareness of the theatrical elements in our everyday existence and an expanded sense of how to become engaged in the art form itself.

SUGGESTED ASSIGNMENTS

These questions may be used simply for reflection. They might also be handled as short writing assignments or discussion topics shared in small groups.

1. Have you ever been in an audience and known that your reaction and that of those around you was actually influencing and changing the performance itself? Describe the experience.

2. What is your earliest memory of an encounter that could become the first scene in the play of your life?

3. As an audience member, what is your most memorable live theatre experience so far? Your most memorable media experience? How do they compare to each other?

4. What, so far, has been the best (offstage, personal theatre) performance of your life? Why do you consider it a personal triumph?

5. What has been the worst? What caused you to bomb?

6. What is your most memorable experience of seeing someone only on film and then experiencing that person live?

7. Interview an acting student (or, if you can find one, a professional actor) and ask what he or she loves most and least about practicing this art form.

8. Pick a movie or personal theatre event and discuss it with friends following some of the guidelines provided in this chapter. Alternatively, discuss with friends your shared experience of time, space, values, pleasure, structure, and the senses.

9. Examine each of the major topics chosen for dramatic conflict (life themes). Which of these have you already experienced in your own life that might provide the basis for a play someday?

10. Survey your own key relationships in life. Which of these people are you more likely to act for or to pretend to feel other than you really do? With which persons are you most authentic and real when you are around them?

SUGGESTED ACTIVITIES

1. **Individual:** Make a list of five to 10 films that have had a profound impact on you at various times in your life. Choose one or two from early childhood, grade school, middle school, high school, and the current year.

2. **Group:** Make an entire evening out of going to the theatre with several friends or with classmates you have just met. Agree to have dinner together before the play and dessert and coffee afterward. Discuss your anticipation beforehand and share your collective responses to the production.

3. **Long-term:** Start a Personal Theatre journal. At least twice a week, note a performance that you observed and one that you gave. That is, write down instances where the behavior exhibited (yours or another's) would have been entirely different if some kind of "audience" had not been involved.

4. **Large lecture:** Form the class into groups of 10, and then share the list you created in Exercise 1 with your group. Do a quick assessment of the films that had the most impact on the group. Select a spokesperson to share your group results as others in the room do the same.

KEY WORDS AND IDEAS

theatre = actor, audience, space, story
imagination
impulse
comic/tragic
suspension of disbelief

aesthetic distance
theatre protocol
the world of the play
three kinds of theatre: live, media, and personal

chapter 2
ORIGINS

A group of Korean women perform as part of Chinese New Year celebrations on the streets of Beijing.

African masked Dogon dancers from Igbo tribe in ritual performance; Mali.

Peter Adams/Bridge/Corbis

Lesson Objectives:

Upon completion of this chapter, you will be able to:

1. Compare oral and written storytelling traditions, recognizing the importance of translation in interpreting meaning.
2. Identify four theories of the origins of the theatre and determine what makes sense to you.
3. Recognize the importance of ritual in your communal and private life.
4. Identify and say "yes" to any production's conventions.

Introduction

How did theatre begin? For many years, historians claimed that it started in Athens in the fifth century B.C.E., with the first reported tragic playwright being Aeschylus, and then the genre developed in Europe and spread to the New World. We call this the Dead European White Guy (DEWG) syndrome, a perspective that has afflicted many disciplines. We now recognize that theatre is immeasurably older than 2,500 years and far more geographically diverse than one peninsula on the edge of Europe. We also now know more about how early contributions from women and non-Europeans have influenced global theatre.

Why was Western theatre scholarship dominated by cultural chauvinism for so long? Eurocentric scholars came from a patriarchal literary tradition that had little or no knowledge of other cultures grounded in oral traditions. Knowledge was based on what was familiar to the scholars themselves. In all fairness, it is far easier to research available evidence than to pursue less tangible sources. Our intention is not to show disrespect or ingratitude to the DEWGs. They have given us towering genius and profound wisdom. Some of the greatest works of dramatic art and some of the most meaningful insights into the human condition have come out of their tradition and perspective. They were presenting the truth as they knew it. Most of us would have not done any better in their situation. We will turn to them constantly for information and inspiration. We have all been DEWGs in some aspect of our lives, seeing through our own limited lenses and responding with inherent bias. The term is created with affection, gratitude, and a bit of irreverence. Our goal in this book is to expand beyond their insights to embrace a wider perspective not available to them but revealed by more recent research.

This chapter will present varying cultural perspectives, share some of the very earliest theatrical offerings, identify major theories about how theatre came to be, demonstrate the importance of ritual in our personal and theatrical lives, and establish the rules of make-believe that we all accept as part of the theatre experience.

Translation Power

Here is a vivid example of how cultural bias can alter meaning. One of the more common shared experiences among Christians is the recitation of the Lord's Prayer in unison in a place of worship. This event has theatrical elements, where all present usually stand and take part in a public performance of worship. But what exactly are we saying? Here is the version from the King James Bible (Matthew 6:9–13):

Our Father which art in heaven, Hallowed be thy name.

Thy kingdom come, Thy will be done on earth, as it is in heaven.

Give us this day our daily bread.

And forgive us our debts as we forgive our debtors.

And lead us not into temptation, but deliver us from evil: For thine is the kingdom, and the power, and the glory, for ever. Amen.

Here is the original Aramaic version:

Abwoon d'bwashmaya

Nethgadash shmakh

Teytey malkuthakh

Nehwey tzevyanach aykanna d'bwashmayo aph b'arha

Hawvlan lachma d'sunganan yaomana

Washboglan khauboyn (wakhtahayn)

Aykana daph khnan shbwogan l'khayyabayn

Wela tachlan l'nesyuna. Ela patzan min bisha

Metol dilakhie malkutha wahayla wateshbukhta l'ahlam almin

Ameyn.

When material is translated, the translator can't help but filter the words through a cultural bias that is so ingrained that he may not even notice it. What follows is a careful attempt to translate the words as closely as possible to their original meaning rather than imposing values from another time, place, and perspective:

O Source of wisdom and life,

Carve out a space within us where your Presence can abide.

Fill us with imagination to be empowered on our mission.

Endow us with the wisdom to produce and share what each of us needs to grow and flourish.

Untie the tangled threads that bind us, as we release others from the entanglement of past mistakes.

Do not let us be diverted from our true purpose, but let us ever be aware.

For you are power and fulfillment, as all is gathered and made whole once again and for all time.

Amen.

(translated by M. Shani Illahan)[1]

---

[1] NOTE: Biblical translations are challenging and controversial. The Syrian Aramaic texts that survive are not in the dialect spoken by Jesus or his followers. Published English versions are often adaptations, not translations. The above is offered not as a claim to historical authenticity, but simply as an example of how the same passage can change when filtered through different contexts.

Erich Lessing / Art Resource, NY

AUTHOR'S INSIGHT

ROBERT: Whenever some of my students claim to dislike a great classical play that has been translated, I always urge them to look at two or three other translations because of the power of the translator to profoundly change the work itself.

★★★★★

ANNIE: When I finally found a superb translation (by Seamus Heaney) of *Beowulf,* it not only changed my view of the work itself, but I suddenly understood some parts of my family, especially those from northern Europe. I felt I had discovered a heritage!

FIGURE 2.1 This riverboat carving from the tomb of Meketre, held at the Metropolitan Museum of Art, is typical of carvings from the time of the *Abydos Passion Play.*

Not only are the words different, but the meanings have changed as well. It would be absurd to conclude that the original English translators got it "wrong" because what emerged is one of the most powerful, beautiful, profound, and inspirational documents in Western history. This does not, however, make it any less intriguing to imagine translation with fewer cultural filters.

Time, translation, and perception can transform writing beyond its original context.

If the written word, which is at least captured on the page, can change so much with interventions, what about the unrecorded and ever-elusive spoken word?

The First Plays

What really was the first play? The first recorded drama is not from Greece but North Africa. Fragments of a work called the *Abydos Passion Play* have been traced back at least 1,500 years before Athenian drama emerged. It was elaborately staged on boats, stopping at various locations along the Nile and concerned the murder, mourning, and resurrection of the wheat god, Osiris. It is our first documented production through literary testimony. Plays of the **oral tradition** existed even earlier, although that tradition, by its very nature, resists empirical evidence. Two things are likely to be true about the first play:

1. It was about the changing of the seasons, an explanation of why we have to endure winter to experience spring.

2. It was about the relationships of gods and humans and how what was going on between them may have influenced these seasonal shifts.

Why are these issues likely to have been central to a play? One or both of them emerge in every discovered work from times gone by. These are the two overwhelming concerns. Much preliterate evidence has been neglected and now, sadly, is lost. But scholarship is finally finding, recording, and preserving rich theatrical heritages of cultures with sophisticated oral traditions. A growing body of archaeological artifacts also reveals contributions from women and non-European artists. A more global and inclusive view of the art form continues to emerge.

Because we cannot with certainty identify the first play, we will share two contenders that are so old, their origins are lost in the mists of time. One example preserved by oral tradition is *Uzume's Trance*, a Japanese folk comedy that has been performed in one form or another for many centuries and continues today. This theatrical ritual is enacted each year on the winter solstice and is designed to ensure and celebrate the return of spring, regardless of scientific evidence that seasons are brought by annual rotations of the earth around the sun. It features a woman performer known as a ***miko***, or female shaman, who plays the title character, a young mischievous goddess named Uzume. What follows is the story in a bare-bones outline.

Uzume's Trance

Once upon a time, Amaterasu, the sun goddess, was so offended by a remark her consort made about her beauty that she shut herself in a cave. Suddenly the sun was gone from the sky. The entire world turned dark. The people began to suffer. Crops died. The village elders tried to coax her out of the cave, but she would not budge. Suddenly a young playful goddess, Uzume, leaped in front of the cave, danced in a wild and funny way, sang bawdy songs, and flung her skirts over her head, making everyone laugh. Intrigued by the laughter of the people, Amaterasu came out of the cave, returned to the sky, and light and warmth were returned to the people.

Your first response might be that *Uzume's Trance* is a story, not a play. In oral-performance tradition, a narrator has memorized the basic story, without setting the words. Others are selected to enact various named characters. The performance includes the core narration, pantomimed action by other actors, and interludes where improvised **dialogue** is inserted. Many lines will be spontaneous, while some may also be considered important enough to be passed on exactly from one generation to the next. The "script" often does not exist on paper, but in the imaginations and memories of the performers and the audience.

Each year, as the sun hides herself in the long nights of December, people gather together and let a *miko* play the role of Uzume and make them laugh, knowing that the sun will soon return to her place in the sky. In this early piece of theatre, we find the healing power of comedy, the link between sex and comedy, the necessity for female energy in many performance traditions, and the satisfaction derived from ancient and enduring traditions.

What follows is an adaptation that might be performed by an American acting troupe. Because the oral tradition continually adapts

FIGURE 2.2 *Amateratsu Appearing from the Cave* by Yoshitoshi in Japan's creation myth, from the series *Dai nippon meisho Kagami,* "Mirror of Famous Generals."

and evolves, performances—while respecting traditional ideas—may involve contemporary dialogue, and if the story is basically comic, it may include slang and pop culture references. The following script provides a starting place from which a contemporary company can build and expand.

Uzume's Trance*

Gift of Tarō Yamamoto/Morikami Museum & Japanese Gardens

FIGURE 2.3 As the embodiment of springtime, joy, and renewal, Uzume dances to entice Amateratsu, the sun goddess, out of her cave.

(to be performed by 10 actors)

CHARACTERS:

Narrator
Amateratsu, Sun Goddess
Consort/Boulder

*English adaptation by Annie McGregor and Robert Barton

Villagers (Elders)
Children
Uzume

NARRATOR: Once upon a time, long, long ago, Amateratsu, the sun goddess, was travelling in her usual course across the sky when her consort made an unforgivably rude remark about her beauty. (*Amateratsu and her consort appear.*)

CONSORT: You're looking old today, baby.

AMATERATSU: What????!!!! (*She strikes him hard enough that he falls down, then kicks him, and he curls into a ball, becoming a boulder.*) Let's see how you like life as a boulder! I cannot shine under these conditions. I'm going to go in that cave and never come out. (*Two actors form an arch, like the entrance to a cave.*)

NARRATOR: Amateratsu was so angry that she retired to a cave and rolled an enormous boulder across the mouth of the cave.

AMATERATSU: Get over here, Boulder, and cover my entrance! (*The "consort" rolls across the stage and fills the entrance created by the other two actors.*)

NARRATOR: Suddenly the sun was gone from the sky and the people began to suffer. Their crops died in the fields. The children cried from hunger and cold. All the village elders went up to the cave where Amateratsu was sulking, and they tried everything they could think of to coax her out of the cave.

VILLAGERS: (*ad-lib moaning, pleading, and supplicating*) Please come back and give us light! We miss you so much! We brought you rice and sweet treats! You are so beautiful!

AMATERATSU: Not everyone seems to think so(*kicks the boulder*).

VILLAGERS: Your consort is a jackass!!!

AMATERATSU: Well, now he's just a boulder. Okay, maybe a jackass boulder. But I am here to stay.

NARRATOR: They wept and wailed, but Amateratsu sniffed imperiously and ignored them. The cold and dark continued, and the suffering of the people grew. Soon the whole village gathered in front of the cave, begging and praying.

VILLAGERS: (again, largely ad-lib) We will do anything. Anything! We cannot live without your light! Have mercy! You are the most beautiful goddess ever!

NARRATOR: But Amateratsu, still angry in her cave, only harrumphed.

AMATERATSU: Go away and stop bothering me!

NARRATOR: The people were in despair, and they simply sat in a circle in front of the cave and waited to die. (Actors form a circle and sit.) Suddenly, a young goddess named Uzume jumped into the center of the circle and began to dance and sing. (Uzume leaps from offstage into the middle of the gathering.) At first, the people were too sad to notice her. But she only danced more wildly and sang more raucously until the people stared at her in amazement. She began to twirl in place, round and round, until all were dizzy watching her. She danced and twirled and sang bawdy songs until the people slowly began to smile, and a few clapped their hands in time to her song.

UZUME: (singing; she may also improvise dialogue between her ventures into song)

Roll me over in the clover.

Roll me over and over and do it again.

I'm just a girl who can't say no.

I'm in a terrible fix.

I always say come on, let's go, just when I ought to say nix!

I want your sex. I want your sex. I want your sex!

(Uzume, in an inspired state, continues to sing snatches of racy songs, perhaps encouraging the audience to shout out requests.)

NARRATOR: Finally, she picked up her skirts, flinging them over her head, showing Amateratsu and everyone else her underpants . . . and the people began to laugh. (Uzume has, under her very full skirt, petticoats and bloomers or some other amusing kind of underwear, so what she shows is funny and not particularly revealing.) They laughed and laughed as she twirled with her skirts over her head until Amateratsu heard the laughter.

AMATERATSU: All right, what is so damn funny, anyway?? Move it, Boulder. Let me take a look. (Boulder obligingly rolls out of her way.) Oh my God, that is hilarious!! (She doubles over with laughter.)

NARRATOR: She laughed so hard, she almost missed the small mirror Uzume had placed in a nearby tree. (One actor "holds" a mirror toward Amateratsu, who can't resist her own beauty, and the actor with the mirror begins to tease her with it.) Finally, Amateratsu left the cave, and before she knew it, the other gods and goddesses grabbed her and pitched her back up into the sky, and the warmth and light of the sun shone down on the people again.

(Some of the actors lift her up and twirl her and pass her around. Finally she and everyone onstage are dancing. Boulder returns to his consort state.)

CONSORT: You're lookin' good, baby!!

AMATERATSU: Yeah, well, I don't need you to tell me that. (Villagers cheer her on. She ad-libs lines about her own beauty, perhaps culminating with a claim like "I am the original bling!") Come on, Uzume, let's leave this loser and dance! (She and Uzume join in a joyous dancing circle, with all the other actors doing the same movement in unison.)

NARRATOR: And so Uzume once again teased Amateratsu out of her cave and twirled her way into the hearts of the people, proving once again that a girl with a mirror and a great pair of underpants can accomplish anything!

Ogun's Sacrifice

A second drama, this one from West Africa, transmitted orally between generations for thousands of years, helps us understand the early traditions of tragedy. The following is *Ogun's Sacrifice,* one part of a large body of works known collectively as *Ogun's Mysteries.* In Yoruban culture, the *Mysteries* detailed the many adventures of Ogun. While the culture of ancient Greece identified the first actor as Thespis of Icaria, for the Yoruban people of West Africa, there is no doubt that the first actor was someone named Ogun. (Note: The terms **griot/griotte** are French words meaning male and female *praise singers.* The title denotes both a storyteller and something much more sacred. The *griot / griotte* is the living memory of the people, the keeper of the communal consciousness.)

This ancient ritual drama holds many essential elements of tragedy: the suffering of a people, the rise of a **hero**, the willingness to sacrifice for the good of others, and ultimate redemption. Many hundreds, perhaps even thousands, of years later, Aristotle would describe this process in his work *Poetics.*

Ogun's Sacrifice*

(to be performed by 10 actors)

CHARACTERS:
    Griot (narrator)
    Obatala
    Babalu Aye
    Ogun
    Other gods
    Humans

GRIOT: In the beginning, there was only the One, encompassing all Creation in divine harmony. One day, as he tended his garden, his slave rebelled and rolled a huge boulder down upon him, sending him crashing into the abyss, where he shattered into 1,001 pieces. (*Other actors enact this event in an abstract way, coming tightly together and then bursting apart and collapsing at various points on the stage.*) From these shards of the One came all things, including the gods. One god was Obatala, who became the Creator. (*Throughout the following, the actors often use large, stylized, dance-inspired movements to represent the eternal qualities beyond everyday behavior that identify them as gods.*)

OBATALA: I am the fabric that binds the universe together. Each day, my hands form new children to be born into the world. (*As he speaks, he spreads his legs and moves his hands as various actors emerge from beneath him and are released by his hands into the world.*) All the people are made by the hands of me, Obatala.

GRIOT: Obatala is the essence of passive creation, serene, unchanging, and unmoving. Sadly, Obatala's great weakness is drink. (*Obatala mimes rapidly downing huge quantities of alcohol.*) When he is drunk on palm wine, his creations become a little wobbly, so that some among us are blind or lame. (*He begins swaying. Actors now appear to limp or struggle to find their way when released by his hands.*) Obatala, in his serene composure, goes on making children. Babalu Aye is the god of suffering.

BABALU AYE: I am the god who teaches the people to cope with misfortune, to learn patience and forbearance without despair. I am calm in the face of all the tides of fate. (*He/she embraces each child as he/she is born.*)

GRIOT: Ogun is the warrior god, the first actor, the dispenser of justice both gentle and harsh.

OGUN: I am the embodiment of force, energy, and most of all, the power of Will.

*English adaptation by Annie McGregor and Robert Barton

GRIOT: Long ago, as the ages passed, Ogun noticed discontent and sadness in his fellow gods. (*Other actors mingle around Ogun.*)

OGUN: What ails you, my friends? What is the source of this overwhelming grief?

OTHER GODS: (*divide and ad-lib the lines as needed*)
We feel lonely for human men and women.
The great abyss separates us from the people.
We wish we could have them in our lives.
But the abyss saddens and frightens us.
It is a place of chaos, terror, and annihilation.

OGUN: Let us go through the abyss and see our little brothers and sisters. Let's go right now.

OBATALA: I would go with you, my old friend, but the business of Creation itself is in my hands. It is my destiny to remain unchanging.

GRIOT: Simple consciousness was all Obatala could manage. Or maybe he was drunk that day. I don't know. What did Babalu Aye say?

BABALU AYE: Suffering is to be endured. It cannot be avoided, so maybe it would be better to just be quiet.

GRIOT: Babalu Aye believed one could only wait and endure, that we simply must manage with our lot. But Ogun, warrior and first actor, felt differently.

OGUN: I cannot stand it anymore. I will do whatever it takes to bring us all—gods and humans—together. I will go to the worst possible place and find out.

GRIOT: And as the other gods watched in horrified amazement, Ogun poised on the edge of the abyss, and gathering all of his Will, he threw himself in. (*Ogun thrusts himself forward to the ground, where he is barely caught by other actors. All the actors continue to act out the chaos that surrounds him, pummelling him, then lifting and even throwing him high into the air.*) The terrors he experienced in the chaos can only be imagined. The pain he suffered was not to be imagined. He was torn and shredded, but he endured and struggled on. At last, one day at the end of long days and ages of pain and hardship, he landed at the bottom of the abyss and shattered into 1,001 pieces. (*The actors lift him high above the ground, from which point he jumps down and falls to the ground and appears to be dead.*) Then slowly, agonizingly, Ogun began to pull the pieces of himself together again (*the actor performs a painful resurrection*), and he began the long and painful climb up the other side of the abyss, cutting a path through the terrible abyss and called for his fellow gods to follow him. From that day until this, we, the people, live among the ancestors and the unborn. (*The other actors form a wide circle, and, slowly, all go down on their knees to pay homage to Ogun, who stands in the center.*)

OGUN: We will all now live together, the gods and the demons, the good and the evil, the strong and the weak, all living fully in the universe with all that exists available to us if we only have the Will to act.

GRIOT: And we all now know the power of our own will, thanks to the hero-god, Ogun.

How Did Theatre Begin?

Identifying the first play, while an enjoyable quest, is ultimately a purely academic one. We know that plays existed long before Western tradition and that we can move beyond our known canon to include the world at large. We have only theories about the origins of theatre. Here are four of the best.

1. Spontaneous Inspiration

Robert Edmond Jones's seminal work, *The Dramatic Imagination*, offers a possible story of the first play:

Let us imagine ourselves back in the Stone Age. It is night. We are all sitting together around a fire—Ook and Pow and Pung and Glup and Little

Pierre Colombel/Fine Art/Corbis

FIGURE 2.4   Do cave paintings such as this support the theory that the first performances entailed a switch from *telling* about a hunt to *showing* what happened in a hunt? *Rock Painting of a Hunt With Dogs*, 4000–1500 B.C.E.

Zowie and all the rest of us. We sit close together. We like to be together. It is safer that way, if wild beasts attack us. A lion has been killed today, and it is all anyone wants to talk about. The lion's skin lies close by, near the fire. Suddenly the leader of the tribe jumps to his feet. "I killed the lion! I did it! I followed him! He sprang at me. I struck at him with my spear! He fell down! He lay still."

He is telling us. We listen. But all at once an idea comes to his dim brain. "I know a better way to tell you. See! It was like this! Let me show you!" In that instant, drama is born.

The leader continues, "You, Ook, over there, you stand up and be the lion. Here is the lion's skin. You put it on and be the lion and I'll kill you and we'll show them how it was. . . ." And now these two men—the world's first actors—begin to show us what the hunt was like. They do not tell us. They show us. They act it for us. The lion growls. The hunter poises his spear. The lion leaps. The spear is thrown. The lion falls and lies still. The drama is finished.

Now Ook takes off the lion's skin and sits beside us and is himself again. Just like you. Just like me. Good old Ook. No, not quite like you or me. Ook will be, as long as he lives, the man who can be a lion when he wants to.

Jones theorizes a spontaneous "light bulb" moment when the tribe leader decides to *show* the lion hunt rather than tell about it. Theatre is then born in pure inspiration. The Ooks of the world were unable to send out mass e-mailings to share their discoveries and are unlikely to have had direct contact with more than a few hundred people during their whole lives. The notion of just getting up and performing stories must have inspired countless actors in different places and times. Could it be that the need and ability to create theatre is inherent in each of us?

2. Imitation to Ritual

Internationally renowned mythologist and anthropologist Joseph Campbell, inspired by a fascination with Native American culture in his youth, sought to unify all myths. His theory, the second that we will discuss, says that the human capacity to imitate and fantasize leads to the creation of myth and ritual.

Campbell observed that children everywhere need to imitate behavior, learning to talk, walk, play, read, and sing by watching and mimicking. As our imitations become more complex, we practice playing "house," "school," or "war." We may then create long dramatic scenarios, like television series, returning to the same game (and exploring behaviors and consequences) in episode after episode.

We then move to complex dramatic situations, beyond our known worlds. Campbell noted that once children are engaged beyond their own living room, tent, or cave, they begin to fantasize about worlds that are partly real and partly invented. Did you play "Ninja Warrior," act out stories with a My Little Pony™ collection, or play in a fort in your backyard or under the dining room table? You probably went beyond imitation to playing out roles that existed only in your imagination.

Combining imitation with fantasy is universal. In Dakar, Senegal (West Africa), every boy has a ball, bundle, or tin can with which he plays soccer endlessly, dreaming of one day becoming star of the Senegalese national soccer team. Boys may not have player cards to collect or a television to watch the games, but they can recite the names of current and former team members and their vital statistics. Girls play house in courtyards and enclosed spaces, dreaming of being the first (and hence the most important) wife of a rich man. (In Senegal, a man can have up to four wives if he can afford to care for them.) Less popular girls have to play second or third wives. A favorite war game for all is still "rebellion against the French," which exerted colonial control over the country into the 1970s. An actor who pretends to be Hamlet, prince of Denmark, existing purely in imagination, is only a more sophisticated version of children playing El Hadji Diouf (the great soccer star), Mom, Fidel Castro, or SpongeBob SquarePants.

Campbell understood that for the childhood impulse to construct drama to become the art of the theatre, community engagement is crucial. Childhood games explore the mysteries of life, but long after childhood,

Robbie Jack/Corbis Entertainment/Corbis

FIGURE 2.5 Early Greek drama consisted of one actor and a chorus. The actor impersonates a mythological or historical figure, and the chorus represents the community, as in this performance of *The Oedipus Plays of Sophocles*, directed by Peter Hall.

we still want answers. The mysteries—our purpose in life, our relationship to higher powers, why we suffer, and whether true justice exists in this world or the next—simply grow more complex. We imagine answers through myth, ritual, and community—moving from childhood imitation to theatre art.

The source of all mythology is *need*. Long before science and technology, we depended on the autumn harvest to see us through winter, with meat brought home by hunters and roots and plants harvested by gatherers, preserved to prevent starvation during the lean months. But what if one year, the hunters come home empty-handed time and time again? They have roamed far and wide but have seen no sign of the much-needed herds. The community is afraid. We gather together to decide why this is happening. An elder suggests that the animals have left us because our creator is angry with us. What could we have done? Can we appease the anger and bring back the herds? Someone suggests an offering of something precious to us. We agree, we make the offering, and within days, the hunters return loaded with meat for the winter, and we can see the returning herds from our own home. Coincidence? Maybe. Maybe not.

According to Campbell, a mystery like the absence of animals will cause us to *do* something. If that something has the desired results (bringing the animals back), we repeat it. To make the mystery plausible, we evolve stories about the creator/spirit, the people's response to divine anger, and heroes who solved the mystery. We continue the behavior that worked the first time we needed it. Each generation may make the event bigger, developing elaborate stories of life and death, seasonal renewal, plenty, and starvation—called **myths**—our way of comprehending the unknowable. Long after we evolve past the hunter/gatherer stage, our myths and rituals are preserved and passed on. A sacrifice that involved five minutes and minor effort in the beginning may now include elaborate effects and community-wide participation with many roles to be cast. Cultural identity is reaffirmed through mythic reenactment, with diverse peoples creating drama dealing with the same essential mysteries.

3. Stepping Out

Our third theory is from **Aristotle**'s fourth-century B.C.E. document *Poetics,* the first known Western analysis of a body of dramatic literature. His essay is often used to define the very nature of Western theatre. While he wrote of a specific culture, place, and time, his theory can be applied to any community. (More about Aristotle and Greek tragedy can be found in Chapter 7.)

Aristotle believed that theatre evolved out of religious rituals known as **dithyrambs**. The dithyramb involved the entire community gathering on occasion to sing songs and recite words in unison. One day, according to Aristotle, a man named Thespis stepped forward and began speaking to the community and letting the community respond in unison. This changed the nature of the event. Instead of a group **monologue**, a dialogue was created between speaker and community. The dynamic of a man standing alone on the stage speaking to the community is changed. Now the man is impersonating a mythological or historical figure (a character), and the community is represented by a group of actors known as the chorus.

Thespis has been immortalized in Western theatre culture. His name has been adopted to represent not only actors but also members of any dramatic society, who are called **thespians**. The likelihood is strong that performers in other, earlier cultures also one day stepped outside the group and created dialogue. Thespis was the lucky one whose name is remembered.

4. A Divine Gift

A fourth theory comes from ancient India and encompasses much of the Asian theatre-dance tradition. The Hindu theorist **Bharata** wrote even earlier than Aristotle about what theatre is and should be. The god Brahma ("the breath of the world") is one of a triumvirate of primary gods, including Shiva and Vishnu, and is believed to have commanded the first drama. When humans desired to imitate the experience of the gods, Brahma confided his secrets to Bharata, whose seminal work is ***Natya Shastra,*** or the *Canons of Dance and Drama.* He was trying to identify the crucial components of Sanskrit drama.

Dallas and John Heaton/ree Agents Limited/Terra/Corbis

FIGURE 2.6   Puppets act as symbols and can lend great power to a performance. This is a Wayang shadow puppet performance in Bali province, Indonesia.

Plots for many plays in this tradition were originally based on two epic poems: *Ramayana* and *Mahabharata*, religious and ethical works that still are primary sources in classical and modern dance dramas, including contemporary filmmaking in India.

Music and dance are required in much of Asian drama, and according to Bharata, language must be poetic and plots should be familiar. Additionally, narrators must define the outline of a performance while actors perfect **gesture** and physical nuance to express the writer's intent. Sometimes the use of puppets allows the expression of something beyond the capacity of human performers.

Acting, dancing, and puppetry, according to the *Natya Shastra,* attempt to reach beyond the natural world, and in this effort, trance states are sometimes induced. The puppet (in some ways akin to a mask) cannot act poorly or tell a lie, but rather represents "the symbol of man in the great ceremony of life and eternity." The puppet can teach the actor simplicity, precision, and a lack of affectation, just as a character may teach the actor how to expand her view of life in general. Appreciation of the divine gift and magical transformative states gives theatre its profound power.

The theories of Jones, Campbell, Aristotle, and Bharata are plausible and compatible. The sudden spontaneous "Ook" impulse is common among adults and children in the midst of discussion or at play. Rituals are often fully communal. Participation in them is a crucial rite of passage. Each culture's Thespis could easily make the inductive leap from stepping up around the fire, recreating the beast, to stepping out of the chorus to create character. The magical components of theatre, its trancelike moments, and the fusion of the actors with any and all around them may indeed be divine gifts.

Rituals of Life

Each of these four origin theories focuses on ritual. Rituals are central to the theatre, just as they are to everyday life. A **ritual** is any act that is repeated over and over in a very specific way. When you wake up, you may begin a series of ritualistic preparations for your day: which foot you put in which slipper first, the way in which you brush your teeth, and the way you gather what you need to venture into the world. Rituals center us. The more difficult the day ahead or behind, the more we value comfort rituals.

A ritual with an audience, even an audience of one, becomes a performance. In your offstage life, you may have repeatedly performed private rituals, such as a particular way of putting on your socks or taking off your jeans. When you do any of these in front of a new roommate, it suddenly turns theatrical. Your audience may comment on the weird way that you do it and make you realize that not everyone else in the world handles socks and jeans as you do. So you reconsider your choices. You may decide to (1) only change clothes in private from now on, (2) change how you do it, or (3) enjoy your own individuality, maybe even flaunt it, encouraging other comments from your roommate, in fact "performing" on a regular basis. If you choose (3), you might consider becoming a theatre major.

We have official rituals from birth to death. Most cultures have some kind of ceremony welcoming and/or naming a newborn child in the village, followed by other religious and secular celebrations, graduations, and other rites of passage, games, pageants, sports events, dances, awards ceremonies, weddings, public hearings, presentations, debates, trials, and finally, funerals and memorial services. These all have strong theatrical elements and defined performer and audience roles. Sometimes we skip or reject rituals and then regret it deeply later, saying how much we now wish we had shown up. Why? Because the ritual may have allowed us to let go, gain peace, and move ahead.

Theatre people are often superstitious. Backstage rituals abound. Many actors arrive at the theatre at precisely the same time each day; put on their makeup in an exact, perfected pattern; and converse with others in the cast in a predetermined sequence. Many athletes have their own set of rituals, all aimed at maintaining a sense of continuity.

Ritual Growth

In the theatre of our lives, rituals can be not only our comfort but sometimes our salvation. The Wounded Knee Massacre is an example of how the elements of theatre have formed an annual event of great healing, which is described here.

BRIAN COLLINS
THEATRE MARKETER

Digital entertainment is convenient, but it's not as emotionally charged or socially driven as a live theatre event, not as communal with not nearly as strong a sense of ritual.

GORDON COX
JOURNALIST

In a world where most entertainment is delivered on increasingly convenient screens, the ritual and social connections of live theatre are increasingly valued by people. It gives them powerful memories.

Wiping Away of Tears

In 1890 at Wounded Knee Creek in South Dakota, the U.S. Cavalry opened fire on and exterminated almost 350 women, children, and elders, all members of the Lakota Tribe. One of their chiefs, Big Foot, was attempting to bring them to shelter after the assassination of their leader and greatest war chief, Sitting Bull, who had defeated the cavalry repeatedly in the past. They had traveled hundreds of miles to seek refuge at Pine Ridge Reservation and were just 20 miles short of their destination before being rounded up and shot. This incident remains one of the most questionable events in our military history in terms of judgment and compassion.

RON HIS HORSE IS THUNDER

SITTING BULL'S GREAT-GREAT-GREAT-GRANDSON

This massacre broke the back of our nation, and it continues to stand as the most potent symbol of the American Indian genocide.

After this, tribal elder Black Elk predicted, "seven generations of anguish and then regeneration." The remaining Lakota were stripped of their lands and placed on reservations, beginning a downward spiral of despair, poverty, and unemployment. Similar conditions permeated the lives of other tribes on the 314 reservations in our country, but no single incident exemplifies total devastation as does Wounded Knee. Many descendants believed such conditions were simply their destiny. An enervating sense of futility pervaded a population that felt stuck and without hope.

As the 100-year anniversary of the massacre approached, something remarkable happened. Tribal elders decided they needed to break the cycle. They revived an old public ritual, called "Wiping Away of Tears," to release

Ken Marchionno

FIGURE 2.7 Rituals can help a culture grieve and heal, as with the American Lakota tribe's Future Generations Ride. A lone white horse leads a procession that retraces the route to Wounded Knee.

the collective grief of their people. Tribal members now repeat the long, cold ride of their ancestors with eagle feathers on the staffs they are carrying. Because the wind chill factor makes temperatures dip well below zero, the ride is grueling. Other tribal members observe and assist at various places along the journey.

Each of the six days of the original ride began in a specific prayer for members of the tribe: day 1, children and orphans; day 2, the elderly and shamans; day 3, the physically and mentally sick; day 4, prisoners; day 5, women; day 6, the spirits of those who have died and the hope for an end to war. The ritual has expanded to 14 days, focused more and more on children and has been renamed "Future Generations Ride." Those who have taken part report a renewed sense of hope and a greater commitment to education and success.

It is as if many Lakota felt trapped by a single moment in history and were released by acting it out. It was not enough to tell the story. It had to be fully ritualized. It had to be experienced and felt. It had to be performed. Many of us experience this phenomenon in our personal history, but in this case an entire population felt an identical and overwhelming frustration, ritual absolution, and release. Sitting Bull's direct descendant, Ron His Horse Is Thunder, not only serves as one of the leaders of the ride but is president of one of 37 tribal colleges, spearheading a campaign to build a new educational and financial future for young and newly ambitious tribal members. A new generation of American Indians is turning the event into one of healing and redemption.

You may ask if this is a theatrical performance or a spiritual event. Is it theatre? We believe that, yes, this is theatre functioning at its most serious and spiritual level. We have performers playing the roles of their ancestors, audiences participating fully in the event, a designated space (vaster than most conventional theatres but still a performance space), and a story. As *Uzume's Trance* is performed as a comic expression about serious issues of survival, the Future Generations Ride is performed as a tragic expression of regeneration and renewal.

VINA WHITE HAWK
TRIBAL ELDER

The grieving helps the children to accept who we are and to grow from that.

ALEX WHITE PLUME
TRIBAL MEMBER

This journey has helped us rebuild in the seventh generation. It has allowed us to find the peace within ourselves and to extend that peace to others, even those who have hurt us.

MELANIE KUNTZ
TEENAGE RIDER

I didn't really want to do it, but my Dad wanted me to, so I did. Then I got to talk to the older people who know the history of this place. They told me our ancestors were watching as we rode through the hills—and you know, I truly felt it. Now I'm interested in learning more about my heritage. And I feel like maybe I can do a lot more things with my life than what I thought before.

Embracing Womanhood—The Quinceañera

Rituals may include an entire culture or be focused on the life stages of an individual. The transition out of childhood is honored by Jewish bar and bat mitzvahs for 13-year-old boys and 12-year-old girls, as does the Vision Quest embarked on by some Native Americans on the brink of adulthood. However, there is probably no more vivid ceremonial transition than the *Quinceañera*, which celebrates the 15th birthdays of young Latina women. This event often involves formal wear and up to eight young men in attendance, men designated as guardians—or *chambelanes*—for the honored young woman. It may also include a court of young female attendants called *damas*. Events move from the solemnity of Mass, prayers, ceremonial gift giving and vows, through a formal procession, to festive banqueting and dancing. The *Quinceañera* starts with a deeply spiritual ritual and ends with a vibrantly secular fiesta celebration.

While the specifics vary among communities, traditional elements include a special headpiece worn by the honoree, known as a *diadema* (much like a tiara), ornamental altar pillows, pastel colors, a birthstone ring, and a *libro y rosario* (a missal and a rosary).

The *Quinceañera* can be traced all the way back to the first encounters between Spanish explorers and Aztecs in Mexico over 500 years ago. Both of these cultures already had ceremonies recognizing the coming of age of young women. The two traditions intermingled and evolved into a daylong celebration. While not all elements of the *Quinceañera* are readily understood by those outside the culture, at least two of the key rituals can be universally appreciated. At one point in the ritual, the honored young woman gives away a doll to a younger girl; at another, she accepts the gift of a pair of high heels.

DAN WOJCIK

FOLKLORE SCHOLAR

Most Caucasian Americans fail to recognize this key rite of passage, making a challenging life transition even more difficult and confusing for all involved.

PANCITA DAVILA

QUINCEAÑERA PLANNER

From this important day on, the sweet-15 girl can find a good path to become a better person with new ideas.

MARLOWE VELEZ

RECENT QUINCEAÑERA CELEBRANT

It's an opportunity to express your maturity and to be thankful. Every girl should have that, whether she's Hispanic or not.

AP Photo/Hobbs News-Sun, Kimberly Ryan

FIGURE 2.8 Some rituals focus on the individual's rites of passage, as in the *Quinceañera* ceremony, a tradition for Latina women on their 15th birthdays.

Evolving Rituals—The Japan Divorce Ceremony

Rituals must be suited to each culture or they become empty gestures. We need to adapt old rituals or invent new ones that have contemporary relevance. One example in Japan is the divorce ceremony. According to journalist Paige Ferrari, this is "a new, niche ritual for commemorating failed marriages." Participants report finding comfort and closure from the formal ceremony. The popularity of this ritual has led to the creation of a new career path in Japan: the divorce planner. Rituals are scheduled on days considered too unlucky for weddings. Representing extended family and friends of each former spouse, anywhere from 30 to 50 guests may attend and partake of a buffet meal. However, some couples choose the most private of ceremonies. One ritual had only one guest and was held in an abandoned house called by the divorce planner "his House of Divorce." With no power, no plumbing, peeling paint, and sagging timbers, "It is a building which represents a husband and wife's relationship—about to collapse."

The divorce ceremony is not the legal end to a marriage, but instead is seen as the beginning of the healing process after the legal work (involving petitions, lawyers, judges, and courts) is done. According to Hiroki Terai, a divorce planner based in Tokyo, the earthquake and tidal wave of 2012 caused people to reassess their priorities. Since those natural disasters, more than 200 couples a month have sought his services.

Couples often make speeches, promising to continue to raise their children well and to attempt to remain friends. A ritual within the ritual may involve husband and wife taking a hammer and smashing his wedding ring together, then sending it in a container out to sea. This ritual is beginning to fill a void felt by many people who believe that ending a marriage deserves a respectful and formal acknowledgment.

Theatre versus Ritual?

The Future Generations Ride, the *Quinceañera*, and the Japanese divorce ceremony all have the basic elements of theatre: performers and audience, costumes and props, and a definite progression from a beginning to a symbolic final curtain. Most important, lives are touched by the event.

Because of the profound connection between ritual and theatre, the question inevitably arises, "What is the difference?" When is one not the other? While there is some disagreement among theatre practitioners, our bias is in favor of not quibbling. We would say that it is possible to argue that a ritual is not theatre if it is private or unobserved (no audience), if the participants remain entirely themselves with no hint of dressing up or role playing (no actors), and if the ritual act is functional, utilitarian, or both, rather than narrative (no story). We would say theatre may not be a ritual if it is a single, one-time-only event, particularly if presented with largely improvisational elements. Repetition of the kind that occurs in rehearsals

Erich Schlegel / Dallas Morning News/Corbis News/Corbis

FIGURE 2.9   Native American Tewa Dancers of the North perform the ritual Eagle Dance.

and multiple performances is essential. The one-shot ritual is an oxymoron. The Future Generations Ride will extend its run with new casts. While each young woman will experience her own *Quinceañera* only once, the ritual, with many of the same participants shifting roles, will occur over and over again within the community.

It is often said that theatre is built on illusion, on things not being what they seem. It is also based on an agreement to pretend, to choose to see or not see, which we will now discuss.

Conventions

In each piece of live theatre, we are asked to accept theatrical *conventions*, which are conditions of make-believe that demand our willing suspension of disbelief. Some conventions are so familiar to us that we don't even notice them. We often use the term **realism** to describe a play in which people act much the way we do in life and *style* or **stylization** for those in which they do not. In a modern realistic play, presented in a traditional theatre space, the setting, the performances by the actors, and the way the story unfolds might seem very like our own everyday experiences. But the most realistic performance is still subject to conventions. We may look through an opening called a **proscenium arch**, the frame (much like a picture frame) that defines the acting space. The space within that arch is called the **fourth wall**, which has been left open so we can peek through it. We act as if this fourth wall has magically opened for us or that we are flies on that wall. In either case, we pretend that the wall is there and that we are not.

CLOSE-UP

Speech as a Second Language—Darren Fudenske on Broadway

Sign language is in itself a convention, with visual signals substituting for auditory ones. When American Sign Language (ASL) is employed by a company of deaf actors, audiences readily accept the convention of using their eyes to "hear." But when a deaf actor speaks, the convention is broken. This is an issue of some controversy within the deaf theatrical community, many of whom feel that it is not just broken but violated.

In 2006, Darren Fudenske, a deaf actor, was cast as Tilden in the Nicu's Spoon Theater Company's production of *Buried Child,* by Sam Shepard. In this case, the production team made the decision that if Tilden were born deaf, the family would not insist that he be educated in sign language, and they would never learn it themselves. The family would just force him to speak as best he could. This family is beyond dysfunctional, with dark secrets including incest, alcoholism, murder, and, of course, the ominous implication of the title. No accommodation is made for any family member—ever. According to director Stephanie Barton-Farcas, "This choice underlies the family's state of denial. No one here would speak ASL. There was no deaf community for Tilden." But not everyone was happy about casting a deaf actor in a role that required him to speak.

For decades, opinion has been divided sharply between those who believe in *manualism*, or the teaching of sign language as the primary means of communication, and *oralism*, or teaching spoken-language skills through speech production and lip-reading. According to New York Deaf Theatre board member Dave Bowell, "There are many people who feel that all deaf people should embrace and use ASL in every facet of their lives. Many nondeaf people do not believe deaf people should speak at all. But many deaf people also feel that way."

Darren Fudenske saw being cast in this role as a chance to move beyond the confines of signed productions, with such theatres as the National Theatre of the Deaf and Deaf West, or traditional productions where he would always play a character written deaf.

For this role, it was a challenge for him to improve his enunciation so other cast members and the audience could understand him, as well as for him to lip-read in performance so he could understand them, especially if a fellow actor had a moustache. He ended up having to learn the parts of the other actors as well as his own to keep up with cues.

Itai Erdal

FIGURE 2.10 Darren Fudenske, a deaf actor, was considered by some a controversial choice to play a deaf role in Sam Shepard's *Buried Child* in the Nicu's Spoon Theater Company production, directed by Stephanie Barton-Farcas, 2006.

Because only a few performances of the play were scheduled to be ASL-interpreted, some of his compatriots felt the excitement of the Broadway debut of a fellow deaf actor was diminished by their not being able to understand or follow the production.

It will be interesting to see how this issue plays out in future productions. Jim Williams, with whom Fudenske had most of his scenes, made a constant effort to keep his moustache trimmed. Fudenske says, "I have to keep working to make myself understood without hands. I am so used to using my hands. I love to use my hands. That's my first language. But at the same time I'm an actor, so I have to separate the two and learn to speak."

Since *Buried Child,* Fudenske has continued work as an actor, writer, and director with Nicu's Spoon, The New York Deaf Theatre, Clubbed Thumb Theatre, the TV show *Rescue Me*, and the comedy troupe Funny Zero, of which he is a founding member.

Along with other members of the New York deaf theatrical community, he was involved in an active protest when, in a recent production, a hearing actor was cast in a deaf role.

On stage, everything represents something else. Iced tea may stand in for bourbon, a blinding light for God, a specific hand gesture for love, a sharp light and sound change for a character's emotional distress, a wild dance for a character's ecstatic inner thoughts, or ketchup for blood. Blood may also be a red ribbon suddenly revealed, a scarlet sheet dropping over a victim, or a wash of crimson light on the back wall. We accept these symbols.

The more unfamiliar the style of a play, the more we are asked to say yes to new conventions. The actors are playing "dress up and let's pretend," and we are joining in the "let's pretend" part. In less realistic plays, we accept the convention that the actors may ignore us for much of the evening and then occasionally turn to us and comment (called **asides**) or speak their thoughts aloud with no one else on stage able to hear them (called **soliloquies**). In some plays, we accept a constant interweave of actors speaking directly to the audience, acknowledging our presence for a time, and then going into intimate, private scenes where they ignore us. And we have no problem being there and then not being there. In theatres around the globe, audiences readily pretend that masks are faces, men are women, extravagantly bewigged and painted actors are animals, precise synchronicity among many actors is natural, percussive instruments are the human heart beating, and mortals are gods.

Photostage

FIGURE 2.11   One widely accepted convention is the fourth wall, which allows the audience to observe the scene without being acknowledged by the actors. The set of *Noises Off* by Michael Frayn, shown here at the Birmingham Repertory Theatre in England, is a good example.

JM11 WENN Photos/Newscom

FIGURE 2.12 Musical theatre audiences will accept strange conventions. After all, how often do people spontaneously break into song and dance in real life, a commonplace occurrence in musicals like this production of *The Book of Mormon* at the Eugene O'Neill Theatre.

If conventions of other cultures are challenging to us, we need to remember that our own theatre can be as strange as any in the world. Musicals are widely believed to have originated in the United States, and yet musical theatre is a feast of outrageous conditions of belief that is readily accepted by the audience. When we go to a madcap musical, we agree to pretend, for example, that it is perfectly normal to wear tap shoes and even sequins to the office and to totally color-coordinate your shiny outfit with that of all your coworkers, and that the most reasonable behavior in the world, when someone says, "I've got an idea!!" is for everyone in the office to lean way into him suddenly and shout in unison "What???" We accept that his idea (perhaps for improving sales for the company) will naturally be expressed in song.

If his idea goes over, the whole office staff will of course join in that song and naturally start dancing on the desks and file cabinets to express their joy and relief at the brilliance of the plan. As an audience member, you agree to pretend that this is reasonable behavior, even though you would (and should) have serious second thoughts about trying it in your own workplace. In subsequent chapters, we explore a variety of conventions from different cultures and time periods.

THEATRE IN MEDIA

Conventions of Film and Television

The range and power of the conventions we accept from media are growing at a phenomenal rate. Many films are now available in 3-D, adding a layer of visual "reality" to the experience. In both film and television, we pretend that life has a musical underscore that swells up to stir our emotions. We pretend that everyday people played by our favorite superstars can naturally wear the hottest designer clothes to their minimum-wage job and rent a huge Manhattan or Parisian apartment without any predictable, constant source of income.

We adjust our sense of reality to serve our desire to be swept away, at least temporarily. Have you noticed the haircut transformation phenomenon? In almost any film, if a character decides to change her hair, she or a friend will just cut randomly away, perhaps with kitchen shears, and the result is always fabulous. Has anyone ever had this experience in life?

The many media technical developments can seem to bypass live theatre through sheer extravagance. While some stories are better told in media venues, that doesn't mean that live theatre is "less than." Rather, its conventions lend themselves to stories that are visceral, intimate, and magical in their own peculiar ways. And as a critic recently pointed out, live theatre is always in 3-D.

THEATRE IN YOUR LIFE

Conventions of Daily Life

What about personal theatre? How often have you laughed politely at what was supposed to be a funny story or joke, but you just didn't get it, or you got it but found it lame? How often have you and a whole roomful of people done this? We accept the convention of responding as we *ought* to rather than as we want to. And you may live with family conventions that dictate how you are expected to respond to any news. In some families, only polite reserve is acceptable, while in others, unbridled, gushy enthusiasm or confrontation is the norm.

We usually adjust to our space being invaded and pretend it's okay. When on a crowded elevator, with personal space at a premium, a common choice is to pretend that the other people aren't there, avoiding any kind of eye contact to compensate for the fact that some stranger may actually be pressed physically against our privates. The art of public privacy is highly developed in parts of China, where masses of people push together when a scarce commodity like transportation becomes available. The more crowded the space, the more intense the rules of make-believe. When someone says or does something reprehensible in the grocery store, the most common choice is to pretend that it did not happen and hope the offender will just go away. This may go on for some time as the offensive behavior escalates. Finally, someone's patience vanishes, at which point the convention is dropped and confrontation occurs.

The conventions of daily life are as many and varied as those in a theatrical production. We all pretend so we can make life better. If it is disappointing, we pretend to make it bearable; if it is good but not great, we do what we can to convince ourselves that it is full of magic, passion, and wonder.

SUMMARY

For years, the origins of theatre were believed to be a distinctly Western, male, literary phenomenon. Now scholars are looking to other cultures, the contributions of both sexes, and oral traditions to find universal impulses that lead and have always led to theatre everywhere. Four major theories of how theatre began include (1) spontaneous inspiration, the acting out of the day's events to make them come alive again; (2) imitation to ritual, the impulse of children acting like adults evolving into repeated acts and expanding beyond the home to embrace the community in an act of communion; (3) stepping out, the practice of someone taking part in a group activity, emerging from that group one day, and turning a choral monologue into a dialogue where ideas are not merely expressed but also exchanged and a character emerges; and (4) divine gift, the idea of accepting magic, trance, and communion with inanimate objects as a reality far beyond ordinary life. Theatre grows out of an intense desire for ritual in all aspects of our lives, from the mundane daily comforts to life-changing ceremonies. In performance, something always represents, stands in for, or symbolizes something else. Performance is defined by ritual conventions, which are the rules by which we all play make-believe at the theatre and in everyday encounters.

SUGGESTED ASSIGNMENTS

For reflection, short writings, and discussion:

1. How do the image of the deity being addressed and the specific requests being made alter between the English King James version of the Lord's Prayer and a more direct translation from Aramaic? What shifts in values appear to have occurred?

2. What are the most crucial rituals in your life, the ones you could not possibly live without?

3. Now that you're learning more about how theatre started and starts, what was the biggest misconception you brought into this course? How is actual theatre most unlike what you expected?

4. What was the most memorable moment in your life when you found that your ritual choices were not those that very many other people make? What was your response?

5. What is your strongest superstition, and how does this influence your behavior? How does this become a ritual? Are any of these rituals done with observers? How do they then become theatre?

6. In your personal theatre, what is the most consistent performance you give? Where are you most in the pretend mode?

7. In your own public life, where do you have the largest set of conventions? At what kind of occasion or group gathering is there the most agreement about what is real and what we are going to pretend is real for this event?

8. Does your family have any rituals that are unique? When did you discover this, and how did you react?

9. As a child, when you role-played based on TV shows or movies, what were your most popular choices?

10. How did you take the basic details of the shows that you listed in Question 9 and embellish them into fantasy?

SUGGESTED ACTIVITIES

1. **Individual**: Go back and look over the list of childhood game enactments shown earlier in this chapter. Make your own list of what you acted out most often.

2. **Group**: In groups of five, agree on a role-playing childhood event that several of you took part in earlier in life. Take 10 minutes to cast the roles, play out the event, and present it as closely as possible to your best memory of how you did it back then.

3. **Long-term**: Start a ritual journal, with sections such as private, public, theatrical, ceremonial, and communal. Observe and record the degree to which ritual is a crucial part of life.

4. **Large lecture**: Identify and perhaps even change a ritual annoyance in your community. Find a ritual that the class can identify with, such as standing in line at the registrar's office or dealing with nasty roommates. Figure out together what your specific goal is and what is blocking you from that goal. Get four or five volunteers to act out the usual response. Is it passive or self-defeating? Have the whole class shout out alternative approaches. Act them out to discover the results. Continue until a truly viable alternative is found. If you have an idea, join the volunteers. Work as a community to solve a problem. (This exercise is adapted from the works of Augusto Boal, who is featured in Chapter 11.)

KEY WORDS AND IDEAS

Abydos Passion Play
oral tradition
miko (Uzume's Trance)
dialogue
griot/griotte (Ogun's Mysteries)
hero
myth
Aristotle (*The Poetics*)
dithyramb
monologue
thespian

Bharata
Natya Shastra
gesture
ritual
conventions:
   realism
   stylization
   proscenium arch
   fourth wall
   asides
   soliloquies

Love

Featured plays:

Much Ado About Nothing by William Shakespeare (1598)

M. Butterfly by David Henry Hwang (1988)

(NOTE: The scripts for these plays, along with additional background information, are available in the companion anthology to this text, *Life Themes: An Anthology of Plays for the Theatre.*)

Love. It makes the world go 'round and it's never easy. It may be intoxicating and enthralling, but most of us live out the old adage, "The course of true love never did run smooth." Some of us do not dance and twirl toward love. We stumble and limp. *Much Ado About Nothing,* one of Shakespeare's most delightful and popular plays, explores not just the joy but the agony, not just the rewards but the risks of falling in love. Although over 400 years old, it is strikingly contemporary in its portrayal of how our defenses and neuroses can prevent us from openly connecting from the heart. *M. Butterfly* also explores the complexities and unexpected turns of love. Because a man falls into a deeply intimate relationship with another man (masquerading as a female Beijing Opera singer) and never realizes it for many years, a masterful deception occurs. To what degree do all of us agree to be deceived for love?

Much Ado About Nothing (1598)

Setting: Messina, a seaport town in Sicily

Major Characters:
Benedick, a lord of Padua, in a battle of wits with Beatrice
Beatrice, niece to Leonato, in verbal combat with Benedick
Don Pedro, Prince of Aragon, recently victorious over his brother in battle
Don John, his bastard brother, looking for vengeance
Claudio, a lord of Florence, in love with Hero
Leonato, governor of Messina, host to all the visiting soldiers above
Hero, daughter to Leonato, in love with Claudio

In this romantic comedy, every kind of love goes awry— that between brothers, friends, colleagues, and parents and children, but most of all, lovers. Why? Because characters succumb to lying and spying. They are constantly overhearing others, believing slander, jumping to conclusions, and making a fuss over imagined facts with nothing to support them. Elizabethans pronounced "nothing" very much like "noting," a word they used for "paying attention" (as in "note me"), so the title's pun envelops both our capacity to fail to note and our willingness to react to nothing.

FIGURE D1.1   In the end, Benedick and Beatrice, portrayed here by Jimmy Smits and Kristen Johnson, admit their love for one another, but they're still "too wise to woo peaceably." *Much Ado About Nothing,* directed by David Esbjornson at New York's Public Theater, 2004.

Michal Daniel

Much Ado also satirizes the ridiculous extremes of chivalric love to which many of Shakespeare's contemporaries succumbed. Elaborate rituals of poetic courtship prevailed, many of them a lot of fancy nothings in which suitors, caught up in the act, failed to really note the object of their affection. Unlike Shakespeare's other romantic comedies, which are heavy on verse (with its strict rhythmic structure and elevated language), this one is nearly 80 percent prose; therefore, it is far more blunt and down to earth. At the center are two of Shakespeare's most famous battling lovers, who have been waging a war of words for years. At one point, he says to her, "*Thou and I are too wise to woo peaceably.*" They are the first in a long line of "oil and water" partners (eventually perfected onscreen by Spencer Tracy and Katharine Hepburn, among others) who spit and spar until something makes them collapse into love.

The avowed central plotline involves another younger, naive couple, Claudio and Hero, who fall in love without any knowledge (or genuine "noting") of each other. Hero is then falsely accused of being unfaithful, is rashly rejected by Claudio, and only when the truth of her innocence is revealed are they reunited. Their relationship is overshadowed, however, by their more worldly and combative companions.

When they run into each other, these two very strong personalities say things such as:

BEATRICE: I wonder that you will still be talking, Signior Benedick. Nobody marks you.
BENEDICK: What, my dear Lady Disdain! Are you yet living?
BEATRICE: Is it possible disdain should die while she hath such food to feed it as Signior Benedick? Courtesy itself must convert to disdain, if you come in her presence.
BENEDICK: Then is courtesy a traitor. But it is certain I am loved of all ladies, only you excepted: and I would that I had not a hard heart; for, truly, I love none.
BEATRICE: A dear happiness to women. I thank God, I am of your humor for that: I had rather hear my dog bark at a crow than a man swear he loves me.
BENEDICK: God keep your ladyship still in that mind! So some gentleman or other shall escape a scratch'd face.
BEATRICE: Scratching could not make it worse, if 'twere such a face as yours.

The way they talk *about* each other is even worse than what they say *to* each other. Here is an example of Beatrice describing Benedick:

He is the prince's jester: a very dull fool; his only gift is in devising impossible slanders: he both amuses men and angers them, and then they laugh at him and beat him.

Benedick in turn describes her thusly:

Every word she speaks stabs: if her breath were as terrible as her words, there were no living near her; she would infect to the North Star. While she is here, a man may live as quiet in hell as in a sanctuary and I would sin on purpose, because I would rather go to hell than endure her!

Only when their friends conspire to trick them by getting Beatrice to overhear her women friends talking about how hopelessly in love with her Benedick is, while Benedick's male friends are playing the same trick on him about her, do they succumb. Then they sound quite different. When they are apart, they say:

BEATRICE: What fire is in mine ears? Can this be true? Stand I condemn'd for pride and scorn so much? Contempt, farewell! and maiden pride, adieu …! And, Benedick, love on; I will requite thee, Taming my wild heart to thy loving hand: If thou dost love, my kindness shall incite thee To bind our loves up in a holy band.
BENEDICK: Love me! Why, it must be requited! I will be horribly in love with her! I may chance have some odd quirks and remnants of wit broken on me, because I have rail'd so long against marriage: but doth not the appetite alter? A man loves the meat in his youth that he cannot endure in his age. The world must be peopled! When I said I would die a bachelor, I did not think I should live till I were married!

And when they are alone together, they have this exchange:

BEATRICE: Will you go with me, Signior?
BENEDICK: I will live in thy heart, die in thy lap, and be buried in thy eyes.

This last tribute from Benedick is one of the most romantic of all time. Elizabethans used the term *die* to mean orgasm, so the sexual implications make the speech even more wholeheartedly and aggressively loving. Their bumpy ride from cynically denying romance to this moment is rough, hilarious, moving, and exhausting. One can easily imagine Beatrice and Benedick, indeed "too wise to woo peaceably," engaging instead in joyous loving combat for the rest of their days.

Here is a combined scene from *Much Ado*, edited and adapted by Robert Barton, excerpted from the companion anthology to this text, *Life Themes: An Anthology of Plays for the Theatre*.

BENEDICK: I do much wonder that one man, seeing how much another man is a fool when he dedicates his behaviours to love, will, after he hath laugh'd at such shallow follies in others, become the source of his own scorn by falling in love: and such a man is Claudio. I have known when there was no music in him but the drum and the fife; and now had he rather hear the lute and the pipe. I have known when he would have walk'd ten miles to see a good armour; and now will he lie ten nights awake, carving the fashion of a new doublet. He was wont to speak plain and to the purpose, like an honest man and a soldier; and now is he turn'd orthography; his words are a very fantastical banquet, just so many strange dishes. May I be so converted? I think not. Love shall never make me such a fool. One woman is fair, yet I am well; another is wise, yet I am well; another virtuous, yet I am well; but till all the graces be in one woman, one woman shall not come in my grace. Rich she shall be, that's certain; wise, or I'll none; virtuous, or I'll never cheapen her; fair, or I'll never look on her; mild or come not near me; noble, of good discourse, an excellent musician, and her hair shall be what colour it please God!

[Enter BEATRICE]

BENEDICK: Lady Beatrice, have you wept all this while?

BEATRICE: Yea, and I will weep a while longer.

BENEDICK: I will not desire that.

BEATRICE: You have no reason; I do it freely.

BENEDICK: Surely I do believe your fair cousin is wrong'd.

BEATRICE: Ah, how much might the man deserve of me that would right her!

BENEDICK: Is there any way to show such friendship?

BEATRICE: A very even way, but no such friend.

BENEDICK: May a man do it?

BEATRICE: It is a man's office, but not yours.

BENEDICK: I do love nothing in the world so well as you: is not that strange?

BEATRICE: As strange as the thing I know not. It were as possible for me to say I loved nothing so well as you: but believe me not; and yet I lie not; I confess nothing, nor I deny nothing. I am sorry for my cousin.

BENEDICK: I protest I love thee.

BEATRICE: Why, then, God forgive me!

BENEDICK: What offense, sweet Beatrice?

BEATRICE: You have stay'd me in a happy hour; I was about to protest I loved you.

BENEDICK: And do it with all thy heart.

BEATRICE: I love you with so much of my heart, that none is left to protest.

BENEDICK: Come, bid me do anything for thee.

BEATRICE: Kill Claudio.

BENEDICK: Not for the wide world.

BEATRICE: You kill me to deny it. Farewell.

BENEDICK: Tarry, sweet Beatrice.

BEATRICE: I am gone, though I am here—there is no love in you—nay, I pray you, let me go.

BENEDICK: Beatrice.

BEATRICE: In faith, I will go.

BENEDICK: We will be friends first.

BEATRICE: You dare easier be friends with me than fight with mine enemy.

BENEDICK: Is Claudio thine enemy?

BEATRICE: Is he not approved in the height a villain, that hath slander'd, scorn'd, dishonour'd my kinswoman? O that I were a man! What, bear her in hand until they come to take hands; and then, with public accusation, uncover'd slander, unmitigated rancor—O God, that I were a man! I would eat his heart in the market place.

BENEDICK: Hear me, Beatrice—

BEATRICE: Talk with a man out at a window! A proper saying!

BENEDICK: Nay, but, Beatrice—

BEATRICE: Sweet Hero! — she is wrong'd, she is slander'd, she is undone.

BENEDICK: Beatr—

BEATRICE: Princes and counties! O that I were a man for her sake! Or that I had any friend would be a man for my sake! But manhood is melted into curtsies, valour into compliment, and men are only turn'd into tongues. I cannot be a man with wishing; therefore I will die a woman with grieving.

BENEDICK: Tarry, good Beatrice. By this hand, I love thee.

BEATRICE: Use it for my love some other way than swearing by it.

BENEDICK: Think you in your soul the Count Claudio hath wrong'd Hero?

BEATRICE: Yea, as sure as I have a thought or a soul.

BENEDICK: Enough. I am engaged; I will challenge him. I will kiss your hand, and so I leave you. By this hand, Claudio shall render me a dear account. As you hear of me, so think of me. Go, comfort your cousin: I must say she is dead. And so, farewell.

[Exeunt]

M. Butterfly (1988)

Much darker than Shakespeare's vision, though similarly based on deception, David Henry Hwang's play explores the ways in which we fall in love with our own fantasies rather than a human being.

Setting: A Paris prison in the present and, in flashbacks, the decade 1960–1970 in Beijing and 1966–1987 in Paris

Major Characters:
René Gallimard, a French diplomat in China
Song Liling, a performer in the Beijing Opera and Gallimard's lover

Minor Characters:
Helga, Gallimard's wife
Various friends of Gallimard (Marc/Man #2/Consul Sharpless)
Women Gallimard meets or imagines (Renee/Woman at Party/Girl in Magazine)
Chinese contacts of Song (Comrade Chin/Suzuki/Shu Fang)
Men of authority to Gallimard (M. Toulon/Man #1/Judge)

Hwang was inspired by a factual 1986 newspaper brief, but he chose to use fictional names and details to create his drama. When Gallimard meets Song, he is immediately smitten with "her." Song is deliberately courting him under orders from the government, but Gallimard can only see romantic, passionate fantasies coming true through their affair. While Song spies on him, there is an undeniable and powerful love between them. The play begins in 1988 Paris with Gallimard in his prison cell, reliving the 20 years of happiness he experienced with Song, a performer in the Beijing Opera. Through flashbacks, we go to China during the 1960s and follow their intensifying romance. An intentional plot to get political information out of him dupes Gallimard. He believes Song's many deceptions (including gender) because Song's behavior matches his perfect Asian woman stereotype and he wants badly to be the dominating male lover of his imagination. Their first encounter foreshadows much of what comes later. Song has just performed an aria from *Madama Butterfly:*

GALLIMARD: A beautiful performance.
SONG: Oh, please…. You make me blush. I'm no opera singer at all.
GALLIMARD: I usually don't like *Butterfly.* What I mean is, I've always seen it played by huge women in so much bad makeup.
SONG: Bad makeup is not unique to the West.
GALLIMARD: But, who can believe them?
SONG: And you believe me?
GALLIMARD: Absolutely. You were utterly convincing. It's the first time . . .
SONG: Convincing? As a Japanese woman? The Japanese used hundreds of our people for medical experiments during the war, you know. But I gather such an irony is lost on you.

GALLIMARD: No! I was about to say, it's the first time I've seen the beauty of the story. Of her death. It's a pure sacrifice. He's unworthy, but what can she do? She loves him … so much. It's a very beautiful story.

SONG: Well, yes, to a Westerner.

They embark on a long-term affair. At one point, after he has not visited for some time, Song writes him letters. One ends with a phrase repeated over and over in the play: "*What do you want? I have already given you my shame.*"

Shame becomes an ongoing part of their lives. The affair continues with Song employing age-old techniques of deception and never disrobing during their relations. One day, Gallimard demands to see her naked:

SONG: Well, come. Strip me. Whatever happens, know that you have willed it. Our love, in your hands.
GALLIMARD (*moving away, talking to audience*): Did I not undress her because I knew, somewhere deep down, what I would find? Perhaps happiness is so rare that our mind can turn somersaults to protect it.

They move to Paris, living together for some years before both are arrested and tried for espionage. Only at the trial, when Song removes her clothes, does Gallimard realize that the love of his life is a man. Yet his illusions are so central to his identity, he cannot let them go. By the end of the play, he realizes that he did live a *Madama Butterfly* dream life, but he cast himself in the wrong role. When confronted by the male Song, who is still willing to submit to his desires, he is repulsed:

SONG: I'm disappointed in you, René … You really have so little imagination.

Joan Marcus

FIGURE D1.2 The lovers of David Henry Hwang's *M. Butterfly* live an elaborate illusion. Gallimard (John Lithgow) believes Song (B. D. Wong) is a woman, accepting her extreme modesty because it fits his stereotypical view of Asian women. This Broadway production was directed by John Dexter at the Eugene O'Neill Theater.

GALLIMARD: You … accuse me of too little imagination. You, if anyone should know—I am pure imagination. And in imagination I will remain. Now get out!

[GALLIMARD *bodily removes* SONG *from the stage, taking his kimono.*]

SONG: René! I'll never put on those robes again! You'll be sorry!
GALLIMARD: I'm already sorry! Exactly as sorry … as a Butterfly.

He realizes that he was the dominated one, but even after the humiliation, he is so trapped in his illusions that he still can say:

I've become patron saint of the socially inept! Men like that—they should be scratching at my door, begging to learn my secrets! For I, René Gallimard,

you see, I have known and been loved by … the Perfect Woman.

Gallimard takes his own life exactly as Butterfly does in the opera. The play is a harsh indictment of the Western tendency to draw conclusions about the East without going beyond its mask to explore its mysteries. It is also, first and foremost, a story of passionate love.

Here is a scene from *M. Butterfly* available in *Life Themes:*

Setting: M. GALLIMARD's prison cell. Paris. Present.

[*Lights fade up to reveal* RENÉ GALLIMARD, *65, in a prison cell. He wears a comfortable bathrobe and looks old and tired. The sparsely furnished cell contains a wooden crate upon which sits a hot plate with a kettle and a portable tape recorder.* GALLIMARD *sits on the crate staring at the recorder, a sad smile on his face. Upstage,* SONG, *who appears as a beautiful woman in traditional Chinese garb, dances a traditional piece from the Beijing Opera, surrounded by the percussive clatter of Chinese music. Then, slowly, lights and sound cross-fade; the Chinese opera music dissolves into a Western opera, the "Love Duet" from Puccini's* Madame Butterfly. SONG *continues dancing, now to the Western accompaniment. Though her movements are the same, the difference in music now gives them a balletic quality.* GALLIMARD *rises and turns upstage towards the figure of* SONG, *who dances without acknowledging him.*]

GALLIMARD: Butterfly, Butterfly …

[*He forces himself to turn away, as the image of* SONG *fades out, and talks to us.*]

GALLIMARD: The limits of my cell are as such: four-and-a-half meters by five. There's one window against the far wall; a door, very strong, to protect me from autograph hounds. I'm responsible for the tape recorder, the hot plate, and this charming coffee table. When I want to eat, I'm marched off to the dining room—hot, steaming slop appears on my plate. When I want to sleep, the light bulb turns itself off—the work of fairies. It's an enchanted space I occupy. The French—we know how to run a prison. But, to be honest, I'm not treated like an ordinary prisoner. Why? Because I'm a celebrity. You see, I make people laugh. I never dreamed this day would arrive. I've never been considered witty or clever. In fact, as a young boy, in an informal poll among my grammar school classmates, I was voted "least likely to be invited to a party." It's a title I managed to hold onto for many years. Despite some stiff competition. But now, how the tables turn! Look at me: the life of every social function in Paris. Paris? Why be modest? My fame has spread to Amsterdam, London, New York. Listen to them! In the world's smartest parlors. I'm the one who lifts their spirits!

[With a flourish, GALLIMARD directs our attention to another part of the stage.]

[A party. Present. Lights go up on a chic-looking parlor, where a well-dressed trio, two men and one woman, make conversation. GALLIMARD also remains lit; he observes them from his cell.]

WOMAN: And what of Gallimard?
MAN 1: Gallimard?
MAN 2: Gallimard!
GALLIMARD: [To us] You see? They're all determined to say my name, as if it were some new dance.
WOMAN: He still claims not to believe the truth.
MAN 1: What? Still? Even since the trial?
WOMAN: Yes. Isn't it mad?
MAN 2: [Laughing] He says … it was dark … and she was very modest!

[The trio breaks into laughter.]

MAN 1: So—what? He never touched her with his hands?
MAN 2: Perhaps he did and simply misidentified the equipment. A compelling case for sex education in the schools.
WOMAN: To protect the National Security—the Church can't argue with that.
MAN 1: That's impossible! How could he not know?
MAN 2: Simple ignorance.
MAN 1: For twenty years?
MAN 2: Time flies when you're being stupid.
WOMAN: Well, I thought the French were ladies' men.
MAN 2: It seems Monsieur Gallimard was overly anxious to live up to his national reputation.
WOMAN: Well, he's not very good-looking.
MAN 1: No, he's not.
MAN 2: Certainly not.
WOMAN: Actually, I feel sorry for him.
MAN 2: A toast! To Monsieur Gallimard!

WOMAN: Yes! To Gallimard!
MAN 1: To Gallimard!
MAN 2: Vive la difference!

[They toast, laughing. Lights down on them.]
[GALLIMARD's cell.]

GALLIMARD [smiling]: You see? They toast me. I've become patron saint of the socially inept. Can they really be so foolish? Men like that, they should be scratching at my door, begging to learn my secrets! For I, René Gallimard, you see, I have known, and been loved by … the Perfect Woman. Alone in this cell, I sit night after night, watching our story play through my head, always searching for a new ending, one which redeems my honor, where she returns at last to my arms. And I imagine you—my ideal audience—who come to understand and even, perhaps just a little, to envy me.

[He turns on his tape recorder. Over the house speakers, we hear the opening phrases of Madame Butterfly.]

GALLIMARD: In order for you to understand what I did and why, I must introduce you to my favorite opera: Madame Butterfly. By Giacomo Puccini. First produced at La Scala, Milan, in 1904, it is now beloved throughout the Western world.

[As GALLIMARD describes the opera, the tape segues in and out to sections he may be describing.]

GALLIMARD: And why not? Its heroine, Cio-Cio-San, also known as Butterfly, is a feminine ideal, beautiful and brave. And its hero, the man for whom she gives up everything, is—[He pulls out a naval officer's cap from under his crate, pops it on his head, and struts about]—not very good-looking, not too bright, and pretty much a wimp: Benjamin Franklin Pinkerton of the U.S. Navy. As the curtain rises, he's just closed on two great bargains: one on a house, the other on a woman—call it a package deal.

[MARC, wearing an official cap to designate SHARPLESS, enters and plays the character.]

SHARPLESS/MARC: Pinkerton!
PINKERTON/GALLIMARD: Sharpless! How's it hangin'? It's a great day, just great. Between my house, my

wife, and the rickshaw ride in from town, I've saved nineteen cents just this morning.

SHARPLESS: Wonderful. I can see the inscription on your tombstone already: "I saved a dollar, here I lie." *[He looks around.]* Nice house.

PINKERTON: It's artistic. Artistic, don't you think? Like the way the shoji screens slide open to reveal the wet bar and disco mirror ball? Classy, huh? Great for impressing the chicks.

SHARPLESS: "Chicks"? Pinkerton, you're going to be a married man!

PINKERTON: Well, sort of.

SHARPLESS: What do you mean?

PINKERTON: This country—Sharpless, it is okay. You got all these geisha girls running around—

SHARPLESS: I know! I live here!

PINKERTON: Then, you know the marriage laws, right? I split for one month, it's annulled!

SHARPLESS: Leave it to you to read the fine print. Who's the lucky girl?

PINKERTON: Cio-Cio-San. Her friends call her Butterfly. Sharpless, she eats out of my hand!

SHARPLESS: She's probably very hungry.

PINKERTON: Not like American girls. It's true what they say about Oriental girls. They want to be treated bad!

SHARPLESS: Oh, please!

PINKERTON: It's true!

SHARPLESS: Are you serious about this girl?

PINKERTON: I'm marrying her, aren't I?

SHARPLESS: Yes—with generous trade-in terms.

PINKERTON: When I leave, she'll know what it's like to have loved a real man. And I'll even buy her a few nylons.

SHARPLESS: You aren't planning to take her with you?

PINKERTON: Huh? Where?

SHARPLESS: Home!

PINKERTON: You mean, America? Are you crazy? Can you see her trying to buy rice in St. Louis?

SHARPLESS: So, you're not serious.

[Pause.]

PINKERTON/GALLIMARD *[As PINKERTON]*: Consul, I am a sailor in port. *[As GALLIMARD]* They then proceed to sing the famous duet, "The Whole World Over."

[The duet plays on the speakers. GALLIMARD, as PINKERTON, lip-syncs his lines from the opera.]

GALLIMARD: To give a rough translation: "The whole world over, the Yankee travels, casting his anchor wherever he wants. Life's not worth living unless he can win the hearts of the fairest maidens, then hotfoot it off the premises ASAP." *[He turns towards MARC.]* In the preceding scene, I played Pinkerton, the womanizing cad, and my friend Marc from school ... *[MARC bows grandly for our benefit]* played Sharpless, the sensitive soul of reason. In life, however, our positions were usually—no, always—reversed.

Here are examples that expand ideas from the past two chapters. If you were to attend productions of *Much Ado* or *M. Butterfly*, we cannot determine what you may experience. However, we *can* offer observations and predictions based on the scripts and production traditions.

Familiarity

You already know the parameters of both plays from these synopses. You have a basic idea of the plot and can appreciate how the show may develop similarly to or differently from what you anticipated. It would be fun to debate and predict with a friend what the production will be like and see who comes closer.

Story

Beyond the facts and arcs described previously, *Much Ado* is straightforward, and most questions are answered to our satisfaction at the end. *M. Butterfly* leaves certain offstage actions and some of Song's motives a mystery.

Conflict

Both plays deal with the conflict between truth and illusion and between stubbornness and sensitivity. Beatrice and Benedick use conflict as a way of communicating; in fact, they use it as a way of entertaining themselves. Until their last encounter, Gallimard and Song avoid conflict at all costs.

Emotional Mode

Much Ado is largely a rollicking comedy until the exposure of Hero, at which point there is a stretch of dark, *very* serious scenes until all is again released into buoyant comic energy. *M. Butterfly* remains consistently dramatic, intriguing, and thought-provoking with no real comic relief. It probably does not reach traditional tragic levels because Gallimard never has the greatness needed for his downfall to feel profound.

The World of the Play

- **Time:** *Much Ado* is timeless and not tied to any specific historical event. The action takes place in linear fashion over about two weeks. *M. Butterfly*'s narrative takes place in the "present" (1988) with flashbacks over the preceding 20-odd years. While one play was written over 400 years before the other, there is not a sense of a classical versus a modern perspective. In fact, the central characters in the older play support breaking old customs, while those in the newer one cling to them.

- **Space:** Both are set in relatively exotic locales, but productions usually make little effort to represent these through scenic detail. Both are often performed on a large unit set, perhaps with ramps and platforms and lighting being the primary means of suggesting a change in locale. *Much Ado*'s action takes place within (at most) a few acres in Sicily, while *M. Butterfly* veers between multiple Chinese and French locations, so one play feels contained/local and the other expansive/global.

- **Values:** Both plays support our collective beliefs that love is tough but worth it and that lies of all kinds often lead to disaster. *M. Butterfly* challenges the widespread Western belief that we know what is right for other people even when we do not really know them (although we may think we do).

- **Structure:** In both worlds, women are not allowed to be aggressive in demanding their rights. Even someone as strong as Beatrice must ask Benedick to revenge Hero's wrongs. For this reason, *Much Ado*, while presented in many time periods, is rarely set before the widespread impact of feminism.

- **Pleasure:** A great love of beauty permeates both worlds. In *Much Ado*, the greatest pleasure is repartee, the well-turned phrase and brilliant retort. Forthright, bawdy sexual references abound. *M. Butterfly* remains more delicate and elusive, with sex as an art and nakedness in any form is too much. Beatrice and Song represent almost polar opposites in terms of the ideal woman.

- **Senses:** Both plays are likely to be sumptuously produced, with beautiful costumes, music, and striking visuals throughout. Both are likely to make you feel that you have taken a sensual journey with unfamiliar textures, patterns, and delights.

Conclusions

Both writers, while having compassion for those who succumb to deception, present strong arguments in favor of straightforward truth and relationships based on candor rather than denial. Each central love affair is unconventional and, for better or worse, original.

We share some other thoughts related to the past two chapters.

Ritual and Convention

Beatrice and Benedick mock blind, elaborate courtship rituals in favor of confrontation and disclosure. They have probably invented a whole new fight/flirt ritual code of their own. Gallimard believes that he loves Eastern ritual, but he never fully comprehends the culture that so enamors him. Beijing Opera performers live by tradition and illusion and are sustained through ritual. In *Much Ado,* as in all Shakespeare, multiple characters sometimes speak directly to the audience (asides); while in *M. Butterfly,* only when Gallimard is in present-tense narrator mode does this occur (breaking the fourth wall).

Translation

Some consider Shakespeare's language difficult and dense, almost like a foreign language and hard to interpret. Fortunately, this may be his most easily comprehensible play in terms of both words and contemporary values. *M. Butterfly* focuses on the elusive challenge of translating levels of meaning between cultures; in a way, it is *about* a failure of translation.

Stage to Screen

Both plays have been filmed, and both had film versions that were released in 1993. Kenneth Branagh's *Much Ado About Nothing* was a critical and popular success. The script was cut down to well under two hours, adapted to make the language even easier to understand, had a glorious setting and rousing music, and was acted with gusto. (Even though Keanu Reeves was in the cast, he did not have very many lines.) The cinematic *M. Butterfly* was far less successful and panned by several critics, with many citing this movie as probably the weakest film David Cronenberg had directed to date. This was due in part to a bizarre rethinking of the ending, in which Gallimard (Jeremy Irons), in full, grotesque quasi-geisha drag, takes his life in front of hundreds of other prison inmates. Critics also almost universally pointed out that the actor playing Song (John Lone) had a distractingly large bone structure and strong male features, making the onscreen deception unconvincing. A work so strongly invested in illusion may have been doomed from the start from the scrutiny of the camera and the tyranny of the close-up.

DAVID HENRY HWANG
PLAYWRIGHT

I wrote this play as a plea to all sides to cut through our respective layers of cultural and sexual misperception, to deal with one another truthfully for our mutual good, from the common and equal ground we share as human beings.

In this scene from the 2013 West End production of *The Audience,* Margaret Thatcher (Hadyn Gwynne) curtsies before Queen Elizabeth II (Helen Mirren).

part II

Who Does Theatre?

In Chapter 3, we will demonstrate how plays evolved out of oral storytelling tradition and describe the qualities of good plays and ways to analyze them for deeper understanding.

In Chapter 4, we will examine the actor, how acting evolved in the East and West, and the ways in which different actors work. Then we will discuss the role of the director, how it has developed over time, what it entails, influential figures who brought about changes, and ways that actors and directors collaborate.

In Dramatic Interlude 2, we will show how two very different plays—*Arms and the Man* by George Bernard Shaw and *9 Parts of Desire* by Heather Raffo—consider war.

In Expansion 2, we will examine the mood and dramatic structure of both plays, as well as ways in which they might be cast, rehearsed, and performed, applying the principles of Chapter 3 and Chapter 4.

In Chapter 5, we will explore the physical aspects of production, focusing on the work of the designers, including spaces in which theatre occurs and how these spaces are shaped and altered by set, costume, makeup, mask, lighting, and sound design efforts.

In Chapter 6, we will identify the remaining members of a show's team, including the roles of producers, artistic and managing directors, dramaturges, various rehearsal and technical specialists, as well as all those who run the show and promote it to the public.

In Dramatic Interlude 3, we will explore the communication/conflict between generations over vast periods of time and cultures, as reflected in Shakespeare's *King Lear* and Milcha Sanchez-Scott's *Roosters*.

In Expansion 3, we will apply information from Chapter 5 and Chapter 6 to identify the challenges facing all the designers and staff members for productions of these two plays.

The chart below indicates the usual hierarchy within university and professional theatres in the West.

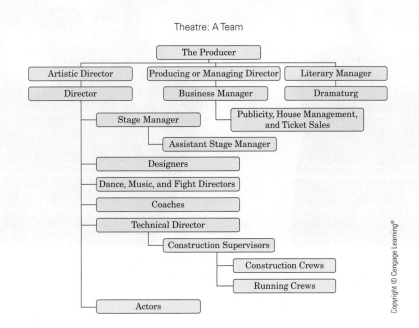

Theatre: A Team

chapter 3

STORYTELLERS AND STORIES

(Left to right) Playwright and V-Day founder Eve Ensler, actor Meryl Streep, and Revolutionary Association of the Women of Afghanistan member Sahar Saba, during a press conference that was part of the Afghan women's summit presenting a proclamation for reconstruction of Afghanistan to the U.N. Security Council.

Keeping the old ways alive: *Griots*, traditional
singer/storytellers, Mali, Africa 2004.

Bruno Morandi/Robert Harding World Imagery/Corbis

Lesson Objectives:

Upon completion of this chapter, you will
be able to:

1. Identify different types of oral
   storytellers.
2. Identify the elements that compose a
   "good play."
3. Explore ideas that might inspire you
   to try playwriting.
4. Analyze plays using dramatic
   structure and character analysis as
   tools.
5. Articulate, in written or verbal form,
   what the playwright is trying to
   accomplish.

Introduction

One of the most powerful human impulses is to tell stories: from our own lives, the lives of others who have touched us in some way, or simply from our imagination. Skilled storytellers are honored in any culture. In this chapter, we will look at the people who create theatrical stories in Africa, Asia, Europe, and the Americas; examine differences between oral and written traditions; and provide methods for analyzing plays in all forms.

Griots/Griottes, Sutradharas, and Bards

The first authors of plays in every culture were masters of oral tradition. In Africa, this tradition continues today as a primary means of communicating stories of the people. Storytellers there are often called ***griots/griottes***

MICHAEL MCCARTY

CONTEMPORARY *GRIOT*

I fight every moment for my place. Because everyone is a storyteller. If I don't get the people's approval and attention, they'll just take the story over.

(or "praise singers"; also see Chapter 2), and they are legendary for their musical skill, dramatic intensity, and endurance. One famous oral narrative from West Africa, called *Ozidi*, is an epic tale of the communal history of the region's people. *Ozidi*, or parts of it, is still used as a foundation for some emerging new theatre in Africa. *Griots* who tackle *Ozidi* must be true masters of their art: it lasts a full 24 hours, and the *griot* plays all the parts.

Most past performers of the oral tradition needed to master the arts of music and dance as well as characterization and narration. In China, Buddhist monks spread the teachings (the *Sutra)* of the

FIGURE 3.1 The village of Kela was offered to the *griots* during the foundation of the Mali Empire in the thirteenth century. Today, the *griots* maintain the living memory of the whole history of Mali through oral tradition.

Sebastien Cailleux/Corbis

FIGURE 3.2 Sutradhara (narrator/director) in a performance of Sanskrit drama.

Lindsay Hebberd/Documentary Value/Corbis

Buddha through memorized song. Later, secular artists added verses, dance, movement, and more songs influenced by contact with Indian and central Asian Sanskrit dance/drama. These narrators are sometimes called *sutradharas* (or "string pullers," from the tradition of puppetry, because the narrator also "pulls the strings" of the story and sometimes guides or manipulates other performers). Not only did the *sutradharas* have to memorize long, intricate texts, but they also had to interpret the work for audiences who did not know Sanskrit as a language but could appreciate the beauty of its sounds. The *sutradhara* was also required to play at least one musical instrument and to guide the dancer/actors into correct visual presentation of their work.

In numerous ancient cultures, including those in Europe and the Middle East, the presence of a **bard** was an essential part of existence. Often associated with the ruling family, the bard was expected to capture the events and stir the emotions of the people, just as Ook did with his recounting the story of the lion (as discussed in Chapter 2). Working with a single musical instrument, playing male and female characters, and sometimes employing song, chants, and narrative poetic forms, the bard helped to inspire and excite the people for an upcoming battle or long journey. At the end of a difficult or significant event, after an evening's meal, the bard would put what had happened in perspective and shape it into meaning through theatrical means. For many, it was as if the events were not finalized until the bard captured them.

Each of these storytellers could function as creator, memorizer, entertainer, and communal historian. Some twentieth-century recordings have

Bridgeman-Giraudon / Art Resource, NY

FIGURE 3.3   A bard before a royal couple in thirteenth-century Spain.

captured the artistry of oral performers. While not being live causes them to lose something in translation, the recordings nevertheless reveal multidimensional performance skills and give us a glimpse into the selection and training of oral storytelling masters.

In Europe, after the fall of the Roman Empire, our best guess is that professional actors and entertainers, having been banished from Rome, spread out across the wilderness that was Europe and made their way beyond the reach of Catholic Rome. If they were lucky, they found patrons to protect and nourish them and became vassals of their liege lords. Displeasing your lordship was a risky business, and many of our most beloved stories, plays, and films are romanticized versions of events created by bards in honor of their chieftains/lords. Training was by apprenticeship, and it is likely that minstrelsy or court performing ran in families as other trades did. Perhaps the best-known use of the term *bard* is in reference to England's beloved William Shakespeare. Even today, he is sometimes referred to as "the Bard of Avon" or simply "The Bard."

In Africa, the *griot/griotte* was trained by the elder storytellers, and selection was based on both suitability and a sacred spiritual calling. Habibu Selemani, a master of the art in Tanzania, died in 1993, leaving no trained survivors to carry on his work. He had learned the art by watching his masters from the time he was five until he started performing himself at age 14. His passage without a successor is felt as a great loss in his culture even though he left many performances captured on audiotape. Some of the stories have survived, but no one now knows everything he remembered, including his mastery of the music, movement, impersonation, and character. One of his eulogists declared that the *griot* tradition is dying out in postcolonial Africa, but others believe that it may simply be changing. Contemporary playwright Ngugi wa Thiong'o of Kenya, for example, has been imprisoned for his plays, which are critical of the dictatorial government of Kenya. Today, his plays are being spread across the country by *griots* and *griottes* who enter a town, recite the script, shape the performance elements, and then slip away to avoid arrest and prosecution.

In India, young girls were dedicated to religious communities where they were raised and initiated by the priestesses into the mysteries of dance/drama. Through exhausting repetition, these girls learned each tiny gesture and sound until perfection was achieved. Into the twentieth century, in some Asian cultures, the tradition of adopting very young children into a sacred or theatrical house continued, sometimes with painful and cruel deprivation as part of the training. In ancient Persian and Arab cultures, female bards were considered essential to the well-being of the empire and of individual clans.

CLOSE-UP

Mark Lewis—Contemporary Storyteller

While Mark Lewis rarely performs around a campfire, in most ways he practices this ancient profession just as the earliest tellers of tales did. He performs in meeting places: community centers, churches, schools, restaurants, parks, and family rooms. He does not use props and rarely appears on a stage. When he does, he demands that all the houselights be turned up, and he is likely to move up and down the aisles, eliminating any distance between actor and audience. The magic is all in the telling. He transforms the space with the power of his ability to challenge the imagination of his listeners.

Mark has won two Emmy awards for his storytelling show *Word Pictures,* has appeared on *The Tonight Show,* and has hypnotized live audiences around the world. When auditioning for traditional roles earlier in his career, he was often told that his performance was too "big." He recognized that the ability to play big is part of the game in storytelling, where it takes a large presence and dynamic choices to captivate an audience. When working Renaissance fairs as an actor, he discovered his current profession. "We performers would gather together at the end of the day and regale each other with tall tales. I realized that this was what I was supposed to do." Mime training and working on character voices and accents (he supplies three of the voices on Disney's "Pirates of the Caribbean" ride) helped, because the storyteller suggests every setting physically, plays all the characters, and needs to create change in an instant.

Can one find sufficient storytelling work living in Eugene, Oregon, a town of 150,000? No, so Mark is frequently on a plane pursuing his motto: *"Carpe per Diem."* While his travels take him far and wide, he primarily works in Los Angeles and, surprisingly, Las Vegas, where some audience members see storytelling as an alternative relative to stand-up comedy. Half of his audiences are children, but a common venue for him is parties for adults where the host has arranged storytelling as the after-dinner entertainment.

Unlike the culture surrounding *griots,* for most of Mark's audiences storytelling is such a rare treat that instead of breaking into the performance, they tend to watch and listen in a state that might start as silent skepticism and then move swiftly to enraptured attention. He employs what he calls "old-wave special effects," often creating astonishing imitations of wind and storms. While he finds audiences who seek most of their entertainment through technology to be increasingly challenging on first contact, once he lures them in, they tend to give themselves up completely. "The most important thing," he says, "is that you have to allow the listeners to make it their own."

The stories may run for just a few minutes, or in the case of some long-form epics, up to an hour and a half. While he writes quite a few himself, his most requested "greatest hits" include "The Highwayman," "Jabberwocky," and "How the Grinch Stole Christmas." For new material, he says, "In my mind there is a house, with a hallway and different rooms. I step into one and the story is all there, characters and details swirling all around me, but in a chaotic way. It is then my job to take what is in the room and create something linear."

FIGURE 3.4   Mark Lewis in performance.

Courtesy, Mark Lewis

NELSON GEORGE

AUTHOR, HIP HOP AMERICA

Hip-hop is all acting. Some are more gangster than others, but it's all about the creation of narrative persona. That's why every rapper uses a fake name. It's an inherently theatrical form.

AUTHOR'S INSIGHT

ROBERT: Observing contemporary storyteller Mark Lewis engage an audience of hundreds of children, I understood firsthand how technology would never supplant this ancient art. He *demanded* that they arouse their imaginations, and once they did, they were all completely enthralled. The reactivation of their (in some cases dormant) creative mind muscles was thrilling and inspiring.

STEVEN SPIELBERG

FILMMAKER

I consider myself first and foremost before anything else to be a storyteller.

AP Photo/Seth Wenig

FIGURE 3.5 Lynn Nottage doing a phone interview after winning a Pulitzer Prize for Drama in 2009 for her play *Ruined*.

Although earliest dramas were developed in the oral tradition, with each culture's stories taught to succeeding generations, the transition to written narrative was inevitable. The balance between written and oral narrative today will vary depending on the traditions of a region or country. Some believe the emergence of rap and hip-hop represent a renaissance of the oral tradition in a new form.

More traditional storytelling has experienced a revival in part due to the National Storytelling Festival in Jonesborough, Tennessee, which attracts 10,000 visitors each fall and features such renowned performers as Emmy-winning contemporary storyteller Mark Lewis. It is a gathering place, not just for those wishing to listen but for those very much committed to keeping the form alive.

In most parts of the world today, some form of playwriting is the starting point for most productions. We will identify key elements of the playwright's work and ways that we can analyze those works to understand them better.

Playwrights

Most productions start with plays, but how do plays start? Some are commissioned, in which case a theatre picks a theme, an occasion, or an issue on which to take a stand and then hires a **playwright** to produce a script. This process begins with those who manage the company itself, so the playwright is second on board.

But far more often the playwright is first, working in isolation, creating something on paper which may or may not end up as theatre magic and which in fact may never be produced. If a theatre company decides to mount a new play, the script can go through a long evolution process, ending with an opening, where critics pass judgment and audiences may flock to the theatre or stay away. The play can close after a single performance or it can run for years.

What about the weird spelling? A "wright" is by definition "a construction worker; a carpenter, mechanic, or manufacturer; a skilled craftsman." Throughout history, there have been boatwrights and also book-, cart-, coach-, gate-, house-, mill-, plow-, ship-, wagon-, and wheelwrights, among others. What does the person who makes plays have in common with these artisans? Another definition is "one who makes or contrives, a deviser or inventor." The playwright is different from the novelist, poet, essayist, short-story writer, biographer, or other literary figures because what is being "wrought" is the first step in a crafting process where these words will not stay on the page for silent reading but will be molded into a living, breathing performance.

The playwright makes a play as the plow-wright makes the plow, crafting ingredients sturdily, readying the product for years of use by others. The playwright shapes words to be spoken by people in costumes and makeup, walking on a stage lit in a particular way, in the presence of other actors, crews, and audiences; in places that the playwright will never visit in any way except through this script. The playwright does not create words to be contemplated exclusively in cozy solitude or the occasional public reading, nor does he create words to be taken in parts at one's leisure and put aside for periods of reflection. The playwright prepares for an event that, once it starts, will proceed with or without intermissions until it is over.

Most writers need to consider only the reader. The playwright needs to consider all participants and elements of theatre as the script evolves. The "wrighter" needs to envision a finished product that will be used, that will in fact *move*, like a boat, a plow, or a wheel. At her desk at home, she needs to hear the words spoken and to see them enacted, projecting forward through

FIGURE 3.6 Playwright Suzan-Lori Parks working with director Michael Greif on *365 Days/365 Plays* at the Public Theatre. From November 2002 to November 2003, Parks wrote one short play a day, resulting in *365 Days/365 Plays*.

collaboration and evolution. Many brilliant writers from other literary backgrounds fail as playwrights. Their words do not leap off the page and across the stage. Their texts have not been built to be used, and used hard, by others.

STEVEN DIETZ

PLAYWRIGHT

There's no fast way to make plays. It takes just as long and is just as hard as it was a thousand years ago.

JOHN PATRICK SHANLEY

PLAYWRIGHT

Theatre is a safe place to do the unsafe things that need to be done.

FELICITY HUFFMAN

ACTOR

If it ain't on the page, it ain't on the stage.

In early theatre models, the playwright (including Kan'ami Kiyotsugu of Japan, Sophocles of Athens, and Shakespeare of England) was often the primary production guide, coaching and cajoling the actors, structuring the event, and steering the play toward its opening. The creator of the script continued to create through the performance. Nowadays, playwrights are often excluded from the final process except when the director needs advice or script changes. So, while they are in some ways the most central figures in the theatrical process, they can also be the ones who feel most outside that process in its final stages. Others may change what they had in mind, shift the emphasis of their words, minimize their themes, and even seem to sabotage their ideas. What they experience on stage may be far from what they envisioned at their laptop or legal pad back home.

A Good Play

It is sometimes difficult to separate a play from its production. Let's examine what constitutes a strong script, which makes for a good story, no matter how it is told.

A successful theatre script must have five essential ingredients:

1. *Action* moves the play forward. A script needs to move. Something important must happen. Sometimes what happens is physical, sometimes psychological. Even in Theatre of the Absurd, a style of theatre in which characters may wait endlessly for something that never happens, it is likely that this is the most compelling *day* in their wait, perhaps the one in which they finally realize that things will never change and they have to deal with it. Plays take place at crucial and *active* life moments.

2. *Suspense* keeps us wondering. In some plays, it has to do with twists and turns of plot. But in many of the great classical plays, the audience knows the entire story, so suspense is about smaller surprises and discoveries, the creative variations that pop up along the journey. A good play keeps us engaged by the possibility that what we think will happen might not.

3. *Believability* makes us accept the world of the play and its inhabitants as enough like us that we recognize their struggles, successes, and failures. No matter how unfamiliar the situation (a well-known Nigerian play features the King of the Cockroaches trapped in a bathtub), we must feel that it is true to its own conventions and experiences. Each person (or

metaphorical being) should be fully realized, whether man, goddess, or cockroach. Many of us can write about people like us, but to write with empathy and truth about those beyond our comfort zone is a true gift.

4. *Fluidity* allows the events of the play to occur smoothly from beginning to end. The playwright considers where actors will enter and exit, where there will be breaks between scenes, where acts will end and intermissions occur. The playwright considers how the evening will shift and turn through various handlings of the text. She must be aware of audience and cultural expectations as to length, tempo, and rhythms in the style of play "wrighting." The best scripts are clear roadmaps for the actor in terms of what is essential to the author's vision and what is open to creative interpretation.

5. *Compression* transforms events into condensed and compelling forms. Because the story needs to unfold publicly over the course of an expected period of time (rarely more than a few hours), the playwright must edit and reduce details to the essential. She needs to consider constantly the mechanics of the theatre and, whenever possible, streamline and make choices that focus our attention on the exact part of the story that is important.

Freedom and Influence

When a new play is being produced, the playwright may be expected to do revisions as the show passes through readings, rehearsals, and even previews. This process can be electrifying and frustrating.

This is, however, the only time the author is obligated daily to meet the scheduling needs of others. For the rest of the process before this, the trade-off for being isolated is that the playwright is the most free of all theatre artists. Unlike the rest of them, she can work when she wants. She can pick the time of day, place, and circumstances, without concern for inconveniencing an army of collaborators. The playwright also has the freedom, if a script gets published, not to be involved in any way with subsequent productions and yet still earn an income. When shows close, most participants' experiences can be put in a single envelope: opening-night notes, congratulatory emails, telegrams, reviews, maybe some pressed flowers, a souvenir program. This huge experience leaves almost no lingering evidence. The only lasting tangible element is the script.

Every other person connected with the show needs to go on to a new job when the play closes. After closing night and strike (the process of tearing down the set), these other participants have only memories. But if the play is successful, it may be published and produced for many years in many places without the playwright even knowing about it except through royalty checks. Just as you

DAVID HENRY HWANG
PLAYWRIGHT

You're under a lot of pressure. If you've spent a year with a play, there's something absurd about rewriting the whole thing in four weeks.

AUGUST WILSON
PLAYWRIGHT

I generally start with an idea, something I want to say, but with The Piano Lesson, I just started writing a line of dialogue and had no idea who was talking . . . at some point I say, "Well, who is this?" and I give him a name. But I usually have no idea what the story line of a play is. It's a process of discovery.

Photostage

FIGURE 3.7 Playwrights' works are often staged without their input—especially when they're dead. Take Shakespeare, for instance. This is a contemporary production of *Hamlet*, with Marty Cruikshank (Gertrude) and Samuel West (Hamlet) at the Royal Shakespeare Company in Stratford-upon-Avon.

are reading this book without the authors having direct contact with you, someone is mounting many playwrights' work without their direct involvement, though their sphere of *influence* continues.

Playwrights also have the power of being listened to. Their ideas are shared, discussed, and passed along. People pay attention and pay to pay attention. They can have profound impact on the thoughts and actions of others. For this reason, we revere our successful playwrights as highly as any artist in the theatre. While the fame of others fades, the playwright has a chance at genuine immortality as scripts live on long after their deaths. Sophocles, Shakespeare, and Zeami Motokiyo (Zeami) are alive again in theatre after theatre and in the pages of this book. Tennessee Williams, Eugene O'Neill, and Thornton Wilder have long ago passed on, but they are at the center of our culture. The more recently deceased Arthur Miller, August Wilson, Wendy Wasserstein, and Augusto Boal have joined them. Living legends like Wole Soyinka of Nigeria, Marie Irene Fornes of Cuba, and Ngugi wa Thiong'o of Kenya are only steps behind. You may not recognize all these names, but you probably recognize some of them, which would be unlikely for other theatre artists, except actors. Playwrights change lives and reinvigorate cultures.

Some claim that the playwright has become less central to the theatrical process as more and more scripts are evolved through improvisation and games or created by entire performance companies instead of a single writer; in addition, texts have sometimes been altered through **deconstruction** (taking the play apart and reinventing it in a particular way) or **problematizing** an isolated issue (making one possibly minor problem in the script major in the production). But these processes and the scripts resulting from them are simply redefining what it means to have "wrought" a play. Even in a work devised through collaborative group play, the entire gang is essentially functioning as collective playwrights. Rather than diminishing the role of the playwright, these theatre groups are sometimes renewing oral and collaborative traditions that long preceded written text.

Getting Started

The oldest and wisest advice in the world is "write what you know." Playwrights need to dig into their own life experiences and imaginations to find what they know that might become electrifying theatre. What you know does not have to be what you have experienced firsthand in an autobiographical sense, but it should be about what you know deep inside so that it may reflect a personal powerful fantasy or an imaginative journey that is as much a part of you as the mundane details of your actual life. It should have happened in your mind and heart. You may just start hearing words in your head.

These possible springboards might be the beginning of a script:

1. A character who fascinates you, real or imagined

2. A family or group whose interaction intrigues you

3. A startling event in the news or the transcript of an actual trial

4. A real or imaginary world or place that seems exotic to the degree that you want to set a story and imagine life there

5. A controversial issue in which you wish to explore various positions and points of view

6. A life-changing event that happened to you or someone close to you

7. A famous person or fictional character whose biography or story intrigues you

8. A brief encounter that you overhear on the street or in a store, which keeps replaying in your head so that you are fascinated enough to create the back story and the rest of this relationship

9. An imaginary encounter between two famous people who probably never met but could have

10. A personal encounter that you wanted to have and never did, but which could happen now as drama

ALAN BENNETT
PLAYWRIGHT

I can't write about any place where I don't understand the social structure as it is expressed through the way people speak. I can write in posh, public school English, but not in American.

Other Writers: Composers and Lyricists

In musical theatre, the play script is traditionally called the *libretto* or *book* and the playwright the *librettist* or *book writer*. While spoken words are important, no one leaves the theatre humming the book. In some musicals, it may be just a way to get from song to song as swiftly as possible. In many parts of the world, the entire play is sung or chanted to musical accompaniment. While all composers conceive music that will be performed by others, the musical-theatre composer, like the playwright, needs to envision and hear (in his head) the collaboration of soloists and chorus and to imagine that what is on paper is being taken to another level by aggressive participation. The lyricist essentially writes poetry to be set to music or to match music already written, with a particularly necessary flair for expressing ideas that rhyme and are revealed through a character, just as Shakespeare has characters suddenly rhyme when they are making a particularly crucial point at the end of a scene or speech. When characters are so full of emotion that mere speech will no longer suffice, they break into song. Both the words and the tune that they perform should reflect who they are, show how they function in the world, and capture an emotional wave to be shared with the audience.

Walter McBride/Corbis

FIGURE 3.8   From left to right, Casey Nicholaw (co-director), Trey Parker (co-director/author/composer), Matt Stone (co-author/composer), Robert Lopez (co-author/composer), and Andrew Rannells (actor) during the Broadway opening night curtain call for *The Book of Mormon* at the Eugene O'Neill Theatre in New York City.

AUTHOR'S INSIGHT

ANNIE: Any collaboration can have unexpected rewards. I worked with a dancer/choreographer on a script we adapted from a novel. Working with someone who inherently understood and "saw" the script in dance sequences was an entirely new and rewarding experience.

These positions are often filled by two different artists, both of which need to virtually personify the word *collaboration* by being in sync with each other. When we think of the legendary partnerships of the American musical theatre (Rodgers and Hammerstein, Lerner and Loewe, Kander and Ebb), it is as if they are one unit. And Stephen Sondheim, perhaps our most revered living writer of musical theatre, does both.

Story Anatomy

All artists use available tools to tell their truth. "True" is not the same as "real." Many use fanciful variations of the real world to communicate their ideas. Their truth may move far beyond facts or evidence. Plays can be realistic or abstract. They may be simple or complex. They may speak in poetry or prose. They may be a combination of any of these elements. Playwrights make choices, each one opening some doors and closing others. By trying to be aware of the choices made, by analyzing the playwright's construction process, we can better understand each script, starting with the choice of medium, mood, and dramatic action.

ARTHUR MILLER

PLAYWRIGHT

What I'm doing is helping reality out. To complete itself. I'm giving it a hand.

Medium

The first choice any artist makes is **medium**, the raw materials (such as oil or watercolor for a painter, or clay or marble for a sculptor), or method of presentation (such as media or live theatre). The playwright choosing live theatre accepts both benefits and challenges. Large epic visual events (the opening scene of the D-Day landing in *Saving Private Ryan* or almost anything in *The Lord of the Rings* trilogy) are not suited to the theatre medium. On the other hand, live theatre gives the playwright a personal connection with the audience, allowing intense and active interaction. Finding communion and connection in film is challenging, in part because of the technology that stands between the performance and the audience. We are not unaffected by film events, but we cannot influence them.

While both mediums allow intensely intimate glimpses into the lives of characters, live theatre will more often demand more dialogue by its very nature. In the film *Lost in Translation,* Bill Murray's character, in Tokyo, receives constant faxes from his wife. Both the content of these messages and his reaction to them are shown in subtle silence. In a live performance of a play, a similar action would require that the messages be read aloud by the actor or projected on a giant screen, changing these moments altogether.

The playwright can expect the play to be produced by living, breathing human beings in a special space designed or designated as a theatre. His audience will probably expect to listen carefully, experiencing the event in a more auditory, less visual way. Because playwrights do not work in watercolors or marble but with words, they have a number of decisions to make about those words. Will some of them be set to music, or will it be a straight text? Will some of them rhyme, appear in some other form of verse, or be prose? Will the words be elevated and formal or street-talk colloquial? Will the language be sacred, profane, or both? Will the characters have the gift of gab or struggle and stumble to say what must be said? Will speakers generally be allowed to finish, or will characters continually interrupt and unsettle each other? Will the language choices be widely shared by all in the play or represent startling diversity? Here is tremendous power and responsibility.

TINA HOWE
PLAYWRIGHT

I have my white-glove plays about aging WASPs recalling better times and my bare-hands plays about women blasting into the light now. I tend to alternate my WASPy plays with my frisky ones.

Mood

Storytellers must decide on the **mood** early in the process: how closely they will be working to comic or tragic space. The comic mood assumes that while something is wrong in the world, the characters are going to struggle through to a new and better place—or at least find a way to tolerate their lives with less strain. The most common plot in comic mode is the love story. Two people fall in love, obstacles make their union seem impossible, but love triumphs in the end. What is wrong is not insurmountable.

Though Chekhov's plays are seldom laugh-out-loud funny, he calls each of his four masterworks comedies, including *The Three Sisters*. The designation "comedy" suggests that by the end of the play, the world will be different, fresh, or maybe even better, but Chekhov's plays have a tendency to end with a sense of melancholy, as few of his characters are able to overcome inertia, social restrictions, or their own natures to succeed. However, they *endure*, go on with their lives, and do the best they can with the little they've got.

Tragic mood assumes that the world (or cosmos) is thrown out of order by the actions of an individual or group. Tragic drama frequently involves characters who have power and use it to make others' lives miserable. In *Antigone,* a young woman challenges the authority of the new king of Thebes, her uncle Creon, and his reactions disrupt the lives of the entire community. He doesn't intentionally bring pain and suffering to his people, but his goal (maintaining an appearance of control no matter the cost) causes the known world to career out of control for a moment. Only when he realizes and attempts to correct his errors can the community, the world, the cosmos return to balance and order. In the tragedy, characters must alter their behavior and relationship with the cosmos to survive and thrive. Sometimes (such as in *M. Butterfly, King Lear,* and *Antigone*) a character must die to restore the natural balance of the universe, but other times (such as in *Roosters, The Piano Lesson,* and *He and She*), a character can learn and change his or her behavior before the final reckoning.

FIGURE 3.9 Anton Chekhov's *The Three Sisters* has a distinctly bleak perspective. This production was directed by Joe Dowling at the Guthrie Theater in Minneapolis, 2003.

FIGURE 3.10 A scene from a Japanese Kyogen play, a light form of drama associated with *Noh*.

The same actual story can be told in either comic or tragic mood, although the choice will alter the result beyond recognition. At times, the two are kept distinctly separate. During the fourteenth century, the venerated, classical Japanese playwright Zeami divided drama into serious or tragic—known as *Noh*—and comic or romantic—known as *Kyogen*. To this day, the two are performed in different types of theatres, use different conventions, and rely heavily on different styles of theatricality. French neoclassicism of the seventeenth century dictated equally strict divisions in content, style, and production venues.

These two still tend to dominate the playwright's range. Comedy is found throughout the world, from biting satire to gentle romance. Tragedy also thrives as we try to make sense of our complex and dangerous world. Increasingly, however, contemporary playwrights blend and distort mood to create tragicomedies or dramedies within a deconstructed, rediscovered, or simply absurd universe. Often works will switch gears and even layer one mood on top of another. The comic/tragic contrast is simply a starting point for increasingly complex, overlapping, and still-evolving forms.

Dramatic Action

The playwright decides on the action of the drama, guided by three major principles.

1. All **dramatic action** involves **conflict**. Human encounters are most interesting when we do not agree. On a normal day in real life, we may be able to avoid conflict in every interaction. But no one writes plays about normal days. Plays are about days when something of critical importance is being confronted. Identifying the central conflict is crucial to understanding.

2. Dramatic action always occurs in the **present tense**. The play must occur before us as if it were happening right now. If a playwright needs us to know something about the past, the characters may talk about previous events or actually experience a flashback where they are not reminiscing but living the earlier event as it happens.

3. Most stories use the same **structural elements**. In *Poetics*, Aristotle claimed that each play must have a beginning, middle, and end. If you write a play or if you are the great storyteller in your family or tribe, knowing where to start, building intensity for exactly the right amount of time, and then ending it with the only possible outcome or the most surprising one is half the battle.

Play Analysis

The arts share a peculiar place in the human heart. Many of us are drawn to them, and some of us want to *be* artists, but few of us have both the genius and the luck necessary for a successful career. Those who choose this path must have a strong need that overwhelms uncertainties and failures. For the playwright, that need might be to give voice to ideas, feelings, or important events. Comedy may offer a chance to satirize idiots and oppressors, while tragedy helps us cope with suffering. The playwright leaves a legacy for us to experience here and now. The text is that legacy.

In the following section, we offer two avenues for analyzing script structure and character.

Dramatic Structure

Ten basic elements define the structure of a dramatic work. While some playwrights may twist or exclude some of them, the act of searching for them gives us insight into the work as a whole.

1. **Point of attack:** Where in the larger story of a life does the playwright choose to start this work? The story of Ogun has many episodes, starting from the moment of his creation and continuing into the present. A playwright working in Nigeria today might want to write a new play that will inspire people to continue the work of moving past the colonial era. He could look at the entire Ogun epic and choose one episode to retell, updating it to reflect current and local events. The point of attack is that choice of where in the longer story to start this play. In Greek tragedy, Sophocles wrote of Oedipus, the king of Thebes, part of a story that is

many generations long. Long before the birth of Oedipus, one of his ancestors offended the gods; the family was cursed through all generations, and Oedipus is the recipient of a fate that he did nothing to deserve. Likewise, his children are cursed, and their misfortunes carry through generations to come. Many plays continue to be written about this family and each playwright chooses a point of attack. Sophocles's *Oedipus the King* starts on the last day of Oedipus's reign. The same playwright wrote *Antigone*, a play about the daughters of Oedipus in which the point of attack chosen is after the exile of their father and a civil war between their two brothers. Both plays tell the same big family story, but different points of attack focus the audience on specific incidents of the playwright's choosing. (For more about *Antigone*, see Dramatic Interlude 4.)

The following three elements, while content-related, help reveal how the work as a whole is constructed.

2. **Protagonist:** Who is the central character in the play? In some forms of playwriting (such as the *Noh* drama and Elizabethan tragedies), the protagonist is the tragic hero defined as a well-born, good man who commits an error from which catastrophe ensues. In modern plays, men and women, low- and high-born, good and flawed, function as protagonist. Which character does the playwright want us to follow? Who changes the most in the play? Which character would you want to hire a top-dollar movie star to play him or her in your movie? Who wins the contest/conflict or loses most spectacularly? More important, who does the playwright think *ought* to win, lose, or change?

3. **Antagonist:** Who is the character most actively trying to prevent the protagonist from achieving his goals? Antagonist does not equal "villain" or "bad guy" except in a simple form of storytelling called melodrama. Maybe the antagonist is trying to protect the protagonist by blocking his actions. Maybe the protagonist's goal is one that the playwright believes should be challenged.

4. **World of the play:** What are the basic facts about the characters and particular universe given to us by the playwright? *Much Ado About Nothing* (discussed in Dramatic Interlude 1) is set in Messina, a vague, exotic, romantic locale in the home of its governor, Leonato. His estate is large and luxurious. The season seems to be spring or summer. The well-to-do characters are experiencing a period of leisure. We identify what is known, without immediate judgment. The basic categories introduced in Chapter 1—time, space, values, structure, pleasure, and the senses—are always worth investigating. (Appendix A offers extensive questions within each of these general topics.)

The playwright may also need to tell us about the past or warn us about the future using the two structural elements discussed next.

5. **Exposition:** Information about past events is given by the playwright through character conversation. One of the challenges of performing

FIGURE 3.11 Hecuba huddles together with her daughters in shock and terror in the opening moments of Anne Bogart's production of *The Trojan Women* by Euripides. In an unusual structural devise, Euripides chose the point of attack to be the moment after the Trojan War, when the few survivors learn what the Greek soldiers will do to them now.

exposition is for the actor to make telling the story active and alive. Telling is inherently less compelling than doing. *"Master Harold"* . . . *and the boys* is an example of a play that relies heavily on exposition. (For more about the play, see Dramatic Interlude 4.) Characters Sam and Hally spend their afternoon together relating stories about the good old days when they lived in the Jubilee Boarding House, telling us critical information about their past experiences together and the evolution of their relationship. But for the characters, these are not simple reminiscences. Sam uses the stories to calm and encourage Hally, or to help him cope. In the hands of a good actor, exposition serves an active function in the present tense as well as clueing us in to past events.

In contrast, Shakespeare uses little exposition in *King Lear* (see Dramatic Interlude 3). We learn nothing about the history of the family, about the mother, childhood, or recent behavior of the three daughters. By not sharing the characters' history with us, Shakespeare forces us to concentrate on their present behavior. We may learn a tidbit, such as that Lear always loved Cordelia best, and we may make connections between that and the current anger of her sisters, Regan and Goneril. But neither we nor they are allowed to spend much time justifying their harsh treatment of their father. Shakespeare seems to want to make them (and by extension us) accountable for each choice made in the present, focusing on *what* they do rather than *why* they do it.

6. **Foreshadowing:** Does the play contain a warning about something in the future? In film, foreshadowing is often accomplished by soundtrack music. In *Jaws,* the heavy heartbeat sound, "baaah-dum, baaah-dum," signals the approach of the shark (or teases us into tensing up only to release us with a fake cardboard shark fin). In our personal theatre, a friend may casually mention, "So-and-so might be at the party tonight," or "Your mom called, she didn't say what about," and in your head, you may hear the traditional "uh-oh" music soundtrack. In live theatre, characters who receive warnings are less likely to be supported by ominous sound cues. More often, they and the audience don't realize the significance of the clue until later in the play, when a jolt of recognition goes through them and us. Both exposition and foreshadowing can occur at any point in a play. The playwright chooses when to reveal or conceal, when to tease or fulfill, to build suspense and sustain conflict.

The following four elements help define the shape of the story.

7. **Inciting incident:** Which event changes the life being portrayed in the play? At some point near the beginning of the story, an **inciting incident** gets things rolling. In *M. Butterfly* (see Dramatic Interlude 1), David Henry Hwang reveals one possible inciting incident in Gallimard's life through a flashback to the first time he laid eyes on the "perfect woman," when Song performed at an embassy function. Until that moment, Gallimard's life had been depressingly ordinary. Only through his involvement with Song did his life become interesting enough for someone to write a play about him.

Sometimes the inciting incident is more difficult to identify. In *The Three Sisters* (see Dramatic Interlude 5), a play characterized less by dynamic than reflective action, the inciting incident that makes this day different from every other day occurs in the first act—but exactly where? It might be Irina's birthday party and the fact that she turns 20 (thereby feeling a need to grow up), or when Masha meets her future lover, Vershinin, for the first time, or when the unsuitable Baron Tusenbach declares his love for Irina. At first glance, any of these might function as the inciting incident, but careful study is needed to ensure that the chosen event leads to rising and falling actions and eventually to the climax when performed. One method for finding or confirming the inciting incident is to identify the climax of the play and work backward from there, tracing the plot back to the beginning to see if the chosen incident is the mechanism triggering the climactic outcome.

8. **Rising and falling actions:** Where does tension build and release in the text? Good storytelling always involves this alternation. **Rising action** is an event that increases tension, while falling action temporarily decreases it, allowing characters and audience a moment to breathe. Identifying rising actions is particularly critical as the central conflict is intensified and complicated. **Falling action** is an event that relaxes us and gives us a moment of respite, but it doesn't drive the action forward. A much-used diagram of basic storytelling structure is shown in the accompanying figure.

In some plays, the playwright challenges the normal storytelling arc, so analyzing structure helps us discover what the organizing principle is.

Joan Marcus

FIGURE 3.12 The inciting incident of *M. Butterfly* is the first meeting of Gallimard (John Lithgow) and Song (B.D. Wong). From the original Broadway production.

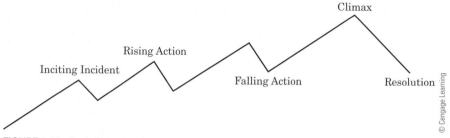

FIGURE 3.13 Basic Story Structure

9. **Climax:** What is the moment of peak struggle or encounter in the central conflict of the play? It is often the final confrontation between the protagonist and the antagonist, when one of them wins and the other loses. The climax is often the place where we learn the purpose in telling this tale. If the play was a comedy, the climax will usually lead to the victory of good over evil. If it was tragic, good may still triumph, but only at a tremendous cost. Particularly in contemporary drama, if the "wrong" side wins, the meaning of the work may be showing us the strength needed to even attempt to overcome evil. Sometimes the meaning of our lives is not found in our victories, but in our willingness to fight unbeatable foes.

10. **Resolution:** At the end, there may be a new world, circumstances, or understanding created by actions of characters. In a standard television

FIGURE 3.14 The resolution of Shakespeare's *Much Ado About Nothing* is a celebratory dance between Beatrice (Janie Dee) and Benedick (Aden Gillett). A Peter Hall Company production at the Theatre Royal, Bath.

drama, the resolution takes place after the last commercial break, when the characters wrap up loose ends, ponder the outcome of the conflict, or move on to a new adventure. In live theatre, we may celebrate the victory of love with a dance (as in *Much Ado About Nothing*), or try to make sense of the suffering of the characters (as in *Antigone*). Some playwrights refuse to give clear, comfortable resolution. In *"Master Harold" . . . and the boys*, Athol Fugard denies us the "ahhh" scene in which Sam and Hally repair their relationship with a hug. Instead, Hally exits before they can make up, and we are left with an uneasy sense that nothing is ever going to be the same for them, but we don't know if that's going to be a good thing or a bad thing. All we are given, perhaps as an antidote to despair, is the vision of Sam and Willie dancing, attempting to keep their hopes alive despite the ugly, destructive climax of Sam's fight with Hally. Fugard refuses to give easy answers to racism and apartheid as complicating factors in loving relationships, but he also refuses to leave us without any hope at all.

Character Analysis

While the 10 elements of dramatic structure help us comprehend the play as a whole, **character analysis** helps us understand the individuals who inhabit it. These inquiries help reveal the *who, what, how,* and *why* of each character.

1. **Given circumstances** (*who*): What are the facts given by the playwright about this character? We might be told that a character named Chata is a woman in her late twenties of Mexican American heritage, sister to the husband of the family and living in New Mexico in the present day; she has lived a rough-and-tumble life as a prostitute among migrant farm workers (see *Roosters* in Dramatic Interlude 3). If we take any of this further and start making judgments like "She's a slut" or "She's immoral," we are no longer considering facts, but only opinions. Another character calls her a tramp, but that too is opinion, not fact.

2. **Values** (*who*): All persons have values, what we believe to be true and important. Conflicts often arise in life and art because of opposing value systems. In *9 Parts of Desire* (see Dramatic Interlude 2), we meet nine women whose values are in conflict. Some are expatriots living in America or England, while some have lived most of their lives in the desert among their Bedouin tribes. Some are highly educated, while others have never entered a school. Some are very modern, even socialist, in their values, while others are extremely conservative. The two values that they all share make this play universal in its impact: they all love their families and their country. One person may value peace at any cost, another winning at any cost. One may value the family or community first, another only himself. With a character whose values are different from your own, try not to dismiss the values, but rather work to understand them. Our most important life lessons can come from exposure to the value systems of others.

T. Charles Erickson

FIGURE 3.15   Boy Willie struggling with his sister Berniece in *The Piano Lesson.* The siblings of August Wilson's *The Piano Lesson* have opposing superobjectives involving the piano. Boy Willie wants to sell it, and Berniece wants to save it.

3. **Superobjective** (*what*): Most of us have a driving ambition that determines our day-to-day choices. You may want to get married, start a lucrative career, or simply graduate on time. This would be called your current superobjective. In a play, the character's superobjective drives her through most of the play. In *9 Parts of Desire,* Layal's superobjective might be "to paint the truth of Iraq" or simply "to survive the Iraq wars." In *King Lear*, Lear wants to retire from the pressures of ruling the kingdom, but he's accomplished that during the first scene of the play, so we must continue searching for his overriding need or want, which might be something like "to shed the burden but keep the privileges of kingship." In some plays, superobjectives of main characters reveal the central conflict. In *The Piano Lesson* (see Dramatic Interlude 6), Boy Willie wants to sell the family piano so he can buy the farm he is sharecropping. His sister, Berniece, wants to preserve the family history, which is carved on the piano. They can't both get what they want.

4. **Actions** (*how*): What are characters willing to do to get what they want, and what strategy and tactics do they employ? Search for verbs that describe each character's "tool kit." Examples might include arguing, whining, sulking, killing, waiting, observing, or accusing. In *He and She* (see Dramatic Interlude 6), both Tom and Ann want to succeed at their careers while maintaining the health of the family, so their actions reveal

the central conflict. While he asserts, rejects, ignores his child, demands, and assumes, she hides, struggles, supports, and finally gives up. He proclaims and she questions. They want the same thing but use different and conflicting actions to achieve that goal.

5. **Motivation** (*why*): We often must engage our intuition to determine why a character makes the choices that she does. Characters seldom discuss their motivations openly, and frequently they seem unaware of them. Why would a king divide his kingdom into three parts? Perhaps he's motivated by a desire to weaken the authority of each child, thereby setting himself up as the better ruler. Perhaps he is motivated by an urge to prove to the world that he is the most fair and honorable father/king ever known. Perhaps he is insecure about his children's love and wants them to make public statements of adoration and loyalty. Applying psychological motivations that were unheard of in the world of the artist and/or characters is dangerous. We now have a tendency to attribute almost all bad or self-destructive behavior to a lack of self-esteem. To an Elizabethan, filled to the brim with self-esteem, the idea of a king making a world-altering decision because he wasn't feeling very good about himself would be incomprehensible.

The Playwright's Plan

For many artists, we can never be absolutely sure what they were trying to communicate. Playwrights themselves frequently can't identify in objective language what message they hoped to share. August Wilson said he often started a new play because of a song he happened to hear or a phrase he overheard while passing someone on the street. The artist has a burning need to communicate truth but may be the last person to ask what that truth is. Her plan may come from a place other than consciousness. Art is born deeper in the heart and mind of the creator than language can articulate. Our work as audience members and as participants in the pageant of life is to try to understand what others are trying to tell us. Identifying the playwright's plan is part craft and part art.

Professional critics, though paid to write or talk about the work of artists, all too often are untrained or too lazy to focus on the artist's plan. We have all read movie or play reviews that are mere plot summaries and personal opinion. Frequently, critics simply stop short of true exploration by listing topics found in the play, such as "this is a play about love, family, and suffering." We would like to challenge such critics to find a play that is *not* about love, family, or suffering. The playwright's plan can be broken down into the following three elements.

1. **Issue:** What are the real subjects being addressed, sometimes lurking below the level of the simple story? What questions emerge out of these subjects? In *"Master Harold" . . . and the boys*, racism and apartheid are

central issues, but so are love and the pain that we cause those we love the most. A play may ask lighthearted questions such as, "What is the very best way to spend your free time?" It may also ask, "How much abuse should you tolerate from someone you love?" or "When is it justified to take someone else's life?"

2. **Point of view:** What is the artist's take on the issue in question? A work of art may declare that love is a miracle worth any sacrifice or that love stinks and is not worth the effort. One artist might explore the enduring and loving bonds of family, telling us that we should always put the needs of our family first, but another might share the awful things that family members can do to each other and encourage us to leave our family baggage behind. To the serious questions asked earlier, one play might answer "None" or "Never" to the issues of abuse and murder, while another might offer a far more complex answer such as, "As much abuse as you can take without having your heart broken or losing hope for change," or "To protect those close to you, but never simply for revenge."

3. **Support from the text:** Are the conclusions drawn in categories 1 and 2 supported by the words and actions of the characters? Examples of well-constructed and poorly constructed arguments follow:

In *"Master Harold" … and the boys*, one of the ideas explored by Athol Fugard is the issue of fatherhood. What makes a good father (*issue*)? Fugard seems to be saying that a good father is one who is sensitive to the feelings and needs of the child, someone who spends time caring for the child and worrying about his or her well-being. The biology of parenthood does not necessarily make one a good father (*playwright's point of view*). This is supported in the play by the consistent contrast between Hally's biological father and Sam. Hally's father is absorbed in and consumed by his own needs. He is in fact absent from the play, as he seems to be absent from his son's life except as a problem. In contrast, Sam is the man who makes sure that Hally eats, does his homework, and grows into a strong, proud man. As Sam relates in the "kite story," he was the one who carried Hally's drunk father home from the bar and then built a kite so that the boy would look up and find something to be proud of after the humiliating behavior of his father. Throughout the play, Sam is actively engaged in raising Hally, while the boy's biological parents are busy dealing with their own problems (*support from the text*).

You may or may not agree with the conclusion reached by this writer, but crucial elements—issue, point of view, and support from the play—are all there.

The play, *M. Butterfly*, is about a French diplomat who falls in love with a Beijing Opera singer and pretends he's a character in an opera called *Madama Butterfly*. He is in jail for treason at the beginning of the play. It turns out that his lover is actually a man, not a woman, which would seem to be impossible to not notice. It makes one wonder if the diplomat was really gay or what. I think

FIGURE 3.16 The central issues of Athol Fugard's *"Master Harold"* . . . *and the boys* are racism and apartheid. Here are Hally (Jonathan Broadbent) and Sam (Edward James Walters) in a production at London's Southwark Playhouse, directed by Joyce Branagh.

he was both wrong and stupid to pass government secrets to a Chinese man pretending to be a woman. It also seems like a very unlikely story to me.

This is an oversimplified plot summary and personal opinion by the author of the argument. Personal opinion is best saved for later. Anyone may find a playwright's plan boring, stupid, or even offensive. Such response, while legitimate, does not belong in the description of the plan itself. In a critical review, it is essential to identify what the artist was trying to do *before* evaluating how well it was done or whether it was worth doing.

Work with an open mind and heart and try to understand the playwright's ideas. Avoid imposing opinions. Understanding another's heart, makes us more aware of our own beliefs and ideas, allowing us to stay open, without losing those parts of ourselves that we cherish and wish to sustain.

> **RACHEL WEISZ**
> ACTOR
>
> *Everyone walking around the planet is the hero of their own story. It is the actor's job to get into people's skin, and not judge them but to see things from their point of view.*

THEATRE IN MEDIA

The Screenwriter

How does the role of the live theatre writer compare with that of the media writer? The screenwriter (notice the difference in spelling from "playwright") has far less need to address how transitions occur and can actually have events juxtaposed in wildly different settings without concern for the limitations of a stage. Many sequences in a screenplay are merely suggested, particularly action scenes involving battles, explosions, aerial shots, and extended chases. Entire scenes where a character reflects silently on what has happened or is observed going on a journey are common. There may be no dialogue at all. Most of the time, film scripts will have fewer words than plays have.

Those words that do exist will be far more vulnerable. While the Dramatists Guild of America (essentially the playwrights' union) requires as part of its standard contract that no changes are to be made in dialogue, no such protection is afforded the screenwriter, whose words may be altered by almost anyone involved on or off the set. The screenwriter is also less likely to achieve legendary status. In the medium of film, it is actors and directors who achieve immortality.

The cinema is indelibly, even profoundly, visual and less tied to text. Unless screenwriters are auteurs (think Ben Affleck, George Clooney, Clint Eastwood, Woody Allen) who also direct and even perform in what they write, they tend to be relegated to a backseat behind their more glamorous colleagues. For how many films can you name the screenwriter? The American Film Institute asked critics to select the 100 best films of the past century, and only six of the winners had started as plays. This may reflect the idea that plays are often too talky for "the talkies" and that the entire experience of primarily listening versus primarily watching is decidedly, blessedly, and vividly different.

TUBE STORIES—SHORT, SHORTER, AND SHORTEST

Plays and films are often highly condensed adaptations of novels or biographies. Entire characters and episodes may be cut or blended. Yet the final product is still comparable, in theatrical terms, to a book, or in television terms, to a short story (sometimes shorter than short, in fact). With the exception of episodic epics like *Revolution* and *Lost,* most tales on television are told in miniature. All elements need to be presented, explored, and wrapped up in hugely condensed time frames. The point of attack needs to be near the climax, the protagonist immediately recognizable, the exposition minimal, and foreshadowing nonexistent. The inciting incident may be the only one, rising and falling action must be without digression, and resolution must be instant and complete. The actions (how) and motivation (why) of central characters must be absolutely clear.

The hour-long (which is often actually 48 minutes, factoring in commercials) crime drama may allow for a few false leads before resolution. However, with some exceptions, here is what has to happen in tight time frames:

- Sitcom: Often 23 minutes (8 minutes of the half hour often will be commercials or credits) for the central character to make a bad mistake, get caught in comic ramifications, somehow survive through the help of friends or family, and maybe even learn an obvious moral lesson.
- Music videos: Usually under three minutes for the pop star to experience loneliness, encounter a hot love goddess who gives life meaning, and be left behind and desolate again so he can write more sad songs.
- Commercials: Often 30 seconds to discover laundry or carpet damage, get advice from a wise friend, try a new product, and experience the sheer ecstasy and enlightenment that comes from something being really clean—maybe for the first time ever.
- YouTube: Viewers make rapid decisions about content. By 30 seconds into an online video, 33 percent have moved on. At one minute, 44 percent. And by the two-minute mark, 60 percent have abandoned the clip.

The limits of time frame and need for instant clarity often lead to overly familiar, cliched characters and situations because confusion and ambiguity do not work well in this art form. When originality appears, we are doubly impressed because of the limited parameters. People who write for this medium consider exposition, character development, and digression to be luxuries outside their universe. We tend to discount their work as lightweight—and certainly not great art—but it does take a certain very specific skill to get everything compact, condensed, and clear to fit into the confines of "tube time."

THEATRE IN YOUR LIFE

Scripting Our Lives

In this epic called *My Life,* when do you tend to write the script? For most of us, it is in preparation for an important encounter with an authority figure (boss, parent, or teacher) or companion (friend, lover, or potential lover), where we do not want to mess it up. Therefore, we may even write out what is to be said or we may just write it in our head and practice saying it over and over. So in many ways we become playwrights in circumstances where we are not comfortable or where the stakes are very high. Unfortunately, the other person, the recipient of these brilliantly crafted words, usually does not respond with the lines that we have written for them. Even if they say what we think they'll say, they might not say it in the *way* we pictured. If only we could control *their* script as well as ours. We also tend to eventually

"script" stories that we love to tell over and over, as we refine the rising and falling action and master the climax or punchline.

A POSSIBLE PLAYWRIGHT?

Are you frequently quoted by others because you have a flair for phrasing things well? Do you have an ear for the rhythms and word choices people make? Can you empathize to the degree that you are able to express the feelings of those whom you may dislike or with whom you disagree? Do you prefer ideas to be expressed by exchanges of dialogue rather than in essay form? When reading the "Getting Started" section of this chapter, did you find yourself eager to try a number of the ways of creating a script? If so, playwriting may be something you should explore.

SUMMARY

Much unscripted storytelling tradition continues to thrive around the world. In scripted work, the playwright is usually the first to struggle in isolation, creating words that must survive the collaboration and intervention of countless others. The more we understand the decisions made by the writer, the better we comprehend the work itself. A medium, mode, and course and pattern of dramatic action are chosen. Decisions are made in terms of the point of attack, protagonist, antagonist, world of the play, exposition, foreshadowing, inciting incident, rising and falling action, climax, and resolution. A storyteller may choose to scramble the order of plot events, leave out structural elements, or create unexpected outcomes to conflicts. When analyzing the play, we assume that every choice has a reason.

We can understand the work more fully by analyzing characters and asking the *who* (given circumstances and values), *what* (superobjective), *how* (actions), and *why* (motivations) questions that define and drive each of them. While some writers cannot identify their intentions, we can make every effort to unearth the playwright's (sometimes unconscious) plan by looking at issues, point of view, and textual support for any conclusions that we may draw.

SUGGESTED ASSIGNMENTS

1. When have you been faced with a challenge to create something artistic and had to choose a medium? Consider not only classroom assignments but social events. What influenced your decision to go with one medium as opposed to another?

2. Consider the comic versus the tragic mood in your day-to-day existence. When have you chosen one over the other? Have you gone through phases where your life was a tragedy and other phases when it was a comedy? Have you experienced other phases where it was a hysterical blend of both? How much of this was caused by external events and how much was due to your own choices? If you could go back and do it all over, how might making a different choice change the events?

3. Both media and live theatre have the potential for overwhelming spectacle and extraordinary intimacy. In a media event, what was an experience you had as an audience member that simply blew you away with the scope, majesty, and detail of the spectacle or the deep, personal connection of the intimacy?

4. Answer Question 3 for a live- or personal-theatre event.

5. Because dramatic action requires conflict, consider your own life. If someone were to create a play or film based on your experiences so far, what would be the primary conflicts that would provide them with an immediate inspiration? What were the main moments in the journey that brought you to who you are now?

6. In this event, *My Life*, what would be your answers to fill in the 10 elements of dramatic structure? To tell your story most effectively, for example, what should be the point of attack, how much foreshadowing is needed, and who is the antagonist (assuming that you are the protagonist)?

7. Take a recent film or play and answer these same questions for an event created by a writer.

8. Because foreshadowing is such a key element in analysis, as you examine your own history, what were the primary clues (alas, minus the hints given by the *Jaws* soundtrack) which, had you recognized them earlier, would have saved you from grief and regret later?

9. Compare yourself with a character in a play or film in terms of the five basic elements of character analysis. Come up with a brief answer for each. How have your insights about the character changed as a result of doing the analysis? What new insights do you have into your own character that you might not have noticed before?

10. Try to find an example of an instance where a critic has successfully examined and revealed a playwright's plan before going on to make judgments about it. Also, find an example where the writer limits himself to identifying the issues and quickly jumps to personal opinion regarding the work itself.

SUGGESTED ACTIVITIES

1. **Individual:** Try your hand at writing dialogue, picking two of your friends and creating a conversation which, to your knowledge, they have not had but could have. Be sure to capture the way each of them uses or hesitates to use language.

2. **Group:** Pick a very familiar story and discuss what it would take to define the event clearly as comedy, tragedy, or a surprising blend.

3. **Long-term:** Using the list of ten ideas in the "Getting Started" section of this chapter, start a play ideas journal, jotting down something each day from your imaginary life, real life, or the news that could be the beginning of a script.

4. **Large lecture:** Have someone who considers himself or herself a skilled storyteller volunteer to be narrator. Let the class vote on a fairy tale or other universal story. Divide the group into four parts: (1) sounds of nature such as wind, (2) interior sounds such as doors slamming, (3) repetition of key phrases in the story to emphasize them, and (4) overt active audience sounds such as gasps, shrieks, and giggles to accompany key plot moments. The storyteller will point to each group during the telling of the tale, at which point the group provides the sound supplement to make it come fully alive.

KEY WORDS AND IDEAS

griot/griotte
sutradhara
bard
playwright
five ingredients of successful scripts:
   action
   suspense
   believability
   fluidity
   compression
deconstruction
problematizing
medium
mood
dramatic action
conflict
present tense
structural elements

point of attack
protagonist
antagonist
world of the play
exposition
foreshadowing
inciting incident
rising action
falling action
climax
resolution
character analysis
given circumstances
values
superobjective
actions
motivation

chapter 4

ACTORS AND DIRECTORS

Kevin Spacey in *Inherit the Wind*, directed by Trevor Nunn, at The Old Vic Theatre, London, 2009.

David Hyde Pierce in rehearsal for *Vanya and Sonia and Masha and Spike,* by playwright Christopher Durang, directed by Nicholas Martin at the Lincoln Center Theatre in 2012. Durang, long known as a master of the absurd, blended Anton Chekhov's best plays, resetting them in present-day Bucks County, Pennsylvania.

T. Charles Erickson

Lesson Objectives:

Upon completion of this chapter, you will be able to:

1. Identify the functions of the actor and director in modern theatre.
2. Compare Western and Eastern traditions in terms of actor training, social status, and freedom of choice.
3. Compare Western and Eastern traditions of the director, or "Who's in charge?"
4. Identify when you are acting in your personal life and how to improve your performances.
5. Identify whether you are the take-charge director-type in your personal life.
6. Identify if you might have what it takes to make one of these professions your career.

Introduction

In this chapter, we will explore the work of two of the most intimately related members of any production team. They are bound, for good or bad, in a symbiotic relationship of great intensity, which may include shared laughter, tears, discoveries, and challenges. They create theatre together. We will examine the details of that process and try to answer the question, "What does it take to be an actor or a director?" We will explore their preparation, skills, and challenges.

Putting a Show Together

Table 4.1 shows the most common production steps of the actor and director. Some shows will include additional steps, and others may skip some listed here. The procedures outlined are traditional from Broadway to your local community theatre.

Table 4.1 | The Production Process for Directors and Actors

THE DIRECTOR	THE ACTOR
1 Casting Calls—producers or directors notify agents and actors of upcoming auditions for single productions or seasons.	**1 Audition Notices**—working professional actors are notified by their agents; novices will see posted notices, posters, and newspaper ads for events sometimes called *cattle calls*.
2 Casting, Round 1—directors see actors, performing prepared monologues, usually in three- to four-minute intervals.	**2 Auditions**—actors perform prepared monologues for the director(s) and producers.
3 Casting, Round 2—directors see only those actors who have sparked their attention. May work with the actors on a prepared piece or a reading from the text.	**3 Callbacks**—actors may have been given a piece of text to work on or advice on preparing for the next round. They can generally expect some kind of direction or interaction with the director(s).
Note: *For musicals, the musical director and choreographer/dance director will follow the same steps as above.*	**Note: *For musicals, the actor must be prepared to audition in all three disciplines: acting, singing, and dancing.***
4 First Company Meeting—sometimes a "meet and greet," sometimes a first reading, often the director reveals the approach to the play.	**4 First Company Meeting**—actors meet the people they will be working with. May include a first reading of the text and the director's approach to it.
5 Show and Tell—an exciting meeting where the director's vision is explored and the designers' work revealed.	**5 Show and Tell**—actors learn what the environment for the play will be, what they'll be wearing, and what world will be created for this production.
6 Read-throughs—work done at the table with the text or script ideas. May last for a week or more with a complex script, or one day for a more accessible one. May involve work with a finished text or evolution of unscripted materials.	**6 Read-throughs**—actors read the full script aloud and explore ideas. Length of table work varies, as does the role of the actor, who may be reading or developing scenarios.
7 Blocking—stage movement and action are developed and carefully orchestrated.	**7 Blocking**—stage movement and action must be written down, learned, justified, and frequently adjusted.

Table 4.1	**Continued**

THE DIRECTOR	THE ACTOR
8 **Design Meetings**—throughout the rehearsal process, the director meets with designers for detail work and problem-solving strategies. Blocking choices must be discussed for safety and ease of movement, as well as time frames for quick costume or location changes.	8 **Costume Fittings**—actors are fitted for clothing, hair, prosthetics, etc., and must be able to envision blocking to discuss safety issues and ease of movement with design staff, as well as strategies for any needed quick costume or location changes.
9 **Actor Coaching**—work focused on assisting the actor in any aspect of their performance. May be individual or ensemble.	9 **Character/Ensemble Development**—actors are guided by the director toward the desired character or ensemble work.
10 **Intensives**—focus on critical details or problem areas (i.e., a fall, a love scene, a difficult entrance).	10 **Intensives**—same as for the director.
11 **Promotion**—selling the production; getting the word out; photo shoots; television, newspaper, and radio interviews; and so on.	11 **Promotion**—same as for the director, possibly also performing preview excerpts from the show.
12 **Technical Rehearsal**—incorporating all technical elements to the production, including lights, sound, special effects, scenery changes, and so on. A very busy time for the director.	12 **Technical Rehearsal**—actors adjust to all technical components that can affect blocking, stage position, and "scale" of performance such as light, sound, and stage changes. Can be a very slow time for the actor as technical problems are solved.
13 **Dress Rehearsals**—add costumes, hair/wigs, makeup, and hand props. Most directors try for one clean dress rehearsal without stopping for adjustments.	13 **Dress Rehearsals**—actors are called in early to put on makeup, costumes, hair/wigs, etc. The process of make-believe goes up a notch, as the actor is transformed physically into another character.
14 **Opening Night**—electric moment of birth as the "baby" is brought before the audience for the first time. In professional theatre, this is the end of the director's involvement.	14 **Opening Night**—same as for the director, except that it is just the beginning of the run and the actor will repeat this performance for days, weeks, or months to come.
15 **The Run**—The stage manager generally becomes the authority figure who works to preserve the director's vision. In some community and educational theatre, the director may attend performances and give notes all the way up to closing night.	15 **The Run**—actors work to balance on a fine line between keeping the work fresh and open to discovery while not ambushing fellow actors or changing the director's vision.
16 **Closing Night**—The end. The stage will be cleared (called the "strike"), and costumes cleaned and stored. A new show will move in and the process begins all over again.	16 **Closing Night**—same as for the director. For successful actors, a few reviews, photos, and mementos are stored and they are off to another theatre, perhaps in another country, state, or city, to start a new production.

The Prologue

The process in Table 4.1 begins once both participants are involved. Long before this (months, sometimes years before) the **director** in traditional Western theatre is involved in script analysis and development, historical or style research, brainstorming sessions with various designers, and subsequent design conferences as the preliminary look of the show evolves. The director is also putting together a core staff for the initial rounds of casting and rehearsal, and he is generally doing enough homework to move confidently to the point where actors will be welcomed into the process.

MARY SELWAY
CASTING DIRECTOR

You need to find actors the director can work with, with the right temperament and with an emotional truth the audience can believe. If you get the perfect cast, then 75 percent of the work is done.

FIGURE 4.1 The production process often involves extensive rehearsal of actors by the director. Here, British director Peter Brook directs a rehearsal of his play *Mahabharata* on stage at Theatre des Bouffes du Nord, Paris.

Julio Donoso/Sygma/Corbis

The Timetable

The average nonprofessional production rehearses four to six weeks, five days a week, for three to five hours. A professional production may have fewer weeks and take longer hours per day. Plays rehearse at least an hour for each minute of performance time, so a two-hour play would rehearse 120 hours. The length of rehearsal expands based on the size of the cast, scale of production, and new skills required of the cast, so a big musical or Shakespeare play could easily rehearse 12 weeks. A contemporary, realistic, small-cast, and simple-set show may rehearse less than the standard minimum, whereas a period piece in which female actors need to, for example, learn to work with fans, corsets, bustles, and trains, would take longer due to the need for extra rehearsals devoted entirely to these skills.

Ethan Miller/ Getty Images Entertainment/Getty Images

FIGURE 4.2 Actor John O' Hurley, actor/writer Eric Idle, director Mike Nichols, and actress Nikki Crawford sing during the curtain call of the premiere of Monty Python's *Spamalot* at the Grail Theater at the Wynn, Las Vegas.

The Actor

While the director is usually on board before the actor in contemporary Western scripted theatre, for much of history, there was no such thing as a director. Today, in some other parts of the world and in improvisational and storytelling theatre, there still is no director. Therefore, we will start our examination with the participant who always was and is present: the actor.

The actor is the heart and soul of theatre. Without actors, we have no theatre. They tell us the story, take us out of indifference, and stir our feelings. They are emotional warriors who put themselves on the line and often take great risks to provide a rewarding—even life-changing—evening at the theatre. No one is more vulnerable in the performance because no one is more subject to the approval or disdain of the audience and the critics. In less civilized times, actors were targets not just of boos and hisses, but of thrown objects such as tomatoes. In places where critical social or political changes are taking place, actors sometimes risk imprisonment, torture, or even execution for doing their work. In less extreme circumstances, actors have been objects of suspicion, awe, disdain, or acclaim; either the "stray cats" or "national treasures" of their society's pecking order.

Despite the vulnerability of their position, actors are often awarded the gift of envy and adoration. When acting works, when the magic happens, it is so exhilarating that almost everyone wants to do it.

Many people find ways to make acting an important part of their lives as an avocation. Tens of thousands find outlets for the actor in their souls while maintaining another viable career and source of income. They may be "re-enactors" who you've seen at historical celebrations, fairs, and festivals. They may be participants in Korean folk drama, where once a year they get to put on the mask of a frog and leap around the newly planted rice fields chasing pretty girls. They may be active participants in a local community theatre group, working not for money but for love of the theatre.

> **AUTHOR'S INSIGHT**
>
> **ROBERT:** Almost always when I meet people and they find out I am an acting teacher, their eyes glaze over and they talk about an acting class they once took or a show they once did and found unforgettable, or how much they wanted to do one of these but somehow never got the courage, either a high point in their lives or one they wished for but never got.

For most of us, it is good to choose something besides acting as our primary means of support. The classic waiter/actor who auditions during the day and waits tables at night is not a myth. So many people want to make acting their life that no profession has a higher rate of unemployment. In any given year, no matter what state the economy is in, boom times or bust, most actors are always underemployed or unemployed. Many are called, few are chosen. Talent, charisma, training, and a wide range of skills are not enough. One also has to be lucky, confident, and able to tolerate rejection. Still, most actors would pay for the chance to perform, and any kind of remuneration thrills them. Their union (**Actors' Equity Association**) is the only union to negotiate *lower* wages for its members to secure them more work opportunities!

Yet in some other countries, actors have no choice but to be actors, the decision having been made for them in childhood. Their livelihood is assured, but their choice is limited. In the *Noh* drama of Japan and the Sanskrit dance drama of India, only those chosen and trained from a very young age will ever be allowed to perform, and no uninitiated person would dream of auditioning for a part. In other places, theatre is so communal, such a social requirement, that all are expected to participate and auditions are a lifelong demonstration of narrative, musical, dance, and interpretive skills.

What exactly do actors do? That depends very much on the tradition that one is pursuing. Looking at all global possibilities is beyond the scope of this book, so we will focus on the more universal aspects of the actor's life in the West (Europe, North America, and the world influenced by the colonial era) and in the East (South and Southeast Asia, China, Japan, and Korea).

The theatre of Africa, Micronesia, and parts of South and Central America is just beginning to throw off the yoke of foreign domination. There, the actor's life is rapidly changing, with dynamic new theatres blending colonial influences with traditional, indigenous forms. New companies and actor-training programs are being formed in countries where oppressive puppet dictatorships followed colonial occupation. During difficult times, the actor was strictly controlled by censorship and the need to toe the party line.

Those who didn't conform were persecuted, driven underground to hit-and-run performances, and then forced to flee ahead of the authorities. During the 1980s, Augusto Boal of Brazil had his actors wear firearms under their costumes to defend themselves if the police burst in during the performance of one of his many projects that were critical of the government. Now emerging nations are demanding a people's theatre. We wait and watch to see what new theatrical world will be invented.

RUSSELL CROWE

ACTOR

Acting is storytelling. Its roots are age-old and part of who we are as humans. It's the same job as the bloke that used to hold the talking stick aloft and talk about when the first canoe arrived.

Evolution in the West

The status, training, and financial and physical security of the Western actor have swung on a pendulum of extremes. A brief survey will take us from ancient Greece into modern actor training.

In Greece, the original actors were the playwrights, but by 449 B.C.E. competitions were held for tragic actors. They were probably semiprofessionals paid by the state as part of festivals like the City Dionysia, which included a tragic playwriting competition as well. Only three actors were allowed for each playwright. Men played all roles and wore masks to indicate character. All needed fully developed vocal skills (in the use of chant, declamation, poetry, and song) to be considered for a role. Our scant evidence of the tragic actor's status points to a respectable position in society and, for a few, fame and fortune. The tragic chorus, probably made of amateurs, performed interludes featuring song, dance, or both. They were rehearsed to move and speak in perfect unison, representing the citizens of the polis. One source speculates that they trained 11 months of the year in addition to their day jobs, much as community theatre actors do today.

Comic actors were distinct and separate from tragedians, most likely professional entertainers, bards, or street performers, and were always granted greater license than their tragic counterparts. The Greeks were serious about drama, but they also had a lively sense of the bawdy, risqué, and funny. As the comedies of Aristophanes show us, sex farces and buffoonery were part of the Greek temperament. Comedies might come at the end of a day of tragedy, like a dessert. Little is known about the societal status of comic actors.

FIGURE 4.3 An adaptation of Sophocles's *Oedipus* plays performed in London—behind the masks are Alan Howard, Clare Swinburne, and Tanya Moodie.

Although much of Roman tradition (c. 250 B.C.E.–100 C.E.) was copied from Greece, Roman actors were generally a despised, expendable commodity—often slaves—bought and sold like gladiators and exotic animals for use in huge outdoor theatres. The free Roman actor usually inherited his position (women were still not allowed to perform except as dancers in private performances) and was required to learn a detailed map of gesture and pantomime to indicate actions when dialogue could not be heard over the milling of the vast audiences.

When the Roman Empire converted to Christianity in the late fourth century, theatre was banned from the Roman Catholic Empire, and the profession of actor/entertainer was outlawed. Some changed professions, while others fled or were imprisoned and killed. The professional actor would not be seen in Europe again for almost a thousand years. During that long millennium, actors were amateurs working on religious dramas sanctioned by local church authorities, where guilds, or trade unions, competed in annual religious festivals.

In the fifteenth and sixteenth centuries, professional drama revived. William Shakespeare (1564–1616) was first an actor, then a playwright, and eventually part owner of the company with which he made his start. Talented performers, while not in high society, could once again make their living performing in the theatre for appreciative

MARTHA FLETCHER BELLINGER

HISTORIAN

Dill [the historian of Roman society] *describes them as showing "an inhuman contempt for a class whom humanity doomed to vice and then punished for being vicious." Legally, the position of the acting class was never essentially changed; but in time the social standing was somewhat improved, and gifted artists, such as Roscius in comedy and Aesopus in tragedy, occasionally rose above their station and enjoyed the friendship of men of high standing.*

Photostage

FIGURE 4.4 Male actor (Mark Rylance) playing female role (Olivia) in Shakespeare's *Twelfth Night* at the Globe. During Shakespeare's time, all actors in England were men, so boys often played female roles.

crowds. Although women performed as members of *Commedia* troupes on the continent, all actors in England were still men. The first female actors would not appear on the legitimate stage in England until the 1660s. Boys were apprenticed to professional companies before puberty and learned by working closely with adults, first just playing female roles, and later, when their voices changed, moving into male parts. Like actors today, some achieved enough financial security to retire to the country. Some did not. Some became stars, and others were always in the background.

The status of an actor in Elizabethan England and the status of an actor in the contemporary West are very similar. The actor was, and remains, an odd duck to those not smitten with the acting bug. We revere our favorites, sometimes granting them more authority than they deserve. At the same time, we are not entirely without suspicion because they are different from others. We adore them, give them license to misbehave, and forgive them their public sins again and again.

Next, we will look at the entirely different world of acting in the Eastern theatre, which has seen less extreme swings of the popularity pendulum and where tradition is the foundation upon which actors build their life's work.

Puppets and Puppeteers

Actors have been acting through and with puppets at least as long as since 3000 B.C.E. Scholars can trace the puppet master art this far back, though it is probably even older. Imagine Ook, Pow and little Zowie (our ancient people from Chapter 2) in their cave, where their spiritual guide takes a token of sacred importance and makes it seem alive through manipulation. If the figure is human-shaped, maybe the spirit guide controls the head and arms with one hand, leaving the other free to cast spells or tell stories (pretty much the same thing). Today, puppet masters continue to weave spellbinding tales all over the world, sometimes with contemporary techniques and sometimes with techniques going back thousands of years. (See Chapter 7 for an introduction to bunraku puppets of Japan.)

Here we will look at two out of the vast number of puppet traditions: one old and one new. The older comes to us from the Middle East, specifically Iran. The newer is a puppet phenomenon found on world-class stages around the globe.

In Iran, for thousands of years, the traditional Persian puppet show, *Kheimeh Shab-Bazi*, has been performed in a small chamber in a portable stage named *Kheimeh* (The Box). There are, according to Iranian puppeteer Salma Mohseni, three key creative performers:

1. the puppeteer inside the tent or box,

2. the storyteller called a *morshed* or *naghal* who narrates, interacts with the puppets, and plays an Iranian percussion instrument, and

3. the musician who plays an Iranian string instrument.

The *morshed* must, according to tradition, be a singer, narrator, actor, and functional director. The puppeteer and musician also must be highly trained in their respective arts. Dialogue takes place between the *morshed* and the puppets. The main hero is a puppet named Mobarak, who is clever, naughty, and sometimes very rude, like his counterparts Punch in England or Pulcinella in Italy.

While the traditional puppet theatre of Iran almost died out in the last few generations, renowned Iranian director Behrooz Gharibpour helped invigorate a renaissance in 2005, with a brand new puppet opera, *Rostam and Sohrab* by Loris Tjeknavorian. Gharibpour also directed a puppet production of poetry by Iran's beloved mystic poet Rumi that is available in its entirety on YouTube with English subtitles. It is highly recommended for its glimpses into both the magic of puppetry and into the heart and soul of a society that is unfamiliar to most of us. In the twenty-first century, Iranian puppeteers have performed around the world from Spain to Poland to Kazakhstan. Today, Tehran boasts one of the world's finest training programs in professional puppetry. Gharibpour believes that puppetry and puppet opera will be Iran's bridge to the world in the years to come.

In 2008, a transformational play, *War Horse,* hit the London stage. When this blend of puppets and live actors came to Broadway in 2011, it took New York by storm, winning five Tony Awards in 2011, including Best Play. In addition, the Handspring Puppet Company of South Africa, which designed the puppets and trained their operators, won a Special Tony Award for its work. The story of a boy, a horse (Joey), and their bond of love during the brutality of the First World War, based on a beloved English children's book, features live actors interacting with full-size puppet horses. The horses are created with steel, leather, wood, fabric, and aircraft cable. They can bear the weight of an adult man. But they are also finely tuned to allow micromovements, nuances that bring the horses to life.

Three to five puppeteers control each animal, depending on their action in a scene. One controls the head, including the micromovements of the ears, eyes, and mouth. One controls the front legs, another the hind legs. If the animal is ridden in a scene, two more artists provide support through the animal's midsection. We will discuss the design and construction of the puppets in future chapters.

Puppeteers are actors with very specific transformative challenges. Transmitting life and feeling from their bodies to those of the puppets is their goal. Anyone visiting the backstage storage area after a puppet show is stunned at how lifeless and flat these figures can be when not animated by their human partners.

Iranian traditional puppet theatre uses marionettes. You may already be familiar with this type as the character, Woody, in the *Toy Story* movies is an example (in Toon form, of course). The marionette convention usually includes the masking of the puppeteers from sight. More than manipulating with their fingers alone, watching these artists from backstage reveals full body involvement with the puppet. They say that it's the only way to achieve emotional truth in their work. *War Horse* employs a different performing convention: all

Handspring Puppet Company

FIGURE 4.5 This production of *Ouroboros*, by the Handspring Puppet Company in 2011, uses a combination of creativity and technical mastery of the puppetry medium to depict the love story of a poet and a dancer.

puppeteers are fully visible to the audience at all times. They must work in perfect harmony with each other and with the puppet. They must come alive in the performance of their character, transmitting physical and emotional truth through the medium of the puppet.

Puppet acting offers unique challenges and opportunities. An actor may feel less scrutinized than others since the audience is largely focused on the puppet. However, since his own facial and body expressions are in service of the puppet character, movement and vocal skills need to be highly developed to compensate and to bring the puppet to full life. Actors who interact with puppets need powerful belief and endowment to make that relationship real.

Sometime long ago, before written records began, artists discovered the power of endowing an inanimate object with life, whether it was for entertainment or spiritual purposes or both. Chapter 2 explores the connection between ritual and performance, and the razor-fine line that separates them. Like the other types of actors in this chapter, puppeteers were there in the beginning and continue to shape the art of performance today.

Evolution in the East

Acting in the East is far more steeped in tradition and repetition than in the West. Precepts guiding status, training, and performance style were established many hundreds, if not thousands, of years ago and did not significantly change until the twentieth century. The influence of India and the

Sanskrit drama was, and is, felt throughout a vast region in Asia, where details articulated in the Natya Shastra (c. 300 B.C.E.) helped shape the perception and training of actors up to the present day.

The *Natya Shastra (The Canon of Dance and Drama)* was the last of five basic guides organizing all aspects of Hindu life. It defined the status of the actor as near the bottom of the caste system, despite the fact that the art form itself was a gift from the god Brahma. According to the *Natya Shastra,* "The same rules shall apply to an actor, dancer, singer, players on musical instruments, a rope dancer, a juggler, a bard, pimps, and unchaste women." In addition, traditional Eastern social custom enforced strict segregation of the sexes more profoundly than most Western societies. So theatre developed as either an all-male or all-female enterprise.

As Sanskrit drama and Hindu distinctions of caste and gender spread through South and Southeast Asia during the third century B.C.E., their influence was absorbed into local customs and beliefs. The spread of Buddhism and Confucianism reinforced status and gender segregation of the actor, while regional and local traditions shaped specific schools of performance. Although the actor was officially lowest on the totem pole, some still achieved fame, fortune, and fanatically loyal admirers. Being a social outcast and idol at the same time went with the job. The actor might never have been admitted to high society, where male actors playing women were suspected of being homosexuals and female actors of being prostitutes. Nevertheless, a male actor in the East might have caused the heart of many respectable matrons to flutter, while a female actor might have been the only literate, well-educated woman in the community, and possibly chaste or married as well.

In ancient imperial China, society stratified into strictly controlled groups. Confucius (551–479 B.C.E.) taught that family and social hierarchy were the primary stabilizing factors in life, placing the actor beyond the pale—along with criminals, bandits, scavengers, slaves, and prostitutes. Actors and their families were forbidden to apply for the much-coveted examinations (in literacy and respectability) that were the only route to success for the Chinese family. Without exam access, actors were not allowed valued stations of conformity, and the result was isolation. No family would accept an actor as a son- or daughter-in-law. Theatre became a closed corner of society, and the actor was born into a family of his own kind.

Segregation of the sexes has also shaped the life of the actor. Inescapably, when men and women were strictly forbidden to appear together on stage, sexuality and acting became entangled. In Japan, the Kabuki theatre (see Chapter 7), though originally an all-female form, quickly became all-male and remained so well into the twentieth century. Young boys born or adopted into theatrical families were chosen at an early age to play male or female roles in their adult careers. Some were trained in the art of impersonating an idealized female called an **onnagata**, undergoing meticulous, painstaking training in every nuance of gesture, posture, and vocal intonation to create the magical appearance of a perfect woman. (See the play *M. Butterfly,* in Dramatic Interlude 1, if you doubt the possibility of this.)

A. C. SCOTT

THEATRE HISTORIAN

In effect, he [the onnagata] says to his audience, here is an interesting character, now watch how perfectly I can act it for you, as my father did and my grandfather before him.

Men playing women is not the only form of gender-bending in Eastern theatre forms. In the **Shanghai Opera,** as popular and enduring a tradition as is the Beijing Opera further north (see Chapter 8), women played both male and female roles. Some critics imply that its popularity was not based on talent, but rather on beauty and assumed promiscuity. However, many talented women achieved star status for the brilliance of their work, not their faces.

Bound together by ostracism and segregation, actors in the East have built enduring traditions that transcend time, race, and the influences of Western imperialism. The minimum training period is about seven years and begins in childhood. The actor begins playing bit parts and walk-ons, learning from masters who play the leading roles. The work is deeply symbolic, combining familiar stories with dance, music, and abstract movement. Innovation from young actors is discouraged. They learn to do it right, and under no circumstances do they ever correct their master's definition of right. If they are among the fortunate few who gain the prestige and skill to play leading roles, they may then begin to—ever so subtly—leave their own signature on traditional roles.

The great masters (male and female) of Sanskrit dance and drama, Kabuki theatre, *Noh* drama, and the operatic forms of China achieve a fan base that rivals anything in Hollywood. A few achieve legendary status, and these few often become the head teachers at the intensely private schools that train the next generation. The revered masters select promising apprentices, and the great life's work begins again as another young boy or girl begins years of labor and training. Sometimes history comes full circle. At present the

FIGURE 4.6 Onnagata (man playing a female role) in a Kabuki play. Kabuki became an all-male form, requiring male actors specially trained to impersonate an idealized female.

Alison Wright/Documentary/Corbis

most popular form of Kabuki is *onna* Kabuki, which is performed entirely by women.

Stanislavski and Character

While Eastern actor training remained prescriptive and traditional, one Russian theatre artist created a revolution in the West. Konstantin Stanislavski (1863–1938) created a complete system for constructing a character, now used in some degree by most reputable Western acting programs.

A brilliant actor, director, and teacher, he co-founded the Moscow Art Theatre in Russia in 1898 and changed the way actors worked forever. He wrote four famous books (*An Actor Prepares, Building a Character, Creating a Role,* and *My Life in Art*), which establish the basic principles for relaxation, concentration, imagination exercises, warm-ups, improvisations, and rehearsal experiments used in classes and rehearsals. When Stanislavski started acting, he was not a natural. He was awkward, ungainly, and ill at ease. As such, he was motivated to study what all the great performers did to calm and focus themselves and then to report the results in a systematic way. He came up with a method to deeply comprehend a dramatic encounter.

The System has two sets of ingredients. Some may be familiar to you from earlier chapters. The first 10 are questions actors ask themselves for any scene they are in:

1. *Relationship:* What is this other character I am acting with to me, and what am I to him?

2. *Objective:* What do I want?

3. *Obstacle:* What is stopping me? What's in the way?

4. *Strategy:* What kind of plan do I have to get past the obstacle(s) and obtain what I want?

5. *Tactics:* What individual maneuvers or changes do I make within my strategy? (*Strategy* is sometimes compared with the overall game plan, and *tactics* with single plays used in sports.)

6. *Text:* What are the words we speak?

7. *Subtext:* What is really going on behind these words and between them?

8. *Interior Monologue:* What is the tape that is running in my head as I constantly and silently talk to myself?

9. *Evaluations:* What do I consider doing but don't do? What alternatives do I reject?

Imagno/Contributor/Hulton Archive/Getty Images

FIGURE 4.7 Konstantin Stanislavski in the title role of Aleksandr Pushkin's play *Don Juan*, Russia, 1889.

10. *Beats:* When do my partner and I change tactics or topics? How does our encounter shift internally?

You can see that any life situation could be analyzed and further understood by answering these questions, especially if you come away reeling from an experience with someone and not really knowing what happened. Or you tend to always have the same run-ins with someone in your life and would like to break the pattern. Stanislavski used the analysis of human behavior to enlighten any scripted encounter.

Like most brilliant discoveries, it seems common sense once you think about it. If an actor does each of these things, his attention will be fully engaged, his instrument will respond honestly, and he will be *compelling* to watch. Tension, stiffness, and self-consciousness tend to fall away because the mind can hold only so much.

The elements above help actors enter an *isolated* encounter. For the entire play (or an entire life), the actor adds 10 more:

1. *Given Circumstances:* What are all the major relevant facts that influence your character's behavior?

2. *Magic IF:* Place yourself in your character's shoes and ask, "What would I do IF I were this person in this situation under these conditions?"

3. *Superobjective:* What does your character want most in life?

4. *Through Line of Actions:* What is the *connection* between all the behaviors of the character?

5. *Score:* Write down the results of the previous questions and mark the script into workable units.

6. *Endowment:* Project onto other actors and objects imaginary qualities that will be helpful when you perform opposite them.

7. *Recall:* Use your five senses to awaken physical and emotional memories of your own that can be filtered into the character's experience. We use the term *recall* to encompass memories of physical sensations (which Stanislavski always supported) and emotional ones (which he grew more skeptical about with time). Also note what a small place (just one tool in an entire toolbox) it had within his total System right from the start.

8. *Images:* Add photos or a film to the interior monologue in your head to "see" what the character does.

9. *External Adjustments:* Change your own tendencies (physical and vocal) to suit those of the character.

10. *Creative State:* Use all the previous research to become free, open, and experimental.

FIGURE 4.8   Based on this image, how might this pair of actors have used Stanislavski's 10 elements to approach this play? Jud Williford (Macbeth) and Stacy Ross (Lady Macbeth) in *Macbeth* at the California Shakespeare Theater, 2010.

The core of all this work is creating a profound empathy for characters so that entering their world is natural and spontaneous. The System offers great potential for a convincing, compelling performance.

Unfortunately, Stanislavski's ideas have suffered from poor translations and delays in the publication of his books; so, more often than not, a distorted version of the System has been used. Nevertheless, his System led to the whole idea of actor training as a curriculum rather than something learned only in apprenticeship.

Happily, in the last few years, a number of publications have advanced information about Stanislavski's life, culture, and ideas, making them all more accessible. It is clear that he paid far more attention to Eastern arts than was previously recognized and that the System is genuinely more holistic (with a mind-body-spirit connection) than has often been acknowledged.

One of the major events in theatre publishing history, *An Actor's Work* [New York: Routledge, 2009, by Konstantin Stanislavski, translated by Jean Benedetti] presents Stanislavski's sometimes dense, florid, challenging prose as clear, vivid, and colloquial language. The book places his major works under a single title and cover, as was the author's original intent. It clarifies countless ideas by including extensive material that was randomly cut from earlier translations. This means that you can now read the book that comes

HILARY SWANK

ACTOR

I get to delve into other lives and express things I would never ever get to express if I did not have this job. What more could I ask for?

EDWARD NORTON

ACTOR

In acting, it is like having a master key to every door. You're granted access to these worlds of experience that most people never get.

as close as possible to the one Stanislavski intended, with language that will be far easier to comprehend than in other editions. Because the second part emphasizes technique so strongly, it will hopefully put to rest once and for all the idea that the System is solely based on emotion.

Benedetti also contrasts Method Acting with the Stanislavski System. Pointing out that the Method is about releasing emotion with almost no textual or dramaturgical analysis, he sums up the difference: "Whereas in the System, each section of the play contains something an actor has to *do*, in the Method it merely contains something an actor has to *feel*." The System allows the actor to portray any person, however despicable at first glance, without judgment. It is based on the most humanizing trait, empathy.

Strasberg, Adler, and Meisner

Much of what Americans know about Stanislavski has been filtered through three famous acting teachers who picked up bits and pieces of his process and left out others. In the early 1920s, the Moscow Art Theatre toured the United States for a year and a half, stunning this country's theatre community with the depth, power, ensemble, and detail of its work. American companies tried to emulate it. The first and most influential of these was the Group Theatre, founded in 1931. Three members eventually became teachers of great consequence.

Lee Strasberg (1901–1982)

Probably the most famous acting teacher of the twentieth century and mentor to film stars from Marilyn Monroe to Robert De Niro, **Lee Strasberg** called his work a "reformulation" of Stanislavski. He developed **the Method** based on a small part of the System, placing emphasis on emotion memory. You may have heard the term *Method acting*. This is Strasberg's invention, a corruption of a much larger concept, the Method of Psycho-Physical Actions developed by Stanislavski and not to be confused with the totality of his System. Strasberg defended and widened the use of emotion memory even as Stanislavski moved away from it. Strasberg's actors have sometimes been accused of displaying emotionalism and of violating a core of privacy within each performer.

Stella Adler (1901–1992)

The most successful actor in the Group Theatre, **Stella Adler** was frustrated with Strasberg's classes, so she went to Paris to visit Stanislavski in 1934. He steered her away from emotion memory because it had led to hysteria in some actors. He provided her with less invasive ways of summoning emotion. Adler focused on character through evidence in the script. She trained actors to do research into the text and the world surrounding it, not unlike an anthropologist, emphasizing the value of the actor becoming the character rather than subduing the character to his own emotionality.

Sanford Meisner (1905–1997)

Founder of the Neighborhood Playhouse, Sanford Meisner was the most respected acting teacher of the past century. He wanted acting to come from the heart, not the head, for actors to always find a connection with each other instead of indulging in their own private emotional reveries. All his work is between partners—based on Stanislavski's concept of "communion"— while most Strasberg and Adler exercises are done alone. His teaching builds trust between actors, and he succinctly defined acting as "the ability to live truthfully under imaginary circumstances."

FIGURE 4.9 Stella Adler (seated) gives direction to a student at the Stella Adler Studio, 1989. Adler encouraged "paraphrasing" of lines to make them feel fresh.

Internal versus External Acting

The great ongoing controversy in Western theatre is whether it is better for actors to approach their characters *internally* or *externally*. Should you burrow into the thoughts and emotions of the character and let the performance emerge from this immersion, or should you plan and calculate your performance, making vocal, physical, and psychological choices based on observations and carefully accumulated details? Should the actor be a deeply intuitive artist or one who constructs his performance? This is sometimes called the argument between *truth* and *technique*.

The international stereotype of the American actor is of a deeply internal

FIGURE 4.10 Sanford Meisner working with Diane Keaton at the Neighborhood Playhouse.

Robbie Jack/Corbis Entertainment/Corbis

FIGURE 4.11   Most great actors combine instinct and craft to lend power to every gesture. Tara Fitzgerald plays the title role in a production of Sophocles's classic tragedy *Antigone* at the Old Vic Theatre in London.

DENZEL WASHINGTON
ACTOR

Acting is both a craft and a privilege.

AUTHOR'S INSIGHT

ROBERT: When my son was about four years old, I overheard him talking with friends and asking them, "Don't you love to visit your Daddy's office?" They all responded, "No!" So he asked, "Don't you like to play with all the masks and stuffed animals and swords and balls and...," the list went on and on. I was reminded that most daddies' offices don't have this stuff, that my job requires toys and I am blessed for that.

performer and of the British actor as a consummate external professional; one is all instinct, while the other is all craft. In the great Eastern schools of actor training, the actor doesn't choose between the two. First, you learn the technique, and then the truth will be found in the most subtle flick of the actor's hand. In the West, too, the reality is that most great actors combine the two. They work to get inside the character emotionally but also design the performance technically. The goal is the same whether you are an actor/dancer in one of India's dramas from the *Mahabharata* or an American playing your first role in a college production—find the truth and support that truth with technique, or more important, let them support each other. No matter where or when the actor is working, given the challenges, it is a true labor of love.

The Modern Actor

Although acting in Western and Eastern traditions may seem more different than alike, the processes of casting, preparing, rehearsing, and performing are similar. Whether it takes years or days, all actors do the same painstaking work: analyzing their characters, taking notes and ideas from the director, memorizing lines and blocking (stage movement), experimenting with different ways to become the character, trying to make brilliant discoveries in rehearsal, and then trying to solidify all this preparation so they can repeat the performance consistently from night to night. Actors should be fit, athletic, and expressive, with fully developed vocal and physical instruments. One of the major tasks of any acting class and rehearsal process is to get the actor back to a childhood sense of wonder and magic. The actor must always be ready to play.

Finding the balance between the sheer joyful playfulness of acting and the grinding hard work can be challenging. Many novices to the theatre are blown away by the amount of time a show demands. Not only are you committed to rehearsals for at *least* 15 hours a week (and many more in professional theatre and many, many more in some Eastern forms), you are also expected to do a great deal of work outside of rehearsal. This is what most actors are required to do *on their own* between formal rehearsals:

1. Conduct an in-depth analysis of the character.

2. Memorize lines, blocking, and script changes.

3. Research the role and the world of the play (both as written and as conceptualized by the production).

4. Apply the director's notes and suggestions from the last rehearsal.

5. Experiment with character approaches.

6. Develop the vocal life of the character.

7. Develop the physical life of the character.

8. Brush up on material that hasn't been worked through recently.

9. Attend costume fittings.

10. Participate in publicity photo sessions and interviews.

For actors pursuing work in the West, the task of marketing themselves in order to secure the next job requires extensive, sometimes overwhelming, time and energy. The business of acting and the art of acting do not mesh easily for some actors. The two are like oil and water. Many discover that while they continue to love the art, they are ill-suited to the business and all it requires.

The Director

While the actor and audience are the essential ingredients for theatre, the director is, in many instances, the vital link in their relationship. In Western theatre, the director is now regarded as so crucial that it is hard to imagine that no such designated position existed 150 years ago. The director, after months of research, consultation, and preparation, guides the event from rehearsal to opening night. She is responsible for envisioning the show and for realizing that vision. No one is more directly involved in every aspect of production. No one will be held more responsible if it does not come off, although many others may be more honored if it does. This is because the director's work will often dissolve from consciousness if all artists shine and the show glows. The director molds a final product that may or may not receive acceptance from the critics and the public at large. The producer is the one person who can take control away from the director. Without a hands-on producer supervising (and perhaps interfering) at rehearsals or filming, the director is the leader.

Although we now believe the director to be essential, no such creature really existed until the late 1800s. The need for a director who was not a playwright or actor doing double duty came about with the advent of a movement called realism, which emerged in the mid-1800s. For the first time, plays were expected to be believable, not just fanciful. Someone who could coordinate the whole event, modulate the performances, and layer in lifelike touches was needed. The director clarified presentation.

While the director is a relatively new phenomenon in Western theatre, in non-Western theatre, the position is still somewhat rare. Instead, the master teacher, author, elders, or *griot*/narrator controls the development of the production. Today, those working as directors in other parts of the world are often trained in European or American universities and conservatories.

Historical evidence points to the playwright as the primary source of production aesthetics from the classical Greek period (c. 500 B.C.E.) through Shakespeare's era (c. the late sixteenth century). For nearly 2,000 years, the playwright was the deciding voice, but actors were active participants in decision making as well. By the mid-seventeenth century, the person in charge of production was the theatre manager/owner, who hired actors and designers, scheduled and supervised rehearsals, arranged promotion or advertisement, and managed the company finances. In terms of artistic guidance, however, the owner/manager had better things to do. A new play was rehearsed for a few days. Old plays were revived with one quick **run-through**. Actors were told to memorize their lines and step into the light to talk. Costumes, props, and scenery were pulled from stock and used repeatedly in different plays.

During the early nineteenth century in England and the United States, the **star system** developed, placing artistic control in the hands of the lead actor. Successful actors could buy the rights to a play in which they would play the leading role. They then toured, arriving in each new city with a trunk full of their own costumes and props. They hired a hall and secondary actors, bought advertisements, and staged the show. Star-actors would arrange the production to suit their own egos. Often, the star was the only person on stage allowed to stand in the light. The play could be cut and shaped to emphasize the star's role and de-emphasize others.

After nearly a century of this, live theatre had become smothered in repetitious, star-oriented melodramas. Something had to change.

Saxe-Meiningen and Unity

Many historians credit **Georg II, Duke of Saxe-Meiningen,** as being the first director. Born in 1826 to wealth, education, and travel, he developed a great passion for theatre. In 1866, he assumed control of the Duchy of Saxe-Meiningen after the forced abdication of his father. When he came to power, the duchy had a court theatre that had long suffered from neglect and mismanagement and had a well-deserved reputation for mediocrity. He immediately instituted programs to improve the theatre. He named himself *indendant* (chief administrative officer) and took direct control. As both the duke and *indendant*, he wielded authority over the company that became known as the Meiningen Players.

Between the years 1874 and 1890, the Meiningen Players became the most admired company in the Western world. Their repertory was not particularly unusual, but their methods were highly innovative and became influential. Georg II was able to institute four practices that have become the model of the modern director.

1. The duke insisted on **play-specific costumes, scenery, and props.** The design team was expected to do extensive research into the time period of the play and to build detailed replicas of whatever else was needed for each production. Prior to that, scenery, costumes, and props were pulled from storage and often had nothing to do with the play being performed. A leading lady might select from stock the most stylish and flattering nineteenth-century dress available and wear it no matter which role she was playing. The duke refused to allow anything incongruous or anachronistic onstage. If the play was set in ancient Rome, everything on stage would be appropriate to that culture. Designers became a vital aspect of the artistic whole and answered to the director.

2. The Meiningen Players **abolished the star system.** The duke fired the old company and hired a group of fresh young actors whom he could train and shape. He made sure that all actors played both major and minor roles, and the entire company participated in the realistic crowd scenes, for which the Meiningen Players became famous. The company became

akg-images

FIGURE 4.12　Georg II, Duke of Saxe-Meiningen, is considered the model of the modern director, due to his introduction of several production innovations.

an ensemble working together without ego for the good of the production. This innovation also established the authority of the director over the actor.

3. Georg II insisted that a production should be **rehearsed for as long as necessary,** occasionally for a year, though normally for several months. Few modern companies can afford to stay in rehearsal so long, but this innovation influenced theatres around the world to extend their preparation periods.

4. A **unified production concept,** grounded in research and analysis, became the domain of the director, who now does research, analyzes the script, and evolves an interpretation. The director must find a means of communicating these themes clearly to the audience. If a unified concept is important to communication, the simplest way to ensure unity is to have one person responsible for developing it. Most modern directors find this both the most difficult and the most rewarding aspect of their art.

The Modern Director

Today's directors often prepare for months—even years—before rehearsals begin, researching, meeting with other staff members, exploring the text and their own ideas for bringing the script to life. Hopefully, analytical homework unleashes inventive, intuitive discovery. This combination of careful planning followed by open-ended creativity makes directing enthralling.

In some ways, directors are also designers and playwrights. They design all the stage pictures that are created, dissolved, and re-created throughout the performance; no matter how imaginative the design work, it will fall flat unless these moment-to-moment visual creations are compelling and varied. A director needs to be a spatial artist. While the playwright provides a score of words, the director determines how that score will be "sung," how it will sound, so he is an auditory artist as well.

Today, there are two major kinds of directors: traditional and conceptual. The **traditional director** sees her job as serving the script and aims to

FIGURE 4.13 Saxe-Meiningen insisted on extensively researched costumes and props. Here, a Saxe-Meiningen actor wears Roman armor and lies against a stuffed horse.

realize the playwright's vision, hoping to enhance that vision. She seeks the best way for the audience to experience the script as written. Any alterations are aimed at taking that appreciation up several levels. The production aspires to illuminate and expand the experience beyond that of a silent reading without violating the intent of the text. While the traditional director serves the text, she is not necessarily subservient to it. There may be many original touches, but none assault the script.

> **ZELDA FICHANDLER**
> DIRECTOR
>
> *I do at least six months of advance research because knowledge releases my imagination. Without knowledge, one's imagination may be too thin.*

Georg II and Stanislavski provided models for traditional directing. For others, the challenge of directing involves a more free and personal approach. For the **conceptual director**, the script is simply a vehicle to express an idea, explore a problem, serve a cause, and achieve something more (alas, sometimes it turns out to be less) or far different than may have been intended by the playwright. The script may be radically cut, rearranged, interspersed with bits of other text, ignored during improvisational interludes, altered from night to night, and generally made subservient to the director's intent. A script may be deconstructed or problematized to place the emphasis on a formerly minor area of concern. Sometimes the

Terrence Spencer//Time Life Pictures/Getty Images

FIGURE 4.14   An actor at the Polish Laboratory Theatre under the direction of Jerzy Grotowski.

JONATHAN MILLER
DIRECTOR

A director should have common sense, tact, and literary sensitivity.

PETER BROOK
DIRECTOR

The great feature of the theatre is that the audience can enter very deeply into contradictions, contrasting points of view. Unlike media-dominated works, theatre has the potential to offer visions that are messy and conflicting, full and complex.

script may not exist but will be evolved through games, experimentation, and group effort.

The major pioneer in this area is **Jerzy Grotowski**, whose work with his Laboratory Theatre in Poland, beginning in 1959, influenced the freedom with which subsequent directors have altered the text. Grotowski trained his actors to be *überathletes*: physically and emotionally tuned to survive great demands of stamina; open to finding the shock, terror, and danger in any moment of a play; and always moving beyond mundane everyday behavior into the extraordinary. He would also rearrange the relationships of actor and audience so that the latter might be looking down into a pit at the action onstage, or be surrounded by the actors, or countless other nontraditional configurations. Other famous directors in this mold include Elizabeth LeCompte, Robert Wilson, and Anne Bogart.

Directing Process

So what do all directors do? They study the play, and then they develop ideas about how best to prepare and present it. They cast the roles, guide actors, create a productive working atmosphere, and oversee the work of a very large team. They serve as both managers and artists, which means that they have a wide range of skills from attentive supervision of others to wide-open, imaginative, and creative impulses.

All directors are likely to do the following:

1. *Analysis:* Some research intensively, while others prefer to come to the script fresh and respond instinctively. At some point, all examine the text for interpretive clues.

2. *Scheduling*: Some directors provide a complete outline of each rehearsal at the first cast meeting, so all participants know when they will be called and what will be done each day. Others feel the need to reconsider each day what might be done at the next rehearsal and post the call that day based on that new perception.

Dereck Jones/FilmMagic/Getty Images

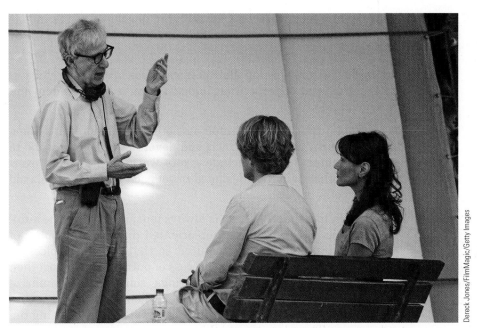

FIGURE 4.15 Some directors, like Woody Allen, shown here working with Carla Bruni-Sarkozy and Owen Wilson on the set of *Midnight in Paris,* work in both film and theatre, two very different formats.

3. *Blocking:* Some directors spend many hours with a model of the set and figures (sometimes chess pieces) standing in for each actor while they meticulously work out the performers' movements before passing these decisions on to actors. Others work organically, encouraging actors to explore how they wish to move and not setting the blocking until well along in the process. Directors and actors use a code or shorthand to write down movement in the quickest way possible and to recognize blocking later at just a glance.

   Some of these include: US (for **upstage,** or away from the audience), DS (**downstage,** or toward the audience), and such variations as DL (near the audience but to the left side of the stage, from the performer's perspective) or UC (away from the audience but in the exact middle of the acting area's width). Scenic elements, entrances, exits, and platforms may be assigned letters or numbers. Additional standards are illustrated in the accompanying figure.

cross – X	table – T	sit – ↴	chair – C
enter – E	exit – Ex	pivot right – ↩	kneel – ↲
face direction – →	fall or lie down – ↓	pivot left – ↪	rise – ↑

FIGURE 4.16 Stage Shorthand

4. *Organization:* While most directors have highly developed skills in this area, a significant number are spontaneous *artistes* who compensate by using assistants.

5. *Coaching:* Helping actors develop their performances in close, careful sessions with experimentation, repetition, and attention to both freedom and detail is a crucial task.

6. *Atmosphere:* Some directors are autocrats, others collaborators. Some expect actors to warm up on their own and devote no rehearsal time to building the ensemble. Others include group warm-ups, sharing exercises, games, and other activities designed to get each participant relaxed and at ease with others in the cast.

ZACH BRAFF

ACTOR

I find that directors who are also actors tend to be really collaborative because they've been in that position where they feel like they're not able to contribute.

MARK LAMOS

DIRECTOR

There is no collaboration if you come to the table and say, "I have this idea—and this is how you will assist me in presenting it." Collaboration is saying, "I have certain potent feelings about the work, but I don't understand everything."

In live theatre, there is always tension between the autocratic and the more group-oriented director. A number of theatres today are structured so that as many voices as possible are heard in the process of putting a show together. The director may chair meetings, solicit and summarize input, and serve as a tiebreaker when there is not a consensus, but may make few decisions without consulting the team. The advantage to this process is that each participant is likely to feel valued and involved. Great minds working together can achieve greater results. The disadvantage is that it takes time, requires more meetings, and can sometimes lead (like some political elections) to compromised rather than inspired choices.

Some directors feel that while their power is lessened in some collaborations, their accountability is not. Their authority to do what needs to be done has been taken away, and yet they are held solely responsible by critics and the public if the reaction to the show is negative. Commercial productions have been less eager to embrace the system because it is so hard to tell where the buck stops. Nevertheless, we will probably continue to experience a trend toward less autocratic and more collaborative leadership. While many directors will not relinquish the right to make the final decision, more and more are finding more inclusive ways of encouraging the best ideas to float to the surface.

CLOSE-UP

Santiago Segura—King of the Gross-Out World

One genre with a steady film life, which rarely invades live theatre, is the gross-out comedy. We Americans tend to feel that we own this form. From *Animal House* to *American Pie* to *Jackass* to *Ted*, from John Landis to the Farrelly brothers to Matt Stone and Trey Parker, we are the masters of tasteless, guffaw-inducing, shameless shockers. Right? No, we are amateurs compared with Santiago Segura, whose films *Torrente 1, 2, 3,* and *4* are among the highest grossing and just plain grossest films in the Spanish-speaking world.

While Segura has started to appear in American films such as the *Blade*, *Cody Banks*, and *Hellboy* series and comedies like *Jack and Jill*, his signature work remains the *Torrente* franchise.

According to journalist Jay Parker, "When you have experienced *Torrente*, you will see all American attempts at the form as quaintly innocent, like the yearbook shot of your bad high school haircut, because Segura's character is an unrelenting fire hose of grossness." The character Torrente is a racist, fascist, gay-bashing hater of foreigners. He has often been described as a pig, an idiot, and a pervert, but most

Carlos Alvarez/Getty Images

FIGURE 4.17 Director Santiago Segura attends the *Torrente 4* premiere at the Capitol Cinema on March 9, 2011, in Madrid, Spain.

agree those do not yet quite do him justice. He is not just bald but has a comb-over—and not just a comb-over but, as Parker describes, "a stringy, clumpy one draped like a greasy black squid atop a dome of glistening skull skin." He sweats excessively and is genuinely obese. Segura is both director and star of the *Torrente* franchise, and so deserves all its credit and blame. For each film, he has gained 80 pounds, and he loses all the weight before beginning the next one.

Naturally, as the least likely person to keep the peace, Torrente is a policeman. In every film, Torrente always makes an untranslatable, sexual suggestion to his new squad partner. This remark, the most notorious catch phrase of his movies, is now shouted to him by seemingly everyone in the Spanish-speaking world wherever he goes. According to director John Landis, "The only person I've ever been out with who was approached like Santiago was John Belushi."

"Torrente is Don Quixote," says Landis, "without the nobility." According to director Oliver Stone, "Everything he does is immoral and despicable. He is not malicious. He is just despicable. In most of our comedy, we tend to poke fun at pretentiousness and normality. Torrente makes fun of everything we find legitimate and respectable."

What finally makes these films exceed ours in the gross quotient? Segura says that they include everything he hates about Spain in one place and suggests that if we ever attempt to adapt them, we will need to "put in whatever you do not like about America, in a rough and brutal way." Our comedies almost always have some element of redemption. It turns out the boob has a secret heart of gold, finds love and vows to change, or is rendered less harmful by some act of kindness. As Jay Parker puts it, "Torrente is redemption-free."

The United States is unusual in that both acting and directing classes are incorporated into college curricula, whereas in most other parts of the world, artists train at an academy or conservatory, keeping academics and art as separate institutions. Alternatively, the custom of apprenticing with a master or a company still survives.

The best actor–director connections are based on enormous mutual respect, affection, and engagement. Each time they meet, they share, exchange, and laugh. They each bring in their individual ideas and emerge with something

AUTHOR'S INSIGHT

ANNIE: I discovered fairly early on that I am no director. I hate being in charge, but I am an excellent lieutenant for the captain of our theatrical ship. Watching the various directors I've worked with over the years, I am always amazed by their ability to juggle many balls at one time and by their single-minded pursuit of excellence.

far more than their isolated solo impulses. They come into the rehearsal with expectations but leave with discoveries beyond what they expected. In the best of these interactive relationships, the actor receives deep support and stimulation from the director, and vice versa. The director receives an "I trust you and am willing to let you guide me almost anywhere" promise from the actor. The director in turn promises, "I will take you on this trip with the best help I can give." The director gives the actor the skill, belief, and will to fly and then watches that flight with deep, profound satisfaction and some regret that the interchange is now over. Both will be richer and ready for the journey—and ready to move on to the next one.

THEATRE IN MEDIA

Screen versus Stage Acting

The first feature film, *The Birth of a Nation*, was released in 1915, and regular television broadcasts began in 1948, so the Stanislavski System has profoundly affected the relatively short history of acting in front of a camera. In early silent films, the intimacy of the camera makes the non-realistic acting seem melodramatic and over the top. What early media actors needed to learn, and what most contemporary theatre actors must as well, is that the primary difference between acting for stage and camera is scale.

Stage actors need to project vocally, physically, and emotionally to the very back of the house, sometimes all the way up to the third balcony, with much of the audience at a considerable distance. In contrast, the camera can scrutinize an actor in extreme close-up, and the boom or body mike can pick up the subtlest sound. There is rarely any need to raise volume and diction, to find gestures that clearly delineate reactions. Even in a small, intimate live theatre, no one is as close as a close-up.

A stage actor can calculate an effect and pull it off impressively, while film exposes an actor's technique and effort. Film acting tends to support internal work, while stage acting demands at least some external attention to detail. Some advise film actors to just "be" because anything more can be too much. The stage actor has to sustain and repeat a performance for two or three hours and then again the next day and sometimes twice on matinee days and again the next week. The film actor needs to be able to do takes over and over, but that is usually over the course of one day and then it is on to something else. The stage actor gets to work scene by scene in performance,

moving through the story in the exact order that it is written. The screen actor shoots wildly out of sequence, sometimes starting with the ending or the most intimate encounter in the whole film, long after the characters have gotten to know each other in the actual story. The stage actor gets constant audience response, while the camera is neutral. Although the camera loves some actors more than others, it never utters this love. In movement and proximity, screen performers are often asked to move closer than would be normal for everyday interaction because the camera creates space. Finally, the stage actor at some point fully memorizes the text and sets it. The screen actor arrives not only having to know today's lines, but also needing to be prepared for rewrites and text adjustments on the spot.

Whether acting for the stage or screen is more rewarding will always be open to debate.

CYNTHIA NIXON
ACTOR

Doing a film, someone picks you up, they get your food, tell you everything you have to do. To be childlike, to be in that place at the spur of the moment— that's what you're responsible for. The business of life, other people do for you. But for a play, you take the subway to the theatre, put on your own makeup, listen for your cues. On stage, you're responsible for the play.

SEAN (P. DIDDY) COMBS
HIP-HOP MOGUL, ON PERFORMING IN *A RAISIN IN THE SUN* ON BROADWAY

Live theatre, if I would've got warned what it was, I don't know if I would've done it. You don't want to be up there for two and a half hours saying the words when you can feel you're being bad.

TYRONE GIORDANO
ACTOR (DESCRIBING DIANE KEATON, COSTAR)

I thought in working on my first film I would miss the chance to do something new each night onstage. Diane taught me that you can do something new each take, making each one like a new night.

ANNETTE BENING
ACTOR

What I enjoyed about acting on stage was the physicality of it. The breathing, moving, just like an athlete. Suddenly in a film you're asked to do a two-minute scene where you're speaking quietly, sitting down. So different!

HUGH JACKMAN
ACTOR

Stage acting sharpens your senses. When I go right from live theatre to working on a film, I go in feeling sharper and more in tune.

SCREEN VERSUS STAGE DIRECTING

While all directors carry tremendous responsibility, there are five striking differences between live and media directing:

1. Focus is a major challenge for the stage director because each audience member can look anywhere on the stage at any given time. The media director, on the other hand, has the flexible power of tight close-up to long shot, bird's-eye view to below sea level, and a myriad of other camera options to control exactly what an audience sees at any given moment.

2. Theatre directors have a rehearsal period for experimenting and developing. Any media rehearsal is rare and costly, so it is far more important to cast actors perfectly and expect them to arrive on set ready.

3. Theatres are relatively controlled spaces. If a film is shooting exteriors, or on location, the potential for natural or physical disasters and surprises (from weather or the local populace) multiply radically.

4. While a theatre staff can be large, media technical demands can multiply staff size many times over and complicate coordination efforts even more. Things move fairly rapidly in live theatre except for technical rehearsals, where there are huge pauses while adjustments are made and cues are set. In a film, every day is tech day, and there are always huge gaps between times when the camera is rolling.

5. The stage director has to let go of the show as it is gradually turned over to the cast and crew, who will be on their own after opening. The film director can continue to tinker and refine the product, often reshooting, reediting, scoring, and tightening, long after filming has ceased and even after initial showings. Some claim that films are largely created in the editing room. While the stage director cannot stop an actor from altering a performance as the live show runs, a film director has that performance "in the can" and can control and transform it by the way it is cut.

CGI ACTING

Should the Academy create a new Oscar for "performance capture" actors? These actors bring computer-generated characters to life. Andy Serkis, who shot to fame playing Gollum in the "Lord of the Rings" trilogy, weighs in on one side of the debate about CGI (computer-generated image) performers with this, "Personally I've never believed there should be a separate category because the essence of the performance is pure acting. It's ultimately whether whoever's voting for the awards thinks the performance is a genuinely moving character." In an industry increasingly dependent on "green screen" and CGI performances, an actor today needs to feel comfortable and confident in these rapidly evolving media. Veteran of stage and screen, Helen Mirren, describes what

her experience was in her 2011 film *The Tempest*. She explained that Ben Whishaw's character, an impish spirit named Ariel, was often represented by an inanimate object during the film's production. "It was a bit of a challenge, he was a tennis ball on a stick for a lot of the time," she said. "But you know that's the way digital effects work and our job as actors is to live in the world of the imagination, so that's what we do for a living. So it wasn't so difficult." Easy or difficult, actors-in-training today need to add these new skills to their repertoire in order to stay competitive.

THEATRE IN YOUR LIFE

Politicians as Actors

Theatre terms frequently enter the political world with politicians compared to performers. During the last presidential campaign, when Mitt Romney traveled to Europe and the Middle East, he made statements that offended both the Brits and the Palestinians. Some of his staff expressed concern about him going "off script." This motivated White House spokesman Josh Earnest to comment on his failure "to rise to the challenges of being an actor on the international stage." In contrast, one of President Obama's nicknames during this period was "No Drama Obama."

Just after our legislators finally reached last-minute compromises at the edge of the "fiscal cliff," this nationally syndicated cartoon appeared, reflecting the

ever widening perception that we are watching performers of highly questionable authenticity. Or actors in desperate need of directors.

AUDITIONS IN OUR LIVES

People sometimes say they are suspicious of actors because they must be great liars to be good at their jobs. In fact, the actor must be truthful, emotionally available, and thoughtful. We all act our lives. We audition for important roles. We decide whether to rely on internal or external techniques or both.

We are auditioning whenever we are in a circumstance that is now temporary and indefinite but may become permanent. So a first date is an audition for a second date, just as flirting is an audition for the first date. Meeting the parents of your partner is a challenging audition to possibly join the family. At each audition, you are deciding whether (or how much) you want the part.

One of the more profound life acting tips is offered by award-winning author Toni Morrison, who says we should all ask, "Does your face light up when your child enters the room?" For years, she fussed over details of how clean, healthy, or prepared they were, thinking her love would naturally be perceived out of this concern. Then she learned otherwise and always vowed to show in her eyes how glad she was to see them. Try this with anyone you

FIGURE 4.18   This political cartoon from the *New York Times* demonstrates society's perception of politicians as actors giving a performance.

love. You may not always be absolutely ecstatic to see them, but you can still send out light.

Whenever we anticipate unfamiliar or uncomfortable events, we prepare ourselves for the event by rehearsing, analyzing the other characters in the event, and accepting or rejecting the advice of someone who might or might not be on our side. Acting isn't about being a better liar than the others around you—it's about being alert and aware, being thoughtful and engaged, and making and rejecting choices from moment to moment.

Job interviews can be a high-stress audition, very much like auditioning for a play. One of the largest employment agencies in the country has reported its greatest success is in placing theatre majors—in nontheatrical jobs! Why? They have skills valued by every organization. They have learned to have social poise, to practice self-reliance, and to be self-motivated, perceptive, and adaptable. Actor training teaches these things by necessity. It teaches fundamental survival and advanced marketing skills as well.

Analyzing your life choices using the Stanislavski System can be revelatory. You may be surprised to find rehearsal, clear objectives, and focus can change the outcome of life encounters in significant ways. Let the actor inside you search for truth, and then figure out how to share that truth with others.

COULD YOU BE A DIRECTOR?

Do you like to plan events? Do details fascinate rather than overwhelm you? Do you love the challenge of molding people into some creative, cohesive whole? Do you love having others ask you how to do it right? Do you love to be in charge? You probably already direct personal theatre events for those around you on a regular basis.

Oddly enough, considering the potential power, authority, and satisfaction of this job, many theatre artists would not touch it. They prefer having their own niche and a tightly defined area of accountability instead of being responsible for the whole theatrical event. Directing requires knowledge of all areas of production. If you are interested, your best first step is to study every position on your potential team so that you can communicate with each member cleanly. It also requires major time-management skills because you are taking the time of so many other participants. You need a strong sense of the visual, timing, analysis, interpretation, management, composition, and a general capacity to get people to work hard for you. Probably the most significant requirement is an elusive capacity to cross brain hemispheres from logic to wonder and back again, to do scholarly research but not get trapped in detail, and to take imaginative leaps but remain grounded. So if you love to be in charge, can attend to details but always see the big picture, can produce on deadline, and do the left/right brain shift on a dime, this may be your destiny.

SUMMARY

The actor and the director engage in one of the most intimate of adventures when they join their talents in production. The actor must bring talent, charisma, and strong training to the relationship. In the East, technique is taught in exacting detail from early childhood to adulthood. In the West, most actors have been influenced by some of the Stanislavski System. In either tradition, the actors are the emotional warriors, putting themselves on the front line—figuratively and sometimes literally.

In the West, the actor works closely with the director, a relatively recent addition starting in the late nineteenth century with Georg II, Duke of Saxe-Meiningen, who insisted on appropriate design elements for each specific production, abolished the star-based vehicles, lengthened rehearsal periods, and established the director as responsible for a unified production concept.

The modern director is responsible for analysis, organization, blocking/focus, scheduling, and the rehearsal atmosphere. Some directors are traditional (serving the text), and others are conceptual (using the text as a springboard). Some are autocratic, and others are collaborative.

SUGGESTED ASSIGNMENTS

1. When have you had an experience closest to that of an actor auditioning for a play? What did you want, and how effectively did you present yourself?

2. Were you ever on the line for something you really wanted and you knew the competition? What did you do to win, or fail to do to fall short?

3. Would you say that you would do better in an audition where you were asked to present polished, memorized material or in one in which improvisation and cold readings will take place?

4. Because theatre involves constant collaboration, how do you measure up as a collaborator? Are you more autocratic or group-oriented?

5. In the theatre, it is unacceptable to drop out of a project once it is launched. In other contexts of your life, when are the best and worst times to withdraw?

6. How much do you rehearse in your life and how much is improvisation? Do you run speeches that you intend to give to someone important in your life over and over until they are perfect? Do you prefer to never prepare and go with the flow? What does this say about you and those with opposite preferences?

7. How does the protocol of your current workplace differ from that in the theatre? What does this teach you about the ways in which theatre is very much like your offstage life and the ways in which it is a whole new world?

8. Because the actors are your direct link to the play's content, when you attend a performance, ask yourself how effectively they accomplished this goal. Could you feel empathetic and connected to them? If not, what was missing?

9. Take either an improvised or written dialogue and ask two or more of your friends or classmates to rehearse with you. Ask them to make adjustments in their physical relationship, movements, line readings, and attitudes to make the scene work better. Did it work? How does it feel to do this?

10. Choose a play that you have seen or read and try to come up with a unified production concept. What ideas do you want to emphasize? How would you use space, color, actors, and so on to realize your ideas on the stage?

SUGGESTED ACTIVITIES

1. **Individual:** Identify two famous actors, one with whom you believe you have some connection, who is perhaps the same type as you, and one whom you consider as far removed from your own tendencies as possible.

2. **Group:** Attend an audition together and observe what you learn from the preparation level and behavior of various actors.

3. **Long-term:** See if you can get permission to visit a play in rehearsal. Sit in on the very first company meeting, and then return once or twice a week up until the opening. Keep a journal of what you particularly notice about how the production develops.

4. **Large group:** Identify a crowd scene, such as a party where someone asks for a date or a crowded terminal where two old friends rediscover each other. Pick the two people with real lines and have a large number go onstage and begin milling about as if it were the real event. Let the teacher guide both the crowd and the featured characters so there is variety, focus, interest, and clarity. Try as a group to achieve satisfactory results.

KEY WORDS AND IDEAS

casting calls
cattle calls
auditions
callbacks
show and tell
blocking
ensemble
read-throughs
intensives
technical rehearsals
dress rehearsals
opening night
director
Actors' Equity Association
Natya Shastra
onnagata
Shanghai Opera

Konstantin Stanislavski
the System
Lee Strasberg
the Method
Stella Adler
Sanford Meisner
run-throughs
star system
Georg II, Duke of
    Saxe-Meiningen
unified production concept
traditional directors
conceptual directors
Jerzy Grotowski
upstage
downstage

dramatic interlude 2

War

Featured plays:

Arms and the Man by George Bernard Shaw (1894)

9 Parts of Desire by Heather Raffo (2013)

(NOTE: The scripts for these plays, along with additional background information, are available in the companion anthology to this text, *Life Themes: An Anthology of Plays for the Theatre.*)

Two playwrights, working a hundred years apart, set their war stories in regions of seemingly perpetual conflict: the Balkans and the Middle East. Both challenge the fragile notion that war is a heroic, noble event, but they do so in very different ways. Shaw uses dazzling wit and satire, while Raffo takes a dramatic, naturalistic approach. In each play, it's not the war itself that is featured, but rather the effect of war on the hearts and minds of the survivors.

Arms and the Man (1894)

Setting: The home of the Petkoffs, "the richest and best-known family in Bulgaria," in a small town near the Dragoman Pass

Characters:

Raina Petkoff, heiress of the Petkoff family, engaged to Major Sarnoff

Catherine Petkoff, Raina's overbearing, excitable mother

Major Paul Petkoff, Raina's somewhat befuddled war veteran father

Captain Bluntschli, on the run after his army has been defeated

Major Sergius Sarnoff, affianced to Raina, recently victorious, full of glory and himself

Louka, household servant, flirtatious and bold

Nicola, another servant, far wiser and more pragmatic than his masters

Into Raina's bedroom comes a Serbian officer on the run after that army's defeat. While initially frightened, she immediately senses the possibility of adventure with someone she perceives to be an intriguing bad boy. After he charms and challenges her, she chooses to save him

from discovery. He then manages to mock all the lofty ideas that she and her family have about the glories of war. However, he disappoints her by not being a real enemy:

RAINA: You are one of the Austrians who set the Serbs on to rob us of our national liberty and who lead their army for them. We hate them!

BLUNTSCHLI: Austrian! Not I. Don't hate me, dear young lady. I am a Swiss, fighting merely as a professional soldier. I joined the Serbs because they came first on the road from Switzerland . . . If I'm caught, I shall be killed. Do you understand that?

RAINA: Yes.

BLUNTSCHLI: Well. I don't intend to get killed if I can help it. (*formidably*) Do you understand that? (*He locks the door quickly but quietly.*)

RAINA: (*disdainfully*) I suppose not. (*She draws herself up and looks him straight in the face, adding with cutting emphasis.*) Some soldiers, I know, are afraid to die.

BLUNTSCHLI: (*with grim humor*) All of them, dear lady, all of them, believe me.

She hides him and helps him escape, even giving him one of her father's coats in which to disguise himself. After the war, he returns to claim her, challenging and unsettling her pompous "hero" of a fiancé and the entire household with his ideas about what it means to be a professional versus an amateur:

SERGIUS: I refuse to fight you. Do you know why?

BLUNTSCHLI: No, but it doesn't matter. I'm a professional soldier: I fight when I have to. And I'm very glad to get out of it when I haven't to. You're only an amateur. You think fighting's an amusement.

Bluntschli always carries chocolates where most soldiers store cartridges and is much concerned about running out of them. In their first encounter, the shocked and disillusioned Raina disdainfully bestows a box of chocolates on him. She then calls him her "Chocolate Soldier" and falls in love.

When he returns to ask for her hand, she still has a romantic vision of him as a poor foot soldier, but it turns out he is a man of vast wealth. This unsettles her and delights her parents, who immediately withdraw their permission for her marriage to Sergius and pass it on to Bluntschli:

PETKOFF: (*with childish awe*) Are you Emperor of Switzerland?

University of Delaware, Office of Public Relations, Kathy F. Atkinson

FIGURE D2.1 Raina learns that the hero of *Arms and the Man*, Bluntschli, is not the warring kind, preferring to carry chocolates instead of bullets, in this University of Delaware production.

BLUNTSCHLI: My rank is the highest now in Switzerland. I am a free citizen.

CATHERINE: Then Captain Bluntschli, since you are my daughter's choice . . . .

RAINA: (*mutinously*) He's not . . . I shall not be sold off to the highest bidder. (*She turns her back on him.*)

BLUNTSCHLI: I won't take that answer. You accepted me as a fugitive, a beggar, and a starving man. You accepted me. You gave me your hand to kiss, your bed to sleep in, and your roof to shelter me.

RAINA: I did not give them to the Emperor of Switzerland!

BLUNTSCHLI: That's just what I said. (*He catches her by the shoulder and turns her face to face with him.*) Now tell us whom you did give them to.

RAINA: (*succumbing with a shy smile*) To my chocolate cream soldier!

(*They embrace and kiss.*)

Shaw makes a strong case that war is not glorious, but brutal. While others have made that argument, he is perhaps the first to point out that on a day-to-day basis, it can often, even more disappointingly, be deadly dull.

Most brilliantly, Shaw offers the perception that one is always better off and more likely to get what one wants by carrying candy instead of cartridges.

Here is a scene from *Arms and the Man*, edited and adapted by Robert Barton. The full text of this edition of the play is available in the anthology *Life Themes: An Anthology of Plays for the Theatre*.

Raina is engaged to a cavalry officer in the Bulgarian army. She is about to encounter a young Swiss mercenary named Bluntschli (identified in the following scene only as "the man") hiding in her bedroom:

[THE MAN (*Bluntschli*) *immediately steps out from behind the curtain, sheathing his sabre, and closes the shutters. Then, dismissing the danger from his mind in a business-like way, he comes affably to Raina.*]

THE MAN: A narrow shave; but a miss is as good as a mile. Dear young lady: your servant to the death. I wish for your sake I had joined the Bulgarian army instead of the other one. I am not a native Serb.

RAINA: [haughtily] No, you are one of the Austrians who set the Serbs on to rob us of our national liberty, and who officer their army for them. We hate them!

THE MAN: Austrian! Not I. Don't hate me, dear young lady. I am a Swiss, fighting merely as a professional soldier. I joined the Serbs because they came first on the road from Switzerland. Be generous; you've beaten us hollow.

RAINA: Have I not been generous?

THE MAN: Noble! Heroic! But I'm not saved yet. This particular rush will soon pass through, but the pursuit will go on all night by fits and starts. I must take my chance to get off in a quiet interval. [Pleasantly] You don't mind my waiting just a minute or two, do you?

RAINA: [Putting on her most genteel society manner] Oh, not at all. Won't you please sit down?

THE MAN: Thanks. [He sits on the foot of the bed.]

[RAINA walks with studied elegance to the ottoman and sits down. Unfortunately she sits on the pistol, and jumps up with a shriek. THE MAN, all nerves, shies like a frightened horse to the other side of the room.]

THE MAN: [irritably] Don't frighten me like that. What is it?

RAINA: Your revolver! It was staring that officer in the face all the time. What an escape!

THE MAN: [vexed at being unnecessarily terrified] Oh, is that all?

RAINA: [staring at him rather superciliously as she conceives a poorer and poorer opinion of him, and feels proportionately more and more at her ease] I am sorry I frightened you. [She takes up the pistol and hands it to him.] Pray take it to protect yourself against me.

THE MAN: [grinning wearily at the sarcasm as he takes the pistol] No use, dear young lady, there's nothing in it. It's not loaded. [He makes a grimace at it, and drops it disparagingly into his revolver case.]

RAINA: Load it by all means.

THE MAN: I've no ammunition. What use are cartridges in battle? I always carry chocolate instead; and I finished the last cake of that hours ago.

RAINA: [outraged in her most cherished ideals of manhood] Chocolate! Do you stuff your pockets with sweets—like a schoolboy—even in the field?

THE MAN: [grinning] Yes. Isn't it contemptible? [Hungrily] I wish I had some now.

RAINA: Allow me. [She sails away scornfully to the chest of drawers, and returns with the box of confectionery in her hand.] I am sorry I have eaten them all except these. [She offers him the box.]

THE MAN: [ravenously] You're an angel! [He gobbles the contents.] Creams! Delicious! [He looks anxiously to see whether there are any more. There are none. He can only scrape the box with his fingers and suck them. When that nourishment is exhausted, he accepts the inevitable with pathetic good humor, and says with grateful emotion.] Bless you, dear lady! You can always tell an old soldier by the inside of his holsters and cartridge boxes. The young ones carry pistols and cartridges; the old ones, grub. Thank you. [He hands back the box. She snatches it contemptuously from him and throws it away. He shies again, as if she had meant to strike him.] Ugh! Don't do things so suddenly, gracious lady. It's mean to revenge yourself because I frightened you just now.

RAINA: [loftily] Frighten me! Do you know, sir, that though I am only a woman, I think I am at heart as brave as you.

THE MAN: I should think so. You haven't been under fire for three days as I have. I can stand two days without showing it much; but no man can stand three days. I'm as nervous as a mouse. [He sits down on the ottoman, and takes his head in his hands.] Would you like to see me cry?

RAINA: [alarmed] No.

THE MAN: If you would, all you have to do is to scold me just as if I were a little boy and you my nurse. If I were in camp now, they'd play all sorts of tricks on me.

RAINA: [a little moved] I'm sorry. I won't scold you. [Touched by the sympathy in her tone, he raises his head and looks gratefully at her.]

RAINA: [eagerly turning to him, as all her enthusiasm and her dreams of glory rush back on her] Did you see the great cavalry charge? Oh, tell me about it. Describe it to me.

THE MAN: You never saw a cavalry charge, did you?

RAINA: How could I?

THE MAN: Ah, perhaps not. No. Of course not! Well, it's a funny sight. First one comes, then two or three close behind him, and then all the rest in a lump.

RAINA: [her eyes dilating as she raises her clasped hands ecstatically] Yes, first one! The bravest of the brave!

THE MAN: *[prosaically]* Hm! You should see the poor devil pulling at his horse.

RAINA: Why should he pull at his horse?

THE MAN: *[impatient at so stupid a question]* It's running away with him, of course. Do you suppose the fellow wants to get there before the others and be killed?

RAINA: Ugh! But I don't believe the first man is a coward. I know he is a hero!

THE MAN: *[good-humoredly]* That's what you'd have said if you'd seen the first man in charge today.

RAINA: *[breathless, forgiving him everything]* Ah, I knew it! Tell me about him.

THE MAN: He did it like an operatic tenor. A regular handsome fellow, with flashing eyes and lovely moustache, shouting his war-cry and charging like Don Quixote at the windmills. We did laugh.

RAINA: You dared to laugh!

THE MAN: Yes, but when the sergeant ran up as white as a sheet, and told us they'd sent us the wrong ammunition, and that we couldn't fire a round for the next ten minutes, we laughed out of the other side of our mouths. I never felt so sick in my life, though I've been in one or two very tight places. And I hadn't even a revolver cartridge, only chocolate. We'd no bayonets, nothing. Of course, they just cut us to bits. And there was Don Quixote flourishing like a drum major, thinking he's the cleverest thing ever known, whereas he ought to be court martialed for it. Of all the fools ever let loose on a field of battle, that man must be the very maddest. He and his regiment simply committed suicide; only the pistol missed fire; that's all.

RAINA: *[deeply wounded, but steadfastly loyal to her ideals]* Indeed! Would you know him again if you saw him?

THE MAN: Shall I ever forget him! *[She again goes to the chest of drawers. He watches her with a vague hope that she may have something more for him to eat. She takes the portrait from its stand and brings it to him.]*

RAINA: That is a photograph of the gentleman—the patriot and hero—to whom I am betrothed.

THE MAN: *[recognizing it with shock]* I'm really very sorry. *[Looking at her]* Was it fair to lead me on? *[He looks at the portrait again.]* Yes, that's Don Quixote. Not a doubt of it. *[He stifles a laugh, then apologetic, but still greatly tickled.]* I didn't laugh, I assure you. At least I didn't mean to. But when I think of him charging the windmills and imagining he was doing the finest thing—*[He chokes with suppressed laughter.]*

RAINA: *[sternly]* Give me back the portrait, sir.

THE MAN: *[with sincere remorse]* Of course. Certainly. I'm really very sorry. *[He hands her the picture. She deliberately kisses it and looks him straight in the face before returning to the chest of drawers to replace it. He follows her, apologizing.]* Perhaps I'm quite wrong, you know, no doubt I am. Most likely he had got wind of the cartridge business somehow, and knew it was a safe job.

RAINA: That is to say, he was a pretender and a coward! You did not dare say that before.

THE MAN: *[with a comic gesture of despair]* It's no use, dear lady. I can't make you see it from the professional point of view. *[As he turns away to get back to the ottoman, a couple of distant shots threaten renewed trouble.]*

RAINA: *[sternly, as she sees him listening to the shots]* So much the better for you!

THE MAN: *[turning]* How?

RAINA: You are my enemy; and you are at my mercy. What would I do if I were a professional soldier?

THE MAN: Ah, true, dear young lady: you're always right. I know how good you've been to me. To my last hour I shall remember those three chocolate creams. It was unsoldierly, but it was angelic.

RAINA: *[coldly]* Thank you. And now I will do a soldierly thing. You cannot stay here after what you have just said about my future husband; but I will go out on the balcony and see whether it is safe for you to climb down into the street. *[She turns to the window.]*

THE MAN: *[changing countenance]* Down that waterpipe! Stop! Wait! I can't! I daren't! The very thought of it makes me giddy. I came up it fast enough with death behind me. But to face it now in cold blood—! *[He drops his head in his hands in the deepest dejection.]*

RAINA: *[disarmed by pity]* Come, don't be disheartened. *[She stoops over him almost maternally; he shakes his head]* Oh, you are a very poor soldier. A chocolate cream soldier! Come, cheer up! It takes less courage to climb down than to face capture. Remember that.

9 Parts of Desire (2013)

Settings: Baghdad, 1993

Characters:
Mullaya
Layal
Amal
Huda
The Doctor
The Iraqi Girl
Umm Ghada
The American
Nanna

God created sexual desire in ten parts; then he gave nine
*   parts to women and one part to men.*
                    Ali b. Abi Talib, fourth caliph after Muhammad

A group of nine women of Iraqi descent struggle with
the damage done by war. The most recent war recounted
in this play is the American invasion of Iraq in 1990
in response to Saddam Hussein's invasion of Kuwait.
Following hard on the heels of the eight-year Iran-Iraq
war of the 1980s, and leading to the Second Gulf War of
2003–2011, this particular conflict may seem like a minor
skirmish in a region that has seen nothing but bloodshed
for three decades. But, of course, that's never the case
for those living it or for those who are terrified
for loved ones living in the war zone. Our primary guide
through the chaos of war is a young artist named Layal:

LAYAL: Leave Iraq?
    [*She giggles oddly as she tries to imagine it.*]
    Well, I could move I suppose –
    My sister wants me to come to London
    and she has a house and an art studio there now
    I could go I have the money.
    I don't know
    maybe I feel guilty
    all of us here
    it's a shame if all the artists leave too –
    who will be left to inspire the people if all the
    artists and intellectuals run?
    Most of them already have
    my sister included.
    I don't judge
    I mean for most
    they feel they cannot express themselves
    because always it is life and death –
    even I should have been dead twice before I tell you
    but I'm not
    death is only teasing me.
    [*She laughs.*]

Maybe that's it, maybe I stay because
I feel lucky, I am charmed, what can touch me?

Layal is a modern, sophisticated, young urban Iraqi woman
who is the curator of the national art museum that is
filled with monumental images of Saddam Hussein. But
sometimes in a small alcove or corner, an artist is allowed
to exhibit work that is new. Layal's art becomes our
window into the lives of Iraqi women:

LAYAL: I did a painting once of a woman
    eaten by Saddam's son
    that's how I describe it.
    A beautiful young student, from University of Baghdad –
    One day he asked her out, she couldn't refuse,
    he took her and beat her brutally, like is his way –
    she went back to campus and
    her roommate saw the bruises and things and asked
        her "What happened?"
    And she so stupid, innocent girl told her the truth.
    Why she talks such things?
    Iraqis they know not to open their mouth not even
        for the dentist.
    Of course one day, he took her back
    with his friends, they
    stripped her covered her in honey
    and watched his Dobermans eat her.

    See in my painting she is the branch's blossom
    leaning over the barking dogs
    they cannot reach
    no matter how hungry they are
    not unless they learn to climb her
    but they are dogs, they never will.
    You see, nobody knows the painting is her
    but I believe somewhere she sees.

    That is me, [*laughing*] my philosophy!
    These stories are living inside of me
    each woman I meet her or I hear about her
    and I cannot separate myself from them. . . .

Next we meet Amal, a Bedouin Iraqi woman struggling
to stay true to her heritage in a constantly shifting
contemporary landscape. She has just learned that she's
considered fat and has put herself and her two children
on a diet. Her first husband, a Saudi Bedouin, took her
to London where he was a successful plastic surgeon.
They had two children together before Amal learned he
was sleeping with her best friend. She left him and in
time became the second wife of an Israeli Bedouin who
promised to take her to Canada. The first wife was not
happy and Amal left the marriage. Then she meets the
third love of her life and they carry on a courtship of two
years by phone. After they meet in Dubai, he suddenly
tells her the engagement is off:

AMAL: I see with my heart
    not with my eyes.
    I am Bedouin
    I cannot tell you if
    a man is fat or if a man is handsome
    only I can tell you if I love this man or not.
    I think you see with your heart like a Bedouin.

    We talk and we say we will get married, third
        marriage, oh!
    He says let us meet in Dubai
    because the war it was then and if he comes back
        home to Iraq
    they may keep him.

    So I left my job, I left everything.
    I telephone to his family congratulations
    he telephone to my family
    and we go to meet in this hotel in Dubai
    we go to dinner
    he says after dinner
    "I am going I will call you later "
    and I waiting in my hotel room so happy to see this
        man I love.
    I telephone hims at two A.M. and he says, "No, not
        now I am drunk" –
    I say, "Let us talk I want to talk
    we spent one year on the phone talking everything
    finally we see each other
    my heart is so full to share" –
    he says, '"No Amal,
    no," he says, "it is over
    do not talk to me anymore."
    I am crying really I don't understand him say this thing
    but him say,
    "You are too pure for me
    what you do with a man like me? I am twenty year
        older than you
    soon I will be very olds man and you have to take
        care of me
    you are too good, too innocent for me."
    I don't understand hims say this thing because I love him,
    and him says, "No,"
    "No," he say,
    "you are not the Amal I love."
    What does this mean?
    I am not the Amal he love?

    How he say this?
    Why can this be?

    I am shamed to my family
    they think he slept with me that night
    we meet in Dubai
    and change his mind.

    I don't have peace.

    Always I am asking myself what he think of me?
    What he seed in me that change him?
    I see now I am fat.
    Now I look for the first time to dress myself more pretty
    I am doing my hair this way –
    but I don't see hims fat, I don't see hims old
    I see hims with my heart not with my eyes
    and never have I love a man this much.

The play goes on to introduce us to Huda, an Iraqi expat communist living in London. She is torn between hating Saddam Hussein and doubting the altruism of American foreign policy. We meet The Doctor, desperately trying to save lives amid filth and without medical supplies. She's not only fighting the immediate conditions of her clinic, but also a millennium of tradition. In the following excerpt from the play, we meet Umm Ghada (Mother of Ghada) the ghostly, dreadful survivor of a bombing raid:

[UMM GHADA *lets the abaya fall; it is a black hole. A
    woman of great stillness and pride, peaceful and
    dispassionate.*]

    UMM GHADA: I named my daughter Ghada.
        Ghada means tomorrow.
        So I am Umm Ghada, Mother of Ghada.
        It is a sign of joy and respect to call a parent by their *kunya*.

        In Baghdad, I am famous now as Umm Ghada
        because I do live here in yellow trailer
        outside Amiriyya bomb shelter
        since the bombing
        13 February 1991.

        Yes I was inside
        with nine from my family
        talking, laughing
        then such a pounding, shaking
        everything is fire
        I couldn't find my children
        I couldn't find my way out
        but somehow I did.

        In the whole day later
        I am searching, searching charred bodies
        bodies they were fused together
        the only body
        I did recognize
        is my daughter Ghada
        so I did take her name [*With so much pride.*]
        I am Umm Ghada, Mother of Ghada.

        I am hard to understand
        why I survive
        and my children dead.

I asked to Allah why?
Why you make me alive?
That night all people died
four hundred three people
and there's nothing we can do. They are dead.
This trailer is my witness stand.
All photos on this wall – and here – are me
with emissaries from the world
who come to Amiriyya shelter to look
what really happen here
not what they read in papers
or see in the CNN.
Here is guest book they all sign,
your name will be witness too.
La, I must show it to you first. Ta'alu.

*[She enters the shelter, it is the first time we see
her subtle limp.]*

This is Amiriyya bomb shelter.
Here they write names
in chalk over the smoked figures.
Here, on the ceiling, you can see
charred handprints and footprints
from people who lay in the top bunks.
And here a silhouette of a woman
vaporized from heat.
This huge room became an oven,
and they pressed to the walls to escape from the flames.
In the basement too
bombs burst the pipes
hot water came up to five feet
and boiled the people.

La, la,
I do not want to show you there
it is too much
the walls are stuck with hairs and skin.

Come, I will take you to the roof
you can see how the hole was made.

*[As she walks towards the hole in the roof we hear
the midday call to prayer off in the distance; she
pauses briefly.]*

Two bombs from U.S. airplane
come to this point of the roof.
The first bomb is drilling bomb
drilled this hole
second one
come inside exactly same spot
and exploded in fires.

The U.S. said they thought this is
communication center for military.

Myself,
I think they were testing bomb –
these bomb had never been use before, but it is special
two bomb design for breaking only a bomb shelter.
It is very purpose.
It is very purpose.

Now look around this hole
wild greens they are growing
life did choose to root
here in this grave of Iraqi people.

All my family is here, Ghada is here
so I am Umm Ghada, Mother of Tomorrow.
My full name is dead with them.

Come.
Now you sign the witness book.

[LAYAL picks up a paint brush.]

LAYAL:
We have a story –
There is a restaurant with a sign
'COME IN, EAT ALL YOU WANT,
FREE OF CHARGE
YOUR GRANDSON WILL PAY THE BILL.'
So a young man, a teenager,
he goes in
happy for the free meal,
he eats, and eats, and eats
when he is done eating all he wants
the waiter brings him a bill.
The young man says to the waiter,
"No, your sign says free of charge,
my grandson will pay the bill."
The waiter says, "Yes, indeed sir,
but this –
this is your Grandfather's bill." *[She laughs.]*

My Grandfather's bill!

You know my house was hit, from Bush's war, aa, aa,
I wasn't there, il-hamdu lillah,
but we lost everything, my paintings for the new
    exhibition
my family's things, everything.
That's why I'm living here, at my sister's house.
It was only eight houses from here –
this neighborhood they bomb, Mansur, can you believe it?
So how smart is this bomb
if it bomb a painter? *[She laughs.]*
Maybe they think I am dangerous?

Maybe I am, I am attached like I will die if I leave.

Expansions 2 | Stories into Performances

Here are examples that expand the ideas of the past two chapters. Both of our featured interlude plays can be analyzed further as dramatic texts and as challenges for directors and actors.

Playwrighting

Heather Raffo provides an obvious opportunity to discuss the process of "wrighting" a play. Her first visit to Iraq as an adult (1993) led to love and trust between Raffo and her many relatives. They opened their hearts and homes to her and in time told her the stories of their lives. Raffo then transformed the reality of those stories into the theatricality of a one-woman show, performed by Raffo. In the edition referenced here (2013), she continues to update material to include the most recent conflicts in Iraq and their effects on the women who live there. Her work involves wrestling with and mastering the non-dramatic material of talks around the kitchen table into the dramatic material that we find in the play.

Influence

Because wars continue today as they have for all recorded history, can we say that these playwrights or plays have *influenced* the world or culture around them? Certainly Shaw was deeply disappointed in the loving reception given to *Arms and the Man* when he realized that audiences were allowing themselves to be charmed by the love story before they were influenced by the antiwar message so firmly entrenched in his intent. He survived to see his beloved country become enmeshed in World War I, during which literally millions of young men eagerly enlisted in the hope of tasting the glories of war. It didn't take long for England and her youngsters to become disillusioned by the horrors and tedium encountered in the trenches of Europe.

Heather Raffo, too, is all too aware that atrocities against women continue in every war-torn region of the world today. Her focus may be on the experiences of Iraqi women—the country has been at war for most of the last three decades and continues to be a scene of perpetual violence—but her message is universal: whenever war strikes, women, children, and other innocents often pay the ultimate price. This is certainly a topic worth considering and discussing. Is that the influence both of these playwrights hoped for—that we would at least begin to discuss the possibility of ending wars?

Medium

If we start with a discussion of a possible film version of *9 Parts of Desire*, the likely differences between the play and the film are numerous. In a film, would we need to see the actual war, the actual atrocities committed, the battlefield and civilian horrors taking place before our eyes? In many ways, the stage script seems too static for film. We seldom see movies that take place in such a limited number of locations and in which the focus of the dramatic action is on interior rather than exterior events. In addition, in most (though not all) productions of this play on stage, Heather Raffo plays all the parts. On the other hand, the stage doesn't lend itself particularly well to battle scenes, large-scale refugee evacuations, or panoramas of destroyed towns, villages, and fields. The stage does, however, give us the opportunity to experience the intimate sharing of interior experience that can be achieved only by living in the same space and breathing the same air as the characters as this exact moment in time is re-created before our eyes. If a generalization can be forgiven, perhaps war itself is best depicted on the expansive canvas of film, while the aftereffects of war are best explored in the intimacy of live theatre.

Mood

We might expect war plays to be violent and tragic, but one is comic and the other contemplative. How do these unexpected moods serve each work? In Arms and the Man, we might consider the love story between Raina and Bluntschli as the spoonful of sugar that makes the medicine of an antiwar message go down. In *9 Parts of Desire*, the focus is not so much on war itself as it is on war's effects on the innocent. Such a contemplative mood might seem to undermine the horrors of war on the battlefield, but for a play about survivors, it seems ideal. As revealed in the text, the women in Baghdad spend their days (and years) waiting—waiting for something to happen, waiting for something to change. They also live in fear and horror, yet with enormous courage make every effort to live a "normal" life. Neither play takes us to the full scale, "you are there" horrors of, say, *Saving Private* Ryan, but because that is not their intent, their moods seem perfectly designed to promote the intent of the authors.

Point of Attack

Both plays begin *after* the war. Why? To what end? Logistically, a stage production is never going to do full justice to the portrayal of a war. Because neither writer is interested in the excitement and spectacle of battle but rather its impact, it serves both plays to deal with the aftermath. It also shakes us out of our complacent tendency to believe that once a truce is made, the war is over; its reverberation goes on and on. Both playwrights are asking us, once all the fireworks have abated, to take part in thoughtful reflection.

Structure

Interestingly, both plays offered analytical challenges in discovering the protagonist/antagonist relationship. In *Arms and the Man*, assuming Raina is the protagonist (the character who changes the most or whom the author wants us to follow through her journey), then who is her antagonist? This depends on what you see as the central conflict of the play. If Raina's conflict is her attempt to continue seeing war as a noble and glorious enterprise, then shouldn't we choose Bluntschli as her antagonist? He is certainly the character who opens her eyes to the truth about war. However, if her desire is to marry her true love, then Sergius is the character most in her way (with the backing of her parents). If the idea of the play is to focus on the stupidity of war, choosing Bluntschli as her antagonist and emphasizing their conflict supports that idea. If the play is a love story, the classic love triangle of Raina–Sergius–Bluntschli provides a time-tested model for overcoming obstacles on the way to love, and emphasizing this structure supports that storyline. Which do you think Shaw would have desired?

Antagonists

9 Parts of Desire, a play that defies most structural conventions, comprises a series of monologues that build in a dramatically engaging way to a climax that is powerful and devastating. But since the characters never interact and presumably don't know each other, searching for a traditional protagonist/antagonist relationship is fruitless.

Playwright's Plans

There are many great antiwar plays, but these two differ from most of the rest. Shaw chooses to use high wit and elegant conversation to pass devastating judgment on war, while in Raffo's play, the focus is entirely on those who are influenced and, in some instances, devastated by the warring actions of others. The point of view shared by both scripts is high skepticism. Imagine either play being produced at a time when the United States is considering or taking the first steps toward another international conflict. The degree to which many audience members share the playwright's perspective is strongly influenced by the state of the world and current public opinion.

Casting

9 Parts of Desire would be a challenge for college theatres because of the maturity of some of the central characters and the need for some women to look and speak believably Iraqi. As mentioned, many productions of this play feature Heather Raffo in all nine roles. In *Arms and the Man*, the challenge for all cast members is to rise to Shaw's elevated, witty repartee and to be convincing as people who lived over a hundred years ago. Actors must move well, speak well, and convey crisp intelligence. Whereas the contrast in dialects is crucial in Raffo's play, in Shaw's, the use of Bulgarian and Swiss accents would just be a distraction.

Rehearsal

Both plays have small casts and are relatively short, so the logistics of rehearsal would be relatively simple. The setting in Raffo's play is described as suggestive of open space and flexibility, so scenery is minimal. While Shaw's play has three different settings, each of which is somewhat detailed, set changes are all accomplished during the two intermissions. Both plays involve intense dialect/speech work. In *9 Parts of Desire,* the work involves

Iraqi speech, while in *Arms and the Man*, the work involves an elevated, nonregional speech with superb diction and a powerful sense of wordplay. Shaw's women characters must master movement in corsets, bustles, and possibly trains, while the men characters deal with the military bearing of another era. The entire Victorian mode of behavior, from hand kissing to bows and salutes, must be mastered.

Internal versus External Acting

If the actors are cast close to age and type, *9 Parts of Desire* would benefit from internal work on the part of actors. The lines are conversational, the situations are real, and good actors should be able to tap easily into the emotions of the characters. Shaw's characters are larger than life and require technical virtuosity. While actors may do some internal work in terms of character motivation, there will be a huge emphasis on the external mastery of unfamiliar modes of speech and behavior.

Directorial Approach

Which script would more readily welcome a conceptual versus a traditional directorial approach? Neither script particularly lends itself to a conceptual directorial vision, although conceptual directors would probably disagree. *9 Parts of Desire* relies on the "reality" of the world of play, as well as the believability of character and dialogue to make its emotional point. Can it be conceptualized into a highly theatrical event? Of course, and the visual/design challenges of the play may lead to the use of theatrical rather than realistic images on stage. *Arms and the Man* also seems grounded in the intimate reality of the characters' interactions. However, can the play be set in modern times or theatre time? Is war a constant that is not confined to any particular place or time? Unfortunately, yes. If the language and wit of Shaw were preserved, this script, perhaps more than the realistic, specific world of Raffo's play, might lend itself to a conceptual approach.

chapter 5

DESIGNERS

The photos pictured here show different productions of Shakespeare's *Hamlet*. Compare this production—featuring David Tennant as Hamlet, a Royal Shakespeare Company Production directed by Gregory Doran at the Courtyard Theatre—with the other shown on the next page. Observe the differences in costume, scenic, and lighting design.

T. Charles Erickson

Hamlet at the Alley Theatre has a darker setting and more vampire-like costume and makeup design, radically different from the Courtyard Theatre production.

Lesson Objectives:

Upon completion of this chapter, you will be able to:

1. Identify the various types of stages used in the modern theatre.
2. Identify the functions of the designer in modern theatre.
3. Compare Western and Eastern traditions in terms of design.
4. Identify the design processes of the four major areas of design: scenery, costume, lighting, and sound.
5. Identify when and how you design your personal life.
6. Identify if you might have what it takes to make one of these professions your career.

Introduction

Theatre is possible without design. It can happen with no sets, lights, costumes, makeup, or sound, and it can be magical. However, without these elements, a performance relies on the power of the actors' skilled concentration to transform and enthrall. Audiences want to be transformed and transported. Actors can manage this without backup if they are so compelling and imaginative that we give ourselves up the same way we did when being read to aloud as children, when words could metamorphose us through our limitless imagination. But sometimes we want the magic without necessarily working all that hard for it to happen.

Designers are wizards who take us out of "same old" into some "special other." They jump-start our imaginations. When we are less than resourceful and need recharging, they give us the juice. The world that they hand us may be more exotic, spectacular, mysterious, threatening, satisfying, complete, or romantic than the one in which we live. It may be so dark and dirty that we are stunned and appalled but compelled. On the other hand, it may be so exactly like some world we know that we lose ourselves in unexpectedly familiar territory and amazing detail. But it will not be what we experienced on the ride to the theatre, in the parking lot, the box office, and the lobby. All that will dissolve, and we hope that it will give us indelible memories.

This chapter offers glimpses into the world of those who design sets, costumes, makeup, masks, and sound. We will try to understand more about how each of them makes the magic happen.

Design Basics

Designers work with five key ingredients and five basic principles. The **design ingredients** are:

1. **Line:** Are the primary lines going to be horizontal or vertical, and within that domain, how straight, curved, angular, zigzagged, or scalloped will they be? What does this suggest to an audience? What shapes will communicate meaning?

2. **Mass:** How much and what kind of space will be filled? How thick and how shaped will it be? What kind of bulk, weight, and size will fill the stage?

3. **Color:** What hue, intensity, and values will be used? Will they be light, dark, warm, cool, tinted, shaded, or in primary or secondary colors?

4. **Texture:** What will the surfaces be like? Will they be rough, smooth, shiny, matte, or grainy?

5. **Decor:** What will be added within the overall scheme in terms of furniture, trim, moldings, fringe, and general ornamentation?

FIGURE 5.1 Viewing this scenic design for the musical *Hairspray*, notice how the design ingredients of line, mass, color, texture, and decor create a clear world of the play.

Erin Patrice O'Brien/Corbis

All visual artists outside the theatre—such as architects, home decorators, painters, sculptors, and clothing designers—consider these same elements. Sound designers take visual ingredients and translate them into auditory components.

Basic design principles include:

1. **Unity:** How do we tie individual components together into a coordinated, harmonious whole?

2. **Variety:** Within this unified whole, how will interest, suspense, and enjoyment be created (and boredom avoided) by diverse and lively choices?

3. **Balance:** How will the weight and size of elements be distributed? In the range between completely symmetrical and asymmetrical, where will the pictures be? What will be the scale of each part in relation to others?

4. **Focus:** What will be disguised and what enhanced? Where do we want to draw the eye and emphasize an element? What will be strong and what will be weak?

5. **Progression:** Will each of the preceding elements and principles stay constant or shift throughout the performance? Which will be repeated, altered gradually, or changed altogether? How will the timing of the event move, segue, or flow?

Theatre Spaces

The type of staging space used affects all design work, and all designers learn to adapt to the variables inherent in each. Five of the most common styles are proscenium, thrust, arena, environmental, and black box (or flexible) staging.

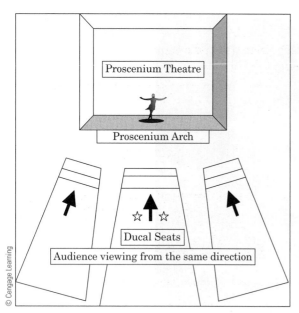

© Cengage Learning

FIGURE 5.2   Proscenium stage.

Proscenium Stages

From approximately the seventeenth century well into the twentieth century, European and American designers were working in theatres with **proscenium stages**. As you can see in Figure 5.2, the proscenium stage resembles an opening in a wall through which the audience looks. That hole, known as the *proscenium arch,* creates a picture frame that controls the point of view of the audience. All audience members are facing the same direction. Designers face both limitations and rewards in this type of space.

The obvious advantage is the ability to control focus. Scenery, lighting, costume, and sound are designed toward the audience, while much of the mechanics of the magic remain hidden. When scenery was primarily made of canvas drops painted to create the illusion of depth with two- and three-point perspective (from the seventeenth through the nineteenth centuries), the starred locations on the proscenium theatre diagram in Figure 5.2 were known as the "ducal seats," which were reserved for the most important audience members. Even today, these seats are set aside for reviewers, major donors, and other VIPs. The proscenium stage works well for producing large, complicated projects and for creating and sustaining the illusion of reality. Proscenium houses also tend to be larger than some other types, serving more patrons, and everyone in the audience can see most of the stage at all times.

The term **sight lines** refers to how much the audience can see and what the arch or other **masking** blocks from view. Masking is anything designed to block the audience's view, to "mask" the mechanics of the backstage area, for example. In a proscenium house, designers often use curtains or flats to accomplish this. While this type of space controls masking and sight lines to a degree, audiences sitting at the outside walls often will not be able to see some action at the very sides of the stage.

The primary limitation of the proscenium stage is achieving a sense of intimacy with the audience. The great European opera master Richard Wagner (1813–1883) called the space between the arch and the audience the "mystic gulf." Sometimes getting past this gulf is difficult. For lighting and sound designers, the challenges include finding ways to model visual and audio elements into three-dimensional experiences. If all the lights point from the same direction, people on stage tend to blend into the scenery. Equally, if all sound emanates from one direction, the effect can be flat. During the second half of the twentieth century, a strong movement away from the traditional proscenium stage occurred.

Thrust or ¾ Round Stages

In moving away from the proscenium stage, focus issues increase and design detail becomes more important. In Figure 5.3, showing the **thrust stage** or ¾ round stage, you can see that the audience sits on three sides of the stage. Only one wall and the stage floor are available for scenic design, and they become essential elements of focus, whether left completely blank or filled with ornate detailing. Now audience members can also see each other. Performers and space have to compete with the unpredictable behavior of human beings.

The single remaining wall in a thrust stage may be architectural, painted, or draped with one or more exit/entrance points for actors. In Figure 5.3, the stars indicate not ducal but "cheap seats," which are usually sold last because the view of the wall and, frequently, the performers is reduced. Thrust stages allow more intimacy with the audience, so costume designers must increase their attention to detail when working in this type of space. Audience members will generally be closer than when the mystic gulf allows a few shortcuts.

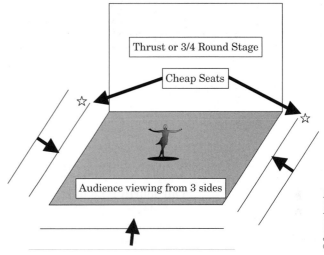

FIGURE 5.3 Thrust or ¾ round stage.

For lighting and sound designers, the thrust stage allows a fuller artistic palette. Light thrown on the stage floor becomes a visual focal point and creates space, time, mood, and patterns as realistic as sunlight through trees or as abstract as swirling blends of color. The challenge lies in lighting all parts of the stage and each actor anywhere on that stage without spilling light onto unwilling audience members. Sitting in stage-light spill can be embarrassing, uncomfortably warm, and can distract focus.

The thrust stage similarly challenges and frees sound designers. They have the opportunity to wrap the audience in sound coming from multiple directions. They must, on the other hand, control and balance that sound so that half of the audience isn't blown away by sound while the other half barely hears it.

Arena or Full Round Stages

In some ways, theatre architecture has come full circle with the **arena** or full round stage. As Ook gathered his clan around the fire to perform his lion hunt (described in Chapter 2), the arena stage gathers the audience in a circle around the stage. In Figure 5.4, the first thing that you might notice is that no place exists for walls, drapes, or large units of scenery because the audience is looking at the stage from every direction. The stage floor becomes more central as a design component, as may scenic elements hung above the stage or very

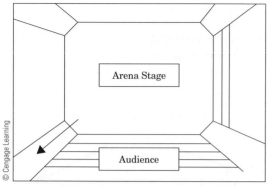

FIGURE 5.4   Arena stage.

strategically placed. The audience tends to be even closer than in thrust stages. The challenge becomes a need for brilliant simplicity in design. Anything of any mass or height blocks sight lines. For the costume designer, the intimacy increases the need for detail. For lighting and sound designers, the challenges of balance and focus become even stronger.

However, increased communion with the audience, a strong sense of being close together physically and psychologically, rewards all these challenges. The audience member can't help but see other audience members on all sides, and this can powerfully increase a sense of community.

Environmental Stages

Our fourth type of stage is as ancient as theatre itself and as cutting-edge as today's news. The **environmental stage** is any space designated by an agreement between audience and performance as a theatre. In fact, in some avant-garde theatre, the audience is left out of the agreement. An environmental space may be as intimate as a private living room or as big as the wide-open prairie. Street corners, alleyways, churches, town halls, marketplaces, warehouses, ruined buildings, mountaintops, and clearings in the forest can all serve as environmental theatres.

The level of design challenge depends entirely on the level of control desired, sometimes with nothing altered and sometimes with an intricate creation built in the found space. Environmental stages can provide some of the most magical theatre experiences. They are certainly the kind of stage used by our primal theatrical ancestors. They are the most fleeting and delicate of the five types of stages because as soon as we leave them, they disappear, reverting to what they were before we arrived to see a play. If the environmental stage is in the town square, just about anyone passing by can see it, so it can be the most egalitarian and communal of stages. On the other hand, if the stage is someone's private home, it may be the most elitist (designed to keep out the riffraff) or the riskiest (if the authorities are watching). Look for theatre events staged in nontraditional spaces, as they are sometimes brilliant and always intriguing.

Black Box Theatres

By far the most popular choice for contemporary production is the **black box** or flexible staging space, which is essentially a large, box-shaped room, usually painted all black. If equipped with versatile, movable, and flexible seating, lighting, and sound, this space can become whatever the production team wants. It can be proscenium (with a frame inserted), thrust, or arena by simply reconfiguring the audience/actor proximity. It can become a stadium or corridor theatre with audiences on both sides of the action, such as in a football field. The audience can be subdivided in countless creative ways, or even move from stage to stage rather than having the scenery change. For many, the black box is an almost limitless theatrical toy for those conceiving a production, and it is an ever-changing adventure for audiences who arrive not quite knowing what to expect.

The two basic approaches in live theatre are to design each element from scratch for each new production or to design elements that will be reused repeatedly. We will look at the basic processes of show-specific design and discuss one example of permanent design in each of the following sections.

FIGURE 5.5 Proscenium stage at Sugden Community Theatre, Naples, Florida.

Dan Forer/Beateworks/Terra/Corbis

FIGURE 5.6 Thrust stage at the Stratford Festival's Tom Patterson Theatre.

Courtesy of Stratford Festival

View pictures LTD/Alamy

FIGURE 5.7   The arena stage offers intimacy and audience involvement in any production.

The Black Box Theatre at Edmonds Community College

FIGURE 5.8   This 11,000-square-foot, 200-seat "black-box" theatre opened in 2008 at Edmonds Community College.

Scene Designer

For thousands of years, the position of scene designer did not exist. Throughout the world, productions occurred in spaces that varied little from show to show. Today, show-specific scenery is still rare in traditional Asian and African theatres.

History

In Europe, it was not until production moved indoors that the responsibility of creating an acting space became constant. **Scene design** pioneers included Italians Sebastiano Serlio (1475–1554) and Bastiano da Sangallo (1481–1551), followed by their countryman Giacomo Torelli (1640–1719). The French designer Jean Bérain the Elder (1640–1711) and Englishman Inigo Jones (1573–1652) experimented in their respective countries. In fact, credit goes to Inigo Jones for introducing the proscenium stage in England.

When the theatre moved indoors in Europe, it became the plaything of the privileged classes, and lavish proscenium theatres sprang up under the patronage of royal or aristocratic families. The designers worked in two dimensions, creating intricate sets of canvas scenery designed in two- or three-point perspective to create an illusion of depth. They often used and discarded these magnificent works of art after one evening's entertainment, despite the outrageous expense.

Later, when theatres became more commercial again, even the most heavily subsidized theatre could afford only a set of stock scenes: perhaps a formal interior, an informal interior, a street scene, and a "pastoral" or outdoor scene. These four designs would be used for each production until they wore out or burned up (a frequent event—canvas plus oil paint plus candles for lighting equals flammable scenery!).

FIGURE 5.9 The box set for Katie Holmes's *Dead Accounts*, produced in 2012 at the Music Box Theatre, New York City.

Christopher Peterson/Splash News/Corbis

By 1800, the scene designer became essential, and with the influence of the Meiningen Players during the nineteenth century (see Chapter 4), play-specific scenery was expected. The **box set**, or a set that is built like a box with the one side open through which we look (the fourth wall), dominated the nineteenth-century proscenium stage until the legendary scenic artists Adolphe Appia (1862–1928) and Edward Gordon Craig (1872–1966) moved the art further forward into imagination. The three most widely renowned artists of the twentieth century include Jo Mielziner (1901–1976), Josef Svoboda (1920–2002), and Ming Cho Lee (b. 1930). Each of these five designers moved design away from a realistic, detailed box set to more abstract and metaphoric settings that carve space fluidly and evocatively without literal limitations. They have moved out of cluttered detail into minimalist, spare, and elegant creations.

Postmodern designers (a movement started in the early twentieth century) now think nothing of combining realistic and abstract scenic elements in the same space. While the box set remains popular because so many "domestic" plays are set in someone's living room, even in these plays we are now more open to experimentation, fragmentation, and scenic surprise. Some designers who describe themselves as postmodern experiment with random design, attempting to avoid pattern, meaning, and concept by literally scattering pieces of scenery on the stage. These designers represent one extreme of the design pendulum. In contrast, some forms of theatre don't use scenic designers at all because tradition defines the space. The stage itself is predesigned to give symbolic meaning to every aspect. At this end of the pendulum, we find the traditional ***Noh* stage**.

The *Noh* theatre of Japan exemplifies tradition that does not embrace the idea of show-specific scenic design. Few stage designs are more firmly rooted in tradition and symbolism than the one for this elegant style of presentation. The stage design was "set" during the fourteenth century, and the only changes are found in the tiniest details, where individual artists disagree on "correct" and "incorrect" designs. Few *Noh* stages have been constructed since the early twentieth century, and one Japanese authority speculates that it may be impossible to build one today—the authentic woods and other materials would be massively expensive, if they are available at all. Figure 5.10 is a diagram of the *Noh* stage. Each *Noh* play fits the space, not the other way around.

The mirror room is the actors' dressing room, and each character makes a first entrance across the bridge of three pines. The entrance is a critical moment, and it can take minutes for an accomplished actor to make the short journey. The audience is on two sides, making this a type of thrust stage, and the chorus, usually composed of eight people, is in full view. The chorus supports the primary actor, narrating the story, singing in accompaniment, and sometimes even speaking the character's thoughts aloud. Most *Noh* plays feature two characters, and the stage space is relatively small. Clay jars hang under the stage (in exact locations dictated by tradition, those exact locations being an insider secret) at 45-degree angles, functioning to amplify sound. Each image, each board in the stage floor, and even the

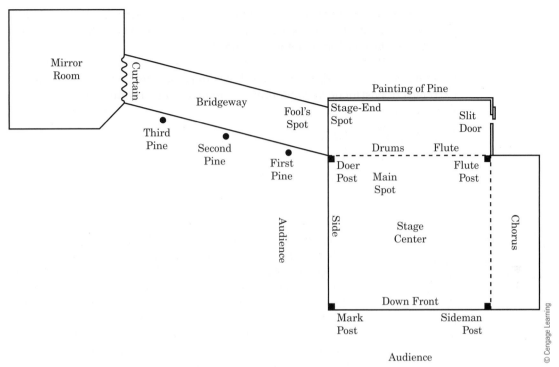

FIGURE 5.10 Diagram of *Noh* stage.

FIGURE 5.11 Here on a *Noh* stage, observe the "bridgeway" and the pine tree painted on the back wall. *Ataka* as produced at the National Noh Theatre of Japan.

style of roof tiles used to house the stage is deeply symbolic and aesthetically unified. The *Noh* drama (see Chapter 8) and the *Noh* stage link inseparably so that one doesn't happen without the other.

In the following section, we explore the basic processes of the scene designer in theatres that produce shows designed somewhere between the extremes of postmodern randomness and *Noh* stage immutability.

Scene Design Processes

The set is the first thing that the audience sees. If the front curtain remains open in a proscenium theatre, they may see it for as much as a half hour from when the house opens until the show begins. This first look can set the tone of the production, reveal the time and locale, set the basic style, establish mood and atmosphere, and introduce the concept. It can suggest a lot about the kind of people who will inhabit this world, even before we meet them.

Scene designers need a strong sense of the history of art and architecture and of the theatre itself to be able to draw on past elements or re-create these eras. They also need to understand construction, carpentry, and all the methods needed to build their creations. Unless they specifically specialize in historical artifacts, designers need to stay on top of developments. Scenery is no longer based just on wood, canvas, and paint, as it was for many years, but it may now involve thermoplastics, Styrofoam, molded Plexiglas, expanded polystyrene (EPS), urethane, vacuforms, and an ever-increasing use of metal alloys. It also may involve projections. Designers must be computer-savvy and up to speed on technology. Designers also need to have strong analytical skills, the ability to read a text or imagine an evolving production, and the ability to see the event in the space provided.

Clearly, the configuration of the theatre itself will strongly influence design. These questions will as well:

1. What number and kind of scene changes are needed for shifts in locale?

2. How many entrances and exits are needed, and what is their placement? How many windows, doors, and any other openings are there?

3. Will the set require levels or platforms, or will all action be at stage level?

4. Will there be isolated items such as trees, columns, or rock formations? Will there be furniture? If so, how much and what kind?

5. Will exits and entrances require escape-step units leading offstage for the actors to return to stage level or to prepare for entrances, and how will this affect backstage space?

6. How will masking block the audience's view of backstage areas beyond the set itself, if at all?

JOHN LEE BEATTY

SCENE DESIGNER

I try to create environments that prove home is where the art is. If I am a decorator, characters are my clients. I often ask the director who's being cast in a role. . . . Sometimes when I hear an actor speak, I can instantly see her furniture.

FIGURE 5.12 New materials like plastic and foam are used in scene design, as in this production of *K2*, with Kevin D. West as Taylor and Tim McGee as Harold. Scenic design by Joel Sass, lighting design by Barry Browning, at the Jungle Theatre.

Michal Daniel

7. Is the set built right on the stage, in a shop a few feet away, or (as is the case for all Broadway shows) will it need to be transported from a studio across town and reassembled on stage?

8. Is the show playing in repertoire or going on tour (so it will need to be taken down and put back up repeatedly), or will it be ensconced permanently?

9. Will set changes need to be made by stage-crew members or actors, or will they be motorized? Which will need to be done by hand, by flying set pieces in and out of the space above the stage, or by moving them on and off via elevators, wagons, treadmills, or turntables?

10. How much, if any, of the set can be pieced together from units already in stock and taken out of storage? How much can be built from scratch?

Three Kinds of Scenery

It helps to break down all the myriad forms of scenery into three components. Much of it is cloth or some variation on a curtain. Hard scenery elements are solid but still one-dimensional units, requiring backing or support of some sort. Finally, some dimensional scenery is about mass.

1. Soft Scenery

Much of what you see is drapes or hanging fabric. At the front of a proscenium stage theater may be the "act curtain," which might pull in from the sides like standard drapes at home or be raised and lowered from above the stage. As this opens, you will note "borders" and "legs." Borders hang horizontally at the top of the opening to mask the **fly space** (where lighting instrument and scenery live when not in use). Legs hang vertically at the sides of the stage to mask the backstage area. They are often called "blacks" because of the usual color of choice. They define the stage in terms of what you can and cannot see (see the previous discussion of masking). At the very back of the stage and covering the entire area, possibly even curving around the sides, may be a **cyclorama**, a huge, white or light gray, tightly stretched curtain attached to pipes at its top and bottom. The "cyc" (pronounced "sike") receives light or other projections. As a play progresses and locales change, various **drops** (pieces of painted canvas) stored in the fly space above the stage may lower onto the stage to represent a new location and fly out when the next change occurs. A **scrim** is a gauze curtain that seems opaque when lit from the front but becomes transparent when lit from behind. These are popular for dream sequences, appearances by ghosts, and other abstract moments. The act curtain and any of the drops may also be scrims, seen as solid at one point in the play and then transparent at another.

Any of the items discussed here may be stock scenery pieces in a proscenium theatre, used in show after show. However, the designer might create them for a specific production, such as an act curtain that has a painted mural of the town in which the play is set, legs that are trees instead of simple blacks, and borders that are clusters of leaves.

2. Hard Scenery

Some set pieces are constructed more solidly so they can stand and support themselves or be stood upon. Traditionally, these are **flats**, frames of wood covered by stretched canvas. Increasingly, flats may actually be lauan (pronounced "lew-ahn"), a thin sheet of wood or some other solid, hard-surfaced material instead of just canvas, so that the entire piece is hard. These have the advantage of not damaging as easily as stretched canvas and not shaking on contact. Flats are put together to create walls, doors, windows, fireplaces, arches, castle walls, prison cells, and anything that must sustain the illusion of constructed surface. Whenever something needs to appear absolutely solid but still needs to take up very little deep space, a hard set unit is likely to appear.

3. Dimensional Scenery

The first two types of scenery are flat. Settings may also use staircases, ramps, or platforms or may require free-standing, three-dimensional forms such as columns, hills, rock formations, tree trunks, porches, or any other "island" formation that may be approached from various sides, needing to be constructed with considerable support. These units may be light and fragile if they primarily are used for scenic effect, or they may require great stability if actors will perform on them.

T. Charles Erickson

FIGURE 5.13 Images projected on a scrim for *Antigone Project*, an adaptation of the Sophocles play at the Julia Miles Theatre, New York, with set design by Rachel Hauck and projections by Nick Schwartz-Hall.

Sketches to Models

The scene designer draws—first in rough **sketches**—to enhance discussions with the director and other designers. She may bring in artwork, including drawings from other sources, for discussion as well. At some point, these will evolve into perspective sketches that begin to look like the actual set and then, once approved, into **renderings** that will look like a painting of the set as it will appear upon completion. Accompanying these will be floor plans, which are essentially blueprints drawn to scale with the exact measurements to guide the construction crew. The combination of these blueprints and elevation drawings (rear, front, side, painters) are needed for each of the three-dimensional set pieces under construction. Often the designer will create one or more scale **models** of the set, which are small replicas like dollhouse versions. The director may use a model to work on blocking the play, or the model may live prominently in the shop as a reminder of what this thing is supposed to become when it's done.

If the designer will be constructing her own set, the precision of these drawings is less crucial than in those instances where a professional designer may visit the "construction site" only a few times in the process, and the paperwork needs to speak for itself. In these latter instances, where the designer may be out of the country and not available, clarity is crucial.

While some scene designers assume responsibility for everything in the acting space, if there are special needs such as a very particular piece of furniture or any handheld item, an artisan with specific skills may be recruited. Therefore, a production may have a separate prop designer and set decorator.

Courtesy Elizabeth E. Schuch

FIGURE 5.14   A set design rendering of Henrik Ibsen's *Hedda Gabler* by Elizabeth Schuch.

Corbis

FIGURE 5.15   A scenic model created by Kurt Söhnlein for Wagner's opera *Tannhauser*.

Media Invades Theatre—
The Projection Designer

More and more live theatre incorporates media. This is attributed to the fact that emerging theatre designers and directors grew up watching television and cinema is their language. With a culture immersed in BlackBerry devices, iPhones, and various other mobile gadgets, screens are everywhere in life, so it was only a matter of time before they hit the stage.

The new trend is so pervasive that the Yale School of Drama now offers a full-fledged projection design program. The technology has resulted in highly efficient and inexpensive software such as Isadora, Eyeliner, and Pandora's Box, which can coordinate 20 or more video projectors and link computers that formerly separately ran projections and moving scenery.

Projections allow the inclusion of performer/creators who are not actually physically present onstage, as in the tribute show *Sondheim on Sondheim* where the composer himself was a constant presence, albeit electronically. Projections are also one of the most flexible parts of a show. Actual sets can take labor-intensive months to design and build; at a certain point, changes need to stop as opening night draws near. Conversely, a projection or video image can be added, deleted, or substituted in the blink of an eye. They are also far less expensive than constructing three-dimensional scenery.

A medium that essentially didn't exist 20 years ago has quickly become an essential storytelling and stage-setting tool for many young directors.

ANITA GATES
JOURNALIST

Lately, it seems, going to the theatre is a lot like going to the movies. There's often a screen upstage, and either film footage, photo stills, or a combination of the two—collectively known as projections—are part of the show.

PETER FLAHERTY
PROJECTION DESIGNER

The liveness of theatre is still the reason that theatre is theatre, but video has an immense power to help tell the story.

THEATRE IN MEDIA

Scene Design in Films

Except in science fiction and fantasy, Western film seldom embraces theatricality where sets look like sets (as in *Nine*, *Moulin Rouge!*, or *Chicago*), so media design is for the most part much less abstract and fanciful. Films often shoot on location using real locations instead of a set. When that is not possible, the set is often a re-creation of the real thing, down to the last detail. Sitcom sets, on the other hand, filmed before a live audience, are often like old-fashioned box sets where we peek into someone's living room and kitchen. The creation of such sets is not unlike that for domestic plays.

In most media settings, detail, texture, and surface treatment become far more important than the overall look because the audience rarely sees everything from a long shot and often sees it so close up that it must pass scrutiny. Because of the cost of moving from set to set, movies are filmed wildly out of sequence. Anything taking place in one location is filmed before moving on to the next, no matter how far afield that is from the progression of the story. Sometimes designers create a set in miniature for what ends up looking like a long shot on film. Increasingly, computer effects enhance or entirely replace spectacular sets so that major construction can be avoided.

Costume Designer

Costumes are like scenery that constantly moves. But they are far more than that. Because the audience experiences the actor and costume as one, **costume design** is the most personal and intimate of design challenges. In a production-specific design, a costume is created for a particular actor playing a role in a particular production. It is inextricably interwoven with the performer who inhabits it. The evolution of this costume requires complete collaboration and trust.

History

Costumes have always been part of theatre, though the earliest ones in any culture were likely to be ceremonial robes for rituals, often religious in nature, or found items such as Ook using the lion skin to become the lion (see Chapter 2). Until the advent of realism in the nineteenth century, costumes in Western theatre were generally more about making a spectacular impression than reflecting the actual life of the character. Actors pulled costumes from the theatre's stock of clothing (perhaps donated by a wealthy patron).

Flamboyance was not restricted to Western theatre. In the *Kathakali* school of Indian dance/drama, a tradition some 300 years old, costumes thrill and transport the audience from the world of everyday life to one of magic, mystery, and eternity. *Kathakali* divides characters and their

FIGURE 5.16 *Kathakali* performers in costume as various character types.

SEPIA / Alamy

costumes into five types rather than specific individuals. The types are green, knife, beard, black, and polished. (For other conventions of *Kathakali* theatre, see Chapter 8.) Their costumes and makeup reveal the internal nature of the mythic character and have no connection to realism. The scene design for *Kathakali* theatre is absolutely minimal: a half-curtain used to delay the impending arrival of certain dangerous character types, a lamp, and a stool. However, the costume designs more than make up for the sparseness of the stage.

It may take as long as four hours to get into these costume and makeup combinations and as many as two hours to take them off. The *Kathakali* traditionally happens outdoors, beginning at dusk and continuing through the night. Actors are mute; the costume tells the audience who and what they are. The chorus, unassumingly costumed in dark colors, sings, chants, and performs the dialogue, while the actor uses the costume to embellish mimed action as the chorus speaks it. Although bound by tradition, each *Kathakali* master is responsible for his own costumes. One contemporary master confessed that one of his costumes could run as high as $25,000! Not surprisingly, when a new costume is required, he sends the old one to the construction artists to salvage any usable fabric or ornamentation.

Processes

Today, it is rare for any production to ignore the impact of costumes. Even a very casual improv troupe is likely to share some unifying element (all may wear black clothing, Hawaiian shirts, or company T-shirts) to separate performers from audience and to create a company identity. Costume designers must consider the practical as well as artistic needs of the production. In addition to all design elements discussed so far, costume designers must ask:

1. Is the play going to be true to its period of origin or an interpretation of that period with some contemporary elements? Will it move to another period altogether or perhaps become a collage where characters from various historical periods meet? To what extent will the same be true of place and style, and how will this influence the costumes?

2. What should costume reveal about each character's job, status, style, age, sex, and the degree to which this person is unique or like others in the play? How will it define her personality and relationship to others, and how might that change as the story progresses?

3. Is the costume going to take focus or blend with others? To what extent should it call attention to itself as a work of art or simply blend in as everyday clothing? Should the costume appear to be shiny new or does it need to be aged in some way? Will it need to look worn and faded and require paint, dye, bleach, staining, brushing, tattering, or other distressing techniques? Will it need to seem to start one way and end another way?

FIGURE 5.17   Here, Haimish Linklater wears a dark costume as Hamlet in a Long Wharf Theatre production.

AUTHOR'S INSIGHT

ANNIE: One of the most critical parts of the process of design is **COMMUNICATION** between director and designers, and between designers themselves. I once worked on a production of *The Rivals* (a period costume comedy). Wonderful costumes and a wonderful set were designed and fully built before we discovered in tech rehearsals that the costumes wouldn't fit through the doors of the set. It all worked out beautifully in the end, but that night was one of panicked adjustments!

4. Will all audience members view the costume up close in an intimate space or at a considerable distance from the actors?

5. Does the costume need to alter the actor in some way? Does it need to emphasize or diminish some feature? Should it make this person more or less attractive/ugly, thin/heavy, old/young, distinct/universal; or is major alteration needed because the character is flora or fauna or some other fantasy creature?

6. Was this costume chosen by the character or imposed in some way, as in uniforms, sexy outfits chosen by a "sugar daddy," or adaptations made to be allowed to join or be accepted?

7. Are there particular movement demands? Do characters dance, squat, fight, faint, or fall? Do they run up staircases or leap off parapets; or should they be restricted, as in a skirt too tight to really walk in or an outfit so oversized that the character is overwhelmed by it and can barely make a gesture?

8. Are rehearsal costumes needed to help the actor learn to work in unfamiliar garments such as corsets, trains, capes, or other variants from standard contemporary clothing?

9. Can any items be rented, borrowed, or drawn from costume storage? Can any be bought at new, used, or vintage clothing stores; or will the costumes have to be created from scratch?

10. Will the actor need to change costumes? If so, will these be quick changes or in any way require assistance?

Basic attributes needed by the costume designer include a strong historical background; rendering skills; knowledge of cutting, draping, patterning, and sewing; and the ability to show in drawing form the placement of seams, darts, pleats, and other details. While staff may include pattern drafters, drapers, cutters, tailors, stitchers, fitters, wardrobe supervisors, and dressers as well as hair and makeup specialists, it may also include few or none of these, so the designer has to be able to do it all. In the same way that the designer attends to details like undergarments and shoes rather than just the major garment, attention goes to the look of the actor from the neck up. The design may include a specific hairdo or wig and makeup for each actor, particularly if the show is extremely stylized and/or actors will look nothing like their offstage selves.

The costume designer's medium is primarily fabric. **Swatches** (small samples of fabric) are crucial in even early conferences, and shopping is a major part of the process. The texture and bulk of the fabric, whether it is sleek or rough, wrinkled or smooth, shiny or flat, or supple or stiff, and how it reflects or absorbs light, drapes, or clings to or hides the body all matter. Even the sound it makes (think taffeta versus corduroy) affects performance.

The process is likely to go from rough sketches through various evolutionary stages to full-color renderings. The fabric is purchased, patterns are drafted, material is cut, parts are basted together, and fittings begin. Once stitching is completed, trim or ornamentation (fringe, feathers, lace, ribbons, etc.) and accessories (purses, hats, belts, umbrellas, gloves, muffs, scarves, and jewelry) are finally added. The actor is rarely called in for less than two fittings and may be involved in many more. A costume chart will finally be prepared to guide changes throughout the performance.

Contemporary Asian theatre often follows the Western model and professional scene and costume designers study in the U.K. or the U.S. In the more traditional theatre forms, because "start from scratch" design is infrequent, key positions such as prop master and wardrobe mistress take on significant status, with many years of training, in history and culture as well as theatre. These highly respected experts are often as much archivists as designers. In the Beijing Opera or *Jingju* (see Chapter 8), for example, construction companies may produce the same costume in 10 colors, plus black and white, as a part of stock and then selectively reuse them. Working even as a *Jingju* dresser (several steps down the ladder from the mistress) requires two to four years of intensive training because costumes have so many layers and ways of being presented. Dressers then specialize in headgear/jewels, inner garments, or outer garments. Until late in the twentieth century, dressers needed to keep hundreds of costume plots in memory because all detail passed on in the oral tradition. Written documentation of this information occurred only in recent years. The wardrobe mistress oversees everything from costume production to storage. The storage system is elaborately codified with costumes placed according to the status of the character and as if the garments themselves have attitudes. For example, tradition requires that the emperor's yellow *mang* is stored third from the top under the red and green *mang* robes so that it (the costume) does not become too self-important.

Richard Feldman

FIGURE 5.18 Actor getting fitted for a costume for *The Changeling* at the American Repertory Theatre.

Richard Feldman

FIGURE 5.19 Actor wearing the same costume in performance.

THEATRE IN MEDIA

Costume Design for the Camera

The intense scrutiny of the close-up influences the work of the media costume designer as it does the scene designer. In fact, partial costuming, like partial nudity, can look complete by the clever use of camera angles. Stage designers may select many fabric patterns that look a certain way from a distance of a hundred feet or more. Some of these would seem overstated, even garish, when viewed up close and personal through the lens. The texture and detail of fabrics become crucial on camera, and subtlety of design here works well, although such costumes transferred to a large theatre might seem hopelessly bland. A costume designer wishing to work in both areas needs to dial up and down quite effortlessly.

Media stars often have their own designers, who are not infrequently from the world of fashion rather than costuming. The designer for everyone else will then need to work around and adapt to these very visible garments at the center of the film and make the whole thing appear somehow unified. Contemporary films are often entirely shopped, so the designer's skill involves finding what's out there that will work rather than creating it. Because many highly successful modern films are not in contemporary realistic style, the opportunity to create fanciful, elaborate, stylized, and period fantasy ensembles is becoming more frequent than in live theatre. Period films, such as *Lincoln*, *Anna Karenina*, and *Argo*, and fantasy films, such as *The Hunger Games*, *The Avengers*, and *Total Recall*, are giving media costume designers fun opportunities to strut their stuff.

CLOSE-UP

Meryl's Magician

Actors get the attention and accolades, though this chapter has demonstrated that even the most gifted of them do not do it alone. When Meryl Streep accepted her third Academy Best Actress Award (from 17 Oscar nominations), after briefly thanking her husband, she went on at some length to thank her "other partner," J. Roy Helland, who has been her hair and makeup artist for 37 years. During that time, they have created all her characters together. He has done her hair and makeup for her television interviews and red carpet events as well, for the theatre in her life.

Their film collaborations started with *Sophie's Choice* in 1982, but they actually began working together earlier in live theatre in a 1975 Broadway production of *Trelawny of the Wells*. They immediately bonded during that show, not only with a sense of mutual creativity and strong work ethic, but Streep admired Helland (whose first career was as a female impersonator) for his gutsy way of protesting the stage-hands' posters of naked women, by wallpapering his own room with *Playgirl* centerfold naked men.

Helland is obviously fortunate to be working with the most revered actor of our time, but Streep is also quick to point out just how blessed she has been "to have this man by my side." "It's a great joy, and we have a really good time, which is why we like to do it, still," says Helland, "It's fascinating to make her look different. A long, long time ago I probably got the best lesson in makeup, which was someone said, 'Don't paint what you see; paint what you want.' So for us— Meryl and I—it's all about not having it be her but having it be whoever the character is." Says Streep, "It's a relationship that I think is unique in our business—the longevity of it. I am so proud of him and have been proud of him for a very long time."

Helland was at long last honored at the same ceremony as Streep with his own Oscar for his work on helping to transform her to portray Margaret Thatcher in *The Iron Lady*. In accepting the award he said, "Thanks, Meryl, for keeping me employed for the last 37 years. Your brilliance makes my work look good no matter what." At this writing, they are collaborating on her look for the film of *August: Osage County*.

Makeup Designer

Makeup design helps communicate the age, condition, and attitude of an individual character, as well as the general style of a production. In large spaces, where lighting can wash out facial features, makeup helps restore color and form to individual faces and aids the actor's expression. As vital as makeup design can be, this is one staff position that many productions do not include. Actors must learn to do their own makeup and to purchase their own makeup kits, whether that means creating the effect of realistic street wear or the stylized extravagance of *Kathakali* makeup. A specialist is likely to be employed for extreme alterations in appearance. In film, in part due to the intense scrutiny of the camera, makeup artists are essential.

JERRY WILLIAMS

MAKEUP DESIGNER

A skilled makeup artist has tremendous power to transform actors, sometimes making them totally unrecognizable. It's like giving them extreme plastic surgery for a few hours of disguise each day.

The basic categories for **stage makeup** are:

1. **Straight**—getting the actor's face to "read" at the back of the house without actually altering his or her features.

2. **Corrective**—making the actor generally more attractive and vivid in appearance, much like the purpose of street makeup.

3. **Age**—adding years to an actor's appearance, a challenge far more common in educational than professional theatre. Directors cast students in roles beyond their years, while pros are more likely to cast actors close to the actual age of the characters.

4. **Character**—changing the actor in a significant way to suggest an entirely different background and personality than that of the performer. This is the most fun category, as false noses, beards, scars, warts, jowls, temporary tattoos, and the entire range of prosthetic devices (think Austin Powers's bad teeth) may be employed for a stunning transformation.

5. **Stylization**—creating a visual impression outside of the natural, where characters may be supernatural, animal, mythical, or abstract rather than real. Non-Western theatre employs this last category at great length, but we can also see it in Broadway hits such as *Cats*.

The basic makeup implements are a base to cover the face, highlight and shadow (lighter and darker tones) to punch up or recede features, liner and mascara to bring out the eyes, rouge to give the face some color, an eyebrow pencil to define brows and create shadow, brushes and sponges to help apply all of this, powder to set it, and cold cream and tissues to remove it at the end of each performance. These elements would be in any actor's basic kit. They may be supplemented by hair whitener, hairpieces to be converted into facial hair or extensions of such, spirit gum to attach hair and an infinite variety of plastic, rubber, and latex materials to exaggerate features beyond what is possible through highlight and shadow. Items such as noses and jowls may be preconstructed or designed specifically for a performance.

FIGURE 5.20 Sean McCourt puts the finishing touches on the elaborate makeup for his role in the Broadway production of *Wicked* as the goat, Dr. Dillamond.

Frances Roberts/Alamy

False eyelashes, colored eye shadow, lipstick, and all the other ingredients employed in offstage "glamour makeup" may also be included.

If an actor's makeup is particularly challenging, the designer or an assistant applies it at each performance. Far more often, specialists instruct the actor during various dress rehearsals and provide a makeup plot; the responsibility then moves to the actor for the actual run of the show. The designer may provide a kit with the nonstandard items the actor needs and possibly a chart with a drawing of a face to remind performers of the specific details. Often photographs are taken of actors in full makeup, and these are mounted on their dressing room mirrors to provide guides during the run.

Mask Designer

Early Western theatre and many forms of Asian and African theatre to this day use masks instead of makeup, or some combination of the two. For many years, actors had no paparazzi or crazed fan problems because their offstage appearance differed so radically from their onstage look. Transformation was the goal, not self-merchandising. Sometimes this is still true today. The American performance group Blue Man Group has played to rave reviews and packed houses on Broadway for over 15 years, and now it has ongoing productions in three other U.S. and several foreign venues. Yet few of us would recognize any of the cast members: three bald men painted entirely blue. Their makeup has become a **mask** that hides their identities and transforms each performer into a creature of myth.

A. C. SCOTT

THEATRE HISTORIAN

As both a sacred object and a means for making the wearer sacred, the mask has a long history. The actor wearing a mask is no longer a prisoner of his own ego or inhibited by the conventions of everyday speech and movement.

In mask theatre, whether classical Greek tragedy from the fifth century B.C.E., ancient Yoruban masked plays about the god Ogun, or the 600-year-old tradition of the *Noh* theatre, one thing binds the work of the designer: the mask itself is seen as a transformative talisman. When the mask is "off-duty," the owner treats it with care and reverence because it contains within it the spirit of the character conveyed. When combined with the power of the actor, the two join in a sort of communion that empowers both mask and actor to leap into the mythic realm.

Most mask designers are artists who have learned from masters who came before them. Some discover on their own that they have a gift for creating inanimate objects that can seem alive when worn by an accomplished actor. Masks may be designed based on long-standing tradition or created for a specific production. They may be constructed from any number of materials and may cover all or only part of the actor's face.

In live theatre, the mask designer remains the closest tie to the ancient idea of magical transformation. The creator of a mask must combine artistry with craft to create the illusion of life in wood, paper, clay, or any other material.

Most of us have experienced the work of the mask designer in events that call for some kind of festival atmosphere such as Mardi Gras, Halloween, and costume parties. In our culture, the mask is sometimes used to take advantage of the anonymity granted the wearer. You may have been at a Halloween party, amazed and dismayed at the behavior of a friend who thought she was hiding behind a mask. We may associate masks with dark characters in horror films such as *Halloween* and *Scream* or with characters who have license to misbehave in films such as *Eyes Wide Shut* or superpowers such as in *The Mask*.

In most live theatre traditions, however, the comic, the lewd, the evil, the heroic, and the virtuous come to life by combining the spirit of the mask with the artistry of the performer who wears it. The actor may remain anonymous,

Otto Lang/Corbis

FIGURE 5.21 A man from the Kuba tribe wears an elaborate ceremonial mask representing a deity for a dance.

but the mask designer creates the means, the tool, that lets us transcend day-to-day life and experience something larger and more universal.

Lighting Designer

"Remember me in light!!" cries the character The Old Actor in the famous musical *The Fantasticks*. This could be the rallying cry for all actors and everyone else who works in the theatre. No matter how brilliant our work, if the **lighting design** is too dark or badly focused, we're dead. **Lighting designers** have the godlike power to plunge us into darkness; to distort, dismiss, or destroy our best efforts; or to enhance, enrich, and enlighten them.

History

There have always been lighting effects. From the earliest moments in history, rituals and ceremonies have been timed to coincide with the rising or setting of the sun, the shape or size of the moon, and the resulting light. Fire has always been used to create light and shadow. Bonfires, torches, lanterns, and candles have always been crucial to create the desired effect. No matter how much technology has intervened, we seek these nature-sourced effects in our lives now as much as the ancients did.

JENNIFER TIPTON
LIGHTING DESIGNER

Light can change the world in a mysterious and compelling way that is not true of directing, set, or costume design. Lighting can confuse or clarify. It is the audience's guide to the story.

In performances during the Middle Ages, shiny metal surfaces were used so that fire could reflect off them. In the Renaissance, stained glass was employed so light could be seen bouncing through it. At that time, fireworks became a crucial part of major celebrations. For many years, theatrical productions were mounted outdoors in the daytime just to capture and preserve the light.

When Western theatre moved indoors during the fifteenth and sixteenth centuries, candles and oil lamps were employed. When gaslight came along in 1803, lighting took a major step forward. Alas, the combination of spaces crowded with people and flammable light sources ended in tragic consequences often enough to create alarm.

With electricity, stage lighting turned into a major art. Not only was it now possible to control effects, but incandescent lighting was clearly safer than fire. Theatre artists jumped on this new and miraculous development. In fact, electric stage lighting first appeared in U.S. theatres in 1879, the same year Thomas Edison invented the lightbulb—and many years before municipal power plants made electric lighting available to commercial buildings and private residences! When the spotlight came on the scene in the twentieth century, the art form came into its own, and computer technology has recently made it soar. In the 1980s, automated lighting emerged, and by the end of that decade, the invention of Intellabeam lighting instruments made it possible for lights to change their focus and color and to move without a person running each of them, requiring instead a single person at a control board.

Throughout the years, lighting has always benefited from new technology—even while much of the labor in other design areas is still painstakingly done by hand. Almost a thousand instruments may be used for a big Broadway show, but even a college production may use hundreds. A thousand light cues is not unusual. If accurately wired into the right circuits, these can all be handled easily now by one person at the control board.

Lighting design involves determining the following qualities:

1. **Intensity:** How many instruments are needed, at how high a wattage? What is their distance from their "targets"?

2. **Direction:** From what angles will light hit objects and characters?

3. **Spread:** How focused or diffused will the light be? How is it distributed across the stage?

4. **Color:** Which filters are being used? Which color sources are being mixed and in what proportion?

5. **Movement:** How is light being raised and lowered, and when? How are various areas of the stage illuminated or cast into darkness and in what rhythmic pattern?

CHRIS PARRY

LIGHTING DESIGNER

I can't paint or draw, so this is how I do it. I use what I call light paintbrushes.

While the large number of women costume designers is not surprising, given their association (at least in public consciousness) with dressmaking, it is noteworthy that some of the most revered lighting designers have been women: Jean Rosenthal, Tharon Musser, Jennifer Tipton, and Peggy Eisenhauer.

A lighting designer can turn technology to art and paint without paint. Questions the designer considers include:

1. How much light will need to seem real, coming from believable sources like streetlights, the sun, the moon, car headlights, lamps, or fires? How much will be about mood and style?

2. How much will light suggest time, weather, or season? How important is this to establishing basic information and moving the plot forward?

3. How will the light change as the fortunes of the central characters do?

4. How much light will be direct, and how much will be broken up by gobos (filters that carve light into casting patterns such as those created by leaves and branches for dappled sun or moonlight)? When will light need to achieve focus, and when can it primarily create atmosphere?

5. How much front-, cross-, back-, and down-lighting will be used, and how bright or intense will each of these be?

6. To what extent do the light sources need to be hidden, or does it not matter that they and perhaps their operators are in full view of the audience?

7. Is the light going to carve the space, or will it be used mainly for general illumination?

8. What (if any) are the special effects needed/wanted? Is there lightning, a fire or fireworks, a snowstorm? Which projections are constant, and which need to move, as in changing rains, clouds, flames, and/or smoke?

9. Will lighting areas generally have sharp, crisply defined edges or soft, undefined, and diffused ones?

10. How will the rhythm of light be used? When will changes be rapid, abrupt, and sharp, with sudden blackouts and equally unnerving sudden full washes of light? When will they be slow, languid segues in which light fades in and out with gentle, gradual deliberation? And when will they be in and out as opposed to cross-fades, where light declines from one acting area as it emerges in another?

Lighting designers need to know something about physics and electronics, the principles of optics; the working capacity of the existing system; limitations of available instruments, lamps, electrical cable, and connectors; what can be done with spotlights, striplights, floodlights, reflectors; and what is possible within an existing budget. They need to master all three kinds of **dimmers**: resistance, autotransformers, and electronic. They need to command preset, master-control, and memory banks. They need to keep up with constantly changing technology and to know when less is more.

Presenting and discussing lighting design with other team members provide unique challenges:

1. Drawings are particularly problematic for the lighting designer when consulting with the director and other designers. How do you draw light? Computers have assisted this process because one can to some degree play with light while in discussion, but many designers still refer to paintings because one can identify a quality of light from such sources, enhancing discussion.

2. How does the quality of light change things? Pure blue may convey cold or night, red may suggest heat or passion, while green often radiates illness or panic. Glaring, stark white light may convey interrogation or clinical sterility. A warm, golden glow conveys warmth, security, and coziness. An important entrance of a major character might bathe that person in light in a doorway, so that her silhouette is vivid but her actual appearance remains a shadow. In a confusing crowd scene, with many people running in many directions, light may pluck out the person to whom we should be paying attention. As a relationship changes, the quality of light may reinforce personal transitions.

JULES FISHER
LIGHTING DESIGNER

Often my job is as much to remove light as to provide it.

THARON MUSSER
LIGHTING DESIGNER

Lighting is such an intangible thing. Art books are a great way to demonstrate to a director the kind of color or texture you're thinking about.

DAWN CHIANG
LIGHTING DESIGNER

Lighting design requires insight, innovation, and motivation. You need to rest and rejuvenate between projects. You cannot fully accomplish this work on an overtaxed schedule and too little sleep.

Photostage

FIGURE 5.22   Compare the lighting in this image with the image in Figure 5.23. Both images are from *The Prince of Homburg,* in a Royal Shakespeare Company production at the Swan Theatre, with Dan Fredenburgh in the title role, sitting at the front of the stage.

Photostage

FIGURE 5.23   *The Prince of Homburg* with drastically different lighting.

In the design process, values sketches, lighting scores, computer simulations, **light plots** (schematics that show instrument placement, direction, and color), and instrument schedules may be employed. While lighting designers begin preparations early, work stops by necessity once initial consultation, research, and drawing are done until the set and costumes are ready to be lit. It is impossible to set lights based on sketches; it is crucial to see how light hits a wall or pillar or a hat or gown before finalizing it. The designer cannot blindly proceed based on an impression of fabric for ball gowns or texture of columns but must experience the results of the other designers' work.

THEATRE IN MEDIA

Lighting in Films

Camera lighting is strongly connected to the work of the cinematographer, who creates a film's visual canvas. Because the audience sees what the camera sees, focus is not as much of an issue. If filming takes place outside a studio, lighting equipment is constantly transported, and every day involves a new setup. Except for action sequences, there is generally less actor movement in film. The camera is more likely to move, so this shifts emphasis.

In addition to the vast knowledge required of the stage lighting designer, the cinematographer (sometimes called the director of photography or camera operator) needs to understand everything possible through the lens, in the developing lab, and increasingly in postproduction, where lighting for a scene may be changed radically after the fact. Super 35-mm cameras require fewer lights, so the process is getting faster and less cumbersome. And more and more "digital doctoring" is taking place.

Cinematographers create an entire lighted world as in the sepia-tone setting of past *Godfather* films (now an almost standard period-piece convention), the painterly light in *Road to Perdition*, the gas lamp–lit world of the period scenes in *Midnight in Paris,* or the cold, stark palette created by Wally Pfister for *The Dark Knight Rises*. A highly qualified cinematographer is often considered essential to give a film weight and power.

Sound Designer

A whole auditory world of the play supports and supplements sound coming from actors. This auditory world is the **sound design**. The sound designer is responsible for:

SHANNON ZURA
SOUND DESIGNER

I think my design work is stronger for having explored and practiced every other area of theatre as well. It is important to secure the broadest range of experiences possible.

1. **Mood music:** From pre-curtain tunes that play as the theatre house opens through intermission musical interludes, possible curtain-call music, and even potential post-show melodies that carry the audience out of the theatre at the end, the sound designer creates, sustains, shifts, and controls mood. His or her work may also involve underscoring certain

stretches of dialogue and action (a convention far more often used in film) to enhance emotional response.

2. **Sound effects:** The script may require cues such as a car driving up and stopping outside, a thunderstorm, a gunshot, an explosion, or a siren, all of which need to be believable. Specific plot events and shifts in conditions need to be supported through sound.

3. **Ambient sound:** This includes other effects, such as background sounds, that can run continuously throughout a scene. The constant noises of big-city traffic or rural crickets and birds may establish and sustain a sense of place.

4. **Internal life:** Sounds of internal life may reflect the mental state of a character—a throbbing heartbeat for nervous anticipation, discordant percussion as a character becomes unsettled or undecided, or the sound of children in delighted laughter when someone experiences childlike euphoria on receiving great news. Sound can punch up a shocking revelation, as in a door slamming (and the slam reverberating over and over as the character realizes that door will not open again), or the sounds of a storm intensifying outside as a relationship grows more stormy inside.

5. **Amplification:** In large theatre spaces, particularly for musicals, the sound designer may need to body-mike or hang amplification so that those who need to be heard can be. In some shows, a ghost or any other unearthly figure may be amplified to help separate them from the mere mortal characters.

The designer's sound system includes at least three recorder/playback units for mixing from variable sources, digital or cassette recorders, equipment to alter sounds, microphones, turntables, a high-quality speaker system, a patch bay for interconnecting sources and amplifiers, computer memory storage, and a control console for efficient operation.

Oddly enough, sound designers have been allowed in the club for a very short time. It was 1986 before the International Alliance of Theatrical Stage Employees (IATSE), the professional stagehands union, added a sound design chapter, and 1993 before designers received standard labor contracts for Broadway shows. It was not until 2008 that sound design was added to the Tony Awards (in two categories: plays and musicals), as full acknowledgment of its importance as an art.

AUTHOR'S INSIGHT

ROBERT: In Shakespeare's *The Two Gentlemen of Verona*, a major problem is how this guy (Proteus) who has always professed love for his childhood sweetheart (Julia) could drop her on the turn of a dime when he meets a new woman (Silvia). A recent production, besides using costume, makeup, and light effects to make Silvia seem like a goddess, used sound. As soon as her name was mentioned, hot bluesy music started, with other characters onstage undulating to it. When she made her entrance, others gasped. Proteus took one look and the clear sound of an arrow piercing a target told us all that his heart had been shot. (These sounds were invaluable in reinforcing his character transition from loyal boyfriend to besotted stalker.)

"Originally we were considered technicians, not design artists," said Scott Lehrer, sound designer and winner of the first Tony Award in this category in 2008 and recipient of three subsequent nominations. "It's taken a long time, but now I feel like we're really considered part of the design team. This is not an award for placing a microphone somewhere. It's about the creation of an aural environment that impacts our relationship to a production."

Prop Master

The property master is responsible for most objects handled by actors during performance. The task may be monumental, involving the design and construction of hundreds of original props or it may be as simple as shopping for a few. It may involve a large crew of assistants or working alone. Unlike other designers who may leave the production once it has opened, the prop master often stays on for the run of the show, taking responsibility for the setup, organization, and running of performances, including prop storage, care and, maintenance.

This job description varies somewhat. In addition to props that are handled, it may also amount to, if a separate set dresser is not involved, securing small items involved in set décor, the details that make a set look as if someone lives there. While the prop master is sometimes called "props god" due to the potential difficulty of the position, Broadway prop master Melissa Erdman refers to herself as a "prop tart," specializing in "fake," everything from fake blood to dead animals to food.

The prop master closely collaborates with the director, actors, and all the other designers, deciding which props need to be bought, rented, or constructed. To succeed requires a precise eye for detail, exceptional organizational skills, and being a great and enthusiastic scavenger/shopper, especially in flea market and garage sale environs. The Public Theatre's prop master Jay Duckworth claims the ideal person would be "extremely intelligent, socially somewhat awkward, an engineer, historian, and autodidact (self-teacher)." Skills needed include sewing, carpentry, fabrication, mold making, antiquing, welding, upholstering, painting, and food styling. It often involves figuring out how something can substitute for something else, as nonalcoholic beverages convincingly standing in for booze, or food that can be consumed far more easily than the authentic original. After considerable experimentation, Melissa Erdman "came up with a killer recipe for vomit: mixed-fruit oatmeal."

The profession has slightly more female than male participants. George Street Playhouse prop master Mary Gragen speculates this may be because "Women multitask very well. They are great artisans and managers because they have to juggle so many balls at the same time."

THEATRE IN YOUR LIFE

Designing Our Settings

In the theatre of your life, to what extent is setting crucial? You have designed your living space whether you are consciously aware of it or not. Look at your current home environment and see what you discover about the scene designer in you. You may find that you embrace postmodern randomness, and you tend to throw stuff around without thought. You may find that you have reconstructed a space based on memories of an earlier time or place in your life. If you were to propose to your beloved, declare your freedom, honor a memory, or declare a significant change in your lifestyle, diet, addictions, or connections, to what extent is it important that this occur in the right setting? Do you envision events in their settings? Are you a feng shui fanatic? Do you have ideas all the time about improving a place with some imagination?

COSTUME DESIGN IN OUR LIVES

To what extent do you plan your outfits and put together all the accessories, as opposed to just throwing something on? Do you change styles and master each new one, or have you developed a distinct look that does not vary until it is time for a major change? Do you make wise and informed predictions about people's behavior based on how they dress? Do you see some people on the street and deeply covet their outfits or feel like the fashion police about to make an arrest? Do you look over any group and make silent judgments about fashion faux pas? Do others tend to seek your advice before making a major garment purchase, or do all these questions leave you somewhat speechless, even clueless? Are you someone who is just glad to find something clean and not too wrinkled as you face each new day? Either way, you are designing yourself each day by your choice of attire.

LIGHTING DESIGN IN OUR LIVES

Are you someone who lights 100 candles around the tub or arranges candlelight dinners for romantic encounters? Do you use a dimmer switch or wish that you did? Do you select soft or tinted lightbulbs and savor the glow of the fireplace even if it's not cold outside? Do you make every effort to avoid harsh, overhead neon lights in favor of softer mood and area illumination? When you think of an idealized circumstance, is the quality of light always part of the picture? Do you try never to miss the sunset if you can catch it and savor it? Do you crave light to the degree that you always open the curtains in any room or space under your control or do you never even think about or notice such things? Some of us are constantly designing our life light whenever we can and revering it even if we can't change it. Some of us barely register it as part of our existence.

SOUND IN OUR LIVES

How sound-sensitive are you? Are you part of the group who gets asked to leave a restaurant or bar because you are getting way too boisterously big for the space you inhabit, or are you one of those who ask to have that group over there shut up or be thrown out? Are you bothered by background noise while you study (unless it is exactly the music you have selected), or are you indifferent, even preferring the white noise of radio or television while you work? Are you very fussy about the quality of your sound system for playing your digital music or CDs and unable to comprehend how others can survive with low-grade systems and careless use; or are you pretty much satisfied with that bargain unit? To what extent is the soundtrack of life important to you? Do you like your life supported by sound, and how important is it that you decide what that sound is; or do all these questions make you ask what the fuss is all about?

COULD YOU BE A DESIGNER?

Until they are successful enough to have others execute their creations, all designers need to have both vision and the mechanical skill to execute that vision in concrete, practical ways. They are both artists and artisans. Are you a scene designer? Have you always been interested in buildings and decor? Do you have some natural aptitude for drafting, construction, sculpture, architecture, conceptual space, or projections? Are you a costume designer? Have clothes always fascinated you, and can you identify the main differences in clothes from various decades and periods in history just because you have always noticed such things? Do you have knowledge of or interest in fabrics, dyeing, cutting, and sewing? For each of these, can you draw and paint? Can you show your ideas to others before they are finalized? Are you a possible lighting designer? Have you always been interested in mood lighting, levels, and the effect of light on any space or event? Are you light-sensitive? Do you understand electrical work, control boards, and programming? Are you maybe a sound designer, with knowledge of music, sound effects, and recording equipment and amplification, and a general fascination for mixing just the right party playlist? Do you have a highly developed auditory awareness of the world around you?

Review the sections of this chapter describing the work of each of these artists. In the theatre of your life, how important are any of these elements to you, and how much skilled attention do you pay to them? Is your apartment furnished with great care and skill? Do you sometimes sketch your future dream house? Does your wardrobe reflect an artist's sense of personal presen-

tation? Do you always adjust light levels and produce background music for any social occasion, from a wild open house to private seduction to even a casual gathering of pals?

If you have the intense fascination but not the skills for execution, consider taking a few courses in your area of interest. Many skills can be learned. Some students may find that they cannot make the leap from their head to their hands, but the most important ingredient is extreme interest.

Believe it or not, in many theatres, one person does almost all the jobs described in this chapter. High school, small college, community, and struggling professional theatre companies often have a single, dedicated (and frequently exhausted) person who drives the whole program and shapes each production. If you connect in any way with these one-person theatre phenomena, recognize and honor all that they do.

SUMMARY

Some theatre artists start their work long before the show goes into rehearsal. The designers (scene, costume, makeup, masks, lighting, and sound) create the world in which all the directing and acting will occur. Their work is heavily influenced by the kind of theatrical space (proscenium, thrusts, arena, environmental, black box) in which they work. They all share basic design principles (unity, variety, balance, focus, progression), yet each is unique in the process. They each must be both artist and artisan, with a unique capacity to envision and the practical skill to accomplish. Dramatic Interlude 3 considers some of the design decisions required by a classic Shakespeare play and a contemporary play that moves between dream and reality.

SUGGESTED ASSIGNMENTS

1. Examine the living room in your apartment or your room in the dorm and imagine it as a stage setting. Which wall should become the open fourth wall? What shifts in location of furniture and other props should occur for this to become a set?

2. On what occasions have you so altered your own or a friend's appearance that it could actually be called costuming and makeup? What was it like to have others respond to it?

3. Try to identify who in your life are the idea people and who are the can-do people. Do you know anyone who combines these qualities? What alignments make the vision and application possible? Do you know anyone at either position who is looking for that collaborative hookup?

4. After examining the work of all these designers, what was the single event in your personal theatre where you filled as many of these jobs as possible to make it all happen?

5. Which design position intrigues you most as one you might consider for pursuing further training and experience? If you chose to have a life in the theatre, which of these would you wish to be?

6. Take any play being read but not viewed as part of your class. Do one or more of the following and write a justification for the choices you have made. Create:
   A. A costume for one male and one female character, drawing the clothing on the models provided.
   B. Makeup plots for the same.
   C. A floor plan or a sketch of what you believe the set might look like, giving attention to staging and movement requirements.
   D. A sound design with a listing of essential effects, music to underscore, and pre-curtain and post-curtain interludes.
   E. A description of how the light might be generally and how it might shift, including any special effects and moments when a transition in character development and story can be reinforced through light.

SUGGESTED ACTIVITIES

1. **Individual:** Pick a famous designer identified as a leader in the profession in this chapter. Research the person and write a brief report on his or her career and ideas.

2. **Group:** Choose a play and have each person in the group design a floor plan for a different type of theatre space. Discuss the challenges and how the sets adapted to the space.

3. **Long-term:** See if you can get permission to sit in on the production meetings for a production, where each of these designers and their staff check in with each other weekly. What did you learn about how their work progresses?

4. **Large group:** Take a production or film that the entire class has seen. Divide the class into five groups, each of which will be charged with coming up with a strong argument why sets, lights, costumes, makeup, or sound was the most important element. Have the teacher select the team with the strongest argument.

KEY WORDS AND IDEAS

design ingredients (line, mass, color, texture, decor)
design principles (unity, variety, balance, focus, progression)
proscenium stage
sight lines
masking
thrust stage
arena stage
environmental stage
black box
box set
Noh stage
fly space
cyclorama
drops
scrim
flats

scene design
  sketches
  renderings
  models
costume design
  sketches
  renderings
  swatches
makeup designer
stage makeup (straight, corrective, age, character, stylization)
mask
lighting design (intensity, direction, spread, color, movement)
  lighting designer
  dimmers
  light plots
sound design (mood music, sound effects, ambient sound, internal life, amplification)

chapter 6
THE PRODUCTION TEAM

The scene shop at the California Institute of the Arts.

A lighting technician focuses an instrument during the light hang/focus at the University of Reading.

University of Reading, Department of Film, Theatre & Television

Lesson Objectives:

Upon completion of this chapter, you will be able to:

1. Identify the various roles of behind-the-scenes professionals in the modern theatre.
2. Identify the functions of the members of the production team in modern theatre.
3. Identify the procedures and skills of people like the producer, stage manager, and technical director, and how they vary between stage and film.
4. Identify when and how you function as a member of the production team in your personal life.
5. Identify if you might have what it takes to make one of these professions your career.

Introduction

A huge production team may be behind a show. The past few chapters have been about those who, if they do well, receive attention and acclaim. Most theatergoers can name some playwrights, some directors, and many actors. While designers are not exactly household names, when we see a show, we can identify their choices and respond to their contributions. The work of all these team members is in the foreground, and they are, for better or worse, highly accountable.

This chapter is about the background team, the unsung heroes who make vital contributions without public acknowledgment. Their work is crucial, but they labor almost entirely in obscurity. If you can name three people in any one of these professions, you are far more knowledgeable than the theatergoing public at large. These positions are found in some form in all the theatre traditions of the world. Job titles and duties shift with time, place, and custom, but in Brazil, Nigeria, England, or Japan, the same "behind the scenes" artists create, produce, manage, build, and hold theatre together.

Some would argue that these theatre-makers are the ones who have the most fun, getting to take part in theatre magic without overwhelming scrutiny. Their work is seldom mentioned in reviews. They get no cheers, standing ovations, or raves, but they also receive no jeers, pans, or public humiliation. Theatre production cannot function without them. Some are involved long before a show goes into auditions, some as late as opening week. They carry the play on their shoulders. On the opening pages of Part II, the chart "Theatre: A Team," shows the organization of all the people necessary to put on a play—from the producer to actors and crews. Dramatic Interlude 3 considers the different demands that a classic play like *King Lear* and a contemporary play like *Roosters* put on the various members of the production team.

DARYL ROTH

PRODUCER

Producing is like an important birth, as a new play is brought into the world. I advise producing only the works that speak to you, not the work that you think will speak to someone else. This is too hard a business not to feel deeply passionate about your show.

The Producer

As the song says, "There's no business like show business!" and the **producer** is the business side of the show. While others may be more immediately involved in the artistic process, the show will not happen unless funds can be raised, contracts negotiated, script rights secured, royalties paid, staff hired and supervised, budgets set and enforced, rehearsal space rented, weekly payroll accomplished, investment reports made, performance space booked, promotion and publicity assigned and executed, posters and fliers printed and distributed, media ads designed and booked, tickets sold, and bills paid. In professional theatres, the producer may need to negotiate with 11 different unions and individual agents to iron out employee salaries and contract details. The producer is everything that is pragmatic about the art, and yet great taste is essential for picking the right project.

CLOSE-UP

Daryl Roth—New York's Finest

Because of the spelling, many audience members reading producer Daryl Roth's name on a theatre program do not realize she is a woman. Because few theatergoers follow the careers of producers, few also realize that she is probably the most successful producer in New York, if not in box-office receipts, undoubtedly in rave reviews and awards.

Plays she has produced have won the coveted Pulitzer Prize an unprecedented seven times. These include Bruce Norris's *Clybourne Park*, Tracy Letts's *August: Osage County*, Nilo Cruz's *Anna in the Tropics*, David Auburn's *Proof*, Margaret Edson's *Wit*, Paula Vogel's *How I Learned to Drive*, and Edward Albee's *Three Tall Women*. Three of these plays were also winners of the Tony Award for best play. Her most recent triumph, as of this writing, is the best play award for the musical *Kinky Boots*. Her *Old Wicked Songs* is one of the most produced plays in the United States. Her productions include not only some of the most lauded of the past decade, but also numerous ventures into edgy, thought-provoking new territory. It is hard to overpraise this quality in our age of safe, corporate-based choices.

Roth's acclaimed production of Nora Ephron and Delia Ephron's *Love, Loss, and What I Wore* has been presented in New York, Los Angeles, Toronto, Australia, and Argentina. A U.S. national tour will be followed by future international productions in France, Mexico, Brazil, Germany, Scandinavia, and the Philippines.

If you could pin down two qualities that unite the wide variety of shows that she chooses to produce, it would be intelligence and risk. None of her plays is lightweight. They expect audiences to enter the theatre ready to go somewhere new with their brains challenged. "Good theatre," she says, "is about risks. That could almost be part of its definition. Risk is the reason theatre is stimulating and often thrilling."

As if her producing ventures were not enough, Daryl Roth also owns two theatres in New York. Both have contributed alternative, unusual spaces to the New York theatre scene. The Daryl Roth Theatre, converted from the old Union Square Savings Bank, is a completely open, vastly high, and entirely versatile space. Her production of *De La Guardia*, a total sensual experience free of linear plot, played for five years in the theatre named for her. The DR2 Theatre, in the former bank's annex, offers 99-seat intimacy, serving small, subtly detailed works, including children's plays, requiring close audience proximity.

She also gives back regularly, serving on major theatre boards such as that of Lincoln Center and the Sundance Film Festival. She created the Daryl Roth Creative Spirit Award, given annually to theatre artists who have demonstrated exceptional quality and promise in their fields.

She sometimes coproduces with her son Jordan. She says, "Theatre offers you the chance to challenge yourself in a safe way. You enter a space, think about new things, open up, but in the end, you can leave the theatre safely and with a richer point of view."

FIGURE 6.1 Daryl Roth and her son, producer Jordan Roth, at the American Theatre Wing's annual gala in New York.

Walter McBride/Corbis

There have always been producers because there has always been a need for money. In various contexts, the producer might have been or may still be a chorus leader, a guild, a royal patron, an actor/manager, or a government agency. A producer may now be a single freelance entrepreneur (in the commercial theatre), a whole board of directors (in a regional repertory company), a set of faculty members (in a university), or elected officers (in a community theatre). In these settings, usually someone is still the lead peer in the decision-making process. This job can be done solo or shared by an entire collective, but more and more often, it is shared. On Broadway, in recent years, it has been rare for there to be only one producer; more often, there is a team of coproducers with a retinue of investors.

The producer needs strong artistic instincts and intuition, even if she is always one level away from direct participation, because the choice of the right show, the right staff, and the day-to-day decisions about whether any element is worth the investment requires taste and aesthetic judgment as well as an ongoing sense of what will sell. The ability to balance bucks and beauty, vision, and practicality is crucial. Common management wisdom is to hire the right people and then leave them alone to do their job. How alone the producer can leave them depends on how right she was to hire them.

Theatres may be commercial, for-profit organizations, or not-for-profit resident companies, which receive some tax breaks. These are roughly comparable to television networks versus the Public Broadcasting System (PBS). For a freelance producer, crucial costs involve the rental or booking of a space and raising backer capital. For a resident theatre that owns its own space, these costs shift to building and equipment maintenance and the wooing of donors, grants, and endowments. Otherwise, their producers' responsibilities essentially remain the same. Many artists have dreams and great ideas for starting a theatre or mounting a show. The producer has the job of grounding those dreams in the fiscal world of facts, figures, and fund-raising.

Artistic Director/Managing Director

In many resident theatre companies, the **artistic director** and the **managing director** (sometimes called the executive director or business manager) share producing responsibilities. In these situations, creative and fiscal components are sharply divided.

The artistic director is responsible for the overall image and vision of the theatre, for selecting the season of plays and the artists who will mount them and perform in them. The artistic director chooses directors, designers, actors, and other creative personnel. He offers guidance as each of these artists makes decisions along the road to opening night, and he often directs at least one play per season.

THEATRE IN MEDIA

Film Production

Media production is expensive. Staff sizes can quadruple for all the increased technical components. While many concerns are the same for live and media production, everything escalates for the latter. The film producer needs a more complex understanding of marketing because the target audience is not a specific, geographic cultural market but potentially the whole world. This also means that marketing costs alone may match the film's budget. While some Broadway musicals have major costs and financial risks, it ramps up for almost any film.

The managing director determines budgets and makes sure everyone stays within them. She may be involved in determining salaries and production expenditures for scenery, costumes, lighting, props, or music. She is ultimately the supervisor for all business, promotional, **box office**, and "front of house" staff.

These personnel may intersect, for example, when the artistic director believes that a costume or set piece is not working and needs to be replaced. This creative judgment has to be processed by the managing director, who must decide if the artistic change is worth the investment or if the show can survive relatively unscathed with the original choice. Often negotiation is involved.

FIGURE 6.2 Lynne Meadow has been Artistic Director of the Manhattan Theatre Club since 1972.

Michael Weschler/Corbis

Dramaturg

Dramaturgy is often traced back to 1767 Germany, when Gotthold Lessing became an "in-house critic" for the Hamburg National Theatre, and the position has gradually become standard throughout Europe, particularly in government-supported theatres. This is by far the newest member of the U.S. team, not a standard position here until near the end of the twentieth century. This staff member is least likely to end up praised or panned in reviews because the work of dramaturgy is largely invisible. It involves doing research, asking questions, and troubleshooting to help the script reach its full potential in performance. A **dramaturg** may:

1. Explore different translations or adaptations of the script (if it first appeared in a foreign language) to help the director select the one most suited to this production's concept, or possibly assist in creating a new translation and in cutting the text as well.

JEANNINE WOO
DRAMATURG

As a dramaturg, you have a wonderful opportunity to take the script from a piece of literature to something that breathes with dynamic life.

2. Research the author's life and other plays to provide background and perspective for the script.

3. Help the director with script analysis and the actors in character analysis by providing challenging questions and background information.

4. Conduct historical research on the period and country in which the play is set and the culture surrounding the play to create a rich context for the work.

5. Summarize critical essays written about the script and reviews of previous productions, so past responses can be scrutinized by the company efficiently while the production moves forward.

6. Attend rehearsals periodically and take notes, mainly with questions for the director about decisions that may appear unclear and interpretive choices that may not be those that the director actually intends.

7. Prepare a study guide that will be sent out to instructors if school groups will be attending a performance to provide background and generate excitement prior to the field trip.

8. Provide program notes that will help educate the audience with a framework that will allow them to get the maximum experience from watching the show.

9. Organize question-and-answer sessions after some performances or during visits by the actors to classes and organizations to discuss and present excerpts, extending the influence of the ideas of the show.

10. Prepare and supervise site visits for the director, designers, and actors when a play deals with unfamiliar circumstances.

AUTHOR'S INSIGHT

ANNIE: I was dramaturg for a production of *Death of a Miner,* a play set in an Appalachian coal community. We made arrangements to tour a working coal mine. It was so dark, cold, and stifling; I know none of us were unchanged by the experience. The lives of the characters were much more real and visceral to us after spending time in their environment.

The role of dramaturgs as educated observers is frequently their most valued contribution. Having someone on the team who knows the play as thoroughly as the director but who is not involved in every moment of every rehearsal provides much-needed objectivity. The real danger in any rehearsal is that we forget the audience member, who was not there when we discovered all the glorious stuff we love which may or may not be worth keeping. An informed observer who was not there for all those work sessions helps the company stay clearheaded. A good dramaturg does not get caught in the loop but keeps coming back from the perspective of a first-time audience member and asks those kinds of questions.

In many theatres, the dramaturg is too expensive a luxury for the budget. In an academic setting, a director often selects a play more than a year before production and may choose to do the dramaturgy work herself. Because a campus is a hospitable setting for scholarly research, however, this is also the best environment for nurturing a student dramaturg in training. However, in a professional repertory company, where a director

Movement and voice or speech coaches may also help a cast achieve accomplishments that have not been part of their previous training. If a play takes place in a historical period with particular etiquette and movement conventions, a coach will be brought in to help everyone appear to have lived in another time. There may be instruction in how to breathe in a corset, how to maneuver a hoop skirt, how to keep a sword elegantly at your side (and not accidentally injure fellow cast members), how to hold a staff as an experienced shaman would, and a whole range of other actions out of the immediate comfort zone of the actors.

If a director has no experience in classical speech, a coach may be brought in to help actors speak in a timeless, elegant fashion (or just the opposite if actors cast

FIGURE 6.4 Actors study fight choreography during a summer intensive training course at Rosebud School of the Arts in Canada.

as farmhands have no sense of how to sound genuinely rural). Probably the most common use of a speech coach is for **dialects**. Mastering how to sound Irish, British, Jamaican, German, or Zimbabwean in a way that is comprehensible to audiences is a highly specialized skill. Stage dialect coaching amounts to choosing evocative changes rather than re-creating authentic accents that could result in performances that few could understand. In both movement and voice, it is not enough to know what is historically accurate; history must be converted and modified into theatre. In traditional Eastern theatre, every syllable, every step, and every movement of the eye, hand, and foot are rigorously trained, bringing a single actor into perfect alignment.

At this point in the production process, we shift from those who started it to those who are compelled to continue it. All of those identified up to now (except for the actors, of course) can and sometimes do leave town on or before opening night. Everyone who follows is essential in seeing the production through to the end. There is a tremendous shift in energy and responsibility as the planners of the event phase out and the players of it step forward. The technical director, who has been involved in nearly all phases of production, represents the major transition.

Technical Director

The most crucial and least acknowledged participant in the whole event is the **technical director (TD)**. Usually this person runs the scene shop, sets schedules for design and construction deadlines, coordinates communication between design teams, troubleshoots every emergency, assigns crew heads and crew members, trains backstage personnel, and generally guides

FIGURE 6.5 This theatre technician is working in the scene shop, building a piece of a set.

JANET ROSE

TECHNICAL DIRECTOR

A TD needs many construction techniques, but most important is the skill to plan ahead, knowing what pieces are needed for rehearsals first, the painting schedule, and the logistics of how the pieces go together. This has to be balanced with the variety of skill levels found in construction crews.

all production activities surrounding the actors. The crews do not get curtain calls and applause, and the TD will get little or no acclaim if all goes smoothly—beyond the satisfaction of knowing that it did. In educational theatre, the TD must often train crew members with virtually no experience. In these settings, she is responsible for the safety standards for the entire theatre and is often present at rehearsals and performances to troubleshoot any emergencies.

While connected to all designers, the TD is most strongly associated with the set designer, and the TD's duties include planning and managing construction, installation, running, and striking of scenery. The TD also keeps track of all stock units in storage and of those needing to be drafted. Often this position involves drafting working drawings, setting a construction schedule, purchasing equipment and supplies, and supplementing the master schedule with daily shop work lists. The TD will supervise load-in (moving the scenery from the shop to the stage), load-out (the reverse operation, also known as "striking"), and keep strict accounts of scenic expenses and supervision of all shop personnel. In educational theatre, the TD is likely to be involved with assigning and training personnel in props, lighting, and sound as well. Because of the huge technical component of moviemaking, no direct parallel to the TD exists; those duties may be divided among a half-dozen positions, such as location manager, unit production manager, key grip, foreman, and postproduction supervisor.

Props

Properties may involved a large number of participants with separate designers, builders, and crew members who work the actual running of performances. It may also involve just one person who does it all. In professional and large educational theatres, the prop master is often a dual occupation blending design, construction, and leadership over the props crew during the production. Sometimes, when the props are complex, the prop master must be on hand for every performance in case something goes wrong. And it happens. Never knowing what's going to happen is part of the thrill of live theatre. The prop master must always be available in such emergencies. For more information on prop masters, see Chapter 5.

In addition, the prop master often functions as the prop crew head, training prop handlers and acclimating them to the specific demands of each production. The prop master organizes the crew and assigns them in such a way that the exact prop is where it needs to be when it is needed. Actors in a quick-change situation reach for their prop on a table backstage and expect and need it to be there. They simply don't have time to run around looking for it. In some ways, the prop master is similar to the TD—in on the process from beginning to end and always on call in case of emergency.

Stage Manager

The **stage manager (SM)** will eventually take over from both the director and TD and run the show. No one is more crucial once a production is in dress rehearsal and performance. The SM usually "calls" the show from the light booth or a place just offstage in the wings, on headphones, communicating electronically with crews, alerting them to upcoming cues, and calling each one when it is time. A modest production can have hundreds of cues because each change in lights, sound, scenery, costumes, and actor position must be timed and coordinated carefully for the show to run smoothly. The SM makes countless judgment calls, from determining when the house manager should start flicking the lights in the lobby to beckon the audience to be seated, to when the house lights should come up at the end of the show to signal that it is time to leave—and everything in between. The traditional symbol for the SM is the "ghost light"—a single bare bulb on a pole that stands onstage in an otherwise dark theatre, providing the only illumination in the cavernous space. This "ghost" beckons the SM into the theatre, often before anyone else arrives. Sometimes called "Stanley," the ghost light has often been replaced by just turning on a breaker switch for ambient low light. For those theatres still employing it, however, the final ritual of the day will be the SM returning this sole light to its spot before plunging all else back into darkness until tomorrow.

Most SMs join the production team just before casting takes place, often running the auditions themselves; handing out, collecting, and collating forms; calling actors' names when it is their turn; timing and cutting off those who run overtime; and answering questions so that the director can remain free to concentrate on each audition. Sometimes the SM will be asked to read with an actor when no scene partner is present. Professional stage managers are actually members of the same union (Actors' Equity Association) as actors.

After casting, the stage manager will then be responsible for the physical details of each rehearsal, making sure the space is unlocked, lights and heat or air-conditioning are turned on, necessary rehearsal furniture and props are set up, as well as making sure all who are supposed to be

MARTHA KING
STAGE MANAGER

You will get more work as a stage manager than as an actor. This is a good job for someone who really likes being in the middle of everything. Keep track of all the details and know how long it is before the next break, because that is the most asked question!

FIGURE 6.6 A "ghost light" on stage. The stage manager is the first to arrive and the last to leave the theatre, and traditionally returns this light to the stage before closing up for the night.

present are. She creates a daily sign-in list and will be in charge of tracking down those not present when they are due. She will create something called the promptbook, which will include the script and all relevant printed material, including notes on blocking and cues as they accumulate. As actors struggle to memorize their parts, she may prompt them and correct errors in lines. Eventually, this book will become the guide by which she calls the cues.

Throughout rehearsal, the SM is liaison among the director, the cast, and each of the shops, setting up costume fittings, communicating special needs to designers as they arise in rehearsal, and sometimes booking actors for interviews or other sessions where their presence may be required outside actual rehearsal. The SM helps determine actor call times, scheduling those with extensive hair and makeup demands early and gradually working in the timed arrivals of others.

As crucial as this position is, a student often fills the role in educational theatre. This person needs to have enough respect among peers to be able to lead and coordinate them. Self-confidence, high organizational skills, tremendous diplomacy, and the willingness to "kick butt" when butts need to be kicked are all crucial. The SM deals most directly with actors who have been late, missed cues or fittings, or have jeopardized the coordination of the production in any way. In the professional theatre, the SM is responsible for enforcing union regulations, which include scheduling a break every 55 minutes, being in charge of food delivery, making sure standards are being upheld if a rehearsal runs past a certain length, and enforcing a whole bookful of additional rules that keep actors and crews from being taken advantage of. The professional stage manager also conducts rehearsals for understudies or replacement casts.

Usually at least one assistant stage manager (ASM) is the eyes, ears, and legs of the SM backstage during performance, when the SM needs to stay in the booth on headphones. For example, the SM may communicate to the ASM that it is time for actors to take their places, and the ASM in turn will make that announcement backstage. The ASM may tell the SM via headphones that an actor has completed a quick costume change so the SM can call the next cue. The ASM provides a vital connection to onstage and backstage activity. Often he is incorporated into the rehearsal process, sometimes being on book, calling latecomers, and sharing other tasks with the SM. Both the SM and ASM positions require organizational and people skills. Many of the same questions about whether you are suited to become a director can determine if these jobs are for you. The crucial difference is that you would have to feel rewarded with just the work and knowing you did it well, because SMs, like TDs, remain largely unacknowledged—no glory, just the satisfaction of a job well done.

Musicians

For much of Eastern theatre, and most particularly for Kabuki and *Noh*, the presence of live musicians is an essential part of the theatrical event. Musicians also play an important role in Native American performances and, of course, in traditional musical theatre, where an entire orchestra may be employed. The decision to use recorded or live music may be part of a production plan. Some shows even have performances with both kinds of musical support, generally with reduced ticket prices for the former. In Eastern theatre, the coordination of movement with music, especially the use of percussion, is so vital that the musicians are likely to be an integral part of the rehearsal process. For Western musicals, a rehearsal pianist will be employed in all stages of rehearsal, but the other musicians will not be brought in until very close to opening. These may be musicians for hire, with no particular interest in theatre. The level of involvement in the process can therefore vary from complete integration to last-minute adjunct participation.

The orchestra for a Western musical is often not seen or only partially visible in the pit. Only the conductor can be seen by the audience, and only she is the potential recipient of a curtain call acknowledgment. Conducting the orchestra for a musical requires exceptional skill and sensitivity. Coordinating the singers and musicians who have been rehearsing separately into a cohesive whole is a great challenge. In general, a theatre musician is a distinct artist from one who just creates music. Each moment is about supporting the actor's performance rather than expressing the musician's personal interpretation. Just as a male ballet dancer primarily

WING LONG
PIT MUSICIAN

Playing for a theatre production is way different than playing at a concert. The fact that you are usually hidden from the audience should give you a clue. It is not about you or even the music. It is about how the music supports the acting.

FIGURE 6.7 The musicians on the *Noh* stage are clearly visible to the audience.

Luca Tettoni/Corbis

presents, lifts, and enhances the presentation of his ballerina partner, this art is about supporting someone else.

Musical underscoring is sometimes used in nonmusical live theatre, though less frequently in Western theatre than in some other traditions. In media, however, the musical score is a major tool in shifting mood and attention. A musician employed to play a film score may have no contact of any kind with the production. Rough cuts of the film might be projected during the scoring session, but that will be as close as the musician gets to the core action. You could play on the score of a film and have little idea of what it was actually about until you saw it in a theatre with everyone else.

At the other end of the spectrum, an Asian production may involve musicians as extensions and interpreters of each actor's every movement and shift in emotion. An actor's entrance may be punctuated by percussive accompaniment, pointing up each step taken. Key shifts in awareness and expression may receive similar treatment. The actor's movement into dance or stylized reactions will have powerful and interpretive sound support. A combat scene may involve unrealistic weapons that never actually make contact with each other or with the actors' bodies, stopping just inches short of such contact when a percussion artist produces a sound that represents the contact that might have been made. In situations like this, there are a full integration and communion between musician and actor.

There may be no other area of theatre with a wider degree of involvement from central to peripheral than that of a theatre musician.

CLOSE-UP

Handspring Puppet Company: *War Horse* from Novel to Stage

"An actor struggles to die onstage, but a puppet has to struggle to live. And in a way that's a metaphor for life."
Basil Jones

Handspring Puppet Company was founded in 1981 by four graduates of the Michaelis School of Fine Art in Cape Town, South Africa. Two of the co-founders, Adrian Kohler and Basil Jones, continue to run the company. Originally, they created shows for children, and then later began developing works for adult audiences. Arguably one of the greatest puppetry companies in the world, the company provides an artistic home and professional base for a core group of performers, designers, theatre artists, and technicians who collaborate with them on a project-by-project basis.

In 2007, the National Theatre in London approached them with a really big idea: put a novel about horses in World War I on the National's big stage. They chose the children's novel *War Horse* by Michael Morpurgo, adapted the text for the stage, and imagined the action of the play starring puppet horses. (For more information, see the Chapter 4 section, "Puppets and Puppeteers.") When Morpurgo first heard the idea of puppets, he reacted, "I thought 'are you stupid? Puppets?!' In my head I'll tell you what I couldn't stop thinking of, do you know what a pantomime horse looks like? I mean laughable! All of it seemed to me to be ridiculous, so I said 'Honestly, it doesn't sound all that brilliant.' He said 'Would you come up? I'm going to show you a video of the work of Handspring Puppets.'" Invited to London, Morpurgo saw an example of Handspring's work. "It was a giraffe, more than life sized, operated by three people. And when I saw that on this little screen, I knew that something magical would happen."

And so, the Puppet Factory back in South Africa got to work. Each puppet in *War Horse*, handcrafted by artisans and apprentices, took months to build. Cane formed the "frame" around each puppet, steamed into shape before being bound with rope and wire cables. A full video exploration of the Puppet Factory is available at http://www.warhorseonstage.com/puppetry. The same website features detailed looks at the articulation of the head and legs on each puppet. We highly recommend this site, as it provides interviews with the artisans as well as a visual journey through the social landscape of South Africa today.

Catapulted to world attention with *War Horse,* the Handspring Puppet Company continues to explore the boundaries of adult puppet theatre within an African context. Now considered the center of the revival of the art of puppetry, HPC supports the design, construction, and performance of puppetry in all its many guises around the world.

Handspring Puppet Company

FIGURE 6.8 Handspring Puppet Company's best-known work is *War Horse*, produced by the National Theatre in London in 2007 and in constant performance since. Here Joey the horse reveals the cost of war to creatures great and small as he stumbles exhausted through the barbed wire nightmare of a WWI battlefield.

CHRISTINE SMITH-MCNAMARA

COSTUME SHOP MANAGER

I find management as fulfilling as any part of the costume world. I remember back in high school, I would listen to Broadway recordings and long to be part of that world. Twenty-five years later, I am. The more you understand about how the technical work gets done, the more it will help your relationship with a shop.

Crews

Just as there are those who plan a show and those who actually play it, there are also staff members who *coordinate* the technical elements and others who *execute* them. In educational theatre, during the day, there will be crews making costumes, building sets, searching out and constructing props, hanging lights, recording sound—basically putting together the show. These people may or may not stay on board once the show opens, or they may in fact be replaced by a whole *other* group of people who work each performance, in which case the distinction is made between **construction crews** and **running crews**.

In any theatrical setting, there are **shop supervisors**, who oversee the implementation of designs. These positions require extraordinary skill in interpreting what the designer has presented and coordinating the efforts of all artisans who will be engaged in achieving it.

The costume-building crew does the sewing, fitting, trimming, and construction of all costume elements, while running crews inventory costumes each day and may serve as dressers for actors with fast or difficult changes. They may also then repair, replace, launder, and iron costumes as needed after each performance. An electrics crew, often under the supervision of a **master electrician**, hangs and focuses lights, while the light board operator actually runs them during the show, usually from a booth at the back with the sound operator and SM. There may also be special lights such as follow spots, which are operated by individual crew members from the back of the theatre or in the grid. The scenery is built under the supervision of a **shop foreman** and perhaps a **master carpenter**, but then a **key grip** may supervise the changing of scenery, props, and furniture during the show. This pattern follows through each of the other design elements. Ironically, running crews often have no idea how the construction process was accomplished. One of the great advantages for participants is that those who are employed at another job, whether during the daytime or at night, can still take part in the theatre process because it goes on all day long.

FIGURE 6.9 In the Berkeley Repertory Theatre's costume shop, Kitty Muntzel and Janet Conery consult a pattern as they work on a period blouse.

THEATRE IN MEDIA

Movie Public Relations

If you are alive and well in this country today, you almost can't avoid the extensive public relations (PR) used in media to boost ticket sales for every new movie, television show, and video game. In fact, if you start to pay attention, you'll begin to notice that some media are awash in publicity for weeks and even months before opening day. In late 2012, publicity for the film *Les Miserables* began in earnest. Like a campaign in war, strategically released trailers "leaked" online and in the media in different regions of the world so that fans in the United States (for example) could keep watch on UK and European websites for the latest bits of news. The film didn't open until Christmas day that year, but by then, most people in the United States and Europe (along with other strategic areas of the world) were poised and ready to see this big-budget musical. In contrast, many new films receive very little commercial attention, and some even go straight to video without a whimper. Someone is deciding exactly how much money to spend on promotion. This person decides, based partly on the cost of the project and partly on the producer's judgment, whether you will hear about it. Preopening hype may not mean a quality product. Many aggressively marketed films are mediocre, and films that appear quietly with little fanfare may be some of the best of the independents.

Public Relations (PR)/Promotion

You cannot do a show and know that "they will come." The word needs to get out. Few experiences are more depressing than to put forth all the effort that goes into a production and then have the cast outnumber the audience. While an individual production may have a publicity director, a permanent theatre company is more likely to have a director of **public relations (PR)/promotion** or development. The most visible parts of promotion are posters and print ads, which need thoughtful design to catch attention and reflect the production concept while staying within a limited budget. Other standard tasks are writing press releases to submit to local publications and supervising the taking of photos to accompany these articles. Developing a positive working relationship with the local press is essential. The posters and perhaps smaller flyers need to be distributed, displays and signs created, businesses contacted to sell program advertising, and the theatre's website constantly updated and maintained. Increasingly, social networking sites are being used to reach target audiences. The PR director may also keep production records, including preview and review articles as well as archival materials. They may also organize special performances for schools, senior citizens, or other special-interest groups. Countless details are involved just in preparing the program given to audience members. Cast and staff members' bios, and possibly photos, need to be included, and each cast member's hometown newspaper contacted as part of the process.

A great deal of the promotion process is not about calling attention to a single production but rather gaining long-term support. In educational settings,

AUTHOR'S INSIGHT

ANNIE: I read a film review in *Rolling Stone* magazine that said, "we have been led to expect terrific stuff from this director, but this piece is just a tired re-hash . . . etc." The very next day, the ads on TV for the same movie quoted *Rolling Stone* as saying "Terrific!" The coincidence reminded me that advertising can be very deceiving.

FIGURE 6.10   Terence Keane, director of public relations (at right), greets a journalist on opening night at the Berkeley Repertory Theatre.

ADAM MAYNARD
PUBLICIST

I feel as if I am the force that releases the show from being a private, intimately shared experience to becoming one that includes countless others. If a tree drops in the forest and is not heard, did it happen? Well, a show that isn't seen and heard did not happen.

BETH CARLTAN
HOUSE MANAGER

I feel almost like a mother tucking her children in and making sure they are comfortable. If the house does not run smooth, the experience of these "children" will be unsettled. We want them to bask in the warmth of the show.

this involves keeping alumni happy and interested in giving back, as well as reaching out to parents of currently enrolled students. It includes wooing new donors, or "angels," as they are sometimes called. A theatre's support base includes getting and expanding season subscribers—those who buy a full season of tickets and provide a measure of financial stability—so each season's campaign is crucial. Subscribers usually receive reduced-price tickets in return for purchasing the entire season, and they are considered a substantial support base. Making contact with each support group may involve planning special fund-raising events, reunions, and workshops, as well as writing and distributing a newsletter to make everyone feel part of that theatre's extended family. Increasingly, on Broadway, publicity is being handled by marketing agencies such as The Marketing Group and Situation Marketing and group sales by companies such as Group Sales Box Office.

House Manager

The SM finds a counterpoint in the person who runs the theatre's public areas. The **house manager (HM)** handles those parts of the theatre space that the stage manager does not. He is primarily responsible for the safety of the audience and the smooth functioning of all "front of house" (lobby, box office, public restrooms, lounges, and auditorium) activities—all that is not onstage or backstage. The HM organizes ushers to seat the audience in the most efficient way and works closely with the stage manager to coordinate the event. The job requires skill in organizing others and being assertive yet friendly. It may involve checking in at the box office regarding ticket sales and accessibility problems, coordinating lobby and restroom cleanliness, picking up items left on seats or in aisles, adjusting seating, supervising the folding and organizing of programs, putting out parking signs, training ushers, setting up lobby display panels, and checking the hearing assistance system.

The HM is in contact with the SM to coordinate opening the house and starting the performance, determining, for example, if there needs to be a delay because someone will be late or because the show may be sold out but many tickets have not yet been picked up. These two managers also consult about intermission length and the procedures for starting each act. A few minutes before curtain, the

HM may be asked to count empty seats and organize standby ticket holders, close the doors at curtain time, turn off the hall and inner lobby lights, and then return to the outer lobby to meet with any latecomers or deal with any other problems that might come up. Once the play is started, he may count tickets and arrange the seating of late arrivals as unobtrusively as possible. This process repeats itself for each intermission.

The HM blinks the hall lights when it is time for the audience to enter the theatre or return to it. At the end of the play, he may coordinate ushers for general cleanup, store ticket stubs, close up the outer space, and turn out interior lights and the marquee lights outside the theatre. An HM needs to be very good at troubleshooting, diplomacy, and finding quick solutions for such issues as disgruntled or suddenly ill patrons or extended delays.

While specific employment statistics are not available for the positions we've been discussing, there is general agreement than unlike acting, one has a reasonable chance, if sufficiently trained, to find and sustain work in these less flashy but vital areas of employment.

Audience

Is the audience, who joins the production last, actually part of the team? We would say they are because without them, there is no game. The actor is one of the two core ingredients for theatre, and the audience is the other. No audience, no theatre. Who are these people who attend? For media, the audience embraces entire cultures. In our culture, the number of people who attend films is vast. It is difficult to find someone who never watches movies. Despite dire predictions that the video, DVD, and home theatre phenomenon would destroy the cinema, the cinema continues to thrive. Watching a film in the cozy seclusion of your home clearly offers a different type of satisfaction than venturing into the darkness of a movie house among strangers. Media, in all forms, is so omnipresent that its audience does not really have a clear identity. And this is true in most areas of the world. In 2004, media artists from both Iraq and Afghanistan began making films again before the wreckage of war settled. In India, famous for its Bollywood style of extravagant filmmaking, hundreds of millions of people flock to movie houses regularly.

LOIS LEBON

REGULAR THEATRE AUDIENCE MEMBER

I go to the theatre to be taken out of my own life. I want to be transported. I don't mind if the play is about a life like my own, but I at least want to learn something and still feel like I have left my own home for some reason. I want the show to either take me away or give me more reasons to stay where I am.

What are the actual figures of attendance? While global statistics are not available, in our country, it is estimated that about 200,000 people each day attend a live theatre production; 50 times that number (10 million) will be watching a movie, and 400 times that number (80 million) will watch television.

Public, ceremonial, and personal-theatre events are dictated by existing connections among participants. For ritual events—from christenings to funerals—the audience is going to be made up largely of those who already have some strong tie to the featured subjects. Huge public ceremonies

FIGURE 6.11 Audiences gather outside the box office to pick up tickets for a performance at Berkeley Rep.

Patrick Cheatham. Courtesy Berkeley Repertory Theatre

(some weddings and commencements, for example) expand to include those not among the near and dear, but there is almost always a traceable connection to explain the presence of each audience member. Some are enthusiastic participants, while others are only fulfilling obligations. The only element that varies is the degree to which cultures (and families within those cultures) embrace each opportunity to ritualize life events through public theatrical occasions or shun such events in favor of more private, reflective rituals.

The audience that is the most difficult to pinpoint is that for live theatre. While no absolutely reliable statistics are available, a common estimate is that less than 5 percent of Americans attend plays on any kind of regular basis. Live-theatre audiences tend to live in large cities, where there is simply greater access to a variety of live-theatre companies and high-quality professional work. Aside from Broadway (New York City) and the West End (London), the cities require sufficient resources to support an arts or a community center with space, seating, and equipment for touring productions beyond local offerings. Such audiences are often relatively affluent because ticket prices demand disposable income. Ironically, this is less true in many cultures where theatre is either subsidized by governments or is created by the whole community and therefore available to all.

Because live theatre is magical and mysterious, there are numerous small companies that defy the odds and thrive and are in no way elitist in

MAUREEN STAPLETON

ACTOR

I've been asked repeatedly what the "key" to acting is, and as far as I'm concerned, the main thing is to keep the audience awake.

FIGURE 6.12 A Chinese audience attending a performance by the Travelling Theatre.

ZENG NIAN/Corbis News/Corbis

either content or availability. A small theatre company or community may target a specific, underrepresented audience, such as Theatre By The Blind in New York City or the bilingual Spanish/English theatre produced in the Guadalupe Cultural Arts Center in the heart of the barrio in San Antonio. Depending on where you are in the world, the audience may include everyone or only a specific few.

When we talk about majority attendance in this country, what kinds of theatrical works lure U.S. audiences regularly in large numbers? There are two. The first will not surprise you. Musicals (covered in Chapter 10) are the mainstay of live theatre. When the entire community shows up, it is likely to be for a big musical. Often summer theatres are devoted entirely to them. When a touring house books shows, musical theatre will be second only to pop music concerts. In any given Broadway season, musicals will outnumber straight plays by as much as five to one.

The other, perhaps more surprising, box office champion is Shakespeare, the single most produced playwright in the world. Almost every state has its own Shakespeare festival, and even though they may be in remote destinations, audiences show up in droves. In addition, Shakespeare is considered a draw across all spectrums of professional and educational theatre and is one of the only playwrights likely to have multiple New York productions within any season.

These two audience favorites strike some as being at opposite ends of the cultural spectrum—from populist

TOM JONES
MUSICAL WRITER, COMPOSER
I realized early on that musicals in their presentational form were much more like Shakespeare than like realistic plays. From large to small, serious to comic, poetry to prose, and back again, Shakespeare's use of heightened language, direct audience address, extreme theatricality, and wonderfully modulated "breathing" was like the structure of some great musical work.

lowbrow to elitist highbrow—but they have much in common. Audiences hope to be thrilled, and both favorites have what it takes to deliver. Both are likely to have large casts, blend intimate scenes with spectacular ones, be set in exotic, fascinating worlds and even remote time periods, and deliver sweeping pomp, spectacle, and ritual, providing a vast adventure. More important, both have moments when characters pour their hearts out, and both demand powerful emotional commitment from performers who need to be both big and honest. Shakespeare's speeches can have an impact similar to musical numbers because the gorgeous language, poetic imagery, and musicality of his verse can stir emotions as strongly in soliloquy as a song may in a musical.

Probably the major misconception preventing more audiences from venturing to the theatre is the belief that it is tied to a "culture vulture" perspective often placed on ballet, opera, and classical symphonies. Theatre actually embraces all cultural levels and topics. After learning more about it, you may consider joining that 5 percent of regular theatergoers.

Audiences affect film in obvious ways such as box office figures and whether we are subjected to a series of sequels. However, at any individual showing of a film, nothing that happens alters what comes off the screen. As a live-theatre audience member, however, your laughter, gasps, sighs, applause, and weeping all affect the performance. From something huge, such as a standing ovation, to the subtle effect of actors looking out on a sea of smiling faces, you alter productions through your connection and communion with the actors.

THEATRE IN YOUR LIFE

Could You Be a Producer?

You may have mounted a few major events in your time: some big parties, fairs, or celebrations. Perhaps you have been involved with fund-raising. But very few of us have much in our offstage lives to prepare us to produce live theatre or media beyond understanding finances, investments, and budgets. There is no official training program or degree in producing, and those who succeed come from a diverse set of backgrounds. Training in business and in all aspects of theatre is useful. Because the producer needs to filter requests from all other staff, it helps to have walked in their shoes at one time or another, so taking classes and gaining production experience in each area helps. It gives you a stronger sense of the validity of each request or complaint. It also helps if you are known for your objectivity, for not getting swept up in volatile emotional or inconsequential causes. The producer needs to be a solid voice of reason, even when surrounded by extravagant artistes who may be just the opposite.

PRODUCING IN OUR LIVES

Are you a regular producer of life events? You probably know this already because if you are, everyone always asks you to help put together the next big shebang. Do people who want to do things ask you if they can afford it or if you have any tips? Are you constantly recognizing where your friends' ideas have no backup, but instead of telling them to forget it, you are interested in exploring ways to make it happen? Are you good at cutting corners but still producing an impressive display? When others sink in despair in preparation for occasions, do you step in and offer concrete solutions that get them all back on track? Do you understand that art and commerce must always balance and coexist without getting bent out of shape over that simple fact? You may be a producer.

COULD YOU BE A DRAMATURG?

Do you have dramaturg potential? If the list at the beginning of the "Dramaturg" section earlier in this chapter sounds appealing to you and you like to do research in general—in fact, if you prefer it to production activity—you may be suited to this position. It is also essential that you be good at doing the research without getting caught up in it, allowing you to recognize what will and will not be noticed by an audience. It helps if you have a knack for asking questions rather than telling people what to do.

Are you the person who always does research on a project, while others will just jump in without it? Do you feel compelled to learn as much about the history and facts of any new undertaking, not just to protect yourself from rash choices but because this adds pleasure and depth to your experience? Do you actually enjoy going to the library on a treasure hunt, delighting as one piece of information leads to a clue that leads to another? And when you share this information, do you tend to do so with contagious enthusiasm but without inhibiting the less scholarly among your friends? Are you more comfortable behind the scenes than on stage? Do you have a keen sense of detail? Are you genuinely satisfied if you can make any event better by the research you did and do not really care if others get the glory? Do you always tend to ask probing questions that others may not even have considered, but once they do, they realize how valuable these may be? Are you able to provide insights and alternative points of view without making others feel threatened? When you become fascinated with a person or period in history, do you almost automatically collect clippings and memorabilia to create lasting images? You may be the dramaturg of your group even when there is no "drama."

COULD YOU BE A TECHNICAL DIRECTOR?

Are you someone who likes to build things? Are you the person your friends always call upon to help them realize their dreams in a tangible way? Do you actually know how to make and fix things? Are you the person who, once everyone gets done brainstorming, begins to question, explain, examine, and explore pragmatic solutions? Are you perfectly willing to tell the fanciful, high-flying visionaries in your life that what they want cannot be done with what they've got, that the money and resources will not match their vision? Do you generally thrive in organizing work parties to do construction and actually enjoy the practical challenges of galvanizing a group of unskilled workers to create and sustain a project? You are the TD of your group if, after their breathless ecstasy over discovering an idea, your friends come to you, often in the cold light of the next day, to ask if and how it might be done.

COULD YOU BE A PR PERSON?

Working in PR requires a healthy, positive aggressiveness. Your show or theatre is competing for print and media coverage with countless others. You need to prepare convincing publicity packages and be able to follow up with even more convincing personal (often phone) pitches. You must believe in what you are promoting and be constantly inventive in how you get others to share your enthusiasm. When the houses are packed, you need to feel enormous satisfaction just in seeing all those people because chances are that others involved in the production will not notice your efforts. Getting them to show up ("butts in seats" is the promotional mantra) is your goal—and ultimate reward.

SUMMARY

Theatre's unsung heroes are neglected when it comes to attention, but the jobs have deep challenges, satisfactions, and employment potential. The producer must manage the business end. The technical director is probably the most essential link between the ideas of the planning team and their realization, holding together all concrete and practical aspects of production. The stage manager is the glue that binds the daily running of rehearsals and ultimately performances; he calls the shots, and at a crucial juncture in the process, takes over for both the director and technical director. Many shows require special skills and equipment, so experts are brought in. Perhaps one team of crew members constructs a show and then another team altogether runs it in performance. These two groups may be entirely separate entities. The public relations person has the challenge of making sure that all potentially interested audience members know about the show, and all potential long-range supporters and investors feel connected to the theatre company. The house manager takes care of all the business out front, while the stage manager monitors onstage and backstage activities. The audience is the essential final ingredient. While media and personal audiences are vast, only a small percentage of the population makes live theatre a regular, constant part of their lives.

SUGGESTED ASSIGNMENTS

1. Next time you attend a play, notice how well or poorly managed the production is. Were any cues confusing? Did light, sound, and set changes happen fluidly? Were there any obvious errors?

2. Notice the same for the house management. Did the show start on time? If not, was there an obvious good reason, such as a last-minute line of people wanting tickets? Were ushers available to help you? Could they actually answer questions? Did the intermission last the amount of time that the program said it would? Were you effectively warned in time to get in your seat for each act?

3. How demanding was this piece of work to produce and run? Were significant demands placed on those backstage, onstage, and in the front of the house? If yes or no, what evidence do you have for this conclusion?

4. What constitutes an effectively promoted production? Begin to notice posters, flyers, ads, and feature stories, and make comparisons among your local theatre groups as to which are more and which are less effective at getting the word out.

5. What skills do you possess that could be called upon by a theatre with special production needs?

6. As you examine the program from a recent theatre event, ask yourself how well put together it is in terms of serving your theatre experience. Is there enough information to divert and entertain you while you wait for the show to begin? Are there any questions that could have been answered in program notes but are not?

7. Examine the list of staff members in this chapter. Do you feel that you now understand what each person on that list does? If a crew seems very large, can you determine from the performance itself why so many people were needed? Are any positions still unclear to you?

8. As you imagine yourself taking part in a production, where do you see yourself fitting in, provided you have more training and experience? Are

you absolutely a potential performer, or would you find a more comfortable niche among those less publicly exposed?

9. The next time you experience theatre with music, consider what the event would have been like without it, and evaluate the degree to which the musicians' involvement enhanced or distracted from your engagement in the event.

10. Can you tell, as you look around at a performance, the demographics of this theatre's audience? Are they an older, more formal crowd, or are they young, hip, and incredibly eclectic? From the nature of the play itself and the season of which it is a part, can you find a reason for the nature of the audience?

SUGGESTED ACTIVITIES

1. **Individual:** Interview a music, fight, or dance director and report on the specific contributions the person believes she brings to any production.

2. **Group:** Volunteer as a group to help with the promotion of a production about to open. Meet with the publicity director, who may eventually assign you places to put up posters and may also involve you in other aspects of publicity.

3. **Long-term:** Meet with a TD at the start of production and once a week throughout rehearsal. Identify specific challenges at the beginning and how they change as the show gets closer to opening.

4. **Large group:** Select a production or film that the entire class has seen. Divide the class into five groups, each of which is charged with coming up with a strong argument why the role of the producer, dramaturg, TD, running crew, or publicist was the most important element. Have the teacher select the team with the strongest argument.

KEY WORDS AND IDEAS

producer	technical director (TD)
artistic director	stage manager (SM)
managing director	construction crews
box office	running crews
dramaturg	shop supervisors
literary manager	master electrician
music director	shop foreman
fight director	master carpenter
choreographer	key grip
coach	public relations (PR)/promotion
dialects	house manager (HM)

Generations

Featured plays:

King Lear by William Shakespeare (1605)

Roosters by Milcha Sanchez-Scott (1987)

(NOTE: The scripts for these plays, along with additional background information, are available in the companion anthology to this text, *Life Themes: An Anthology of Plays for the Theatre*)

There comes a time in some families when a son feels the need to challenge his father at arm wrestling. No matter what the outcome, there is poignancy and sadness around this encounter because someone must win and someone must lose. The encounters in *Lear* and *Roosters* are not as simple or direct, but both plays have much intergenerational "wrestling" over power.

When children become adults, how does their relationship with their parents change? To what extent do they remain obedient, and to what extent do they assert themselves? When is the right moment to break free—or are they ever free? There are as many answers as varieties of families. The transition is rarely painless or satisfactory to all involved. In these plays, it is often catastrophic. *Lear* is set so far back in time as to be beyond recorded history, yet the dilemma of a powerful man about to retire and dividing his wealth among his offspring is universal and timeless. The ways in which parents misjudge their children, perhaps even favoring those least loyal to them, is a sadly common phenomenon as well. In *Roosters*, set in the late twentieth century, the struggle between father and son is connected to ancient ideas about what it means to be a man.

King Lear (1605)

Setting: Ancient Britain

Major Characters:

Lear, King of Britain, about to divide his kingdom among his children, "every inch a king," though "a foolish, fond old man"

Goneril and Regan, his elder, married daughters, "she foxes" and "gilded serpents"

Cordelia, his youngest, favorite unmarried daughter, an "unprized, precious maid"

FIGURE 6.13 The storm scene from *King Lear.* Kent (Christopher Benjamin, Edgar (Michael Maloney), King Lear (Nigel Hawthorne), and Lear's Fool (Hiroyuki Sanada) are battered by the storm. Directed by Yukio Ninagawa.

The Earl of Gloucester, Lear's patient, longtime adviser, an equally credulous, rash old man

Edgar, his legitimate son, "whose nature is so far from doing harm that he suspects none," later disguised as Mad Tom

Edmund, his "bastard" son, "rough and lecherous"

The Duke of Albany, wed to Goneril, "a man of milky gentleness"

The Duke of Cornwall, wed to Regan, a villain "whose disposition will not be stopped"

The Earl of Kent, Lear's most loyal subject, "noble and true-hearted," first a lord in Lear's court, later disguised as a servant

The Fool, Lear's "bitter, all-licensed jester"

Oswald, arrogant steward to Goneril, "a knave and rascal"

At an elaborate retirement ceremony, Lear, before dividing his kingdom among his three daughters, asks each to tell him publicly how much she loves him. His two elder offspring extravagantly fawn over him, but Cordelia, his youngest and favorite, cannot bring herself to do so:

LEAR: What can you say to draw a third more opulent than your sisters? Speak.

CORDELIA: Nothing, my lord.

LEAR: Nothing!

CORDELIA: Nothing.

LEAR: Nothing will come of nothing. Speak again.

CORDELIA: Unhappy that I am, I cannot heave My heart into my mouth.

Lear angrily disinherits her altogether. One of her suitors, the king of France, offers to marry her without dowry, and Lear in essence says she is dead to him. It immediately becomes apparent that his other daughters actually bear him no love. His situation is paralleled by that of the Earl of Gloucester, one of his courtiers, who fails to realize which of his sons loves him and which merely uses him. In one of the most famous speeches in all Shakespeare, Edmund the "bastard,"* alone onstage, wonders why he should be "deprive[d]" because he is the younger and illegitimate of two brothers:

EDMUND: Thou nature art my goddess; to thy law
My services are bound . . . . Wherefore should I . . .
   permit
The curiosity of nations to deprive me,
For that I am some twelve or fourteen moonshines
Lag of a brother? Why bastard? Wherefore base? . . .
Well, my legitimate, if this letter speed,
And my invention thrive, Edmund the base
Shall top the legitimate—I grow; I prosper—
Now gods, stand up for bastards!

Edmund plots to make it appear that his brother aims to assassinate their father, forcing Edgar to flee and to disguise himself as a madman. Through a complex series of events, both old men are betrayed by "trusted" family, are thrust out into a violent storm, experience a slow dawning of awareness, and are reunited with those whom they can trust. While they experience profound insights and increased compassion for all creatures of the world, this wisdom comes too late for them to be able to live it out into productive change.

This is one of Shakespeare's most violent plays. At one point, Gloucester has his eyes ripped out, and at the final curtain, there have been nine deaths of major characters, with only Edgar (who has beaten his brother in battle) and Goneril's husband, the Duke of Albany, alive. The pain experienced by his elders is summarized by Edgar:

EDGAR: The oldest hath borne most; we that are young
Shall never see so much nor live so long.

Here is a scene from *King Lear*, from the adaptation by Robert Barton found in *Life Themes: An Anthology of Plays for the Theatre*, in which the evil Edmund begins unfolding his plot against his brother, Edgar, the loyal son who stands by his father through thick and thin:

[EDMUND *stands alone.*]

EDMUND: I should have been that I am, had the maidenliest star in the firmament twinkled on my bastardizing. Edgar! Ha! He comes like the catastrophe of the old comedy; my cue is *villainous*

melancholy, with a sigh like Tom o' Bedlam. *[Enter EDGAR.] Fa, so la mi.*
EDGAR: How now, brother Edmund! What serious contemplation are you in?
EDMUND: When saw you my father last?
EDGAR: The night gone by.
EDMUND: Spake you with him?
EDGAR: Ay, two hours together.
EDMUND: Bethink yourself wherein you may have offended him. Forbear his presence till some little time hath qualified the heat of his displeasure.

EDGAR: Some villain hath done me wrong.
EDMUND: That's my fear. Retire with me to my lodging, from whence I will fitly bring you to hear my lord speak: pray you, go; there's my key: if you do stir abroad, go arm'd.
EDGAR: Arm'd, brother!
EDMUND: Brother, I advise you to the best. Pray you, away.
EDGAR: Shall I hear from you anon?
EDMUND: I do serve you in this business. *[Exit EDGAR.]*
A credulous father! And a brother noble.
Whose nature is so far from doing harms,
That he suspects none; on whose foolish honesty
My practices ride easy!—I see the business.
Let me, if not by birth, have lands by wit.
All with me's meet that I can fashion fit.

[Exit.]

*While Edmund behaves like a "bastard" in our contemporary usage of that term, in this instance, it refers to the fact that he is the result of his father's affair outside his marriage (probably with a non-aristocrat), while Edgar's mother was probably titled and wed to Gloucester, so Edgar is the rightful, legal heir to his father's estates.

Roosters (1987)

Like *Lear*, *Roosters* involves a father who was so absent and distant in the crucial growing-up periods of his children that he really does not know them in adulthood. But there are significant differences as well. Whereas *Lear* has no mothers of any kind, *Roosters* is filled with the force of both mother and aunt, actively engaged in raising children. Whereas *Lear* has only grown children, *Roosters* features a teenage girl clinging to childhood and still in need of guidance. The play has much female energy surrounding the machismo. While it is no surprise that Shakespeare has speeches of power, poetry, and extraordinary eloquence, Milcha Sanchez-Scott also has characters frequently launch into breathtaking poetry. Both plays alternate between the most direct down-to-earth language and soaring elegant imagery.

Setting: Exterior of the Morales house, somewhere in New Mexico

Characters:

Gallo, patriarch of the Morales family, just released from prison

Juana, his wife, hardworking, patient, exhausted

Hector, his son, who currently works in the fields

Angela, his daughter, who wears angel wings and often prays aloud

Chata, his sister, brassy, boozy, sarcastic

Adan, Hector's friend

Shadow 1, Shadow 2, mysterious figures who come looking for Gallo

Zapata, a rooster

San Juan, a rooster, each represented alternately by actual roosters and by actors portraying them

The play begins on the day that family patriarch Gallo, a legendary rooster fighter, returns home. It is also the day that his son is scheduled to take his own rooster into the ring for the first time. Gallo shows his intense involvement with the rooster Zapata:

> GALLO: Take my blood, honey. . . . I'm in you now. . . .
> Morales blood, the blood of kings and you're my
> rooster . . . a Morales rooster.

Hector is probably not that far off the mark in this harsh judgment of his father:

> HECTOR: Whatever happens, Papi will still only care
> about the rooster. That's his son, that's who gets it
> all.

Hector's buddy, Adan, tries to talk him out of fighting because he really doesn't have it in his heart:

> ADAN: Why? Why you do this for? You no even like bird
> . . . You just want money to go from the fields . . .
> HECTOR: How could you think I just wanted money?
> I want him to see me.

When Hector and Gallo finally encounter each other for the first time in seven years, they simply stare at each other for a long time, followed by this tense exchange:

> GALLO: Well . . . you are taller. This offshoot . . . this
> little bud has grown.
> HECTOR: Yeah, well . . . that must be why you
> seem . . . smaller.

Chata has always been disappointed in men. "They're all shit," she keeps repeating, whereas Juana tends to blame herself for life's letdowns. Angela wears

FIGURE 6.14   The angel ascension scene in the Illinois State University School of Theatre production of *Roosters*.

wings, longs for innocence and transcendence, prays continuously, and often hides under the porch.

Gallo gets in trouble with some men who go back to his rooster days before jail and plans to leave again even though he has just gotten home. Both Hector and Angela interfere. Hector has plotted a way to give up roosters altogether to keep his father at home and to keep him safe, but it takes a miracle in the form of Angela's ascension to actually make this happen. As the play ends, Gallo drifts off to sleep as his children speak of journeys yet to come.

Here is a scene from *Roosters*, starting on the day Gallo returns from seven years in prison for killing his neighbor over a rooster. His children await him with different emotions. Hector, now 20 and supporting his family, is filled with anger and distrust. Angela wants so badly to be her daddy's little girl that she tries to reverse the clock that has led her to the brink of young womanhood:

[ANGELA *slides out from under the house, wearing her wings. She carries a white box which contains her cardboard tombstones, paper and crayon, a writing tablet, and a pen. She too sniffs the air. She runs to the little cemetery and looks up, as HECTOR appears at the window behind her.]*

ANGELA: Tres Rosas . . . Did you hear? Sweet Jesus, Abuelo, Queen of Heaven, all the Saints, all the Angels. It is true. It is certain. He is coming, coming to stay forever and ever. Amen.

HECTOR: Don't count on it!

ANGELA: *[To Heaven]* Protect me from those of little faith and substance.

HECTOR: I'm warning you. You're just going to be disappointed.

ANGELA: *[To Heaven]* Guard me against the enemies of my soul.

HECTOR: Your butt's getting bigger and bigger!

ANGELA: And keep me from falling in with low companions.

HECTOR: Listen, little hummingbird woman, you gotta be tough, and grown-up today.

[ANGELA *digs up her collection can and two dolls. Both dolls are dressed in nuns' habits. One, the St. Lucy doll, has round sunglasses. She turns a box over to make a little tea table, on which she places a doll teapot and cups.]*

ANGELA: As an act of faith and to celebrate her father's homecoming, Miss Angela Ester Morales will have a tea party.

HECTOR: No more tea parties.

ANGELA: Dancing in attendance will be that charming martyr, St. Lucy.

HECTOR: He will not be impressed.

ANGELA: Due to the loss of her eyes and the sensitivity of her alabaster skin, St. Lucy will sit in the shade. *[She sits St. Lucy in the shade and picks up the other doll.]*

HECTOR: Who's that?

ANGELA: St. Teresa of Avignon, you will sit over here. *[She seats the St. Teresa doll.]*

HECTOR: Just don't let him con you, Angela.

ANGELA: *[Pouring pretend tea]* One lump or two, St. Lucy? St. Teresa has hyperglycemia, and only takes cream in her tea. Isn't that right, St. Teresa?

HECTOR: He's not like Abuelo. *[ANGELA animates the dolls like puppets and uses two different voices as St. Lucy and St. Teresa.]*

ANGELA: *[As St. Teresa]* Shouldn't we wait for St. Luke?

HECTOR: Stop hiding. You can't be a little girl forever.

ANGELA: *[As St. Lucy]* St. Luke! St. Luke! Indeed! How that man got into Heaven I'll never know. That story about putting peas in his boots and offering the discomfort up to God is pure bunk. I happen to know he boiled the peas first.

HECTOR: I don't want you hurt. It's time to grow up.

ANGELA: *[As St. Teresa]* St. Lucy! I can only think that it is the loss of your eyes that makes you so disagreeable. Kindly remember that we have all suffered to be saints.

HECTOR: Are you listening to me, Angie?

ANGELA: *[As St. Lucy]* Easy for you to say! They took my eyes because I wouldn't put out! They put them on a plate. A dirty, chipped one, thank you very much indeed! To this day no true effort has been made to find them.

HECTOR: Excuse me! . . . Excuse me, St. Teresa, St. Lucy. I just thought I should tell you . . . a little secret . . . your hostess, Miss Angela Ester Morales, lies in her little, white, chaste, narrow bed, underneath the crucifix, and masturbates.

ANGELA: Heretic! Liar!

HECTOR: Poor Jesus, up there on the cross, right over her bed, his head tilted down. He sees everything.

ANGELA: Lies! Horrible lies!

HECTOR: Poor saint of the month, watching from the night table.

ANGELA: I hate you! I hate you! Horrible, horrible, Hector.

JUANA: *[From offstage]* Breakfast! *[HECTOR leaves the window. Angela sits on the ground writing on a tombstone.]*

ANGELA: *[Lettering tombstone]* Here lies Horrible Hector Morales. Died at age twenty, in great agony, for tormenting his little sister.

JUANA: *[Offstage]* You kids . . . breakfast!

HECTOR: *[Pops up at window]* Just be yourself. A normal, sex-crazed, fifteen-year-old girl with a big, gigantic, enormous butt. *[He exits.]*

ANGELA: *[To Heaven]* Send me to Alaska
Let me be frozen
Send me a contraction
A shrinking antidote
Make me little again
Please make my legs
Like tiny pink Vienna sausages
Give me back my little butt.

Here are examples that expand ideas of the past two chapters.

General Design

Lear is a massive undertaking, an epic tale demanding a fully realized production, a large cast, and innumerable design challenges. *Roosters* is a far simpler undertaking, with a single modern location, a small cast, and no huge technical demands.

Scene Design

Lear takes place all over England, from palaces to hovels, moving constantly between tamed interiors and wild exteriors. *Roosters* takes place in a single family setting. The challenge in *Lear* is creating a large, flexible space that can adapt through light to suggest various locales and conditions; in *Roosters,* the challenge is creating a detailed, believable sense of a home where people have actually lived for many years. The effort in *Roosters* will lie in the detailed surface, set decoration, and props.

Costume and Makeup Design

Unless *Lear* is relocated to a recognizable later time period (which is often the case), the challenge is to create a world that we have never known, believably ancient and yet spectacular. Given the number of characters, the play will be a massive costume design and construction endeavor. While most of the *Roosters* costumes can be purchased rather than built, the roosters themselves, in their human manifestations, present really creative challenges. Two males need to clearly *represent* the roosters; they must be able to move with great agility and to fight viciously in these costumes. Angela must actually ascend above the stage in the final moments of the play. How will her costume be constructed so that she can be flown upward?

Lighting and Sound

Both plays have sequences where reality is altered in a way that must suggest supernatural forces at work, so the world will need to change largely through the power of light, music, and sound effects. The storm in *Lear* is one of the most technically difficult feats in theatre to pull off because the actors must appear to be in the midst of a blinding, violent storm with convincing eruptions of wind, rain, lightning, and thunder (without soaking the audience). At the same time, the actors' lines must be entirely clear to the audience (as they never would be in the midst of a real storm). These cues need to be planned and executed with great flair and precision.

The Producer

Roosters can be performed in a very small space on a miniscule budget. However, many theatres will need to recruit appropriate actors who may be outside their usual casting pool and to expand publicity to gather members of the community who do not necessarily regularly attend live theatre. *Lear* will also demand a significant investment in time, money, and highly skilled participants. It will, however, benefit from being extremely well known and will probably not require nontraditional promotion.

Dramaturgy

There are difficult, ambiguous passages in both scripts that will really benefit from the kind of investigation that a dramaturg can offer. The dramaturg on *King Lear* will be essential in deciding which edition or adaptation of the script to use, and in helping interpret the more difficult passages of poetry. In addition, references in the script to events or slang that were current in Shakespeare's lifetime will need illumination. The dramaturg on *Roosters,* while dealing with a contemporary American script, will still need to have a deep understanding of magic realism, life in the American Southwest, and the culture of Mexican American families.

Other Directors

Both plays require skilled fight directors who also have choreographic abilities. In *Roosters,* the rooster fight needs inventiveness and power because it could easily appear comical (men in tights prancing and pecking at each other). The degree to which battle scenes are placed on stage will vary among *Lear* productions, but the big fight between the two brothers (Edgar and Edmund) is so keenly anticipated by the audience throughout the play that it cannot be shortchanged. It needs to be brutal, impressive, and satisfying.

Stage Manager

Both plays will have many cues to call and require a highly efficient and tightly organized stage manager and well-trained crews, so running the shows will be challenging. While the plays are still in rehearsal, *Roosters* will be less demanding, simply because it is so small in scale, while for the stage manager of *Lear*, just making sure that all cast members are present and accounted for will be a challenge. Ironically, *Lear* will probably involve fewer props and set pieces to be set each evening because it does not depend on the detail (such as at a family dinner) that permeates the world of *Roosters*, including someone who always takes care of the real roosters.

Audience

Both plays are highly regarded and can attract a wide range of patrons. *Roosters* has particular appeal to the Latin American community but speaks to us all. Some audiences are intimidated by Shakespeare, particularly a great Shakespearean tragedy, and may avoid *Lear* not only because they doubt they will be entertained but because they fear not understanding or being able to follow the action. Both plays will benefit from effective marketing strategies designed to make it clear that they are universal, comprehensible, and deeply human.

An Indian dancer dressed as a
Hindu deity in Calcutta, 2004.

part III

How Did Theatre Evolve?

In various locations around the world, theatre developed in astonishingly similar ways. Part III explores how Indian, Greek, Chinese, English, Japanese, French, and African theatres all found their own strong, early voices and how they evolved.

In Chapter 7, we will address theatrical forms of Sanskrit drama, Chinese opera, *Noh*, Kabuki, Bunraku, African Yoruban ritual, as well as ancient Greek and Elizabethan drama.

In Chapter 8, we will scan the seventeenth and eighteenth centuries and such forms as *Kunqu, Kathakali, Jinguju,* Restoration and Georgian comedy, neoclassicism, *Commedia dell'arte,* melodrama, and the effects of diaspora on African theatre. The changing nature of performance space and the influence of theatre moving from an open-air to an inside event will also be explored.

In Dramatic Interlude 4, following these chapters, we focus on the issue of rebellion as manifested in Sophocles's *Antigone* and Athol Fugard's *"Master Harold"* . . . *and the boys* and explore the differing consequences within these dramas.

In Expansion 4, we apply the historical concepts of the preceding two chapters to the featured plays.

The Historic Parallels table shown here identifies some phenomena of global similarities.

Chapter 7 | Historic Parallels

ASIA	EUROPE	AFRICA
	ORIGINS	
Indian Sanskrit Drama (700–200 B.C.E.)	Greek Tragedy/Comedy (5th century B.C.E.)	"Functional" Communal Drama
	CONQUEST AND RETREAT	
Chinese *Zaju* (*Xigu* 1–900s)	Medieval Mystery/Passion Plays (900–1400)	Coptic Christianity—Ritual (3rd century)
Japanese *Noh* (1350s)		Islam—Bards, Pageants, Puppetry (640)
	RESURGENCE OF POPULAR DRAMA	
Japanese Kabuki (1600s)	Elizabethan Drama (1590s)	Colonial Impact (1600s)
Bunraku and Other Puppetry	Jacobean and Carolingian (17th century)	
	ELITISM	
Chinese *Kunqu* (*Xigu* 2—17th century)	English Restoration Comedy (17th century)	Submission and Survival
Indian Kathakali (1650s)	French Neoclassicism (17th century)	Diaspora—Slavery and Colonialism
	Molière	
	RETURN OF THE PEOPLE	
Chinese *Jinguju—Xigu* 3—Beijing Opera (1790)	English Georgian Comedy (18th century)	The Americas—Minstrelsy
	Melodrama	

chapter 7

EARLY STAGES

Scene from the Greek tragedy *The Oresteia* by Aeschylus, with actors in traditional costume. Olivier Theatre/National Theatre, London.

Yoshida Tamao, one of Japan's Living National Treasures, exhibits a traditional Bunraku puppet.

Lesson Objectives:

Upon completion of this chapter, you will be able to:

1. Explore unfamiliar styles of theatre from various global communities with a basic understanding of the history and conventions of each.
2. Identify the names of major theatrical movements and playwrights from the beginnings of scripted drama through the Elizabethan period.
3. Recognize how theatre has moved from an elite to a popular art form in continuous swings on a continuum.
4. Recognize that forms of theatre around the world have shared similarities that are difficult to explain logically.

Introduction

The Historic Parallels table preceding this chapter shows us how theatre has swung back and forth from an inclusive event involving the entire community, to a restricted luxury for the elite few, and back again to embrace the people, in what may be an inevitable pendulum as part of its evolution. Intriguingly, the same pendulum swing was occurring in separate parts of the world.

Each section of this chapter begins by looking at the foundation theatres: Sanskrit dance-drama in the East, Greek scripted theatre in the West, and the oral traditions of Africa. As we progress to the theatre that follows the early brilliance in various regions of the world, we will be able to see the continued influence of the Indian, Greek, and African worldview on their respective parts of the world. Because theatre is a way to respond to prevailing ideas, we begin each survey by looking at the dominant worldview of each culture, followed by the drama, theatre practice, and influence of these early masterpieces on world theatre today. Rather than repeat those ideas, we point out only critical changes or divergences in thought that influenced the theatre of a particular place and time.

First Scripted Theatre: Indian Sanskrit Drama

The first fully documented, scripted theatre originated in India, where **Sanskrit dance-drama** influenced its evolution throughout Asia. We will examine Sanskrit theatre, and then trace a few of the many forms of Asian drama that followed, showing how the swing between popular and exclusive theatre occurred. We will contrast elitist Sanskrit with popular *Zaju* and exclusive Kabuki with popular Kabuki.

Sanskrit dance-drama was formalized in written form around 2,600 years ago. Before that, the drama flourished as an oral tradition for centuries. As the dominant theatre of the Indian Empire, Sanskrit dance-drama lasted until at least the 1200s. Its influence continues today. Sanskrit theatre reflects the worldview of the Indian culture and its prevailing attitudes.

Worldview

India was and is predominantly Hindu. For the Hindu, time is an eternal cycle with infinite wheels of experience coexisting in celestial harmony. The passage of time is an illusion, and this life is only one incarnation of the infinite cycles of the soul. In the most influential Indian story, *Mahabharata*, a god asks a great hero, "What is the greatest wonder of the world?" With the lives of his four brothers at stake, this calm and wise hero correctly answers, "The greatest wonder is that death is everywhere, we see it every day and yet we each live as if death will never touch us."

The Hindu social system was set down in four great works called the *Vedas*, describing a male-dominated system, celebrating the victory of gods over demons, describing the creation of humanity, and establishing codes for behavior. The *Vedas* encourage not only physical strength, courage in battle, and skill with weaponry, but also the pursuit of peace, serenity, and happiness in the mind. Rash behavior is discouraged, love is central, and men must protect and cherish women. Family is essential. The many gods and demons of the cosmos provide daily temptation and redemption. Both evil and good are necessary for the harmony of creation. The ultimate destination of each soul is enlightenment, perfect peace, and happiness. But this can only be achieved through many cycles of life, or reincarnations. With enlightenment comes release from the eternal cycles of time and space, birth and rebirth, into oblivion.

The caste system gives form to Hindu society. In spiritual terms, each soul is bound to seek harmony and enlightenment and each caste is responsible for the well-being of other castes. In actual social reality, the caste system evolved into a complex and sometimes cruel system that allowed great luxury and pleasure to a few and hardship and hopelessness to the many. Whatever their caste, women submitted to fathers, then husbands, or to brothers, uncles, or other male relatives. And yet, in Sanskrit drama, women are often central figures, objects of love and devotion, and powerful figures that change the nature of the world.

Epic stories or poems are lengthy narratives that celebrate the adventures of a legendary or historical hero. The epics of India teach that true pleasure comes through kindness, humility, duty, love, and correct behavior.

Beyond India

About 556 B.C.E., a young prince named Siddhārtha Gautama left his life of riches and power and set out to find the meaning of the suffering that he saw in the world. After six years of training with spiritual masters, he sat under a tree and entered a state of profound meditation until he achieved enlightenment. He became the **Buddha**, and he and his disciples began a lifelong journey of teaching, spreading the ideals of **Hinduism** and **Buddhism** through vast reaches of the Asian continent. In the process, they used theatre as a teaching tool and so spread the conventions of India to the rest of Asia.

The Drama

While the oral tradition is the starting point of all drama, the recording of two epic stories and one book of rules—all three grounded in antiquity— still influence Indian theatre today. Sanskrit tradition says that the gods invented theatre and gave it to humans through an ancient sage whose

Date

Date		
Prehistory	▲	Storytellers and actors
	■	*Uzume's Trance* (see Ch. 2)
	■	*Ogun's Mysteries* (see Ch. 2)
2500 B.C.E.	●	Earliest *written* accounts of human creation, c. 2300–2100 B.C.E.
2000 B.C.E.	●	*Abydos Passion Play*—Egypt (see Ch. 2)
1000 B.C.E.		
800 B.C.E.	▲	Homer, *The Iliad* and *The Odyssey*, 8th century B.C.E.
	●	Oral traditions continue—*griots*
	▲	Thespis, the "first actor," Greece (see Ch. 2)
	■	The Buddha spreads Buddhism and Hinduism through Asia, c. 550 B.C.E.
600 B.C.E.	■	*Mahabharata*, c. 5th century B.C.E.
	▲	Athens—Play contests begin, c. 534 B.C.E.
500 B.C.E.	▲	Aeschylus (*The Oresteia*), 525–456 B.C.E.
	■	Sophocles (*Oedipus Rex, Antigone*), 496–406 B.C.E.
	■	Comedy introduced to play contests in Athens, c. 487 B.C.E.
	■	Euripides (*Medea, The Bacchae*), 484–406 B.C.E.
400 B.C.E.	▲	Aristophanes, "Old Comedy" (*Lysistrata*), 448–385 B.C.E.
300 B.C.E.	●	*Ramayana* by Valmiki, c. 300 B.C.E.
	▲	Plautus, Roman comic playwright, 254–184 B.C.E.
200 B.C.E.	■	*Natya Shastra*, c. 200 B.C.E.; Sanskrit drama flourishes until 1200s
100 B.C.E.		
1 C.E.	▲	Seneca, Roman tragic playwright, c. 3 B.C.E.–65 C.E.
100		
200	■	Sanskrit dramatists Kàlidàsa (3rd century), Shudraka (dates unknown), and Bhàsa (c. 275–335)
300		

Date

Date		
400	▲	Rome banishes theatre, c. 400
	▲	Fall of Roman Empire, 476; theatre in the West declines
500	■	Muhammad lives and preaches, c. 570–632
600	●	Islam arrives in North Africa—bards, dancers, 640
700		
800		
900	▲	*Quem Quaeritis*, dramatic interlude, inserted into Easter Mass, 925
	■	*Zaju* begins in Sung Dynasty, China, 900s, thrives into 13th century
1000	■	Decline of Indian Empire
1100	●	Shadow puppets in North Africa
1200	■	Guan Hanqing, *Zaju* playwright, Yuan Dynasty, c. 1241–1320
1300	■	*Noh* drama evolves during Samurai period; still performed today
	■	*Noh* playwrights Kan'ami Kiyotsugu, 1333–1384; Zeami Motokiyo, 1363–1443
1400	●	Benin Empire (modern Nigeria), 14th to 17th centuries; court societies support performing arts
	▲	*Commedia dell'arte* starts in Italy, 1400s; continues into 17th century
1500	●	European incursions into West Africa; slave trade begins, 1500s
	▲	Elizabeth I rules England, 1558–1603
	▲	Tudor drama, c. 1550–1600
	▲	Christopher Marlowe, 1564–1593
	▲	William Shakespeare, 1564–1616
	▲	Elizabethan Drama, c. 1590–1615
1600	■	Kabuki theatre begins, Japan, 1600s, still performed today
	▲	Jacobean drama, c. 1603–1625
	■	Takemoto Gidayû sets up Bunraku theatre, 1684

KEY: ▲ The West   ■ The East   ● Africa

name was **Bharata** (see Chapter 2). Bharata transcribed the will of the gods into the *Natya Shastra* or *Canon of Dance and Drama*, a 37-chapter, detailed description of theatrical presentation. The book's author and its date are the subject of much debate. Bharata (who, like Homer, may have been one oral storyteller or many) created the current form of the *Natya Shastra* between 200 B.C.E. and 200 C.E.

The *Natya Shastra* outlines theatre spaces, training of performers, and "appropriate" material for performance. To this day, the great epics provide the model, if not the actual source material for much Indian theatre and film. *Mahabharata* (translation: *The Great Story of the Bharata Family*), the most influential, is an epic poem that has 100,000 stanzas for the narrator to memorize!

The story begins 7,000 years ago, before humans became corrupt through idleness and greed. It is the story of two great families, one with 5 brothers and the other with 100 brothers. The two families are torn apart by jealousy, greed, and betrayal. The 5 brothers are heroes, sons of gods, possessing all that is good. Their 100 cousins are not evil; they are simply weaker than their cousins. Sages, visionaries, gods, demons, spirits, and women are active characters. After many adventures, the families fight a great war, and the heroic brothers defeat their cousins.

Styles

Sanskrit dramatists found many **points of attack** (see Chapter 3) within the epic stories. Most plays blended the comic and serious, with every character type included. The clown figure is often central as a comic counterpart to the hero. The often-flawed hero must suffer and learn to achieve success. Sanskrit drama never separates the sacred from the profane or the comic from the cosmic. Love and restoration is the unifying principle. Romance and heroic quests are the two dominant themes. In *Ramayana*, for example, a king searches for his stolen wife for 10 long years before they are reunited. The concept of tragedy is absent. This does not mean that no suffering, death, or loss occurs. Rather, since this life and these trials are part of the great harmony, the chance of rebirth and redemption follows suffering and death.

As Sanskrit drama spread across the Indian Empire, the Sanskrit spoken language fell into disuse, becoming the language of elite poets and scholars. Audiences in the far reaches of the empire spoke no Indian languages, yet everyone knew the stories. As time went on, the plays evolved into an increasingly visual form. Performers danced, gestured, and spoke Sanskrit, while a narrator translated the play into the language of the audience. Music and dance provided universal languages that crossed cultural boundaries.

The Playwrights

The "Big Three" classical Sanskrit playwrights are **Śhudraka** (dates unknown), **Bhàsa** (c. 275–335), and the most honored of them all, **Kàlidàsa** (third century), who is credited with writing the "perfect" play.

Śhudraka's play, *The Little Clay Cart,* is a complicated 10-act love triangle. It is the story of a priest who falls hopelessly in love with a beautiful courtesan, who in turn is in love with a poor merchant. After many trials and tribulations, lovers are united, lives are spared, and balance is restored.

Bhàsa's most respected work is *Vasavadatta's Dream*, which tells of a king pressured by his minister of state to marry the daughter of a powerful ruler in order to strengthen his reign and protect his kingdom. The king, however, is too devoted to his wife to consider such a marriage. Instead, the queen, ready to sacrifice her own happiness to save the kingdom, fakes her death in a palace fire and then secretly returns to wait upon the new queen and to be near her husband.

ANDRE FERDINAND HEROLD
___
TRANSLATOR/ADAPTOR AND DIRECTOR

. . . the Shakuntala [is] a masterpiece that appears once every two thousand years.

The most revered of the three is Kàlidàsa, whose *The Recognition of Shakuntala*, called by some Indian scholars the "perfect play," tells the romantic story of King Dushyanta, who falls in love at first sight with Shakuntala, a beautiful maiden he meets while hunting in the forest. She returns his love and they agree to marry, but, burdened by a strange curse, the king forgets her as soon as he returns to his palace. Time passes and Shakuntala leaves her family to journey to the palace. En route, she loses the ring that the king gave her as a token of their marriage. Rejected at the king's palace, she soon gives birth to the king's son. Magically, the ring is found, the gods restore the king's memory, and, to borrow a Western phrase, they all live happily ever after. This play had a profound impact when discovered by European audiences in the late eighteenth century. It was translated 46 times into 12 different languages, and it literally forced Europeans to question their presumed racial superiority, at least in the area of the arts.

FIGURE 7.1   A scene from the great Indian playwright Kàlidàsa's play *Shakuntala* performed in Urdu in Pakistan, January 2010.

Kaushik Roy/India Today Group/Getty Images

The Theatre

Stage Spaces—From Temples to Village Squares

The theatre "handbook," the *Natya Shastra,* includes detailed outlines of the stage space. The appropriate space for the great epic dramas is the temple, featuring marble-pillared halls with large sweeping roofs. The building is rectangular with separate entrances for men and women. Between the two entrance doors stand two large copper drums.

As the Sanskrit drama spread across Southeast Asia, many smaller communities didn't have ornate marble temples but tried

FIGURE 7.2 Indian dancers using traditional hand gestures and steps, a convention of Indian drama.

to adhere to the basic teachings of the *Natya Shastra*. A rectangular area was marked in a central location such as a marketplace or simple place of worship. Even today, the large sweeping roof (which may be made of canvas or palm fronds) protects the playing area. The audience might get drenched, but not the actors! This basic style of theatre space spread throughout Asia, and we find remarkable similarities to theatre spaces in use today.

Theatre Conventions

The multitude of non-realistic conventions in Indian dance-drama can be daunting. Among the most obvious and unfamiliar are:

- **Masks/Makeup/Costume:** A traditional mask or makeup and costume identify each *type* of character. Heroes wear certain colors and makeup, while villains wear others. Demons and gods use masks in styles dictated by tradition for easy recognition.

- **Dance and Gesture:** The performer moves and gestures in abstract rather than realistic ways. The actor learns each step, finger gesture, and expression of face or body to communicate *essence* rather than everyday *reality*.

- **Narrator:** Narrators sing, chant, and describe in local dialects the details of the story.

- **Music:** Music, inseparable from the dance drama, employs instrumentation, key, rhythms, and tempos to express meaning.

- **Time/Length of Performance:** Sanskrit drama can last several days or even weeks. Performances start at sunset and continue all night, taxing the strength and endurance of both performers and audience.

Decline and Rebirth

Over the course of centuries, the Indian Empire declined, Sanskrit language died out even among the aristocracy, and peoples previously conquered by India embraced their native forms of theatre. By the tenth century, setbacks in China and Southeast Asia drove the Indian Empire back into the region it now occupies in South Asia.

Sanskrit drama survived in many new forms grafted onto local performance traditions. From Malaysia to Japan, for example, puppet theatre was and is enormously popular and distinctively regional. In fact, the puppets themselves look suspiciously like the imperial kings and queens of old India, and the stories tell of love, valor, and heroism.

In folk drama throughout the region, local and Hindu deities melded, as did theatrical spaces and the model of Sanskrit drama. Dance and music continued to be inherent, as did the essentially optimistic point of view. With the spread of Buddhism, ideals of time as illusion, cosmic justice and redemption, duty and family, and love as the path to happiness continued to be the dominant values. But each community grafted their local gods and demons, native languages and musical styles, and local conventions of mask, makeup, and costume onto the foundation built by artists of the Sanskrit theatre.

Influences on Theatre Today

We can see the influence of Sanskrit theatre in today's Western musical, twentieth-century anti-realism movements in Europe, and the booming film industry of India, dubbed "Bollywood." Although Western musical theatre as we know it today is only about 100 years old, the path from Sanskrit drama to the American musical is long and winds through centuries of adaptation and change. Today, we (just like the audiences of ancient India) love the beauty and power of music, dance, and story blended to tell us of love found, lost, and re-found; heroes who suffer, struggle, and win; and villains who seem to prosper but pay in the end.

In non-realistic theatre styles of the last century, Western theatre artists have drawn experimental forms directly from the influences of the Far East. Samuel Beckett, a giant in twentieth-century Western theatre, experimented with language and gesture as pure symbols, going so far as to compose plays entirely without words. Before him, August Strindberg, a nineteenth-century master of non-realism, attempted to address the cosmic mysteries of love and pain and birth and death, and he even used Hindu symbolism and deities in several of his works.

Next, we will look at three descendants of Sanskrit theatre as they developed in Asia: China's first popular operas and Japan's *Noh* and Kabuki theatres.

CLOSE-UP

It's a Bird, It's a Plane, It's *Krrish*

Even in the most contemporary Indian theatre and cinema, some vestiges of Sanskrit influence can often be seen. Mythology and the great epics *Mahabharata* and *Ramayana* are filled with heroic figures, and the exploits of gods like Hanuman and Krishna have captivated Indians for centuries. Given that Bollywood (a Western name for this style of popular Indian film) is already a hybrid of traditional Indian and glitzy Western show business conventions, it was probably only a matter of time before another key element was added to the above combination—that of the comic-book style superhero. In the film *Krrish*, another hybrid comes to Hindu cinema.

Krrish features a hero who can dance, woo beauteous women, and defeat bad guys, all at the same time if necessary. The name of the central character is Krishna (note the godlike association), whose quiet life in a remote village communing with

animals is unsettled when an alluring television reporter arrives to learn hang gliding. He rescues her after an accident and romance blooms. He follows her to Singapore, encounters an arch villain who happens to have murdered his parents, and transforms into Krrish so he can save the world. Krrish is a sleek, black-leather-clad flying machine who can leap like Spider-Man among skyscrapers, just as he did at home among trees, but without the need for webs.

Released in the summer of 2006 and instantly becoming one of the biggest hits in the history of Indian film, *Krrish* was actually a sequel to *Koi . . . Mil Gaya,* the first film to add sci-fi, *E.T.*-like elements to a Bollywood musical. The *Krrish* franchise continues to flourish with the release of *Krrish 3* in 3-D in 2013. All directed by Rakesh Roshan, these films star his own son, Hrithik, who, with the requisite chiseled handsome features and body, is one of India's biggest stars.

After testing nearly 70 masks, a zigzag half-mask was chosen, one that is even less convincing at hiding the hero's true identity than Clark Kent's glasses. There is also no Peter Parker meager alter ego in these films. Krishna is strength personified and just gets more so as Krrish.

A second innovative combination (Bollywood and Chinese martial arts) characterizes the films, with poetic fight sequences staged by the legendary Tony Ching of *House of Flying Daggers* and *Hero* fame.

According to director Shekhar Kapur, it has been no surprise that *Krrish* captured the Indian film market "because Krrish can dance and sing and Spider-Man cannot." Krrish can also, incidentally, walk on water.

Bollywood films have an enormous world market, with an estimated annual audience of more than three billion. Who knows how many formerly isolated genres will find new fusions in the future? We can certainly look to Indian cinema and particularly Bollywood for more possibilities. In the meantime, we can marvel at a Sanskrit superhero.

Film Kraft/The Kobal Collection

FIGURE 7.3 Scene from Indian Bollywood film *Krrish*.

The First Chinese Opera: *Zaju* (*Xiqu* 1)

Sanskrit drama became serious theatre for serious people, satisfying the need for ritual and continuity, but what about the need for sheer exuberant fun? In the tenth century in China, an extraordinary form of theatre emerged, called *xiqu.* Chinese language symbols do not invite exact phonetic transcription, so English translation invariably results in multiple spellings, but *xiqu* can be broken down as *xi* (pronounced "shee")—theatrical entertainment, and *qu* (pronounced "chyoo")—music or tune, so it means "tuneful theatre." (A capitalized name indicates the name of its city or region of origin; if not capitalized, it's a general label.) Later, we will describe *xiqu*'s current manifestation (Beijing Opera or *Jingju*), but here is where it all began.

Worldview

Early China embraced the teachings of Confucius (551–479 B.C.E.), creating a most striking contrast between Indian and Chinese values. The *Analects,* or rules of Confucianism, also stand in deep contrast with Western thought, which was developing at the same time.

Confucius was born into a time of war and chaos. In response, his vision emerged as a path to order and benevolence. Each individual owed absolute obedience to the hierarchy of family and empire. Those in power must rule with benevolence (kindness) and justice in exchange for this obedience. Filial piety, or the near worship of parents, grandparents, and ancestors, created a society in which the needs of the individual were unimportant when in conflict with those of the family, community, or government. Adoption of the *Analects* resulted in a less chaotic society, but during some periods, the rules were used to enforce stifling conformity and control.

Zaju, the first form of *xiqu* (and thus "*xiqu* 1"), emerged in the tenth century during the Sung dynasty, but its peak popularity occurred during the rule of the invading Mongol emperor Kublai Khan in the thirteenth century. Perhaps in response to the severity of Mongol rule, this form of theatre is one of the lively arts. Vivid and alive with spectacle, the plays of the *Zaju* also served as forums for political thought. Many deal with social injustice and the suffering of the masses, using myths and legends as the subject matter to conceal their political agenda.

The Drama

Guan Hanqing was the founder of *Zaju* and the author of 67 plays, 18 of which are still performed in contemporary *xiqu*. His works focus on the darker aspects of life, yet with a sense of possibility. He wrote about historical peasant rebellions and common people of history or legend who rose up against their fate. *Saving the Prostitute* depicts a prostitute willing to take up cudgels for a just cause. She is sympathetic, intelligent, and courageous. In *The Injustice to Dou E,* he wrote about a girl named Dou E who becomes the target of a local tyrant's lust. When she refuses to marry him, she is falsely charged with murder and convicted. Before her death, Dou E predicts snow in midsummer and a three-year drought—both of which happen. Years later, cleared of the charge, her final words endure: "Those who are kind are poor and die young, while evildoers enjoy wealth and longevity. Heaven and earth both bully the weak and fear the strong, not daring to go against the flow."

Under the Khan regime (aka the Yuan dynasty), Guan Hanqing and his fellow dramatists suffered severe oppression. But as Huo Jianyi, a modern scholar, states, "It is worth recalling that although the Yuan rulers and the . . . scholars were at opposite ends of the social scale, and waged life-and-death struggles, they all had the same eventual destination—the grave. Yuan *Zaju* has, however, survived to this day."

According to historical records, 450 *Zaju* plays were written during the period. To date, 160 texts survive. Many of these scripts turn up again in *Kunqu* or *xiqu* 2, forming a quarter of that theatre's repertoire.

Styles

This theatre is based on comedy, drama, music, and dance; is interspersed with clowns and acrobatics; and is highly physical and filled with spectacle. *Zaju* is definitely popular entertainment, as it embraces juggling, puppets, tumbling, jokes, and riddles—and of course, lots of songs. The more farcical productions had "rude comic effects," including farting and burping. A head clown served as troupe director for companies of four to seven actors. This director (*ts'anchon*) might also have served as master of ceremonies and led musicians onstage. Sometimes he was called "the bamboo stick," a label referencing his baton.

The Theatre

Stage Spaces: The Continued Influence of Sanskrit

No authentic *Zaju* theatre space survives, so we have to turn to other sources. One *Zaju* play that survives is *A Country Bumpkin Knowing Nothing of the Theatre* by the Yuan dynasty poet Du Renjie. It describes a *Zaju* performance through the eyes of a farmer coming to the city for the first time. Between this text and the stage demands of others, we can begin to imagine the *Zaju* theatre space.

As in Sanskrit, performances would be on a stage open on three sides, with an open ground area

FIGURE 7.4 Chinese terracotta figurine of an actor whistling, from Yuan dynasty.

Giraudon / Art Resource, NY

surrounded by raised seating and possible balconies. Because companies would also tour, these theatres were often mobile. A wooden fence covered with colorful banners surrounded the theatre, re-creating courtyards in much the same way Elizabethans would later take a familiar courtyard inn as the model for theatres such as the Globe.

At one point in the late 1200s, *Zaju* grew to have such popular support that a single amusement park (picture an early Disneyland) in a northern capital city had up to 50 *Zaju* theatres, one housing at least 1,000 people. Areas in large cities featuring *Zaju* theatres called "tile districts" were often huge fenced enclosures with flags and banners flying high above them.

Theatre Conventions

In *Zaju*, conventions of Sanskrit theatre and local custom blended, incorporating local gods, demons, heroes, and myths.

- **Dance and Music:** *Zaju* was representational rather than realistic.
- **Makeup:** Flamboyant makeup was used as a masking technique to identify character types.
- **Spectacle:** As the play progressed, interludes of acrobats, magicians, and musicians provided entertainment between acts. Even the most serious plays included elements of farce and magic. *The Country Bumpkin* ends with the sight of the farmer running around the stage to find a toilet and, when he can't find one, leaving in disgust.

The *Zaju* theatre ended 600 years ago. Its vibrant appeal lives on in the texts and in its influence on today's Beijing Opera. But as *Zaju* was disappearing, a deeply insular and elitist form of theatre was developing across the sea in Japan.

Japanese Medieval and Renaissance Theatre: *Noh,* Kabuki, and Bunraku

Noh

Worldview

During the twelfth and thirteenth centuries, Japanese culture emerged as a distinct entity after centuries of Chinese domination. By the fourteenth century, the royal family still practiced Chinese arts in their centralized palace, but in the countryside, warriors ruled under the code of the samurai. The samurai was an aristocratic warrior who dominated his territory in the same way that feudal barons of Europe were controlling their fiefdoms during the same period. The samurai ruled from the eleventh to the nineteenth centuries, and during the height of the samurai period, **Noh** drama evolved, with the majority of plays focused on the exploits of warrior heroes. *Noh* evolved as a surprisingly restrained and even fastidious art, considering it came out of a world of chaos, bloodshed, and war. You can go to Japan today and see a *Noh* drama performed. It is the oldest continuously performed drama in the world.

The Drama

We credit one father–son team with the creation of *Noh*. **Kan'ami Kiyotsugu,** a professional actor, began training his son, **Zeami Motokiyo,** at the age of six to follow in his footsteps. In 1374, the shogun (head samurai warrior) ordered the two to appear in a command performance. The shogun was so impressed that he took them into his service. Kan'ami, a skilled musician, composer, and playwright, began the work of refining *Noh* performances, which had been a hodgepodge of song, dance, and bits of story, juggling, gymnastics, and stilt walking similar to *Zaju*. He gathered stories, songs, and epic poems about the warriors and heroes of the past and structured them into the elegant dramas of the mature *Noh* theatre. Zeami continued his father's work, writing about 240 of the surviving plays, all now designated as national treasures.

FIGURE 7.5 A *Noh* actor performs a female role at Tokyo's Sensoji temple.

YURIKO NAKAO/Reuters/Corbis

Styles

Noh drama is ceremonial, mysterious, and tragic. Impregnated with Zen Buddhist concepts of enlightenment through meditation and personal insight, it focuses on symbolic images and the struggle to escape the realities of time and place. Shinto beliefs also play a role, as ghosts and gods haunt the stage while mortal men struggle to understand the mysteries of life.

The plots are slim. The focus is on the precise, choreographed movements and vocal inflections. The protagonist is the *shite* (pronounced "shtay"), meaning the "doer." He may be a god, a ghost, or an animal, but most often he is a legendary warrior. Always played in masks and costumes, tradition dictates every detail of this role to allow instant identification of the character. Questioned and challenged by secondary characters who may be ministers, commoners, or priests, the *shite* responds at length, defending, explaining, describing events, or chastising the others.

Werner Forman/Corbis

FIGURE 7.6 An early *Noh* mask of a woman turned into a demon.

Conventions

- **Stage:** You can find a detailed description of the *Noh* stage in Chapter 5.
- **Performers:** All actors in the *Noh* drama are male.
- **Music:** On stage are four musicians playing a flute, a small drum, a large drum, and stick drums. A chorus of six to ten singers lends vocal accompaniment to the actors and musicians.
- **Masks:** This is a masked drama that allows instant character recognition.
- **Costumes:** Flamboyant costumes are designed by tradition.

The *Noh* drama is essentially unchanged from its development 600 years ago. Its appeal has fallen and risen over the centuries, but it has never faded completely. A highly revered art form today, it holds a special appeal to the intellectual and the connoisseur. Interest and attendance is on the rise again. Perhaps its grace and beauty, its ephemeral dreamlike quality, and its stately ancient conventions provide a welcome respite from the hectic pace of modern life.

FIGURE 7.7 Actors in traditional *Noh* costume.

Toshiro Morita / HAGA / The Image Works

Kabuki

Worldview

The Tokugawa shogunate ruled Japan with a feudal military dictatorship from 1603 to 1868. The Tokugawa family inherited a world of civil war and provided the first centralized stability in many years. They imposed a strict class hierarchy, with the samurai at the top, followed by farmers, artisans, and traders. Barred from *Noh* by tradition and inclination (who wanted to watch boring samurai strutting around a bare stage?), the common folk turned to the **Kabuki** theatre. Kabuki is one of the most exciting and spectacular of theatres still performed around the world today.

The Drama

In 1603, a shrine dancer in Kyoto set in motion a series of events that led to a new form of theatre that defied the refined dignity of *Noh*. **Izumo no Okuni,** the outrageous and eccentric female dancer, performed in a temple wearing male garments and a wooden cross around her neck. Her adaptation of religious dance (*nembutsu odori*) included an erotic interlude. Her audience called her *kabuku* and *kabukimono*, meaning weird and flashy, which would be true of such a show even now.

FIGURE 7.8 A scene from a popular Kabuki performance.

Michael S. Yamashita/Documentary/Corbis

She soon had a crowd of followers who capitalized on her innovations and expanded on them. All-female dance companies began performing stories, and the term *kubuku,* meaning "askew," described the cross-gender extravaganzas in which women played both male and female roles. The government soon issued a decree banning women from the stage in the interest of public order. Because the show must go on, men began playing women's roles, forcing a concentration on the skill of the actor that continues in the Kabuki theatre to this day.

Unlike *Noh,* Kabuki drama was committed to an ever-changing repertoire of plays. Each company had a team of professional playwrights, and new plays evolved based on the needs and fashions of the day. The plays are epic, and they play fast and loose with history and historical personages. Kabuki involves lightning-fast costume changes, freezes, and poses, juxtaposed with rapid, energized moves. The actor always comes first in Kabuki, so the play must offer opportunities for performers to "strut their stuff."

Performances always rely on dance, music, and elaborate vocal effects. A guiding principle is *yatsushi*, in which the old story is presented but at the same time modernized and parodied. Famous characters may appear in outrageous modern garb and predicaments.

Styles

Two main types of plays are histories and domestic plays. Most involve conflicts between love and duty, and they often end in suicide. Always highly emotional, the plays appeal to passions more than intellect. They are also very long. Audiences expect to spend the whole day in the theatre, so playwrights use every trick in the book to keep them happy.

Kabuki is popular because it deals with the joys and sorrows of common people living in a remote and fascinating past. It blends tragedy, comedy, realism, and romanticism into one performance. Kabuki delighted the common folk with a more spectacular and accessible style, often gaudy and always exhilarating. By 1700, the basic conventions of Kabuki were in place, and the actors were the center of its appeal.

The Theatre

Stage Spaces

The Kabuki stage evolved from the influential *Noh* stage. Over time it changed, most importantly with the extension of the bridge (**hanamichi**) through the audience to the back of the theatre and a small room for the actors—popularly known as the "hen coop." This convention made the actor–audience relationship much more direct and intense by bringing them into the same space.

Conventions

The theatrical conventions remind us of Sanskrit and *Noh*:

- **Music:** Central to each play, follows Asian traditions in notation, key, and instrumentation, but constantly evolving to stay current with popular styles.

- **Performers:** All performers are male. Acting style veers from the stylized to the realistic.

- **Masks:** Performers are masked.

- **Dance:** Choreography is essential to the storytelling; however, the exuberance and athleticism of the actors contrasts with the controlled gestural language of Sanskrit and *Noh* traditions.

- **Narrator:** We would probably not see a narrator, as the plays needed no translation.

No film star of today commands a more adoring and loyal fan base than the Kabuki actor. The strange paradox is that

AUTHOR'S INSIGHT

ROBERT: The first time I saw the Grand Kabuki in performance, I was astounded at the stunning, strange, almost nonhuman sounds the actors produced. Western actors trying this would do their vocal cords serious damage. It was a lesson in how the actor's instrument can be slowly trained over time to accomplish almost any feat.

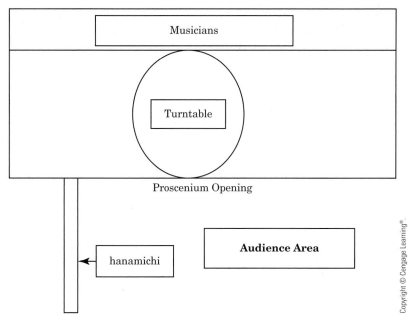

FIGURE 7.9 Kabuki stage line drawing.

at first, actors were at the bottom of the social ladder—outcasts with no civil rights. Adored by the public and scorned by the government, Kabuki actors closed ranks and became self-governing within the restrictions of their class. Eleven families produced all the Kabuki actors.

All the actors must know infinite rules, necessitating a long and arduous training period. An **onnagata** character (a female character played by a male actor) is seated a half-pace behind an actor in a male role, and an actor always faces the audience for an important speech. Male characters always start with the left foot, females with the right. They seek great beauty of stage picture, each scene ending with a striking pose. Frequent poses are preceded by energetic motion that is then offset by the sudden stillness. This convention crystallizes the striking contrast within the form, between intense drama and utter tranquility.

Bunraku

This is a good time to rexamine one of the most delightful and magical of theatre styles: the puppet theatres. Around the world, from Egypt to China and from Malaysia to Korea, folk theatre includes masters of puppetry. Many styles evolved, depending on local preferences and traditions. One popular theatre of puppets that developed simultaneously with Kabuki, influencing it greatly, is the **Bunraku.**

The puppets are controlled by men dressed all in black, and such is the intensity of the performances that these puppet masters become all but invisible to the audience. The stories often tell of love and/or suicide, and the power of these puppet theatres sometimes influenced young lovers to actual acts of double suicide. Other stories are about the joys and sorrows of the merchant classes or about duty to the emperor. The two-way influence between Bunraku puppet theatre and Kabuki theatre is clear when the performances are seen side by side.

Decline and Rebirth

Although Kabuki has seen its share of hard times over the centuries, like *Noh,* it clings tenaciously to life. The form changed continuously until after World War II, when it froze for about 30 years. Today, the leading Kabuki artist, Ennosuke Ichikawa III, is again stretching the limits, reviving lost traditions of clowning and audience interaction, and adding new and spectacular stunts, and all-woman companies are the rage.

Sadly, the theatre that evolved for common people has become prohibitively expensive to produce and attend. Corporate sponsorship is necessary to cover costs, and the most common Kabuki audience today is a group of business VIPs. On the upside, international attention paid to touring Kabuki troupes and renewed national interest in preserving the spirit of Kabuki makes its continuing survival certain. And everywhere across Asia, the Bunraku puppet theatres thrive, offering their performances to both privileged and poor alike.

Michael S. Yamashita/Documentary/Corbis

FIGURE 7.10 A scene from a Bunraku play showing puppets and onstage puppet masters dressed in black.

Influences on Western Theatre

American actors rarely perform Kabuki scripts, but the style can be used to mount Western scripts, especially Shakespeare and Greek tragedy, which already involve a mixture of drama, poetry, music, and dance. Kabuki and Shakespeare share sweep, grandeur, and sheer size. For Shakespeare scripts involving magic, storms, and high ritual (*The Tempest, Macbeth, A Midsummer Night's Dream, King Lear,* and *Titus Andronicus,* among others), the form offers an ideal way of handling these elements through striking theatrical conventions instead of high-tech. A forest is suddenly created and dissolved by *koken* (stage assistants) and a wind by swirling chiffon. These are simple, highly theatrical possibilities.

As the early brilliance of theatre in the East spread and adapted to the currents of change, Western theatre was experiencing its own burst of brilliance. We will turn now to some of the most famous and influential Western theatres, starting with the Greeks and ending with the English Renaissance and its most favored child, William Shakespeare.

First Scripted Western Theatre: The Greeks

Between the first major drama festival in 534 B.C.E. and the defeat of Athens in 404 B.C.E., the Greek theatre achieved immortality. Only 3 percent of all drama written in that century remains: 33 tragedies, 11 comedies, and one satyr play. Yet that 3 percent has affected Western theatre to this day. These 45 plays have had such impact on so many styles and eras of Western theatre that the fifth century B.C.E. is often referred to as the "Golden Age" of Greek theatre. To understand their enduring influence, we again begin with the culture itself.

Worldview

Unlike the Hindu faithful, the Greeks perceived time as linear, starting with a creation point and moving forward toward an inevitable end. Because a Greek citizen stood firmly in the present, the plays of the fifth century B.C.E. explored historical events, but they taught appropriate behavior in the present.

The average Greek experienced the most important events of his life in public. He was an active citizen and aired his views in public forums. His private life remained enclosed behind walls (as was the case for the women, too, by the way). He had to earn and keep his place in public venues for his life to have any real importance.

Essential values of Greek society are reflected in the words *patriarch, warrior, intellectual, balanced,* and *service.* Only a *citizen* had value or power in a Greek city. Citizenship was usually a birthright (although an outsider

Vanni / Art Resource, NY

FIGURE 7.11   The Parthenon on the Acropolis in Athens. The most important events in Greek life occurred in public, reinforcing the individual's identity as a citizen.

might earn it), and only men received it. A citizen's duties were simple: first, to the city; second, to his male companions; and third, to his family. A citizen received an education in logic, mathematics, and rhetoric (the art of public speaking).

The social and political structure of Athens in the fifth century B.C.E. was a democracy that divided citizens into four categories based on wealth. It was a direct democracy rather than a representative one. The two relatively low-level categories received voting rights only after approval by the two richest. The hierarchy was inflexible, preordained, and determined at birth. Ancestry, wealth, and gender determined one's place on the social ladder.

When the Golden Age of Greek drama began, Athens was at the height of her glory, wealth, and power, but she had endured nearly half a century of war with Persia. During the lifetimes of three of our major Greek playwrights, she fought a ruinous civil war with her rival, Sparta, that lasted more than 20 years and ended with her defeat. Perhaps the plays turned to the glories of the heroic past as inspiration during a dangerous and uncertain present.

The Drama

Sources

The sources for most surviving tragedies can be traced to a long history of oral storytelling that culminated in such epic poems as **Homer**'s *The Iliad* and *The Odyssey,* which carried forward the history of ancient civilizations that had colonized the region before 1500 B.C.E. Like Sanskrit dramatists, playwrights in Athens had a rich storehouse of material. For centuries, scholars believed that the stories were pure myth, invented by oral storytellers and eventually recorded around the eighth century B.C.E. We now know that many of these stories are based in historical fact, while mythic truth adds magic and mystery.

The Iliad tells the story of the Greek war against Troy. (The 2004 Brad Pitt film *Troy* took major liberties with the story.) *The Odyssey* is the story of Odysseus, one of the heroes of the Trojan War, as he tries to make his way back home after the Trojan War. In this epic, the foundation of Sophocles's three tragedies dealing with the royal house of Thebes is told, including the marriage of King Oedipus to his mother. All these sagas, born from the oral storytelling of centuries, involve the rise and fall of great powers; dynastic crime and punishment; and sex, power, greed, and vengeance. They proved to be fertile fields for the tragic playwrights to plow. Drawing tales from a long-ago age distinct from the day-to-day suffering of real life allows the aesthetic distance necessary for rational discourse. At the same time, the extreme nature of the characters' behavior ensures the emotional impact and the willing suspension of disbelief. The great tragic playwrights took episodes from what they thought of as their own Golden Age, when men and gods walked the earth together. The comedies, on the other hand, were about everyday events in the city, with subjects fresh from current gossip. The past held a sacred place in the minds of Athenians, while their own "modern" world deserved mockery and laughter.

Styles: Aristotle's Poetics

We are fortunate that one of the great philosophers of Western thought became interested in theatre and created a sort of *Natya Shastra* handbook about the great tragedies of Athens. We discuss in Chapter 2 his ideas on the origins of Greek tragedy. **Aristotle** wrote his *Poetics,* an analysis of the art of tragic drama, in the century after the Golden Age of Greek tragedy, and his work is a source of much of our knowledge.

Aristotle tells us that tragedy and comedy were kept separate, performed at different festivals at different times of the year. We have no reason to believe that a tragic playwright competed with a comic or vice versa. Yet that constant striving toward balance between the dark and light, rational and irrational, the timeless and the everyday is reflected. Tragic playwrights finished their tragedies with a satyr play that satirized their own efforts, and comedy could be savage and dark behind the mask of a simple sex farce. The tragic playwrights competed at the annual Dionysian Festival, with three plays chosen for the competition. (In Table 7.1, the term "Victories" refers to how many times a playwright won the competition as best tragic playwright.)

According to Aristotle, the ideal tragedy focused on a great man, a hero who, while attempting to serve the community, commits a grave error. In time, he sees his mistake and recognizes the solution. Aristotle preferred plays in which recognition comes too late for change. Throughout the play, the chorus, a group of singer/dancers, represents the community, watching and commenting on the choices of the hero, with their survival often at stake.

The only remaining complete comedies are all by the same playwright, **Aristophanes.** They are satire and farce, and often mock the behaviors of VIPs, criticize the government, and fully explore the erotic. From a few remaining fragments, a shift toward domestic comedy seemed to follow, so the satire/sex farce is now known as **Old Comedy,** and the later domestic romantic comedy is called **New Comedy.**

The Playwrights: Aeschylus, Sophocles, and Euripides

Richard Feldman

FIGURE 7.12 Scene from the American Repertory Theatre's performance of *The Oresteia.* Orestes has just killed his mother, Clytemnestra.

The three playwrights shown in Table 7.1 stand as the giants of tragic drama. **Aeschylus** lived long enough to remember tyranny but died in a democracy. His contributions included:

- Introducing the second actor, allowing character interaction
- Reducing the chorus from 50 to 12 members
- Inventing the **trilogy**, a set of three tragic plays on a related theme
- Increasing the importance of the dramatic part of the performance
- Writing the most magnificent choral odes, song-poems performed by the chorus
- Developing wildly effective satyr plays, the fourth play in a set that satirized the three tragedies in a trilogy

He was the author of our only complete trilogy, *The Oresteia,* in which he recounts a particularly nasty episode from *The Iliad,* but in a way that affirms the concepts of faith, justice, and Athenian law, considered by Aeschylus to be a gift from the goddess Athena.

We honor **Sophocles** for:

- Introducing the third actor and later the fourth in *Oedipus at Colonus*
- Increasing and standardizing the chorus at 15 members
- Discovering serenity in tragic vision

- Adding subtlety and suppleness to drama
- Achieving the most poignant and moving of climaxes
- Developing the arts of plot and characterization
- Developing scenes into full acts with choral divisions

Some Western scholars call his *Oedipus the King,* "the perfect tragedy." His *Antigone* (see Dramatic Interlude 4) is probably the most widely produced Greek tragedy in our time.

Euripides, the youngest of the three, is known for:

- Increasing the number of characters and roles (but not actors)
- Showing that drama can focus on the individual and on specific social questions
- Developing interest in abnormal psychology and its origins
- Disconnecting the chorus from the main action
- Combining realism and pathos in one event
- Breaking traditions and embracing controversy, innovation, courage, and independence

FIGURE 7.13 Bust of Sophocles.

bpk, Berlin/Musei Capitolini, Rome, Italy /Alfredo Dagli Orti./ Art Resource, NY

Medea, a strange and empathetic story of a woman who kills her children to punish their father for the crime of casting her aside, and *The Bacchae,* his chilling look at the fate of a man who interferes with the worship rites of Dionysus, are his most frequently produced plays today. *The Trojan Women,* dealing with the aftermath of that war, is considered by many to be one of the greatest antiwar plays ever written.

Aristophanes (c. 448–385 B.C.E.) is our master of the Old Comedy, a style that focuses on political/social satire and farce. Of his 40 documented

Table 7.1	Greek Tragic Playwrights		
	AESCHYLUS	**SOPHOCLES**	**EURIPIDES**
Dates	525–456 B.C.E.	496–406 B.C.E.	484–406 B.C.E.
Plays	90	123	92
Extant	7	7	18
Victories	13	24	4
Died at age	69	90	78

comedies, 11 remain today. He sharpened his wit on political figures, philosophers, military leaders, and his fellow playwrights. Absurd, fanciful, angry, and sometimes downright raunchy, his plays stand in testimony to the Greeks' willingness to laugh at themselves and each other. His comedy *Lysistrata*, where the women decide to withhold sex from their husbands until they end the war, is considered by many to be another of the greatest antiwar plays ever written.

Near the end of the great period of Greek theatre, comedy seems to have shifted away from the biting farce of Aristophanes. We have limited evidence of a phase known to scholars as Middle Comedy (a transitional form), followed by a poet named Menander, who is given credit for introducing New Comedy. New Comedy was a kinder, gentler form of comedy, in which raunchy humor and attacks on living people were avoided. In New Comedy, we see the beginning of the romantic or "domestic" comedy of later playwrights. Of Menander's 108 plays, only eight won the prize for comedy, which may be why he killed himself at the age of 52 by throwing himself into the sea.

The Theatre

Spaces

By the fifth century B.C.E., the basic standard for the Greek theatre space was set, although scale and grandeur would grow in the centuries to come. Productions were held in the open air before a crowd of up to 30,000 seated on stone bleachers in a hollowed-out hillside surrounding two thirds of the stage. In front of the stage, a circular area called the **orchestra** was the performance area for the **chorus.** Behind the stage, the **skene,** or scene house, provided three entrances/exits and a changing room for the actors.

Conventions

Some of the conventions of Greek drama are going to be strangely similar to those of Sanskrit. Why? No one knows. Maybe actual contact between the two traditions occurred. Maybe these shared conventions arise out of the shared human need for ritual and ceremony. Our evidence about Greek theatre conventions is thin, based primarily on pottery drawings and the texts themselves. Some of the likely conventions include the following:

- **Competition:** Perhaps unique among the great theatre movements of the world is the Greek concept of theatrical competition. Each tragic poet/dramatist was a competitor, producing his three tragedies, plus satyr play, in the course of a full day. During a given festival, three playwrights might compete for top honors, chosen from a long list of rival submissions. To be allowed to produce at the annual festivals was a great honor in itself, and to win was to achieve a sort of immortality.

- **Performers:** All performers were male. The primary two or three actors may have been professionals. Scholars believe the chorus was a dedicated group of volunteers.

- **Masks:** When actors put on the mask, they assume the power of the gods and that of other actors who have taken on this character before. There are only seven surviving vase paintings known to show fifth-century masks. They appear to be soft and quite natural. The mouths are slightly open. Their expressions have endlessly shifting meanings. Comic masks are not very different from what we think of as clown masks today—with buffoons, gluttons, and lechers as ridiculous then as now.

- **Dance/Music:** Both music and dance were central to the production. Many scholars believe that the entire performance was more like watching a dance and listening to songs than like realistic behavior.

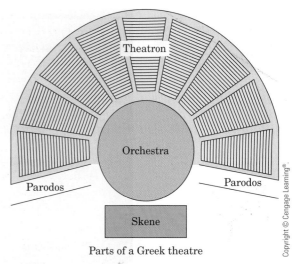

FIGURE 7.14 Diagram of Greek theatre, showing orchestra and skene.

- **Chorus:** Perhaps the strangest convention in Greek tragedy (to us) made it more moving and involving for the original audience. The chorus and chorus leader are the ideal spectators for the event, representing *us* while the heroes struggle through their trials. The chorus expresses the conventional attitude of an average citizen of this community,

FIGURE 7.15 Greek theatre at Epidaurus, a typical example of a Greek performance space, meant to accommodate a very large audience outdoors.

Robbie Jack/Corbis Entertainment/Corbis

FIGURE 7.16 Vanessa Redgrave in the title role with the Greek chorus in the Royal Shakespeare Company's production of *Hecuba*.

introduces new characters and questions them, chastises characters behaving inappropriately, offers comfort to characters who are victims, and clarifies motives.

- **Length:** Surviving scripts are generally *much* shorter than those of India. The theatre *event* might have taken all day, beginning at dawn and ending with the evening, but they produced four plays during that day. The comedies of Aristophanes are also quite compact, generally lasting much less than two hours in modern productions.
- **The Unities:** Unlike Sanskrit theatre, with epic adventures spanning decades, Greek plays tend to take place in "real time," located in a single place, and they tend to tell one story about one event, usually starting near the end (a late point of attack) so that all necessary action can believably take place in the time allowed.

Decline and Rebirth: Roman Theatre

By the end of the fifth century B.C.E., the glory days of Athenian drama had passed. Greece continued to be the home of beauty, philosophy, and devotion to the arts, but within 50 years of the deaths of Sophocles and Euripides, she ceased to exist as an independent state, conquered first by the Macedonians and then the Romans.

The Romans were the great "borrowers" of Western history. They happily copied anything they found useful or attractive, and one of the things they found attractive in Greece was theatre. They built huge theatre spaces that copied the Grecian style but dwarfed them in size and grandeur.

They copied the tragedians, too, and at least one playwright, **Seneca the Younger** (c. 3 B.C.E.–65 C.E.) achieved a stature that has endured. He wrote dark tragedies and is considered one of the primary influences on the Renaissance tragedies of Shakespeare and his contemporaries.

On the other hand, comedy was not only borrowed but redefined in the hands of one Roman comic playwright **Plautus** (c. 254–184 B.C.E.). Adapted from Greek New Comedy, his plays avoided the critical, satirical tone of Aristophanes but instead featured middle- and lower-class characters and were written in the language of the common people. He created **stock character** types, such as the braggart warrior and the old miser, that we would see returning to the European stage a full 1,500 years later—first in the Italian *Commedia dell'arte* of the fourteenth century, then in the works of Shakespeare and Molière (see Chapter 8).

With the fall of the Roman Empire, Western civilization and the theatre entered a period of long decline and stagnation. Actors and playwrights disappear into the wilderness. The tradition of bards, troubadours, and poets who returned to the oral traditions of their ancestors is our only evidence of their survival and our continued need to create performance art.

Shakespeare's Comedy of Errors, Stratford Shakespeare Festival, June 2007. Bruce Dow & David Snelgrove on stage.

FIGURE 7.17 A scene from contemporary performance of Shakespeare's *Comedy of Errors* at the Stratford Festival. This is a good example of Roman comedy's influence on later plays.

Theatre in the Middle Ages

Throughout most of Europe during the centuries following the destruction of the Roman Empire, the primary authority was the Catholic Church. In the fourth century, the church outlawed theatre—and with good reason. Christians had been a target of mockery in the "entertainments" of the late Empire, sometimes sold into slavery and forced to perform, sometimes killed outright as the audience cheered. A long dormant period followed, and not until the ninth century do we find our first scrap of evidence that the church began to use theatre as a means of teaching biblical ideas to their largely illiterate converts.

By the thirteenth and fourteenth centuries, many European towns held annual festivals that included performances of stories from the Bible. Sanctioned by the church, though sometimes grudgingly, trade groups organized these pageants, with each in charge of one section of the story. Our

Table 7.2	The Seven Virtues and Vices		
VIRTUES		**VICES**	
Love/Charity	Caritas	Lust	Luxuria
Hope	Spes	Gluttony	Gula
Faith	Fides	Avarice/Greed	Avaritia
Temperance	Temperantia	Sloth	Acedia
Justice	Iustitia	Wrath	Ira
Courage	Fortitudo	Envy	Invidia
Wisdom	Sapientia	Pride	Superbia

documentation of these events is spotty, but competition between guilds clearly led to some spectacular effects and occasional episodes of secular humor. Many included **allegory,** the use of characters that represent one of the seven vices and virtues (see Table 7.2). Others drew from the Bible and transformed the whole into a long series of pageant wagon/theatres. Each wagon, or "station," told one part of the biblical story, from creation through redemption and/or damnation. Damnation stations provided opportunities for creative pyrotechnics and fierce competitions for the "Hell's Mouth" project occurred.

Individual medieval plays are often designated by one of three types:

- **Miracle Plays:** These present an account of the life, miracles, or martyrdom of a saint recognized by the Catholic Church. They appear to have evolved out of church services devoted to the saint's day in the liturgical calendar during the tenth and eleventh centuries. Also called "Saint's Plays."

- **Mystery Plays:** These recount an episode from the Bible, at first under the auspices of church services, but by the thirteenth century, removed to other venues, such as the pageants described previously.

- **Morality Plays:** The last of these three types to evolve (fifteenth and sixteenth centuries), they use the allegorical character types seen in Table 7.2 to teach moral lessons.

Although these events were not a return of professional theatre, they eventually evolved into and influenced the next period of truly exceptional Western theatre—the Renaissance.

The Print Collector / Alamy

FIGURE 7.18 A group of courtly ladies is entertained by performers playing "Dance of the Wodehouses." Notice the lower clergy in the lower right corner, and the musicians in the upper right corner.

Commedia dell'arte

The term *renaissance* means "a rebirth or revival, for example, of culture, skills, or learning forgotten or previously ignored." In Europe, the period ranging roughly from the fourteenth to the sixteenth century is known as the **Renaissance** because of explosive and wide-ranging cultural and artistic changes that mark the end of the Middle Ages. Of course, this rebirth didn't happen in one day, or even in one year, but over decades and at various stages in different parts of the West.

Theatrically, one of the earliest hints that the long period of drought was over was the re-emergence of a professional theatre. This was the ***Commedia dell'arte*** ("comedy of art" or "comedy of the profession") that first entered the historical record in the fourteenth century in Italy. But it must have been around for generations before that, because the first family troupes of *Commedia* players were well established by the time they gained official recognition.

At first, the *Commedia* troupe was a family business, a traveling band of relatives who created performances on the wing, staying a few days in any town willing to receive them, and then traveling on to the next. Their "scripts" were really outlines, though carefully orchestrated outlines, known as **scenarios,** within which each performer was expected to show verbal or physical brilliance as the moment inspired them.

KARL MANTZIUS
THEATRE HISTORIAN

The [Commedia] actors had to find the proper words to make the tears flow or the laughter ring; they had to catch the sallies of their fellow-actors on the wing, and return them with prompt repartee. The dialogue must go like a merry game of ball or spirited swordplay, with ease and without a pause.

FIGURE 7.19 From fourteenth–sixteenth century, image of *Commedia* stock characters, Capitan Bombardone and Capitan Grillo.

Scala / Art Resource, NY

The *Commedia dell'arte* style of scenario and improvisation was built on the use of character types or "stock" characters, like the ones created by the Roman Plautus. Like costumes pulled out of "stock" or storage, stock characters can be pulled out as needed. Stock characters were developed by members of the family and used repeatedly in different stories. Some of these stock characters can be found today in modern incarnations. They included young lovers (***innamorati***); the elders, usually male, who block the young lovers' attempts to be together (known collectively as "Masters"); and the servants (***zanni***, pronounced "ZAH-nee"), who assist the *innamorati*. In a typical scenario, two young people fall in love, her father/uncle/guardian forbids their marriage, and the servants help the not-too-bright lovers devise a scheme for thwarting the old man.

Into the scenarios, actors were expected to insert bits of physical or verbal virtuosity known as ***lazzi*** (pronounced "LAH-tsee"). *Lazzi* might have nothing to do with the story but were simply to amuse and amaze the audience.

The *Commedia dell'arte* troupes traveled Europe for 400 years, influencing many of the major stars of Western theatre, including Shakespeare and Molière. But we also celebrate them for another major accomplishment: the introduction of women to the professional stage in Europe. In each family, everyone had to pull his or her weight, so the *zanni* (servant) named Colombina might be played by Mom, while the young female lover, or *innamorata,* might be played by her daughter. In fact, when the *Commedia* visited England during the early seventeenth century, response indicates that this inclusion of women on stage raised many eyebrows and brought them into general disfavor. It may be noted here that the *Commedia* did not thrive in England but was generally confined to the continent.

Meanwhile, however, England was in the midst of its own renaissance, a period of shining rebirth called the Elizabethan Age.

AUTHOR'S INSIGHT

ANNIE: I once knew a young actor who would take off his gold necklace, swallow it, and pull it out of his nose, on a moment's notice. He did it in an audition once when the director asked him if he had any special skills. This would be a prime lazzi for a *Commedia* troupe!

THEATRE IN MEDIA

Twentieth-Century *Commedia*

Finding the influence of *Commedia dell'arte* in film and television today is easy. The Cowardly Lion in *The Wizard of Oz* is a perfect Capitano. Capitano is a type of stock character who is also known as the Braggart Warrior, actually a holdover from Roman comedy. The Lion begins his adventure with Dorothy and her friends by threatening first to eat them, then to beat them up. But when Dorothy slaps his nose, the Lion begins to cry and we learn that he has no courage. This is the Capitano personified. Also, if you are a fan of the television show *The Simpsons,* the character Mr. Burns is a Pantalone (pronounced "pant-ah-loan-ay").

Mr. Burns even looks like a Pantalone, who is shown in old drawings as having a long, skinny, crooked nose, a potbelly, and thin, bent legs. Pantalone is also usually rich, greedy, and powerful but is always hungry for more. Sounds just like Mr. Burns. Other contemporary versions of *Commedia* characters in recently ended television series include Dwight Schrute (*The Office*) as a Capitano and Jack Donaghy (*30 Rock*) as a Pantalone.

Elizabethan Drama

After the brilliance of the ancient Greeks, more than 2,000 years passed before unquestioned greatness returned to Western theatre. Plague, war, and famine wiped out much of Europe's population and, for a time, theatre itself. Then a mighty England emerged as ruler of the known world, and the English language exploded, with more than 10,000 new words added in less than a century. Not before or since has a language grown so astonishingly quickly. Drama is where the new words became part of London's lexicon.

The term *Elizabethan* usually refers to the reign of Elizabeth I (r. 1558–1603) and the reigns preceding and following her. Because her father (Henry VIII) broke with Rome and created his own church, Elizabeth, at her coronation, became both head of state *and* head of the church. She had no higher allegiance than her own vision. While the Renaissance began in Italy, in an emancipated England, it flourished.

Strongly influenced by the rediscovery of classical Greek and Roman texts, the worldview of Elizabethan England was similar to that described earlier in this chapter. Here we discuss only those elements that were different from the classical worldview.

Elizabeth I, Armada Portrait, c. 1588 (oil on panel), Gower, George (1540–96) (attr. to) / Woburn Abbey, Bedfordshire, UK / The Bridgeman Art Library

FIGURE 7.20   George Gower's *Armada Portrait* of Elizabeth I, 1588.

Worldview

Much like Athens 2,000 years earlier, the English of the late sixteenth and early seventeenth centuries believed they could do no wrong. Sir Francis Drake's voyage around the world, Sir Walter Raleigh's exploration of North America, and an astonishing naval victory over the Spanish Armada seemed like miracles. Elizabethans had already found "more things in heaven and earth" than ever previously dreamed. Like the Greeks, the Elizabethans experienced time as linear and finite. Nurtured in the teachings of the Christian faith, they believed that Creation led to an inevitable Armageddon. But the known universe was growing and shifting under their feet. A new world had been discovered—a round world at that. The telescope challenged the immutability of heaven itself.

The majority practiced a Protestant state religion that was all but Catholic in its ceremonies and liturgies. At the same time, new sects bent on purging the faith of any taint of Catholic ritual (Puritan, Calvinist, and Anabaptist) held secret services. No one wanted more bloodshed over religious doctrine. After decades of bloody conflict and shifting official faiths, many Elizabethans turned to secularism. The classical humanists of Greece and Rome became their models.

For all their innate optimism, they knew that life was short. The average life expectancy was 27 years—with 65 percent dying by the age of 16. So much to do, so little time! Much like the Sanskrit ideal, the perfect Renaissance man was a warrior, scholar, philosopher, dancer, musician, and poet. The well-educated person in this period (meaning of the privileged class) could read Latin and maybe Greek; sight-read music; debate philosophy, theology, and history; and write love sonnets to his unattainable mistress. Of course, most people lived short, brutal lives in the slums of London or as peasants on the great estates of the aristocracy. But almost every Londoner, from high to low, had the chance to escape through the magic of professional public theatres crowded among the prostitutes and bear-baiting pits across the Thames River from London proper.

The Drama

The era named for Elizabeth actually spans several monarchies and includes Tudor, Elizabethan, and Jacobean drama—related styles named for the monarch in power. **Tudor** plays (named for Henry Tudor, aka Henry VII, Elizabeth's grandfather and founder of the dynasty) evolved in the universities and broke from the control of the church. Elizabethan plays (named for Elizabeth Tudor, aka Elizabeth I) shone as the pinnacle of the era. Everyone attended, from the queen herself to stableboys and kitchen maids. **Jacobean** plays (named for James Stuart, aka James I, Elizabeth's heir) are much darker and more cynical. England was careening toward yet another civil war, and dramatists focused their gaze on the grim life of the common people of London.

Tudor Playwrights: Christopher Marlowe

Tudor plays mark the transition from medieval to Renaissance drama and showed from the start that English drama would not be constrained by European classical rules. The plays included elements of morality play and farce and ignored the unities of time, place, and action. While not graced with the beauty of language and depth of character of their descendants, they reintroduced secular and mythological stories and set the stage for the brilliant playwrights to come.

No one showed greater promise than the brilliant young **Christopher Marlowe.** Writing about heroes whose very greatness leads to their fall, he wrote in blank verse "with a rhetorical brilliance and eloquence superbly equal to the demands of high drama." The son of a shoemaker, he was educated at Cambridge and might have challenged Shakespeare as the greatest Elizabethan playwright if he had not been murdered in a barroom brawl at the age of 29. His grand tragedies include *Tamburlaine the Great* (1587), *The Tragical History of Doctor Faustus* (1588), *The Jew of Malta* (1589), and *Edward II* (1592). Notice how quickly he wrote. As a professional living on a very limited income, he *had* to produce. In addition to writing plays that command universal respect 400 years after his death, he also wrote pamphlets, poetry, and song lyrics.

FIGURE 7.21 While no conclusive evidence has been found that this portrait is, in fact, Christopher Marlowe, it is universally believed to be him. The inscription in the corner reads, "That which nourishes me, destroys me."

The Granger Collection, New York

Elizabethan Playwrights: William Shakespeare

The Elizabethan dramatists (see Table 7.3) lived and worked in the shadow of the greatest of them all, **William Shakespeare.** Born in 1564 as the son of a tanner in the village of Stratford-upon-Avon, he was forced by youthful indiscretion into marriage and fatherhood by the age of 19. He later hitched his wagon to a theatrical star and went to London, where he lived and worked well into his forties. He eventually returned to Stratford, living as a prosperous landowner until his death in 1616. No Western playwright commands so much adoration, attention, criticism, and continued production as he. His poetry intrigues even when his plots are trifling, and his works delve into the full range of human experience. He is often called the "greatest playwright who ever lived." He wrote romping farce

FIGURE 7.22   Portrait of William Shakespeare.

(*The Comedy of Errors*), agonizing tragedy (*Romeo and Juliet* and *King Lear*), shimmering romance (*As You Like It* and *Twelfth Night*), and challenging experimental forms that defy labels (*Measure for Measure* and *All's Well That Ends Well*). We discuss two of his plays, *Much Ado About Nothing* and *King Lear,* in some detail in Dramatic Interludes 1 and 3, respectively.

Oddly, from our perspective, Elizabethans did not consider plays worthy literature, so less than half of Shakespeare's plays made it into print in any form during his lifetime; his literary reputation was based on his epic poems and sonnets. In 1623, seven years after his death, two of his former theatrical colleagues published *The First Folio*, a collected edition of his dramatic works that included all but two of the plays now recognized as his. It contained 36 texts, including 18 printed for the first time.

He is considered the world's greatest playwright because he changed us back then and continues to change us now. Shakespeare created numerous innovations in the ways plays were shaped. Prior to his work, most were written entirely in verse. Shakespeare mixed verse (elevated topics and classic line form) and prose (down-to-earth subjects and conversational style) to reflect contrast and changes between characters. Writers who used direct audience address soliloquies tended to do so to simply provide information, while Shakespeare used them to explore the character's deepest thoughts and feelings and to create a sense of intimacy with those present. Previously, romance was presented almost exclusively as tragedy. However, Shakespeare offered varied comic romantic perspectives and in works such as *Romeo and Juliet*, even dared change the form as the play progressed, moving from light comedic to deep tragic content. He also worked the reverse in plays that begin in sorrow and find their way to light. His work influenced and changed ideas about characterization, plot, genre, language, grammar, and more.

His profound influence went beyond theatre and literature, including words themselves. He is credited with inventing more than 1,700 words. Examples include accused, addiction, advertising, amazement, arouse, assassination, backing, bandit, bedroom, bet, birthplace, blanket, blushing, bump, buzzer—just to sample the first two letters of the alphabet! Because he used a total of 17,677 words in all his writings, this means he made up a tenth of those. He also invented hundreds of phrases that are still in use. (A small sample: all of a sudden, a forgone conclusion, a sorry sight, dead as a doornail, it's all one to me, fight fire with fire, pure as the driven snow, we have seen better days, out of the jaws of death.) He not only produced lasting theatre works, but gave us many ways to more effectively express ourselves in both the privacy and the theatre of our daily lives.

Aside from his astonishing eloquence, perhaps the single strongest reason for his lasting impact is that he wrote with deep, profound empathy for every character he created. Shakespeare seems to have been incapable of disliking his characters, even the most vicious and villainous. And in turn, he causes us to also find something to care about in every single one of them. According to scholar/author Harold Bloom, he can even be credited with "inventing the human," giving us our first definitions of what it means to be a fully formed human being.

In Interlude 3 in this text, we discuss one of Shakespeare's most honored tragedies, *King Lear.* Bloom reminds us that the full title of the play is *M. William Shakespeare: His True Chronicle Historie of the life and death of King Lear and his three Daughters. With the Unfortunate Life of Edgar, sonne and heire to the Earle of Gloster, and his sullen and assumed humor of Tom o' Bedlam . . .* The title gives us the hint that the double plot of this complex tragedy highlights not only the king, but also his three daughters, and especially Edgar and his father, the Earl of Gloucester, the center of the second plot line. With the parallel plots of families who define the term "dysfunctional," we are witness to characters who are fully and uniquely human.

Looking at one character, Lear is enough to illustrate Shakespeare's genius. The king is and must be awe-inspiring at the beginning of the play, although he is very old and makes a very bad choice in trying to provoke a *quid pro quo* love-fest with his three daughters. He must be capable of loving deeply and being deeply loved, since whatever he becomes, he has been a powerful king worthy of the allegiance of his Fool, Cordelia, Kent, and Edgar. As he descends into petulance and impotent rage, then into madness, he is still "every inch a king" to those who love him. It is Lear himself who ironically says this as he stands in rags with weeds in his hair for a crown. He is delusional, and our hearts can't help but go out to him in his suffering. If the subtitle above seems a bit strange, when Shakespeare is translated into other languages, various subtitles are often added. *The Shakespeare Newsletter* reported a Japanese version of it subtitled "An Unfortunate Case of Early Retirement."

If we look at Shakespeare's contemporary poets and playwrights, we see nothing like this level of humanity and complexity in their characters. Christopher Marlowe's *King Edward II, Tamerlaine,* and *Barabas* are vehicles for a single humor: King Edward is a weak king, Tamerlaine is a merciless pagan warrior, and Barabas is so evil he becomes almost a comic figure. In Shakespeare's earliest works we see some of these traits. But even in these earliest plays, he couldn't help but create more than simple stereotypes.

Asking "Why Shakespeare?" is a reasonable question. Why should we continue to produce thousands of performances, books, and articles on one single playwright? The answer is that we continue to study Shakespeare 400 years after his death because no one in the English language has ever continued through the centuries to teach us what it means to be human, to make tragic mistakes, to fall in love, to feel anger, remorse, dread, and delight. No other playwright has given us material so rich, so complex, that our finest artists come back to his work again and again. As theatre people, we share this need, this drive to test ourselves against the very best. Google Shakespeare in production and see how many of his plays are being produced this month alone all over the world in dozens of languages. Then Google any other playwright, living or dead, and compare. And that's "Why Shakespeare"!

Other playwrights who gained some success and popularity at the time include George Chapman (*All Fools*, 1599; *The Gentleman Usher*, 1606; and *Bussy D'Ambois*, 1607), and Shakespeare's friend and rival Ben Jonson (*Volpone*, 1606, and *The Alchemist*, 1610). Although he wrote in a style that was the opposite of Shakespeare, designed to appeal to the educated elite, Ben Jonson was very successful during his lifetime, being named poet laureate of England in 1616, with a substantial annual allowance.

Jacobean Playwrights

In fact, Shakespeare's talents continued to shine well into the Jacobean period. From the death of Elizabeth in 1603 to his own retirement in 1613, he wrote some of his masterpieces, including *Macbeth*, *Othello*, and what some consider his finest work, *Hamlet*. Other Jacobean playwrights created plays with increasingly sensational bouts of violence and mayhem. Lacking the literary talents of Marlowe and Shakespeare, they compensated by entertaining audiences with buckets of gore. Their plays (even the comedies) tend to be horrific, obscene, and deeply cynical. Sadly, their plays offer us a more realistic view of seventeenth-century London than the beautiful fictional worlds of Shakespeare. See Table 7.3 and Table 7.4 for more-complete lists of playwrights and plays of these periods.

FIGURE 7.23   Illustration of the interior of the Swan Theatre (a competitor of the Globe Theatre) during a performance. Sketch by Johannes de Witt, 1596.

CLOSE-UP

Sor Juana Ines de la Cruz: The "Tenth Muse"

Although male artists dominate most of the early history of theatre, an intriguing woman worked to international acclaim as a poet, playwright, essayist, and champion of women during the seventeenth century in New Spain. Sor Juana Ines de la Cruz (Sister Joan Agnes of the Cross) was born in 1651 (disputed) and died in 1695, but in her relatively short life, she accomplished marvels of wit, intelligence, and imagination.

At the time of Spain's farthest reach as a colonial Empire under Charles V, 400 million square kilometers of the world were under his personal control. One corner of his far-flung territories was Mexico, and it is here that we meet an intellectual giant, celebrated throughout Europe and the Spanish Empire, dubbed by her contemporaries "The Tenth Muse."

Her life was dramatic in and of itself. She was the illegitimate daughter of a *criolla* (a Spanish woman born in Mexico) and an unknown father. As a child, she wished to dress as a boy so that she could attend school. Her mother nixed this plan but sent her to live with her maternal grandfather, an educated, wealthy man whose villa was near Mexico City. His library numbered in the thousands, and Juana began there a journey of self-education. Her intellect caught the attention of the viceroy and vicereign (his wife) and she was brought to court, tested by the acknowledged scholars of the day, and declared a prodigy. She became a lady-in-waiting to the vicereign and lived a worldly, fashionable, and intellectual life until she was 20. Then the pressure increased upon her to marry, and rather than follow what she saw as the road to dependency and

drudgery, she entered a cloistered convent. Little did she know she was merely trading one cage for another.

She had some very good years in the monastery, befriended and protected by no less than four viceroys and vicereigns. She wrote prolifically in many genres including sacred and secular plays that spoke out against the violent excesses of the Conquest and the treatment of women of all classes. Her essays and poems were greeted with wonder and delight in Enlightenment Europe, but the Catholic Church in Mexico was not amused. At last, she wrote her most famous essay fighting for a woman's right to education, and the Archbishop of Mexico (who had been waiting for his chance) pounced. He denounced her for "defiance" and "waywardness," potentially capital crimes within the Church. She was forced to relinquish all of her books and scientific instruments, her writings were burned, and she had to do public penance declaring herself, "I, the worst of all women." It was either that or face charges of heresy before the Inquisition.

Shortly after her condemnation, the plague struck the convent and Sor Juana nursed as many as she could back to health. After the plague had eased, she became infected and died. But her last great friend, the vicereign of Mexico, retrieved as many of her writings as she could and smuggled them out of Mexico. We can only thank her in retrospect for saving the work of this remarkable young woman, a nun, a poet, a playwright, musician, and scientist: a true seventeenth-century Enlightenment woman in an unenlightened Catholic Mexico.

The Theatre

Stage Spaces

Located on the south bank of the Thames River, the popular outdoor theatres shared their neighborhood with other shady (but very popular) entertainment venues, such as brothels, taverns, and baiting pits. Indoor theatres were built to house the **boy companies,** a special company of young male actors, but these theatres were smaller and more expensive than the outdoor ones. Theatre companies also toured the country during the summers and when the theatres were closed due to plague. Command performances for the queen could be performed in her palaces. But the major venue of the

FIGURE 7.24   Members of the Afghan theatre ensemble Rah-e Sabz performed Shakespeare's "Comedy of Errors" in the Iranian language Farsi at the 22nd Shakespeare Festival, June 2012. This was the first time in 25 years that Shakespeare was performed in Afghanistan.

Daniel Naupold/dpa/Corbis

London public was the open-air theatre. The open courtyards of inns, where carriages pulled in off the street to deposit passengers and cargo, provided the models for both the theatres and baiting pits.

The **Globe Theatre** had a great, open stage nearly 40 feet wide and 29 feet deep, with up to seven entrances and exits, surrounded on three sides by seating and standing room filled with up to 3,000 spectators, none more than 60 feet away and some close enough to touch the actors. Most productions made no attempt to suggest locale.

Conventions

- **Performers:** All actors were male, with boy apprentices playing the female roles until their voices changed.
- **Music:** Musical interludes entertained between every act or scene. Plays almost always included one or more songs (even the really grim plays). But unlike the Greek and Asian early theatres, plays were not performed through dance and song. The word became the Thing.
- **Masks:** No masks were used to indicate character.
- **Costumes:** Costumes were pulled from stock and used over and over again. Nothing was designed for a specific play or character.

Plays and Playwrights

Table 7.3 and Table 7.4 list the scripts most likely to find life in a modern production. Almost any play by Shakespeare is more likely to enter your life, whether in live theatre, on television, or at the movies, than any single

Table 7.3 | English Dramatists

TUDOR DRAMATISTS	ELIZABETHAN DRAMATISTS	JACOBEAN DRAMATISTS
John Lyly *Endymion* (1591) **Robert Greene** *Friar Bacon and Friar Bungay* (1591) **Thomas Kyd** *The Spanish Tragedy* (1592) **Christopher Marlowe** *Tamburlaine the Great* (1587) *The Tragical History of Doctor Faustus* (1588) *The Jew of Malta* (1588) *Edward II* (1590)	**Francis Beaumont/John Fletcher** *The Knight of the Burning Pestle* (1607) *The Maid's Tragedy* (1610) *A King and No King* (1611) **Thomas Dekker** *The Shoemaker's Holiday* (1599) **Ben Jonson** *The Alchemist* (1610) *Bartholomew Fair* (1614) *Every Man in His Humour* (1598) *Volpone* (1605) **William Shakespeare (see Table 7.4)**	**John Ford** *'Tis Pity She's a Whore* (1625) **Thomas Middleton** *The Changeling* (1623) **Thomas Heywood** *A Woman Killed with Kindness* (1603) *The English Traveller* (1638) **John Webster** *The White Devil* (1608) *The Duchess of Malfi* (1612) **Cyril Tourneur** *The Revenger's Tragedy* (1607)

Table 7.4 | William Shakespeare (dates are approximate)

COMEDIES	TRAGEDIES	HISTORIES	OTHER
The Comedy of Errors (1590)	*Titus Andronicus* (1590)	*Henry IV, Part 1* (1597)	*All's Well That Ends Well* (1604)
The Taming of the Shrew (1591)	*Richard III* (1592)	*Henry IV, Part 2* (1598)	*Measure for Measure* (1604)
The Two Gentlemen of Verona (1593)	*Romeo and Juliet* (1594–1596)	*Henry VI, Part 1* (1590–1592)	*Pericles, Prince of Tyre* (1608)
Love's Labour's Lost (1594)	*Richard II* (1595)	*Henry VI, Part 2* (1590–1592)	*Cymbeline* (1609)
A Midsummer Night's Dream (1594)	*Julius Caesar* (1599)	*Henry VI, Part 3* (1590–1592)	*The Winter's Tale* (1610)
The Merry Wives of Windsor (1597)	*Hamlet* (1601)	*King John* (1596)	*The Tempest* (1611)
As You Like It (1598)	*Othello* (1603–1604)	*Henry V* (1599)	
Much Ado About Nothing (1599)	*King Lear* (1605)	*Henry VIII* (1612–1613)	
Twelfth Night (1600)	*Macbeth* (1605)		
	Antony and Cleopatra (1606)		
	Coriolanus (1608)		
	The Life of Timon of Athens (1605–1608)		
	Troilus and Cressida (1602)		

script by any other writer of the period. Do not discount his brothers, however. Some genuine thrills and chills exist in the rest of Elizabethan drama. Naturally, the lives and works of these artists overlap, so keep in mind that these tables denote the period of their best work or of their strongest association.

In 1642, the English Civil War broke out between the supporters of King Charles I and the Puritan army of Oliver Cromwell. Although the age of English dramatic greatness waned prior to the war, theatre came to an abrupt end in 1642 and would not be seen on the English stage again until 1660.

First Theatre in Africa

When discussing theatre in Africa, we must be clear about several key issues:

1. Africa is a vast continent with distinct nations, languages, histories, and traditions. We will focus on the West African culture of **Yoruba,** as it is one of the most fully documented of ancient African cultures, but we include a variety of regions when possible.

2. The oral tradition was and still is central to the theatre of much of sub-Saharan Africa. This means that dating the first play or playwright, even identifying dates of origin, is meaningless. As one contemporary Africa scholar puts it: "In contrast to written 'literature,' African **'orature'** is orally composed and transmitted, and often created to be verbally and communally performed as integral part of dance and music. Oral arts and traditions of Africa are rich and varied, developing with the beginnings of African cultures, and continuing to flourish today."

3. Much of the research about African theatre traditions is highly controversial. When scholars disagree vehemently, we will attempt to honor their points of view.

As with Sanskrit and Greek theatre, we will begin by discussing the Yoruban worldview, relying on the scholarship and life experiences of West Africans such as internationally acclaimed playwright/scholar Wole Soyinka (winner of the Nobel Prize for Literature), *griotte*/scholar Adaora Nzelibe Schmiedl, and African American actor/scholar Charles Dumas.

Worldview

Think of the Yoruban sense of time as a lake. All time exists simultaneously. One's life is a drop of water in that lake. All that has been, is, and ever will be coexists in the lake of time. The lake of time encompasses four states of being: the unborn, the living, the ancestors, and the gods. As all four states of being exist in simultaneous time, communication is possible and sometimes required. Recall the story of Ogun and his fight to reunite with the people; his effort and sacrifice broke the barriers of time and space that kept the gods apart from the people (see Chapter 2).

In the prosaic world of day-to-day life, the family home in the village of their birth was the central space where work, play, learning, and teaching took place. Unlike both Indian and Greek culture, the Yoruban community did not define itself by warrior values. The epic stories passed down through the generations did not glorify an ancient time of wars and heroes. Instead, the people of West Africa valued family, community, and peaceful consensus. This is not to imply that violence never occurred, only that the communal history celebrated peaceful resolution of conflict.

The ancestors were worshipped, the elderly respected, and children cherished. The concept of "it takes a village to raise a child" was (and is) a working reality in West Africa. Resources were shared; gift giving and receiving was a part of daily life. The gods, spirits, and demons that shared time and space with the living were consulted, appeased, and exorcised through communal effort.

The elders, who consulted, debated, and argued with each other until they reached consensus, led the community. A single leader usually made day-to-day decisions, settled disagreements, and navigated social interactions. This position was earned and could be kept only by consultation with the other elders. Age was the defining organizational model, with those who survived childhood and adulthood into their elder years moving up in authority through the years. Each child learned the history and lessons of the community through the traditional theatre events that were literally a functioning part of each day. The faster they learned, the sooner they would achieve respect and authority within the communal structure.

Dance, music, storytelling, and theatre were deeply honored pleasures, in part because they were communal by nature and in part because they were simply so much fun. The arrival of a *griot* or *griotte* was a cause for feasting and celebration. Even the preparation of the evening meal was a time for teaching children and entertaining adults through these performance arts. At the end of a hard day's work, the adults took turns and competed with each other while the children looked on and waited for the day that they could tell the next story or act a part in the next performance.

FIGURE 7.25 A *griot* with his *Kora* (Mande harp).

Hemis / Alamy Limited

The Drama

Because Yoruba's traditional theatre is quite distinct from the formalized drama of India and Greece, we have to explore the form from a new perspective. The "text" of the plays resided in the communal memories of the people. This is not because the people of West Africa had no written language. (How could they carry on international trade without some means of recordkeeping?) It's because the source, style, and *function* of theatre was so different from the other cultures we've discussed.

The Source

The source of theatre was very simply the memory of the people. No one has attempted to date the beginning of the theatre in West Africa because the stories go back to the "time before" and the "time to come" and contain the history of the people through hundreds of generations. *Ogun's Mysteries* (see Chapter 2) were only one part of an enormous body of work carried forward generation after generation.

Styles (and Function)

The style of West African drama is linked to its function. Its function is linked to the event. Sometimes the function is educational (which does not mean entertainment is neglected!).

DR. MALAIKA MUTERE

KENYAN SCHOLAR AND ARTIST

African oral arts often combine religious, artistic, as well as social functions: e.g., to convey wisdom, teach ethics and social codes of conduct, teach religious beliefs and communal values, celebrate cultural heroes and revered ancestors, and explain the origins, history, and development of states, clans, and other important social organizations.

Some artists call African oral arts "art for life's sake." An individual volunteered to tell a story. She may then select younger people to act out the parts in the story. A young person may then be challenged to tell a new story, and he could choose to play all the parts himself or recruit others to perform. This kind of theatre was an ongoing part of daily life. One didn't buy a ticket, go to a theatre, sit in a seat in the dark, and watch others perform a play. The entire community participated, playing audience one moment, actor the next, and narrator the time after that.

Comedies, tragedies, ghost stories, history lessons, and moral lessons could be combined in endless variety. Though less formal than some of the styles we have looked at, never think that this was a free-for-all improv either. The child learned from the adults, the adults learned from the elders, and those who were gifted in their dramatic abilities were honored. Making it up as you went along, violating the communal memory, or deciding to "correct" a narrative was simply unacceptable. Because everyone participated, everyone also felt free to critique the performance.

Three stylistic tendencies emerge (though not without debate):

- West African theatre strives to interpret reality rather than realistically represent it.

FIGURE 7.26 Story Workshop performs traditional West African drama, which involves the community via call and response.

- West African drama offers its audience a quality called *efe*, translated as indulgent enjoyment. The suffering of a King Lear or a Greek tragic hero, even in a performance of one of those plays, must reflect the African sense of forward-looking, solution-seeking positivism and joy.
- The drama must not only allow or encourage audience response but must demand audience participation.

The Theatre

As noted previously, very little in Sanskrit or Greek theatre prepares one for the traditional theatre of West Africa. The theatre space is anywhere, any time, every day. From the kitchen to the marketplace, the world itself is the stage and life itself is the drama. The conventions depend entirely on the function and nature of the event. We can safely identify some tendencies:

- **Allegory:** This involves the use of symbolic characters that have become associated with certain human qualities. For example, many plots feature Rabbit, a trickster and thief, who can illustrate the canny solution to a problem or the punishment coming to the thief.
- **Mask/Costume:** In sacred events, gods, spirits, and demons are performed in masks and costumes designed to bond the performer to the character. These masks and costumes are deeply spiritual artifacts that allow transcendence between the living and the ancestors, the unborn and the gods.

KOLE OMOTOSO
NIGERIAN THEATER ARTIST
The streets of my hometown . . . in Nigeria, constituted the ever-moving theatre in which my eyes first saw the rituals of my Yoruba culture, history, and rituals.

- **Music/Dance:** Both music and dance are central to any performance event. The accomplished performer uses song, dance, and strongly percussive, polyrhythmic music to build tension and release tension.

- **Call and Response:** The actor expects the audience to support the performance vocally. Community involvement is so important that only by hearing the shouts and praises of the people can the actor feel secure. Silence is very bad news. Shouted criticisms and corrections are worse. The performers often talk directly to the audience, and, unlike most Western theatre, they expect the audience to talk back.

- **Optimism:** However sad or harrowing a plot may be, the resolution is usually profoundly optimistic. Because the universe is operating in harmony, even death is a transition from one plane to the next. (Despite centuries of colonial oppression, this profound faith that things are moving in the right direction continues to inform modern African drama.)

Decline and Rebirth

Enter Islam: Bards, Pageantry, and Puppetry

Traditional theatre in North Africa almost (but not quite) ceased to exist with the invasion of conquering Arab armies bringing Islam and a new dominant culture to the region. Today, only a very few hidden sanctuaries of indigenous African populations can be found (and finding them is not for the faint of heart or weak of body). Islam arrived in Egypt during the mid-seventh century, and in Egypt, we can trace Islamic influences most easily because of the wealth of source material.

Although Alexandria fell to an Arab army in 640 C.E., transformation did not occur overnight. Islam encourages tolerance of other faiths, so as its empire expanded, conversion was not the first priority. For the next 200 years, in fact, the official religion of Egypt was Christianity. Ultimately, conversion did take place and the performance traditions of nomadic Arab tribes melded with ancient Egyptian styles.

The Arab traditions included the importance of bards, who retained the tribal history and interpreted all important events. Music and dance flourished as performance arts that were part narrative and part abstract expression. Egyptian tradition centered around religious and seasonal celebrations, marking community-wide participation in and observance of key events. Elaborate processionals were performed, often on the Nile River, the lifeblood of Egyptian

FIGURE 7.27   An illustration of Karagoez and Hacivat, two popular recurring figures in early Turkish shadow plays.

culture. Islamic rulers encouraged the continuation of these age-old festivities and added about 50 Muslim festivals to the calendar, including the Muslim lunar New Year, the birth of Mohammed, and the feast of Ramadan.

By the Middle Ages (the thirteenth and fourteenth centuries), travelers to Egypt reported seeing dancers, storytellers, bards, and even trained fleas and camels as an ongoing parade of performers. They also reported finding shadow puppets, imported from Asia but given a distinctively Egyptian flavor.

The first recorded shadow puppet play, *Ajib wa Gharib*, is a comedy satirizing both performers and con men, perhaps universally suspected of being the same thing. Later, shadow puppet plays supported the birth of the Ottoman dynasty and even told stories of the Crusades.

The Arrival of Europeans

The arrival of European colonizers and missionaries deeply affected the traditional theatre of West Africa. In their attempts to exploit and "civilize" Africa, Europeans imported Western theatre traditions and styles as well. For centuries, traditional oral theatre was displaced from the center of the community and replaced by Western institutions. It did not die out completely, though. It continued in the memories of the communities, in the lessons taught to children by their elders through song and dance, and in performances conducted away from the disapproving eyes of the colonizers.

SUMMARY

Early theatre moves through some remarkably similar patterns of emphasis in cultures widely separated and without direct interaction. These can be divided into three periods: (1) origins, (2) conquest and retreat, and (3) resurgence of popular drama. Beginning with highly spiritual and profound Sanskrit and Greek dramas, important principles were established for the theatre as a force in all our lives. Theatre was used to explore the major questions about the meaning of life itself. There then followed a period of less brilliant but intriguing theatrical productivity around the world, in some cases being used to indoctrinate and in others simply to have a wildly good time. Late in the sixteenth century, Elizabethan drama, led by Shakespeare, burst upon the world with a sweeping energy not unlike that of Japanese Kabuki. Suddenly theatre not only embraced all the people but also captured imaginations in tales of power, wonder, and adventure. Early African theatre was unlike anything found in Asia or the West. Grounded in a unique perspective, it pervaded everyday life, from the simple kitchen stories at the end of a workday to the high ritual ceremonies invoking the protection of gods. Islam brought a new set of aesthetic values that gradually blended with local customs, resulting in theatre unique to North Africa and grounded in the traditions of the bard, dancer, singer, and shadow puppetry. European colonization and slavery, beginning in the sixteenth century and continuing for centuries, nearly doomed Africa's theatre.

SUGGESTED ASSIGNMENTS

1. What do you find most and least similar about the earliest periods of recorded drama?

2. Why do you believe theatre moves in and out of brilliance at various times?

3. Is there any possible explanation for similar events occurring in theatrical communities with no direct interaction?

4. What characteristics would you pick to distinguish European, Asian, and African theatre during their early periods of development?

5. What can you identify as the concerns of early drama, no matter what the culture? How many of these concerns are still major for all of us, and which seem to have receded with time?

6. To what extent do you believe early prevailing cultural standards and beliefs limited or set up free theatrical expression?

7. What would you identify as the greatest similarities between early styles of theatre and our own, and the greatest difference between them?

8. How would you answer Question 7 for the years 1590–1620 as compared with our own era?

9. Which cultural values seem to have most separated parts of the world in terms of their theatrical expression? Where do you feel there is the most potential to meet in accord?

10. Which of the earliest theatrical achievements have had the most profound influence on theatre today?

SUGGESTED ACTIVITIES

1. **Individual:** Choose one ancient tradition from any part of the world and gather any visual, written, or recorded images that you can find. Present this to your class, or create a "montage" that shares and preserves your findings.

2. **Group:** Choose a topic of interest to the group (greed, lust, politics, dorm food, roommate troubles). Elect a *griot,* bard, or storyteller. Rehearse a performance with other group members playing roles as the storyteller narrates or sings the tale.

3. **Long-term:** Outline key events in your life that involve a spiritual, cosmic, or social concern of magnitude. Develop a means of dramatizing

those events into one essential story line. Choose a Western, African, or Asian tradition to provide the style of storytelling used.

4. **Large group:** As a community, create a traditional dramatic celebration. Decide what issue to address, what style to use, and what conventions (music, dance, puppets, and masks) to use. Decide how the audience will participate actively. Try your best to create the whole event.

KEY WORDS AND IDEAS

Sanskrit dance-drama
Vedas
epic
Buddha
Hinduism
Buddhism
Bharata
Natya Shastra
Mahabharata
points of attack
Shudraka, Bhàsa,
    Kàlidàsa
xiqu
Zaju
Noh
Kan'ami Kiyotsugu and
    Zeami Motokiyo
Kabuki
Izumo no Okuni
hanamichi
onnagata
Bunraku
Homer
Aristotle
Aristophanes
Old Comedy
New Comedy

Aeschylus, Sophocles, Euripides
trilogy
orchestra
chorus
skene
Seneca the Younger
Plautus
stock character
allegory
Miracle, Mystery, and Morality
    Plays
Renaissance
Commedia dell'arte
scenarios
innamorati
zanni
lazzi
Elizabethan
Tudor
Jacobean
Christopher Marlowe
William Shakespeare
boy companies
Globe Theatre
Yoruba
orature
griotte

chapter 8

MIDDLE STAGES

A Kunqu Chinese Opera performance.

Minstrelsy is alive and well and back in the hands of the people who created the form. This young performer is participating in the Cape Town Minstrel Festival, South Africa. The festival acknowledges the city's slave heritage.

MIKE HUTCHINGS/Reuters/Corbis

Lesson Objectives:

Because this chapter is a continuation of the history portion of this course, your learning objectives will remain the same:

1. Explore unfamiliar styles of theatre from various global communities with a basic understanding of the history and conventions of each.
2. Identify the names of major theatrical movements and playwrights from the seventeenth century to the early nineteenth century.
3. Recognize how theatre continued to move from elite to a popular art form in continuous swings on a continuum as discussed in Chapter 7.
4. Recognize that forms of theatre around the world have shared similarities that are difficult to explain logically.

Introduction

During the seventeen and eighteenth centuries, theatre again repeated the strange pattern noted in Chapter 7. At first, new forms that welcomed audiences of all classes continued to develop. Then a middle phase of exclusivity restricted theatre to courtiers and aristocrats. Finally, there was a sense that enough was enough! People burst back into the theatre and have remained there ever since.

By the seventeenth century, *Noh* became the exclusive domain of the warrior samurai class with common folk not invited—not that they were all that interested in the now slow-paced drama that was utterly disconnected from their lives.

By the mid-seventeenth century, the people's theatre of Shakespeare and his contemporaries had also been taken over by elitist aristocrats, who not only didn't welcome the commoners but used them as the butt of their jokes.

During the same period, the rollicking, flamboyant *Zaju* of China evolved into *Kunqu.* Confined to the imperial courts, this formalized and elitist theatre lost its former connection to the folk drama that had inspired it.

Meanwhile, in Africa, the long and interminable domination of European colonial powers discouraged the traditional theatre of the people and drove it underground, while European imports were performed for the governing elite. But in the Americas, although struggling under the yoke of slavery, Africa's cherished traditional theatre forms found new means of expression.

In spite of these strange parallels in history, the people's need and desire for theatre never died, as it never will. New invigorating and accessible forms saved theatre from becoming the dull plaything of the rich and famous. In this chapter, we follow this pattern in Asia, Europe, and Africa. We look at the elite theatre of the Chinese *Kunqu,* and then we will examine the people's theatres of the Indian *Kathakali* and of the *Jingju* (Beijing Opera) of China. We will also explore elitist theatres of the English Restoration and the French neoclassicists, followed by the European people's theatre of the *Commedia dell'arte,* the genius of Molière, and the return of the middle class in English Georgian dramas. We introduce the most enduring form of Western theatre, the melodrama, which is as popular today as it was over 150 years ago. Finally, we look at the continued suppression of traditional theatre in Africa and discover the ways that people kept their inherent love of performance alive. (The Historic Parallels table at the beginning of Part III provides an overview of these historical phenomena.)

Chinese Opera *(Xigu 2)—Kunqu*

Kunqu (pronounced *kwin-chu*) replaced the earliest form of Chinese opera, *Zaju,* by the mid-seventeenth century. Unlike *Zaju,* with its ribald, acrobatic clowning, *Kunqu* ("Songs of Kunshan," its town of origin) is stately, poetic, and genuinely aristocratic. Refined and subtle rather than obvious and exciting, it quickly gained favor in the imperial court.

Kunqu evolved during the Qing dynasty (1644–1912), which was founded by the Manchu, the second ethnic group to rule the whole of China, after the native Chinese Ming who gave us *Zaju*. The last feudal dynasty in the country's history, the Qing led imperial China to its zenith of power and influence, but its rulers were autocratic and despotic, persecuting many intellectuals and banning or destroying works that did not meet their approval. In this atmosphere of strict feudal control, *Kunqu* evolved under close supervision of imperial agents. Concurrently, the educational and social level of those in the theatrical profession rose, and theatre actually received scholarly support. This combination brought new status and respect, but it also limited contact between the most brilliant practitioners and the people.

The Drama

Based on the Kun melodic system, *Kunqu* depended on a small orchestra of wind and percussion instruments, with the flute used for primary accompaniment. Its language is an artificial stage language, written in eight tones (all Chinese dialects use tone as well as pronunciation to indicate meaning), making composition of the libretto highly complex. Authors continuously had to refine libretto and music until the two fell into "harmony." Because *Kunqu* playwriting presented such a challenge, almost all playwrights were poets whose work today stands as an example of high Chinese literature.

Kunqu evolved out of very early regional musical styles. It was not until the Qing dynasty that the court musician Wei Liangfu codified a new style of delicate singing called "water mill tunes." He and his collaborators standardized rules of rhyme, tones, pronunciation, and notation, which helped this regional form become a national standard. By the end of the sixteenth century, *Kunqu* had spread across China and became the most prestigious form of Chinese drama for the next 200 years, during which nearly its entire repertoire was created.

Date

1600	■ *Kunqu* (*Xiqu* 2), China, 1600s
	● The Diaspora—Slavery sends West African theatre traditions to the New World
1650	▲ Neoclassicism, France, seventeenth century
	▲ Restoration Comedy, England, seventeenth century
	■ *Kathakali,* India, 1650s
	▲ Molière, France, 1622–1673
1700	■ European colonization of India and Asia, introduction of Western theatre forms, eighteenth century
	■ Traditional theatres in Asia struggle to survive colonial rule
1750	▲ Georgian Comedy, England, eighteenth century
	■ *Jingju* (Beijing Opera), China, 1790
	● Colonizers divide Africa and attempt to destroy the foundations of society: language and the arts, 1800s
	● Imposition of Eurocentric forms of theatre in Africa, 1800s
1800	● Traditional theatre in Africa driven underground
	● Early slave entertainments in America
	▲ Melodrama (all of Europe and North America)
	▲ First plays by African American playwrights, 1820s (see Chapter 11)
	▲ The minstrel show—white performers co-opt African performance traditions, 1830s
1850	■ *Noh* and Kabuki (Japan), Beijing Opera (China), shadow puppet and puppet theatre, folk drama all continue to the present day
1900	▲ U.S. Civil War and freedom for slaves, 1861–1865
	▲ The modern theatre with competing styles/genres begins

KEY: ▲ The West   ■ The East   ● Africa

Though basic rules of musical form were established by 1530, it was not until the famous playwright Lian Chenyu used its music as the foundation for his play *Laundering the Silken Yarn* that *Kunqu* was elevated to the status of "Official Melody." Collaborative teams of poets, scholars, musicians, and artists then created new compositions. In its own fashion, *Kunqu* was as much courtly theatre for aristocrats as was English Restoration comedy (discussed later in this chapter), requiring an educated appreciation for nuance and literary finesse that makes it inaccessible to many audiences.

Styles

Kunqu scripts have complicated rules of versification, and their formality suits classical plays. None have military themes. Two styles of text form the script: arias and prose. Arias—elaborate and complex poems of high literary quality—are sung and accompanied by the orchestra. Prose is neither spoken nor sung but chanted in stylized fashion. Sometimes the two are performed simultaneously, with one actor singing an aria and the other chanting a prose response.

The Theatre

Theatre Spaces

As in all traditional Chinese theatre, *Kunqu* uses minimal stage scenery. Stages are flat and bare, allowing for full expression of dance and movement

Francis Loney/ArenaPAL/The Image Works

FIGURE 8.1 The Kunqu Opera Company performs *The Peony Pavilion*. The character in the foreground wears water sleeves.

Marc Garanger/Documentary/Corbis

FIGURE 8.2 Kunqu character types: female, male, painted face, and clown.

by the actors. No curtains or sets hamper the flow of movement from place to place or from time to time. These pieces were performed in the imperial courts rather than separate theatre buildings. As in Shakespeare's theatre, *Kunqu* performers conjure time and place by appealing to the imagination of the audience through poetry, music, and gesture.

Theatre Conventions

- **The Actors:** Like the Sanskrit theatre convention, *Kunqu* theatre relies on abstract and symbolic movement, dance, and gesture. Actors assume statuesque postures that change for each word or beat of the dialogue. Because there is a movement for every shift in verse, the association between dance and poetry grew even stronger than in the past. Some theorize that the term *foot,* eventually employed to describe a single unit of verse in the West as well, originated from the idea that a *Kunqu* actor would be likely to shift the placement of the foot at each rhythmic transition in the dialogue.

- **Character:** The meaning and accessibility of *Kunqu* performances rely on the use of well-defined character types. The four major types are male, female, painted face, and clown, with subcategories of each. Stylized movement associated with each role constitutes an art form in itself. These same character types occur in the wildly popular Beijing Opera, discussed later in this chapter.

- **Costumes:** The costumes are elaborate, exaggerated versions of dress worn during the Ming dynasty and do not attempt to fit the time or place of the action. In many roles, the actors wear robes with extremely long white sleeves called "water sleeves," which essentially serve as props to emphasize the performer's movements. One sign of an accomplished *Kunqu* performance is the skilled manipulation of water sleeves.

- **Props:** Few props clutter the *Kunqu* stage. A chair and table might appear, but they rarely do. Props might help identify characters. For example, a young man with peonies on his robe might indicate a playboy, and an actor carrying a magnifying glass might indicate social blindness. A Buddhist nun always carries a feather duster to ward off evil spirits.

Influences

Many audience members found (and still find) *Kunqu* just as baffling as some in our culture find opera and classical ballet. Concurrent to this exclusive form, a more popular theatre of the people, called "Clapper opera," developed in many regional cities. The name comes from a loud clapping of drumsticks on wooden blocks. It would be another century before the most famous Chinese opera, *Jingju,* or Beijing Opera, evolved, combining elevated and accessible theatre into an indelible form.

Despite the challenges of *Kunqu*, it is still a dynamic form in modern China, with six currently active professional companies, each consisting of 600 to 700 performers, musicians, and related support personnel. Each has its own school for training future performers. Many of the performance traditions and texts of *Kunqu* contributed to the evolution of Beijing Opera, when the theatre moved out of imperial courts and back to the people.

Imagery India/Alamy

FIGURE 8.3   A *Kathakali* actor in performance.

Indian *Kathakali*

Long after its demise, the influences of formal Indian Sanskrit dance-drama lived on, giving inspiration and fire to a form of popular drama known as ***Kathakali*** (meaning "story play"), which evolved in the rural villages of the southern province of Kerala in the mid-1600s. *Kathakali* has clear connections to classical theatre, but it is also designed to delight the commoner. Today it is the most internationally familiar style of Indian dance-drama.

FIGURE 8.4   A drummer accompanies a *Kathakali* Story-Play, performed on stage with a traditional flame in a theatre in Trivandrum, Kerala, in India.

The Drama

Based on stories from the *Ramayana* and the *Mahabharata*, the two great epics that inspired Sanskrit drama, the repertoire consists of about 50 plays which feature kings and heroes in the constant struggle between good and evil, gods and demons. Their mood is mysterious, cosmic, and often frightening. Though good wins in the end, the power of evil forces is fully realized.

The Theatre

Theatre Spaces

Kathakali evolved as open-air performance, performed on a 16-foot square framed by four poles, one at each corner. A single, large oil flame issues from a metal cauldron placed in front of the playing area. Traditionally performed at night, the sense of mystery and shadow of *Kathakali* is enhanced by this fire. Costumes and extreme makeup identify character types and add to the mystery and suspense in the flickering light of the oil flame.

Theatre Conventions

The Actor: A distinctive feature of *Kathakali* is that the actors remain mute. They communicate through gesture and mime as a small chorus of two or three singers forcefully underscores their movements. Training is long and arduous, beginning around age 10 and with actors often not achieving mastery until they are in their forties. Extraordinary and powerful movement skills are required. *Kathakali* involves great strength and majesty, alternating huge leaps with perfectly still poses. The eyes express forceful emotion. One custom is that of placing a tiny pepper seedpod in each eye, turning an actor's eyes blood red while doing no lasting harm. According to Asian theatre scholar A. C. Scott, "The use of such devices adds a particular dramatic emphasis to the charged silence of the actors, who are no longer human beings but dream characters from another world, the gods descended to earth."

Created by and for the common people in rural towns in southern India more than 300 years ago, *Kathakali* is internationally known and respected today. Its continued popularity is a testament to its power to lift audiences out of their daily lives and transport them to a place of magic, mystery, and suspense.

Chinese *Jingju*, or Beijing Opera

Lindsay Hebberd/Corbis

FIGURE 8.5   A male character in the Beijing Opera.

One of the most famous and beloved of Eastern theatres was founded in 1790. ***Jingju,*** or **Beijing Opera**, restored theatre to the common folk after the aristocratic *Kunqu* excluded them. During frequent hunting expeditions in south China, the emperor developed an interest in local operas. In 1790, to celebrate his 80th birthday, he summoned opera troupes from different regions to perform for him in the capital. They amazed the imperial court with their combined singing, dancing, acrobatics, and martial arts. In time, several regional styles blended to form a new genre, known as Beijing Opera. With the exception of a 13-year hiatus during the Chinese Cultural Revolution of the 1960s, Beijing Opera has been in continual production ever since.

The Drama

Like Kabuki in Japan, Beijing Opera encouraged constant development of new plays. Drama usually explored stories of legendary heroes or military feats. Using an extravagant performance style, the plays depict larger-than-life heroes overcoming "monsters" that threaten the people. This dynamic theatre form never catered to strict rules. Audiences expected innovation and risk-taking. Most texts drew inspiration from well-known tales, such as

FIGURE 8.6 A Beijing Opera performance of *The Carp Fairy of the Green Pond*. Note the character types distinguished by their wardrobe and face painting techniques.

the Monkey King, the Water Margin, and the Romance of the Three Kingdoms, along with countless well-known Chinese fairy tales and legends. Adventure, romance, and mortal combats feature strongly in the traditional texts.

The Theatre

Theatre Spaces

At first, the imperial courts controlled performance spaces, limiting theatres to those allowed by the emperor. As a result, many actors would sneak away and bribe court officials to allow them to perform in courtyards and inns among the common people. In time, the court relinquished the strict controls, and the Beijing Opera bloomed into almost any performance space of adequate size. The stage was usually bare, with no limit in space, time, or action. The actors' footwork, gestures, and body movements symbolized the actions of opening a door, climbing a hill, going up stairs, or rowing a boat. When a girl did needlework, she had neither needle nor thread in her hands. Four generals and four soldiers could represent an army of thousands.

Theatre Conventions

- **The Actor:** Beijing Opera is a comprehensive performance combining music, singing, dialogue, pantomime, acrobatics, and martial arts. Actors must meet more requirements than those for other performing arts, usually taking more than 10 years of training to learn singing and acrobatic skills. Until very recently, only men performed.

CLOSE-UP

Takarazuka: All Women, All the Time

Given the historical restrictions on participation of women actors in Asian theatre, it is ironic that one of the best sources of employment for contemporary performers is *Takarazuka*, wherein every role is played by a woman. The shows also draw a predominantly female audience, with nearly 3 million patrons flocking to the tiny spa town for which the company is named to take in the spectacular productions.

There are more than 400 members of the acting company. *Takarazuka* also plays in huge theatres in Kansai and Tokyo and tours widely with five long-running touring productions.

Asian theatre scholar Barbara Sellers Young has described *Takarazuka* as "a little like Las Vegas meets Broadway with a nod to classical Japanese performance." Some of the shows are revues, styled on those made famous in the West at the Parisian Moulin Rouge. Others are massive productions of musicals such as *West Side Story, Singin' in the Rain,* and *The Phantom of the Opera,* and even adaptations of epic novels/films such as *Gone with the Wind* and *War and Peace.* A production may focus on a single story line or present a series of sketches, short plays, and musical numbers. Enactments of traditional Asian folk tales are interspersed with highly Western pieces. Costume and set designs are incredibly lavish, and the performance style is melodramatic in its intensity.

In response to the ancient prejudice against women on stage and the association of actresses with prostitutes in the minds of many in the culture, *Takarazuka* performers are sequestered, chaperoned, and isolated almost as if they had joined a nunnery. Great efforts are made to project the company as wholesome and unworldly in every sense.

A documentary film *Dream Girls* (not to be confused with the Broadway and Hollywood musical of the same name) demonstrates the elaborate system of training involved for all performers and the huge reaction and support of women fans for the company. James Michener featured *Takarazuka* in his best-selling novel *Sayonara,* though when it was adapted into an Academy Award–winning film, the company name was changed to *Matsubayara.*

According to Jennifer Robertson, author of a book about the company, "The greatest attraction is undoubtedly the stage presence of the tall, slender, handsome *otokoyaku,* women who play male roles." These performers are not limited to male roles, however, but are likely to be cast whenever a strong female character (such as Scarlett O'Hara) is needed.

Except for some special wartime productions, all dramas and revues may be set in any country and time *except* modern Japan. All performers must therefore at some time play non-Japanese or what Robertson calls "cross-ethnicking" roles. This might also be considered an ironic payback for all the times in history when Asian actors were not cast in Asian roles.

TOSHIFUMI KITAMURA/AFP/Getty Images

FIGURE 8.7   A scene from the Takarazuka Revue performance of *The Rose of Versailles,* a show about a female disguised as a Palace Guard during the French Revolution, based on a 1970s cult manga cartoon.

- **Character:** The form relies on stock characters. Actors were chosen at a very early age to specialize in male (*sheng*), female (*dan*), painted face (*jing*), or clown (*chou*) roles. Very few actors mastered more than one type of character role.
- **Music:** The music of Beijing Opera uses typical Chinese musical instruments, including two-stringed fiddles, reed pipes, mandolin, lute, drums, bells, gongs, and hardwood castanets.
- **Face Painting:** This theatre genre is color-coded. Facial painting shows the character's age, profession, and personality by using different colors: for example, red for loyalty and uprightness; black for a rough, stern, or honest nature. More than 1,000 painted facial patterns are used. Each actor is challenged to make subtle and interesting changes within the fixed facial pattern without contradicting the code.
- **Costumes:** Costumes impress audiences with their bright colors and magnificent embroidery. Some used in present performances resemble the fashion of the Ming dynasty (1368–1644). Again, colors indicate social status: yellow for the imperial family, red for high nobility, and white for old officials. Besides gorgeous clothes and headdresses, jeweled girdles for men and hair ornaments for women are also used.

Considered today a national treasure in China, Beijing Opera has become not only a true people's theatre but also an international ambassador to the rest of the world. It is one of the best-known and beloved forms of theatre. The use of pantomime, gesture, and symbolism overcomes language barriers. Amazing acrobatic and martial artistry combined with passionate and heavily percussive music delight the eye and the ear. Stories are universal, and the appeal has endured for 200 years.

English Restoration

While Shakespeare's death alone did not send the English theatre into a state of mourning, his demise coincided with a downward spiral from theatrical greatness. Politics replaced art. Those for and against the monarchy struggled for power. The extravagant and decadent Charles I was executed in 1649 after a long and bloody civil war. Oliver Cromwell and the Puritans took control and established the Commonwealth, under which a repressive, joyless atmosphere pervaded. Theatre was officially called corrupt and eventually outlawed in 1642. With Cromwell's death, the Puritans were no longer strong enough to control those loyal to the monarchy. In 1660, Charles II, who had been living in comfortable exile in France, was invited back to reclaim the throne for the Stuart dynasty. After years of self-denial, Londoners burned with a longing for diversion and indulgence, and what followed was the reign of a king far more wild and corrupt than his father ever was.

While many dismiss the theatre of this **English Restoration** era as trivial, seldom in Western history has drama been the instrument for such

FIGURE 8.8   Portrait of King Charles II (Stuart) of England in full regalia. The monarch was a living example of the decadence that marked the era.

a strict distinction among social classes. It is an example of Western theatre gone berserk in celebrating one class and ridiculing all others. We might call this "country-club theatre," written by, played by, and presented to the elite in exclusive environs, safely remote from the ill-informed and unwashed masses.

Fundamentally grounded in Western worldviews, some peculiar points of view evolved in England under the rule of Charles II and his cronies. The Restoration worldview is one in which the lives of the audience and the plays created to entertain them are virtually inseparable. Theatre became the playground of Charles II and his social set (famous or infamous for their insatiable appetites), and the meeting place for those wannabes seeking to get closer to the wealth, power, and freedom of those at the top of the food chain. In fact, according to many diaries of the time, a better show was going on in the audience than onstage.

Worldview

Among the elites of the royal court, values underwent a profound shift to individual gratification. No longer much concerned with state or family, courtiers wanted to enjoy life. Wit, beauty, money, and youth offered the ticket to the inner circle of power. Satire, mockery, and profound cruelty reigned, creating a vicious but outwardly pretty world.

Structure and hierarchy returned to a Western model of monarchy; the brief period of the Commonwealth was no more than a political blip on the royalist screen. Royal privilege and absolute license were reflected in the authority of fathers in the families. Tensions between wild young men (and women) and the all-powerful fathers played out again and again. The father controlled the family's purse strings and arranged marriages to strangers for his offspring; the father's arrival in town caused dismay.

The Drama

Restoration comedy reveled in repeating the same essential plot. The elegant but poverty-stricken young man of fashion pursued a beautiful, witty young lady, either to steal her virginity and dump her (just for fun) or to marry her and steal her fortune (also just for fun). Frequent use of second and third plotlines allowed playwrights to mock the lower classes, the overly serious, the Puritans, the Irish, the guardian, and the unfashionable country cousin.

The Playwrights: Aphra Behn

Playwrights pushed the boundaries of propriety, many writing plays that would shock a modern audience with their sexuality and promiscuity. Because the audience was limited to the fashionable elite, new plays were needed every few days. Only two theatres operated in London, so a decent playwright (or a sufficiently witty/dirty one) could make a reasonable living cranking out formulaic plays on a regular basis. Playwrights got paid only if the play ran for a third night; most did not.

FIGURE 8.9 Portrait of Restoration playwright Aphra Behn, the first woman to earn a living as a playwright in England.

The era did produce at least one major innovation: the woman as a professional playwright. **Aphra Behn** (1640–1689) was the first woman to make her living as a playwright in England, and she would remain one of the very few, proud, and brave women who would attempt and succeed at playwriting until well into the twentieth century. Her plays were successful, perhaps because she followed the mood and tone of the times and wrote plays very much like those of her contemporaries. Although she was not overtly "feminist" or even "female" in her writing style (her works would never have been produced and she would have starved!), she did feature strong, smart, witty central female characters who were at least a match for their male counterparts.

Some playwrights wrote comedies that stood the test of time as examples of universal humor, but most sunk into well-deserved obscurity. Below is a list of playwrights who worked above the vulgarity and elitism of the era. Their work is still produced on the modern stage:

Aphra Behn—*The Forced Marriage, The Town Fop,* and *The Rover*

William Congreve—*The Way of the World* (perhaps the masterpiece of the era)

George Etherege—*The Man of Mode or, Sir Fopling Flutter*

William Wycherley—*The Country Wife* and *The Plain Dealer*

The Theatre

Theatre Space

The two licensed theatres were intimate and small. Notice in the ground plan for the Theatre Royal, Drury Lane that the whole building is only 80 feet long. With over 50 percent of that space taken up with lobby, scenery, and stage, the audience area was 20 to 25 feet deep. The **apron**, an extension of the stage floor beyond the proscenium arch, was the invention of this time period. It was used constantly as a

APHRA BEHN
PLAYWRIGHT

One hour of right-down love is worth an age of dully living on.

VIRGINIA WOOLF
AUTHOR

[A]ll women should let flowers fall upon the tomb of Aphra Behn, for it was she who earned them the right to speak their minds.

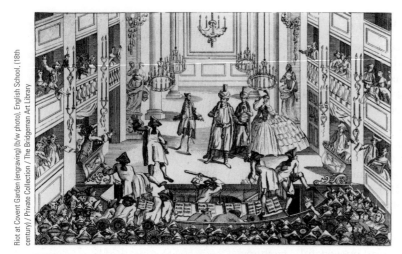

Riot at Covent Garden (engraving) (b/w photo), English School, (18th century) / Private Collection / The Bridgeman Art Library

FIGURE 8.10 Print of a Restoration-era theatre performance. Note the proximity of the audience to the actors.

special space to allow the actor closer proximity to the audience. All entrances were made through stage doors built into the right and left sides of the proscenium arch. All scenery was relegated to the upstage area, which was employed for little more than background decoration. However, this was the introduction of painted perspective scenes to the English theatre, and a new set of scenery, though costly, provided a reason to advertise a play. Many diaries refer to trips to the theatre to see the new "scenes"— the painted backdrops, not the scenes created by playwrights and actors. The theatre might own four sets of basic scenery (street scene, pastoral scene, etc.). These were all used in every play. And they were used no matter the play, so once the "newness" rubbed off, the actor, and particularly the first actresses on the English stage, were fully and closely scrutinized and even joined onstage by audience members.

Theatre Conventions

- **The Actor:** The Restoration actor, though not as restricted as in the theatre of Asia, was certainly cast according to type. Some men played "bad boys" or rakes, while others played buffoons. Some women played ladies of seductive wit, and others played prudes. These are essentially stock characters whose names revealed a dominant characteristic, such as Sir Clumsey, Constant, Lady Fanciful, Lady Fidget, Horner, Mr. Smirk, Mrs. Squeamish, and Lady Wishfort. Each character had a function (gallant, rogue, prude, fop, courtesan, wit) that followed a tradition. An actor or actress might "mature" from one role to another, but this was quite rare.

- **Breeches**: At some point, most Restoration plays feature the leading lady in male disguise, called **breeches roles**, so that all may see her hips, calves, and ankles. This was the first inclusion of the actress in the professional theatre in England. Although their social status was little higher than a prostitute, they were a big hit with men in the audience and on occasion made fortunes for themselves. One of them, Nell Gwyn, became the king's mistress, and her illegitimate son became the Duke of St. Albans. She specialized in breeches roles.

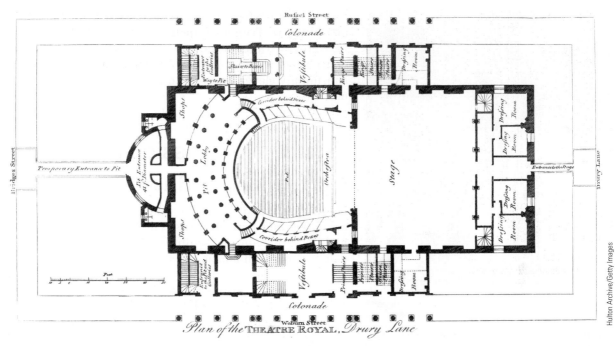

Plan of the THEATRE ROYAL, *Drury Lane*

FIGURE 8.11 Floor plan for the Theatre Royal, Drury Lane. Notice that half of the building length is stage and stage machinery.

Decline and Rebirth

The audience came to the theatre as much to be seen, hunt for prey, socialize, and pass the time as to see the play. The Restoration period was relatively short lived, having passed its heyday with the death of Charles II, and faded as the throne was occupied by more serious-minded monarchs. By 1700, the raucous and racy comedies fell into disfavor, and the Georgian dramas that followed would appeal to a much broader audience, bringing the middle class back into the fold. The days of theatre by, for, and about the English aristocracy drew to a close.

Influence

Restoration comedy did influence the subsequent arch and wicked drawing-room comedies during a number of eras. Certainly the privileged, self-absorbed, and often cruel characters of Oscar Wilde and Noel Coward are reminiscent of that era. To this day, the heartless, devastating wit may show up in any number of plays

FIGURE 8.12 Portrait of Nell Gwyn, a Restoration actress who specialized in breeches roles.

FIGURE 8.13 The ridiculous meets the sublime in George Etherege's comedy *Love in a Tub*.

FIGURE 8.14 Joanna Roth and Toby Stephens in Jean Racine's *Phèdre*, a Neoclassical drama.

as a kind of Restoration ghost. The acrid comments often attributed to Truman Capote and the sort of character that Hugh Grant specializes in (in such films as *Bridget Jones's Diary* and *American Dreamz*)—the heartless but charmingly clever roué—all owe something to this form of theatre.

French Neoclassicism: Corneille and Racine

Neoclassicism refers to a renewed interest in classical Greek and Roman works. The movement stimulated architecture, painting, sculpture, clothing, and even garden design. An emphasis was placed on balance, harmony, elegance of line, and dignity of design. None of this was a bad thing, but in the realm of theatre, the ***Académie Française*** took things a bit further. Except for the singular genius Molière, the French theatre of the seventeenth century became so caught up in rules and regulations that playwriting became a sort of academic exercise. The common people had little interest in the intellectual elitism of neoclassicism, and today, the plays seem so mechanical and so devoid of emotion or pleasure that they are seldom produced with any success.

The *Académie Française* was established in 1635 as the oversight committee of French language and literature—and its primary aim was to protect them from corruption and foreign influences. **The Academy** also became the style police in dramatic literature. New plays had to be submitted for approval before they could be produced. Censorship of content was part of the process, while censorship of style also began to stifle the creative imagination of artists. The Academy began treating the *Poetics* by Aristotle as a rulebook rather than the analytical survey it was. In time, it began to create rules that Aristotle wouldn't have recognized. Here is a list of just a few of the restrictions placed on the playwrights.

1. **The Unities:** The action of the play had to take place in a maximum of 24 hours, using only one location and telling one story on a classical theme. From Aristotle's logical sense that a play should have a beginning, middle, and an end, The Academy made the Unities into absolute rules.

2. **Genre:** Comedy and tragedy were strictly separated, with tragedy being the higher art. Comedy had to be in prose, and tragedy had to be in verse. No exceptions!

3. **Verisimilitude:** "Believability" dictated no flights of imagination, no mysterious or unexplained events. A king acts like a king, always. Dramatic conventions, like asides, violated the rule against "unnatural sentiments" because they didn't happen in real life.

4. **Decorum:** A sense of dignity and restraint had to be employed. Even agony and ecstasy must be confined within restrained poetic language. The rational was to be celebrated; the irrational was eliminated.

5. **Act structure:** This required a strict rationale for the progression of the plot, taking Aristotle's structure analysis and formalizing it into a restrictive list of rules. The five-act rule was created.

Two playwrights achieved enduring respect under the stringent guidelines of The Academy. One was **Pierre Corneille** (1606–1684) whose tragic masterpiece, *Le Cid* (1637), was an enormous popular success, but it drew the ire of The Academy, which declared it defective and ignited a bitter debate among the literary elite of Paris. He had a long and distinguished career, focusing thematically on the repression of passion in favor of duty.

Corneille's old age was marred by bitterness after he was eclipsed by the rising star of **Jean Racine** (1639–1699). Racine achieved fame and fortune with his third tragedy, *Andromaque,* written when he was only 28 years old. Considered a masterpiece, it earned him the patronage of King Louis XIV. Such plays were designed to please the intellectual elite of Paris and are seldom produced today—they are more often studied as literature than as theatre. Racine himself became disillusioned with his work later in life and seems to have regretted his involvement in the theatre.

The forms of theatre that brought the common person back into the fold began first with *Commedia dell'arte* and Molière in Europe. Then Georgian comedy evolved in England, and finally melodrama swept the European and American stage.

> **PIERRE CORNEILLE**
> PLAYWRIGHT
>
> *To win without risk is to triumph without glory* (Le Cid).

> **JEAN RACINE**
> PLAYWRIGHT
>
> *For a long time past, God has graciously permitted that the good or evil that may be said of my tragedies scarcely moves me, and I am only troubled by the account of them I shall one day have to render to Him.*

Molière and *Commedia dell'arte*

As introduced in Chapter 7, *Commedia dell'arte* (meaning "comedy or theatre of artists") is a colorful and extremely theatrical art form based on the interaction of traditional stock characters in improvised scenarios that facilitate a comic plot to arrive at a humorous climax. It originated in the streets and marketplaces of the early Italian Renaissance, although its roots can be traced as far back as ancient Greece.

> **MOLIÈRE**
> PLAYWRIGHT
>
> *One dies only once, and then for such a long time!*

FIGURE 8.15 French comic genius Molière, in a portrait by Nicholas Mignard (1658).

FIGURE 8.16 Louis XIV performing as Apollo in *Le Ballet Royal de la Nuit*. Molière was strongly influenced by Louis XIV's love of pageantry.

In France, many scenarios were scripted into *Commedia*-style plays. In the mid-seventeenth century, the *Commedia* influence met with the comic genius of one man, Jean-Baptiste Poquelin, also known by his stage name, **Molière**, easily the second-most-produced playwright in the West and most scholars' choice for second-greatest. While Shakespeare was surrounded by a half-dozen other brilliant writers, Molière stands alone. Like Shakespeare, he stole or borrowed plots everywhere, using them merely as something to which to attach his ideas. Also like Shakespeare, he embraced characters from the aristocracy all the way down to country bumpkins, sometimes making the play *about* the bumpkin. And like Shakespeare, he died in his fifties after creating more than 30 plays, working primarily with one established company under royal patronage. Both were investors in, or part owners of, their companies, and both were actors: Molière even acted on the night of his death in 1673 playing, ironically, the title role in *The Imaginary Invalid*. No one in his time and place touched his genius. And *absolutely* no one shares his particular voice. Today, the world famous *Comédie-Français* theatre in Paris is rightly called "The House of Molière."

Three important influences make Molière's work unique:

1. Molière managed to work within the neoclassical framework and still write comedy. He was the first to give comedy true respectability, raising it to the level of esteem previously reserved for tragedy. He surprised audiences with the idea that comedy could actually be polite. He created social satire as we know it today.

2. Molière also wrote out of the *Commedia* tradition that employs the very broadest comic and improvisational ingredients in performance. Molière observed and used the great precision of the Italian *Commedia* performers, carefully refining it and giving it sophistication.

3. Molière was strongly influenced by Louis XIV, a monarch with an incomparable ego and great love for pageantry, laughter, and dancing. After first performing for the 20-year-old Louis at the Louvre on October 24, 1658, Molière spent much of the rest of his life creating plays interspersed with music and dancing, featuring His Radiance, who loved to make guest appearances.

Imagine a contemporary playwright managing to draw from vaudeville and the circus to serve the whims of a tycoon who believes himself the center of the universe, while honoring the strictest etiquette books and most

T. Charles Erickson

FIGURE 8.17 Comic scene from *Molière Impromptu*, directed by Christopher Bayes at Trinity Repertory Company. Molière's plays adopted many *Commedia dell'arte* conventions, including clowning and stock characters.

repressive lobbying groups, and still writing strong satire in the process. This was the genius of Molière. His company, first called the *L'Illustre Théâtre*, knew humble days touring the provinces, and he never lost the common touch. His comedies remained human and universal despite his elevation to courtly status, and they account for his continued and constant production over the last 300 years to this day.

Georgian Comedy

Molière, the Restoration playwrights, and the Georgians all wrote variations on a style called Comedy of Manners (**Georgian** refers generally to the eighteenth-century reigns of the Kings George in England, and to George III in particular (r. 1760–1811). While the Restoration theatre involved elegant corruption, its two closest relatives were considerably more wholesome. Both Molière and the Georgians were interested in not simply what behavior *works* but what behavior was morally *right*. They were interested in the overall good of society as much as in the individual. They found in this struggle of self versus society a strong source of laughter. The Georgians followed the Restoration by nearly 100 years, during which time enough sweeping changes had taken place in the world to bring about a distinct type of comedy involving the middle class. The Georgians could be called the grandchildren of the Restoration. A little embarrassed by their profligate ancestors, they became *very* concerned with what is proper and much less concerned with aristocratic privilege.

A woman's purity became the "jewel in her crown," but more than that, a mere hint of sexual scandal could

AUTHOR'S INSIGHT

ROBERT: Georgian comedies have always seemed to me the direct ancestors of classic early sitcoms. The kind of innocent, ridiculous predicaments in which characters find themselves are very much like those of Lucy and Ethel (*I Love Lucy*) or Ralph Kramden and Ed Norton (*The Honeymooners*).

FIGURE 8.18   An example of ladies' fashion with wide panniers or hoops under the skirts to add size and "weight" to the appearance.

RICHARD BRINSLEY SHERIDAN
PLAYWRIGHT

Through all the drama—whether damned or not—Love gilds the scene, and women guide the plot.

ruin a woman literally—for the rest of her life. Adultery was no longer a fit subject for discussion. Middle-class Georgians spent a good deal of time moralizing and attacking the morals of others, but they were not without a sense of fun. Diversions included horse races, fox hunting, and golf. Gambling became so popular that even at a ball, a gaming room was provided for those who preferred the table to the dance floor. Ladies danced, sang, played instruments, and practiced various fine arts. These values and behaviors were reflected in Georgian comedy.

The Drama: Sheridan and Goldsmith

The comedies of the period often drip with cloying sentimentality, but two writers represent the period's true strengths. **Richard Brinsley Sheridan** and **Oliver Goldsmith** both reacted against the preachy sweetness of the times and in so doing created plays of lasting appeal.

In 1772, Goldsmith published his famous "An Essay on Theatre," which decried sentiment and cried out for "laughing comedy." He did more than criticize. The next year, he produced what he demanded in *She Stoops to Conquer*. That play had so little in common with others of the time that only through the influence of the powerful and popular Samuel Johnson was it produced at all. *She Stoops* and Sheridan's plays *The Rivals* and *The School for Scandal* define Georgian theatre for modern audiences. Both placed more emphasis on character than did the Restoration writers but retained some of the biting wit. They identified the difference between real and feigned virtue. By our standards, there is plenty of sentiment left in both playwrights' work. Goodness is inevitably rewarded and gentility supported.

The Theatre

Theatre Space

The performance space expanded considerably. Huge new theatres reduced the apron, and lighting was much improved. The actors moved upstage, creating a much larger distance between actor and observer. Scenic wonders evolved with many cutout set pieces and much painting that actually had something to do with the time and place of the play. Sets became lavish, just like the middle-class homes of the audience.

Conventions

- **The Actor:** Portraits from the period reveal that an actor had to be able to maneuver artfully in clothing that might have weighed as much as 20 pounds. They also had to master the intricacy of "manners," a mind-boggling and constantly changing pattern of social behaviors designed to distinguish class difference. Both men and women continued to perform, with women often achieving a level of stardom.

- **Music and Dance:** Music in the form of interludes (played between scenes and acts) became common, and all performers needed to be familiar with the latest dance crazes such as the waltz. Couples embraced and did turns about the room for the first time. Moralists were quick to point out the danger of a dance that allowed young women to be grasped by their partners, thrown into the air, and twirled about. Another similar and even livelier partner dance, the polka, became popular.

- **Masking:** While the wearing of literal masks declined in popularity, the new social mask of choice was middle-class respectability. A solid outward show was employed, with lewd and power-mad impulses carefully concealed and/or suppressed in favor of good-hearted decency.

FIGURE 8.19 Performance of Richard Brinsley Sheridan's *The School for Scandal*, with Geraldine McEwan, Charles Lloyd Pack, Peter Barkworth, Gwen Ffrangcon-Davies, and Meriel Forbes.

John Dominis/Contributor/Time Life Pictures/Getty Images

Melodrama

The century following the Georgians was so dominated by one woman and her large family that it is named after her—Victoria, Queen of England and Ireland and Empress of India. Her reign, the longest in English history, spanned most of the nineteenth century, and her values were embraced across Europe, the United States, and the British colonies. The Victorian era saw the triumph of the middle class over the landed aristocracy. Respectability became the all-powerful goal. Take the social constraints of the Georgian era, multiply by 10, and you've got the Victorian age.

Increasingly complex social rules defined respectability. All the money in the world couldn't buy it. Only years of careful and painstaking social climbing, never taking a misstep, and never taking eyes from the prize could achieve that goal. Even those who were considered respectable lived in a precarious state of rigid, social order. For women especially, restrictions were intense, and the price to pay for defiance was very high.

The **melodrama** was designed to soothe and reassure the middle class, to keep telling them, "Yes, everything is right with the world, and you are right in everything you do." Evil was punished, while goodness was rewarded; wealth was a sign of God's favor and poverty a sign of His disfavor. Manners and social positioning were essential to an orderly universe. Melodramas were written with predictable structures and themes. Designed to appeal to emotions, not intellect, they promoted the status quo. A middle-class matron could be moved to gasps of fear, tears of pity, and groans of horror by melodrama and then go home content and a bit smug, assured of her well-earned superiority and God-given purity of mind and heart. In a society completely ordered around convention rather than honesty, the theatre could only follow suit.

FIGURE 8.20 Young Queen Victoria, near the beginning of her reign.

Conventions

- **Plots** involved a good man or woman tempted or tormented by villainous forces. For a young man, it might have been alcohol, dishonesty in business, or a woman of bad reputation. For a woman, it was almost always her virtue under siege. After lots of action and emotion, the plot was eventually resolved with the salvation or ruination of the protagonist. If temptation was resisted, a happy ending, and if not . . .

- **Good and evil** were simple and uncomplicated. The hero was all good, the villain all bad. No complexity of character or motivation muddied the melodramatic waters.

- **Class distinctions** were strictly adhered to. A servant could never be a lady. A street urchin would never rise to servant class, let alone anything else. An outsider trying to pass as a lady or gentleman of the middle class was the worst of criminals.

- **Action/adventure** required big scenery and big theatres. In one American melodrama called *Under the Gaslight,* the heroine was thrown into the New York Harbor, rescued her friend from an onrushing train, broke free of a burning shed by using an ax, and fought off a midnight attack in her boudoir by the villain—all vividly portrayed onstage.

- **Music** was an important component (it's the "melo" part of melodrama). Music underscored action sequences, raised tension, identified character types, lapsed into love songs, and kept the emotions swinging from one extreme to the other.

Influences

The popularity of melodrama has never waned, although it was often disparaged by the elite. We still love to believe that good overcomes evil; that we are always right and the opposition is always wrong. In media theatre in particular, the action film is often just a big, expensive, violent melodrama. The *Star Wars* epic film series and the *Lord of the Rings* trilogy, for example, are comforting to us because of their clearly defined good and evil characters and the eventual triumph of good. On a more reduced scale, melodrama thrives as soap opera. We will compare melodrama with other modern styles of theatre in Part IV of this book, as for the first time in the West many types of theatre compete for audiences and revenue.

Africa—Diaspora

One of the enduring legacies of European involvement in Africa is the Diaspora (the "scattering") brought about by the hunger for free labor in the New World. Whole communities disappeared into holds of cargo ships to be sold in the Americas. Many survivors, both those taken into slavery and those left behind, lived as shell-shocked remnants, struggling from one day to the next. What the colonizers and missionaries didn't succeed in destroying, the centuries of Diaspora nearly did.

The essential strength and optimism of African culture did not die, however. In the Americas, enslaved peoples used the tools of the theatre—storytelling, dance, music, and narrative—not only to survive emotionally but also to preserve their cultural heritage. Elements of African theatre lived on in American and Caribbean descendants of slaves, giving rise to the American musical theatre, Caribbean dance and music, and a tradition of telling stories and using theatre to create hope, change, optimism, balance, and proportion.

FIGURE 8.21   A map of Africa divided between European powers after the Berlin Conference 1884–1885.

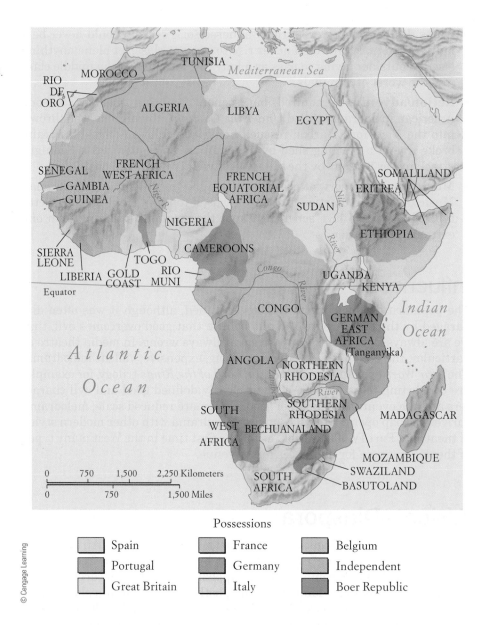

Possessions

Spain
Portugal
Great Britain
France
Germany
Italy
Belgium
Independent
Boer Republic

© Cengage Learning

In 1801, the first European-style theatre opened in Africa in the Cape of Good Hope, and 1866 is the year in which the first European-style play was performed by Africans. None of these in any way acknowledged African tradition but rather simply imposed Western concepts. The colonizing nations of Europe met during 1884–1885 at the Berlin Conference, where they carved Africa into chunks and devoured it. Those created "nation-states" still endure, but with the same critical problems now as then. Some have as many as 250 tribal nations within their borders, while others have only two or three. Each tribal nation speaks a distinct language, making national and even regional theatre almost impossible. The only shared language is that of the oppressor, often English or French. Theatre, which had always functioned as an active mechanism of justice and social cohesion, no longer worked in "nations" that weren't nations. Much of contemporary suffering in Africa traces its roots to the forced separation of families and communities from the same nation on the one hand, and the forced proximity of unrelated tribal communities on the other.

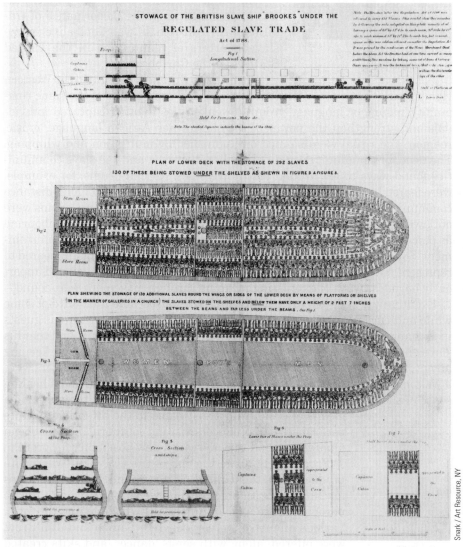

FIGURE 8.22 This floor plan of the British slave ship *Brookes* shows how slaves were transported to the Americas in the holds of ships.

FIGURE 8.23   Anonymous American folk art depicting music, dance, and performance as a means of surviving slavery.

The Americas—The Minstrel Show

In the Americas, however, a revolutionary form of theatre was developing almost from the very beginnings of slavery. This form would become the full-fledged **minstrel show**, or minstrelsy, by the 1830s when white performers wearing burnt cork on their faces (also known as **blackface**) would co-opt African traditions for use in comic mockery of African Americans. But in the beginning, the performance of traditional African rituals was kept alive in the slave quarters of plantations in the United States and the Caribbean.

When slaves were sold in ports in the Western Hemisphere, they were intentionally separated from people of the same community, nation, or language group to weaken ties to other captured individuals and strengthen the power of the slaveowner. African language, music, religion, and ritual were banned and punished by mutilation and whipping. The need for community couldn't be killed, however, and the slave communities found ways to get around restrictive rules. African drums, for example, were feared by white populations because they were a means of long-distance communication that didn't depend on the spoken word. Therefore, drums were outlawed. Instead, slaves used spoons, bells, and eventually the tambourine as percussion instruments. The banjo became associated with slave entertainment. Songs were composed that secretly mocked the masters but appeared to represent submission. When traditional dance was forbidden, new and apparently harmless ways of expressing meaning through movement were found.

Eventually a style of performance evolved that became a favorite of some white audiences. A master might invite favored slaves to entertain his guests in exchange for a shirt or a pound of cornmeal. The master might find that his slave entertainers were in demand by neighbors and rent them out, keeping any profit for himself. For the slaves, the entertainments in the quarters were a welcome holiday from the misery of daily life, providing grace and a healing sense of shared community to the people. For the slaveowner, they became a means of profit. Minstrelsy came to the attention of white performers and producers visiting southern and Caribbean plantations, and they too saw a new possibility for profit.

From the 1830s to the end of the U.S. Civil War, white producers in the United States found ready audiences for slave entertainments that were made over to create parodies of the African Americans who invented the form. Various offensive stereotypes, like Sambo and Jim Crow, were offered, along with songs, dances, and skits created by slaves but exaggerated into mocking shows.

JASON H. LEE
SCHOLAR

The content of minstrel songs worked to reinforce the racial ideology of white superiority—a system where "whiteness" allowed for full citizenship rights to the American body politic, while "blackness" and "yellowness" implied inferiority and exclusion.

FIGURE 8.24 Al. G. Field Greater Minstrels Poster, c. 1900. Notice that the form has now been co-opted by white performers, pictured at the top of the poster.

FIGURE 8.25   Despite performing humiliating caricatures of the original minstrel character types, African American performers used this type of show as their only gateway to the stage.

After the Civil War, African American performers found some of their first opportunities for employment in the minstrel shows. Eventually, minstrelsy became one of the earliest American contributions to the development of American musical theatre. Sadly, the minstrel shows continued well into the twentieth century.

Decline and Rebirth of Traditional African Theatre

Meanwhile, back in Africa, a new mechanism was set in motion that nearly succeeded in destroying the traditional theatre of sub-Saharan Africa. Promising young African artists and scholars were sent to Europe to be trained in Western theatre. When this educated elite returned, they were isolated from their roots and often given high-paying government jobs, writing and producing theatre for Europeans. In the meantime, the old stories and performance traditions were starting to die with the elders who carried them in their heads. Fortunately, many of the old stories finally began to be recorded, and these now survive. Artists, scholars, and playwrights of the past two decades have re-embraced the traditions of African theatre and are finding ways to encourage a renaissance.

SUMMARY

Following the brilliance of the Sanskrit, Greek, and West African classical periods, theatre went through a series of phases, moving outward toward the people, inward to an elite circle, and then outward again. Elitist forms include *Kunqu* in China, where popular opera was confined to the aristocratic court; the English Restoration comedy, when the aristocracy took over and used the theatre as a toy; and neoclassicism in France, where the *Académie Française* applied strict rules that stifled creativity. As always, the people simply developed new forms for themselves: the *Kathakali* in India, *Commedia dell'arte* in Europe, and regional operas in China. Enduring theatre for the people evolved: the Beijing Opera, the plays of Molière, the Georgian comedy of England, and the melodrama. In Africa, the forced dispersal of traditional communities and the imposition of European theatre traditions nearly destroyed the traditional theatre of the people. However, slave entertainment in the Americas grew into the influential minstrel shows that became one of the foundations of the American musical theatre. Postcolonial efforts are succeeding in saving some of the oral history of African communities in traditional performance forms.

SUGGESTED ASSIGNMENTS

1. What cultural factors may have contributed to theatre being widely available or entirely exclusive at various points in history? Can you predict any trends based on historical evidence presented here?

2. What do you find most similar about theatrical activity during each period in this chapter? Given that the cultures identified here were separated by vast distances and had minimal interaction, what may explain similar theatrical trends?

3. What would you say made each culture unique or distinct from the others? What characteristics would you pick to distinguish European, Asian, and African theatre during these developments?

4. Why is it so much more difficult to pin down changes in Africa during this time?

5. The Chinese opera moves through three very distinct phases. What distinguishes each, and what ties them all together?

6. How did the concerns of drama change from those identified in Chapter 7 to this later period? Which of these concerns remains an important part of theatre? Have any receded with time?

7. To what extent do you believe early, prevailing cultural standards and beliefs limited or set up free theatrical expression within each culture during this period? While we do not know enough about theatre outside our own culture to identify influences, we can do so with English Restoration, Molière, and English Georgian comedy. How has each of these theatrical forms influenced contemporary theatre and film? What are examples of works that might never have existed without their influence?

8. The English Restoration inspired all devastatingly witty drawing-room comedy, from the plays of Oscar Wilde to the television show *Will & Grace*. What else?

9. Molière and the *Commedia* tradition have inspired satire, improv, and target theatre generally. What are some examples?

10. The Georgian comedy is an ancestor of the sitcom. The path from *She Stoops to Conquer* to *Everybody Loves Raymond* is fairly direct. What are the essential characteristics of middle-class comedy, and how have they evolved?

SUGGESTED ACTIVITIES

1. **Individual:** Compare the visual extravagance of Beijing Opera with Restoration or Georgian period dress. Explore the worldview that encouraged such "large" characterizations on the stage.

2. **Group:** Choose any play that you have studied together and prepare to produce it in a style covered in this chapter. Assign someone to direct, someone to design costumes and scenery, and performers to act in the play. What happens when you shift your chosen play into one of these grand styles of theatre?

3. **Long-term:** Do the group activity in Question 2 as an individual project. For example, choose a play and decide to perform it as Beijing Opera. Gather or create images and ideas to present to your class as if you were selling this idea to a board of directors or artistic director.

4. **Large group:** Seek out an opportunity to see a type of theatre (or a film like *Farewell My Concubine* or *Casanova* that is set in a long-ago time) presented in this chapter. Most campuses have cultural celebrations, visiting performance groups, and foreign film events. Period plays may be playing on your campus this term. Early in the semester share your suggestion, vote as a group on which event to attend, then set out to experience something that may be new or unusual as a group.

KEY WORDS AND IDEAS

Kunqu

Kathakali

Jingju (Beijing Opera)

English Restoration

    Aphra Behn

    William Congreve

    George Etherege

    William Wycherley

    apron

    breeches roles

Neoclassicism

    Académie Française, aka The Academy

    Unities

Pierre Corneille

Jean Racine

Molière

Georgian

    Richard Brinsley Sheridan

    Oliver Goldsmith

melodrama

minstrel show

    blackface

dramatic interlude 4

Rebellion

Featured plays:

Antigone by Sophocles (441 B.C.E.)

"Master Harold" . . . and the boys by Athol Fugard (1982)

(NOTE: The scripts for these plays, along with additional background information, are available in the companion anthology to this text, *Life Themes: An Anthology of Plays for the Theatre*)

When is it appropriate to go along with rules with which you disagree to keep the peace? When is it time to defy the powers-that-be to create change and bring about a better life? Rebellion may be as simple as resisting a restrictive parental policy, with limited reverberations

within the family, or as catastrophic as the collapse of a government and establishment of a new regime. Or one may lead to the other. Maturity has often been defined as "knowing which battles are worth fighting." In both featured plays, the maturity of the central character is a subject of debate. In both, the characters' actions involve family and household members, but the reverberations go far beyond. In *Antigone*, state security and life and death are at stake. In *"Master Harold,"* a three-person encounter represents what is going on in South Africa as a whole.

Antigone (441 B.C.E.)

Setting: The city-state of Thebes, some centuries earlier

Characters:

Antigone, daughter of Oedipus and Jocasta
Ismene, her sister
The Chorus of Theban Elders
Creon, newly crowned king of Thebes, brother to Jocasta
Haemon, his son, fiancé to Antigone
Eurydice, Creon's wife
Tiresias, a blind prophet
Guard
Messenger

As in most Greek tragedies, much has occurred before the first scene, which is about characters having to process those prior events. Antigone and Ismene have survived the horrific realization that their father had unknowingly married his own mother, making him their brother/father. When he learned this, he gouged out his eyes, left his position as king, and went into voluntary exile, where he died. At this point, however, Antigone's life should be more joyous. She is now engaged to Prince Haemon (he is her first cousin, a common occurrence in ancient monarchies) and on track to be the next queen of Thebes. But a new horrible event has just devastated her. One of her brothers was part of an army that attempted to overthrow the current ruler, her uncle Creon. Her other brother fought

FIGURE D4.1 A scene from Sophocles's *Antigone*, with Jonathan Hyde as Creon, directed by Declan Donnellan and produced by The Old Vic Theatre.

ArenaPal / Topham / The Image Works

on Creon's side and both were killed in battle, but only one will be buried:

> ANTIGONE: Sister, Creon has buried our brother Eteocles with full ceremony and honors, ensuring his place among the dead below. As for our poor Polyneices, however, he has ordered that no one shall bury him or mourn him, but instead leave him lying in a field, a feast for scavenging birds.

She seeks her sister's help in burying Polyneices. But Ismene is a very different person. She has always been more traditionally frail, feminine, and passive. Antigone was more likely to have been a headstrong tomboy who sought ways to assert her will in the world. She has always been resolute. When it comes time to make this very risky decision, Ismene declines, and Antigone is on her own. Her actions help elevate the conflict of the individual versus the state. What is the right of a single person to reject a human edict that she feels violates a higher law? When she is captured, Creon is aghast at her actions:

> CREON: And yet you dared defy the law!
> ANTIGONE: Yes, since it was not God's edict. The final justice, dwelling below makes no such law.
> CREON: But Polyneices died ravaging this land, while Eteocles fell in its defense.
> ANTIGONE: We must honor the dead, nevertheless.
> CREON: But the good man deserves more than the wicked.
> ANTIGONE: Who knows what the gods hold wicked?
> CREON: You do not love someone you have hated, not even after death.
> ANTIGONE: It is not my nature to join in hate, but in love.

The great irony is that both are trying to do the right thing. The question that is impossible to resolve easily is determining when it is better to make decisions for the good of the whole and when it is better to follow one's own heart and personal beliefs. Although his son begs him to spare Antigone and the blind prophet Tiresias warns him to do so, Creon stubbornly insists on her death as an example to any who might further threaten Thebes.

At the end of the play, Creon has maintained his lawful state and there are no more threats of rebellion in sight. He has also lost everyone he loves and has no one with whom to share this "peace." The play ends with our needing to contemplate the effects of the obstinacy of a tyrant versus the inflexibility of a rash young woman. The Chorus, representing the people of Thebes, speaks first to Antigone:

> CHORUS: Your reverence for the dead is a virtue, but the city is strong by the rule of the law. Your willful disposition is what has destroyed you.

Then, Creon enters with his dead son and realizes the depth of his error:

> CREON: Nothing you can say can touch me anymore. My own blind heart has brought me from darkness to final darkness. Dear God I have learned a bitter lesson. Too late!

Finally, the citizens of Thebes reprise the bitter lesson:

> CHORUS: There can be no happiness without wisdom, no wisdom without submission to the gods. The pride of man is harshly punished, until in their suffering, men learn to be wise.

Creon displays the worst kind of inflexibility in a mortal leader. He rejects the counsel of the elders of the city. He spews only venom on the arguments of his niece. He asserts harsh parental authority over his only surviving son. Then, and perhaps worst of all, he rejects the sage advice of the blind prophet Tiresias. Like Oedipus before him, he becomes so single-minded, so blind to alternate points of view, he becomes the instrument of his own tragic destiny. Here is the scene in which his son, Haemon, tries to temper his father's anger with logic and wise counsel (from the translation by Annie McGregor published in *Life Themes: An Anthology of Plays for the Theatre*):

Episode 3

[Enter HAEMON.*]*

> CHORUS: But here is Haemon, the last of your offspring. Does he come grieving for Antigone, his promised bride?
> CREON: We will soon know better than seers could tell us. My son, do you come in rage against your father, having heard my judgment on that girl? Or do I have your love and loyalty, act how I may?
> HAEMON: Father, I am yours, and you are my guide. No marriage is more important than your continuing wisdom.
> CREON: Good, my son, this is the spirit you should maintain in your heart—to stand behind your father's will in all things. This is what men pray for: children who are obedient. Oh, the misery of a man who raises ungrateful sons. Then, my son, do not lose your head over this evil woman. The pleasures of her bed would soon grow cold.

No, spit her out as if she were an enemy, let her go find a husband in Hades. She has shown contempt for the law and for me, and so she will die. If I permit my own kin to defy the law, I will show myself weak before the people. For whoever controls his own household will manage his city as well. Whomever the city chooses to govern, that man must be obeyed in matters small and great and in matters just and unjust. For there is no evil worse than disobedience. This destroys cities; this overturns homes; this scatters armies. Good lives are made by discipline. Therefore we must defend those who respect the law, and we cannot let a woman defeat us. It is better to fall from power by a man's hand, rather than be called weaker than women.

CHORUS: Unless time has stolen our wits, what you say seems wise.

HAEMON: Father, reason is God's gift to man, the highest of all things that we call our own. To say that you are wrong is beyond my power and my desire, yet other men, too, might reason wisely. It is my duty to watch on your behalf all that men say, or do. Fear of you forbids the ordinary citizen to speak such words as would offend your ear. But I can hear these murmurs in the dark, how the city moans for this girl, saying: No woman ever merited death less—none ever died so shamefully for deeds as glorious as hers. They say: Does she not deserve honor? Such is the rumor shrouded in darkness that silently spreads. Father, nothing means more to me than your happiness. What more could any child want? Do not, then, think that your word and no other must be right. Any man who thinks that he alone is wise—such a man may be empty. No, even when a man is wise, he can learn from others. Father, give way and do not cling to your rage. For even from me, a younger man, you may learn good advice.

CHORUS: My king, he is right, that father and son can learn from each other. On both sides there have been wise words.

CREON: Am I then to be taught by the wisdom of a boy?

HAEMON: Not in anything that is not right. But you should look to my thoughts, not to my years.

CREON: Honoring treason is worthy thought?

HAEMON: I would not advise anyone to show respect for treason.

CREON: And did she not commit treason?

HAEMON: The people of this city say no.

CREON: Shall Thebes teach me how to rule?

HAEMON: Now you speak like a child.

CREON: I am the ruler of this city.

HAEMON: No city belongs to one man.

CREON: Does not the city belong to the man in power?

HAEMON: Only if the city is a desert.

CREON: You are fighting on the side of a woman!

HAEMON: Only if you are a woman; *my* concern is for you.

CREON: You traitor, attacking your father in public!

HAEMON: Because I see you making a mistake and committing injustice.

CREON: Am I making a mistake when I respect my own authority?

HAEMON: Yes. You do not have the authority to trample on the rights of God.

CREON: Fool! Taken in by a shameless woman!

HAEMON: You will never see me plead for anything wrong.

CREON: You do. Your every word pleads her case.

HAEMON: And yours, and mine, and God's.

CREON: You can never marry her, not while she is still alive.

HAEMON: Then she will die, and in death destroy another.

CREON: What! Is that a threat?

HAEMON: If you were not my father, I'd say you are insane.

CREON: You woman's slave!

HAEMON: I am sorry. You prefer mute obedience.

CREON: Is that so? I swear by all the gods, you will watch her die. Bring out that hated thing, so that she may die right now!

HAEMON: No, she will not die here—do not even imagine it. Nor shall you ever set eyes on my face again. Indulge in your madness now with your friends who can endure it. [*Exit HAEMON*]

"Master Harold" ... and the boys (1982)

Setting: The St. George's Park Tea Room, Port Elizabeth, South Africa, 1950

Characters:

Hally, a 17-year-old white boy attending a local prep school

Willie, a black man in his forties employed by Hally's family

Sam, a black man also in his forties, who has been with the family longer, is generally wiser and a far better dancer than Willie

Joan Marcus

FIGURE D4.2   A scene from "*Master Harold*" ... *and the boys*, Roundabout Theatre production.

A short play without an intermission, "*Master Harold*" takes place on a blustery late afternoon in a teahouse owned by Hally's parents. It moves from pleasant daily routine through joyous reminiscence to a startling and disillusioning climax, to an ending sufficiently ambiguous to parallel the future of South Africa itself.

In the opening sequence, with Hally returning from a day at school and the "boys" beginning to consider closing up shop, we learn how symbiotic and productive their relationships have been. Sam in particular has mentored Hally and in the absence of his drunken father has provided wisdom. Hally has included Sam in his lessons, helping him to read and explore large and important issues.

However, we get an early glimpse of how little it takes for Hally to snap, pull rank, and become the white "master" of the play's title. Sam has been teasing Willie, who lets fly at him with his slop rag that accidentally hits Hally:

HALLY: [*furious*] For Christ's sake, Willie! What the hell do you think you're doing!

WILLIE. Sorry Master Hally, but it's him . . .

HALLY: Act your bloody age! [*Hurls the rag back at WILLIE*] Cut out the nonsense now and get on with your work. And you too, Sam. Stop fooling around!

Hally has visions of a vastly improved South Africa, with equality and brotherhood and great hopes. He has been living in a dream world of philosophy even though his day-to-day existence has been painful. He continually looks for heroes of social change, honoring rebels, including Gandhi, who brought about change.

HALLY: There is something called progress, you know. We don't exactly burn people at the stake anymore.

SAM: Like Joan of Arc.

HALLY: Correct. If she was captured today, she'd be given a fair trial.

SAM: And then the death sentence.

HALLY: . . . One day somebody is going to get up and give history a kick in the backside and get it going again.

SAM: Like who?

HALLY: They're called social reformers, Sam. My history book is full of them.

SAM: So where's ours?

HALLY: Good question. And I hate to say it, but the answer is I don't know. Maybe he hasn't even been born yet.

Sam tries to explain the allure and joy of the ballroom dancing event in which he and Willie intend to compete:

To be one of the finalists on that dance floor is like . . . like being in a dream about a world in which accidents don't happen.

They dream of such a world, and Hally even intends to write an important essay assignment for school on the ballroom competition. But then he gets a fateful phone call.

At the climactic moment, Hally, realizing that his father is returning home though ill and still desperately alcoholic, takes out the anger he can never express to his parents on the available but undeserving Sam. He rejects the project they have been working on. He even demands that Sam start calling him "Master Harold," as Willie has done for some time. Sam warns him that if this happens, their closeness will end forever and he will never call him Hally again:

HALLY: My mother is right. She's always warning me about allowing you to get too familiar. Well, this time you've gone too far. It's going to stop right now. You're only a servant in here, and don't forget it.

Hally had earlier recalled an idyllic day when Sam made him a kite, helped him fly it, and then for some reason deserted him to go back to work. Only later do we realize that Sam and Hally had to fetch his dead-drunk father from a hotel and carry him home in the humiliating sight of the entire town and that he devised the kite to bring Hally back to cheerful life. We also discover that Sam had to leave him and the bench since it was designated "for whites only":

SAM: You know what that bench means now, and you can leave it any time you choose. All you've got to do is stand up and walk away from it.

The remarkable accomplishment of this play is that it re-creates in microcosm the struggle and dilemma of

South Africa. Like Hally, many desire enlightenment and liberation. They claim to be ready for effective rebellion. They even designate heroes and plan. However, when it gets tight and sticky, the white man resorts to old habits in a knee-jerk response from fear and insecurity that keeps blocking progress.

At the end of the play, Hally is quiet and perhaps deeply regretful and seeking change, but we do not really know. He has been silenced with shame, but he leaves the stage without letting us know if he will move forward toward change or, with the next conflict, reflex back into the sins of his fathers. We don't know if he will get up off that bench or not.

Here is a scene from "*Master Harold*" ... *and the boys* (taken from *Life Themes*):

[HALLY *has just mocked his crippled father; frustrated and ashamed, he lashes out at* SAM *and* WILLIE, *who remind him that he loves his father and should respect him.*]

HALLY: What goes on between me and my Dad is none of your business!
SAM: Then don't tell me about it. If that's all you've got to say about him, I don't want to hear.

[*For a moment* HALLY *is at loss for a response.*]

HALLY: Just get on with your bloody work and shut up.
SAM: Swearing at me won't help you.
HALLY: Yes, it does! Mind your own fucking business and shut up!
SAM: Okay. If that's the way you want it, I'll stop trying. [*He turns away. This infuriates* HALLY *even more.*]
HALLY: Good. Because what you've been trying to do is meddle in something you know nothing about. All that concerns you in here, Sam, is to try and do what you get paid for—keep the place clean and serve the customers. In plain words, just get on with your job. My mother is right. She's always warning me about allowing you to get too familiar. Well, this time you've gone too far. It's going to stop right now. [*No response from* SAM] You're only a servant in here, and don't forget it. [*Still no response.* HALLY *is trying hard to get one*] And as far as my father is concerned, all you need to remember is that he is your boss.

SAM: [*Needled at last*] No, he isn't. I get paid by your mother.
HALLY: Don't argue with me, Sam!
SAM: Then don't say he's my boss.
HALLY: He's a white man and that's good enough for you.
SAM: I'll try to forget you said that.
HALLY: Don't! Because you won't be doing me a favor if you do. I'm telling you to remember it.

[*A pause.* SAM *pulls himself together and makes one last effort.*]

SAM: Hally, Hally . . . ! Come on now. Let's stop before it's too late. You're right. We are on dangerous ground. If we're not careful, somebody is going to get hurt.
HALLY: It won't be me.
SAM: Don't be so sure.
HALLY: I don't know what you're talking about, Sam.
SAM: Yes, you do.
HALLY: [*Furious*] Jesus, I wish you would stop trying to tell me what I do and what I don't know.

[*SAM gives up. He turns to* WILLIE.]

SAM: Let's finish up.
HALLY: Don't turn your back on me! I haven't finished talking.
[*He grabs* SAM *by the arm and tries to make him turn around.* SAM *reacts with a flash of anger.*]
SAM: Don't do that, Hally! [*Facing the boy*] All right, I'm listening. Well? What do you want to say to me?
HALLY: [*Pause as* HALLY *looks for something to say*] To begin with, why don't you also start calling me Master Harold, like Willie.
SAM: Do you mean that?
HALLY: Why the hell do you think I said it?
SAM: And if I don't?
HALLY: You might just lose your job.
SAM: [*Quietly and very carefully*] If you make me say it once, I'll never call you anything else again.
HALLY: So? [*The boy confronts the man.*] Is that meant to be a threat?
SAM: Just telling you what will happen if you make me do that. You must decide what it means to you.
HALLY: Well, I have. It's good news. Because that is exactly what Master Harold wants from now on. Think of it as a little lesson in respect, Sam, that's long overdue, and I hope you remember it as well as you do your geography. I can tell you now that

somebody who will be glad to hear I've finally given it to you will be my Dad. Yes! He agrees with my Mom. He's always going on about it as well. "You must teach the boys to show you more respect, my son."

SAM: So now you can stop complaining about going home. Everybody is going to be happy tonight.

HALLY: That's perfectly correct. You see, you mustn't get the wrong idea about me and my Dad, Sam. We also have our good times together. Some bloody good laughs. He's got a marvelous sense of humor. Want to know what our favorite joke is? He gives out a big groan, you see, and says: "It's not fair, is it, Hally?" Then I have to ask: "What, chum?" And then he says: "A nigger's arse" . . . and we both have a good laugh.

[The men stare at him with disbelief.]

HALLY: What's the matter, Willie? Don't you catch the joke? You always were a bit slow on the uptake. It's what is called a pun. You see, fair means both light in color and to be just and decent. [He turns to SAM.] I thought you would catch it, Sam.

SAM: Oh ja, I catch it all right.

HALLY: But it doesn't appeal to your sense of humor.

SAM: Do you really laugh?

HALLY: Of course.

SAM: To please him? Make him feel good?

HALLY: No, for heaven's sake! I laugh because I think it's a bloody good joke.

SAM: You're really trying hard to be ugly, aren't you? And why drag poor old Willie into it? He's done nothing to you except show you the respect you want so badly. That's also not being fair, you know . . . and I mean just or decent.

WILLIE: It's all right, Sam. Leave it now.

SAM: It's me you're after. You should just have said "Sam's arse" . . . because that's the one you're trying to kick. Anyway, how do you know it's not fair? You've never seen it. Do you want to? [He drops his trousers and underpants and presents his backside for Hally's inspection.] Have a good look. A real Basuto arse . . . which is about as nigger as they can come. Satisfied? [Trousers up.]

Now you can make your Dad even happier when you go home tonight. Tell him I showed you my arse and he is quite right. It's not fair. And if it will give him an even better laugh next time, I'll also let *him* have a look. Come, Willie, let's finish up and go.

[SAM and WILLIE start to tidy up the tea room. HALLY doesn't move. He waits for a moment when SAM passes him.]

HALLY: [Quietly] Sam.

[SAM stops and looks expectantly at the boy. HALLY spits in his face. A long and heartfelt groan from WILLIE. For a few seconds, SAM doesn't move.]

SAM: [Taking out a handkerchief and wiping his face] It's all right, Willie. [To HALLY] Ja, well, you've done it . . . Master Harold. Yes. I'll start calling you that from now on. It won't be difficult anymore. You've hurt yourself, Master Harold. I saw it coming. I warned you. But you wouldn't listen. You've just hurt yourself *bad*. And you're a coward, Master Harold. The face you should be spitting in is your father's . . . but you used mine, because you think you're safe inside your fair skin, and this time I don't mean just or decent. [Pause. Then, moving violently toward HALLY] Should I hit him, Willie?

WILLIE: [Stopping SAM] No. Boet Sam.

SAM: [Violently] Why not?

WILLIE: It won't help, Boet Sam.

SAM: I don't want to help. I want to hurt him.

WILLIE: You also hurt yourself.

SAM: And if he had done it to you, Willie?

WILLIE: Me? Spit at me like I was a dog? [A thought that had not occurred to him before. He looks at HALLY.] Ja. Then I want to hit him. I want to hit him hard! [A dangerous few seconds as the men stand staring at the boy. WILLIE turns away, shaking his head.] But maybe all I do is go cry at the back. He's little boy, Boet Sam. Little *white* boy. Long trousers now, but he's still little boy.

Expansions 4 | Sophocles versus Aeschylus and Euripides

Here are some explorations of terms introduced in Chapter 7 and Chapter 8 in terms of these two plays:

Sophocles versus Aeschylus and Euripides

Sophocles frequently bested both his senior, Aeschylus, and his junior, Euripides, in dramatic competitions. He was the all-time festival champion, with 18 victories. During his own lifetime, *Antigone* was regarded as his greatest work. Contemporary critics tend to place his "prequel" to that play, *Oedipus Rex* (in which the tragic events of Antigone and Ismene's parents are delineated), as the greatest Greek tragedy of all. But from the point of view of critical acclaim and frequency of productions, *Antigone* is unquestionably the most-produced Greek play in our own time owing in part to the universal issues involved and even more to the playwright's superb balancing of questions, which will never be fully resolved.

The Chorus

While the Greek chorus is intended to provide a link between story and audience, it is such a strange device for many of us that it can actually be the most off-putting part of a production. Who are all these people, and why do they keep hanging around and sometimes speaking in unison? Sophocles's choice to cast them as Elders of the city works far better for a modern audience than some other choruses. These are people who would logically be present to advise and offer good counsel. They have a stake in the future of Thebes and vivid memories of its past. They offer wise advice (if only the major characters would take it), and when they speak as a whole, it is a tribute to the playwright's genius that these are ritual words of wisdom that Elders might indeed memorize and chant as one.

The Unities

While it is no surprise that *Antigone* can be held up as a perfect example of Aristotle's view of how a play should be structured, ironically, *"Master Harold"* also adheres strictly to the Greek Unities.

Both plays take place in real time and in one single locale of a somewhat public nature (the fact that no customers appear in the tea room does not mean that they could not appear at any moment). They feature three central characters, including a young headstrong protagonist. They are comparatively short and very likely to be presented without intermission. While Fugard has never stated an intention to model his play on ancient Greek tragedies, in every structural way it qualifies. It even spends the requisite huge amount of time processing what went on in the past, revealing the events to have a different meaning than when they are first presented.

African Diaspora

The separation of South Africans from their own cultural roots and often their homes is presented in a highly intriguing way in *"Master Harold."* While they are still waiting for a major black African playwright to attempt to find reconnections and a full honoring of native traditions, Fugard, a white playwright, remains perhaps the most eloquent chronicler of events and predicaments. However, he is/was Hally, and that is the character whose history and circumstances are most fully delineated. We know nothing about where Sam and Willie came from or how they ended up working for this family. Did they journey to the city from small villages? Have they always lived here? We know nothing of their roots. Their spare time is spent playing and fantasizing about Western ballroom dancing. Their idyllic images are Fred Astaire and Ginger Rogers, Count Basie and Sarah Vaughan, all distinctly Western (in fact American) cultural icons. What is uniquely African about these men we will never know. It is left up to the actors to flesh out distinct and powerful identities. This was something that was accomplished vividly in the first New York production of the play, wherein the roles were played by James Earl Jones and Danny Glover, two of America's greatest African American actors.

Glinda (Lucy Durack) and Elphaba (Amanda Harrison) in the musical *Wicked* during a preview in Sydney.

part IV

How Does Theatre Vary?

In the past 150 years, various theatre forms began to stabilize and compete, while European influences spread around the world. In Part IV, we will look at the ways in which the styles of theatre vary, including their origins, intentions, and continued influence today.

In Chapter 9, we will discuss how realism, our dominant style of performance, came into being. Romanticism, naturalism, and magic realism, which share many of its elements, are also discussed.

In Chapter 10, we will examine more stylized and "less real" theatrical conventions, including a number of influential "Isms" and the most popular Western entertainment form that is least like realism: musical theatre.

In Dramatic Interlude 5, which follows these two chapters, we will explore dreams as manifested in *The Three Sisters* by Anton Chekhov and *Bitter Cane* by Genny Lim, instances of realism and magic realism. These plays share a concern with telling the truth, but it is not the same truth.

In Expansions 5, we apply the concepts laid out in the two chapters to the two featured plays.

This Comparisons of Forms table summarizes some of the key differences between the styles that we'll be exploring in the next two chapters.

Comparison of Forms

	ROMANTICISM	REALISM	NATURALISM	"ISMS"
Time	Epics, perhaps covering lifetimes	Present or recent past; usually a period of a few days or weeks	Present or recent past; scenes or entire play in actual time	Distorted, irrelevant, slippery
Space	May be exotic, elaborate, fanciful, or vast	Seems like actual living spaces but angled for sight lines, moderate detail	Total, detailed recreation of actual settings	Distorted, symbolic, poetic or nightmarish
Values	Freewheeling, emotional expression	Solving problems	Life unedited; complete truth	Interior life of the artist; some anger; rejection of "normal" experience
Structure	Unpredictable, epic	Well-made play with clear progression from definite start to finish	"Slice of life"	Completely subjective; variable
Pleasure	Wild, over-the-top, fantastic adventures	Honest, frank portrayal but discrete, conventional	Unedited, even conspicuously perverse, clinical, unhampered by social conventions	Wildly varied, depending on whim of the artist
Senses	Extravagant visuals, bright, varied, larger than life; speech may include poetic tones and extravagant language	Appearance of life; everyday speech pattern but with sharper diction and intent	"Warts and all," common speech, gritty; usually dark	Assaulted by images; appeal to unconscious

chapter 9

VARIETIES OF REALISM

Hedda Gabler, featuring Cate Blanchett in the title role, produced by the Sydney Theatre Company in 2004.

Marlon Brando (Stanley) kneeling before Kim Hunter (Stella) in a scene from the original Broadway production of Tennessee Williams's *A Streetcar Named Desire*.

Eliot Elisofon/Time Life Pictures/Getty Images

Lesson Objectives:

Upon completion of this chapter, you will be able to:

1. Apply the revolutionary thinking of the nineteenth and twentieth centuries to art in any medium, particularly to the performing arts.
2. Identify the differences between melodrama, romanticism, realism, and naturalism, and apply critical analysis to plays and films that you see.
3. Identify the early pioneers of each new style.
4. Identify American masters of realism and naturalism that followed in the footsteps of these pioneers.

Introduction

By the mid-nineteenth century, new experiments in style transformed the theatre from conformity to the challenge of finding each artist's unique vision of the truth. In the next two chapters, we look at the modern theatre and its many distinctive varieties, first realistic or semirealistic styles, then varieties of theatre that are overtly non-realistic, or even anti-realistic. These varieties are found in almost infinite combinations throughout the world today. Theatre styles from all corners of the globe have become available for artists to mix and match, creating their own visions for their audiences. In these chapters, we will look at the "call for change" (what made the new variety necessary or attractive) and then discuss the look, sound, acting, and major early plays and playwrights of each style.

Global Impact of the European Worldview

Realism, romanticism, naturalism, and magic realism—styles first created in Europe and the Americas—had enormous impact on theatre throughout the world, even in places where traditional theatre had never for a moment attempted to depict gritty daily life. So why the global impact? Colonialism. By the nineteenth century, most of the known world was under the control of European and American powers. The old saying "The sun never sets on the British Empire" was true. France, Germany, Spain, and Portugal had colonial empires nearly as vast as Britain's. Nineteenth-century Western ideals infiltrated these far-flung areas of the world, and few places escaped the "gift" of European civilization. Along with armies and governments, colonists imported every possible aspect of daily life in their attempt to transform ancient cultures into mirror images of their own. This import of forms included theatre.

Nineteenth-Century Changes

Realism and its alternate forms did not develop in a vacuum. Political rebellion was rampant in nineteenth-century Europe. The American Revolution of 1776 was only the first in a series of revolutions aimed at overthrowing monarchies and ensuring the rights of the common person. In 1789, the French began one of the longest and bloodiest revolutions, culminating in terror when the revolutionaries began killing their own in a cycle of manic violence. Belgium, Italy, and the German provinces all revolted against their monarchies in 1848. The philosophies of democracy were growing stronger each year, but the price was often bloodshed and suffering.

Revolutionary thinking in science and philosophy fed those in economic, social, and political arenas. Four of the most influential reformers were Auguste Comte, Karl Marx, Charles Darwin, and Sigmund Freud. All were the product of earlier innovations, including the development of the "scientific method," which argued that knowledge grew out of a process of observation, hypothesis, experimentation, and analysis. Unlike many Victorians, these men did not look around them and assume that all was right with the world—they saw a world that needed changing.

Auguste Comte (1798–1857), a French philosopher, was the founder of modern sociology. He became convinced that the application of the scientific method to social concerns would result in the beneficial, moral, and intellectual reorganization of society. He rejected all ideas of God or metaphysical explanation, believing that application of the scientific method could result in the perfection of human society. This theory deeply influenced the development of realism, which also called for social reform.

Karl Marx (1818–1883), in partnership with Friedrich Engels, created a revolutionary philosophy called "scientific socialism," articulated in their famous work, *The Communist Manifesto*, in 1848. Marx believed that human history was organized around a system of exploiters and the exploited, oppressors and the oppressed. He believed that only revolution would overthrow the capitalists who profited from the labor of the working class, now mired in poverty. Only organized violence could displace those in power, and then a new classless society could emerge in which all were equal. His vision of a society with no preferential "birthright" had a profound effect on political and literary developments. The twentieth-century Communist revolutions in Russia and China led to the development of strongly realistic and naturalistic "People's" art under the critical eye of the censors there. Non-realistic art, in all media, was condemned as "anti-revolutionary," the corrupt art of a corrupt class system.

Charles Darwin (1809–1882) was perhaps the most influential thinker of the period. His book *The Origin of Species* (1859), published after 20 years spent collecting data, argued that species evolve through variation and natural selection ("survival of the fittest"). He theorized that the two primary factors influencing evolution are heredity and environment. The theory of evolution challenged every traditional belief system, including biblical accounts of creation, divine intervention, and a covenant between humans and a supreme deity. It also challenged the belief in destiny and free will; instead, we are essentially all victims of circumstance whose choices are determined by forces over which we have no control. On the other hand, if species evolve through survival of the fittest to higher levels of the evolutionary scale, so can society. In the drama, the naturalist movement focused on the idea of individuals trying to cope with environments that they could not control, while the realist movement was interested in using theatre to help society evolve into a higher state of being.

Sigmund Freud (1856–1939) was the most shocking and controversial pioneer of them all. His theories of the unconscious mind, sexuality and repression, and dark and unconscious motivations influencing behavior were frightening to the Victorian middle-class mindset. He attacked the very heart of respectability, appearance, and female "virtue" (lack of sexuality) that ordered the Victorian world. His work would also help revolutionize theatre, by encouraging exploration of the reality that hid behind the mask of social convention.

These revolutions, occurring throughout Europe and the United States, led social themes and scientific inquiry to the theatre. By the mid-1800s, the extravagant characters, repetitive plots, and callow insights of melodrama were losing their appeal to young theatre artists raised in an atmosphere of revolution. Romanticism grew out of the turbulence of the late eighteenth century, and evolved side by side with melodrama. Romanticism was a call for change A group of young writers searched for a new theatre espousing the rights of the individual, the glory of nature, and the power of emotion.

Romanticism

The segue from full-blown melodrama to realism comes through the transitional movement called **romanticism**. In this style, feelings were more important than thoughts. Anything natural was good. Appearance meant nothing; emotional truth meant everything. A true hero, forced to stand outside society, lived life as passionately and fully as it should be lived. Beyond mere earthly life lies, a higher truth, which was found through art and feeling, and where spiritual happiness was to be pursued. The sublime in nature and art were to be worshipped. Everything exotic, picturesque, and grotesque had value.

Berlin/Hamburger Kunsthalle, Hamburg, Germany/Elke Walford/Art Resource, NY

FIGURE 9.1   Caspar David Friedrich's *The Sea of Ice*, also known as *The Wreck of Hope*. This painting can remind one of the final chapters of *Frankenstein*, a novel of the romanticist movement, by Mary Shelley.

The hero often needed to die by the final curtain after following his heart in an uncomprehending world too full of reason, machines, and rules—a world spoiled by moving too far away from its natural state. Still, to die and leave the physical world was not too great a price to pay for being true to oneself.

Ironically, Asian theatre for centuries had embraced many of the production components taken on by romanticism, but without its agenda.

The Look

Romantic works could be as grand and sweeping in scope as the biggest opera or musical. Large casts and spectacle were common. Settings were often long ago and/or far away. While romanticism was influential in bringing historical accuracy in costuming, the look is likely to be *flamboyantly* historical. The vision of nature tended toward glorious sunrises and tornados, not just a blah day with a few new weeds in the garden. This theatre style sympathized with the paintings of Caspar David Friedrich, John Constable, J. M. W. Turner, and the famous Hudson River School of dramatic landscape painting.

AYN RAND
AUTHOR AND ESSAYIST

To a Romanticist, a background is a background, not a theme. His vision is always focused on man—on the fundamentals of man's nature, on those problems and those aspects of his character that apply to any age and any country.

FRIEDRICH SCHILLER
PLAYWRIGHT AND PHILOSOPHER

[N]othing is so unworthy of man than to suffer violence, for violence undoes him. Whoever offers us violence calls into question nothing less than our humanity; whoever suffers this cravenly throws his humanity away.

Tate, London/Art Resource, NY

FIGURE 9.2 John Constable's *Hadleigh Castle,* 1829. This would make a wonderful setting for a gothic romanticist drama.

Rischgitz/Stringer/Hulton Archive/Getty Images

FIGURE 9.3   Sarah Bernhardt as Napoleon II and Benoit-Constant Coquelin as Flambeau in a production of *L'Aiglon* by Edmond Rostand at Her Majesty's Theatre, London, in 1901.

The Sound

Romantic plays used verse or poetic prose on a grand level, with a great variety of expressiveness. Freewheeling, lengthy, and passionate speeches were common and demanded a large vocal range as well as a delivery that could be defiant and sentimental without becoming strident and cloying. Language reflected the music of Frédéric Chopin, Franz Liszt, Richard Wagner, and Pyotr Ilyich Tchaikovsky; and the poetry of William Blake, Percy Bysshe Shelley, Mary Shelley, and George Gordon Byron (aka Lord Byron).

The Acting

Pulling off romanticism required great bravado and expressiveness. Actors needed a willingness to hit operatic heights. Acting was tour de force, bravura playing, both soulful and expansive. Training in classical ballet and great beauty of vocal tone helped. This was full-blown drama, and it was not for those who tended toward half-hearted presentation.

Early Major Plays and Playwrights: Schiller, Goethe, and Hugo

Major playwrights of this genre were Germans **Friedrich von Schiller** (1759–1805) and **Johann Wolfgang von Goethe** (1749–1832). These two men defined what became known as the ***Sturm und Drang*** or "Storm and Stress" style of romanticism. In their plays, we generally find a disillusioned and highly emotional central character in conflict with a corrupt and conventional society.

Schiller's quintessential romantic play, *The Robbers*, pits two brothers against each other in alternating scenes. One pursues wealth and power, while the other attempts to lead a revolution against Germany's tyrannical class structure. This highly emotional play, with elevated and at times bombastic language and much onstage physical violence, is considered by some to have achieved the pinnacle of romantic ideals.

Goethe's most famous play, *Faust* (1808), is episodic and vast in scope, as the old tale of a learned man who sells his soul to the devil is retold to explore the romantic vision of redemption through individual human struggle. This play covers many years of the protagonist's life as he travels all over the globe and even into the realms of supernatural beings.

In France, **Victor Hugo** (1802–1885) wrote *Hernani* (1830), a play so controversial that it led to rioting in the theatre between Hugo's supporters and the classicists, both groups having filled the theatre at the express invitation of Hugo himself. *Hernani* tells the story of a beautiful young noblewoman who captures the hearts of the king, her noble uncle, and a handsome, rebellious bandit, Hernani (guess who she falls for?). After much adventure and hair-raising escapes, the bandit and his true love are united. They discover

FIGURE 9.4 Johann Wolfgang von Goethe, the giant of European literature in the nineteenth century, paved the way for the movements that continue to captivate us today.

JOHANN WOLFGANG VON GOETHE
PLAYWRIGHT

He only earns his freedom and his life who takes them every day by storm.

MICHELLE FRAM COHEN
AUTHOR AND ESSAYIST

[T]he [romantic] heroes rise above hereditary and environmental influences. Instead of following a path prescribed by outside forces, the characters pursue their convictions and accept the consequences.

THEATRE IN MEDIA

Romanticism Today

Our current, disillusioned age tends to be unreceptive to romanticism and its flights of fancy. Some claim that musicals (such as *Les Misérables*, *Miss Saigon*, and *The Phantom of the Opera*) are now the almost-exclusive purveyors of this form, though many of the elements are present in *Tree of Life*, *Melancholia*, and *Hugo*. Many films tend to some degree to romanticize the human experience. Romantic comedies, melo-dramatic romances, some soap operas, and so-called "chick flicks" include some of the elements, but in watered down form. But who knows? We may see a full-blown revival once audiences get bored with post-modern skepticism.

that he is in fact a nobleman, and they receive her uncle's blessing to marry. But on the very night of their marriage, the unrepentant king orders the death of Hernani, who in honor must obey the summons. His lovely wife joins him in draining the poisoned cup, and they die together in an "ecstasy" of devotion and sacrifice. This emotionalism and pathos were naturally anti-thetical to the aims of the neoclassicists (see Chapter 8) who wanted all behavior controlled by reason, not passion.

Even Henrik Ibsen, considered by many the "Father of Modern Realism," dabbled in romanticism early in his long and prolific career. His plays, *The Vikings at Helgeland* (1858), *Brand* (1866), and *Peer Gynt* (1867), followed the romantic manifesto in using the historical epic, vast scale, and unre-strained passion to underscore the individual's quest to find a place in a corrupt world.

Unrestrained by the rules of neoclassicism, the romantics often created works that were almost impossible to stage, but they broke free of the rigid guidelines that were stifling dra-matic creativity throughout Europe.

Robbie Jack/Corbis

FIGURE 9.5   Before moving on to realism, Henrik Ibsen dabbled in romanticism as in his *Peer Gynt*. Gerry Mulgrew plays Old Peer in the National Theatre of Scotland's production at the Barbican Theatre in London.

Realism

Freud's work on the clinical analysis of personalities, Ibsen's scripts of carefully crafted social import, and Konstantin Stanislavski's System of acting (see Chapter 4) all reflect an interest in seeing life portrayed onstage as it is lived off-stage. The Moscow Art Theatre named its Fourth Studio "The Realistic Theatre." For the first time in history, plays did not focus on people who were exceptional by title, power, beauty, intellect, or eccentricity of personality. Now, the characters onstage could be the people next door.

FIGURE 9.6 Anton Chekhov's masterpiece of modern realism, *The Seagull*, performed by the National Theatre, London, featuring Hattie Morahan as Nina and Ben Whishaw as Konstantin.

Call for Change

Like most theatre movements, **realism** begins with a manifesto or a call for changing the status quo, proposing that it was time to reject the impractical and visionary drama of the romantics. Instead, theatre should show how everyday people react to their environments. Characters should be multidimensional, internally motivated, and believably portrayed. Plays need to explore relationships onstage through psychology, environment, and the five senses. Only drama that has direct relevance to the life of the viewer has genuine *meaning* to the viewer. We all experience social and domestic problems, and so the stage needs to illuminate them.

The Look

Conscientious effort at accuracy is made in all scenic elements, allowing some editing of irrelevant details and some partial or skeletal sets. Settings look like modifications of actual locales. An attempt is made to create the feeling of a real living space, with considerable use of props. Largely through the influence of Émile Zola, the box set develops (see Chapter 5), although sometimes several settings are represented with a cinematic overlapping of action. Costumes and properties try to be true to both historical period and character personality.

The Sound

Realistic plays revolutionized the sound of theatre through the use of pauses, nonverbals, incomplete thoughts, and informal sentence structure—all the characteristics of speech on the street or in the home. Scripts are prose, barely heightened from normal conversation. They reject any hint of declamatory artifice in delivery while maintaining clarity.

The Acting

Performers need a capacity for "public solitude" (behaving in front of others as if they are actually alone so that we really feel we are eavesdropping on their lives) and a strong sense of natural interaction with other actors, props, and setting. They must have believability and the ability to tap internal resources to find truth. Stanislavski's system was developed to assist realistic portrayal. Actors need an eye for contemporary detail, shading, and nuance. At the same time, they must have emotional availability and the capacity to play with depth of feeling at will.

FIGURE 9.7 Influential Norwegian playwright Henrik Ibsen experimented with many styles, but his realistic period had the greatest impact on Victorian life.

HENRIK IBSEN

PLAYWRIGHT

The spirit of truth and the spirit of freedom—they are the pillars of society.

Early Major Plays and Playwrights: Ibsen, Chekhov, and Shaw

The earliest and most influential realist playwrights were Henrik Ibsen, Anton Chekhov, and George Bernard Shaw. Their examinations of the real lives behind social masks were extremely controversial and almost universally loathed by the Victorian middle class. But their work set the world on fire for young people, social reformers, and progressive thinkers and became the groundwork for the dominant style of Western theatre today.

Norwegian **Henrik Ibsen** (1828–1906) was probably the most influential figure in modern theatre. Over his long career, he worked in many styles, including romanticism and non-realism. But his realistic period from 1877 to 1890 produced plays that sent a tidal wave through the smug conventions of Victorian life. Deeply affected by the revolutionary developments that he witnessed, Ibsen chose to see drama as a means for social change. He tore the mask off the middle class to reveal the suffering and corruption just beneath the surface. He wanted his plays to change society for the better.

In his first realist play, *A Doll's House* (1879), Ibsen takes a scathing look beneath the surface of the perfect Victorian family. His heroine, Nora, a mother herself, is little more than a child, having transferred her dependence on her father to her husband. She believes that he will protect her and defend her at any cost, as she has tried to do for him. When she learns that he is more concerned about social appearances than the truth, her disillusionment is so profound that she decides to leave him and learn to live as an adult. In what has been called "the door slam heard around the world," the play ends with Nora's exit, leaving her befuddled husband behind.

This play was so controversial that it was banned in his native Norway, creating a firestorm of angry criticism from audiences and critics alike. His response was the second of his realist plays, *Ghosts* (1881), inspired by the idea of what became of the woman who *didn't* leave her husband, who stayed no matter what he did because social convention demanded it. The play features a mature woman with a grown son, who only after the death of her abusive husband begins to think for herself and regret the wasted years of her marriage. Tragedy envelops the family as the ghosts of the past are revealed as destroyers of the present.

Ibsen's next and most scathing social attack was *An Enemy of the People* (1882), in which the doctor of a spa resort town attempts to close the public baths when they become contaminated. Although he believes that he is working for the good of the community, that same community turns on him, reviling him as a traitor to their economic interests. Ultimately, the doctor is completely ostracized from the community as "an enemy of the people." This play has been in constant production since its nineteenth-century introduction, with a variety of adaptations. One striking adaptation was that of American playwright Arthur Miller in the 1950s. In 1989, it was also made into a popular Bengali film titled *Ganashatru*, literally meaning "the enemy of the people," by Oscar-winning Indian filmmaker Satyajit Ray.

Because Ibsen's stated intention was to change society, his plays are called social realism. **Anton Chekhov**, a Russian writing nearly 20 years later, created four masterpieces of modern realism. With the winds of the Russian Revolution already blowing, his plays seem gentler, more nostalgic than Ibsen's, as though he knew that change was coming for his characters whether they were ready for it or not. *The Seagull, Uncle Vanya, Three Sisters* (see Dramatic Interlude 5), and *The Cherry Orchard* all look into the quiet desperation of an elite class of Russian society. They are not scathing criticisms but rather compassionate glimpses, reminders that privilege does not necessarily mean happiness. Characters find their lives restricted and their options limited. Their wealth is fading away, and their social worlds shrink daily. Chekhov himself was dying of tuberculosis as he wrote his final plays. Is it possible that he sensed that within only 13 years, his families and their kind would all be swept away in the Revolution? His unique plays defy characterization, except as Chekhovian realism.

Bettmann/CORBIS

FIGURE 9.8 Modern realist playwright Anton Chekhov.

ANTON CHEKHOV
PLAYWRIGHT

I try to catch every sentence, every word you and I say, and quickly lock all these sentences and words away in my literary storehouse because they might come in handy.

FIGURE 9.9   George Bernard Shaw (seated) surrounded by cast members on the set of the BBC's 1937 production of *How He Lied to Her Husband,* an early television broadcast in the realistic style.

GEORGE BERNARD SHAW

PLAYWRIGHT

My method is to take the utmost trouble to find the right thing to say, and then to say it with the utmost levity.

George Bernard Shaw (1856–1950) was more closely allied with Ibsen's approach than with Chekhov's, bringing Ibsen's "obscene" realism to England. A socialist, Shaw wrote to criticize society and inspire change, sometimes through charm and wit, sometimes through savage satire. His early plays were first published in an anthology titled *Plays: Pleasant and Unpleasant* (1898). Among the "pleasant" plays was *Arms and the Man,* a charming, witty attack on the glorification of war (see Dramatic Interlude 2). Among the "unpleasant" ones was *Mrs. Warren's Profession,* a scathing look at Victorian hypocrisy about prostitution. In his long career, Shaw produced many volumes of work, both fiction and nonfiction.

Following in the footsteps of these three great innovators were some of the giants of American theatre: Eugene O'Neill, Arthur Miller, Lillian Hellman, and Tennessee Williams. These in turn inspired the contemporary works of Wendy Wasserstein, Michael Weller, Lanford Wilson, Marsha Norman, Tina Howe, A. J. Gurney, Aaron Sorkin, Beth Henley, and August Wilson (see Dramatic Interlude 6 for more on Wilson).

THEATRE IN MEDIA

Realism in Film and Television

Most dramatic cinema attempts realism. When receiving negative reviews, films are often criticized for their lack of reality or believability. The slow demise of the traditional sitcom probably has something to do with increasing discontent with how different most of them are from the lives of viewers. The recent hit in the traditional sitcom category, *Modern Family,* while updating the participants, stays close to the everyday family conflicts experienced by much of the viewing public. While television comedies will probably revive in some form, they will also likely need to reinvent themselves.

Our vision of what is "real" changes with time. Some films of the 1940s and 1950s, thought then to be gritty in their realism, seem overwrought now—too much dramatic background music, too much overtly tortured acting, and too much telegraphing of danger. We have grown far more critical than prior generations of any onscreen behavior perceived as inauthentic. James Dean remains an icon of realistic performance to this day, with only three films as proof.

If a film departs from real life in a genuinely imaginative way, it will attract attention, and theorists are always predicting the death of realism as passé. But the reflection of our own lives, minus the mundane distracting details, is a subject of which we never tire. Of the nine films nominated for Academy Awards for Best Picture in 2012, all but two dealt with realism and the two that were not were magic realism.

Naturalism

Call for Change

For artists of **naturalism**, realism only *begins* to oppose artificial theatricality; it does not go far enough. It chooses which elements of life to present, often suggesting solutions to social problems. What is needed instead is stark reality, with no compromise—life with details, including the ugly, distracting, and irrelevant. The keys to all truth are scientific method and scrutiny. Individuals cannot be responsible for what they do because heredity and environment overwhelm them. Plays should be more human and less social in orientation. No characters are specifically sympathetic; they just act and react, like any other organism. Plays do not need to progress rapidly or have clear climaxes. Endings can be pessimistic, ironic, cynical, and even disappointing, just as life is. Actors should *live* the life of their characters onstage rather than just *play* them.

The movement had a decidedly pessimistic tendency and rarely focused on the positive details that are every bit as "natural" as the dark side. And some would argue that some choices are essential for a work to be called art. Perhaps the pioneers of naturalism are dancing in their graves over the current glut of reality shows on television. Eventually, filmmakers adopted the detail necessary for naturalism, but its impact remains in the theatre today.

Image statements might include: "warts and all," "don't look away," "all are victims," "the uncensored mind," and "who needs an ending?" This is theatre eavesdropping on the dark side of human nature. Naturalism is the alley behind realism's street.

The Look

Phenomenal set detail may be employed, so that water runs and stoves cook. In a famous André Antoine production, real

HENRIK IBSEN
PLAYWRIGHT

(Contrasting his realistic writing with that of naturalistic writer Êmile Zola.) Zola descends into the cesspool to take a bath, I to cleanse it.

FIGURE 9.10 An example of a naturalistic production, *Of Mice and Men* by John Steinbeck, presented at the Mermaid Theatre, London.

© Photostage

flies buzz around real beef hanging in a meat market scene. A highly contained box set is likely. Real clothes are better choices than costumes, which will require minutely accurate detail to pass naturalistic muster. The environment is a major character. It has more influence than any human does in the play. Movement needs to seem spontaneous. The fourth wall is very much in place, and the audience is never acknowledged. Actors are less likely to cheat out to the audience. They are more likely to turn their backs to the house and generally drop theatrical conventions in favor of accuracy.

The Sound

Speech may be muffled or even mumbled if it is true to character. Language is basic, gritty prose, often lower class in syntax. Conversations do not necessarily go anywhere. Snatches of dialogue may be lost or drowned out by background noise or distractions. Just as very few of us in life say exactly what we mean, characters tend to circumvent and talk around their issues.

The Acting

Naturalistic acting needs great subtlety and a complete lack of artifice. A simplicity that belies technique is essential. Because most actors are so accustomed to editing or exaggerating themselves for performance, naturalistic acting is much more difficult than it first seems. A complete concentration and absolute ability to play *in* the moment and to go *with* the moment is needed. A deeply rooted psychological comprehension of character is essential, as well as strong empathy and ability to play the complexity of personality. There are no stars in naturalism, so a strong sense of ensemble or group consciousness is needed along with a willingness to "let it all hang out." One actor referred to his role as a "scratch and itch and belch and fart" part. He meant naturalism.

Early Major Plays and Playwrights: Zola, Strindberg, and Antoine

In the 1870s, French writer **Émile Zola** (1840–1902) coined the phrase **"slice of life"** (perhaps realism was merely a bite or sip of life) and wrote *Therese Raquin*, the first naturalistic drama. His introduction for that play was the complete manifesto of the movement. His work depicted society in minute, often sordid detail.

August Strindberg (1849–1912), the Swedish playwright who later rejected naturalism, wrote several influential naturalist plays, including *The Father* and *Miss Julie.* Like Zola, he refused to beautify human behavior and never suggested an alternative to the pain and misery of life. In *The Father* (1887), he dissects a family in crisis, as the parents tear each other apart emotionally over the fate of their only child.

Strindberg believed that men and women were destined to mortal combat, and the play ends on a disturbingly unresolved note of agony. Equally, in *Miss Julie,* class struggle and sex intersect in a fatal combat between a young upper-class woman and her father's servant. Another servant simply observes, expecting nothing but disaster and being glumly content when it occurs. With no solutions, no happy endings, and no chance at redemption, Strindberg's naturalist plays are dark and disturbing but powerfully real.

André Antoine (1858–1943) founded *Théâtre Libre,* or "Free Theatre," which was devoted to naturalism and became the model for experimental theatres around the world. His absolute commitment to minute detail and his refusal to cater to entertainment values had an impact on much of Western theatre, in part by making all realize how much they had been selecting and omitting from performance.

FIGURE 9.11 Swedish playwright and novelist August Strindberg.

FIGURE 9.12 Caroline Cave as Miss Julie and Kevin Hanchard as Jean in the Vancouver Plays Theatre 2009 production of Strindberg's *Miss Julie.*

AUGUST STRINDBERG
PLAYWRIGHT

Family . . . the home of all social evil, a charitable institution for comfortable women, an anchorage for housefathers, and a hell for children.

THEATRE IN MEDIA

Naturalism in Film and Television

Robert Altman's film *Short Cuts* contains countless naturalistic moments, including a man urinating facing the camera instead of turning away, a wife squeezing a pimple on her husband's neck, a phone-sex employee who is actually a housewife changing her baby's diapers while panting to her customer, and a "naked bottom" scene (played by Julianne Moore) that is not remotely sexual. The character has an argument with her husband while expecting guests: she spills wine on her skirt and takes it off to rinse and blow dry while the argument continues. At one point, he stops the fight to say, "You're not wearing any panties!" She rolls her eyes and the fight goes on.

Of recent films, *The Sessions* is a primary example of naturalism.

One of the most vivid touches of naturalism in television history took place in the classic 1970s television series *All in the Family,* when the sound of Archie Bunker flushing the toilet was heard. This was not a naturalistic show, but that was a naturalistic moment. When a flush is heard on network television, we think about all the offstage noise and life sounds usually edited out of a performance. When *Roseanne* was first broadcast, audiences realized that it had been a long time since they had seen anything but tidy kitchens and svelte families on the tube.

Naturalism has largely been circumvented in recent years by documentaries and reality shows. It is much easier to show real-life detail than to re-create it. For both fictional and actual filmed events, there is a tendency to locate the action in areas of poverty and crisis. Ghettos, housing projects, hospitals, prisons, and areas of extreme poverty, drug abuse, isolation, and danger are often chosen. The life that is sliced is rarely one the audience would choose to live. Of course, this can all change depending on the point of view of the artists.

JOHN AUGUST
SCREENWRITER

I just saw a woman driving a van with a man desperately holding on outside. As a screenwriter, I said to myself, "If you put Will Ferrell in the role, it's a comedy, Hugh Grant and it's a romantic comedy, Sean Penn and it's a dark thriller."

Bettmann/Corbis

FIGURE 9.13   American dramatist Eugene O'Neill.

Twentieth-Century Masters: O'Neill, Williams, Hellman, and Miller

Eugene O'Neill, Tennessee Williams, Lillian Hellman, and Arthur Miller did not limit their work to realism and do not constitute a complete accounting of American masters. Nevertheless, their plays have become standard works in the American repertoire. They enjoy global respect as well.

Eugene O'Neill (1888–1953) is regarded by many as the foremost American playwright. The son of an actor, he walked away from the theatre at a young age and spent years as a seaman, prospector, derelict, and newspaper reporter—all experiences that he would use later in his plays. His realistic works depict the lives of the down and out, bordering sometimes on nihilistic despair. He won four Pulitzer Prizes (including one for *Beyond the Horizon,* his first full-length play) and the Nobel Prize for Literature in 1936. His last two plays, *A Moon for the Misbegotten* and *Long Day's Journey into Night,* are strongly autobiographical, focusing on the difficult and tempestuous relationships in his immediate family.

Tennessee Williams (1911–1983) was born Thomas Lanier Williams in Columbus, Mississippi. His realism is more closely aligned with that of Chekhov than Ibsen in that it is lyrically poetic. His plays are delicate, about fragile and lost souls. Often nostalgic, his early (and most successful) plays look at lives of faded beauty and faded hopes. Two of his masterpieces are *The Glass Menagerie* and *A Streetcar Named Desire.*

Lillian Hellman (1905–1984) was a political activist whose plays are remarkable for their tightly woven plots and her ability to explore depths of psychological weakness while maintaining sympathy with flawed characters. Her political leanings were socialist, and she traveled the world as an outspoken critic of fascism and the oppression of minorities and women. Her most frequently produced plays are *The Children's Hour,* a study of the destructive power of corruption, rumors, and bigotry set in a girls' boarding school, and *The Little Foxes,* the story of a family of ambitious, unscrupulous, and cruel siblings who stop at nothing to achieve success.

The work of **Arthur Miller** (1915–2005) was social and political, as was his life. His most famous and enduring plays focus on the struggles of the common man to find a place in a world dominated by commerce and industry. His long life and career spanned most of the twentieth century, and his masterpieces include *All My Sons,* the story of a man who sold defective airplane parts to the U.S. military during World War II; *A View from the Bridge,* an exploration of immigrant poverty and despair; and *Death of a Salesman,* a modern tragedy blending expressionism and realism that focused on the life of a little man overwhelmed by the failures of his life.

Realism is of course a distinctly Western concept, and most indigenous theatre in other parts of the world is far removed from the form. Its impact on world theatre, however, was profound, not in changing homegrown theatre elsewhere but rather in its universal importation and presentation as an alternative. Ironically, when other cultures present works common to our culture, they most often represent two extremes: the comparatively brutal honesty of realism and the fanciful extremes of the musical.

FIGURE 9.14   American playwright Tennessee Williams.

FIGURE 9.15   American playwright Lillian Hellman.

FIGURE 9.16   American playwright Arthur Miller.

CLOSE-UP

Uncommon Woman—Tribute to Wendy Wasserstein

Wendy Wasserstein was one of the most beloved realist playwrights of our time; her plays struck a profound chord with women struggling to reconcile desires for romance and companionship with the urge for achievement and independence. Her death in 2006 from complications of lymphoma at age 55 left a significant void, although fortunately she was quite prolific. According to André Bishop, who frequently produced her works, "In Wendy's plays, women saw themselves portrayed in a way they hadn't been onstage before—wittily, intelligently, and seriously at the same time. We take that for granted now, but it was not the case 25 years ago. She was a real pioneer."

Her characters were largely feminists who wanted change but did not choose stridency; in fact, they used humor as a primary tool for survival and communication. Wasserstein, who frequently attended Broadway productions growing up in Brooklyn, produced her first play in 1973 with *Any Woman Can't*. Her first big hit was *Uncommon Women and Others*, a play about the reunion of a group of women who went to college together that dissolves into flashbacks of their pasts together. *New Yorker* critic Edith Oliver described it as "funny, ironic, and affectionate. Under the laughter, there is a feeling of bewilderment and disappointment over the world outside college, which promised so much." It helped launch the careers of both Glenn Close and Meryl Streep and became for years a standard production at colleges around the country.

While other major hits included *Isn't It Romantic* and *The Sisters Rosensweig*, probably her defining work was *The Heidi Chronicles*, which covered two decades during which the rules on relationships between men and women were being rewritten, as were those between women. After the first exhilarating rush of feminism settles, the character Heidi observes, "I feel stranded. And I thought the whole point was that we wouldn't feel stranded. I thought the point was that we were all in this together." Starring Joan Allen, *The Heidi Chronicles* won the Tony, the New York Drama Critics' Circle Award, and the Pulitzer Prize. Wasserstein became the first woman ever to win the Tony Award for Best Play for a solo written script.

Because her plays have so much humor and she showed such affection for all her characters, her scripts were sometimes undervalued and underestimated. "My work is often thought of as lightweight commercial comedy," she said, "and I have always thought, 'No, you don't understand: this is in fact a political act.'"

Sarah Jessica Parker, who acted in her works, recalls, "She spoke at my niece's graduation. And I thought, 'Oh, how lucky you women are. This is what sent you out into the next chapter of your life: Wendy Wasserstein's words.'"

AP Photo/Gino Domenico

FIGURE 9.17   Wendy Wasserstein

FIGURE 9.18 Philip Seymour Hoffman, Brian Dennehy, and Robert Sean Leonard in Robert Falls's production of Eugene O'Neill's *Long Day's Journey into Night.*

Magic Realism

Cuban writer Alejo Carpentier used the term *lo real maravilloso* (roughly "marvelous reality") in the preface to one of his novels to describe the heightened sense of reality found in his work. **Magic realism** is a term first used in the 1920s to describe a growing body of art (including painting, playwrighting, and fiction) that challenges the very definition of "what is real." Magic realism is characterized by two apparently contradictory perspectives, one based on a belief in an objective reality and the other on the acceptance of the supernatural as prosaic reality. Contradictory as these two perspectives may seem to a Western audience, many cultures around the world accept this as normal. In fact, those who don't are in the minority!

One of the first writers to gain international acclaim using this style was Colombian novelist **Gabriel García Márquez**, whose *One Hundred Years of Solitude* (1967) and *Love in the Time of Cholera* (1988) exemplify the qualities of magic realism. In his Nobel Prize–winning novels, Márquez embraces both objective, three-dimensional reality and apparently miraculous or absurd events as fully compatible elements of the same truth. Although some Western critics describe his style as a blending of fantasy and reality, Márquez considers himself to be a pragmatic realist telling the truth as he experiences it.

AUTHOR'S INSIGHT

ROBERT: Every era tends to produce theatre that reflects how people *feel* they are. If the term "realism" existed earlier, theatres in all periods might claim that what they were doing was realistic, because the plays were about how people *believed* the mselves to be, even if that is not what we see from the comfortable perspective of time.

FIGURE 9.19 Colombian writer and Nobel Prize winner in Literature Gabriel García Márquez.

Controversy swirls around the use of the term *magic realism*. For some critics, the term assesses a work as blending fantastic, miraculous, or absurd elements in what is essentially realistic work. But others, including the authors of this text, disagree. For some, the term *magic* implies a trick (as in the illusions of a stage magician) or the childlike "let's pretend" of a Peter Pan. But the artists in this style say that they have no intention of creating either illusions or pretend; rather, they are speaking of reality as they experience it in all its richness and mystery.

AUTHOR'S INSIGHT

ANNIE: My first attempt at magic realism was in the novel *One Hundred Years of Solitude* by Gabriel García Márquez. And I must confess I was both confused and annoyed by it and put the book away for several years. The mix of real life and weird stuff was just too hard to follow. Then I fell in love with the play *Kiss of the Spider Woman* while working on a production of it, and a big "aha!" happened. I went back to the novel after that and fell in love all over again.

The idea that only concrete, three-dimensional reality has validity dates from the eighteenth-century European and American philosophy also known as the Enlightenment. Influenced by rationalism and the growth of science, this movement rejected experience that could not be explained through rational, scientific inquiry. Most of the world didn't accept this limited view of reality. Central and South America, as well as all of Africa and Asia, simply were not affected by this philosophical movement and continued in their own traditions of thought, including the simple acceptance that much of experience is a mystery, that spiritual beings exist, and that the miraculous and unexplainable are in fact an expected part of life.

Thus, works from outside the Enlightenment tradition, including Asian, African, Hispanic/Latino, and their American counterparts, assume the existence of beings and events that seem impossible or fantastic to the rationalists. The term *magic realism* is therefore criticized as being a Eurocentric one, focused on making the realistic experiences of much of the world into little more than fairy tales. However, so far, no one has agreed on a more appropriate and inclusive term. Sometimes the term *realismo* is applied to works from the Spanish-language tradition, such as the play *Roosters* by Milcha Sanchez-Scott (see Dramatic Interlude 3). This term seems to exclude the works of the Asian and Asian American traditions, such as *Bitter Cane* by Genny Lim (see Dramatic Interlude 5), and African and African American traditions such as *The Piano Lesson* by August Wilson (see Dramatic Interlude 6). In all of these plays, ghosts, ancestors, and mysteries play an essential part, not distinguished from the gritty, almost naturalistic style of the works. The magic isn't in conflict with the reality of the world of the plays—it is an essential fact that informs that reality.

The Look

As the name *magic realism* implies, the look is generally realistic, sometimes even naturalistic. In *Roosters*, the setting is the dusty yard in front of a weatherbeaten little house in a New Mexican desert. The characters eat meals, hang laundry on a clothesline, fight, and tend roosters in this space. But sometimes the roosters are real birds (a stage manager's nightmare), and sometimes the fighting rooster Zapata is portrayed by an actor/dancer as an almost Mayan deity. Similarly, the fight between father and son over the rooster at the end of the play must be real, gritty, and dangerous. But when the daughter Angela prays for a miracle, she gets one in the form of a literal ascension into the sky, which must be handled with great delicacy and artistry by the director and design team.

The Sound

The sound of magic realism is frank, honest, and even vulgar everyday language, suddenly mixed with passages of lyric poetic imagery. Both sounds are true. Both are real. The characters are able to shift between the two modes without difficulty. In *The Piano Lesson*, the family members can talk of money, sex, and work in one scene and then tell stories of beauty and musicality in the next. Doaker, one of the elders of the family, can cook breakfast, criticize family members in one breath, and tell the heartbreakingly poetic story of the family's heritage in the next.

Early Major Plays and Playwrights: Manuel Puig

The advent of magic realism on the theatrical scene began about the midtwentieth century, although there was no manifesto or declaration of intent published. Playwrights from outside the post-Enlightenment tradition simply began writing plays about their own experiences. As their work achieved international success, the form defined itself.

One influential playwright was **Manuel Puig** (1932–1990) of Argentina. As a gay man with leftist politics, Puig foresaw the wave of right-wing military coups on the horizon and fled to Mexico where he lived and worked until his death in 1990.

Although primarily known as a novelist, his play *Kiss of the Spider Woman* (1976) achieved international acclaim and became both a film and a Broadway musical (1993). *Kiss* tells the story of two men confined in an Argentinean prison, one as a political prisoner, the other because he is a gay man. They create the Spider Woman and other stories as a means of surviving the harsh conditions of the prison. Although the political prisoner hates and fears his cellmate for being gay, he comes to rely on the other man's imagination as a way to escape the torture and sickness that are his daily lot. He also comes to love his cellmate as a fellow sufferer and as a human being, learning at last to see past the man's sexual orientation. The play is infused with scenes that blur the line between reality and fantasy. The characters and the audience

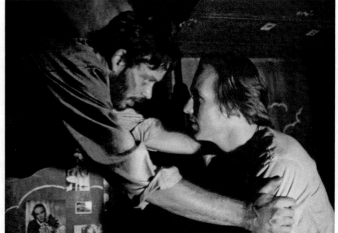

FIGURE 9.20 Raul Julia and William Hurt as cellmates in the 1985 film of Manuel Puig's *Kiss of the Spider Woman*.

Courtesy of the Everett Collection

THEATRE IN MEDIA

Media Milestones

The advent of film lent itself completely to romanticism (with the potential for sweeping camera angles and majestic musical scores), realism (with its sense of minute detail), and naturalism (where gritty slice of life could be achieved in close-up). Here a different breed of masters took technology and found a new and compelling way to tell stories. Here are the high points.

Film

1888—First motion picture camera invented by Thomas Edison

1895—First screen projection system developed by the Lumière brothers

1903—First plot/storyline film introduced (*The Great Train Robbery*)

1915—First major film (*The Birth of a Nation*)

1927—First "talkie" introduced (*The Jazz Singer*)

1930—Establishment of the studio system

1946—Top box office attendance of all time is marked (90 million)

1948—Television is marketed, competing with films

1960s—Emergence of independent film movement

1968—Motion Picture Association of America (MPAA) ratings warn and restrict attendance

1977—Big-budget blockbuster concept takes off, modeled on *Star Wars*

1980s—Home VCRs in general release

1995—First major computer-generated animated film (*Toy Story*)

1995—Stadium seating multiplexes

1997—DVD introduced

1999—Netflix flat-rate rental introduced

2007—D2D theatres

Television

1925—First television transmission

Late 1940s, early 1950s—Television's "Golden Age"

1950—Nielsen ratings system initiated

1953—Color television introduced

1956—Dominance of three major networks

1967—Public Broadcasting Act

1970—FCC limits network prime time access

1972—Cable approved by the FCC

1975—HBO available on satellite, VCRs introduced

1976—First basic cable service introduced (TBS)

1984—Cable Act integrates wireless technologies

1996—Mergers motivated by Telecommunications Act

1997—Flat-panel television

1998—Networks lose dominance

1999—TiVo

2004—Reality television exceeds scripted shows

2008—Transition to digital television

Computer Viewing

1994—Netscape Navigator

2003—MySpace

2005—YouTube

2007—Hulu

ultimately find it difficult and even unnecessary to differentiate between the reality of the prison and the reality of the Spider Woman. Puig also wrote the plays *Under a Mantle of Stars* and *Mystery of the Rose Bouquet*, along with a number of screenplays and teleplays in Mexico.

Magic realist playwrights write without any sense that they are doing anything but writing realism, if not naturalism. These include many American artists from non-Eurocentric cultures, like Genny Lim, David Henry Hwang, Milcha Sanchez-Scott, and August Wilson (to name only those playwrights discussed in this text's Interludes).

SUMMARY

During the nineteenth century, neoclassicism faded, and the new melodrama was busily appeasing the middle class. The works of Comte, Marx, Darwin, and Freud triggered radical changes in politics and thought. Theatre artists searched for new ways to address a rapidly changing world. The romanticists looked back to nature for solace, creating epic dramas about the struggle of individuals to free themselves from the corrupting forces of society. Early romanticist playwrights included Goethe, Hugo, and the first plays of Ibsen. Realism attempted to change society for the better by focusing on cause and effect and the influences of heredity and environment on behavior. Ibsen, Chekhov, and Shaw were early masters of this style. Naturalism takes realism one step further, sparing nothing, and offering no solutions. Zola, Strindberg, and Antoine were early champions of naturalism. Twentieth-century American masters of realism include O'Neill, Williams, Hellman, and Miller. A twentieth-century development has been the explosion of magic realism (for lack of a better term) onto the international stage. Blending the gritty, objective reality of realism and naturalism with the equally truthful mysteries of ghosts, ancestors, saints, and the imagination, magic realism emerged in the mid-twentieth century as the cultural expression of non-Eurocentric playwrights. Especially noted first in plays and novels from South American artists, the style is inclusive of many playwrights from Asian, African, and South and Central American backgrounds.

SUGGESTED ASSIGNMENTS

1. Because realism now dominates as a form, why do you think the world seemed to get along fine without it for so long before it evolved?

2. Which of the four "great thinkers" (Comte, Marx, Darwin, or Freud) identified in this chapter do you think has had the greatest impact on your own view of the world?

3. Why is it that for more than 2,000 years, playwrights seemed unconcerned with writing about the average person?

4. Of recent theatre or films you have attended, which came closest to pure realism?

5. Of recent theatre or films you have attended, which came closest to romanticism and naturalism?

6. What is the most naturalistic detail you have experienced as an audience member?

7. What has been the most sweeping, romantic moment you have experienced in the theatre?

8. Consider someone writing or directing the story of your life so far. Which of the four (realism, romanticism, naturalism, or magic realism) would be likely to be chosen for the style or treatment? Why?

9. Do you determine any trend in films at present to favor one of the four forms examined in this chapter?

10. To grasp magic realism more fully, identify the weirdest thing that ever happened to you—an encounter with the paranormal, or even a miracle that cannot be explained within the confines of realism. Place this experience in the context of the more mundane events of that day and allow yourself to say "yes" to these everyday juxtapositions.

SUGGESTED ACTIVITIES

1. **Individual:** Identify a moment of importance in your own life. Think about your story as a romantic epic, a realistic social drama, and a naturalistic "slice of your life." How does it change the meaning of this event to look at it through these three different lenses?

2. **Group:** Choose a world news event of interest to you and prepare a naturalistic docudrama report of it for presentation to class. Then dramatize the event by applying romantic or realistic selectivity to it. Which style best represents the story that you really want to tell?

3. **Long-term:** Follow an event unfolding in the world around you, whether that is your personal drama or the global stage. Keep a journal in which you try to report just the facts, naturalistically, and then render it as social realism intending to solve a problem. Finally, see what happens if you set this event on the epic stage of the romantic vision. Does your participation in the event change depending on your approach? Does the outcome or meaning of the event change?

4. **Large group:** Watch a news story together and determine if it is being reported in true "slice of life" fashion or not. Are parts of the story actually dramatized as social realism? Does any part of it seem to follow the ideas of the romantics? Should news reports include anything but the facts?

KEY WORDS AND IDEAS

Auguste Comte
Karl Marx
Charles Darwin
Sigmund Freud
romanticism
    Friedrich Schiller
    Johann Wolfgang von Goethe
    Sturm und Drang
    Victor Hugo
realism
    Henrik Ibsen
    Anton Chekhov
    George Bernard Shaw

naturalism
    Émile Zola
    slice of life
    August Strindberg
    André Antoine
Eugene O'Neill
Tennessee Williams
Lillian Hellman
Arthur Miller
magic realism
    Gabriel García Márquez
    Manuel Puig

chapter 10

VARIETIES OF STYLIZATION

Alan Cumming starred as the Emcee in the Tony Award-winning 1998 Broadway revival of *Cabaret*.

Fiona Shaw as Anna Fierling, Mother Courage, in the production of Bertolt Brecht's *Mother Courage and Her Children* directed by Deborah Warner at the National Theatre in London.

Robbie Jack/Corbis

Lesson Objectives:

Upon completion of this chapter, you will be able to:

1. Discuss the possible reasons why realism and naturalism seemed like failed styles to some artists after the world wars.
2. Identify the key ideas and conventions of the major anti-realist movements and track their influence on contemporary theatre and media.
3. Engage in the conventions of a variety of musical theatre forms, both traditional and contemporary in format.

Introduction

In realism, behavior comes close to what we believe to be our own. **Stylization** is the process of taking a play beyond reality through distortion, exaggeration, or some other stretch of convention. The more stylized a production is, the more conventions that it asks its audience to embrace. This chapter examines the styles, called in this chapter by their common nickname, the "Isms," that emerged as a result of crucial world events in the twentieth century. It also examines our most highly stylized and popular entertainment, the musical. As in Chapter 9, we look first at the call for change, and then we will examine the look, sound, and major early works of each style. We explore the contemporary impact on stage and film of these Isms.

Although realism is often serious, even grim in its examination of life and society, there is an optimism embedded in the way it advises us to look at things objectively, ferret out problems, and search for solutions. It suggests we might evolve into something better, fairer, and more humane. Realist plays often challenge our sense of the world around us by saying, "You think you know what it's like out here? You don't. Let me show you." Realism seems to imply that if we understand the problem, we may be moved to address it, if not politically, at least in our own hearts. Given the events of the twentieth century, many began to despair of this optimistic assessment of humanity and to embrace the bizarre absurdity of life.

Holocausts—The World at War

World events in the first half of the twentieth century made many doubt the possibility that rationalism, science, and technology provided solutions to social problems. In 1914, the assassination of an Austrian duke and duchess in Sarajevo ignited the first global war. Europe, its colonies around the world, and the United States became involved. New technologies (including chemical and biological weapons, air bombing, and tanks) made death and destruction possible on an unprecedented scale. The final toll was 8.5 million killed, 21 million wounded, and 7.5 million prisoners or missing. During the final months of the war, the Russian Revolution sparked a civil war that wreaked devastation on a population that was already suffering. It ended with the establishment of the first Communist government in the world and sent the imperial powers of Europe into a dither. On October 28, 1929, the U.S. stock market collapse triggered a global economic depression that would last for almost a decade. Germany, having

FIGURE 10.1   World War II concentration camp prisoners, one source of motivation for the anti-realistic "isms" of the twentieth century.

Popperfoto/Getty Images

FIGURE 10.2 The town of Hiroshima, Japan, after it had been devastated on August 6, 1945, by the first atomic bomb used in warfare, dropped by the United States during World War II. The bomb killed more than 75,000 people.

lost World War I, was severely punished in the Treaty of Versailles, an agreement designed to ensure that Germany and the German people would never rise from the ashes.

Adolf Hitler gained power in a Germany facing crisis after World War I. Using propaganda and charismatic oratory, he appealed to the economic needs of the lower and middle classes, while sounding resonant chords of nationalism, anti-Semitism, and anti-Communism. With the establishment of a restructured economy, a rearmed military, and a fascist regime, Hitler pursued an aggressive foreign policy with the intention of expanding German *Lebensraum* ("living space"). This triggered World War II.

This time, the destruction was even more devastating. By 1945, 35 million had died globally, along with another 10 million in concentration camps. In Hiroshima and Nagasaki, a new weapon of unbelievable force was unleashed: the first and (so far) only use of nuclear weapons. Suddenly, it was clear that the human race now had the technology to destroy itself. Tension filled the decades that followed, as the Cold War led the Soviet and U.S. governments to stockpile world-annihilating supplies of nuclear weapons. One wrong move by one very human leader, and it could have been the end of everything.

AP Photo/U.S. Air Force

FIGURE 10.3 An infamous image of the mushroom cloud rising more than 20,000 feet into the air after the second atomic bomb dropped by the United States exploded over the Japanese port and town of Nagasaki, on August 9, 1945.

The holocausts of the first half of the twentieth century had a profound impact on the worldview of the survivors. Science and technology had failed to make the world a better place—they had only created more efficient killing machines. The idea of society moving toward a more just and humane system was fragile. Many theatre artists did not escape the overwhelming sense of anxiety and despair. For them, realism, with its basis in science, reason, and optimism, no longer made sense. They began to create theatre reflecting the world as they experienced it.

Anti-Realism

Throughout the twentieth century, realistic and anti-realistic theatre had an uneasy and often downright hostile relationship. The objections to realism included its emphasis on heredity and environment as controlling factors in human existence. For many, this seemed too limited. Realism did not account for spiritual and cosmic forces and tended to discount ineffable, deeply personal experiences and psychological/emotional realities. Faith in the ability of science, technology, and reason to guide the evolution of society in positive directions seemed, to many, unsupportable.

The "Isms"

There is a tendency to name styles of theatre by adding the suffix "-ism" to its root name, such as expression*ism* and symbol*ism*. We will continue this tradition. Here we list the progression of Isms over a period of 200 years, including those we have already identified:

Romanticism (early 1800s)

Explore history and destiny against all odds, idealize nature, and reject corrupt society, epic in scope.

Realism (1850s+)

Just tell the truth in the hopes of making the world a better place.

Naturalism (1873+)

Reveal everything, warts and all. Don't expect things to change.

Impressionism (1874+)

Theatre should attempt to capture the moment through feeling, mood, and atmosphere. A higher world, artificially created and emotionally sublimated, is ideal.

Symbolism (1890–1920)

Poetic, dreamlike theatre seeks the profound or mysterious in life. Mood and atmosphere are far more important than plot or action.

AUTHOR'S INSIGHT

ANNIE: I clearly remember my first introduction to the Isms as a freshman, when I was assigned a paper on the bizarre play *Dionysus in '69*. I read it and hated it, researched it and still hated it, and in fact, probably still hate it today. But I was forced to deal with my own biases and to look at the art of the theatre in a new way—not just as a way to tell realistic stories, but as a way to tell the infinite variety of human stories.

Expressionism (1910+)

Life is seen through the artist's subjective emotions. Theatre should be forceful, urgent, and emotionally charged. The use of dream/nightmare distortion.

Futurism (1910–1940s)

The actor is a machine subjugated to totally integrated theatre. Reject the past and glorify progress. Anticipate a great industrial future.

Dadaism (1916+)

Contradict all expectations. Nothing is sacred. Theatre should take a nihilistic approach to life and a revolutionary attitude towards art. A totally pacifist rejection of futurist proclamations.

Constructivism (1921+)

Build a story; don't tell it. Sentimentality and individual feeling have no place here. It is time to strip away theatrical illusion and show the bare bones.

Surrealism (1924+)

Freed from morals or esthetics, the artist is finally capable of creation. Theatre artists should seek spontaneous creation without interference from reason. Insanity is often true sanity.

Didacticism (1927+)

Narrative theatre should be for the intellect rather than the emotions. Also called *Epic* or *Brechtian* theatre.

Absurdism (late 1940s+)

Theatre must reflect an irrational world where truth is unknowable and life is nonsensical. Understanding is impossible. Because everything is meaningless, action is cyclical, repetitive, and unproductive.

Feminism (late 1960s+)

Women have a voice, too long neglected and pushed aside, that must be released and heard through theatre that is by, for, and about them.

Postmodernism (1980s+)

Play with the past without nostalgia for it. Theatre should juxtapose the new and the old, one masking, disguising, or hiding itself within or behind the other.

We will discuss six Isms that have most influenced theatre styles. In Chapter 11, we will explore feminist and postmodernist theatre.

FIGURE 10.4 Mary Garden as Melisande in the 1902 operatic adaptation of Maurice Maeterlinck's symbolist play, *Pelléas et Mélisande*.

Symbolism

Poetic, dreamlike theatre seeks the profound or mysterious in life.

Developed in France during the later years of the nineteenth century, **symbolism** profoundly influenced writers in Britain, Ireland, and the United States such as Edgar Allan Poe, James Joyce, William Butler Yeats, and Eugene O'Neill. Belgian Maurice Maeterlinck (1862–1949) is the pre-eminent symbolist playwright, and he was influenced by the French poets Stéphane Mallarmé and Paul Verlaine. Paintings by Paul Gauguin, Henri Rousseau, Henri de Toulouse-Lautrec, and Giorgio de Chirico reflect the basic values. Adolphe Appia and Max Reinhardt explored these values in theatrical lighting and set design. Wagnerian opera tried to fuse all the elements (music, dialogue, color, light, shape, and texture) in performance.

Call for Change

Symbolists called for us to turn our backs on objective reality and move strongly into the subjective and intuitive. Mood and atmosphere are more important than plot or action. Characters need not have personalities of their own because they are symbols of the poet's inner life. Something onstage is not necessarily a *clear* symbol, which the audience will recognize; rather, it is symbolic of the author's *consciousness*. Suggestion is more powerful than explicit representation. Theatre should seek the profound and the unfathomable. Life shown in realism should be either changed or transcended. The autonomy of art frees it from any obligation to deal with social problems in political terms. Art needs to move beyond the real and into the truth.

STÉPHANE MALLARMÉ

SYMBOLIST PLAYWRIGHT

The poetic act consists of suddenly seeing that an idea splits up into a number of equal motifs and of grouping them; they rhyme.

Symbolists argue that realism misses the ultimate experiences of life—the immediate, unique, emotional response of the individual to an event. Language is the primary tool, deemphasizing scenery, action, and character. The primary theorist, Stéphane Mallarmé, felt that drama was "a sacred and mysterious rite which, through dream, reverie, allusion, and musicality, evokes the hidden spiritual meaning of existence."

By challenging the stilted, domesticated, scientific philosophy of the realists, the symbolists seldom achieved any commercial success. But, they gave inspiration to others whose work could be poetic and popular, non-realistic and accessible.

The Look

Repeated symbols include water (symbolizing both life force and death), moonlight, dark forests, and castles that never get warm. Symbols can be arranged in juxtaposition, with projected light and mood music. Static poses may alternate with ritualized slow-motion passages. The space may be undefined and dreamlike, full of shadows, mists, and possibly mirrors. Costumes, often draped and gauzelike, draw on wide-ranging tribal and cultural influences. Much modern dance, in the Isadora Duncan tradition, relates to symbolism.

The Sound

New Age music suits symbolist production. Dialogue may be full of mysterious references, perhaps simple nouns with adjectives rather than complete sentences. Lines are likely to be rhythmic and poetic, with hypnotic use of cadence and intensity to build emotion.

FIGURE 10.5 A scene from Maurice Maeterlinck's *The Blind,* directed by Lina Abyad at Lebanese American University, 2008. Notice the shift away from naturalism and realism toward the symbolic.

The Acting

Performers need to be able to function on a high level of abstraction and to play situations associated more with dreams than waking experience. The ability to play larger than life, to personify a single quality or trait, and to function at times like a puppet is essential. Clarity, practicality, and definition need to give way to a willingness to distort and exaggerate for effect.

Early Works

Elements of symbolism appear in the following works:

Andreyev, Leonid: *The Life of Man*

Claudel, Jean: *The Golden Head*

Jarry, Alfred: *Ubu Roi*

Maeterlinck, Maurice: *The Blind, The Bluebirds, Pelléas et Mélisande*

Mallarmé, Stephane: *Hérodiade, The Faun*

O'Casey, Seán: *Within the Gates*

Wedekind, Frank: *Spring Awakening*

Wilde, Oscar: *Salome*

Futurism

The actor is a machine subjugated to totally integrated theatre.

In 1909, Italian poet Filippo Tommaso Marinetti (1876–1944) wrote an impassioned manifesto on the front page of an important Parisian newspaper, outlining the tenets of **futurism**. Beginning as a strictly literary movement, it quickly spread to visual arts and music as well. The movement ran from about 1910 to 1930, when it was absorbed into the propaganda wing of the Italian Fascist Party. Eventually, Eugene Ionesco employed some of the techniques, as does performance art today.

Call for Change

Futurists urged us to reject the past, glorify progress, and anticipate a great industrial future. Theatre gave expression to the energy and movement of new machinery. Technology "rescued" theatre from a deadly museumlike atmosphere and literary, logical bias. Machines and wars could be a source of great beauty. War was, in fact, the world's hygiene, cleaning out unfortunate vestiges of the past.

Futurists deplored any veneration of the past, seeing it as a barrier to progress. Marinetti wrote in praise of fast cars as a new ideal of beauty, wanting museums and libraries torn down because they had value for only the old and the dying. No futurist was over 40. Their ideal man was an aggressive young warrior, deploring the past and charging full steam ahead into the future, apparently without women. The movement, though it did not produce any great plays or playwrights, influenced future anti-realist artists by promoting modern technology to create multimedia performances, encouraging direct confrontation between audience and performer, and advocating fresh, untried approaches to the arts.

FILIPPO TOMMASO MARINETTI

FROM FOUNDATION AND MANIFESTO OF FUTURISM

We want to glorify war—the only cure for the world—militarism, patriotism, the destructive gesture of the anarchists, the beautiful ideas which kill, and contempt for woman. We want to demolish museums and libraries, fight morality, feminism, and all opportunist and utilitarian cowardice.

The Look

Actors often move among the audience. Simultaneous events take place in various parts of the performance space. Kinetic sculptures; utilitarian objects; leather, chains, steel, and cement; multimedia; high-tech; multiple focus; and simultaneous action may be used. Costumes with straight lines, metallic surfaces, and loose fit turn the human silhouette into a mechanical one, although the face, arms, and legs are often left uncovered. Actors are integrated into the setting, which may be controlled or street theatre. The look is macho-mechanical.

The Sound

Language is blunt, simple, direct, masculine, and militaristic. Lines may involve ideological diatribes, manifestos, shouting, and mechanical noises, delivered in presentational fashion. Sound can be just noises. "Music" may be created out of sirens, machine guns, and other war sounds.

The Acting

The actor, the director's robot, may be asked to perform in a highly geometric, machinelike fashion. Strong masculine attacks, as well as sustained violent, high-energy, and repetitive sequences can occur. Using highly developed technical skills, having great patience, and letting go of the desire to portray realistically are needed, along with the ability to eliminate the actor's own idiosyncratic behavior in favor of total integration into surroundings.

Early Works

Balla, Giacomo: *Disconcerted States of Mind*

Cangiullo, Francesco: *Detonation*

Marinetti, Filippo Tommaso: *Feet*

Settimelli, Emilio: *Sempronio's Lunch*

Dadaism

Contradict all expectations.

Dadaists also rejected traditional forms, but they were stunned and dismayed by the outbreak of war and declared the world insane. They sought to infuse their art with calculated madness, discord, and chaos.

Inspired by the writings of Franz Kafka, the movement was conceived in Zurich by Tristan Tzara and, led by Hugo Ball, spread to France. **Dadaism** itself defies the keeping of records, so its progress was only randomly transcribed. The Dada Gallery was established in 1916, and the ideas were prominent until 1922. More a means of creating a theatrical event than of writing scripts, Dadaism did not produce a body of work. It tended to be favored at private entertainments or happenings.

Dada art reflects the belief that the world makes no sense. Rather than talk about chaos and madness, Dadaists performed it. Often, conflicting performance events occurred simultaneously, as in the futurists' works, employing multimedia and audience confrontation.

Call for Change

Dadaism subscribes to the philosophy that nothing is sacred. Theatre should take a nihilistic approach to life and a revolutionary attitude toward art. Anti-art is the way to think because "creative" acts are worthless. Audiences should be moved beyond rationality to the ridiculous. All beliefs are false. The future smacks of death, so the moment is all that matters. Spontaneity is the closest anyone can come to creating— the more shocking the better.

FIGURE 10.6 A.C.T. production of Tom Stoppard's *Travesties,* featuring Tristan Tzara (Gregory Wallace) defending his Dadaist ideas of art to James Joyce (Anthony Fusco, seated).

American Conservatory Theatre

FIGURE 10.7 The set of *Travesties*—with Henry Carr (Geordie Johnson), center, narrating the tale—designed by Douglas W. Schmidt.

The Look and Sound

Space tends to be bare and abstract but may be buried in irrelevant items. Dialogue may be incongruous, full of non sequiturs, shouting, singing, berating, gibberish, and obscenities. Laughing at the audience is a common mode of attack.

The Acting

An ability to improvise aggressively is essential, as is the actor's willingness to humiliate himself and others. An imaginative sense of what will strike others as obscene and sacrilegious helps. Audacity and a confrontational, defiant nature are needed.

Early Works

The concept discourages scripting. Some elements appear in these works:

Cummings, E. E.: *HIM*

Shepard, Sam: *The Unseen Hand*

Stein, Gertrude: *Four Saints in Three Acts*

Stoppard, Tom: *Travesties*

Expressionism

Life is seen through a single set of subjective emotions.

The **expressionism** movement originated in the paintings of Hervé Auguste Faye, exhibited in 1901 under the title *expressionisms*, and eventually influenced all the arts. The term describes work that vigorously reflects the mood or inner life of either the artist or the object portrayed.

Expressionists believed that fundamental truth lies within the soul, spirit, and vision of the individual. Reacting strongly against an increasingly mechanized world, they felt that external reality must be shaped into harmony with our interior life. In some ways, the expressionists bridge the gap between the realists and the anti-realists. They rejected the heredity/ environment argument of the realists but embraced their desire to shape and improve human society. Expressionists embraced many stylistic ideals of the anti-realists while rejecting their elitist lack of concern with the lives of average people.

Shared qualities of expressionist theatre are as follows:

1. Rather than a linear, cause-and-effect plot, the play will center on a theme, idea, or motif.

2. Action often takes the form of a quest in which the protagonist searches at various "stations" for what is often a vague or elusive prize.

3. The action is often cyclical, reflecting a pessimistic view of the human condition.

4. Characters represent types rather than individuals (often having no names other than the Student, the Husband, or the Prostitute).

5. Often a Christ-like protagonist is slowly destroyed or absorbed by a mechanistic, materialistic world.

6. Distortion is found in every element, portraying a personal rather than objective vision of reality.

7. Dialogue is often short, simple, and staccato, with gesture and pantomime used to communicate emotional intensity.

The influence of the expressionist movement was so profound that finding contemporary drama without some element of expressionism is difficult. Whenever we see a work in which what the mind knows is more important than what the eye sees, we are experiencing its influence.

Call for Change

Expressionists believe that most other Isms are too elitist and specialized. They thought theatre should be forceful, urgent, and emotionally charged, capturing the inner struggle that each of us experiences to develop into The New Person of the future. Nightmarish, anti-industrial, deliberate distortions of reality are ways to deliver a harsh truth.

Dreams are a major source of truth. Portrayal of the dreamlike state may illuminate life so that the subjective can be objectified. The real heroes are hidden among the common workers, stifled by a system that is dangerous, dehumanizing, and deadly. The values of the older generation are useless. It is time for fresh subjectivity that mirrors inner psychological realities instead of outer physical appearances.

AUGUST STRINDBERG
PLAYWRIGHT, FROM *A DREAM PLAY*

Earth is not clean
life is not good
men are not evil
nor are they good
they live as they can
a day at a time
The sons of dust
in dust must wander
Born of dust
To dust they return
they were given feet to plod
Not wings.
Is the fault theirs or yours?

The Look

Moody, atmospheric lighting dominates. Diagonal lines, leaning panels, sharp angles, colored light, and nightmarish images may be employed. Walls may slope, windows and doors may be out of square, and dark shadows may

Oracle Productions, NFP | 2010 | Chicago. Angela Glyda (photographer)

FIGURE 10.8 A production of August Strindberg's expressionist masterpiece *The Ghost Sonata*. Produced at Chicago's Oracle Theatre, 2011.

be juxtaposed with shafts of bright light. Platforms, ramps, scaffolding, and unexpected elements (such as a trapeze) may enter the playing space. Geometric images dominate. Movement may involve stark groupings of actors and choreographed histrionic business. Actions may be fragmentary or disconnected. Some use of masks and Asian stage technique may be employed. Costumes and props may be grotesquely exaggerated.

The Sound

Explosive language is employed, with a startling contrast between lyrical passages and staccato. Full range of sound, including inhuman noises, shouting, chanting, and barking may be used. Like the movement, dialogue may be repetitious and mechanical, with tempos shifting dramatically.

The Acting

Highly theatrical, sometimes flagrantly presentational playing that represents the subconscious and the spiritual is required. Actors need to be able to portray volatile emotions as well as an alienated state of abstraction. They may be asked to work in two extremes, sometimes removing a human quality (such as greed or lust) from their characterizations and at other times becoming these same qualities incarnate.

Early Works

Ĉapek, Josef and Karel: *Pictures from the Insects' Life, R.U.R. (Rossum's Universal Robots)*

Kaiser, Georg: *From Morn to Midnight*

O'Neill, Eugene: *The Emperor Jones, The Hairy Ape*

Rice, Elmer: *The Adding Machine*

Shaw, Irwin: *Bury the Dead*

Strindberg, August: *A Dream Play, The Road to Damascus, The Ghost Sonata*

Treadwell, Sophie: *Machinal*

Absurdism

An irrational world where truth is unknowable and life is nonsensical.

The term *Absurd* is used here in a broader, sadder sense than "ridiculous." It is derived from the original musical term for "out of harmony." While absurdist plays were written in the 1940s, Samuel Beckett's *Waiting for Godot* (1953) was the first major success. Philosophers Albert Camus and Jean-Paul Sartre began to influence the thinking of playwrights.

Their philosophy of **existentialism** called for using *will* instead of *reason* to deal with problems arising from a hostile universe. Continental Europe had experienced great devastation; massive human, economic, agricultural, and architectural loss; fatigue, famine, disease, and finally disillusionment. Memories of the concentration camps and gas chambers were vivid. This was the canvas for **absurdism**.

Silent film comedians of the period (Buster Keaton, Charlie Chaplin, the Keystone Kops, and, later, Laurel and Hardy and the Marx Brothers) employed absurdist elements, with their characters often existing in a nightmarish black-and-white world beyond their comprehension. The movement was most popular in the 1950s and 1960s, but absurdist elements are present today in some of the works of Sam Shepard, David Mamet, and David Rabe.

JEAN-PAUL SARTRE
PLAYWRIGHT, PHILOSOPHER

If man can recognize and accept the simultaneous existence of his absurdity and his responsibility to give himself definition through choice and action, there is hope.

AUTHOR'S INSIGHT

ROBERT: Because an alarming number of people regard life as nightmarish and ridiculous, we are seeing more and more elements of both expressionism and absurdism integrated into productions, even those that at first glance appear realistic and then change.

Call for Change

Playwrights of absurdism believe understanding is impossible. Space, linear time, and conventional structure are abandoned. All laws of probability and physics are suspended. Because he is in a state of moral paralysis, man's *only* freedom is the exercise of his conscious mind. There is no light left in the universe. There is only metaphysical anguish. Life has lost reason. Man has lost touch with his roots. Existence is useless and meandering. Laughter is a coping tool, often the only coping tool for dealing with deep pain. It is difficult to communicate with others, so we need to fill time, as if life is spent in a waiting room with no inner office, with games, jokes, dances, songs, silly routines, or escapes. Plots are often circular (everything that happens has happened before), with the play ending exactly where it began.

Bob Adelman/Corbis

FIGURE 10.9 Samuel Beckett was among the first of the playwrights of the Theatre of the Absurd to win fame, and was awarded the Nobel Prize in Literature for 1969.

Richard Feldman

FIGURE 10.10 Perhaps the best-known absurdist production is Samuel Beckett's *Waiting for Godot*. This production was staged at the American Repertory Theatre.

The Look and Sound

Plays may be realistically mounted so that absurdity comes out of setting up false expectations or may be staged in a cartoonlike way. Because humans, animals, and objects are interchangeable in this world, they may be given each other's qualities. Characters may be complex and multidimensional or completely stereotyped. Casts are mostly small and effects minimal. Speech is disconnected, noncommunicative, and rambling. People never seem to listen to each other. There are rushes of sound followed by unexpected and sometimes interminable silences. Just as a mood appears to establish itself, it changes.

The Acting

An ability to make rapid-fire changes and come up with surprising use of pauses and silence is essential. Having many voices and attacks, high energy, and imagination are important. Movement demands may include acrobatics, silent-film technique, song and dance, vaudeville, circus tricks, and quick breaks between presentational and nonpresentational audience relationships. The capacity to be real and unreal is in sharp juxtaposition. It is no accident that a major Broadway revival of *Waiting for Godot* in 2009 featured three of the world's most brilliant clowns: Robin Williams, Steve Martin, and Bill Irwin.

T. Charles Erickson

FIGURE 10.11 An absurdist production, Jean-Paul Sartre's *No Exit*, as staged by the American Repertory Theatre, featured a pivoting stage that rose and fell in time with the changing balance of power among the characters, Inez (Paula Plum), Estelle (Karen MacDonald), and Garcin (Will LeBow).

Early Works

Albee, Edward: *The American Dream* and *The Sandbox*

Beckett, Samuel: *Waiting for Godot, Krapp's Last Tape, Happy Days, Endgame, Footfall, Act Without Words*

Camus, Albert: *Caligula*

Genet, Jean: *The Maids, The Balcony, Deathwatch, The Blacks*

Ionesco, Eugene: *The Bald Soprano, Rhinoceros, The Chairs, The Lesson*

Kopit, Arthur: *Oh Dad, Poor Dad, Mama's Hung You in the Closet and I'm Feelin' So Sad; The Day the Whores Came Out to Play Tennis; Chamber Music*

Pinter, Harold: *The Dumb Waiter, The Birthday Party, The Caretaker, No Man's Land, Old Times, The Homecoming*

Pirandello, Luigi: *Six Characters in Search of an Author*

Sartre, Jean-Paul: *No Exit, The Flies*

Shepard, Sam: *Buried Child*

Didacticism: Brechtian and Epic Theatre

Narrative theatre for the intellect, rather than the emotions. Also called Brechtian *or* Epic *theatre.*

Erwin Piscator conceived of the idea of a "proletarian drama." The term **didacticism** is used to describe the blend of education and entertainment conceived by Piscator, but perhaps perfected by **Bertolt Brecht**. Brecht became the movement's main theorist and dramatist. He developed a dramatic economy, simplicity of language, mature vision, and depth of expression seldom seen on the stage before. He refined his work through his own company, the Berliner Ensemble. He defined *delight* as the pleasure that comes from discovering new truths about yourself and the world, which he called the perfect reconciliation between teaching and pleasing. His theories have been subjected to many conflicting interpretations but continually stimulate directors throughout the world.

Artists subscribing to didacticism believe that theatre should make you think and act. The stage is meant to narrate (not embody), to demand decisions (not feelings), to communicate knowledge (not experience), to present arguments (not suggestions), and to appeal to our reason (not instincts). Actors should *present* characters instead of inhabiting them. Audiences should stay aware that they are watching a performance instead of losing themselves in the lives of the characters. "Alienation" (*Verfremdung*) destroys theatrical illusion by frequently interrupting the action, so the audience can remain emotionally disengaged and capable of viewing the work intelligently. The *subject matter* is what is alienated. (The term does not mean to be "offended" or "angry." The original German word, *Verfremdung*, means to see things in a new light, to step back and look again at what has become familiar.) Audiences should feel they have the power to change society if it is not working. Critical watching discourages passivity. Drama should deal with a human being caught in the midst of social or political conflict. The best theatre spreads social ideology. Naturalism is rejected because it fails to portray man within the general

Bettmann/Corbis

FIGURE 10.12 Playwright Bertolt Brecht, a champion of the Epic theatre style.

landscape of the whole society. Other forms of theatre encourage audiences to idealistic attitudes with no relevance to real life.

The Look

A proscenium space is preferred with a blank screen used to project images. Signs may describe scenes before they happen and thereby remove suspense. Auditorium lights may be left on. Conspicuously, theatrical props (such as a paper moon) may indicate time. Scenery is likely to be constructivist—simple stairs, scaffolding, or possibly revolving stages. In our era, any constant reminder (cameras, amplification, and multiple screenings) that the event is a theatrical one and not real life may replace traditional choices. The movement runs the spectrum from realistic to highly stylized. Changes in time and place are frequent and abrupt.

The Sound

Clear, distinct, often harsh, and strong language is employed. Dialogue is mixed with narration and vaudeville-like singing interludes. Instead of intensifying emotions, music is used to neutralize them, the opposite of its usual function in theatre. Dialogue may be blunt and colloquial, full of both

FIGURE 10.13 Didacticism, or Epic theatre, a style perfected by Bertolt Brecht, wants the audience to think and act, rather than to passively observe. It is often alienating and disruptive, forcing the viewer to engage with the content, as in this stark, arresting Brecht production.

Richard Feldman

malice and wit. Strident prologues and epilogues are common. Direct address of audience is frequent, and a wide range of dialects may be employed.

The Acting

Actors must have the capacity to step in and out of character, to comment and "demonstrate" character with some flexibility. Training in mime, clowning, and Asian acting techniques is useful. Brecht recommended that actors develop the ability to think of their characters in the third person and to "quote" the behavior of the character with the same immediacy as someone who has experienced an accident and now feels compelled to re-create the event for listeners. The distancing therefore is by no means the dropping of commitment.

THEATRE IN MEDIA

"Isms" in Film

Expressionism has its greatest presence in film because one of the great gifts of cinema is that it can take us completely inside the emotional state of a character—seeing, hearing, and feeling exactly what that character is experiencing. Probably the most expressionistic instances are in horror films, where camera angles, lighting, focus, and sound track all escalate the terror a character experiences, and we are terrified, too. Some watered-down elements of futurism exist in action movies and even more so in video games. Dadaism is such a live event that it defies transfer to film and is most often manifested in strident rock performances where audiences are confronted and even vilified. The common vision of reality has moved in the direction of absurdism in recent years as the world seems to have grown more incomprehensible and laughter seems the only way to deal with it. A distinctly absurdist film movement does not exist, but sequences in many films likely embrace absurdist elements. Didacticism may be employed in certain educational or training films, but is almost unheard of in fictional cinema, where dispassionate objectivity is the last thing a filmmaker wants an audience to experience.

Early Works

Brecht, Bertolt: *Mother Courage and Her Children, The Good Person of Setzuan, The Threepenny Opera, The Caucasian Chalk Circle, Galileo, The Resistible Rise of Arturo Ui*

Kipphardt, Heinar: *In the Matter of J. Robert Oppenheimer*

Tabari, George: *Brecht on Brecht*

Weiss, Peter: *The Persecution and Assassination of Marat / Sade*

Musical Theatre

There is no more popular form of contemporary theatre in the United States than the **musical.** The vast majority of plays on Broadway are musicals, and the chances are great that your first exposure to live theatre was a musical produced by your high school, a local community theatre, or a professional touring production. Why do musicals play to packed houses every day around the world? Because they have the capacity to stir our emotions to the fullest heights. Can you think of a single, major public event in which music is not a crucial ingredient, whether it is one of celebration or mourning? The impulse to break into song when feelings are so strong that they need some expression, even explosion, is one we all understand deep in our bones. The impulse to dance when emotion cannot be contained in stillness is universal. Combining these two actions into a single theatre form allows us tremendous release and excitement.

Musicals may at first glance seem to have little in common with the Isms featured earlier in this chapter. What they share, however, is intense stylization, wherein characters do not behave as they do in everyday life. (See Chapter 2 regarding the extreme conditions of make-believe involved in musical theatre.) Not only can characters wear fully color-coordinated, sparkly costumes and tap shoes to work, but when someone has an impulse to break into song and dance, everyone nearby catches the same impulse and miraculously just happens to know the tune, the lyrics, and the moves to express this ecstasy in complete synchronicity. And just to provide enough room, the walls of the building might disappear until the end of the number and then return. Not every musical is *that* stylized—many have realistic sequences—but at the magic moment when everyone bursts into song and dance, we are transported to a world vastly different from realistic everyday behavior.

If the Isms tend to distort the world in an inverted and convoluted way, musicals tend to do so in embracing exaggerated and unlimited possibilities. For example, all high school glee clubs in small towns with severe budget crises nevertheless have a virtually unlimited costume and set budget. Wasn't that true at your school?

Origins

Music has always been a vital part of theatre. Most non-Western productions integrate it into performance. From Greek tragedy to Shakespearean comedy, Western classic theatre forms have long had elements of song and dance. But when we refer to "The Musical," we mean a peculiar combination of light opera, ballet, music hall, minstrel show, and vaudeville that is a distinctly American contribution to world theatre. And one that has been around for only 150 years.

The first musical is believed to have been an accident! A play called *The Black Crook* was playing in New York in 1866. By itself, it was a lackluster melodrama. However, a French dance company found itself stranded in New York, and the producers decided to add their songs and dances to the show to give it some oomph. Audiences were suddenly enthralled by the combination. It turned out that a mediocre script could be transformed into something magical through music and dance, even if, as in this case, the show lasted an astonishing five and a half hours. Many of the ingredients (chorus girls, elaborate production numbers, lavish costumes, some nice songs, some naughty ones with flirtatious innuendo, and huge dance numbers) in *The Black Crook* survive in musicals today. The same year, a show called *The Black Domino* became the first to actually bill itself as "a musical comedy."

While the musical truly flourished on the New York stage, there were other global contributions to the form. The British light operas of Gilbert and Sullivan demonstrated that a story and music could make a delightful combination. French and Viennese composers, such as Jacques Offenbach (whose *Orpheus in the Underworld* introduced the world to the cancan) and Franz Lehár (*The Merry Widow*), did the same.

Two early American geniuses of musical theatre were Victor Herbert (*Babes in Toyland* and *Naughty Marietta)* and George M. Cohan (*Little Johnny Jones*), whose hits were not only tremendous theatrical successes but contributed songs that became popular on their own. These include "Ah Sweet Mystery of Life," "The Yankee Doodle Boy," and "Give My Regards to Broadway." Cohan in particular created a distinctly American musical in its settings, characters, and song styles, as well as colloquial lyrics and dialogue involving native slang. A pervading American spirit of brashness and unlimited energy defined his works.

The twentieth century saw two major phases in the development of musical theatre, first comedy and then drama. At the start of the century, the **musical comedy** continued and flowered. This format usually involved a madcap, zany plot, lots of young love, choruses featuring lovely chorines never wearing more clothing than was absolutely necessary, jazz or ragtime orchestrations, and tons of dancing with almost always a big, climactic tap number—or maybe a half dozen of them. These were mindless, cheerful celebrations with many memorable songs, the best by brothers George and Ira Gershwin or Richard Rodgers and Lorenz Hart, which are still beguiling

FIGURE 10.14 George M. Cohan's *Little Johnny Jones,* an early American musical, which introduced the popular hits "Give My Regards to Broadway" and "The Yankee Doodle Boy."

Werner Wolff/Contributor/Time & Life Pictures/Getty Images

us today. This form of musical, while moving out of dominance, has never really left us, as evidenced by the recent successes of *Legally Blonde* and *The Drowsy Chaperone.*

The second dramatic phase is that of **musical drama,** considered to have begun with *Show Boat* in 1927, a musical that dealt with racial issues in a serious and profound way. It was a true musical play, with a consistent and credible story line, authentic atmosphere, and characters of genuine complexity. The other major, serious work of this period was the Gershwins' *Porgy and Bess* (1935), which had considerable influence on musical theatre with its powerful, moving lyricism and the blending of opera with musical theatre. In 1940, Rodgers and Hart's *Pal Joey* shocked theatergoers with a gigolo central character, an intellectual stripper, sexually candid lyrics, and a far more adult perspective than audiences were used to. The following year, *Lady in the Dark* dealt with psychoanalysis! Then there was no turning back.

While the works of **Richard Rodgers and Oscar Hammerstein** may seem relatively tame today (and their final work, *The Sound of Music,* certainly is), it is important to realize how often they were the first to push the musical into showcasing other important social issues. Before their production of *Oklahoma!,* dance was primarily a diversion. Suddenly, it was used to tell the story and to explore characters' darker emotional states. The play dealt with significant conflicts between settlers, featured a very troubled major character, and involved an onstage killing, formerly unheard of in a musical. Their subsequent musicals took on subjects such as physical abuse, racial prejudice, and cultural ignorance with courage and relevance.

Each of the forms discussed here are also sometimes called **book musicals**, where the story is told largely through dialogue or the **book** and the emotional explorations of characters come through music and **lyrics,** which constitute the show's **score.**

American dominance of musical theatre faded away during the 1970s. The hits of French composers Alain Boublil and Claude-Michel Schönberg (*Les Misérables* and *Miss Saigon*) and the British phenomenon Andrew Lloyd Webber (*Jesus Christ Superstar, Evita, Cats, Starlight Express, Sunset Boulevard,* and *The Phantom of the Opera*) are still playing decades later in theatres around the globe. Lloyd Webber has never been as popular with critics as with

Robbie Jack/Corbis

FIGURE 10.15 Maureen Lipman as Ado Annie in the 1998 production of *Oklahoma!* at the Royal National Theatre, London. This musical seems tame today, but in 1943, this Rodgers and Hammerstein production innovated by using dance to tell a story and explore the characters' darker emotional states, rather than acting as a simple diversion.

audiences. Many denigrate his work as derivative, some even suggesting he just revises Giacomo Puccini opera scores, but the public remains enthralled.

The role of the critic's darling goes to American **Stephen Sondheim,** the most respected living composer/lyricist. He writes music and lyrics and does both with a complex brilliance, head and shoulders above his peers. Each of his works (*Company, A Little Night Music, Sweeney Todd, Sunday in the Park with George, Into the Woods, Assassins,* and *Passion*) has pushed the boundaries of musical content with ambiguous, adult thought and an almost total disregard for the traditional happy ending. His music is so complex that actors are often warned not to attempt it at auditions because few accompanists can successfully sight-read it.

Unfortunately, his box-office record reflects the fact that many audiences find his work too challenging, ironic, and downright melancholy.

Landmarks

In addition to the events mentioned here, several creators and musicals took the form to new heights and raised the bar for all who followed.

West Side Story

This contemporary *Romeo and Juliet*, with warring gangs, a Polish Romeo (Tony), and a Puerto Rican Juliet (Maria), puts dance at the very center of the theatrical event, no longer secondary in any way and every bit as important as the music. Jerome Robbins elevated the potential of musical dance forever. (By the way, this musical was Stephen Sondheim's Broadway debut as lyricist.)

FIGURE 10.16 In a classic scene from *West Side Story*, these young men are a gang calling themselves the Jets. This 2008 production at the Sadler's Wells Theatre in London used the choreography of the original production by legendary choreographer Jerome Robbins.

Robbie Jack/Corbis

My Fair Lady

After countless musicals got along with meager books or highly watered-down versions of classics, Alan Jay Lerner took George Bernard Shaw's brilliant original *Pygmalion*, pared it down without in any way diminishing its power, and most important, wrote lyrics that matched the wit, intellect, and style of the original. Suddenly the song could be as brilliant intellectually as it has always been emotionally.

A Chorus Line

Many consider this musical the first and most successful example of the **concept musical.** These are shows that take a single idea, event, or location as a dominant factor. They do more than tell a story; they often create a strong sense of environment as well. Opening in 1975 and running for 6,137 performances, this musical held the record for longest continuous run on Broadway until it was passed by *Cats*. The concept is that a Broadway producer is casting a chorus for a new musical. He asks dancers to tell him something about themselves, and so they do. The throughline is the audition itself, rather than the well-made plotline of the book musicals of the previous decades.

Cabaret

This show evolved the concept musical to new heights, creating a total environment that dominated the action. In the original production, slanted mirrors above the action always reflected the audience. Recent revivals re-created the entire Kit Kat Klub so audience members feel they are there in a here-and-now way, intimately engaged.

Company

While every Sondheim show is to some extent a landmark, this was the first to tackle the issue of committing to one partner for life, with all the problems involved in that challenge. It could be called the first truly grown-up musical in addressing the fragility of marriage and of adult relationships in general. It also broke new ground by eliminating the **chorus.** In the place of large unnamed background singer/dancers, the 14 principal performers constituted the entire cast, providing backup in big numbers. *Company* therefore opened up a world of possibility for the small musical.

Billy Elliot: The Musical

While the importance of dance evolved strongly in both *Oklahoma!* and *West Side Story*, *Billy Elliot* takes dance far beyond story and deep into the hearts and minds of characters. Instead of the usual single dream sequence, there are a dozen. The story itself stops while we go through dance into the memories,

FIGURE 10.17 Billy dances with a future version of himself in one of the many dream sequences in this production of *Billy Elliot* at the Victoria Palace in London.

fears, or hopes of individual characters. There is even an extraordinary sequence where Billy, a young boy from a coal mining community who aspires to a career as a ballet dancer, performs a *pas de deux* from *Swan Lake* with his future adult self, showing us where he is now and where he will be someday simultaneously, in a way that the audience finds electrifying and powerfully moving. Over and over, it is dance that provides an overwhelming emotional power, and according to *New York Times* critic Alastair Macaulay, "In these moments *Billy Elliot* brands the eye and mind with scenes that extend our idea of what the musical can mean."

Next to Normal

Only the eighth musical in history to win the prestigious Pulitzer Prize, this play was described by the judging committee as "a powerful rock musical that grapples with mental illness in a suburban family and expands the scope of subject matter for musicals." Who knew that a bipolar disorder could provide the core for a show the *New York Times* called "brave" and "breathtaking"? It also involves a small cast and no traditional glitzy production values, and yet it has been one of the major hits of recent Broadway seasons, proving that a show with big ideas and great music but a small budget can push the musical theatre envelope in new and exciting ways.

Conventions

How do musicals compare with other forms of theatre we have studied?

Time

Most musicals are set in some kind of "long ago" or in a timeless, encapsulated world. They run long compared with straight plays, often three hours or more, with one intermission and the first part somewhat longer than the second. Musicals move swiftly between songs and generally cover a short period of time. Characters rarely age. However, they may come to a standstill, plotwise, when the need to sing and dance pops in or a character needs at least five minutes to tell us how wonderful it is to have met "a girl named Maria." At the other extreme, musical numbers can allow time to race forward, as when Eliza's weeks and weeks of elocution lessons in *My Fair Lady* are condensed into a single song.

Space

Musicals generally play in large proscenium houses (most Broadway theatres seat 1,000 or more), which can accommodate large casts and audiences. Yet unlike straight plays, they are hardly restricted to the stage itself. In *Cats* and *The Lion King,* animals actually roam the aisles; in *The Music Man,* the band marches through the house; in *Peter Pan*, the title character flies out over the audience; and in *The Phantom of the Opera,* a gigantic chandelier does the same. At the end of the show-stopping, first-act number, "I Am What I Am," in *La Cage aux Folles,* the drag-queen singer whips off his wig and storms angrily down the aisle and out of the theatre. In fact, performances often move back and forth between ignoring the audience in a representative way and then turning to them either in asides or to share big presentational musical numbers.

Values

The majority of musicals come down on the side of celebrating life, cutting loose, not wasting precious moments, and getting back in touch with your joyous child. The song "I Am What I Am" is about coming out of whatever closet you may be trapped inside and joining life. There may be anger and protest in the songs themselves, but there will almost inevitably also be hope and redemption. Musicals that address social issues come down squarely for tolerance, forgiveness, and fighting bigotry at all costs—and all but the most somber favor the impulse to party.

SUSAN BIRKENHEAD

LYRICIST

Real genius in writing for a musical is knowing how to say something very, very complicated, in a simple but eloquent way.

Structure

Most have a healthy balance of ballads, character songs, solos, duets, and big group numbers. There is a recognizable, internal structure that often separates a show tune from the kind of pop music on the charts. It is very rare not to have a major musical moment just before intermission, and frequently this is reprised somewhere in the second act. There may in fact be four or five reprises of songs introduced in the first act. If the entire cast is not singing the final number, it is very unusual.

Pleasure

While many of us may burst into song and dance when hearing good news, we are usually talking a few bars of music and a little gyrating at most. And in life, most of us just do this in happy times. In a musical, both good news and bad can send you into verses and leaping up into the air. Those around you may just suddenly feel the same way, singing your words and dancing your moves with you in perfect harmony. So the pleasure or rapture of the moment spreads rapidly to others onstage and then of course embraces everyone in the audience in a celebration of empathy.

Senses

Musicals are often a feast for the eye and ear via their color, fabric, dazzling movement, and glorious sounds from orchestra and singers. Even though we don't get to go onstage (usually) and dance with the cast, we feel as if we have because the empathy component is so strong. And while some songs require magnificent voices, it would be a mistake to assume that you have no future in musicals if you can't sing. Many of the major stars are marginal singers at best. Lauren Bacall has twice won the Tony Award for Best Leading Actress in a Musical, and she has about four notes. What is required is an oversized, exuberant personality that can fill the theatre with contagious energy and sell a song.

Contemporary Forms

Musicals fall into a number of categories beyond comedy or drama, as even those classifications are now often blended. The forms discussed here are arbitrary, and it is common for a single show to bridge several of them. It does, however, provide a way for us to break this huge theatrical form into subcategories of reflection and analysis.

The Concept Musical

We have already identified some of the landmark concept shows in the previous sections. For these plays, a world is created wherein the entire cast may be felines (*Cats*) or even trains (*Starlight Express*), or the audience may be transported into an identity other than the one they had as they entered the theatre. In a concept musical, the show's metaphor or statement is more important than the actual narrative. They emerged strongly in the 1960s and dominated for much of the 1970s. While some claim earlier examples, *Fiddler on the Roof* is considered by many to be the first truly popular concept musical. It created an entire culture of a Jewish village in 1905 czarist Russia, and everything in the show served the central metaphor: tradition. Most works of Stephen Sondheim fall into this category.

Rock Musicals

The **rock musical** *Hair* made history for more than its nude scene (or, for that matter, the moment when a nearly naked actor swings on a rope into the audience to land on the arms of the seat of an elderly female patron and asks if she wants to look down inside the front of his loincloth). It brought rock into legitimate theatre and was revived with tremendous success in 2009. Rock musicals have attitude, of course. They also reject Tin Pan Alley–style show tunes in favor of the blended influences of blues, swing, gospel, R&B, folk, and country and the dominant use of guitar, drums, and keyboard instrumentation.

Grease and The Who's *Tommy* are considered landmarks, and *Rent* has become a theatre classic. Jonathan Larson's stunning work takes Puccini's nineteenth-century opera *La Bohème* into contemporary New York's East Village and a world of HIV and homelessness. Rock musicals fell off in terms of productions in the 1980s, and then came roaring back with such offbeat

FIGURE 10.18 The cast of the film production of *Dreamgirls*, a contemporary African American musical. Here Jennifer Hudson, Beyoncé Knowles, and Anika Noni Rose perform at the 79th Annual Academy Awards.

Gary Hershorn/Reuters/Corbis

entries as *Bat Boy* and *Hedwig and the Angry Inch*. Recent significant productions include *Passing Strange, Next to Normal,* and *Spring Awakening*.

African American Musicals

There is a long tradition of all–African American musicals, a notable early one being *How Come?*, which introduced the Charleston, the dance craze that virtually defined the 1920s. Shows featuring and exploring the lives of African Americans have included *Sophisticated Ladies* (with the music of Duke Ellington), *Ain't Misbehavin'* (Fats Waller), and *Eubie* and *Bubbling Brown Sugar* (Eubie Blake). These shows all work with small casts and dynamic musical talent. Another classic is *Dreamgirls*, which tells the story of a girl group much like the Supremes but also explores the African American culture of the era. *The Color Purple* took the traditional book musical into an exploration of black American heritage. Each of these drew audiences far beyond their targeted subject and offered major cultural insights and connections.

Family Musicals

The Disney franchise has almost singlehandedly turned what used to be largely an adult outing into a theatrical event that embraces the presence of children. While some parents have always brought their offspring to the theatre, it was generally an invitation to enter their world rather than vice versa. Disney has systematically taken their hit animated musical films and converted them to live theatre. While their *Beauty and the Beast, The Little Mermaid,* and *Mary Poppins* are fairly straightforward re-creations of the films as closely as can be done in a live space, Julie Taymor's brilliant reinvention of *The Lion King* is a totally new experience, with genuinely unexpected connections to both Asia and Africa; universal myths, stunning puppetry, mask, and prop work; and dazzling theatricality. She draws on the genius of all sorts of world theatre—African masks, Javanese rod puppetry, Balinese headdresses, and South African Xhosa click language—to produce a theatre experience so stunning that if you have not yet seen it, expect your breath to be taken away. Disney's franchise had also reversed the long tradition of creating a musical for the stage and transporting it to film later; now we see the exact opposite phenomenon, with numerous non-Disney films following the same path (*Billy Elliot, Legally Blonde*).

Jukebox Musicals

This form uses previously released popular songs rather than original scores. The songs share a connection with a particular singer or group because they were written by or for the artists or were covered by them earlier in their careers. They may also be a collection of songs from an era (such as the 1960s) and/or a center of musical activity (such as Motown). The songs are placed into a story, which may be the biography of the performers whose music is featured (such as *Jersey Boys* or *The Buddy Holly Story*) or it may be entirely invented and bear no resemblance to the lives of the performers (as with *Mamma Mia!*).

Using familiar songs, with or without new lyrics, in a stage production was common in Greek and Elizabethan drama, as well as John Gay's *The Beggar's Opera* of 1728. Jukebox musicals are sometimes called Karaoke Theatre because audiences come to the theatre already highly familiar with the songs and, in some instances, will actually be encouraged to join in and sing along.

Mega Musicals

The phrase "and then it ran forever" is of course "music" to any producer's ears. As musicals have gotten more and more expensive to mount, rather than spreading the money around, mounting numerous shows, and hoping most of them enjoy a modestly profitable run, Broadway producers now sink more money into fewer projects and hope that one of them will be the Broadway Mega Musical of the future. The Mega Musical is a live theatre phenomenon similar to the Hollywood film blockbuster—a large production, usually with an element of flash or special effects, that sells an extraordinary number of tickets and basically blows all the competition out of the water. The champion Megas are *Cats* (18 years on Broadway alone), *Les Misérables, The Phantom of the Opera, Miss Saigon, Rent, Chicago, The Lion King,* and *Mamma Mia!*

It is less likely today that a sole producer, such as Cameron Mackintosh or the late David Merrick, backs a production. Corporate sponsors dominate Broadway, and alliances are formed to come up with the investment of $10 million or more that is usually required to mount a musical. In 2002, the credits for *Thoroughly Modern Millie* listed 10 producers, and some of these were group entities.

The newest Mega phenomenon is *Wicked*, a "prequel" to *The Wizard of Oz* which has broken box-office records around the world, holding weekly-gross-takings records in New York, Los Angeles, Chicago, St. Louis, and London, and the record for biggest opening in the London West End (£100,000 worth of tickets sold in the first hour). Both the West End production and the North American tour have been seen by more than 2 million patrons, and it is still going strong. While many Megas rely on spectacle, it does not always work. Musical adaptations of *The Lord of the Rings* in London (2007), billed as the biggest stage production in musical theatre history, and *Gone with the Wind* (2008) lost money for their investors.

Musical Revues

While most musicals tell a story of some kind, however light and fragile the tale may be, some musicals are actually an excuse to celebrate the work of a single composer, composing team, or a group of talented performers. Revues have their roots in variety shows, vaudeville, musical halls, and minstrel shows. Early in the last century, they tended to be lavish productions, with sketches interspersed with music. Contemporary revues tend to be far simpler in staging, and many forgo or modify sketch diversion for a strong musical throughline. Examples are *Closer Than Ever*, *Tom Foolery,* and *Five Guys Named Moe*. Sondheim-based revues range from *Side by Side by Sondheim* (first produced in the 1970s) to *Putting It Together* (2000) to *Sondheim on Sondheim* (2010). The revue format is common to school and organizational celebratory and fund-raising productions.

Sing-Throughs

In some musicals, there is no actual spoken dialogue and music runs through the entire event, with all lines sung. This form comes closest to opera, with the exception that much of the music is popular rather than classical in form, and even if some of the music is quasi-operatic, the style of attack is often "pop-like." Unlike opera, the performance will inevitably be in the native language of its audience and may be amplified, a practice generally unheard of in opera. *Dreamgirls*, *Jesus Christ Superstar,* and *Les Misérables* are significant examples.

Postmodern Musicals

Economics have made it necessary for small musicals that would formerly have played only off-Broadway to move to Broadway instead because a large house is increasingly essential for recouping investments. While a big risk with many failures, this has also resulted in delightful, miniature works reaching a much larger audience—none more so than the Tony Award-winning Best Musical *Avenue Q*. In true postmodern fashion, this show does not go for big emotions but rather charmingly reflective ones and affectionately juxtaposes the old and the new. *Avenue Q* is a young-adult version of *Sesame Street,* with Muppet-like puppets mingling with the major human characters. Television screens at either side of the stage often feature exactly the kinds of graphics used on the children's show. The musical is both tender and sassy. The opening line of the first song, "What Do You Do with a B.A. in English?" engulfs the audience in laughter because so many have found out they need to ask themselves that question. There are also lots of racy dialogue and one very explicit scene of a night of Muppet carnality. In a striking example of the blurring of old on- and off-Broadway distinctions, after a considerable run on the Great White Way, *Avenue Q* moved back to its off-Broadway origins for a more extended run.

Another big postmodern hit was *Urinetown*, which takes on the unexpected crisis connected to citizens having to pay to use public toilets. As the title suggests, this show brings the exact opposite of our traditional expectations for the focus of musical theatre. It satirizes not just our legal system, capitalism, social irresponsibility, populism, bureaucracy, corporate mismanagement, and local municipal politics, but the Broadway musical itself as a form. In recent years, it has become one of the most popular titles to be produced by colleges and high schools.

CLOSE-UP

Broadway Babies: A New Generation of Musical Fans

The Disney Channel children's program *Johnny and the Sprites* is significantly different from other preschool broadcasts. There are, of course, songs, but instead of the "I Love You" Barney-style simplistic ditties, these numbers are written by a dozen major Broadway composers, including Stephen Schwartz (*Wicked*), Mark Hollmann (*Urinetown*), Michael Patrick Walker (*Altar Boyz*), and Robert Lopez (*Avenue Q*).

How did such accomplished adult composers sign on for such a very young audience? The musical supervisor Gary Adler solicited contributions "by offering composers a chance to help create the future Broadway babies and have people listen to music by writers they may not necessarily have been exposed to. We are hopeful that through this show, we can start training young people's ears to a different kind of music."

For many years, songs from Broadway musicals made top-ten airplay lists, albums were best sellers, and a significant part of the U.S. population knew most of the songs from most of the great musicals. Newer styles and trends in music have since displaced this style of song, and there are many now who have never heard a show tune.

So Adler and the program's creator, executive producer and star John Tartaglia, stepped up and decided to rectify this situation. They had already had great success with *Avenue Q* (Adler as musical director, Tartaglia as star), which showed that many adults would enjoy a show with puppets, childhood references, and good music. This also meant a return to the simple charms of puppets for Disney, which had been entirely forsaken for years in lieu of animation. Tartaglia has worked with puppets since becoming a *Sesame Street* and Muppet operator at age 16 and decided "that I missed the layered storytelling of real musicals and disliked the fact that music in much of children's television is very simple and dumbed down."

None of these composers "write down" to their audience. Stephen Schwartz, who wrote the theme song for *Johnny and the Sprites,* says, "I make no adjustment beyond subject matter for age difference. . . . I basically always approach it from the point of view of writing the best song I can. I try to tell the best story, get across the emotion, and if there is a vocabulary word that the children might not know, that's okay, because now they will."

Even if this does not create a whole new generation of Broadway musical fans, it is a no-lose situation. Children are being exposed to some of the smartest, brightest, and best music available. No new episodes have been filmed for several years, but due to a large viewer petition to "Big Mouse" to Bring Johnny Back, reruns of past episodes are now broadcast on the Disney Junior channel, and are available in DVD form.

Frederick M. Brown/Getty Images

FIGURE 10.19   Actor John Tartaglia of the television show *Johnny and the Sprites* with Ginger, one of the star puppets. The show encourages love of musical theatre in children by featuring songs written by major Broadway composers.

Global Production

While India is best known among the non-Western world for its musical productions, South Africa also has an active musical theatre scene, with revues like *African Footprint* and *Umoja* and book musicals, such as *Kat and the Kings* and *Sarafina!* touring internationally, as well as local successful productions such as *Vere*, *Love and Green Onions*, and *Over the Rainbow*.

THEATRE IN MEDIA

Musicals on Film

For much of the early part of this century, musicals were a major part of going to the movies, defined most vividly by all those madcap, dancing delights of Fred Astaire and Ginger Rogers. The definitive musical created entirely for film is *Singin' in the Rain*, and the defining number here is the title song, with Gene Kelly splashing merrily through the wet streets after he realizes that he has fallen in love with Debbie Reynolds. Broadway hit musicals used to be filmed almost as a matter of course, and most of these adaptations did well at the box office.

But the skepticism and even cynicism of our current age has not been entirely receptive to song and dance. There was a long, dark period between the last truly successful movie musicals, *Cabaret* and *Dirty Dancing*, and *Chicago*, which knocked it out of the park for the first time in many years. Granted, *Chicago* itself is skepticism and cynical, but the success of the movie was almost entirely due to director Rob Marshall, who found a way to take a big, splashy musical into the mind of its central character, Roxie Hart, so that musical numbers emerged from her imagination and fear instead of out of thin air. He also connected the musical rhythms to visual ones so that there was a constant pulse to the film. And in an almost-unheard-of strategy, he gathered the cast long before filming started and rehearsed the show much like a play. This success led to a flurry of musical film adaptations, including *Les Misérables*, *Dreamgirls*, *Hairspray*, *The Producers*, *Mamma Mia!*, and *Sweeney Todd*. This is no magic formula, however, as Marshall's attempt to repeat his approach with *Nine* was considerably less successful, both critically and at the box office. Nevertheless, movie musicals tend to work better now if they are reconceived for film itself. The adaptation of *The Phantom of the Opera*, while opulently produced, generally fell flat because most scenes just had highly traditional camera setups and little visual innovation. It is also true that *Phantom* has fewer ideas to stimulate the imagination, and it is a largely in-person theatrical event, with many moments of "I can't believe they did that live!" On film, all these special, spectacular effects are expected—even commonplace.

Also, musicals have largely been superseded by music videos, which now often tell stories and provide similar diversion in a fraction of the time. It seems as if traditional musical theatre will continue to thrive far more live than in celluloid re-creation in our culture. However, in contemporary India, over 800 films, many of them musicals, are produced each year, making that country by far the world's leader in musical productions. Bollywood directors Bimal Roy, Mehboob Khan, and Guru Dutt are as famous as any Western auteurs. While certain characteristics of their particular musical form can be traced all the way back to Sanskrit, it is the Urdu Parsee theatre of the 1930s that is often cited as the start of the phenomenal interest in the form in India. It is perhaps true that the transition to musical film has been far more comfortable within Asian cultures, where song and dance have always been key to the theatrical event and stories have always been presented in stylized forms far removed from our concept of realism.

The *High School Musical(s)* and *Glee* and *Smash* phenomena show a renewed interest, particularly among young audience members, in experiencing fully staged musical numbers on film, as have musical episodes of such series as *The Simpsons*, *Family Guy*, *Buffy the Vampire Slayer*, *South Park*, and *30 Rock*.

Japan has experienced a huge surge in the growth of an indigenous form of musical theatre and film, both animated and live-action, usually based on anime and manga, such as *Kiki's Delivery Service* and *Tenimyu*. A popular series, *Sailor Moon*, has produced 29 musicals spanning 13 years.

The first modern musical produced in Hong Kong, in both Mandarin and Cantonese, is called *Snow.Wolf.Lake*. Cameron Mackintosh has actually set up production offices there to produce indigenous Chinese musical theatre.

THEATRE IN YOUR LIFE

A Stylized Existence

If you are actually existing day to day in a musical, you are either living a charmed life or you are delusional. However, it is worth noting the degree to which you require music to be a part of your life, so that if there is no sound track or accompaniment, you are discontented. Also, are you that person always trying to get a group to sing, even if not to "Happy Birthday," or to dance, even if there isn't a conga line handy? Or do you often just, as the old adage goes, "sing and dance as if no one is watching"? Even if you are not a regular musical theatre audience member, it may be that you are somehow addicted to its components.

Of course, if you are living in one of the Isms, you may really be in trouble, aside from those interludes of absurdism that seem to invade all our lives. For self-awareness, however, it may be useful to ask if you tend to embrace any of the Ism manifestos or stumble into their point of view. And then also ask how that is working out for you.

For most of us, the elements of stylization discussed in this chapter are best left for brief forays outside the tedium of the realistic world.

ENGAGING IN MUSICAL THEATRE PRODUCTION

Because musicals often require a large number of participants, they can provide a great entrée into the world of the theatre. The simple constructing and then running of the show, given the level of spectacle, number of costume and set changes, and other demands, offer a number of opportunities to sign up for crew work, many of which do not require experience or skill but can be a diverting first step into this world. If you have instrumental skills, maybe you can employ them in the show's orchestra or band.

The same possibilities are often available for onstage action. If you have any singing or dancing skills but do not feel ready for a major role, auditioning for the chorus may be an enjoyable and nonthreatening way to engage in the process. Studying singing and dancing can be a great release, and many departments offer musical survey and musical performance classes if training interests you. If you happen to have acting, singing, and dancing skills (what is called in theatre "a triple threat"), you have a chance to actually make a living because performers who specialize in musical theatre have the greatest likelihood of finding employment.

An old African proverb says, "You sing when you can no longer just speak. You dance when you can no longer just stand." Successful musical theatre productions find this organic connection, in which songs and dances are not layered into the action arbitrarily; rather, the actors are so filled with emotion that they simply seem to have no choice but to kick it up many notches. When this happens, their transformation is contagious, and we all get to experience the rapture of the musical.

SUMMARY

In the aftermath of devastating events in the first half of the twentieth century, the theatre began exploring new ways to present its ideas in styles that we have come to call the Isms. A variety of influential though short-lived movements, such as futurism, Dadaism, and symbolism, evolved simultaneously. Among the most important and influential of the Isms are expressionism, which lets the playwright's subjective view of life be expressed; didacticism, or Epic theatre, defined by Bertolt Brecht as "theatre of the intellect meant to teach and stimulate political and social action"; and absurdism, a reaction to the holocausts of World War II, in which all meaning is ludicrous and the only appropriate choice is to laugh. One of the most popular and well-known styles of non-realistic theatre is the musical, an American contribution to world theatre. Early musicals tended to be light, comic, and heavily dance-oriented. Richard Rodgers and Oscar Hammerstein were among the major composers who brought more serious ideas to the musical. Stephen Sondheim is the reigning king of the American musical, although many of the biggest hits on Broadway now come from Britain in the works of Andrew Lloyd Webber and others. Productions may now fall into one or more of the following categories: concept, rock, African American, family, Mega, review, sing-through, and postmodern musicals. The need to make song and dance an inevitable choice is the key to integrating these elements effectively in any performance.

SUGGESTED ASSIGNMENTS

1. How did the crucial changes in the world during the first part of the last century make realism seem less than adequate for expressing universal concerns?

2. Which of the Isms do you believe have had a lasting impact on theatre and film, and which have faded after their initial impact?

3. For which of the Isms do you feel the closest natural affinity? Which expresses a view of the world that is somewhat akin to your own? If you were to put together a personal manifesto, how would you alter that of the Isms to suit your beliefs?

4. Conversely, which of the Isms do you find most removed or outside your own thinking? What do you find off-putting about this theatre form?

5. With greater and greater frequency, plays and films that are basically realistic are being infused with elements (or at least sequences) of absurdism. Why do you feel this is the case?

6. In your own experience as an audience member, what have been the five nonrealistic productions you have seen that have had the greatest impact on you?

7. Why is it that musicals seem to stir up and excite the emotions of audiences more than any other form of theatre?

8. How is it that audiences often are challenged by trying to adjust to strange, new theatrical conventions, yet they have no difficulty accepting those of musicals, even though it could be argued that those are the strangest conventions of all?

9. Why is it that musicals, once a mainstay of films, faded from popularity? What circumstances may be making them ripe for a comeback?

10. Given the current trends identified in musical theatre, what would you predict might be the next direction of musicals?

SUGGESTED ACTIVITIES

1. **Individual:** Write six lines of dialogue that represent, to the best of your knowledge, symbolism. Do the same for futurism, Dadaism, expressionism, didacticism, and absurdism.

2. **Group:** Divide the task above among individual members of the group. Have each writer cast your interlude with others in the group, rehearse briefly, and present them to the class.

3. **Long-term:** Re-imagine each of the plays you are studying or attending this term as one of the featured Isms. What would be the primary changes involved, and how would this affect audience response?

4. **Large group:** Agree on a nonmusical play or film that everyone knows well. How would it be adapted into a musical? Hold a competition for best song title and song description (give extra points for actually singing a snippet of the imaginary song). Have the audience vote for the winning entry. For a variation, have groups compete for solos for individual characters (such as "Darth Vader's Lament," "Chewbacca's Ragtime," or "Yoda's Rap").

KEY WORDS AND IDEAS

stylization
symbolism
futurism
Dadaism
expressionism
existentialism
absurdism
didacticism (Epic theatre)
Bertolt Brecht
musical

musical comedy/drama
Richard Rodgers and Oscar
    Hammerstein
book, lyrics, score
Stephen Sondheim
chorus
musical forms:
    book musical
    concept musical
    rock musical

dramatic interlude 5

Dreams

Featured plays:

The Three Sisters by Anton Chekhov (1901)

Bitter Cane by Genny Lim (1989)

(NOTE: The scripts for these plays, along with additional background information, are available in the companion anthology to this text, *Life Themes: An Anthology of Plays for the Theatre*

What we dream for ourselves may barely resemble the lives for which we settle. But even if none of them come true, dreams get us out of bed and into the world, suffering what Shakespeare calls "the slings and arrows of outrageous fortune" each day. If we did not believe things could get better (and dream that they will get way, way better), many of us could (and do) sink into stagnancy and despair. In both of these plays, people are stuck someplace they do not want to be, doing jobs they do not want to do, and tolerating people they do not want to see, but holding on to the possibility that if they try harder, they will free themselves of these deadly circumstances. In *The Three Sisters,* the dream is to leave a dead-end town for the bright lights of the big city, where magic and opportunity awaits. In *Bitter Cane*, it is to make money in a faraway country and return home secure. If the nature of drama is conflict, watching these characters take their dreams and bump them up against their realities is the stuff of theatre—occasionally inspiring, more often heartbreaking, and always compelling.

T. Charles Erickson

FIGURE D5.1 The realistic style of Chekhov's *The Three Sisters* asks only that the audience accept the fourth-wall convention and doesn't venture into more unconventional territory.

The Three Sisters (1901)

Setting: A remote small town in Russia, around the turn of the century

Characters

The Prozorov family, brother and sisters:
Andrey, male heir, in charge of the family property
Olga, eldest, unmarried, teaching
Irina, youngest, still open to possibility
Masha, middle sister, caught in a loveless marriage
Anfisa and Ferapont, faithful old family servants

Natasha, Andrey's girlfriend, later his wife
Kulygin, Masha's husband and teacher at the same school as Olga
Army officers stationed at the local outpost:
Baron Tusenbach
Tchebutykin
Solyony
Fedotik
Roday
Vershinin

The Prozorovs' dream is to move to Moscow, which has come to represent all that is sparkling, refined, and engaging in life. Even the weather there is better:

> OLGA: Today we can keep the windows wide open, but there are no leaves on the birch trees yet. In Moscow, by this time, everything is in bloom. I remember everything there, even if it has been eleven years.

The play opens on Irina's 19th birthday, which comes exactly a year after the death of Colonel Prozorov, the family patriarch. The lives of all the family have been altered, and not for the better, with feelings of restlessness and sadness dominating:

> MASHA: When father was alive, there were as many as 40 officers at our birthday parties. It was loud and joyous, but now, here's only a man and a half.

All the sisters are smarter than their beloved brother, Andrey, who unfortunately, due to the tradition of the times, controls the family budget. Over the course of the play, he succumbs to the questionable charms of a vixen (Natasha) who at first seems merely ignorant and vulgar:

> MASHA: Oh, how she dresses! Not just unattractive or ugly, but—pathetic. Colors you've never seen together before. And things like—fringe. And her cheeks! Andrey isn't in love—I can't believe it! I just can't. Andrey has taste.

But he is in love. He marries Natasha, and she gradually turns into something of a tyrant, taking over the house, carrying on a flagrant affair with another man, throwing the beloved old servants out into the cold, and, upon the birth of her child, constantly claiming he is a prodigy:

> NATASHA: Bobik understands everything! I say "Good morning dear!" And he gives me a special look. You think I'm only a mother talking, but no! No! He's an unusual child.
> SOLYONY: If this child were mine, I would have fried him in a skillet and eaten him.

All the other characters are living lives of quiet sadness and desperation. Andrey mortgages the house to pay gambling debts, limiting the possibility that anyone will ever escape this town. Olga works her way up to headmistress at her school, but she finds little genuine satisfaction in her work. Masha plunges into a briefly joyous but dead-end affair with Vershinin. Irina accepts a proposal of marriage from the Baron Tuzenbach and briefly glimpses a life of contentment (though not love)

until he is killed in a duel by a rival. All long for something better, often beginning to believe it will not happen in their lifetime, sentiments effectively capsulated by Vershinin:

> VERSHININ: Oh, I think a better life just has to come. We won't share in that life of course, but we are living for it now, starting to create it, I think it's going to grow out of our suffering. I have to believe that.

Perhaps the most brutal blow to whatever has been diverting and pleasing in the sisters' lives is the removal of the military base and an end to that kind of companionship:

> MASHA: The military are in this town, at any rate, the people who are most decent, educated, and honorable. . . . But most of the people in this town are crude and unfriendly.

The play ends as it begins, with only the three sisters alone together, embracing each other and trying to face the future:

> OLGA: Oh dear sisters, our life isn't over yet. We'll live! The music plays so joyously, and perhaps tomorrow—or the day after—we'll know why we live and why we suffer. If we only knew, if we only knew!

Here is a combined scene from *The Three Sisters*, as translated and adapted for the stage by Robert Barton in *Life Themes: An Anthology of Plays for the Theatre*:

In Act Three, the sisters' lives are becoming ever more restricted as Andrey's wife, Natasha, takes over the house. Outside, the whole town is on fire and the sisters wait helplessly for news. Masha's bumbling husband, Kulygin, has joined them.

> MASHA: *[lying down]* Are you asleep, Fyodor?
> KULYGIN: Huh?
> MASHA: You ought to go home.
> KULYGIN: Dear Masha, sweet Masha.
> IRINA: She's tired. Let her rest, Fedya.
> KULYGIN: I'm going, I'm going. My magnificent wife. I love you, my one and only.
> MASHA: *[angrily]* Amo, amas, amar, amamus, amaris, amant.
> KULYGIN: *[laughing]* No, really, what an amazing woman. Seven years we've been married, but it seems like only yesterday. An amazing woman. I am content, content, content.
> MASHA: I'm bored, bored, bored. *[She sits up.]* There's something I can't get out of my head. I can't stay silent. I mean about Andrey. He's mortgaged this house to the bank and his wife has grabbed all the

money! But the house doesn't belong just to him, but to all four of us! How could he?

KULYGEN; Well, he owes a lot of money.

MASHA: But it's outrageous. [She lies back down.]

KULYGIN: You and I aren't poor.

MASHA: No, I don't need anything. It's the injustice that makes me furious. [pause] Go home, Fyodor!

KULYGIN: [kissing her] You're tired, rest a bit. I'll sit and wait for you at home. Sleep . . . . [going] I'm content, I am content, I am content. [He goes out.]

IRINA: Our Andrey has grown petty and small. He's dried up and aged since he married that woman! He has no spark. He's stopped preparing to become a professor altogether. Yesterday he was actually bragging about being on the county council, which is run by Protopopoff. The whole town's talking and laughing and he's the only one who knows nothing and sees nothing. And now, even during the fire, he just sits in his room and plays the violin. [nervously] It's a nightmare. [crying] I just can't bear any more! I can't! [sobbing aloud] I can't . . .

[OLGA enters]

OLGA: [alarmed] What is the matter, what is it, my darling?

IRINA: [sobbing] Where's it all gone? Where is it? Oh, my God, my God! I've forgotten everything. I've forgotten. It's muddled in my head. I don't remember what the Italian word for window is, or the ceiling there. I'm forgetting it all, life's slipping away and we will never go to Moscow. I realize that now—we'll never go.

OLGA: Oh my sweet love . . . .

IRINA: [restraining herself] Now I know misery. I thought that answer was work, but I'm sick of it! First telegraph operator, now council secretary, and I despise everything they give me to do. My brain's dried up. I'm getting thin, ugly, and old, and there's no satisfaction of any kind. Life no longer has any sense of possibility. Why haven't I killed myself? I can't understand why . . .

OLGA: Don't cry, my little girl, don't cry.

IRINA: I'm not crying. I'm not. I'm sick of it. All that is over.

OLGA: My angel, I'm talking to you as a sister and friend, if you want my advice, marry the Baron!

[IRINA weeps silently.] You respect and value him. He's not good looking, but he's decent. I myself would marry without love. I'd marry anyone who proposed if he was an honorable man. I'd even marry an old man. I would.

IRINA: I kept believing I'd meet the real one in Moscow. But it's no more than a silly dream . . .

OLGA: [embracing her sister] My dear, beautiful sister. I understand it all. When the Baron left the military and came to see us in civilian clothes, he seemed to me so homely that I actually cried. He asked, "Why are you crying?" How could I tell him! But if God grants that he marry you, I'll be so happy.

[NATASHA crosses the stage from the right door to the left, without speaking, a candle in her hand.]

MASHA: [sitting up] She walks about as if she was the one who started the fire.

OLGA: Masha, you old silly! You are the silliest one in our silly family. [a pause]

MASHA: I need to confess, my precious sisters. I'll die if I don't say it. [quietly] And you know it before I speak it. [a pause] I love . . . that man . . . Vershinin.

OLGA: [going behind her screen] Stop it. I won't listen.

MASHA: What can I do? First I thought he was strange, then I felt sorry for him. Then I began to love him . . . to love his voice, his words, his little girls, even his misfortunes.

OLGA: [behind the screen] I'm not listening!

MASHA: Oh, Olga, you're the silly one. I'm in love—that's my fate. And he loves me. Is it wrong? [taking IRINA by the hand and drawing her nearer] You read novels and think you understand all about love, but when you fall in love yourself, you begin to see that you know nothing. My loves, my sisters. I've confessed to you, now I'll be silent. I will.

IRINA: What a night! [a pause] Olga! [OLGA looks out from behind the screen.] Did you hear? They're taking the brigade away from us.

OLGA: That's only a rumor.

IRINA: We'll be all alone . . . Olga!

OLGA: Yes?

IRINA: I respect the Baron, I value him, I'll marry him, all right? Only let's go to Moscow! I beg you, let's go! There's nothing in the world like Moscow! Let's go. Olga! Please! Let's go!

[CURTAIN]

Bitter Cane (1989)

Setting: Hawaii in the 1880s

Characters:

Lau Hing Kuo, the ghost of a middle-aged cane cutter
Li-Tai, a prostitute in her mid-thirties
Kam Su, a cane cutter in his early thirties
Wing Chun Kuo, 16-year-old son of Lau Hing
Fook Ming, a middle-aged Chinese *luna* (foreman)

Wing's dream is the same as that of his late father and thousands of other Chinese workers: travel to Hawaii, earn enough to buy land back home, return, and start a better life. He leaves China with the haunting message of his mother ringing in his and our ears:

> VOICEOVER OF HIS OLD MOTHER: Now it is up to you, my son. Do not kill me with shame, as did your father. Will you break the cycle of pain or will you pursue another grievous lifetime?

The lure to work in the cane fields has been largely a false one, with salaries and working conditions much worse than they have been represented and saving money nearly impossible. To keep the workers passive, the owners actually provide them with packets of opium. Wing tries to avoid all that, but an older worker, Kam, is dubious:

> KAM: I give you a month before you're as depraved as the rest of us. Disciples of the golden poppy. . . . If opium is evil, the white man's the devil. He gave it to us and it's him who's keeping us here. . . .

Throughout the play, the ghost of Wing's father appears to us but not to him. Wing feels great bitterness toward his father for deserting his mother:

> WING: She died. He lied to her. He lied to her every month for two years! When he got tired of lying, he stopped writing altogether. She didn't hear from him again. Then one day she gets a letter saying he's dead. . . . You want to know what killed him? Opium. . . . His body was never recovered they said because he had drowned in the ocean. That's why I'm here. To redeem a dead man.

He becomes involved with Li-Tai, the plantation prostitute, exactly as his father had before him:

> LI-TAI: Sometimes I wonder which is more oppressive—the heat of the sun or the lust of a man. . . . You see this body? It's not mine. It belongs to Kahuku Plantation. My skin even smells like burnt cane!

> WING: And what about your heart?
> LI-TAI: I cut it out. Long ago.
> WING: Tell me one thing. I've got to know. Do you love me, Li-Tai? Or is it my father you love?
> LI-TAI: When you didn't come, I wanted to die. Is that love?

Wing does avoid the drug, which is eating others alive, and becomes the most admired worker on the farm. Kam still fears he will go the way of his father:

> KAM: In ten years, he had gone from top cutter at Kahuku to a skeleton. They blamed you for his suicide, Li-Tai.
> LI-TAI: *[bitterly]* Of course. If a man is weak, it's the fault of the woman. Do you think I have the power to change men's lives?

Li-Tai is officially being kept by Fook, the obsessively possessive foreman:

> FOOK: Li-Tai is mine! I own her. Every hair on her body, every inch of her flesh and bones is paid for in gold.
> WING: You don't own her soul.

Just before her own death, Li-Tai reveals that Wing's father's remains have not really disappeared. She urges him to leave the impossible dreams here and to return home. For her, home means death:

> LI-TAI: Now you have a chance to be free. Return these bones to where they belong. They are part of you, Wing. Part of me. Home, I am ready to go home.

Here is a scene from *Bitter Cane*:

Sixteen-year-old Wing has been in the cane camp for a few weeks when his friend Kam takes him to visit the camp prostitute Li-Tai, a foot-bound, opium-addicted woman who was in love with Wing's father.

> LI-TAI *[abruptly]:* Look. I know you're not here to gossip. You have two dollars? *[He fumbles in his pocket and without looking hands her several bills. She smirks at his naiveté and quickly tucks it in her kimono pocket.]*
> LI-TAI: Sit down. *[He sits.]* Want something to drink?
> WING: Some tea would be nice, thank you.
> LI-TAI *[amused laugh]:* Tea? How old are you?
> WING: Twenty.
> LI-TAI *[frowning]:* You're lying.
> WING *[embarrassed]:* Sixteen.
> LI-TAI: This your first time? *[He nods with embarrassment. She takes a whiskey bottle, uncorks it, pours a glass, and hands it to him.]*

LI-TAI: Drink it. It'll give you confidence. *[He takes a big swallow and chokes. She laughs at him.]*

LI-TAI: Slow down. What's your hurry? *[smiling]* Talk to me.

WING *[still embarrassed]*: About what?

LI-TAI: About you.

WING *[blushing]*: There's not much to tell.

LI-TAI: Why not?

WING *[takes a gulp. then blurts]*: My name is Wing and I like to eat duck gizzards. *[She bursts out laughing, then he laughs, too.]*

WING: On the first day of school, I remember the teacher asked us to introduce ourselves.

LI-TAI: And that was what you said.

WING: I couldn't think of anything else!

LI-TAI *[mockingly]*: You still can't.

WING *[frustrated]*: I don't know why I'm so tongue-tied. *[finishes his glass]*

LI-TAI: Talking is not important. *[refills his glass]* There are other ways to communicate. *[pours herself one, clicks his glass. then slumps on the bed with her glass in a provocative manner.]* Your parents have a bride picked out for you yet?

WING: No. *[pauses.]* My parents are dead.

LI-TAI: I'm sorry.

WING: My father died here. At Kahuku.

LI-TAI: Oh? *[surprised.]* What was his name?

WING: Lau Hing. Kuo Lau Hing. *[She freezes at the recognition of his name.]* He was one of those Sandalwood boys who never made it back.

LI-TAI *[trembling]*: How old were you when he left?

WING: I was just a baby.

[Struck by the resemblance, she cups his face with her hands.]

LI-TAI: Let me look at you!

WING *[embarrassed]*: What's the matter? Why are you looking at me like that?

LI-TAI *[marveling]*: You remind me of someone.

WING: I'm as good as any man on Kahuku.

LI-TAT *[disdainfully]*: The average man here is a pig. You don't want to be like them, do you?

WING: One flop in the family is enough. It's no secret. Lau Hing was a bum.

LI-TAI: How can a son talk about his own father in that way?

WING: And how can a father treat his family that way? Why should I pretend he was somebody he wasn't? *[somberly]* He was nobody to me. Nothing.

LI-TAI *[stung with guilt]*: Your mother? She loved him?

WING *[disgustedly]*: She died. He lied to her. He lied to her every month for two years! When he got tired of lying, he stopped writing altogether. She didn't hear from him again. Then one day, she gets this letter saying he's dead. *[bitterly]* You want to know what killed him? *[pauses]* Opium. The money he should have sent home, he squandered on himself. *[pauses]* They shipped his trunk back. She thought it was his bones. When she opened it, she fainted. The box was empty except for his hat and a few personal belongings. His body was never recovered they said, because he had drowned in the ocean. *[with cruel irony]* That's why I'm here. To redeem a dead man.

LI-TAI: You think you'll succeed?

WING: I'm not sending my ghost in an empty box home. Life is too short! *[listening to the sound of rain]* It's raining again.

LI-TAI: It's always raining. There's no escape. *[with a sense of foreboding]* You do what you can do to forget. And survive. *[picks up a fan and begins moodily fanning herself]* I can't decide what's more boring. Living out here in the middle of nowhere or raising chickens in a puny plot back home.

WING: Why did you come here?

LI-TAI: A lady in the village told me that Hawai'i was paradise. She said there was hardly anything to do there but suck on big, fat, juicy sugarcane—sweeter than honey. I was crazy for cane and waited for the day to come here. When my mother died, my father remarried. My new mother didn't like a girl with bound feet who talked back. So I told her to send me to Hawai'i. She sold me to a rich old merchant on the Big Island. I cried and begged to go back home. But I was his number four concubine. His favorite. Four is a bad luck number. So when the old man suffered a stroke in my bedroom, they, of course, blamed it on me. Number one wife, who was always jealous of me, picked up my red slippers and threw them at my face. Then she beat me with a bamboo rod and called me a good-for-nothing slave girl! *[laughs bitterly]* They lit firecrackers when Fook Ming took me. To rid my evil spirit. Some paradise.

The Three Sisters is as perfect an example of early realism as exists, so much so that it is difficult for us to imagine a time when events such as these were not dramatized.

Call for Change

Just as Stanislavski called for a different, more honest approach to acting than had been common before, Chekhov said, "A play should be written in which people arrive, go away, have dinner, talk about the weather, and play cards. Life must be as it is and people as they are—not on stilts! . . . Let everything on the stage be as complicated and at the same time as simple as it is in life." This may seem naive to you unless you realize how unreal everything was before he made this revolutionary statement.

The Look

Each act of this play takes place in a distinct and spacious setting: Act One, the dining and living room of the family; Act Two, bedrooms and hallways upstairs; Act Three, the porch and exterior of the house. In contemporary productions, these locales are not likely to be represented in minute detail. Isolated set pieces and portions of walls or ceilings are likely to suggest the whole and encourage the audience to fill in the gaps with their imaginations in the tradition of realism, which most often gives you selected reality. Actors will be dressed the way people did in the actual time and country, with some attempt at historical accuracy.

The Sound

Actors will sound like real human beings, and speeches will often trail off into incompletion, as do most of ours in life. However, depending on the space, it is likely that diction will be sharper than in life to have all be understood. In actual life, it is estimated we lose about 30 percent of what is actually said and fill in the rest. In this instance, all the dialogue is important.

The Acting

While in life we may hide our intentions, the actors will be asked to hide them from other characters sometimes but at the same time make them clear to the audience. This involves a double level of concentration. While most scenes will appear to be real and we will be allowed the "fly on the wall" sensation of eavesdropping, it will also be true that the performance will actually be pitched forward. Actors will cheat out to the audience to be seen and understood at key moments; actions might stop or go into slow motion on other parts of the stage when we should be looking at a particular exchange or piece of business. All will be truthful, though projected.

Stylization or Reality?

In keeping with the tradition of magic realism, *Bitter Cane* has stark and believable dialogue— some of it blunt, profane, and perhaps on the cusp of naturalism. But unlike *The Three Sisters*, where every action is as it would be in the lives of European cultures without discernible magic, consider these shifts in "reality":

- At the opening, only the audience and Wing actually hear the voice of his mother charging and warning him.

- A ghost of his father appears immediately and gives a poetically charged speech.

- The ghost continues to shadow his son, sometimes repeating the boy's lines right after him, following him into his most intimate encounters.

- When the son performs an action (such as whittling), the ghost will do the same in pantomime, without the props.

- The ghost speaks only to the audience and always in a heightened way. He allows himself to be seen only once by Li-Tai.

At any given moment, a character may leave behind realistic dialogue and burst into highly metaphoric, lyrical, and abstract imagery in some of the same ways that characters in musicals shift reality by breaking into song:

> WING: I was lying in the dark, unable to sleep, so I listened to sounds. The soft feet of rain, the rustling of boughs and leaves, ten thousand voices of crickets . . . I heard the grass talk to the wind. I heard the cicada's song.

Bitter Cane asks us to agree to more "conditions of make-believe" than *The Three Sisters*. We can watch the former, and in the tradition of realism, we can mostly just pretend that we are not in a theatre and peek through the fourth wall. In the latter, we are constantly asked to accept supernatural and whimsical extensions of life. Does this mean the action is actually stylized? The originators of magic realism would maintain that these elements are simply part of everyday "real" life within the culture being represented.

Blue Man Group, a wildly popular performance art production involving percussion, food stunts, and many rolls of toilet paper.

part V

Where Is Theatre Now?

Theatre is moving toward exciting diversity and variety.

In Chapter 11, we will identify international trends, the range of American ethnic theatre, gender-related theatre, unscripted performance for social change, as well as new forms such as performance art, fusion, and devised work. We will also explore the surge in regional theatre creativity.

In Chapter 12, we will offer guidelines for taking the ideas developed in this text into writing critical reviews and offer some final considerations regarding working in the theatre.

In Dramatic Interlude 6, we will offer *He and She* by Rachel Crothers and *The Piano Lesson* by August Wilson as ways of exploring the issue of Values.

In Expansion 6, we will identify how these plays reflect current trends and essential considerations in writing informed reviews of performances, as well as sample critical reviews of productions of the featured plays themselves.

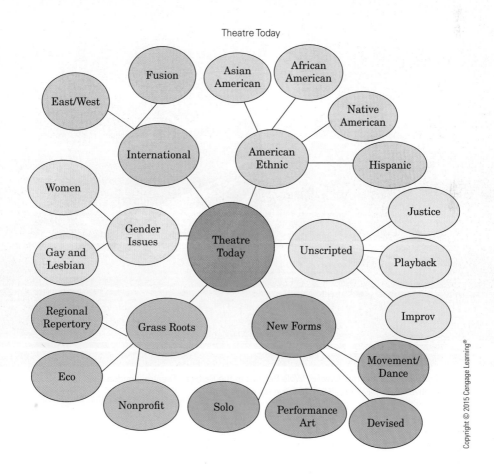

Theatre Today

chapter 11

CONTEMPORARY VOICES

The masquerade scene from *The Lion and the Jewel* by Wole Soyinka at the Barbican Theatre, London.
Soyinka's politically provocative works have forced him to leave his native Nigeria.

Rick Najera, Eugenio Derbez, and Rene Lavan in the play
Latinologues by Rick Najera at the Helen Hayes Theatre in New York.

Lesson Objectives:

Upon completion of this chapter, you will
be able to:

1. Define the conventions of contemporary global theatre and new fusion
   movements.
2. Enjoy the conventions and voices
   of theatre from ethnic American
   communities.
3. Appreciate movements focusing
   on gender identity and equality,
   especially in the United States.
4. Consider ways that unscripted theatre
   might be a tool for you to use in your
   future profession.
5. Define the conventions of new
   performing art genres that push the
   boundaries of traditional theatre.
6. Consider involvement in grassroots
   organizations that may exist in
   your area, or consider creating one
   that addresses the concerns of your
   community.

Introduction

Amazing theatre is happening everywhere, with many innovative attempts to redefine the theatre experience. Today's theatre challenges our very sense of what it means to go to the theatre and what we expect to take away from it. Some of these innovations have highly select and narrow advocates, but others have received far-reaching validation. Sometimes combinations of old ideas have resulted in a new theatrical experience.

In the first half of this chapter, we will explore theatre based on being part of a group of people, whether an entire culture or a specific ethnicity, gender, or sexual orientation. In the second half, we will examine theatre based on form, from the absence of a script to original devised works and the formation of theatre companies with regional roots as a source of new theatrical life.

Eastern and Western Theatre

More and more Western theatre is being produced in Western format in Asian countries. The reverse, alas, has not been true. However, Asian culture now has a profound impact on actor training and practice, particularly in the United States, where physical awareness disciplines such as aikido, tai chi, yoga, and chi gong are often integrated in theatre curricula and in programs in which professional theatres strive to maintain actors' well-being. Eastern wisdom about how body, breath, and mind work together has offered a deeply effective process to the way Western actors prepare themselves to perform.

Although these regions of the world have often reached out to influence each other's theatre practice, some fascinating distinctions remain in contemporary performance. While there will be exceptions to the generalizations discussed here, these theatrical preferences tend to dominate within each culture.

1. Time

    Western: Plays are plotted tightly and often criticized for not moving swiftly enough to hold the audience's attention.

    Eastern: Pacing is far more leisurely, is less based on plot development, and is more given to digression and diversion.

    Western: One may embark on a theatrical career even into middle age.

    Eastern: Most performers are trained from early childhood, and it is all but impossible to break into the profession in another way.

    Western: The vast majority of plays are contemporary, set in the time in which they are written. Even Shakespeare and other classical writers are constantly updated to "now" in production.

Eastern: Almost all are still set either in the distant past or in a universally recurring phenomenon, such as the shifts between seasons.

2. Space

Western: Twenty percent of the world's population is considered Western.

Eastern: Eastern regions constitute 60 percent of people of the world, so our lack of knowledge of theatrical traditions is surprising.

Western: While some plays are based on spectacle, theatres attempt intimacy far more often, trying to get audiences physically closer to the action and more involved in the internal lives of characters.

Eastern: Plays are generally performed broadly and in a highly stylized manner that would be considered over the top in the West.

Western: In realistic drama, often performers ignore the audience altogether, leaving the impression that observers are eavesdropping.

Eastern: Performances are almost invariably presentational and directly involve audience members.

Western: When the audience is acknowledged, performers may ask them to participate, react, or even enter the performance space.

Eastern: Audience is a constant presence but rarely directly challenged or asked to take part in any way not already ritualized.

3. Values

Western: Most plays are judged on how realistically or honestly they portray human experience, or how cleverly they reframe our familiar experiences. Plays aspiring to greatness are judged by what they mean or say about the lives of audience members and their potential for profound impact on those lives.

Eastern: Plays are judged for sensuality of experience, rhythm, melody, beauty of expression, and the degree to which audiences are transported and diverted.

Western: There is great interest in innovation for both performers and technicians; with new interpretations, technical advances are pursued and honored constantly.

Eastern: Highly traditional and deeply connected to religion, folktales, and myths, Eastern theatre is slower to embrace or even respect change.

Western: A great actor is capable of emotional nuance, empathy, and striking originality.

Eastern: A great actor is a great athlete, singer, and dancer and highly respectful of those who have come before him, with subtly nuanced original choices rather than revolutionary changes.

4. Structure

Western: Drama is a significant part of literature; plays are often read rather than seen.

Eastern: Drama is almost exclusively a total theatrical experience, with few scripts published and almost none read as part of standard education.

Western: Many actors train briefly, with no universally recognized pattern to achieve recognition. Some achieve success with no formal training at all.

Eastern: Actors are often born into a theatrical family or adopted by one. They then embark on an intense and standardized training based on apprenticeship and move up through the ranks.

5. Pleasure

Western: Diverse theatrical forms, from naturalistic (going to the theatre to see our own lives reflected) to escapist (a fantastic better version of our lives), make for a virtual smorgasbord of choices when one decides to go to the theatre.

Eastern: A great love of spectacle dominates, with brilliant colors, graceful movement, and no interest in realistic portrayal, but great concern about stunningly beautiful theatricality, visual perfection, and dazzling and sweeping movement.

6. Senses

Western: Except for musicals (and some of them are "sung through"), the text is almost entirely spoken with great effort at making the speech seem natural. Even in classical productions, an attempt is made to have the elevated speech and period-style movement appear natural to the performer.

Eastern: The text is almost never just spoken but sung, danced, chanted, and pantomimed; the theatrical event demands more suspension of disbelief to enter a highly stylized universe.

Western: The appeal is to the intellect and the emotions, with surprise often presented in plot twists, sudden reversals, disclosures, and unexpected climaxes. Audiences expect to be stimulated by ideas, stirred to feel powerfully, or both.

Eastern: The appeal is to the senses. The basic story is likely to be known by the audience, so surprise lies in the moment-to-moment theatrical delights. The event is more likely to be judged by its moments of beauty and esthetic pleasure than shocking details.

Western: Actors may rely on props or pieces of business to enhance their performance, but they largely turn to their own inner recourses.

The more classical the production, the less detail, but it is rare for a performance to be about more than the actor herself.

Eastern: Puppets, stilts, and other extravagant extensions of the actor's art, including hugely challenging, gorgeous costumes, may support the performances. At any moment, the individual performer may step back and allow the theatrical effect to step into focus.

Global Theatre and Fusion

The format of Western drama has influenced a number of global playwrights, and sadly, so have some of our customs of repression. Numerous Asian countries have developed censorship boards. For example, in 1998, the Chinese government shocked the world by canceling a much-anticipated American tour of a Chinese opera called *The Peony Pavilion*, judging it too erotic and not genuinely representative of *Kunqu*.

The Market Theatre in Johannesburg continues to offer theatre that formerly confronted apartheid and now confronts its aftermath. The most prolific and eloquent spokesman regarding this issue is a white man, **Athol Fugard**, who wrote six other apartheid plays besides *"Master Harold" . . . and the boys*. His post-apartheid works, including *Valley Song* and *The Captain's Tiger*, deal with the efforts to heal after a long term of injustice.

Wole Soyinka of Nigeria, often jailed for his political activism and now living in political exile in the United States, has nevertheless created scripts that could never be produced in his own country. His works address government corruption, inept officials, and other forms of post-independence chaos.

In Ghana, traditional African theatre blends with modern techniques and content in a growing phenomenon called the **Concert Party**. In a Concert Party, the traditional Joker or **Ananse** (the spider) has evolved into a character known throughout the country as simply "Bob," named after the first master performer. The Concert Party melds traditional stories and storytelling techniques with ragtime music, minstrel show, tap dance, African American sea shanties, and stand-up comedy. Famous Concert Party performance groups include the Two Bobs, the Axim Trio, Bob Cole's Dynamic Ghana Trio, and the Fanti Trio. The evening usually consists of music performance and comic plays, generally performed by three men who compose the most common form of the Concert troupe. As the play titles suggest (*The Jealous Rival* and *The Ungrateful Husband*, for example), one member of the trio always needs to specialize in drag or cross-dressing roles.

ROSLYN SULCAS
JOURNALIST

Despite South Africa's peaceful transition from the apartheid regime to democracy in 1994, the country is still dealing with the difficulties of racial integration, a population ravaged by AIDS, domestic violence, high unemployment, and an elevated rate of violent crime. The performance arts are a world unavailable to millions who live in poverty.

ESIABA IROBI
THEATRE SCHOLAR

Whereas good Western dramatists are often given prizes and awards, enterprising African dramatists are often imprisoned, sent into exile, or simply killed by their governments.

John Stanmeyer/VII/Corbis

FIGURE 11.1   Street theatre with a purpose in Tanzania. This project is called "Malaria Is Not Acceptable," and performers travel from place to place to share prevention techniques.

In Ghana, as throughout Africa, women are creating powerful new opportunities for their voices to be heard, often in issue-based theatre. AIDS and malaria epidemics cause stress within families that is particularly borne by the women. New plays and performance styles address those stresses in new ways. Women shout, fight, and hurl insults at their abusers in ways unheard of only a decade ago. Single motherhood creates another economic and familial stress factor finding outlet in new theatres. Emerging playwright **Tess Onwueme** may have said it best when she remarked about the growing feminist movement in African theatre, saying simply, "Who can silence her drum?"

In Niger, **Hausa** theatrical troupes are moving slowly but inevitably toward a re-emergent national theatre. The typical Hausa troupe features 30 to 40 members, the majority of which are young to middle-aged men. In this predominantly Muslim country, where seclusion of women is still the ideal, each troupe now has five to ten women in its membership. Most are young unmarried women who leave the troupe when they marry, creating a constantly changing pool of actresses. This pool may yet stabilize because, as one Hausa actor expressed, "*Kansu ya hwara waiwaiye* (They are beginning to awaken)." Hausa plays develop around a theme just as devised works do. Themes may be historical, religious, or political, but they always represent something of immediate importance to the community. The plays expose wrongdoers, suggest solutions, and uniquely let the criminals know that the community is on to them. This is theatre at its most immediate level of community involvement: sometimes scathing, sometimes risky, often comic, and always personal to the audience.

The term **total theatre** is used to identify a contemporary mix of Western and traditional African ritual performance. This theatre renews a connection with Africa's past, honors those cultural heritages long suppressed, and confronts important political issues. It also holds accountable European intervention. In presentation, it fuses the two dominant theatre forms rather than choosing between them.

Fusion, a term for blending theatrical conventions from different cultures into a single production, is an exciting and probably inevitable result of our becoming a global culture. The most noteworthy directors fusing international concepts into their productions are **Peter Brook** and **Ariane Mnouchkine**. We focus on Mnouchkine because she has received less recognition. Mnouchkine, artistic director of the *Théâtre du Soleil,* is particularly known for blending Eastern production traditions and Western texts. She searches for a new language of theatre and blends influences of Antonin Artaud, Bertolt Brecht, and improvisation. She has brought North African Islamic fundamentalism to an innovative production of Molière's *Tartuffe,* which is already a study of religious hypocrisy. She has directed four Asian-themed (Cambodian, Indian, Tibetan, and Chinese) plays by Hélène Cixous. She constantly finds ways to use the old to illuminate the new. *Drums on the Dyke* is based on His Zhou's 400-year-old work on the relationships between humans and nature. It employs masked actors manipulated like puppets. In the original ancient Chinese version, characters try to contain rampaging rivers. However, in Mnouchkine's version, many farmlands are flooded, with no warning to the inhabitants.

THEATRE IN MEDIA

Chinese Influences on Western Films

In the screen world, a powerful new overlap between China and the West amounts to a steady stream of remakes of Asian-language films (such as *The Ring, The Grudge,* and *Dark Water*). We are also seeing a higher international profile for Chinese actors such as Ziyi Zhang, Michelle Yeoh, and Li Gong; far more worldwide distribution of Chinese films; and Western masters acknowledging inspiration from the East. In 2006, Martin Scorsese's *The Departed* was released, a movie based on a trilogy of Chinese gangster films. Quentin Tarantino honors Chinese director Kar Wai Wong as his primary artistic influence. As *Variety*, with its antennae always out for industry trends, states: "There has been much jumping over the Great Wall."

DREAMWORKS IN CHINA

For Hollywood, replacing a boy's silhouette with a panda is no joke. Steven Spielberg's DreamWorks has created the Shanghai Oriental DreamWorks Film & Television Technology Company, signaling its intent to move beyond simply selling to the Chinese market from the outside. Some of America's biggest studios are moving away from the idea of a "domestic" box office by creating long-term joint enterprises across borders.

Four other Hollywood companies, including Walt Disney and Marvel Studios, are also pursuing joint Chinese ventures. When Chinese Vice President Xi Jinping visited the United States in February 2012, he helped develop a proposal to allow more foreign movies to play in Chinese theaters. China is now the second largest international market with $2 billion in sales, just behind Japan's $2.3 billion. Pimin Zhang, the deputy director-general of the State Administration of Radio, Film, and Television of China, in a press release announcing the Oriental DreamWorks's new headquarters in Shanghai, called the move "a creative exploration of Chinese and foreign cultural exchanges. Our shared dream is to make full use of precious cultural resources, develop a world-class production team, create world-class animated films, and thus contribute to the exchange of Chinese culture throughout the world."

One of the most vivid current examples of fusion is in the work of the Contemporary Legend Theatre of Taiwan, which has taken the plots of major works of Shakespeare (*Hamlet, The Tempest,* and *Macbeth*) and ancient Greek tragedy (*Medea* and *The Oresteia*) and placed them in the form of the Beijing Opera. They perform in Mandarin verse with (when touring the West) English subtitles. While both forms employ verse and a relatively sparse stage, the differences provide considerable fusion excitement.

WEI HAI-MING
ACTOR

Beijing Opera portrays beauty. Western drama depicts life.

When Wei Hai-ming portrays Lady Macbeth in the adaptation of Shakespeare's *Macbeth*, renamed *The Kingdom of Desire*, she emphasizes vicious words with lashing movements of her dress, moving it so that her train is like the tail of a snake. Her Lady Macbeth does not just do battle. She does a backflip from the top of a 10-foot wall! The blending of conventions is breathtaking, and everything old becomes new.

Ethnic Theatre in America

Long before Caucasian Europeans brought theatrical forms to this continent, there was North American indigenous theatre. Native American theatre in various forms existed before other races even visited this continent, and Mexican theatre in the Southwest can be traced back over 400 years. Over the years, as various other ethnic groups arrived, a number of immigrants created productions based on customs from their homelands. Many others, particularly Jewish immigrants from both Eastern Europe and Russia, became integrated into the fabric of mainstream American theatre.

C. W. E. BIGSBY

THEATRE HISTORIAN

In mainstream theatre, they [minorities] were effectively excluded from national myths which turned on white supremacy. They found their own lives reflected, if at all, only as stereotypes, as comic caricature or simply villains. In the central plot of American history—the invention of the nation—they had been presented as either merely observers or dangerous impediments.

The view of minorities expressed in white theatre, however, was not always welcoming or respectful. Until the civil rights movement in the 1960s, underrepresented peoples' lives were rarely accurately portrayed, if indeed they were portrayed at all.

Fortunately, one of the results of the political activism of the 1960s was a surge of ethnic pride beginning with African Americans but spreading quickly to include all Americans of color. Almost 40 years later, the result is now a genuine rainbow coalition theatrical scene.

Ethnic American theatre groups have formed over the years for five pervasive purposes:

1. **Coping:** At first, theatre was a way for minorities to cope with their confusion regarding the language and culture of mainstream America until they were able to assimilate or at least comprehend the culture around them. It pulled them into a place of comfort in the midst of myriad, unfamiliar stimuli. Theatre provided that campfire around which we can all gather to tell our stories and feel we are not alone.

2. **Memory:** Theatre also acted as a way of keeping alive memories of homelands left behind. It helped traditions to stay constant and renewed. In a way, it represented a tangible means of transporting the old country to the new. The magic of performance allowed memories to deepen and traditions to go beyond ceremonial ritual into fully acted stories that were told again and again.

3. **Protest:** Eventually, ethnic theatre became politicized. Theatre became a means of protesting mistreatment and exclusion and of demanding equity. New plays served as a rallying point where rage and hurt were turned into something powerful and focused to bring about change.

4. **Sharing:** After the first wave of protest, ethnic theatre also evolved into a way of showing audiences outside these cultures what it was like to be part of them, revealing lives that those outside had rarely experienced firsthand. Allowing audiences into the daily struggles of minorities gave them opportunities not only to appreciate cultural distinctions but also to be reminded of the ways in which we are all essentially the same.

5. **Assimilation versus Identity:** Finally, as new American identities inevitably emerged, some drama became about the unique predicament of having ties to another country while being very much based in this one (for example, being neither Asian nor mainstream American but distinctly Asian American). Because new generations within each culture had no actual firsthand experience of the motherland, it became even more important to deal with the phenomenon of being bicultural.

We will now discuss some of the beliefs, customs, and conventions that distinguish various ethnic theatre productions. There are many exceptions to these generalities, but when a play or production strays from these standards, it is almost invariably because of mainstream influence. We present the theatre forms in their most extreme and uninfluenced contexts.

Native American Theatre

Actual records of Native American drama emerged out of a period of almost astonishing repression followed by neglect. The first collection of plays, *New Native American Drama* by Hanay Geiogamah, was not published until 1980. Nothing comparable to the events described in Chapter 2 (see the "Wiping Away of Tears" section) continued into the past century, but pressure to curtail drama still came with official sanctions.

General characteristics of indigenous American Indian theatre include:

1. Stories are not necessarily linear and are often not told chronologically. There may be no specific beginning, middle, or end.

2. Drama is not necessarily based on a clearly defined conflict but rather on dance, rites, celebrations, and spiritual beliefs being explored.

3. Audience and performers are not separated but considered a single, unified element.

4. Rather than specific settings, performances are likely to take place in a dimensionless sacred space.

5. Theatre is likely to reflect the values of the specific tribe presenting the performance, not necessarily aspiring to universal connections.

> **WILLIAM S. YELLOW ROBE JR.**
> PLAYWRIGHT
>
> *My parents both asked me if I was serious about the kind of writing I was doing. When I said yes, they each gave me courage and strength by saying in slightly different ways "You'd better leave, then. Because there isn't anything for you here on the rez." They were right. . . . Now after writing 30 plays, I have only one regret, that Stanley and Mina Yellow Robe never had a chance to see them.*

MARSH CASSADY

THEATRE AUTHOR/EDITOR

Often the government, in the form of the Bureau of Indian Affairs, banned religious dramas such as the Sun Dance, common to all Northern plains tribes. In 1923, the government even limited "Indian dances" to one a month and declared that only those over the age of 50 could participate.

Prominent companies have included the Native American Theater Ensemble, which has presented off-Broadway productions. Other influential, early regional companies included the Santa Fe Theatre Project at the Institute of American Indian Arts, the Navajo Theatre, and the Thunderbird Company in Ontario.

In 1975, three sisters, Lisa Mayo, Gloria Miguel, and Muriel Miguel, wanted to create theatre free of "grand-mothers and medicine women." They formed a group called the **Spiderwoman Theater**, named after the Hopi household god Spider Grandmother Woman, who taught her people the art of weaving; the group calls their technique "storyweaving." Their first production to achieve widespread attention was *Women in Violence*, which weaves stories around a tribal leader who fights for his people's rights while ironically brutalizing the women in his own life. Spiderwoman's work is notable for handling highly serious subjects, sometimes using slapstick humor.

Another defining production has been ***Black Elk Speaks***, produced by the Denver Center Theatre Company, a collaborative effort between Native Americans from around the country and company personnel. Focusing on a healing vision experienced in 1863 by Nicholas Black Elk, this was perhaps the first mainstream production to honor the culture's emphasis on vision, spirit, and transformative dreaming.

Ned Romero as Black Elk in the Denver Center Theatre Company world premiere production of Black Elk Speaks (1994). Photo by Dan McNeil.

FIGURE 11.2   Ned Romero as Black Elk in the Denver Center Theatre Company world premiere production of *Black Elk Speaks*, a work involving Native Americans from all over the country.

Hispanic Theatre

We can actually trace early Spanish-speaking performances to southeast America (in what emerged eventually as Miami) in the late 1500s, but the earliest professional productions in the Southwest were first recorded in the early 1800s. Actors from Mexico and Spain toured coastal cities in southern California and northern Mexico, and then the companies migrated to Texas. Hispanic theatre companies were common throughout this region during the nineteenth and twentieth centuries, performing the classic plays of Pedro Calderón de la Barca and Lope de Vega as well as new works. **El Teatro Campesino**, "the farmworkers' theatre," which emerged in 1965, was probably the single most noteworthy producing group of the past century. It developed several works that advanced it from grassroots evolution all the way to Broadway. El Teatro's founder, **Luis Valdez**, created theatre for and about migrant workers and went on to great acclaim for plays such as *Zoot Suit* and his film *La Bamba*.

Cuban American theatre evolved in Tampa in the 1890s. Those who had emigrated from Cuba during its War of Independence created theatre specifically for newly established populations in Florida. Two forms of popular theatre that continued to thrive were Spanish *zarzuelas*, a form of melodrama, and Cuban *teatro buffo*, a vaudevillian blend of stock characters in farcical context with much music and dance. After the Cuban Revolution of 1959, another huge surge in immigration to the United States resulted in plays that focused on the problems of adjusting to life in a new culture. A major step was taken in 1966, when Cuban Americans and Puerto Ricans formed International Arts Relations (INTAR) to develop indigenous new works.

In the 1930s and 1940s, both Emilio S. Belaval and René Marqués had their work successfully produced. The Spanish Civil War resulted in a considerable increase in immigration to New York, resulting in a parallel increase in both conventional theatre companies and *teatro popular*, a form of street theatre concerned with social justice. Countless theatrical oases serve their communities.

Nilo Cruz's play, *Anna in the Tropics*, won the Pulitzer Prize in 2002. Playwrights whose works have received prominent productions include Eduardo Machado, Maria Irene Fornes, Josefina Lopez, Carlos Morton, Omar Torres, Yvette Ramirez, and **José Rivera**.

LUIS VALDEZ
PLAYWRIGHT, DIRECTOR

In a Mexican way, we have discovered what Brecht is all about. If you want unbourgeois theatre, find unbourgeois people to do it. Our theatre work is simple, direct, complex, and profound, but it works.

FIGURE 11.3 *Anna in the Tropics*, a 2002 Pulitzer Prize–winning play by Nilo Cruz, at the Royale Theatre in New York City.

T. Charles Erickson

JOSÉ RIVERA
PLAYWRIGHT

All my family, my siblings, mother as well as my abuelo [grandfather] and abuelita [grandmother] tell stories and that is where my plays start. We embellish, we lie, we fib, we fabricate, we alter, we amend, we misconstrue, we misremember, we misstate— we do everything a good journalist is not supposed to do. That's what makes it art.

AUTHOR'S INSIGHT

ANNIE: While touring U.S. regional theatres, I found that visiting the Center for the Arts in San Antonio, Texas, involved crossing railroad tracks and passing through the literal wall that surrounded the Hispanic center of the city. In the middle of the *barrio*, I found a beautiful haven for the arts and learned that the artistic director had chosen to live here, despite drive-by shootings and gang warfare, because "the arts are necessary to heal my community." This vibrant performing arts venue (which has drawn the likes of Edward James Olmos) has played an active role in reducing gang-related violence by bringing leaders of rival gangs to the theatre to watch new plays!

A distinct and important part of Latino theatre is **Nuyorican** performance. Pronounced "new-yuh-REE-can," it represents the unique blended experience of nearly 1 million persons of Puerto Rican heritage (second- or third-generation) living in the New York area. Nuyorican dates from at least 1975, from the first public sessions at the Nuyorican Poets Café, and includes poetry slam; dance theatre that may blend hip hop, salsa, and soul music; and the Nuyorican comedy troupe that "aims to dispel negative Latino myths by representing alternatives to the usual stereotypes." Its drama is sometimes traced to Miguel Piñero's plays *Short Eyes* and *Sideshow* and is vividly represented by Hector Rodriguez in works such as *Hoe Stroll* and *Lonely Lives*. Theatres associated with the movement include The Family, El Teatro Ambulante, Aquarius Theatre, and Teatro Quatro.

African American Theatre

In some sad way, it is possible that the theatre of African Americans began on the slave ships, where they were often forced to sing and dance to entertain the whites on board. In the early 1800s, a phenomenon called the minstrel show (see Chapter 8) featured not only white actors in blackface but black actors in blackface as well. The brilliant Shakespearean actor Ira Aldridge, unable to find suitable work and support in the United States, moved to Europe where racism was less prevalent; he toured England, Russia, and Poland to great acclaim and never returned. The African Grove (1821–1826), a theatre founded by William Brown and James Hewlett, presented Shakespeare and original works but was closed five years into its work due to attacks by white mobs.

In the 1920s, a movement called the **Harlem Renaissance** resulted in numerous theatre companies exploring the nature of African American life. The custom of blackface by white musical performers and the perpetuation of stereotypes were slow to dissolve, however. The latter was perhaps most vividly represented by the play *The Green Pastures,* a well intentioned and at the time much-honored work, which featured a heaven entirely populated by "Negro" residents. Langston Hughes's *Mulatto* was probably the more noteworthy effort by an African American playwright in the 1930s.

The landmark production of an African American playwright was **Lorraine Hansberry's** *A Raisin in the Sun*, which achieved extraordinary success in its Broadway run and subsequent filming. The play, revived to great acclaim in 2004, consistently sold out performances (perhaps in part because of the presence of Sean "P. Diddy" Combs in a central role). This is probably the most successful play to date at letting audiences outside the culture appreciate differences, while being astonished at how much we all share.

Table 11.1	Some African American Theatre Firsts

James Hewlett (1820)	First African American actor to play Othello
King Shotaway (1825)	First play written and performed by African Americans
Bob Cole (1897)	Founder of the first African American repertory company
A Trip to Coontown (1898)	First African American musical comedy
In Dahomey (1902)	First Broadway production in which African American actors appeared without burnt-cork makeup, spoke with a dialect, and wore fashionable clothes
Paul Robeson (1943)	Set undisputed record for longest run (296 performances) as Othello
Gold through the Trees (1952)	First play written by an African American woman (Alice Childress) to be produced off-Broadway
Lloyd Richards (1959)	First African American director on Broadway

Clearly, the civil rights movement influenced a great expansion of African American theatre to include regional companies throughout the nation. A landmark shift came with the Ford Foundation's support for the **Negro Ensemble Company** in the 1960s. Amiri Baraka (formerly Everett LeRoi Jones) wrote confrontational plays such as *Dutchman*, *The Slave*, and *The Toilet*, powerfully confronting the origins of racism. In 1970, Charles Gordone won attention and the Pulitzer Prize for his powerful and clearly titled *No Place to Be Somebody*. Other landmark works were created by Adrienne Kennedy, Lonne Elder III, and Ntozake Shange, whose magnificently poetic (she calls it a choreopoem) *for colored girls who have considered suicide when the rainbow is enuf* continues to move audiences with a very specific treatment of women of color that speaks to women everywhere. This script is often cited as the first hip-hop creation.

A phenomenon from the 1970s to the present is the African American musical, starting with *Purlie* and moving through *Bubbling Brown Sugar, The Wiz, Ain't Misbehavin', Dreamgirls, Sophisticated Ladies, Five Guys Named Moe,* and *Bring in 'da Noise, Bring in 'da Funk,* just to name a few. **George C. Wolfe** has produced some of the most powerful and intriguing scripts, including *Bring in 'da Noise, Bring in 'da Funk*, but most vividly in *The Colored Museum*. In this production featuring 11 exhibits of African American life, Wolfe satirizes both black stereotypes and those who fall into them, while in other exhibits, he strongly defends his people. One segment satirizes *A Raisin*

FIGURE 11.4 The cast of the 2008 Claremont School of Theatre Arts production of *for colored girls who have considered suicide when the rainbow is enuf,* by Ntozake Shange.

Photograph by: Charles Enscoe. Courtesy of Pomona College Department of Theatre and Dance

Joan Marcus

FIGURE 11.5   Scene from the recent Broadway revival of *A Raisin in the Sun,* a landmark African American theatre work.

in the Sun for its stereotypical characters (a strong, faith-based matriarch and her ever-blaming, never-accountable, male offspring) that have subsequently been perpetuated, challenging his audiences to move beyond these characters to full humanity.

AUGUST WILSON

PLAYWRIGHT

Last year I said, "Man, I don't wanna write no play." And I was so glad when it was over. But now I'm, "What's next?" I have lots of new ideas for what I call "a dramatic and poetic, cultural history of black America."

Highly respected contemporary writers include Suzan-Lori Parks, Regina Taylor, Charles Randolph-Wright, and Kia Corthron and their predecessors, Alice Childress, Ed Bullins, Leslie Lee, and Charles Fuller. Recent distinguished achievements include the Pulitzer Prize in drama for *Topdog/Underdog* by African American playwright Suzan-Lori Parks and the National Black Arts Festival, under the leadership of Stephanie Hughley, finding a permanent home in 2002 in Atlanta.

The most highly acclaimed playwright is unquestionably **August Wilson,** who died in late 2005. The winner of seven New York Drama Critics' Circle Awards, he would probably be most critics' choice for the leading American playwright of the late twentieth, early twenty-first century. He completed an almost Shakespearean cycle of plays, depicting the African American experience over each decade of the twentieth century:

1900s—*Gem of the Ocean* (premiered 2003)

1910s—*Joe Turner's Come and Gone* (premiered 1986)

1920s—*Ma Rainey's Black Bottom* (premiered 1984)

1930s—*The Piano Lesson* (premiered 1990)

FIGURE 11.6 Playwright August Wilson and his frequent director Lloyd Richards with piano. Wilson, the best-known contemporary African American playwright, passed away in 2005, shortly after completing his 10-play cycle chronicling the African American experience in the twentieth century.

1940s—*Seven Guitars* (premiered 1995)

1950s—*Fences* (premiered 1987)

1960s—*Two Trains Running* (premiered 1990)

1970s—*Jitney* (premiered 1996)

1980s—*King Hedley II* (premiered 1999)

1990s—*Radio Golf* (premiered 2005)

Most of his plays are set in the Hill District of Pittsburgh, the slum community where he was born in 1945. His genius expands this neighborhood to become Black America itself.

> **PHYLICIA RASHAD**
> ACTOR
>
> *August's plays were a haven for disregarded souls. He saw greatness, beauty, and ability in the lives of the people he wrote about, and he was acutely attuned to their individual rhythms, not just of their speech but also of their souls.*

Asian American Theatre

The voices of Asian Americans were the last of these cultures to be fully heard in the United States. Even the Federal Theater Project of the 1930s, which provided opportunities for other ethnic minorities, neglected the Asian American voice.

For many years, Asian characters in professional American productions were portrayed by non-Asian actors. The Broadway musical *A Chinese Honeymoon* (1902) had an all-white, British cast. Comedies and musicals of the 1950s (prominently *The Teahouse of the August Moon, The King and I,* and *South Pacific*) all featured non-Asian performers in key roles. However, as much as we may now regard their work as naive or reductive, **Rodgers and Hammerstein** were in their time among the only writers to focus on issues confronting Asians and to create characters that moved beyond unidimensional stereotypes. In casting the film roles of these shows, often just being a person of color seemed enough. For example, Rita Moreno, a Hispanic, was cast as the Asian character Tuptim in the film *The King and I*. There are countless ludicrous examples of Hollywood actors impersonating minority cultures (both John Wayne and Rock Hudson made appearances as Native Americans), but the defining gross-out, racial-slur performance of all time may be Mickey Rooney's take on Mr. Yunioshi, a character with full buckteeth and a wildly exaggerated accent, in *Breakfast at Tiffany's,* released in 1961. A major Hollywood film could still be produced with no attempt to cast an actor of color in an Asian role, much less one culturally appropriate.

Again, credit is due to Rodgers and Hammerstein. Their 1958 musical *Flower Drum Song* was a historical landmark, as it featured an all-Asian cast and was adapted from a novel by a Chinese American writer, C. Y. Lee. Sadly, it was not an artistic success. Recently, **David Henry Hwang,** author of *M. Butterfly,* has updated the book of this musical for contemporary production. Hwang remains a leading playwright, most recently with his semi-autobiographical work *Yellow Face.*

Two landmark events occurred in 1965 and 1973. First was the formation of the **East West Players** in Los Angeles, wherein actors of Korean, Japanese, and Chinese heritage combined their resources. This company presented both mainstream Western works and adaptations of the works of Asian novelists. Second was the **Asian American Theater Company** (with founding

FIGURE 11.7 Actors of the East West Players perform a love scene, Los Angeles, 1983. East West Players is a landmark Asian theatre company, presenting mainstream Western works and adaptations of works by Asian writers.

Michael S. Yamashita/Documentary Value/Corbis

directors Frank Chin, Janis Chan, and Jeffrey Chin), which developed the first major play by an Asian American, *The Chickencoop Chinaman,* by Frank Chin.

While *M. Butterfly* remains the best-known work by and about Asian culture, Asian American writers such as Genny Lim, Velina Hasu Houston, Elizabeth Wong, and Philip Kan Gotanda have also risen to prominence as playwrights. New perspectives are always on the horizon.

Non-Asian writers and directors, including Bertolt Brecht and Antonin Artaud, have long incorporated Asian theatrical techniques into their work. More recently, French director Ariane Mnouchkine and English director Peter Brook have been responsible for exposing American audiences to Asian forms.

KAREN HUIE
PLAYWRIGHT

In Yasuko and The Young S-S-Samurai, I wrote a farce about a reluctant samurai trying to convince a dewy-eyed maiden that gutlessness is next to godlessness in a country rife with honor, hara kiri, and Hondas. . . . I think it is time to explore the history of Asians in America in a comedic way.

Trends

The last 40 years have seen an incredible surge in grassroots, multicultural theatre. In a media-dominated society, it is fascinating how often live theatre has been chosen as the medium of expression. Scholars of international theatre have designated the United States as the most prominent laboratory for cultural hybrids and convergences in the theatre. Often the introduction of very old theatre customs into a new context results in amazingly vigorous writing and in finding new ways to tell stories.

The plays often take us into the houses and families of peoples previously viewed by the nation at large only when urban violence has erupted after total failure to comprehend the conditions that escalated into that violence. Theatre has provided a way for cultures to dig in and reestablish old identities in new settings but also for cultural blending, fusion, and the discovery of newly forged identities. We are clearly becoming a culturally pluralistic society, and the sooner dramatic works speak to all races, the better. It has given us ways to reach across cultures and to provide empathy and understanding of how we are different and yet the same.

Gender Issues Theatre

While issues of ethnicity provide the center of the four previous sections and much of what might be called the theatre of underrepresented peoples, our next two deal with exclusion and identification based on gender roles, being born a woman or with a nonmajority sexual orientation. The phenomena cross all ethnic lines and yet in some ways are similar in starting with a feeling of isolation, leading to group unity, and finding a voice that needs to be heard. In Chapter 10, we introduced feminism as an issues-related Ism. There is unquestionably an overlap between that category and our next one, although here we deal with the simple phenomenon of being acknowledged, whether there is an additional agenda attached or not.

Women's Theatre

Although the terms **women's theatre** and **feminist theatre** may seem at least parallel, if not synonymous, they are not the same thing. Women's theatre refers to any work by and about women. It may or may not be contemporary, political, activist, or in any way challenge the status quo. Feminist theatre, a type of women's theatre, generally has a clear social/political agenda meant to challenge and change existing gender dynamics. The feminist playwright or producer uses theatre as the means for achieving goals inherent in that agenda.

Many playwrights who were largely neglected during their own time are now being rediscovered and acknowledged in revivals—and some are being acknowledged for the first time. One of the most prolific writers of the English Restoration theatre was Aphra Behn, all but ignored by history until a recent rediscovery of her works (see Chapter 8). Zoe Atkins, Rachel Crothers, Sophie Treadwell, and Susan Glaspell are other women's voices of past generations that are now being heard in productions. Going even farther back, the person believed to be the first-known woman dramatist is **Hroswitha** (935–975), a German abbess who was so taken with the Roman comedies of Terence, though worried about their potentially immoral influence, that she converted the ideas into six rhymed Latin plays about Christian martyrs or chaste women whose chastity is unsuccessfully challenged. Only recently has one of our "founding mothers," **Mercy Otis Warren,** received acknowledgment for her plays, including *The Adulateur* (1772) and *The Defeat* (1773). These were considered major propaganda efforts in encouraging patriots to pursue the American Revolution.

It is increasingly acknowledged that women's voices, previously pushed aside, must be released and heard. Less than 15 percent of plays are written by women, and less than one-fourth of the roles in plays are for women. Old plays are being reexamined, and new works are being generated from a feminist perspective. Many regard the moment when the character Nora walks out the door and leaves her family (in Ibsen's *A Doll's House*) as the first step for the movement in theatre.

At this writing, the most widely known work is probably **Eve Ensler's** *The Vagina Monologues*. Ensler continues to address women's issues in *The Good Body* and war atrocities in *The Treatment*. Each play, in its own way, brought forth subjects formerly thought unsuitable for mainstream theatre and demonstrated otherwise. Writers who have achieved major success creating plays specifically focused on women include Marsha Norman, Wendy Wasserstein, and Beth Henley. Others with similar focus in their work include Tina Howe, Constance Congdon, Paula Vogel, Naomi Wallace, Theresa Rebeck, Caryl Churchill, and Lisa Loomer. Deconstructionist production, performance art, choral plays, and dramatic collages are also common forms.

More and more productions are carefully considering women's perspective and voice. There are likely to be more women in any cast as all roles are re-examined and alternative casting (gender blind or gender bending) is considered, and there are likely to be a larger number in key staff positions as well. A huge power has been untapped.

NTOZAKE SHANGE
PLAYWRIGHT
I found god in myself and I loved her . . . I loved her fiercely. . . .

Gay and Lesbian Theatre

Those dealing with issues of sexual orientation also began to find a voice after the first stages of the civil rights movement. However, there has always been some debate about how to define this category. Is the presence of a gay character sufficient? How many need to be in a play? Must they be sympathetically portrayed? Does it include work of gay playwrights who do not necessarily present gay characters? Does the play need to have a serious, political agenda or can it be merely satiric or hilarious? Some feel the category should disappear as characters of all variants of sexuality are integrated into the total theatrical scene. While the term *gay* is often used as an umbrella, the Association for Theatre in Higher Education employs the designation LGBTQ (Lesbian, Gay, Bisexual, Transgender, Queer) to designate its forum devoted to issues of members with these sexual orientations.

From the seduction of Pentheus by Dionysus in Euripides's *The Bacchae* (405 B.C.E.) to the relationship of Achilles and Patroclus in Shakespeare's *Troilus and Cressida* (1601), both homoerotica and gay characters existed long before it became a politicized theatre movement. A long tradition of cross-dressing and drag has been part of the theatre scene for centuries and across cultures.

In the twentieth-century United States, **Lillian Hellman's** *The Children's Hour* (1934) was the first commercial play to explore the possibility of a lesbian relationship, albeit in such a way that a central character (Martha) shoots herself due to her guilt about her feelings for her female roommate.

Mart Crowley's *The Boys in the Band* (1968) was a landmark play and film in portraying a significant segment of gay culture with empathy. Ironically, the play generated a great deal of criticism in the gay community itself due to the self-hatred experienced by several of the major characters. Nevertheless, it was considered a milestone in getting large numbers of audiences to experience a deep, emotional connection to gay characters.

Gay activism is often traced to the patrons of the Stonewall Inn in New York City's Greenwich Village fighting back against police officers attempting to close the bar in 1969. Many consider this the official beginning of the contemporary gay rights movement.

Gay companies such as The Glines (New York) and Theatre Rhinoceros (San Francisco) formed in the 1970s. **Charles Ludlam** founded the Ridiculous Theatrical Company after 1967. He was the author of such plays as *Camille* (1973), *Bluebeard* (1970), and *The Mystery of Irma Vep* (1984) and a performer, often in drag, of several roles in each of his plays. After his death in 1987, he was succeeded by Everett Quinton. Charles Busch has also written and starred in similar drag vehicles such as *Shanghai Moon*.

FIGURE 11.8   Harvey Fierstein and Matthew Broderick in *Torch Song Trilogy,* a groundbreaking gay theatre work of the post-Stonewall era.

Harvey Fierstein made a significant impact as both playwright and star of *Torch Song Trilogy* (1981) and the book author to the musical *La Cage aux Folles* (1983). Fierstein is currently known primarily as a performer, recently playing Edna Turnblad in *Hairspray* as well as Tevye in a Broadway revival of *Fiddler on the Roof.*

In 1978, the **Gay Theatre Alliance** was formed among various regional companies, some of the foremost being TOSOS (The Other Side of the Stage) and Triangle Theatre Company (Boston), Diversity (Houston), Lionheart Gay Theatre Company (Chicago), Alice B. Theatre (Seattle), The Glines, Meridian Gay Theatre, Stonewall Theatre (New York), and Theatre Rhinoceros (San Francisco).

The AIDS crisis reached epidemic proportions in 1980, leading eventually to what are sometimes referred to as "The AIDS Plays." These include *The Normal Heart* by Larry Kramer and *As Is* by William Hoffman, both first produced in 1985. Later plays include *Before It Hits Home* by Cheryl West, *Love! Valour! Compassion!* by Terrence McNally, *Baltimore Waltz* by Paula Vogel, and both *Jeffrey* and *The Naked Truth* by Paul Rudnick. Some would place **Tony Kushner's** *Angels in America* (subtitled *A Gay Fantasia on National Themes*) as an AIDS play, though it deals with so many other issues so eloquently that it is the choice of many as the single best play of the 1990s.

Lesbian troupes, such as Split Britches, emerged in the 1980s, and an important historical moment was the founding of WOW (Women's One World) in 1981. Landmark productions include *A Late Show* (1974) and *Last Summer at Bluefish Cove* (1980), both by **Jane Chambers**, and *The Well of Horniness* by Holly Hughes (1985). Lesbian companies have included Red Dyke Theatre (Atlanta), Lesbian-Feminist Theatre Collective (Pittsburgh), and WOW Café Theatre (New York).

In the 1990s, the advent of the **Queer Theory** movement rejected sexuality labels of the kind that we are discussing here. It proposed that sexual and gender identities are largely socially—rather than biologically—constructed so that broad terms such as "homo or heterosexual" or even "man or woman" are insufficient to describe individuals. It instead tends to look at what is "queer" (meaning strange or different) in any behavior that does not fit within rules.

On a more basic level of public awareness, tolerance has been a long and slow journey. Yet there has probably been no more single distinct sign of widespread acceptance of non-straight characters in drama than the 2005 Oscar nominations. The two leading contenders for best actor each played a gay character, one historical and one fictional (Philip Seymour Hoffman in *Capote* and Heath Ledger in *Brokeback Mountain*, respectively), and one of the nominees for best actress played a "transgendered" male in the process of "regenderfication" (Felicity Huffman in *Transamerica*).

By virtue of group identification, theatre constitutes much of what is exciting about contemporary performance. However, in a number of instances it is the mode of presentation, not necessarily the membership of the presenters, that provides the source of innovation. We will now focus on that set of contemporary trends.

Unscripted Theatre

While there are no scripts in the oral storytelling tradition, there is an effort to keep the thread of the event the same from generation to generation. Variances seep into the material as it moves from one narrator to another or from one region to another. Another kind of unscripted theatre has had a surge in popularity in the last decade—improvisation.

Improvisation

Beginning with the legendary **The Second City** improv troupe in Chicago (which has launched the careers of a number of Not Ready for Prime Time Players on *Saturday Night Live*) and fanning out across the country, many communities and colleges support improv troupes, and the activity is a standard part of actor training. **ComedySportz**, combining theatre with the rules of an athletic event, has franchises all over the country. Clubs that used to feature musicians and stand-up comedians are now likely to have improv evenings as well. Cast members from the improv television show *Whose Line Is It Anyway?* had a successful national tour performing live after the show was no longer on the air. The appeal of this format *is* much

AP Photo/Joshua Lott

FIGURE 11.9   Rachel Dratch and Amy Poehler perform during the twenty-fifth anniversary reunion show for the iO improv comedy troupe at the Chicago Theatre.

like that of watching an athletic event, especially a fast-paced sport like basketball, where there are constant surprises and the energy and focus can change in an instant.

Few activities are as liberating as **improvisation.** It channels playfulness and helps renew a sense of spontaneity. It aims at tapping into intuition and knowledge that does not rely on reason or rational processes. It can help sharpen insight and the capacity for guessing accurately. It can help participants dare to decide quickly and dive in, without wasting time speculating or reflecting unnecessarily. All of us would like to make better decisions faster, without mentally debating an issue to death.

Improv Ground Rules

While seemingly freewheeling and open, improv has a number of rules to give it structure. Those rules, which keep it from chaos, become more important as the game gets wilder and more freewheeling. There are several areas of agreement:

1. **Always Saying Yes:** Everyone needs to accept whatever another actor brings into the scene as true. No one says no. All new information is accepted.

2. **Just Doing It:** All participate without instantly evaluating and judging. This is exploration without judgment. Actors listen and respond spontaneously.

3. **Staying Honest:** Performers, for the most part, play to solve the problem, not to find clever lines or cute endings. The more ridiculous the situation

ends up being, the more it needs to appear to be taken seriously. Actors who always crack themselves up do not thrive in this form.

4. **Staying in the Game:** All remain fully involved until the session is over, either because the situation has resolved itself or because a coach calls an end to it. Actors do not step outside the action or drop their concentration. Side-coaching is accepted without breaking focus, and everyone lives in the moment.

5. **Giving Up Control:** Actors need to resist preconceptions or the desire to plan ahead. No one person tries to run the scene or dominate others. They are not playwrights but rather people in a predicament.

Once actors have the basic outline, questions and discussion stop. Improv never bothers with excessive exposition, starting in what might normally be the middle of the scene instead of the beginning. Props are kept to the barest minimum. Answers are kept short and sweet, with lots of chances to stop and listen. Scenes work best if kept physical and active, with more action and less talk. When at a loss for words, actors turn to their senses. How do they feel? What do they smell? Taste? Hear? See? Nothing that happens is regarded as a mistake, just an interesting turn of events. All the actors try to keep filing away twists and turns in the scene for possible later connections as these elements might emerge again.

Improv is also used in connection with scripted works as part of the rehearsal process. Actors might improvise the first time their characters meet or various events that are referred to in the script but that happen offstage. A cast may create a party where they attend as their characters, or an interview show where their characters are questioned. Being able to stay in character outside the script makes performing scripted lines all the more comfortable.

> ### AUTHOR'S INSIGHT
>
> **ROBERT:** Great acting always has an element of improvisation. The *script* may not change, but the best actors are open to a new line reading, a new look, a change in timing, or some fresh and unexpected connection that keeps the performance vital and unexpected. The longer a show runs, the more precious this capacity to improvise it to freshness.

Playback Theatre/Therapy Theatre

A somewhat more serious use of improv is employed in **playback theatre**, in which performers ask an audience member to tell a story from his own life. Actors quickly assume various other characters and play the story back, so the storyteller has a chance to actually view a crucial life event and have it take on greater meaning. These events are not only entertaining but also profoundly illuminating for those whose stories are chosen. The participants have only the basic outline, but it is astonishing how frequently they capture the event in a way that is moving and meaningful not only to the featured subject but to all present and sharing.

In a counseling movement known as **therapy theatre**, participants may be asked to re-create painful moments in their lives with others in the group acting as other participants. Because these encounters sometimes paralyze the "actor" and keep her from acting her life with freedom and creativity, the reenactment can sometimes be cathartic and freeing. If she were unable to say something important back during the actual event, being able to say it now, even in this acting environment, is sometimes liberating. Often the issue is resolved to some extent, and there is no need to confront the offender. The power of theatre is present in that almost anyone can stand in for the offender, and the mere act of much-needed confrontation being acted out is often quite enough. However, if the patients/actors do feel the need to pursue confrontation to experience closure, they now have the confidence of rehearsing what they wish to say in this improvisational context. Such exercises are also sometimes part of actor training, based on the belief that actors who deal with their traumatic encounters and move on will have more emotional availability and confidence to tackle challenging roles and the competition inherent in the profession.

Theatre for Justice

Augusto Boal

While theatre is often intended to divert and entertain as a more polished version of "dress up and let's pretend," it can also be used to address serious social issues and to bring about needed changes in people's lives. While many companies deal with societal issues, **Augusto Boal** was very influential in bringing theatre, and particularly improv, into the realm of social consciousness, providing tools for change. For him, acting had a double definition. It is not just about performing but also about taking action.

He developed methods for combating oppression through theatre. His work breaks down barriers between actors and audience. Observers become active spectators (whom he calls "spect-actors"), offering ideas and even stepping into roles. Boal used theatre to confront problems, with particular emphasis on those (sexual harassment, homophobia, racism, etc.) where one group oppresses another.

Boal saw theatre as a forum designed to analyze problems (usually of the misuse of power) and to explore group solutions. Seeing a problem enacted and debated and then seeing solutions enacted can have a high and lasting impact. He established numerous participatory companies that develop community-based performances for those engaged in the struggle for liberation. Most are called Centers for Theatre of the Oppressed (CTOs). The work is a blend of developed scripted work and improvisation. Activities are of three kinds, which will be discussed below.

Forum Theatre

In **forum theatre**, short scenes represent unsolved problems of a community. Audience members are invited to suggest, interact, and enact, sometimes by replacing characters in scenes and improvising new solutions.

AP Photo/Sucheta Das

FIGURE 11.10 Brazilian director and Worker's Party activist Augusto Boal talks with Narmada Bachao Andolan activist Medha Parker at the International Forum Theatre movement in Calcutta, India. Boal was influential in trying to improve social consciousness.

Sometimes the "problem" scene (often called the "anti-model") is presented once and then again (possibly speeded up) until someone yells, "Stop!" and steps in. It may be repeated several more times as others step into the role of protagonist. The events are presided over by someone called the Joker, named for the joker in a deck of cards—not because she will play jokes on participants. The Joker defines and enforces the rules of the game in the manner of a stage manager/referee. This person may often stop a scene saying, "That's magic," meaning that the actors have contrived a solution that does not involve step-by-step problem solving but rather the waving of a wand or incredible good fortune.

Image Theatre

In **image theatre**, bodies and tableaus are used to sculpt events and relationships. Human forms are employed to create images, helping participants explore power relations and collective solutions. As much as possible, the process is done without words, although it may begin with an individual recounting a personal story of some kind of oppression, or a group discussion on the issue that will be explored. Titles are suggested, and then individuals mold participants like clay to form an intense, visual representation of the power relationships, and other tableaus are created to change the status quo. Two major tableaus emerge: one is the "real image" of things as they are now, and the other is the "ideal image" of things as they could become.

Invisible Theatre

As in Forum Theatre, rehearsed scenes are used to stimulate action. In **invisible theatre**, however, they are performed in public spaces for an unsuspecting audience that does not recognize the event as theatre. In addition to the actors in the scenes, others may infiltrate the crowd as provocateurs, stimulating debate and discussion. For example, a scene is created and rehearsed regarding a cross-dresser. The actors enter a store, and one of the men tries on women's clothing. Another actor responds by being overtly appalled at what he is doing, while another defends his rights. Everyone present is drawn into a discussion about the parameters of individual rights.

The three techniques may overlap, and all Boal's processes share three characteristics:

1. Problems are always presented in an objective form, without the suggestion of a solution in the initial scene.

2. As solutions evolve, the issues always move outward to include a larger group, rather than inward to individual or smaller groups. The oppression is examined in a larger context.

3. Debate or discussion never stays for long in verbal exchange or what Boal calls "radio forum." Instead, participants are frequently asked to stop talking, get up, and express their intentions or interventions in theatrical forms. Actors need to be extremely comfortable with improv, socially and politically aware, able to play opposing points of view without bias, and be, according to Boal, "dialectical and free of narcissism, with a strong sense of give and take."

Actors are not the only people who participate in this activity. Social service workers, labor and union organizers, educators, and community activists may be involved as well. It employs classic improv techniques as well as those of sociodrama and playback theatre. Those learning Boal's techniques will all have the tools, in whatever community they might find themselves, to offer the art of acting as part of a solution, making a huge contribution to that populace. The techniques are equally useful for solving problems within an acting environment or theatre company, where power issues often abound.

Performance Art

An often electrifying theatre form, **performance art** rejects plot, character, suspense, and sometimes even theatres in favor of other spaces such as art galleries. Most portray a striking set of experiences, usually around a central theme, with an emphasis on set design, music, dance movement, and improvisation. Sculpture, lighting effects, poetry, and painting may also be involved. Some consider it a descendant of Dadaism (see Chapter 9), and the influence of the ideas of Jerzy Grotowski and Antonin Artaud are clearly present.

It began to be identified in the 1960s with the work of artists such as Yves Klein; Allan Kaprow, who coined the term *happenings;* and members of the Feminist Studio Workshop in Los Angeles. In 1970, the British-based pair Gilbert and George created "living sculpture" performances. Others pioneered combining video with other media to create experimental works.

In performance art, usually the audience is challenged to think in new and unconventional ways about theatre and performing. An effort is made to break the conventions of traditional performing arts and break down conventional ideas about "what art is." The performance may be scripted, unscripted, or improvisational. It may incorporate music, dance, song, or complete silence. Performance may occur in transient spaces or in auditoriums. It often shocks audiences into reassessing their own notions of art and its relation to culture, to be a spectator of ritual and its distinct community, and to be surprised by the unexpected, unorthodox presentations that the artists devise. Performance art has increasingly incorporated technological media into pieces, mainly because we have acquired exponential amounts of new technology. These artists will no doubt find ever new ways to combine live experience and technology, with the constant goal to offer experiences that are memorable.

Some big names in performance art include Laurie Anderson, Richard Foreman, Robert Wilson, Martha Clarke, Ping Chong, Meredith Monk, Tim Miller, Michael Counts, Annie Miller, and Guillermo Gómez-Peña. Groups specializing in this form include the evocatively named Electronic Disturbance Theater, Guerrilla Girls, Poetry Slams, and Survival Research Lab.

FIGURE 11.11 *The End of the Moon* is one of performance artist Laurie Anderson's touring projects, combining storytelling with electronics and violin music.

Robert Wilson often works with Suzushi Hanayagi, a Kabuki and *Noh* expert, so his works reflect an Asian sensibility, including a slow, deliberate tempo. Michael Counts produces massive undertakings in his warehouse.

Performance art is likely to experiment with multimedia and projections, reducing both the quantity and specific detail of constructed scenery, though with a powerful visual impact. The presentations are often, though not always, highly personal and confrontational.

Because you don't have to try to follow the story, performance art is both intellectually challenging and yet comforting. You are free to find your own way into the experience.

Some of the most exciting work in this area has been done by English artists Leslie Hill and Helen Paris through their company, which they named "curious" because "what drives us as artists is an intense curiosity about the world in which we live." They have become known for edgy, humorous interrogations of contemporary culture and politics. Their investigations involve intimate, personal journeys alongside public research and have led to collaborations with a multitude of people ranging from truck-stop waitresses to nuclear weapons experts to sex workers. They always encourage dialogue with audiences and participants, and their resulting work is sometimes intimate, frequently challenging, often humorous, and always authentic.

Whereas others in this group direct but do not necessarily perform and often work with a large group of actors, **Laurie Anderson** is a solo performer and therefore provides a segue to our next category, known for its stunning imagery and strange electronic sounds. During a performance, she will sing music of her own composition; speak (a variety of voices, though not necessarily characters); play the violin, keyboard, and guitar; and operate electronic equipment, producing both visual and sound effects.

Solo Performance

From Hal Holbrook's *Mark Twain Tonight* to Lily Tomlin's *The Search for Signs of Intelligent Life in the Universe*, the one-person show has been a main feature of professional theatre for years. In the 2005 season alone, Jackie Mason, Billy Crystal, Dame Edna Everage (the alter ego of comedian Barry Humphries), and Whoopi Goldberg all filled Broadway houses. Most, however, involve playing a character and/or making humorous observations. They are (relatively) safe. What is newer, however, is an intensely confessional, autobiographical form of solo work characterized by such performers as Eric Bogosian, Anna Deavere Smith, Karen Finley, Sherry Glaser, Danny Hoch, John Leguizamo, and Mario Cantone.

The most vivid example may be **Sherry Glaser's** *Family Secrets,* where she plays five characters: herself, her mother, father, grandmother, and sister. The secrets are often about sex, religion, mental illness, and birth.

They are both funny and painful—sometimes at the same time. Because of increased costs, even nonsolo new plays are ever more frequently inhabited by very few characters.

Movement/Dance Theatre

The director/choreographer has always been a major force in groundbreaking musical theatre productions. Jerome Robbins, Gower Champion, Bob Fosse, Michael Bennett, and Tommy Tune all demonstrated that when one brilliant mind guided both acting and dance, there was a far more organic and totally integrated sense of dance emerging out of character need, with flawless transitions. A number of artists in recent years have taken this combination a step further to create a new form of theatre.

With *Contact,* multiple award-winning director/choreographer **Susan Stroman** created what was called a **dance play.** There are no songs, no original music, and very little dialogue. Dance tells the three stories.

Matthew Bourne reinvented the ballet *Swan Lake* as a homoerotic dream, with the swans being played by muscular men with bare chests and buzz cuts. He also reinvented the opera *Carmen* as *The Car Man: An Auto-Erotic Thriller*, a bloody, violent, loud, and rampantly sexual dance theatre experience. While innovative, each may have been influenced by earlier, similar adventures on the parts of Pina Bausch and Martha Clarke. In these works, dance is not a supplement or a digression. It is the very center of the experience.

Both **Stomp** and **Blue Man Group** have similarly set audiences afire with enthusiasm using movement and no dialogue. These projects share with performance art a rejection of traditional story and character in favor of pure kinesthetic impact. Stomp, created by English percussionist/composer Luke Cresswell and actor/writer Steve McNicholas, uses garbage can lids, brooms, and other common objects instead of drums, and creates athletic, rhythmic theatrical excitement. In Blue Man Group, three men with shaved heads all painted shiny blue have captured the imaginations of audiences across the country, including Las Vegas, where more traditional fare is generally expected. When it came to New York, Blue Man Group started as street theatre, moved into a small off-Broadway space and gradually moved

Michal Daniel, 2000

FIGURE 11.12 Anna Deavere Smith in one of her one-woman shows, *House Arrest*, at the Joseph Papp Public Theatre, part of the New York Shakespeare Festival. Smith's work is often confessional and autobiographical.

ELIZABETH MCMANN
PRODUCER

Economics almost force playwrights now to write small, often with only two or three characters. This also means trying to find new ways to tell the story.

Joan Marcus

FIGURE 11.13 The Swans from Matthew Bourne's version of *Swan Lake*, a reinvention of the classic ballet with homoerotic overtones. The show premiered at Sadler's Wells Theatre in London, and has toured several times.

up to major runs in big cities, television appearances, and major concert halls. Almost impossible to describe, the shows involve homemade instruments, food fights, extravagant clown routines, marshmallows, audience cue cards, and very risky audience interaction, so you might want to think twice about it if you are invited onstage.

Perhaps no other theatrical sensation of the last several decades has had more impact than Cirque du Soleil, a blend of storytelling, circus arts, dance, and spectacular visual effects. Cirque is a Canadian troupe that began touring in 1980. Initially, even as they grew into an international sensation, they continued to tour in giant tents. Growing rapidly through the 1990s and 2000s, they now produce 19 shows in over 270 cities on every continent except Antarctica.

Delving into myths and themes of contemporary importance, they have created events around the myth of Icarus, the joy of life (*Saltimbanco*), a neglected child's fantasy world (*Quidam*), *Love*, and *Delirium*. At the time of this writing, their most recent show opened in May 2013, *Michael Jackson ONE*. According to Cirque's press release, "*Michael Jackson ONE* is a theatrical evocation of Michael's creative genius. Guided and inspired by his music, four misfits set out on a transformative adventure. By journey's end, they will personify Michael's agility, courage, playfulness, and love."

LIEBE WETZEL

DIRECTOR/DEVISOR

Why devise now? Why not now? The world hungers for original, immediate emerging work that is fresh and vibrant.

Devised Works

Devised works—collaboratively created ensemble pieces—have increasingly attracted the attention of both professional and academic communities. Any team member might be involved in researching, collating, writing, experimenting, and decision making. Instead of beginning with a play, this process may begin with a problem or a topic of fascination. All participants gather materials, have constant input, and are always part of the process. Devising may also begin with an existing piece of literature, ready for reinvestigation and rediscovery, or with a body of literature around a central theme. In most instances, an effort is made to translate literary text into physically active, theatrical interpretation. It is as if these documents, after years of silent reading, long for a fuller life and are released in the theatre.

Some projects begin with an issue of concern to the collaborators who then generate a combination of existing and original material. To devise is "to invent, contrive, to plan, to scheme, to form in the mind by new combinations of ideas." It may involve classic or traditional materials, songs, themes, current events, news reports, or repeated historical phenomena. The final product may include personal testimony, agitprop sketch work, and improvisational sequences. In these instances, the performance may feel like a giant collage. An increased sense of ownership is one of the big payoffs for participants.

Perhaps the best-known devised work of recent years is the Tectonic Theater Project's ***The Laramie Project***, under the guidance of Moisés Kaufman, which took available printed materials and testimony regarding the brutal murder of Matthew Shepard (for being gay) and created a riveting theatre experience. Many of the original collaborators behind *Laramie* have recently created *The People's Temple,* which first opened at the Berkeley Repertory Theatre in May 2005. It focused on the Reverend Jim Jones–led mass suicide of 914 American religious cult members in the Guyana jungle. You may not remember either of these events, but at the time that they occurred, they dominated the news for months. *Variety* described the latter as "a news event of so high a profile that public awareness was compared to that following Pearl Harbor or the Hiroshima and Nagasaki bombings." These were each aberrations in terms of what we believe about ourselves, and the devised productions addressed our collective struggle to resolve our collective sense of horror and shame.

Devising is a complex and labor-intensive process requiring considerable time, effort, and patience. Prominent figures in the professional world include Crystal Brian of The Lost World, Norma Bowles of Fringe Benefits Theatre, Liebe Wetzel of Lunatique Fantastique, John Schile of the Dell'Arte Company, and Stacy Klein of Double Edge Theatre. But devising has, in the opinion of many, found its most appropriate home in educational theatre, where it provides an opportunity for student actors to find a voice.

MARY ZIMMERMAN
DIRECTOR/DEVISOR

The real reason I devise theatre, instead of working from a completed script, is because I believe in the unconscious, and I believe in the will of certain texts (great pieces of literature not yet scripts) to reach the air and our need to submit to them in a way that I find ravishing.

JOHN SCHMOR
DIRECTOR/DEVISOR

On student-devised projects, the director is required to commit to the project as it develops, which demands a position of faith instead of privilege.

PETER BUCKLEY
DIRECTOR/DEVISOR

In theatrical terms, devising places the actor in a central role in the creative process—that of a creator as opposed to an interpreter of someone else's creativity.

Contemporized Classics

Much exciting new theatre comes from old plays. In an effort to help modern audiences relate to the classics, many theatre artists are re-inventing them. One of the big hits of the 2012 London and Broadway seasons was re-imagining of Goldoni's 1743 Italian comedy *The Servant of Two Masters* as a very British version set in 1963 titled *One Man, Two Guvnors*. Replacing aristocrats with gangsters and criminals, the play, by Richard Bean, has been described by many critics as the funniest they had ever seen and won numerous awards including the Tony for best actor for its leading man James Corden.

A leader in innovative updates has been the Oregon Shakespeare Festival, which produced its own improv-based version of *The Servant of Two Masters* as well as a mod, disco rendition of Moliere's *The Imaginary Invalid*, both adapted by Tracy Young. This version was just wacky and silly enough to be a perfect match for Moliere's lopsided universe. Even more recently, OSF presented a Shakespeare send-up called *The Very Merry Wives of Windsor, Iowa* and a startlingly original blend titled *Medea/Macbeth/Cinderella*. The *Cinderella*, in this instance, was Rodgers and Hammerstein's musical version. The idea was to take what many consider the high points of Western theatre—Greek tragedy, Elizabethan drama, and American musical theatre—and have them intersect with one another. So all three plays were presented, though each for no more than a scene at a time, before one of the others invaded it. Each of these old plays was illuminated by juxtapositions with the others.

Original Practice (OP)

One way to make an old play seem new is to go to the other extreme and produce it in an old way that is now largely unfamiliar to audiences. At Shakespeare's Globe Theatre in London, largely under the leadership of multiple award-winning actor Mark Rylance, visitors have packed the house for the chance to see Shakespeare performed "as was," most notably male actors playing all characters, including female roles. This is a new experience for most observers, as has been a rehearsal process that is very close to that employed by Shakespeare's company for the very first productions of his plays. As director Tim Carroll reports, "With OP, there is that excitement of not quite fooling yourself that you have recreated everything exactly as it was, because we'll never be able to do that, but the shared attempt to imagine ourselves back in time. It's very theatrical. It's an intense form of make-believe." For actors and audiences, the layers of interpretation imposed over time have been stripped away and everyone has an experience as close as possible in the twenty-first century to what it must have been like when these plays were presented for the very first time.

Grassroots Theatre

While Broadway remains a powerful force in mainstream theatre, it is no longer the primary source of new and challenging work. Broadway has become primarily a haven for musicals and revivals of tried-and-true straight (non-musical) plays. There is little commitment to innovation. The exciting new play, surmounting all the financial and critical pressures involved in finding a home in the Great White Way, is an increasingly rare phenomenon.

When Broadway audiences have been surveyed, less than one-fifth indicated any interest in productions that were not musicals. More than one-third of those interviewed indicated that only the presence of a major star would lure them to see a straight play. This point of view does not reflect theatergoing tastes elsewhere.

ISAAC BUTLEY
DIRECTOR

Broadway is a place for big musicals and the occasional British import; with the economics of the place being what they are, that is unlikely to change anytime soon.

Eco-Theatre

An increasing number of productions and festivals are exploring environmental issues, not in New York or in large regional theatres, but at the grassroots level. For many years, only Ibsen's *An Enemy of the People* (about a town's refusal to acknowledge water contamination because that would affect its tourist industry) was a consistently performed play in this subject area, until Robert Schenkkan's Pulitzer Prize–winning nine-play *The Kentucky Cycle* (focusing on environmental violence) emerged in 1992. But most works have been local, some addressing specific issues such as logging or pesticides, others more general concerns of sustainability. Ecodrama encompasses plays that illustrate the bond between the human and nonhuman world. In true grassroots fashion, works often are rooted in the problems of an immediate locale. Quite a few employ high theatricality, puppetry, masks, *commedia dell'arte,* pageantry, and direct audience engagement—elements that lend themselves to the sizeable ideas that the environmental crisis engenders and the changes it requires.

The ancient Greek root *eco* means "home." Ecology promotes connectedness, rootedness, and holistic approaches to problems, so it is no surprise that environmentalism is local. The dramatic battle between ecology and economy is "brought home," so that ordinary men and women in small towns or urban neighborhoods are the protagonists. The outcome is neither utopia nor dystopia, but gritty reality combined with "down-home" activism. When artists intervene in the discourse of ownership of natural resources, the distinctions between activism and performance blur.

Particular to the places they were created, recent works by the Seattle Public Theater and the Ukiah Players Theatre of northern California have striking similarities in their localized looks at one of the most publicly volatile arenas for the economy/ecology battle: logging. Each play seeks a compromise solution, that is, "selective cutting" with quick reforestation—a strategy serving the needs of both economy and ecology. Seattle is a hub of the Washington timber industry, and Ukiah is a California town deep in the midst of redwood forests. These communities are polarized over logging, and the theatre companies' expressed goals promote full communication, consensus-building, and healing. Ecodramas draw both subject and spectator into a conversation in the same time and space, and they engage their audience's imaginations and motivate spectators to action.

Regional Rep

In 1965, only four professional **nonprofit theatres** in the United States were operating year round, with their own staffs and a season of plays. In 2010, there are more than 400! Every major city in the country has its own resident company. What happened? There appears to have been a widespread growing awareness that turning to a single center as a source of theatre was no longer proving satisfactory. After all, Broadway is not at the center of the United States but at its extreme Eastern shore. Many found its lack of proximity frustrating, and its sensibility did not seem universal. Also, its economics simply took it beyond the budgets of many theatergoers. The various ethnic groups, improvisation troupes, and innovators of form and gender issue advocates featured earlier in this chapter began to seek an expression that often grew out of a specific region, with its own history, heritage, and culture.

The term **repertory** is often used to indicate the range of selections an artist or theatre is prepared to present. In these instances, the term may be expanded to imply a "rep company," which is a group hired for an entire season and often renewed for years to put on a variety of plays. The value of theatre personnel who have time to get to know one another and develop working relationships over a variety of productions and seasons cannot be underestimated in terms of the depth, detail, and new forms of collaboration that may come out of long-term association.

Regional theaters often produce new plays and challenging works as well as revivals. Most have a loyal and predictable base of audience members or season subscribers that can give the company latitude to experiment with a range of unknown or "non-commercial" works. Regional theatres have profoundly enriched the theatre culture in the United States.

Many resident theatres operate at least two stages: a main stage for shows requiring larger sets or cast, and one or more other stages (often studio theaters or black box theatres) for smaller, more experimental or avant-garde productions. In addition to box-office revenue, regional theatres rely on donations from patrons and businesses, and grants. As each accommodates the demographics of their subscribers and donors, they may develop a specific reputation.

Some regional theatres commit to developing new works and premiering new plays that may move eventually to New York. They also educate young audiences through outreach programs that teach the basics of the dramatic arts. Cooperative programs with nearby university theatre programs are also common at regional theatres. The two major organizations that help to maintain the general welfare of resident theatre in the United States are the League of Resident Theatres (LORT) and the Theatre Communications Group (TCG). These organizations encourage good relations between members and their communities, as well as promoting a larger public interest in regional theatre. LORT acts on behalf of its members in collective bargaining with unions and government agencies on problems of labor relations. TCG members benefit from opportunities to receive grants, attend workshops and conferences, and research into the not-for-profit industry. TCG also publishes the "American Theatre" magazine, the ARTSEARCH online employment bulletin, and dramatic literature.

The roots of the regional theatre movement go back to the second and third decades of the twentieth century. This development, known as the Little Theatre Movement, was started by theatre artists who were concerned that not enough emphasis was being put on the expression of individualism and social issues through the dramatic arts. The desire for more artistry and less commerce drove this movement, which ultimately altered the face of the American stage and allowed room for new works and new audiences.

In recognition of the importance of such theatres in America, a Tony Award is given to one regional theatre each year during the awards ceremonies.

ROBERT FALLS
DIRECTOR

Actors need to feel safe. And Broadway is the least safe place to work because it's so scary and the pressure is so high and there's so much fear factor around it. One must move elsewhere to achieve any kind of comfort zone.

Photo by T. Charles Erickson. The outdoor Elizabethan Stage/Allen Pavilion, Oregon Shakespeare Festival, Ashland, Oregon. HENRY V (2011, Ensemble).

FIGURE 11.14   Actors performing on the outdoor Elizabethan stage at the Oregon Shakespeare Festival.

THEATRE IN MEDIA

Theatre Apps

With the rapidly growing selection of smartphone apps, theatre fans and participants have information (and diversion!) at their fingertips at all times. Some popular theatre apps are described below.

1. **Rehearsal**
   Tool for actors to organize scripts, highlight lines, make notes. Memorization tools including recording other characters' lines so you can run lines with yourself.

2. **Scene Partner**
   An even more advanced memorization program wherein you can upload a script, convert it to speech, play back lines, cues, entire scenes, record your voice and voices of other actors, and merge them with the TTS (text to speech) playback.

3. **Broadway Music**
   Of particular interest to musical theatre fans, with lists of musical numbers within shows, history of notable other productions, cast lists, awards, discography of recordings, and suggestions for further reading.

4. **Theatermania**
   Information for 11 U.S. cities and London, including synopses of shows, play times, prices, and theatre addresses with map locator options.

5. **Theatre Trivia**
   A great learning tool in which you can compete with yourself or others in tracing facts. You can take multiple-choice challenges, save favorite questions and answers, and send questions to other theatre geeks.

   Other theatre-specific apps are almost always tied to New York City, but will no doubt expand. For your trip there consider:

1. **(heart) NYTheater**
   This easy-to-use Broadway League sponsored app includes show descriptions, casts, playing schedules, ticket prices, curtain times, running times, theatre locations, and video clips as well as Facebook page links, Twitter feeds, and YouTube channels regarding current Broadway productions.

2. **BroadwayWorld.com**
   The biggest theatre site on the web includes some regional theatre information as well, plus features "Pick a Broadway Show," which offers advice based on your personal preferences.

3. **TKTS**
   Gives continually updated heads-up on the Theatre Development Fund discount ticket booth in Times Square (see Chapter 1), a listing of shows currently available, and the discount amount for their tickets, plus access to stories published in TDF's online magazine *Stages*.

4. **NYC ARTS**
   Developed by the Alliance for the Arts to get patrons to sample more cultural offerings, this offers guidance to theatre and other arts in terms of category, location, and organization. It is possible to find lists of all the events within a mile radius of your current location.

5. **At the Booth**
   Much like TKTS, but with the addition of telling you how long the ticket buying line is plus offering links to headlines for stories about the shows and lists of restaurants near each theatre.

Regional theatres can often provide actors, directors, and designers with something akin to a "normal" life as they settle into the community, buy homes, and experience benefits such as health care. In addition to a rep company in place, plays are often scheduled to "run in rep." While various configurations exist, a company might present seven plays at once, with a different play every night of the week, or a play might be in the repertory for a few months and then be revolved out and return several months later.

This provides a richly varied experience, not only for audiences but also for participants. Rep actors often report that simply having a few days away from a role, while performing others, causes new insights upon returning. And because they might be playing a role off and on again for nearly a year, there is an opportunity to find layers and dimensions in a performance, which might not be as likely in a shorter run.

Nonprofit

One of the motivating factors for the popularity of regional theatres was the *nonprofit* designation, which allows funding resources (grants, foundation, corporate, and private donation support) beyond box-office receipts, giving theatres tax exemptions. While this made it financially viable, there was a nearly universal desire to move away from being considered the boondocks where very cool New York productions occasionally toured, to being a place where theatre originates and thrives.

Some of the most successful regional nonprofit theatres include:

Cambridge, Massachusetts: American Repertory Theatre

Chicago: Goodman Theatre, The Second City, and Steppenwolf Theatre Company

Los Angeles: Mark Taper Forum

Louisville: Actors Theatre of Louisville

Minneapolis: Guthrie Theatre

New Haven: Long Wharf Theatre

Seattle: Seattle Repertory Theatre, Intiman Theater, Empty Space Theatre, and ACT–A Contemporary Theatre

Washington, D.C.: Arena Stage

These theatres have local loyalty and often produce original scripts that may eventually make it to New York or be optioned for films. But they are just the big guns. This means that wherever you live, there is probably a major professional company doing very sound work and, perhaps even more important, discovering new works each year. There has been a tremendous change in energy, as communities no longer have to wait for Broadway shows to make their way across the country but instead may have their own homegrown plays make their way to the Great White Way. This category, however, also applies to nonprofit professional theatres on Broadway such as Roundabout Theatre Company, Manhattan Theatre Club, and Lincoln Center.

In addition to resident regional companies, there are now more than 100 Shakespeare festivals in the United States.

CELISA KALKE
DIRECTOR OF NEW PROJECTS FOR THE ALLIANCE THEATRE

We have to dream nationally (with ambition, creativity and excellence) but produce locally (inviting audiences to help nurture new work and innovative artists). Then American theatre can dramatize a changing America, neighborhood by neighborhood, city by city, region by region, in the twenty-first century.

THEATRE IN MEDIA

Screen Blends

The authors' material in this section has been supplemented by Megan C. Hakes of Penn State University.

Contemporary films are ever more likely to combine conventions from opposite sides of the world, blend several distinct plots into a single work, and eschew linear narrative for more challenging relationships to time and place. However, there are a number of other interesting trends in screen action.

VIDEO GAMES

Video games are becoming increasingly more complex, detailed, and individualized to each player. Gone are the days of the simple platform or side-scrolling game where the objective was simply to get a character through a complicated maze. Many games are beginning to include artificial intelligence (AI), which provides players with a completely individualized experience, essentially allowing them to create their own dramatic saga in which each one is the protagonist. Games like the *Mass Effect* series and the *Fallout* series allow the player to make multiple decisions that affect not only the game-play (the player's stats, what becomes available to them, and story elements), but the final outcome of the game. The aim of these games is to encourage the player to become emotionally connected to the character that he or she has created. The leading designer in this genre, Brad McQuaid, incorporates filmlike experience and detail into the gaming atmosphere beyond offering richly detailed virtual universes. These games provide a richer experience then simply watching a movie. "I realized," says McQuaid, "that unlike watching a movie, where you're just following the protagonist, in a game you could actually *be* the protagonist."

MMORPGs

MMORPGs (Massively Multiplayer Online Role Playing Games) burst on the scene in the late 1990s, but their roots go back to the 1970s with games like *Maze War* and *Adventure*. In MMORPGs the player is immersed in an online world alongside other players. In the earlier days of online gaming, communication with other players was limited, mostly through text or chat windows. However, now that gaming consoles can be connected to the Internet, communication between players is a seamless element of the game. Players can connect with others all over the world to create a social group that is working together—or as opponents—within the game. In online-only games such as *EverQuest* and *World of Warcraft (WoW)*, both designed by Brad McQuaid, the intention was to create a filmlike experience of a virtual universe. That idea has now expanded, and console video game developers have embraced it. Included in most current video game releases is a multiplayer element in addition to single-player game-play. A player can play through the single-player mode and then continue his or her experience of the game by joining the multiplayer world, essentially allowing players to write their own narrative into the larger interactive world of the game.

WEBISODES

Used first in the early 2000s as a marketing tool, webisodes are now becoming a driving force in the entertainment industry. Webisodes were born out of a need to reach out to audiences that were drifting away from traditional television and looking for new sources of entertainment. Websites such as FunnyorDie.com have come to the forefront and created thousands of original comedy sketches specifically for the Internet. Many popular television shows, such as *The Office*, have begun making webisodes to continue to appeal to audiences that are transitioning to the Internet in search of fresh entertainment. These short episodes follow minor characters, or expand a particular scene that was broadcast, or show a scene from a different character's point of view than what appeared in the original show. Webisodes are also allowing independent artists to create entire series without being hampered by the restrictions of television network broadcasting. Websites like YouTube.com, WebisodesNetwork.com, and Vimeo.com are providing a veritable creative playground for writers, directors, actors, and anyone with a camera to explore this new offshoot of the entertainment industry.

GRAPHIC NOVELS AND COMICS

A massive commercial success in recent years, graphic novels offer the reader an experience unlike any other. The genre features the combination of pictures and words, much like watching stills from a film with subtitles. Some of the most popular graphic novels are beginning to bleed into other media as well with film and television adaptations. One of the most successful graphic novels of the past few years, *The Walking Dead* by Robert Kirkman, Tony Moore, and Charlie Adlard, has been produced by AMC as a television series of the same name. Comics have, for decades, provided inspiration for television and film. The recent superhero movie boom, such as the reboots of *Batman, Spiderman* and *Superman*, has seen great success. This is due not only to filmmakers' creative respect for the original source material, but also to the very nature of graphic novels and comics which allow artistic expansion and reinterpretation. Drawn & Quarterly (D&Q), one of the most successful publishers in the field, offers a wide range of "cartoons," often with serious literary intentions. However, according to D&Q intern Andrew Barton, "Many literary cartoonists cite classic and silent films as their major sources of information." Now graphic novels in turn have inspired films such as *300* and *Sin City,* which try to emulate their source material's visual style.

AUDIOBOOKS AND PODCASTS

Audiobooks and podcasts embrace dramatic elements to create theatrical experiences for your ears. Audiobooks can range from having one narrator to having a cast of voice actors, and even to full-blown audio dramas with huge casts and sound effects. Podcasting has become an extremely popular form of artistic expression. Podcasts come in many forms. There are talk shows, authors reading their novels, stand-up comics performing sets, and even serial audio dramas. Writers and other artists find the medium of podcasting freeing since they are completely in charge of what is produced. They don't have to answer to any editors or censors.

DRAMA/REALITY GAMES

Some film festivals now include competition for prizes among video games with cinematic efforts. These not infrequently have links to earlier theatrical forms.

Façade, a winner of the Slamdance Film Festival Grand Jury Prize for Best Game, was billed as an "interactive drama about a marital crisis" and inspired by Ingmar Bergman's film *Scenes from a Marriage* and Edward Albee's play/film *Who's Afraid of Virginia Woolf?* This is also an area where boundaries are being tested. A creation called *Super Columbine Massacre RPG (Role Playing Game)!* was withdrawn from the festival after receiving complaints regarding the appropriateness of participating, on any level, in an event as horrifying as a school shooting. Peter Baxter, the festival director, says, "Games take the level of participation to a whole other level. You are actively engaged in the outcome of your actions. Games are going to affect us in different ways—in ways you don't fully understand yet."

FILM HOMESCHOOLING

More and more independent filmmakers are not just working alone; they are also training that way. Disillusioned with film schools where, according to director David Tomaric, "classes are out of date and you are often taught by an academic who has never made a movie, let alone had one distributed," a whole new market in home instruction has emerged with such bestselling DVDs as *Film School in a Box, Hollywood Camera Work, The Ultimate Filmmaking Kit,* and *Make Your Own Damn Movie!* These are short on film theory and history but astonishingly comprehensive on practical advice.

YOUTUBE TO BOOB TUBE

Getting a contract for a television series by simply posting videos on a website is a great shortcut when compared with more cumbersome career pursuits. In his early 20s, David Lehre became an Internet phenomenon with popular postings on his site (davidlehre.com), the most famous of which was *myspace: the movie,* a film that satirized the social-networking site that doubles as a place of self-promotion. This led to Fox producing his half-hour late-night television show, "an open-ended, sketch variety show with music videos, short videos, and comedy skits." Fox threw in a film contract as well.

Oral Tradition and Shrinking Tongues

While the oral tradition continues to thrive, the languages in which stories are being told and enacted are shrinking in number. There are approximately 6,800 languages in the world, but 3,000 have the same risk factor as endangered species because only living adults and no children speak them. Within the last century, at least 400 languages can be classified as dead. The Apache tribe has a language that, at this writing, has only three living speakers. Busuu, the old language of Cameroon, can be spoken by only eight citizens.

While Congress passed the Native American Languages Act to help preservation, it never funded it adequately to have enough impact. One of the very few effective centers is the University of Oregon's Northwest Indian Language Institute, which provides training in regional tribal language, both bringing in fluent elders to preserve their knowledge and, where such speakers do not exist, searching out grammars, recordings, and other artifacts. Even within these efforts, however, there is controversy over whether producing written translations from traditionally oral languages will sap them of their potency.

At the present rate of demise, 90 percent of existing languages will probably disappear within the next 100 years. After this happens, what languages will dominate? Will English be the global language? Possibly, but it is not certain. At present, over one-sixth of the world's population speaks Mandarin Chinese. English is actually a distant second, followed by Hindi and Spanish. It will be interesting to see how the oral tradition develops, as there are fewer languages to speak.

CLOSE-UP

Marrakesh *Griot*

As much as things change, it is comforting to know that some forms of theatre are practiced exactly as they have been for thousands of years. Each workday, Mohammed Jabiri still heads for Jemaa el Fna, the main square of Marrakesh, considered the cultural crossroads for all Morocco. He weaves his way past the chaos of snake charmers, drummers, cymbal players, acrobats, and kebab vendors until he finds a relatively quiet spot. He puts down a stool, hauls out a few colored illustrations, and begins.

Jabiri is a descendant of a time when itinerant narrators brought not only stories but also news from other parts of the world. But he does not feel particularly challenged by this electronic media age. "Some people feel that television is very far away from them," he says. "They prefer making contact, they prefer hearing live stories. They want to be captured and held."

Jabiri holds a crowd with highly theatrical means, his eyes growing wide and hypnotic, his gestures stylized, his voice varying from booming volume to whispers as he tells his tales of real or imagined pasts, ancient battles, sinners, prophets, wise sultans, and tricky thieves.

Do his audiences vary in tastes? Yes. "Young people like stories from *1001 [Arabian] Nights* because there is less religion. Older people like stories about the life of the Prophet and his companions. They like war stories, battles between Muslims and either the Persians or the Christians."

Often he begins beckoning listeners (only men, because women are not supposed to stop on the street and listen to wild or bawdy tales) by invoking a blessing, although he may also pretend to start a fight. One of his legendary colleagues, the late storyteller Sarough, was a strongman who would attract attention by lifting a donkey in the air. As it started braying, people would come running. Jabiri might also employ the trick of evoking a curse such as "All those doomed by their parents must leave." So everyone stays. He weaves his tale up to a suspenseful climax, then stops, and asks for payment from all present. When he gets it, he gives them a blessing and brings all to a satisfying conclusion.

At this writing, Jabiri is in his mid-70s. Does he see himself passing the torch to others? Yes, he is currently training two apprentices, "but they need a lot of work."

SUMMARY

While certain performance conventions continue to divide Eastern and Western theatre, a fusion of traditions often makes for exciting blends of ideas. Theatre originating from various ethnic contingencies or from other group identities constitutes a long-overdue sense of inclusiveness. Carefully scripted theatre has been increasingly suspended in favor of improvisation, which is not only a major diverting entertainment but also is a tool for bringing about social change. Language-centered theatre has sometimes been supplanted by productions based almost entirely on movement and nonverbal communication. Nondramatic source material is increasingly adapted and developed to become devised theatrical works. All other art forms and various adjustments to the traditional theatre experience may be present in performance art. An alarming reduction in the number of languages spoken raises questions about the future of the oral tradition. While there will always be a welcoming environment for a traditionally scripted drama, there also appears to be an ever-widening welcome for more physically based and less linear experimental work, casting a wider net for new ways to create exciting theatre. In the United States, a large shift in theatre has resulted in New York no longer being the center of creativity. An increase in grassroots performance is evolving.

SUGGESTED ASSIGNMENTS

1. How does ethnic theatre in the United States differ most clearly from Asian and African theatre? How do the needs to blend cultural influences in the former distinguish it from the traditions of the latter?

2. As ethnic theatre has moved into being politicized, what patterns can be recognized in its development?

3. How is the theatre of Native Americans distinct from other ethnic theatre traditions? Why do you feel there is this difference?

4. What does interest in improvisation, devising, and performance art indicate about the position of the well-made, scripted drama in theatre?

5. What do these forms suggest regarding the hierarchy or power structure of traditional theatre?

6. While improvisation can be pure entertainment, what are its potential uses of a more serious or significant nature?

7. Identify an area of controversy in your community or campus. How might the processes developed by Augusto Boal be used to help solve the problem or to bring closure?

8. What were the primary factors in the decentralizing of theatre in the United States and the advent of grassroots and regional productions?

9. Some examples of fusion are offered in this chapter. Can you think of any other blends or juxtapositions of conventions that might make for exciting theatre? Given the trends identified here, what would be your predictions regarding the next developments in live and media theatre?

SUGGESTED ACTIVITIES

1. **Individual:** Pick any single artist or theatre group identified in this chapter. Go online to research the topic further and to gain insights into the contributions of this person or collective on contemporary theatre.

2. **Group:** Using the ideas from Question 7 in the "Suggested Assignments" section, agree on a problem of significant enough interest to the whole group to develop it further into a theatrical problem-solving experience. Make sure to use Boal's techniques.

3. **Long-term:** Try to identify the not-for-profit regional theatre closest to where you live. Research its history, development, and sources of funding. If possible, interview someone on the staff regarding the challenges of running a large regional theatre under such circumstances.

4. **Large group:** Use a town hall format to have a public debate over which contemporary theatre movement has the greatest significance. Ask for volunteers to argue for each area discussed in this chapter. Vote on whose argument was most convincing.

KEY WORDS AND IDEAS

Athol Fugard
Wole Soyinka
Concert Party
Ananse
Tess Onwueme
Hausa
total theatre
fusion
Peter Brook
Ariane Mnouchkine
ethnic American theatre
Spiderwoman Theater
Black Elk Speaks
El Teatro Campesino
Luis Valdez
zarzuelas

teatro buffo
José Rivera
Nuyorican
Harlem Renaissance
Lorraine Hansberry
Negro Ensemble Company
George C. Wolfe
August Wilson
Rodgers and Hammerstein
David Henry Hwang
East West Players
Asian American Theater Company
women's theatre
feminist theatre
Hroswitha
Mercy Otis Warren

Eve Ensler
Lillian Hellman
Mart Crowley
Charles Ludlam
Gay Theatre Alliance
Tony Kushner
Jane Chambers
Queer Theory
The Second City
ComedySportz
improvisation
playback theatre
therapy theatre
Augusto Boal:
    forum theatre
    image theatre
    invisible theatre

performance art
Laurie Anderson
Sherry Glaser
Susan Stroman
dance play
Matthew Bourne
Stomp
Blue Man Group
devised works
The Laramie Project
nonprofit theatre
repertory
regional theatres
eco-theatre

chapter 12

CRITICISM AND CONNECTIONS

At the Globe Theatre in London, the audience gets as close as they can to the title character
(played by Jasper Britton) during a performance of Shakespeare's *Macbeth,* directed by Tim Carroll.

Children watch a performance of *Ramayana* at Jahangir Palace in Madhya Pradesh Orchha, India.

Anne-Marie Palmer/Alamy

Lesson Objectives:

Upon completion of this chapter, you will be able to:

1. Consider whether you might make theatre criticism a part of your future endeavors.
2. Evaluate written criticism to determine its value by the system of threes offered in this chapter.
3. Write criticism that is thoughtful and thought-provoking.
4. Begin giving and taking criticism in ways that are positive, supportive, and productive.
5. Decide if, and how, you might be involved in theatre after completing this course.

Introduction

The final, powerful player in the life or death of a production is the **critic.** We have placed the critic last in this text, and at a great distance from the production team, because he is indeed isolated from them and is considered by none of them to be part of that team. The critic does not *do* theatre and has rarely trained or participated in it; rather, he comments on it publicly after the fact. Many participants, fairly or not, consider their relationship with critics to be adversarial and the critics to be the true antagonists in their pursuit of excellence. Yet there is no denying their power.

How powerful are they? We will never exactly know. Producers fear critics and hope for notices that will, as publicists say, "put butts in seats." In New York, the *Times* review alone may influence millions in box-office receipts. Many theatergoers in your hometown wait to read what your local reviewers say before buying tickets. On the other hand, while critics certainly have influence, the public increasingly ignores them and flocks to a work that critics unanimously warn them to avoid. Many believe theatre critics influence attendance far more than film critics do. Clearly there are millions of moviegoers who never read reviews.

How long have critics existed? Probably as long as there have been performances. In Robert's book *Acting: Onstage and Off,* he creates a variation on Ook's story in which Ook enthralls his cave audience with tales of dinosaurs instead of lions (see Chapter 2). After his triumphant performance, all cave couples leave the fire:

> As Ook and his mate head off to their corner of the cave, she says to him, 'Ook, you've got it all over those dumb brutes. You're a real artist.' As another couple moves to their corner, she says, 'That Ook. Isn't he amazing? The way he got just how the dinosaur's head swings back and forth. It was perfect.' Her mate replies, 'Well, it was pretty good. Personally, I wouldn't have swung my head so far. It's more of a circle than a swing, actually.' And so the first actor is born. And minutes later, the first critic.

This chapter explores the critic's role and what it takes to be a good critic. It provides guidelines for writing an informed critical review. It also offers ways of connecting your total theatre exposure thus far to potential future participation.

The Power of Libel

We are all critics, and one of the great "after pleasures" of seeing a play or film is discussing and perhaps heatedly debating its merits, often deepening our experience by each of us sharing insights that the others may have missed. In any theatre department, we critics (and that includes everyone in the department!) gather in small groups in the halls after an opening, debate how our responses may match or contradict those of the reviewers, and generally dissect the entire event. If the reviews were mixed to negative, these huddles get more quiet and deep.

But professional critics are granted something called "the power of libel." Anthony Lane's review in *The New Yorker* of the final installment in the *Star Wars* series, *Revenge of the Sith,* provides an example of this power:

> The general opinion seems to be that it marks a distinct improvement on the last two episodes. . . . True, but only in the same way that dying from natural causes is preferable to crucifixion.

To say that this was a "pan" would be a major understatement. If someone in life writes that you "totally suck" without any real evidence, you can sue. Imagine someone writing or reporting on your local television station that being around you was a picayune distinction between natural death and the cross. But the critic can get away with such a statement. This license is essential in a free society when evaluating art. We may sometimes hate what they say but should vigilantly defend their right to say it. We want critics who are honest. If they are, we should be tough enough to take it, whatever it is. Yet it is devastating when people suggest to thousands of readers or millions of viewers that you are unworthy. Here is a further excerpt:

> R2-D2 and C-3PO? I still fail to understand why I should have been expected to waste 25 years of my life following the progress of a beeping trashcan and a gay, gold-plated Jeeves. . . . But the one who gets me is Yoda. May I take this opportunity to enter a brief plea in favor of his extermination?

FIGURE 12.1 Visually stunning and full of snappy Beach Boys music, *Surf* closed after six weeks at Planet Hollywood, Las Vegas, 2012. Critical reviews definitely shortened the stage life of this lavish musical.

Retna Ltd./Corbis

You may be among viewers who love, maybe even adore, these characters and would rally to their defense. Because they are not real, they do not even have to consider suing. Also, it is not likely that *The New Yorker* reviewers or subscribers had any influence on the track record of this largely positively reviewed film, which achieved record box-office figures.

The first definition for *critic* in *Webster's New World Dictionary* is "one who expresses a reasoned opinion of a work, involving a judgment on its value." But the second definition is "one given to harsh or insidious judgment." Hmm. If you read enough reviews, you learn that there are plenty of both kinds of critics—and some of them have feet in both camps. To attract readers and to be thought worthy of being quoted, critics often sharpen their wit, sometimes with devastating effect. Alas, whether their targets actually deserve such lacerations, however amusing, is often open to debate.

No Turn Unstoned

Excerpts from reviews are often used in ads to promote a show. Full-page ads in *The New York Times* herald the success of the production, with lavish praise from various critics presented in support. Sometimes these quotations have desperately squeezed a few positive words out of an otherwise unenthusiastic review. It used to be that only major influential publications were used. In recent years, however, publicists, when putting ads together, have been willing to cast an ever-widening net, going as far down into less-prestigious periodicals as it takes. No matter how bad a film seems to be in the opinion of most, there are always raves available out there somewhere. Ads will trumpet the work, and then in very tiny print you find out this is not from *The New York Times* but the *Ashtabula Grange Record*.

HELEN MIRREN

ACTOR

I remember the reviewer who first panned me. And he's still out there writing—the bastard.

Every actor receives devastating reviews at some point for some project, and while publicists search out the ads for raves, we could also find negative responses for even generally triumphant productions. This is the nature of individual taste. The smartest actors clip and save their worst reviews and sometimes even keep them in their makeup kits so they stay humble. There is also comfort—once you have been panned in a devastating, personal, and humiliating way—that it will probably never get worse than this.

Almost every great actor has experienced critical devastation. Here are some classics, which the much-praised British actor Diana Rigg compiled in her book, *No Turn Unstoned*:

"Miss Hepburn ran the gamut of emotions from A to B."

"Ms. Stapleton played the role as if she has not yet signed a contract with the producer."

"Peter O'Toole [as Macbeth] delivers every line with a monotonous bark, as if addressing an audience of dead Eskimos."

"Anthony Hopkins [as Macbeth] sweats apprehensively and gives the impression that he is a Rotarian pork butcher about to tell the stalls a dirty story."

"Judi Dench as Regan compensates for her strong scowl with a nervous speech impediment which, no doubt, is all Lear's fault."

"Maggie Smith . . . will not let the words speak for themselves . . . and we never forget for a moment this is a performance."

"The best thing about Ian McKellen's Hamlet is his curtain-call."

"Albert Finney's Hamlet is no prince at all, much less a sweet one. More of a 'Spamlet' really."

And a few more:

- Samuel Pepys in his 1662 diary wrote, "*Romeo and Juliet* is a play, of itself, the worst that ever I heard in my life."
- "*Lestat* (the musical) is not a show from which you leave whistling anything, except for a taxi."
- "Beckett's mordant comic allegory (*Endgame*) is thoroughly travestied. It's just shtick in the mud."
- Telegram sent by writer George S. Kaufman to an actor who he believed was giving a weak performance in his *Of Thee I Sing:* "Watching your performance from the rear of the theatre. Wish you were here."

Sometimes actors get a bit of their own back. For example, take Sir Peter Ustinov's view on the subject of critics: "They search for ages for the wrong word, which, to give them credit, they eventually find."

AUTHOR'S INSIGHT

ANNIE: I sometimes feel that I am in heady company in terms of bad reviews. I once directed a *Julius Caesar* that was reviewed as, "if not the worst production of Shakespeare ever, then pretty close." The message was clear! The critique did put me in some mighty exalted company, since it involved the entire world, but I was angry for the actors and designers who had only followed my lead and ended up being mocked in the same review.

Critical Threes

An alarming number of critics have training in journalism but not theatre. The problem is that when evaluating the work of, say, costume designers, if you do not actually understand how these artists function, the challenges they face, and the standard process of moving from design conferences to renderings to completion, your response is likely to be facile, shallow, and uninformed. The more knowledge that a critic has about the specific demands faced by each participant, the more likelihood for an insightful response. We believe that clusters of threes can be used to determine whether critics have the necessary qualifications required to determine the quality of a theatre production.

Critics Should Be . . .

Critics should measure up in the following areas before presuming to judge the work of others and asking us to read or watch their response:

1. **Knowledgeable:** Critics should know more than we do about the play, the playwright, the period or style in which it is written, and other work by this author, director, and major actors. They should be able to place this event in a historical and artistic context. They should have sharply tuned senses and be able to predict the responses of the average viewer. They should have the writing skills to present their ideas with precision, clarity, and wit. Reading reviews should be like reading *Consumer Reports,* where very informed researchers tell whether this product (which, on Broadway, can be a $130-plus memory) is worth purchasing and offer guidelines to make a wise consumer choice. Because this is theatre, critics should also be entertaining, lucid, and clever.

2. **Demanding:** Good critics hold us to the highest standards, call out bad work as well as lazy, repetitive work, and never pander to mediocrity. At the same time, they honor the best. So much is produced that is unworthy. Critics need to place the blame in the hopes that everyone will aspire to quality next time. They also need to be reminders of the difference between dreadful and merely bad and between pretty good and superb, and they must provide examples for those who aspire to the latter. Critics should never pander to even the most revered writers, directors, and actors when any of them are phoning in their work. Critics are there to keep us all on our toes.

BENEDICT NIGHTINGALE

CRITIC

So often criticism seems to be a courtroom in which theatre practitioners are arraigned. If that is so, then perhaps the critic should think of himself as a court record and defense attorney at least as much as a prosecutor and judge.

3. **Compassionate:** Many critics, alas, come across as vultures, actually seeking open wounds. The best are open-minded, hopeful, empathetic; even when needing to write potentially devastating responses, critics do so in a way that makes it clear how and why such inadequate work could have been avoided. They need to acknowledge how difficult some challenges are and even to honor ambitious failures for attempting to raise the bar. The best critics express their opinions with grace and are ever hopeful that the next work or next season will be better than this one.

Critics Should Ask . . .

Good critics should always ask the following questions:

1. **What was the artist trying to do?**

   It is essential to know what was being attempted. If, for example, a production is trying to update a classic play to connect it to current political events, it is pointless to criticize it for not being traditional and conventionally classical enough. The question should be considered for both the play and the production. What did the playwright want us to think and feel, and how closely did the production adhere to or diverge from these aspirations? What was each artist trying to achieve? If it is difficult to answer these questions, then a valid criticism can be made regarding a lack of clarity of intentions. It is essential for critics to get inside the artist's aspirations before gauging success or failure.

2. **How well did she do it?**

To what degree did the artists accomplish what they set out to do? It is quite likely that some elements of the production came closer to the mark than others did. The perspective of this question allows a clear framework beyond the mood or inclinations of the reviewer. It forces the reviewer to get past deep prejudice. Maybe you don't really care for sentimental, madcap, and mindless musicals that attempt to create nostalgia for bygone days that never were. While it is acceptable to admit this bias, you also need to admit how well or poorly they did what they wanted to do. Were the performances convincing and compelling? Was the same true of the work of the director, designers, the stage manager, and running crew? If it was supposed to provoke outrage and debate, to what extent did it do that? If it was supposed to provide amusement, diversion, and laughter, how well did it succeed? If it was supposed to shock us into taking social action, to what degree did it accomplish this?

> ### ALVIN KLEIN
> #### CRITIC
> *It is important to perceive the intentions from within the work itself, not from any preconceived ideas you bring to it. The critic must guide rather than dictate.*

3. **Was it worth doing?**

Sometimes, even after the most strenuous effort is put into a theatre piece and it largely achieves its aspirations, you have to ask if it was

FIGURE 12.2 The 13,000-person, sold-out audience during the curtain call of the *Les Misérables* anniversary performance at The O2 in London.

Ian West/PA Wire/Press Association via AP Images

Roland Weihrauch/epa/Corbis Wire/Corbis

FIGURE 12.3   Sometimes, an imaginative update of a classic story can become wildly popular, as with Andrew Lloyd Webber's rock musical, *Starlight Express*. A Cinderella story about trains, the actors are on roller skates. The show has been playing at the Starlighthalle in Bochum, Germany, for nearly 20 years.

worth all the time and effort. Critics must now consider if it is worth the price of the ticket for audiences. While the world of theatre may seem unlike that of business, in all activities, it is essential at some point to stop and ask if the investment is worth the payoff.

Trying to connect the rhythmic elements of rap to those of Kabuki in a production set in the 'hood, but integrating *joruri* and *koken* and hypothetically calling it *Gangsta Buki,* could be brilliant—or not. If, after all the fusion work, there are neither insights into either theatre form nor the birth of a new one, and if it was not all that entertaining, then the answer would probably have to be no. However noble the intentions and the success of achieving them, there is always the lingering question of whether all this has any lasting value or reverberation. Were enough people engaged and satisfied? Were there enough new insights, moments of theatrical magic, gasps, bursts of applause, or extended ovations to compensate for the effort on the parts of both actors and audience? Did it probe deeply enough or buoy us high enough? Would we like to do it again—or see it again? Will we tell our friends that they ***must*** experience it? Many *civilians* (a term we sometimes use for non-theatre people) consider those in the theatre "mental" for the amount of time and energy that they are willing to devote to an event that plays a few weekends and then is nothing but a memory. So the question becomes, "Was all the sweat worth the payoff?"

THEATRE IN MEDIA

Stage, Screen, and 'Zine

The relationship between live and filmed performances and the printed media is both symbiotic and tenuous. A film or play may be advertised on television, where we get an impression of its plot. However, we turn to newspapers and magazines to find the details—exactly at what theatre it is playing, at what times, and at what cost—the sort of listings that would go by too fast and be impossible to remember if not in some printed form.

By the same token, reviews are largely in print. The websites Internet Movie Database (www.imdb.com) and Rotten Tomatoes (www.rottentomatoes.com) are increasingly influential for in-depth information that used to be available only on the printed page. They include plot summaries (with "spoiler alerts"), complete cast and crew lists, trailers, and critical judgments from a variety of sources, both professional and amateur. And as an added bonus, a link for major characters and team members (director, producer, etc.) provides access to their specific biography and body of work.

Some broadcasts have capsule notices, but rarely anything detailed or reflective. For any considered examination of a play or film, we will need to turn to the printed page or online version of a periodical. Trade publications, such as *Variety,* aim to review most film releases and major theatrical productions in New York, the regional United States, and London. Magazines ranging from relatively highbrow, such as *The New Yorker,* to the opposite, such as *Entertainment Weekly* or *People,* also include reviews of recent openings in every issue. Some of this has to do with the way we take in information. Just as a list of show times can be too complex to take in and remember when experienced scrolling across a screen, the same is true of an extended opinion. Reviews are taken in more effectively by taking more time and perhaps rereading a sentence or paragraph, the sort of luxury afforded by printed material.

Quoting reviews is a major part of advertising. Again, it takes time to scan the document carefully to pull out (or, in some cases, distort) the one phrase most likely to lure audiences into theatres. Programs for professional theatre productions are often much like magazines, with essays or articles about the play, various features on theatre phenomena, bios of cast and staff members, and advertising and notices of upcoming other productions. So for better or worse, what we see in a theatre is very much bound to what we read—at least for now.

Critics Should Consider . . .

Good critics will raise the following issues for each production: Does it have . . .

1. **Relevance?**

Some plays and films aspire only to provide a diverting good time. Critics sometimes call these films "flicks." There is nothing wrong—and a lot right—with simple diversion if it's done well. But if a work is to be judged as major, even great, and presents itself with high ambitions, these questions arise: Does it relate to concerns of our culture, to issues currently being debated? Does it present these with new clarity or complexity? Does it offer any solutions or at least help bring the debate into sharper focus? Does it awaken the public to something important, help bring about an end to ignorance, and offer a beginning of healing? Does it get everyone at least talking and thinking in new ways? If it is a classic, does it point out how much we are still struggling with these issues, perhaps thousands of years later?

ANTHONY LANE
CRITIC

A critic is just a regular viewer with a ballpoint pen, an overstocked memory, and an underpowered social life.

Joan Marcus

FIGURE 12.4   Playwright Tony Kushner's critically acclaimed, award-winning 1990 play *Angels in America* examined AIDS and homosexuality with sympathy and humor. Here, the Angel (Ellen McLaughlin) descends on Prior Walter (Stephen Spinella) in the final scene of the first part of the play, *Millennium Approaches*. The play is still popular today, with a widely viewed miniseries adaptation on the HBO cable channel that premiered in 2003.

When we call a play great, it usually has a resonance throughout all our lives and for all time.

2. Humanity?

At the other end of the spectrum, how personal is this play? How deeply does it connect—not to the political or social but to private pain, fear, joy, disappointment, or ecstasy? Even if it chooses to savage some of us, does it seem to have any positive intentions for bringing us together after bursting our balloons? How effectively does it make each of us realize that in these private concerns, we are not alone? How much does it make us aware that the hopes, hangups, and conflicts that we face are actually our connections in the family of humankind? How much does it help us discover not only our connectedness but our possible paths to move out of our personal traps? Do we feel a genuine compassion and empathy for each of the characters and, through their journeys, find insights into our own lives?

3. Excitement?

Is this a riveting, "can't leave my seat even though I gotta pee" experience, or is it easy to let go not only during the performance but also after? Does it rev up our emotions? Excite our minds? Are we transported out of our ho-hum lives into a far more desirable or perhaps more appalling world? Were we consistently held captive, or did we sometimes drift off? If the play was live, did it use the theatre space in imaginative ways to remind us why live theatre can be a far greater high than the anonymity of the multiplex? Was there genuine suspense, surprise, spectacle, and a continuous stimulation of our curiosity? Does it have resonance? To what extent were we electrified at the time, and how much does it now resonate in our lives? Are we thinking about it and reliving it in the days that follow, or does it instantly dissolve for us?

Reviewers versus Critics/Scholars

The terms *critic* and *reviewer* are generally used interchangeably, but the differences between media respondents and those who provide thoughtful critical analysis are considerable. Reviewers need to rush back to their computers and pound out an immediate first response with almost no reflection. It is comparable to being handed the conditions for an improv and just going for it. Some now attend final previews of a production just to give them more time before publishing the day after opening. But if the show was in the process of still pulling itself together and there was not the excitement of opening night, didn't they really miss the opening?

Others, writing for scholarly journals, have more time not only to reflect but also to do further research before formulating a response. Publications such as *Theatre Topics, Theatre Journal,* and *Voice & Speech Review* actually solicit reviews that will be published long after a production has closed. These serve as historical records or archival documents rather than consumer advice because the opportunity to see the show is long past.

In dictionaries, to criticize is sometimes defined as "to find fault" but also "to understand and appraise." While the former, if witty enough, can be hugely entertaining, the latter is more likely to contribute to both those who have done the work and those who are considering seeing it. In Samuel Beckett's great Absurdist play *Waiting for Godot,* the two central characters shout insults at each other, such as "Vermin!" "Moron!" "Sewer Rat!" "Cretin!" and finally for the topper, "C-r-ritic!!!"

Many theatre practitioners share Beckett's view. But we ask you, while not denying any of this, to give reviewers a massive dose of empathy for working under such tight deadlines, rarely being given enough print space or broadcast time to explore their responses with any degree of depth, and rising to the challenge of trying to predict how countless others will respond when most of us are not even all that sure how our best friends will. They also deserve points for putting their ideas on the line and then subjecting themselves to a barrage of outraged disagreement. They function in a relatively isolated, outsider context regarding the theatre community; they are not invited to receptions and are possibly confronted and vilified when they meet theatre practitioners. The reviewer must have a strong sense of personal integrity and no real need for the affection of or even interaction with those he reviews.

Of course, occasionally reviewers become celebrities in their own right, and their reviews are read as much for entertainment value as for readers to decide whether to see a show or movie. Roger Ebert in film and Frank Rich in theatre have both published collections of their reviews to be savored after the fact.

> **JAMES CAMERON**
> DIRECTOR
>
> *We need more critics who respect the paying audience who look to him or her for guidance, not for lectures on how stupid they are for liking what they like.*

Writing a Review

You may be asked to write a critical review for a class assignment or even consider offering your services as a critic to your school or local newspaper. Believe it or not, you are more qualified now that you have read the previous chapters in this book than many professionals who step up to pass judgment without a theatre education of any kind. Start by looking at the "Responding to Theatre" section in Chapter 1. Ask yourself which of those elements you would like to include. Then consider some of the additions that are discussed here.

If you cannot actually read the play, try to read *about* it—newspaper articles or interviews that are part of the

> **JOHN SIMON**
> CRITIC
>
> *The most common critical failure is the inability to give the reason for one's opinions. Anyone can have opinions, but until you can convey to the reader why and how you arrived at them, they are worthless.*

THEATRE IN MEDIA

The Blog Must Go On

For many years, a handful of powerful newspaper critics dominated New York theatre. Audiences would avidly await their verdicts, and some were considered able to make or break a show. That situation has altered for many younger theatergoers, who turn instead to blog sites run by "theatre freaks" for instant opinions after shows open. Such potential audience members prefer the feedback of their online peers to that of generally older reviewers in print. They seek screen input to decide whether or not to attend live theatre. Rather than waiting for the newspapers to be published, participants in the website All That Chat (www.talkinbroadway.com) actually review shows DURING the show.

There are even competitions among bloggers for who can see the most shows. At this writing, three such marathon show runners chart their progress at Show Showdown (showshowdown.blogspot .com), which includes links to their individual sites. This competition has very specific rules as to which productions qualify. For example, "No Barbra Streisand concerts are allowed."

Of course, entries on such sites need not adhere to journalistic guidelines any more than Jon Stewart's

The Daily Show needs to emulate network newscasts. Entries range from short campy insider quips to extended trenchant cultural observations.

According to theatre blogger Aaron Riccio, "Broadway shows are not any worse or better than other shows, but they get the most coverage because they have the most money, are backed by critics who feel obligated to cover the show, and have publicists. This can be dangerous." As a result, theatre bloggers tend to extend their targets all the way to include off-off-Broadway, opera, and story ballets. Theatre blogger Christopher, who uses only his first name, says, "I see bloggers as the public editors of New York theatre."

While film audiences have often ignored critics for many years, this represents a turnaround in thinking for theatergoers. Those in the industry have started to notice. While Broadway has yet to extend a hand to bloggers, publicists and directors of smaller shows have begun to extend invitations and complimentary tickets to them. According to one publicist who asked for anonymity, "I don't think bloggers have yet made the impact they have in other industries, but they are ultimately going to start having sway. I don't want to offend any of them now."

publicity, or possibly a summary of it in a study guide. Do the same research on the playwright to get a sense of how this play fits into the body of her work. Examine the lobby display, which is often a source of the dramaturg's research, possibly containing fascinating quotes and insights into the culture surrounding early productions, as well as photos of other performances of this work. Read whatever notes are in the program, which are intended to help shape the experience for audience members. While it can be distracting to take notes during a performance, it is often a good idea to have a small notepad where you can jot down your thoughts at intermission and immediately after the performance while your response is fresh.

Other guidelines include the following:

1. Assume the best about your readers. Write for them as if they are well-educated adults, people of taste and good judgment. Do not patronize them. Write up rather than down to them.

2. Be fair in your expectations. If a theatre obviously functions on a shoe-string budget, complaining about a lack of opulence in the production

is pointless. If the theatre specializes in raunchy satire, why bother to make judgments of taste?

3. If you make a strong, negative criticism, supply an example or evidence to back up this assertion. Select a part of the performance where it failed and try to identify, to the best of your ability, why.

CLOSE-UP

An Ideal Local Critic: Richard Leinaweaver

The reason that there is so much dreadful dramatic criticism is that it is very rare for the person writing it to have any qualifications for doing so. While we might reasonably expect a degree in journalism and theatre, we rarely get either. Reviewers in large cities writing for major newspapers occasionally have credentials, but in smaller towns, the task of reviewing can just as easily be assigned to someone simply because he or she is willing to do it or because the "journalist" has already finished an article on a house and garden show and has some free time.

Richard Leinaweaver is, therefore, the unusual specimen of reviewer whom we would like to offer up as an example for other cities. He is a retired theatre

Richard Leinaweaver

FIGURE 12.5 Eugene, Oregon–based critic Richard Leinaweaver.

professor, so he has not only studied all aspects of the art but taught them as well, and he understands what it is like to educate the reader. As a director, Leinaweaver has worked with each of the other members of the production team, from designers to stage managers, and understands the conditions and pressures under which each of them work. This sense of knowing what each member of the team faces in terms of challenges is crucial for rendering a fair verdict on the results. He has also relocated from a different state, so he has no longstanding ties, obligations, or grudges enmeshing him within the local theatre community.

"In a relatively small town," he says, "the prime consideration should be to support the arts, not to destroy them." Thus, he does not succumb to the temptation to say something devastatingly witty that might be needlessly destructive. "I try to offer an honest assessment of the overall theatrical experience. I always point out what is good and also what is egregious, while generally not bothering to mention production elements that are merely adequate. I believe strongly in using Goethe's three principles because you really need to ask those questions before jumping to conclusions."

His pet peeve about other reviewers, aside from those who are needlessly cruel? "Those who say nothing, just kind of describe the event, with no hint of evaluation." The kinds of assignments that he declines? "Those where I do have relationships with company members. It is better to have objectivity."

One recent example of how he manages to level fair criticism without eviscerating actors was a Shakespeare production with student performers that was not all that well spoken. "The language of the play," he wrote, "was beyond the training of most of the actors. The exceptions were . . ." (and these he named and praised for particular demonstrated skills of delivery). The point was made, and it is likely that everyone survived and learned from the experience.

4. Write with confidence when you are quite sure that you believe other audience members would share your response, but do not hesitate to admit that your response is singular. If the show is constantly stopped by hysterical laughter and applause but you never cracked a smile, admit it. If only you and three others were on their feet cheering at the end, admit that as well.

5. Be sure to include whatever is unusual or noteworthy about this particular production. Examples include if the setting or time period has been changed, if cross-gender casting is being used, if an extensive song-and-dance sequence has been added, or if a radical interpretation of a famous character is being presented. Prepare audiences who may have past familiarity with this script for what they may find unsettling. If they are to experience a musical, drag version of *King Lear,* at least let them know.

6. Identify the names of the actors when describing their performances, and distinguish between actor and character. Make it clear when you are discussing Juliet as written versus Lois Lipschitz's Juliet as presented. This also helps define your criticism. Lois may have gone beyond the character as written in terms of fiery engagement, or she may not have measured up somehow to the role as presented on the page.

7. Make the same distinction between the script and the actual performance. Imagine this play done in a different fashion. Try to gauge the quality of the playwright's initial effort in comparison with what the production team achieved in realizing, transcending, circumventing, or even violating that effort.

8. In keeping with other journalism standards, write in clear, vivid language with relatively short sentences and paragraphs. While responses that are more scholarly are freed from this restriction, the instant response usually needs to be sharp, short, and sweet.

9. Go over the list of theatre participants in Chapters 3–6, review the production chart, and ask if there is a reason to include or exclude any of them from mention in your review. Do not feel the need to mention everyone; rather, focus on those who showed exceptional skill or who dropped the ball in a big and unfortunate way.

10. Try to avoid pure rating phrases like "good job" and "awesome" or "didn't quite cut it," and instead specify in what way something was good or bad. A performance is awesome because the actor takes great risks, has outrageously perfect comic timing, shows astonishing versatility, and shows incredible subtlety and nuance or perhaps outrageous theatrical bravado. A production disappoints because it may be flat and unvaried or it lacks energy and conviction. In terms of the actor, he could be clearly miscast, could fail to find the character's vulnerability and let the audience in, or perhaps could be awkwardly at odds with the work of other actors in the show.

11. Write as if you are discussing the play during its run and allow for change. Write about it as an ongoing activity rather than generalizing from a single performance that you attended. Do not use "The actors never pick up their cues," but rather "The actors at the performance I attended had difficulty picking up their cues, but with more performances . . . ." You are therefore able to allow for potential growth rather than pronounce a sentence.

12. Be sure to let the audience know what kind of a time they will have, if they will collapse with laughter, or if they will be stunned but stimulated to think in a new way or simply diverted in a harmless way. Try to predict their experience.

13. If there are great lines in the play and great line deliveries by actors, do not hesitate to quote them.

14. Do not waste time recounting the entire plot, and do not give away surprise elements. Give the audience the same amount of story that might be part of a preview of coming attractions, and no more.

15. Try to form an opening sentence and paragraph that is striking and somehow crystallizes your response.

16. Consider putting this play in a historical context for readers—the history of plays like this done by this theatre, the evolving work of the playwright, or even the growth of this theatre—as productions have gotten more and more ambitious.

17. If you feel great futures are ahead for any of the participants, say so. All critics have a stake in keeping theatre alive and in encouraging brilliance.

18. If you are writing for a newspaper, conclude with dates and times for the remaining run of the show and contact information for securing tickets.

AUTHOR'S INSIGHT

ROBERT: I directed a production of *Much Ado About Nothing* where the woman playing Beatrice, a strong character, was also very physically strong (she did gymnastics on horseback competitively). At the curtain call, the last two couples came out and we had Claudio pick up and swing Hero around after their initial bows. The final couple, Beatrice and Benedick, reversed this pattern as she lifted him and twirled him to great surprise, laughter, and applause. It was a delightful, final surprise for the audience. The local reviewer, while raving about the production generally, told readers about this. We could have killed her.

What Next?

As an introductory theatre class draws to a close, the question invariably comes up, "Where do I go now with theatre?" For some, this one course is enough. This exposure will make you a more informed audience member for live theatre and media, and you are likely to get more out of future viewing experiences. It may also make you a more acute observer of theatrical elements in your own life and give you some insights into how to make these events go more the way you want. Other readers are going to want to take part in some additional way and wonder how to begin.

We have saved the subject of writing critical reviews for this book's last chapter because to do so with insight, fairness, and clarity requires studying the information in all the preceding chapters. Offering your services to your school or local paper as a reviewer is one way to continue to be engaged in theatre after the end of the class that you are now taking. However, it is only one way. Almost inevitably taking such a position, while it means attending productions frequently, will not mean being involved in them in any way. Critics are isolated from the theatrical process to maintain objectivity and to avoid the growing animosity from a large part of the local theatre community. Let's just say that they do not tend to get invited to the best parties.

DOUG HUGHES

DIRECTOR (ACCEPTING THE TONY AWARD FOR BEST DIRECTION OF A PLAY)

I am overjoyed in the world of the theatre, safe and dangerous, small and infinite. I am overjoyed to have a place in it.

What if you actually want engagement in some aspect of *doing* theatre rather than just evaluating it? Now is a good time to review the various "Theatre in Your Life" sections in previous chapters to solidify which aspects of theatre intrigue you most.

The next place to look may be the theatre department's website, main office, or even a bulletin board where notices of upcoming auditions, opportunities to work production crews, workshops, field trips, or discount tickets are posted. Some departments have an e-mail newsletter, highlighting upcoming activities, to which you can subscribe. Local theatre companies probably have similar resources, and the arts calendar section of the newspaper often lists auditions for productions around town.

If one or more aspects of theatre particularly intrigue you, consider enrolling in a class that focuses specifically on, for example, acting, costuming, or directing. The class that you are taking now is often a kind of funnel for students to discover and then further explore those areas of theatre that especially fascinate them. Find out if there are prerequisites or an application/audition process for admission. You might also explore majoring or minoring in theatre. Most departments have a brochure or student handbook with basic degree requirements, faculty profiles, scholarship and financial aid resources, and production requirements. Theatre is a major that usually requires taking part in the shows themselves beyond class work.

Your parents may express concern over focusing on a subject that does not guarantee employment. While it is true that many theatre majors do not work in the theatre, one of the largest employment agencies in the country has found great success placing them in other types of jobs. This is because theatre teaches you basic skills valued in any organization: meeting deadlines, using time management skills, working under pressure, being comfortable in meeting the public, collaborating, coming up with creative solutions, making presentations in a poised and dynamic way, and taking initiative. Those who have studied acting have a far greater awareness of the first impressions they make; the way they look, sound, and move; and the skills to alter themselves to suit an occasion. These aptitudes are as valued in corporate cultures as they are in the arts.

THEATRE IN YOUR LIFE

Personal Criticism

In your personal theatre, this ongoing play called *My Life,* moments of criticism play a big part. When given and received, there is often tension, discomfort, and conflict—the very heart of drama. One of the major life skills is to offer criticism when it is needed in a respectful way without wimping out (not doing it at all, or doing so in such an apologetic way that is has virtually no impact) or going over the top into explosive anger or grief (so shouting and/or tears get in the way of communicating basic information). Behavioral science has shown that many of us (often women) quickly circumvent anger into grief and that many others (often men) do the exact opposite. Clearly, frightening, enraged shouting and incomprehensible, inconsolable crying can stop communication. If this was not even what the person was really feeling in the first place, it gets even more complex and distracting. In the theatre of your own life, it is crucial to determine the circumstances and probably to rehearse and revise serious criticism.

Learning to *give* criticism gracefully is one of the most desirable skills in life—learning to *receive* it is just as desirable. The same responses noted here often occur. Consider first that people who do not care about you do not *bother* to criticize you. They are too busy. When someone criticizes you, there is always some level of concern and connection. So try to get past the comment and into the intention behind it. Many of us find it useful to write down a particularly harsh criticism, thank the person offering it for being concerned enough about us to give it, and then go off to consider its validity. This is usually a better decision than giving in to an immediate impulse. Receiving criticism is a kind of spotlight. Many receive no attention at all. If anyone is offering you this kind of feedback, it means that you matter to that person, even if that means that you matter to them in a way that has a negative effect on you. Knowing the difference between positive and negative criticism is as important in life as it is in the theatre.

Most criticism is more successful if it is not a public performance done in front of observers, but rather given in private, so that the impact of the audience does not add to the drama.

For those seeking employment in theatre, it is wise to study the full spectrum of theatre arts and to select at least three or four for specialization. Actors who study only acting do not always interact successfully during costume fittings, tech rehearsals, or promotion if they do not entirely understand how costumers, tech directors, and publicists work. Those who have studied the process of all team members have more positive, empathetic communications with each of them, enhancing the collaborative process. Some actors also limit their job options to being actor/waiters, so that when they are not performing, they are far away from the theatre environment they love. It is not essential to divide one's time between a theatre and a restaurant. Training to be an actor, director, playwright, designer, publicist, teacher, or any number of other combinations of positions described in this book increases the likelihood of finding a place in the theatre that allows you to *be* there in varying capacities.

You may wonder after all this how people of the theatre can invest so much time and energy into something that lasts so briefly, may be blasted with critical scorn, and is regarded by much of the population as frivolous. You must understand that we in the theatre consider ourselves to be (on most days when we are not just feeling overworked) the most blessed people alive.

HUGH JACKMAN

ACTOR

Everybody should spend a year training as an actor. You come to know so much about yourself. Acting is life learning.

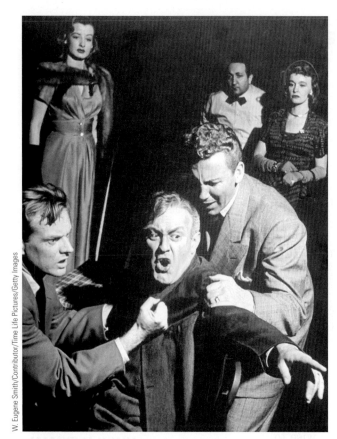

W. Eugene Smith/Contributor/Time Life Pictures/Getty Images

FIGURE 12.6 As Arthur Miller described in his journal, early rehearsals for his new play, directed by Elia Kazan, had him concerned about the abilities of the actor who was assigned the lead role. But Lee J. Cobb gave a mesmerizing performance as Willy Loman in the first production of the classic drama *Death of a Salesman*.

We live in a state of constant bewilderment and compassion for civilians who do not get to play "let's pretend," "dress up," "once upon a time," and "hey, let's put on a show" all the time. We are particularly privileged to rediscover regularly our childhood innocence, to fast-forward into our deep mature peace, and to explore our dark side without ending up in jail or dead, not to mention our hero-lover-wit-wacko-genius-magic-suave-hopeless-inspired sides. We get to enter briefly the lives of almost every kind of person, and to taste every life. Those of us fortunate enough to earn our living in the theatre enter it each day full of possibility, which is the same as feeling fully alive.

Arthur Miller kept a journal of rehearsals for the first production of his legendary play *Death of a Salesman*. Here is a key entry:

Lee J. Cobb, who was playing Willy, sat for days on the stage like a great lump, a sick seal, a mourning walrus. When it came his time to speak lines, he whispered meaninglessly. Elia Kazan, the director, pretended certainty, but from where I sat, he looked like an ant trying to prod an elephant off his haunches. Ten days went by. The other actors were by now much further advanced, but Cobb stared at them heavy-eyed, morose, even persecuted, it seemed.

And then, one afternoon, there on the stage of the New Amsterdam Theatre high above 42nd Street, Lee rose from his chair and looked at Milly Dunnock, and there was a silence. And then he said, "I was driving along, and all of a sudden I'm going off the road. . . ."

And the theatre vanished. The stage vanished. The chill of an age-old recognition shuddered up my spine. A new human being was being formed before all our eyes, born for the first time on this earth, made real by an act of will. A birth was taking place; a man was here transcending the limits of his body and history. A mere glance of his eye created a window beside him, a touch of his hand on this empty stage made a bed appear, and when he glanced up at the emptiness above him a ceiling was there, and there was even a crack in it where his stare rested.

I knew then that something astounding was being made here. It would have been almost enough for me, without opening the play.

There is a certain amount of immortality involved in theatre, created by the knowledge the actor keeps to his dying day that on a certain afternoon, in an empty and dusty theatre, he cast a shadow of a being that was not himself but the distillation of all he had ever observed; all the unsingable heartsong the ordinary man may feel but never utter, he gave voice to. And by that he somehow joins the ages.

One of Robert's former students (Ty Burrell of *Modern Family*) was asked in a *Parade* interview when he realized he wanted to be an actor. He described an exercise the first week in Robert's Acting Shakespeare class where "we had to come up with a Shakespearean type character and improvise for three minutes. I pulled out a wooden box and stood on it to play a guy who thought he was great, who was full of bravado but was a total idiot—a bit like Phil. I got a laugh, and it felt like a love bath. I ran off and changed my major." It *can* feel like a love bath. There may be no more deeply supportive environment than that created by theatre people for their own.

Jordan Roth, a successful New York producer, who often collaborates with his mother Daryl Roth (see Close-Up, Chapter 6, page 183), in accepting the Tony Award for best play, managed to acknowledge all of us who make up the theatre community:

> There are those rare people who can look at the world and see things the rest of us don't see until they show us.
>
> These are the writers.
>
> There are a special few who take that vision and turn it back into the world.
>
> These are the directors and designers.
>
> There are fearless beings who can live in that world and show us who we are.
>
> These are our actors.
>
> There are dedicated people who know why that world matters so very much: crew, theatre staff, producers, investors, managers, marketers.
>
> And then there are the people who step forward and say "Show me this world. I hope it will change me."
>
> These are our audiences.
>
> And when all of these people come together and say "Yes," there is THEATRE . . .
>
> "Thank-you" to everyone who says "Yes."

When the playwright Maxwell Anderson got a letter from a very discouraged young theatre artist considering giving it up, this was his answer:

> If you have truly and deeply chosen to practice this art, be totally proud of it and then, in return, make the art proud of you. If you now hesitate on the threshold of maturity, wondering what rewards are out there beyond feeding, sleeping, and

breeding, turn deep into this art, which has moved you so powerfully. Take what part in it in whatever way you can, as participant, spectator, secret practitioner, or hanger-on and waiter at the door. Neglect no sacrifice at your chosen altar.

It may break your heart, it may drive you half-mad, and it may betray you into unrealizable ambitions or blind you to financial opportunities with its wandering fires. But it will fill your heart before it breaks it; it will make you a person in your own right; it will open the temple doors to you and enable you to walk with those who have come nearest among people to what people may sometime be.

The theatre may or may not be for you. If not, we thank you for spending time with us. If so, welcome to potential torture and infinite possibility.

SUMMARY

Critics have a powerful and ambivalent role in the theatrical process. An astonishing number are not trained in the art that they're evaluating. Critics have the power to say things that could get others sued. We have a right to expect important credentials and insights from those whose reviews we read or watch. Those who have to write instant responses for tomorrow's paper function in an entirely different framework than those writing for scholarly journals with months of preparation. Reviewers should follow certain essential guidelines for writing a critical response to make what they say connect to a large body of potential audience members and to include all those who have contributed significantly to the production. After learning about all aspects of theatre, many readers may wish to become further involved and to consider the options that are offered in this chapter. There are many ways to keep theatre part of your life.

SUGGESTED ASSIGNMENTS

1. Why is it essential that reviewers, however unfair they may be in their assessments, have the freedom to write whatever they want?

2. Why do you think actors are willing to subject themselves to the potential public humiliation of devastating reviews?

3. Examine several reviews by any critic and assess how this writer qualifies in demonstrating the qualities that we should generally expect from someone in this position.

4. What is the fundamental difference between a reviewer and a scholar/critic?

5. Write a review of either a live production or film, following the guidelines outlined in this chapter.

6. If a classmate or someone you know evaluates the same production, examine each other's responses and attempt to analyze in particular the areas in which your opinions differed.

7. What can be learned about the art of criticism in the theatre that might transfer to giving and receiving it successfully in life?

8. Identify how you think you may wish to become involved in theatre at some point in the future.

9. Why are theatre majors often successfully employed outside the theatre?

10. In spite of the hard work and often harsh responses involved, what is it that keeps theatre artists committed and involved?

SUGGESTED ACTIVITIES

1. **Individual:** Locate two different versions of the same dramatic work, perhaps a live production and a filmed version or two different filmed treatments. Using the guidelines from this chapter, write a review that compares and contrasts the productions.

2. **Group:** Have each member of the group interview an actor regarding the impact that reviews have had on her sense of self-esteem and performances. Discuss the range of responses and where the actor's opinions seem to be most strongly shared.

3. **Long-term:** Identify a major theatre or film critic who has worked in the field for a number of years. Examine at least 10 reviews that this person has written over a period of time. What patterns can you determine? What changes seem to have taken place in the critic's written emphasis and preferences?

4. **Large group:** Offer a prize, such as complimentary tickets, and engage the class in a competition to determine who can come up with the most devastating excerpt from a critical review. Note that in addition to major newspapers, almost all weekly magazines (such as *People, Time, Entertainment Weekly,* and *The New Yorker*) feature reviews that might provide your winning entry. Let the class vote to determine the victor.

KEY WORDS AND IDEAS

critic
qualities of a good play:
   relevance
   humanity
   excitement
reviewer
qualities of a good critic:
   knowledgeable

demanding
compassionate
three critical questions:
   What was the artist trying to do?
   How well was it done?
   Was it worth doing?

dramatic interlude 6

Values

Featured plays:

He and She by Rachel Crothers (1910)

The Piano Lesson by August Wilson (1989)

(NOTE: The scripts for these plays, along with additional background information, are available in the companion anthology to this text, *Life Themes: An Anthology of Plays for the Theatre*)

Therapists constantly tell their patients that they must bring their actions into alignment with their values; otherwise, they have little hope for contentment. So, we can change our behavior to match our beliefs, change our beliefs to match our behavior, or modify both so they meet in accord. But they must be aligned. If our values are different from that of the culture around us, it presents a challenge. If they are different from our immediate family or lover, it presents an even greater one because we are likely to confront this issue day after day in close proximity, butting heads and hearts over and over. Both of our featured plays involve families in which values are at odds. They are people who love each other but cannot agree on what is right.

He and She (1910)

Setting: New York City, a comfortable middle-class house

Major Characters:

Tom Herford, a sculptor
Ann Herford, Tom's wife, also a sculptor
Daisy Herford, Tom's sister and secretary
Millicent Herford, Tom and Ann's daughter
Dr. Remington, Ann's father
Keith McKenzie, Tom's assistant
Ruth Creel, Ann's close friend, engaged to Keith
Ellen, a maid

The play begins in the studio shared by Tom and Ann, where their efforts at entering a major competition are considered. All the major ongoing issues faced by the women's movement are handled in this play in a way that, considering its date of origin, is strikingly contemporary. Consider the way this couple discuss the relative talents of Tom and Ann:

RUTH: I've heard you say she has genius—lots of times.
KEITH: So she has—in a way. She has more imagination than the Governor, but great Peter!—When it comes to execution and the real thing, she isn't in it with him. How could she be? She's a woman.
RUTH: Don't be any more anti-diluvian or prehistoric than you can help, Keith.

In his "prehistoric" way, Keith wants Ruth to give up her very successful publishing career to be a homemaker once they wed:

KEITH: I can't bear to see you so tired, dear.
RUTH: I'll be all right when I have some tea.
KEITH: This time next year, you could be in your own home—away from those damnable office hours and this drudgery—if you only would. If you only would.

FIGURE D6.1 Tom and Ann Herford are a married couple up against each other in an art competition in Rachel Crothers's 1910 play *He and She*, in this undergraduate production staged at the Slocum House Theatre in Vancouver, Washington. The story frames the major issues facing the women's movement of the early twentieth century.

Erik Odegard and Slocum House Theatre

RUTH: It never seems to occur to you that I might be a little less tired but bored to death without my job.

Ruth even suggests what seems to her to be a reasonable solution if someone needs to stay at home:

REMINGTON: When you're married, are you going to stay at home and polish up while Ruth goes on running the magazine?
KEITH: It looks as if that's about the way it'll have to be.
RUTH: That's a splendid idea. Keith thinks that somebody's got to do it for a successful marriage—and I won't so (*pointing at* KEITH) why not you dear?

The argument for women seeking their own careers is summarized in capsule form by Ann, while Ruth argues for the importance of motherhood:

ANN: There isn't a single hard thing that can happen to a woman that isn't made easier by being able to make her own living. And you know it.
RUTH: I think being a mother is the most gigantic, difficult, important and thankless thing in the world.

Ann is disappointed by the final version of a sculptural relief that Tom is submitting to a prestigious competition that offers a cash award of $100,000 for the winner. She decides, believing fully that her own ideas are probably too adventurous to be fully considered, to enter the competition herself:

ANN: Since you've been working at this, an idea has come to me. At first I thought the idea was too big for me—that I never could carry it out—and then I said I won't let myself be afraid—and it's grown and grown night and day. . . . Then you know what I'm going to do?
KEITH AND TOM: What?
ANN: Make my models and send them in myself.
REMINGTON: You don't mean it, daughter.
ANN: I do. I mean it with my whole soul.

It becomes clear when Ruth is promoted to editor of a magazine and Keith wants her to give it up that their relationship is over. Keith slowly realizes that Daisy, with whom he has been working all this time, is someone more inclined to be the kind of wife that he desires:

KEITH: I never saw tears in your eyes before. Women are funny things.
DAISY: Yes, we're funny. There's only one thing on earth funnier.
KEITH: What?
DAISY: Men.

Daisy and Ruth are in fundamental disagreement over what now constitutes and will in the future be the average woman:

DAISY: You've got so used to your own ideas you forget that I am the average normal woman the world is full of.
RUTH: Nonsense! You're almost extinct. I'm the average normal woman the world is full of—and it's going to be fuller and fuller.

Ann ends up winning the competition, with Tom coming in second. He has always been supportive of her work and, although he experiences a brief lapse in enlightenment, ultimately wakes up and returns to being both enlightened and honoring her accomplishment. Their daughter, however, returns suddenly home from boarding school with a crisis clearly needing her mother's attention and created by the fact that her mother did not allow her to come home to visit on several vacations because she was so busy working. Ann decides to take her on a trip and gets Tom to agree to execute the winning design for her in their absence, a somewhat ironic compromise because most observers consider her the person with the most brilliant vision and him the one with superior execution. Ann expresses sadness at not being able to realize fully her design herself:

ANN: I've imagined people saying—"A woman did that"—and my heart has almost burst with pride—not so much that I had done it—but for all women.

While many of the lines quoted here could reflect debates going on in households today, we need to remember that this play is 100 years old. While the characters all have strong beliefs, they also express them respectfully and with considerable dignity. Even Keith, the least enlightened of them all, is never less than courteous and thoughtful, and he probably is the sole character to express the dominant values of the year 1910.

Here is a scene from *He and She:*

ANN: [*throwing the other letters on the table*] Come here just a minute, Tom, please.
TOM: [*coming to door*] What is it?
ANN: Shut the door. It's come! [*Showing the letter.* TOM *opens it and reads it. A look of sickening disappointment comes into his face.*] No? Oh, Tom!
TOM: I was their second choice!
ANN: Oh, Tom, don't take it like that. What difference does it make, after all? You know you did a big thing. It's all luck—anyway.

TOM: I'll pull up in a minute. Well, it means taking hold of something else pretty quick. Going at it again.

ANN: Yes, keeping at it—that's it. What a terrible lot chance has to do with it.

TOM: Oh no, that isn't it.

ANN: Yes, it is, too.

TOM: No—I failed. I didn't get it, that's all.

ANN: You'll do something greater—next time—because of this.

TOM: *[taking her hand]* You're a brick! Now, see here, don't you be cut up about this. It's not the end of everything, you know. Stop that! You're not crying, I hope?

ANN: No, I'm not. Of course, I'm not! *[With passionate tenderness]* Oh, my boy. I never loved you so much—never believed in you as I do now. This is only a little hard place that will make you all the stronger.

TOM: Dear old girl! What would I do without you? I'll tell the others and get it over. *[Rising, he stops, staring at one of the letters on the table.]* Ann!

ANN: Um?

TOM: *[taking up a letter]* Ann—here's one for you, too.

ANN: What? *[She tears open the letter.]* Tom! They've given the commission to me! Look! Read it! Is that what it says? Is it? Now aren't you glad you let me do it? You haven't lost! We've got it! Say you're glad. Say you're proud of me, dear. That's the best part of it all.

TOM: Of course I am, dear; of course I am.

ANN: Oh, Tom, I wanted you to get it more than I ever wanted anything in my life, but this is something to be thankful for. Doesn't this almost make it right?

TOM: Yes, dear, yes. Don't think of me. That's over— that part of it. Tell the others now.

ANN: Wait!

TOM: Aren't you going to?

ANN: I only want to be sure that you're just as happy that I won, as I would have been if you had.

TOM: Of course I am. You know that. *[Kissing her]*

ANN: Tell the others, then, Tom—I can't. Say you're glad, dear.

TOM: You know I am, dear. You know that.

ANN: *[with a sigh of relief* ANN *sits at left of fire]* Think how I'll have to work. I can't even go to the country in the summer.

TOM: *[sitting opposite* ANN *at the fire]* And what will you do with Millicent this summer?

ANN: Oh, there are lots of nice things for her to do. The money! Think what it will mean to you!

TOM: Let me tell you one thing, Ann, in the beginning. I'll never touch a penny of the money.

ANN: What?

TOM: Not a cent of it.

ANN: What are you talking about?

TOM: That's your money. Put it away for yourself.

ANN: I never heard you say anything so absolutely unreasonable before in my life.

TOM: If you think I'm unreasonable, all right. But that's understood about the money. We won't discuss it.

ANN: Well, we will discuss it. Why shouldn't you use my money as well as I use ours?

TOM: That's about as different as day and night.

ANN: Why is it?

TOM: Because I'm taking care of you. It's all right if you never do another day's work in your life. You're doing it because you want to; I'm doing it because I've got to. If you were alone, it would be a different thing. But I'm here, and so long as I am, I'll make what keeps us going.

ANN: But I'll help you.

TOM: No, you won't.

ANN: I will. I'm going on just as far as I have ability to go, and if you refuse to take any money I may make—if you refuse to use it for our mutual good, you're unjust and taking an unfair advan—Oh, Tom! What are we saying? We're out of our senses—both of us. You didn't mean what you said. Did you? It would—I simply couldn't bear it, if you did. You didn't—did you?

TOM: I did—of course.

ANN: Tom—after all these years of pulling together, now that I've done something, why do you suddenly balk?

TOM: *[rising]* Good Heavens! Do you think I'm going to use your money? Don't try to run my end of it. It's the same old story—when you come down to it, a woman can't mix up in a man's business. *[He moves away.]*

ANN: Mix up in it? Isn't it a good thing for you that I got this commission?

TOM: No. I don't know that it's a good thing from any standpoint to have it known that I failed, but my wife succeeded.

ANN: I thought you said you were glad—proud of me.

TOM: It's too—distracting—too—it takes you away from more important things.

ANN: What things?

TOM: Millicent and me.

ANN: Oh, Tom—don't! You know that you and Millicent come before everything on earth to me.

TOM: No.

ANN: You do.

TOM: We don't—now. Your ambition comes first.

ANN: [she rises, going to him] Tom, I worship you. You know that, don't you?

TOM: I'm beginning to hate this work and everything in connection with it.

ANN: But you taught me—helped me—pushed me on. What's changed you?

TOM: I let you do it in the first place because I thought it was right. I wanted you to do the thing you wanted to do.

ANN: Well?

TOM: I was a fool. I didn't see what it would lead to. It's taking you away from everything else—and there'll be no end to it. Your ambition will carry you away till the home and Millicent and I are nothing to you!

ANN: Tom—look at me. Be honest. Are you sorry— sorry I got this commission?

TOM: I'm sorry it's the most important thing in the world to you.

ANN: Oh! Why do you say that to me? How can you?

TOM: Haven't I just seen it? You're getting rid of Millicent now because you don't want her to interfere with your work.

ANN: No!

TOM: You're pushing her out of your life.

ANN: No!

TOM: You said just now you were going to send her away alone in the summer. I don't like that. She's got to be with you—I want you to keep her with you.

ANN: But that's impossible. You know that. If I stop work now, I might as well give up the frieze entirely.

TOM: Then give it up.

ANN: What?

TOM: Give up the whole thing—forever. Why shouldn't you?

ANN: Do you mean that?

TOM: Yes.

ANN: Tom—I love you. Don't ask this sacrifice of me to prove my love.

TOM: Could you make it? Could you?

ANN: Don't ask it! Don't ask it, for your own sake. I want to keep on loving you. I want to believe you're what I thought you were. Don't make me think you're just like every other man.

TOM: I am a man—and you're my wife. And Millicent's our daughter. Unless you come back to the things a woman's always had to do—and always will—we can't go on. We can't go on.

ANN: [following him around the table] Tom—if you're just a little hurt—just a little jealous because I won—

TOM: Oh—

ANN: That's natural—I can understand that.

TOM: Oh—don't—

ANN: But—Oh, Tom!—the other—to ask me to give it all up. I could never forgive that. Take it back, Tom—take it back.

TOM: Good God, Ann, can't you see? You're a woman and I'm a man. You're not free in the same way. If you won't stop because I ask it—I say you must.

ANN: You can't say that to me. You can't!

TOM: I do say it.

ANN: No!

TOM: I say it because I know it's right.

ANN: It isn't.

TOM: I can't make you see it.

ANN: It isn't.

TOM: I don't know how—but everything in me tells me it's right.

ANN: Tom—listen to me.

TOM: If you won't do it because I ask you—I demand it. I say you've got to.

ANN: Tom—you can kill our love by just what you do now.

TOM: Then this work is the biggest thing in the world to you?

ANN: What is more important to us both—to our happiness than just that?

Millicent's unexpected return from school interrupts them, and they now must turn their attention to her.

The Piano Lesson (1989)

Setting: A house in Pittsburgh, 1937

Characters:

Boy Willie, a sharecropper

Berniece, Boy Willie's sister

Doaker, Boy Willie and Berniece's uncle

Wining Boy, another uncle

Avery, Berniece's boyfriend, a preacher

Lymon, a friend of Boy Willie's

Maretha, Berniece's daughter

Grace, a woman "dating" Boy Willie and Lymon

Joan Marcus

FIGURE D6.2   August Wilson's *The Piano Lesson* pits the differing values of family members against one another in this performance by the Signature Theatre, New York, 2012.

The parlor of the house shared by Doaker, Berniece, and Maretha is dominated by a 137-year-old upright piano with carvings of masklike figures resembling African totems. Boy Willie has come up north from Mississippi to sell a load of watermelons, and he hopes to sell the family piano as well. His arrival creates mayhem, as it always has:

BERNIECE: What you doing all that hollering for?
BOY WILLIE: Hey, Berniece. Doaker said you was sleep. I said at least you could get up and say hi.
BERNIECE: It is five o'clock in the morning and you come in here with all this noise. You can't come in like normal folks. You got to bring all that noise with you.

The play examines the question, "What do you do with your legacy and how do you best put it to use?" The essential conflict between brother and sister is summarized in these two speeches:

BOY WILLIE: That's why I come up here. Sell them watermelons. Get Berniece to sell that piano. Put them two parts with the part I done saved. Walk in there. Tip my hat. Lay my money down on the table. Get my deed and walk on out.
BERNIECE: Boy Willie . . . you gonna play around with me one too many times. And then God's gonna bless you and West is gonna dress you. Now set

that piano back over there. I done told you a hundred times I ain't selling that piano.

Boy Willie would use the money to buy the land on which the family ancestors served as slaves, therefore building a future. Berniece would cling to the heirloom in memory of the blood that stains its wood, but she will not open it or use it lest the spirits of the past return. Thus, she could hardly be said to be honoring it. This debate goes on in various forms, along with discussions of the relative advantages (or, more accurately, disadvantages) for African Americans living in the South, where they are relative prisoners as sharecroppers, or the North, where pay is so low and expenses so high that moving up economically is nearly impossible.

It eventually becomes clear that the source of ongoing trouble in this family, while symbolized by the piano, is the restless troublesome presence of the ghost of Sutter, the recently deceased owner of the land that Boy Willie covets. Finally, Avery, Berniece's suitor and local pastor, performs an exorcism/blessing:

AVERY: O Holy Father, we gather here this evening in thy Holy Name to cast out the spirit of one James Sutter. May this vial of water be empowered with thy spirit. May each drop of it be a weapon and a shield against the presence of all evil. . . . A new heart also will I give you and a new spirit will I put within you: and I will take out of your flesh the heart of stone and I will give you a heart of flesh.

Sutter's ghost struggles and fights mightily with Boy Willie. As the battle grows more violent and it becomes clear that Boy Willie might lose, Berniece realizes she must unearth the power of the piano, which she finally plays while she sings and beckons each of their ancestors for help. Finally, Boy Willie is calm, free, and about to depart. Berniece begins to chant "thank you":

BOY WILLIE: Hey Berniece . . . if you and Maretha don't keep on playing on that piano . . . ain't no telling . . . me and Sutter both liable to be back. [*exits*]
BERNIECE: [*continuing to chant*] Thank you.

The piano has taught its lesson. It has served as a medium. It is open, and life returns to this house along with a sense of calm. The journey has included music all along—a work song, a traveling song, blues, and boogie-woogie. It has included not just the confrontation with Sutter's ghost but also with the ghosts of Yellow Dog, Crawley (Berniece's dead husband), Cleotha (Wining Boy's dead love), and, of course, the ancestors.

Here is a scene from *The Piano Lesson*:

[The door opens and BOY WILLIE *and* LYMON *enter.]*

BOY WILLIE: Aw hell . . . look here! We was just talking about you. Doaker say you left out of here with a whole sack of money. I told him we wasn't going see you till you got broke.

WINING BOY: What you mean broke? I got a whole pocketful of money.

DOAKER: Did you all get that truck fixed?

BOY WILLIE: We got it running and got halfway out there on Centre and it broke down again. Lymon went out there and messed it up some more. Fellow told us we got to wait till tomorrow to get it fixed. Say he have it running like new. Lymon going back down there and sleep in the truck so the people don't take the watermelons.

LYMON: Lymon nothing. You go down there and sleep in it.

BOY WILLIE: You was sleeping in it down home, nigger! I don't know nothing about sleeping in no truck.

LYMON: I ain't sleeping in no truck.

BOY WILLIE: They can take all the watermelons. I don't care. Wining Boy, where you coming from? Where you been?

WINING BOY: I been down in Kansas City.

BOY WILLIE: You remember Lymon? Lymon Jackson.

WINING BOY: Yeah, I used to know his daddy.

BOY WILLIE: Doaker say you don't never leave no address with nobody. Say he got to depend on your whim. See when it strike you to pay a visit.

WINING BOY: I got four or five addresses.

BOY WILLIE: Doaker say Berniece asked you for three dollars and you got mad and left.

WINING BOY: Berniece try and rule over you too much for me. That's why I left. It wasn't about no three dollars.

BOY WILLIE: Where you getting all these sacks of money from? I need to be with you. Doaker say you had a whole sack of money . . . turn some of it loose.

WINING BOY: I was just fixing to ask you for five dollars.

BOY WILLIE: I ain't got no money. I'm trying to get some. Doaker tell you about Sutter? The Ghosts of the Yellow Dog got him about three weeks ago. Berniece done seen his ghost and everything. He right upstairs. *[Calls.]* Hey Sutter! Wining Boy's here. Come on, get a drink!

WINING BOY: How many that make the Ghosts of the Yellow Dog done got?

BOY WILLIE: Must be about nine or ten, eleven or twelve. I don't know.

DOAKER: You got Ed Saunders. Howard Peterson. Charlie Webb.

WINING BOY: Robert Smith. That fellow that shot Becky's boy . . . say he was stealing peaches.

DOAKER: You talking about Bob Mallory.

BOY WILLIE: Berniece say she don't believe all that about the Ghosts of the Yellow Dog.

WINING BOY: She ain't got to believe. You go ask them white folks in Sunflower County if they believe. You go ask Sutter if he believe. I don't care if Berniece believe or not. I done been to where the Southern cross the Yellow Dog and called out their names. They talk back to you, too.

LYMON: What they sound like? The wind or something?

BOY WILLIE: You done been there for real, Wining Boy?

WINING BOY: Nineteen thirty. July of nineteen thirty I stood right there on that spot. It didn't look like nothing was going right in my life. I said everything can't go wrong all the time . . . let me go down there and call on the Ghosts of the Yellow Dog, see if they can help me. I went down there and right there where them two railroads cross each other . . . I stood right there on that spot and called out their names. They talk back to you, too.

LYMON: People say you can ask them questions. They talk to you like that?

WINING BOY: A lot of things you got to find out on your own. I can't say how they talked to nobody else. But to me it just filled me up in a strange sort of way to be standing there on that spot. I didn't want to leave. It felt like the longer I stood there, the bigger I got. I seen the train coming and it seem like I was bigger than the train. I started not to move. But something told me to go ahead and get on out the way. The train passed and I started to go back up there and stand some more. But something told me not to do it. I walked away from there feeling like a king. Went on and had a stroke of luck that run on for three years. So I don't care if Berniece believe or not. Berniece ain't got to believe. I know 'cause I been there. Now Doaker'll tell you about the Ghosts of the Yellow Dog.

DOAKER: I don't try and talk that stuff with Berniece. Avery got her all tied up in that church. She just think it's a whole lot of nonsense.

BOY WILLIE: Berniece don't believe in nothing. She just think she believe. She believe in anything if it's convenient for her to believe. But when that convenience run out, then she ain't got nothing to stand on.

WINING BOY: Let's not get on Berniece now. Doaker tell me you talking about selling that piano.

BOY WILLIE: Yeah . . . hey, Doaker, I got the name of that man Avery was talking about. The man what's fixing the truck gave me his name. Everybody know him. Say he buy up anything you can make music with. I got his name and his telephone number. Hey, Wining Boy, Sutter's brother say he selling the land to me. I got one part. Sell them watermelons get me the second part. Then . . . soon as I get them watermelons out that truck, I'm gonna take and sell that piano and get the third part.

DOAKER: That land ain't worth nothing no more. The smart white man's up here in these cities. He cut the land loose and step back and watch you and the dumb white man argue over it.

WINING BOY: How you know Sutter's brother ain't sold it already? You talking about selling the piano and the man's liable to sold the land two or three times.

BOY WILLIE: He say he waiting on me. He say he give me two weeks. That's two weeks from Friday. Say if I ain't back by then he might gonna sell it to somebody else. He say he wanna see me with it.

WINING BOY: You know as well as I know the man gonna sell the land to the first one walk up and hand him the money.

BOY WILLIE: That's just who I'm gonna be. Look, you ain't gotta know he waiting on me. I know. Okay. I know what the man told me. Stovall already done tried to buy the land from him and he told him no. The man say he waiting on me, he waiting on me. Hey, Doaker . . . give me a drink. I see Wining Boy got his glass. [DOAKER *exits into his room.*] Wining Boy, what you doing in Kansas City? What they got down there?

LYMON: I hear they got some nice-looking women in Kansas City. I sure like to go down there and find out.

WINING BOY: Man, the women down there is something else. [DOAKER *enters with a bottle of whiskey. He sets it on the table with some glasses.*]

DOAKER: You wanna sit up here and drink up my whiskey, leave a dollar on the table when you get up.

BOY WILLIE: You ain't doing nothing but showing your hospitality. I know we ain't got to pay for your hospitality.

WINING BOY: Doaker say they had you and Lymon down on the Parchman Farm. Had you on my old stomping grounds.

BOY WILLIE: Me and Lymon was down there hauling wood for Jim Miller and keeping us a little bit to sell. Some white fellows tried to run us off of it. That's when Crawley got killed. They put me and Lymon in the penitentiary.

LYMON: They ambushed us right there where that road dip down and around that bend in the creek. Crawley tried to fight them. Me and Boy Willie got away but the sheriff got us. Say we was stealing wood. They shot me in my stomach.

BOY WILLIE: They looking for Lymon down there now. They rounded him up and put him in jail for not working.

LYMON: Fined me a hundred dollars. Mr. Stovall come and paid my hundred dollars and the judge say I got to work for him to pay him back his hundred dollars. I told them I'd rather take my thirty days, but they wouldn't let me do that.

BOY WILLIE: As soon as Stovall turned his back, Lymon was gone. He down there living in that truck dodging the sheriff and Stovall. He got both of them looking for him. So I brought him up here.

LYMON: I told Boy Willie I'm gonna stay up here. I ain't going back with him.

BOY WILLIE: Ain't nobody twisting your arm to make you go back. You can do what you want to do.

WINING BOY: I'll go back with you. I'm on my way down there. You gonna take the train? I'm gonna take the train.

LYMON: They treat you better up here.

BOY WILLIE: I ain't worried about nobody mistreating me. They treat you like you let them treat you. They mistreat me, I mistreat them right back. Ain't no difference in me and the white man.

WINING BOY: Ain't no difference as far as how somebody supposed to treat you. I agree with that. But I'll tell you the difference between the colored man and the white man. Alright. Now you take and eat some berries. They taste real good to you. So you say I'm gonna go out and get me a whole pot of these berries and cook them up to make a pie or whatever. But you ain't looked to see them berries is sitting in the white fellow's yard. Ain't got no fence around them. You figure anybody want something they'd fence it in. Alright. Now the white man come along and say that's my land. Therefore everything that grow on it belong to me. He tell the sheriff, "I want you to put this nigger in jail as a warning to all the other niggers. Otherwise, first thing you know these niggers have everything that belong to us."

BOY WILLIE: I'd come back at night and haul off his whole patch while he was sleep.

WINING BOY: Alright. Now Mr. So and So. He sell the land to you. And he come to you and say, "John, you own the land. It's all yours now. But them is my berries. And come time to pick them, I'm gonna send my boys over. You got the land . . . but them berries, I'm gonna keep them. They mine." And he go and fix it with the law that them is his berries. Now that's the difference between the colored man and the white man. The colored man can't fix nothing with the law.

BOY WILLIE: I don't go by what the law say. The law's liable to say anything. I go by if it's right or not. It don't matter to me what the law say. I take and look at it for myself.

LYMON: That's why you gonna end up back down there on the Parchman Farm.

BOY WILLIE: I ain't thinking about no Parchman Farm. You liable to go back before me.

LYMON: They work you too hard down there. All that weeding and hoeing and chopping down trees. I didn't like all that.

WINING BOY: You ain't got to like your job on Parchman. Hey, tell him, Doaker, the only one got to like his job is the waterboy.

DOAKER: If he don't like his job, he need to set that bucket down.

BOY WILLIE: That's what they told Lymon. They had Lymon on water and everybody got mad at him 'cause he was lazy.

LYMON: That water was heavy.

BOY WILLIE: They had Lymon down there singing:

[Sings.]

O Lord Berta Berta O Lord gal well [LYMON *and* WINING BOY *join in.*]
Go 'head marry don't you wait on me oh-ah
Go 'head marry don't you wait on me well
Might not want you when I go free oh-ah
Might not want you when I go free well
BOY WILLIE: Come on, Doaker. Doaker know this one.

[As DOAKER joins in, the men stamp and clap to keep time. They sing in harmony with great fervor and style.]

O Lord Berta Berta O Lord gal oh-ah
O Lord Berta Berta O Lord gal well
Raise them up higher, let them drop on down oh-ah
Raise them up higher, let them drop on down well
Don't know the difference when the sun go
   down oh-ah
Don't know the difference when the sun go down well
Berta in Meridan and she living at ease oh-ah
Berta in Meridan and she living at ease well
I'm on old Parchman, got to work or leave oh-ah
I'm on old Parchman, got to work or leave well
O Alberta, Berta, O Lord gal oh-ah
O Alberta, Berta, O Lord gal well
When you marry, don't marry no farming man oh-ah
When you marry, don't marry no farming man well
Everyday Monday, hoe handle in your hand oh-ah
Everyday Monday, hoe handle in your hand well
When you marry, marry a railroad man, oh-ah
When you marry, marry a railroad man, well
Everyday Sunday, dollar in your hand oh-ah
Everyday Sunday, dollar in your hand well
O Alberta, Berta, O Lord gal oh-ah
O Alberta, Berta, O Lord gal well

Here are some ways that concepts introduced in Chapter 11 and Chapter 12 apply to *He and She* and *The Piano Lesson*.

Critical Response to *The Piano Lesson*

Unlike most award recipients, *The Piano Lesson* won the Pulitzer Prize before it opened on Broadway, so it came in already having been acclaimed, yet it still attracted some negative criticism. William A. Henry III, in *Time*, called it Wilson's "richest yet," a feeling shared by the *New York Post's* Clive Barnes, who called it "the fourth, best, and most immediate in the series of plays exploring the Afro-American experience during this century." However, Robert Brustein, in the *New Republic*, attacked the play as "the most poorly composed of Wilson's four produced works." John Simon, in *New York*, complained that it was an unwieldy mixture of farce, drama, and musical. This struck some other critics as a strange reservation because the same could be said of many of the plays of Shakespeare. While there were mixed responses to the play's blend of the supernatural and realism, most critics were fascinated by the play's central symbol, the piano. Barnes called it "a living symbol of the family's past—its slavery and its escape, its blood and its tears. . . . The piano is . . . an heirloom of tragic memory and meaning." Frank Rich, in the *New York Times*, appreciated its painful heritage: "Sculptured into its rich wood are totemic human figures whose knife-drawn features suggest both the pride of African culture and the grotesque scars of slavery. The siblings inherit both the pride and scars," and the piano is their key to their reconciliation with their family history and their identity as African Americans. The most negative reviews came from critics who suggested that Wilson's success depended on his ability "to stimulate the guilt glands of liberal white audiences." Simon displayed a similar hostility, attacking the play for having too many subplots and for being repetitive: "It is sincere but overcrowded, overzealous, and, without quite knowing where it is headed, repeats everything three or four times." Nevertheless, most critics expressed appreciation that Wilson was an artist interested in inventing new forms and voices as much as in connecting to voices and traditions from the past.

A sample professional review of *The Piano Lesson:*

THE PAST IS PROLOGUE. THE SHOW: "The Piano Lesson," a drama by August Wilson, at Cygnet Theatre, by Pat Launer, San Diego News Network critic, February 2010. *The piano of the title is practically a character in this Pulitzer Prize–winning play. For Berniece, it's a shrine, a monument to her family's painful past; its carvings present a specter of slavery and a memory of lost loved ones (who were traded in exchange for the instrument). To her brother, Boy Willie, it's a new beginning; if he can sell the piano, he can buy a piece of the land his ancestors worked as slaves. The piano, like its owners, is haunted—by a ghost that makes unnerving, unsettling appearances.*

Ultimately, it's the piano itself that has lessons to teach, about history and legacy, precedent and potential, the delicate balance between reverence for the past and embracing the promise of the future. [At this point, the reviewer launches into an extensive recounting of the plot. Both critics and theatre practitioners are generally divided on how much of the story should appear in a review and how much should not be revealed.]

These harsh realities are played out in and out of Uncle Doaker's, where Berniece lives with her young daughter, Maretha (Madeline Hornbuckle, convincing). Berniece used to play the beloved piano daily, but since her mother died, she can't even touch it. Each character weighs in on the family debate: good-natured, hard-working Uncle Doaker (Antonio TJ Johnson, solid and compelling); and his brother Wining Boy, a hard-drinking piano-man (energetic and amusing Grandison Phelps III). The level-headed preacher, Avery (Keith Jefferson, excellent, especially in his impassioned preaching), wants to set up a church of his own, and take Berniece as his wife. But she's still grieving over the death of her husband, for which she blames her brother; she also suspects he had something to do with the death of the white man who keeps making ghostly appearances. Grace (Tanya Johnson-Herron, pleasant, but usually played more sexy/slutty) is a woman Boy Willie picks up in a bar and brings home, to his straitlaced sister's considerable dismay. And then there's Lymon (handsome, charming Laurence Brown), Boy Willie's genial buddy, who can't wait to get his hands on all these freewheeling Northern women. He's suckered into buying a suit from Wining Boy and goes out on the town. But it's Boy Willie who scores the lady he was eyeing. When

Lymon returns to the house, he participates in the play's most tender, sensual moment, a lovely near-love scene with Berniece, beautifully and sensitively directed, like the rest of the piece, by the gifted Delicia Turner Sonnenberg. The philosophizing and singing of the men—the soulful reminiscences and the gut-wrenching, hard-driving chain-gang chant—add another musical dimension to Wilson's lyrical language.

But ultimately, the play rests on the fraught relationship between this disparate brother and sister. Mark Christopher Lawrence is a force of nature as Boy Willie, an impulsive whirlwind of crazy ideas and crazed energy. It's a huge and outsized role, and Lawrence fills it with brashness, bravado, flimflam, humor, and heart. Monique Gaffney is his ideal foil as Berniece: upright, uptight, determined, unyielding. She's a strong woman who knows what she wants—and doesn't want. And when she softens under Lymon's tenderness, it's heart-wrenching. After all the quarrels and conflict—even some physicality, perpetrated by Berniece, who's tried so hard to move away from the violence of the family's past—it's a very emotional moment when these two finally come together at the end. Turner Sonnenberg has amassed a stellar ensemble and teased from them stunningly authentic performances. Her husband, Jerry Sonnenberg, has given her a lovely home to work with, rimmed in a proscenium of brick, a tasteful, attractive, two-level retreat sporting wood floors, throw rugs, sconces and comfortably worn furniture (property design by Bonnie L. Durben). The lighting (Eric Lotze) and sound (George Yé) contribute mightily, especially to the eerie, otherworldly moments that are such a signature of Wilson plays.

This piece is chatty; it weighs in at nearly three hours. And yet, it moves with the pace and musicality of a jazz riff. At the end, you're reluctant to bid farewell to these folks. You want to know what happens to them next. That's the mark of a captivating play, and confirmation of a dazzling production.

THE LOCATION: Cygnet Theatre, 4040 Twiggs St., Old Town. (619) 337-1525; www.cygnettheatre.com THE DETAILS: Tickets: $17-$46. Wednesday-Thursday at 7:30 p.m., Friday-Saturday at 8 p.m., Saturday and Sunday at 2 p.m., Sunday at 7 p.m., through February 28. THE BOTTOM LINE: Best Bet

Critical Response to *He and She*

It took Rachel Crothers nearly 10 years after writing *He and She* to bring it to Broadway, playing the role of Ann Herford herself. While almost all the contemporary reviews raved about her skills as a dramatist, they disagreed wildly as to what, exactly, she was trying to say. One reviewer declared that *He and She* was a "triumph for the fair sex," and that "Mere man is relegated to his proper place"; another just as clearly announced that "In this play of married life, 'poor old Feminism' never had a chance." Heywood Broun wrote, "The play espouses a side of the feminist question with which we are in the most complete disagreement. We have always found that the soup tastes just the same whether it is opened with loving care or by the hired help. Nor are we convinced that young daughters tend to become entangled in unfortunate love affairs the instant a mother begins to paint a picture or write a book." It seemed as if the play was simply ahead of its time and clearly above the heads of a number of critics. It did not have a major revival until 1980, when it was produced by the BAM Theatre Company. This time, critics united in praising the clear feminist message of the play. Marilyn Stasio went so far as to say, "Its arguments about the relationship between the sexes have a topicality that is downright eerie. In fact, entire lines from this play are probably being spoken at this very moment at Weight Watchers meetings, in department store dressing rooms, grocery store checkout lines, and bedrooms throughout America."

Note: This review ran in the *Champaign News-Gazette* on Sunday, April 4, 2010.

For He and She, *the U of I Department of Theatre reaches out to Bloomington, its neighbor to the northwest. Not only was the play written by Bloomington native Rachel Crothers, but guest director Deb Alley is Associate Professor of Theatre at Illinois State University and Artistic Director of the Illinois Shakespeare Festival in Bloomington.*

It's curious in some ways that Crothers was born and bred in Bloomington-Normal. We don't necessarily think of sophisticated, early-twentieth-century Broadway playwrights springing from the Heartland. But Crothers went in for the kind of upper-class relationship play you might expect from Philip Barry or even Noel Coward. Like Barry, she wanted to examine the role of gender in American society, and what exactly it meant to be a woman or a man within the confines of marriage.

If that sounds dire or dreary, He and She *definitely isn't. It has some heavy issues and some speechifying on whether woman should put family over career or artistry, whether men should make families with women who seek fulfillment in jobs outside the home or only accept happy homemakers, but it's also got some amusing, lighter moments.*

The amazing thing is that Crothers wrote the play in 1911. We have a tendency to think that working women popped up in the '40s when America went to war, and then got shoved back into the kitchen in the '50s. He and She is a valuable lesson that women who yearn for careers and face conflict because of it is nothing new.

Deb Alley does an excellent job keeping the pace moving and creating snap and crackle between her players, and Moon Jung Kim's scenic design creates a lovely studio and even lovelier Edwardian living room inside Krannert's Studio Theatre.

It's often difficult for twenty-first-century actors to acquire the right posture and attitude to properly play these kinds of soignée, society folks from a lost time. Alley's cast does just fine, adding just a tiny bit of today's spirit to yesterday's characters.

As Ann Herford, the sculptress who aspires to the same artistic heights as her husband, Carley Cornelius looks and acts a bit like screen star Norma Shearer, who was exactly the kind of actress who would've taken on a role like that. She has enough fire and intelligence to make Ann seem believable, and she has good chemistry with both Jess Prichard, handsome and properly aristocratic as husband Tom Herford, and Jaclyn Holtzman, who is giddy and charming as their teenage daughter.

Bri Sudia gets some of the best scenes and creates excellent tension as Daisy, Mr. Herford's sister, who can't admit she'd love to fall in love, and she plays well off Tyrone Phillips's clueless Keith McKenzie, who is engaged to the wrong sort of woman for him. Jenny Nelson plays that woman, an ambitious magazine editor named Ruth, and she, too, has good energy and strength.

Doug West rounds out the cast as Ann's father, and although he's clearly too young to take on this Charles-Coburn-meets-Lewis-Stone father figure, he has the right hair and humor to make it work.

By the end, He and She is entertaining and intriguing, offering a window into the world of women in 1911. It's a bit depressing, as well, as we look back and realize a woman of 2011 might face exactly the same problems. Can my marriage last if I'm better than my husband at our shared occupation? Can I follow my artistic vision if it means splitting my attention between my art and my child? Rachel Crothers provides one answer for one woman. Let's hope today's women can find more of a variety of answers.

Innovative Drama

Both plays are traditional in form, being language-centered and linear, highly scripted dramas. Their innovations are in subject matter not widely addressed in American theatre prior to their appearances. While no new barriers are broken in the forms of presentation, each is innovative in terms of ideas.

Women's Theatre

While some would maintain that the voice of woman in Western theatre can be traced all the way back to ancient Greece, when characters such as Medea, Electra, and Antigone railed against the limitations that their cultures placed on women, if we look to the time when plays by, for, and about women actually began, we need to look at the career of Rachel Crothers. Considering the relative scarcity of women playwrights, directors, producers, and characters in plays even today, it is essential to note that Ms. Crothers wrote successfully for the New York theatre for over 30 years, usually with a hit play (popular with both critics and audiences) on Broadway, and that she acted as casting director, producer, and director for almost all the plays that she created.

African American Theatre

The Piano Lesson was the fourth completed script in August Wilson's American cycle of plays. It manages to be a very personal story of a single family and yet explores the lives of African Americans throughout the South and the North during the Great Depression. The reason why Wilson is not simply regarded as the finest African American playwright, but one of the finest American writers, period, is that the play also moves beyond the confines of race to capture essential humanity and conflicts within families everywhere and every time. *The Piano Lesson* received a 1990 Tony nomination and was winner that year of the Drama Desk Award, New York Drama Critics' Circle Award, and Pulitzer Prize for best play of the year.

Qualities of a Good Play

Both plays might be called talky by some, and there is little overt activity (at least until the ghost action in *Piano Lesson*). However, the talk is so strikingly and vitally presented that both qualify as high on the relevance, humanity, and excitement scale.

Three Critical Questions

In analyzing both plays, we reintroduce the questions posed in the "Critics Should Ask . . ." section in this chapter:

1. **What was the artist trying to do?**

   Crothers is attempting to present a fair and balanced discussion of the changing roles of husbands and wives when wives pursue careers. She is also trying to clearly present the challenge for a mother in succeeding at both career and motherhood. Wilson is attempting to reveal life for his people during the Great Depression and to offer a plea for modifying all inflexible positions, for honoring and not closing off our pasts.

2. **How well was it done?**

   It is hard to imagine how either play could more successfully accomplish these objectives.

3. **Was it worth doing?**

   Absolutely, because important ideas and issues are being shared in ways that no other authors at the time of writing were exploring.

After the Play

One characteristic of a great, indelible play is if the events that follow the final curtain can be imagined by readers or audience members because the characters are so vividly etched in their memories. After *He and She,* we can easily imagine the marriage of Keith and Daisy, the European journey of Ann and Millicent, the likelihood of Ann persuading her daughter to abandon her impetuous engagement, and the act of Tom brilliantly executing Ann's designs, as well as the family's achievement of true financial security. We may even consider the possibility that at some time in the future, Tom and Ann could become collaborators rather than competitors. After *The Piano Lesson,* we can sense Boy Willie returning to the South and redoubling his efforts to save his money, Avery proposing again and again to Berniece, and perhaps her accepting him. We feel reasonably sure that laughter and music will return to this house.

World of the Play Checklist

1. Time

- When in history is the play written/organized, set, and performed?
- How do these time facts and choices vary, and how do they interact?
- How far does this production move away from the original time period?
- How do these issues of time interact?
- How rapidly does time move for most people?
- How conscious are characters of the passage of time? Are they culturally trained to view time as linear, cyclical, or eternal?
- How do they record or note time? What is the dominant rhythm/tempo of the world of the play?
- Are these people past, present, or future focused?
- What lengths of attention span are most obvious?
- Is age revered or feared? What is the relationship between youth and maturity?

2. Space

- How is space defined and viewed?
- Is space only literal or do people think in terms of spiritual, philosophical, or abstract space?
- How large of a personal "bubble" do most people carry? What is the accepted comfort zone of interaction?
- Is there flexibility allowed in personal spaces?
- To what degree are private spaces respected?
- How is space violated, and what are accepted responses to personal or public "invasions"?

3. Values

- What beliefs are most widely shared? Which truths, ideals, and traditions are deemed to be self-evident?
- What commitment is made to these values, and what is the punishment for not sharing them?

- What is the predominant mood?
- Who are the role models or idols?
- What fantasies or ideal futures are shared?
- What is the value of money or property?
- What kind of humor is dominant?
- How is fear defined, and is it legitimized or stigmatized?
- How, and to what degree, are emotions of any kind expressed, suppressed, or repressed?

4. Structure

- What is the hierarchy of authority? Who are the leaders and who are the followers?
- Is change possible? Is authority absolute or flexible?
- What is the governance system, and how entrenched is it? Is authority inherited or earned? If earned, what is the mechanism (career, physical strength, beauty, etc.) by which it can be achieved?
- What is the definition and mechanism of justice?
- How are family and marriage defined? How are they related to social structures? How open or closed are familial relationships? Do they change over time?
- To what degree is the individual free within the social and familial structure?
- To what degree is daily life formalized, and how strictly enforced are the etiquette, manners, and tastes of the individual?

5. Pleasure

- What traits are considered beautiful, desirable, or enviable? What are the ideal male and female types?
- Is pleasure primarily sought through physical, social, spiritual, or intellectual pursuits?
- What colors, shapes, textures, or silhouettes give the most pleasure?
- Does comfort have any relationship to pleasure?
- What is the collective attitude toward sex, sexuality, and sensuality? What areas of the anatomy are considered erotic? What areas are forbidden, and what pleasures are taboo? What's hot and what's not?
- What is generally accepted as "fun"? What is the perfect social occasion, vacation, or day?
- What are the shared pastimes or hobbies? What are the favored foods, beverages, or games?
- How much flexibility is allowed for individual taste?

6. Senses

- How do all of the previously listed ideas become manifested in the world of the play?
- Which, if any, of the five senses is most frequently and effectively stimulated?
- What is the quality of light, sound, textures, and patterns that are most prized?
- By what level of stimulation do the senses become overwhelmed or understimulated?
- When people approach one another, how close is too close? How far is too far?
- What skills does one need to maneuver artfully in this world?
- What is the relationship between degrees of nonverbal gestures and verbal skills? Is the gracefulness of speech or of movement more prized? What vocal qualities of tone, pitch, pronunciations, and dialects give the most pleasure to the senses?
- What role does music and dance have? Is the average individual expected to participate or not?
- What smells and tastes are likely to be dominant in this world? Which give pleasure and which simply can't be avoided?
- To what degree are the people aware of the sensory world around them?

The Production

To what extent do any of the above influence the production itself?

1. **Time**—How long does the show run, and how is it divided into intermissions? How tight or leisurely is the presentation? How often does the tempo/rhythm fall into a predictable pattern or timing? How often does it shift and surprise?

2. **Space**—To what degree may the audience be acknowledged, involved, invaded, or even invited to take part? How large is the house, and what degree of adjustment needs to be made to fill it or to go down to subtle nuance based on close proximity? How does the position of audience to actor influence choices?

3. **Values**—Is this show reinforcing generally assumed beliefs or actually polarizing audiences? Is it in sync with what we now seem to consider funny or shocking, or does it stun us and make us reconsider what we believe? Is it welcoming or challenging to what we have formerly valued?

4. **Structure**—Is the play taking place in a time of potential significant change in governance? How does the potential for who rules and who does not influence the action? Is the way the event is structured reflective of the structure in the world of the play?

5. **Pleasure**—To what extent is this a hedonistic or cerebral event? Do the ideas about what is pleasurable match or contradict those in our culture at present?

6. **Senses**—To what degree is this a sensual experience? How have your own senses of sight, sound, and feeling been challenged or enhanced?

Responding to a Production

Event _____   Produced by _____

Place _____   Time _____

Author(s) _____   Respondent _____

You as the Audience

How familiar were you with the text, story, or type of theatre event?

_____

_____

_____

_____

What expectations did you bring with you? Were they met or not?

_____

_____

_____

_____

What was your mood when you entered the theatre space?

_____

_____

_____

_____

What kind of environment was the theatre space? Did it contribute to your comfort or discomfort? Did it seem right for the play?

_____

_____

_____

_____

The Story

What happened? (Just give the basic spine of the story in as few words as possible.)

_____

_____

_____

_____

What was the central conflict?

_____

_____

_____

_____

What was the emotional mood of the event? Did it end happily? Was the conflict resolved?

_____

_____

_____

_____

The World of the Play

(Refer to Chapter 1 or Appendix A for a list of questions to guide you.)

Time: When was the play written? How familiar are you with that time period? Was the production set in the same time or was it changed? What else did you notice about time in this world?

_____

_____

_____

_____

Space: Where was the story set? How familiar are you with that place or type of space? How did the performance space relate to the theatre itself? What else did you notice about time in this world?

_____

_____

_____

_____

Values: Did this story affirm your own values or challenge them? What specific values were addressed?

_____

_____

_____

_____

Structure: What kinds of structure were at play in this world? Were those structures rigid or flexible? Did one or more characters challenge the structures?

_____

_____

_____

_____

Pleasure: What pleasures were the characters pursuing? Were those pleasures taboo or mainstream? How much of the story was about pleasure?

_____

_____

_____

_____

_____

Senses: What senses were stimulated in the world of the play? Did characters seem focused on any one of the senses? How were your senses touched? Did anything surprise you about your sensory experience?

_____

_____

_____

_____

Conclusions

Write one or more clear and concise arguments for what you believe to be the author's intention, message, or project.

_____

_____

_____

_____

_____

_____

_____

_____

_____

Wrap Up

Discuss briefly the essence of your experience—your opinion about the production, your emotional response, and whether you would recommend it to others.

_____

_____

_____

_____

_____

_____

_____

_____

Sample Character Analysis

Here is a sample character analysis. Actors may be asked to answer these questions as the character. Answering from the point of view of a human being other than yourself can be illuminating and unsettling. The playwright may or may not have provided all of this information. The actor is generally asked to *investigate* (checking for facts in the text) first, and only when that search is complete, he moves on to *inference* (intelligent conjectures based on this detective work), and finally moves to *invention* in order to fill in all the gaps.

Character _____ **Actor** _____

For the Play as a Whole

CHARACTER PAST

I come from

My childhood was

The experience that made the most lasting impression on me was

My five most important given circumstances are

The two most powerful members of my private audience and the reasons for this are

The most crucial event prior to my first entrance in the play is

The details of my past history with other characters in the play are

The most significant of these in terms of influencing my attitudes and behavior are

CHARACTER PRESENT

Environment affects me most dramatically when

Other characters and/or the playwright describe me as

I describe others as

In groups, I tend to

I would describe myself as basically

My most distinguishing characteristics are

My favorite things are

The things I loathe are

My temperament could be described as

I am most interested in

I am least interested in

My physical life differs from the actor playing me in that

My vocal life differs from the actor playing me in that

I make the following discoveries in the play

CHARACTER FUTURE

My super-objective in the play is to

If this changes, it becomes

My hierarchy would include these other objectives

The obstacles I face are

The strategy and tactics I most often employ are

My three rehearsed futures are:

    Best possible

    Worst possible

    Wildest dreams come true

FOR EACH SCENE

Major outside forces influencing me are

My immediate objective in the scene is

The major obstacle I encounter is

The strategy and tactics I employ to get what I want include

Fifty Best-Known Western Plays

In our culture the following plays are so familiar that they are referenced constantly in class, auditions, and rehearsal. If you study theatre further, you will want some familiarity with this mix of musical, Shakespeare, classic, and contemporary titles. If reading them all seems too overwhelming, many are on film. All are available as part of study guides or master plots, so that you can at least have an idea of basic story, major characters, and style for each.

A Doll's House (Ibsen)

A Midsummer Night's Dream (Shakespeare)

A Streetcar Named Desire (Williams)

Angels in America (Kushner)

Antigone (Sophocles)

As You Like It (Shakespeare)

Cabaret (Kander, Ebb, Masteroff)

Carousel (Rodgers & Hammerstein)

Cat on a Hot Tin Roof (Williams)

Chicago (Kander & Ebb)

Cyrano de Bergerac (Rostand)

Death of a Salesman (Miller)

Electra (Sophocles)

Fiddler on the Roof (Kander & Ebb)

Guys and Dolls (Loesser, Burrows, Swerling)

Gypsy (Laurents, Styne, Sondheim)

Hamlet (Shakespeare)

King Lear (Shakespeare)

Long Day's Journey into Night (O'Neill)

Lysistrata (Aristophanes)

Macbeth (Shakespeare)

Medea (Euripedes)

Mother Courage (Brecht)

Much Ado About Nothing (Shakespeare)

My Fair Lady (Lerner, Lowe, Shaw)

Oedipus Rex (Sophocles)

Oklahoma (Rodgers & Hammerstein)

Othello (Shakespeare)

Our Town (Wilder)

Rent (Larson)

Richard III (Shakespeare)

Romeo and Juliet (Shakespeare)

Six Characters in Search of an Author (Ionesco)

South Pacific (Rodgers & Hammerstein)

Tartuffe (Molière)

The Bacchae (Euripides)

The Cherry Orchard (Chekhov)

The Crucible (Miller)

The Glass Menagerie (Williams)

The Importance of Being Earnest (Wilde)

The King and I (Rodgers & Hammerstein)

The Misanthrope (Molière)

The Odd Couple (Simon)

The Producers (Brooks)

The Rivals (Sheridan)

The Seagull (Chekhov)

The School for Scandal (Sheridan)

The Taming of the Shrew (Shakespeare)

The Tempest (Shakespeare)

The Three Sisters (Chekhov)

The Trojan Women (Euripedes)

The Zoo Story (Albee)

Twelfth Night (Shakespeare)

Waiting for Godot (Beckett)

West Side Story (Bernstein, Sondheim)

Who's Afraid of Virginia Woolf? (Albee)

Glossary

absurdism   A style of drama that portrays human existence as meaningless and language as an insufficient way of communication. It was made popular after World War II in France by major authors including Samuel Beckett and Eugene Ionesco. There are three types of absurdism: fatalist, existentialist, and hilarious (Ch. 10).

Abydos Passion Play   (c. 2500 B.C.E.) The earliest known example of written theatre, Egyptian (Ch. 2).

Académie Français   The literary establishment that still monitors language and the arts and that controlled the dramatic literature of the neoclassic movement of the seventeenth century (Ch. 8).

Academy   A school for special, specific instruction; a group or society of artists joined to further an artistic or literary end (Ch. 8).

act   To perform a role in front of an audience; a basic division used to separate a play into two or more sections (Ch. 1, Ch. 4).

action   Physical or psychological movement of actors while portraying a character in response to a given circumstance of a play that in turn affects the course of that play; in character analysis, the tactics available to the character in pursuit of their superobjective (Ch. 3).

actor   The essential artist of the theatre, television, or film who creates, portrays, and/or impersonates a character, bringing life to a story through words and gestures; one of the four basic elements of theatre (Ch. 1).

Actors' Equity Association   A union that represents professional stage actors. Abbreviations: Actors' Equity, Equity, or AEA (Ch. 4, Ch. 6).

Adler, Stella   (1901–1992) American acting teacher and a disciple of Stanislavski who based her work on close attention to the text (Ch. 4).

ad-lib   Word or words improvised by an actor during a production usually because the actor has failed to remember his/her line or because something unplanned has occurred on stage. Sometimes a playwright, especially in crowd scenes, may direct an actor to ad-lib (Ch. 11).

Aeschylus   (524–456 B.C.E.) The earliest of the three great Athenian tragedians, author of our only complete trilogy, *The Oresteia* (Ch. 7).

aesthetic distance   The psychological distance between performance and audience that allows for an intellectual response to the work (see **suspension of disbelief**) (Ch. 1).

allegory   Characters representing human qualities, especially used in the Middle Ages to represent the seven virtues and seven vices in religious dramas (Ch. 7).

Ananse   Traditional joker figure (the spider) in African theatre (Ch. 11).

Anderson, Laurie   (b. 1947) American performance artist and a pioneer in personal intimate confessional theatre (Ch. 11).

antagonist   The character that works in opposition to the protagonist's intention (Ch. 3).

Antoine, André   (1858–1943) Early proponent of naturalism, began the Theatre Libre, an experimental theatre that practiced strict recreation of real life on stage (Ch. 9).

Apollo   Classical Greek god representing reason and balance (Ch. 7).

apron   The forward-most structure of the proscenium stage; used commonly during the English Restoration period but also a part of all proscenium stages today (Ch. 5).

aragato   The heightened and bombastic rugged form of acting utilized in certain Kabuki performances (Ch. 7).

arena stage   A theatrical performance area that is usually circular and completely surrounded by the audience (Ch. 5).

Aristophanes   (456–386 B.C.E.) Fifth-century B.C.E. author of our only examples of Old Comedy, a classical Greek style of satire and sex farce (Ch. 7).

Aristotle   (384–322 B.C.E.) Fourth-century B.C.E. Greek philosopher; the first known Western theatre critic and author of *Poetics* (Ch. 2, Ch. 7).

Artha Sastra   The fifth set of precepts guiding the Hindu religion, which placed actors at the bottom of the social ladder (Ch. 4).

artistic director   A member of the producing team, usually responsible for the management of the production season (Ch. 6).

Asian American Theatre Company   A contemporary producing organization, based in San Francisco, which produced the first major play by an Asian American playwright (Frank Chin) (Ch. 11).

aside   Brief lines given directly to the audience that reveal a character's inner thoughts; commonly used by William Shakespeare, often to comic effect (Ch. 2).

audience   The people who agree to experience the enactment with the actors; one of the four elements of theatre (Ch. 1).

audition   An event where an actor engages in the active pursuit of a role. The process can include performing a monologue, preparing a scene, or cold-reading in front of a director or casting director (Ch. 4).

bard   Storyteller, performer, and keeper of communal memory; primary figure in early Western and Middle Eastern traditions (Ch. 3).

Behn, Aphra   (1640–1689) The first professional woman playwright of the English stage. She worked during the English Restoration, from 1660 until her death in 1689 (Ch. 8).

Beijing Opera *(Jinguju)*   A flamboyant style of Chinese opera centered in Beijing, one of the most beloved and enduring of the *xiqu* styles of Eastern performance (Ch. 8).

Bharata   Author of the *Natrya Shastra* or The Canons of Dance and Drama. According to legend, Bharata received the Canons directly from the god Brahma. The Canons describe the elements of Sanskrit and much of Eastern theatre (Ch. 2, Ch. 7).

Bhãsa   One of the three great classical Sanskrit playwrights; author of *The Dream of Vasavadatta* (Ch. 7).

black box   An adjustable theatre space that usually holds fewer than a hundred people (Ch. 5).

Black Elk Speaks   (1932) Native American milestone production, considered the first to illuminate elements unique to this culture. It is the autobiography of an Oglala Sioux medicine man as told to John Neihardt (Ch. 11).

blackface   A derogatory comic African American stereotype portrayed by whites in black makeup with white circles around the eyes and mouth. It started in nineteenth-century American minstrel shows (Ch. 8).

blocking   The actor's movement on stage during a theatrical piece (Ch. 4).

Blue Man Group   Successful dance/movement theatre ensemble masked entirely in blue, employing homemade musical instruments, food fights, and risky audience interaction (Ch. 11).

Boal, Augusto   (1931–2009) Theatre artist, theorist, and creator of Theatre of the Oppressed who designed theatre events for the disenfranchised to encourage and support social change (Ch. 11).

book musical   A musical in which the story is told through words and song, usually in chronological order similar to a well-made structure (Ch. 10).

Bourne, Matthew   (b. 1960) Choreographer credited with innovative dance/movement theatre creations often reinventing ballet and opera (Ch. 11).

box office   A compartment where theatre tickets are sold (Ch. 6).

box set   A set design commonly used in realistic plays where the interior of a room has three sides represented by flats and the fourth wall is removed (Ch. 5).

boy company   A company of young male performers, especially found in the Elizabethan period, who performed special theatre productions at indoor theatres during the late sixteenth and early seventeenth centuries (Ch. 7).

Brecht, Bertolt   (1898–1956) German playwright who embraced Didacticism, breaking traditional stage illusions while attempting to keep the audience aware of the play's message (Ch. 10).

breeches role   Female characters who during the course of the play must disguise themselves in men's clothing. In the English Restoration theatre, breeches or pants allowed audience members a look at a woman's legs (not done in normal circumstances) (Ch. 8).

Brook, Peter   (b. 1925) English director known for innovative international productions (Ch. 11).

Buddha (Siddhartha Gautama)   (see **Siddhartha Gautama**) (Ch. 7).

Buddhism A world religion, founded by Siddhartha Gautama, a Hindu prince who achieved Enlightenment. His teachings spread throughout the Far East and beyond with an estimated 350,000,000 believers today (Ch. 7).

Bunraku The popular puppet theatre originally developed in Japan in the seventeenth century simultaneously with Kabuki and still performed today (Ch. 7).

callback After the primary audition, the director or casting director calls back actors he may be interested in for a certain role for additional readings and/or an interview (Ch. 4).

Capitano A stock character of the *Commedia dell'arte* tradition, meaning the Braggart Warrior or Cowardly Soldier (Ch. 7).

casting call The public advertisement, announcement, or posting of auditions for a play (Ch. 4).

cattle call An audition that is open to anyone. Also known as an "open call," the audition usually brings out big numbers. As a result, actors usually receive less time to perform audition material (Ch. 4).

Centers for Theatre of the Oppressed (CTOs) Places that train and perform in the tradition of Augusto Boal, champion of oppressed people everywhere, who used theatre techniques as a means of demanding social change and empowering individuals to act in their own defense (Ch 11).

Chambers, Jane (1937–1983) Author of landmark lesbian plays such as *The Late Show* and *Last Summer at Bluefish Cove* (Ch. 11).

character analysis A tool for analyzing a play by asking *who, what, how,* and *why* about the characters (Ch. 3).

Chekhov, Anton (1860–1904) Author of early realism who worked with Konstantin Stanislavski at the Moscow Art Theatre. His realism was unique and so delicate that he almost defined his own genre, known today as "Chekhovian realism" (Ch. 9, Dramatic Interlude 5).

choreographer Person who designs the dance and movement in a production (Ch. 6).

chorus In classic Greek plays, an ensemble that moved, spoke, sang, and danced mostly in unison. Their function included providing commentary and narration, serving as a character in and of itself, or representing the mindset of the general public. Originally, the chorus was a large number of about 50 men, then was reduced to 12 or 15. As other playwrights emerged, such as Shakespeare, the chorus became a character who was portrayed by a single actor or a smaller group of actors. In musicals, it is an ensemble that sings and dances in unison or as a series of solos or smaller groups (Ch. 7, Ch. 10).

Cirque du Soleil A dramatic mix of circus arts and street entertainment (Ch. 11).

climax The point of greatest dramatic tension when the conflicts of a play all come to a head. Sometimes it is the moment the antagonist is defeated and/or the highest point of excitement for the audience when watching a play (Ch. 3).

coach Any specialist who assists in a production by training actors in particular skills. The most common are movement and voice coaches (Ch. 6).

comedy A dramatic mood that is usually humorous with a happy ending (Ch. 1).

ComedySportz Improvisational theatre employing the same regulations as athletic events (Ch. 11).

Commedia dell'arte Originating in Italy, one of the first secular theatre movements following the religious domination of the Middle Ages. A style based in scenarios (or basic story lines) fleshed out with *lazzi*, improv, and topical humor (Ch. 7, Ch. 8).

Comte, Auguste (1798–1857) Inventor of modern sociology, heavily influenced the development of Realism in the theatre (Ch. 9).

concept musical A musical, often structured episodically, that is constructed around an idea, motif, or even place, rather than telling one chronological story (see **book musical**) (Ch. 10).

conceptual director A director who sees the text as a starting point for the production but not as the primary inspiration, which comes from within the director's agenda and imagination; to be contrasted with the traditional director (Ch. 4).

Concert Party A contemporary African theatre form melding traditional stories with modern music and stand-up comedy (Ch. 11).

conflict The tension between two opposing forces in a play, key to the movement of the story. It creates setbacks and obstacles for the characters to overcome (Ch. 3).

construction crew A team of workers assembled to build the stage scenery, props, or costumes for a production (Ch. 6).

Corneille, Pierre (1606–1684) Master of tragic French neoclassicism whose plays focus on the need to repress emotion in favor of duty. His masterpiece is *El Cid* (Ch. 8).

costume design The design of all garments worn by actors in a play (Ch. 5).

critic One who evaluates a work of art, often in print (Ch. 12).

Crothers, Rachel (1878–1958) American playwright who broke ground as a successful woman playwright, actor, director, and producer. She was also an early advocate of women's rights in her plays such as *He and She* (Dramatic Interlude 6).

Crowley, Mart (b. 1935) American playwright whose *Boys in the Band* is considered one of the landmark productions in gay and lesbian theatre (Ch. 11).

cyclorama A large white or light gray tightly stretched curtain attached to pipes at its top and bottom. It receives light or other projections (Ch. 5).

cue Something that occurs during the play, technically, physically, or orally, that signals an actor or theatre technician (Ch. 4).

Dadaism European Artisan movement that began after World War I that portrayed the meaninglessness of life and influenced poetry, paintings, and theatre (Ch. 10).

dance play A theatrical piece illustrated through dance minus dialogue in which characterization, narrative, and dramatic conflict are told in choreography instead of words (Ch. 11).

Danjuro family The hereditary "first family" of the Kabuki theatre, starting in 1660 (Ch. 7).

Darwin, Charles (1809–1882) Naturalist whose *Origin of Species* and theory of evolution, heavily influenced the development of Realism in the theatre (Ch. 9).

deconstruction In literary criticism, a movement that challenges the notion of fixed meanings as truths of dramatic text (Ch. 3).

de la Cruz, Sor Juana Ines (1651–1695) The "Tenth Muse," who in a male-dominated age, worked to international acclaim as a poet, playwright, essayist, and champion of women during the seventeenth century in New Spain (Ch.7).

design ingredients Elements making up a design including line, mass, color, texture, and decor (Ch. 5).

design principles Guidelines in the design process including unity, variety, balance, focus, and progression (Ch. 5).

devised works Theatre events developed by a group of artists in a democratic forum, often based around a theme or existing nontheatrical text (Ch. 11).

dialect The variations of a spoken language characteristic to a region or social group (Ch. 6).

dialogue The words spoken by two or more characters in a play (Ch. 2).

didacticism A theatre style, also known as epic or Brechtian theatre, which attempts to lead the audience into an intellectual rather than emotional response (Ch. 10).

dimmer An apparatus that controls the intensity of light. It is run by a dimmer board (Ch. 5).

Dionysus In Greek mythology, the god of theatre, wine, and merriment (Ch. 7).

director The individual in modern Western theatre who steers a stage production (Ch. 4).

dithyramb In ancient Greece, a choral chant to honor the god Dionysus; precursor to the Greek tragedy (Ch. 2).

downstage The part of the stage closest to the audience (Ch. 4).

drama A brand of theatre that expresses a story about people, their actions, and the opposition that results (Ch. 3).

dramatic action Events that occur in a play between the inciting incident and the climax; those deeds or exploits that move the action of the play toward its conclusion (Ch. 3).

dramaturg A member of the production team, skilled in research and analysis, who helps actors, designers, and directors better understand the particulars of the play (Ch. 6).

dress rehearsal The last rehearsals before opening night where actors don their costumes and makeup is added (Ch. 4).

drop Painted canvas or large curtain hung at the rear of the stage to create an atmosphere or indicate a specific locale (Ch. 5).

East West Players Seminal theatre company, based in Los Angeles, combining talents of Korean, Chinese, and Japanese participants (Ch. 11).

eco-theatre the movement for theatres and productions to focus on environmental issues specific to a region or of general sustainability (Ch. 11).

Elizabethan Period referring to the reign of Queen Elizabeth I of England (1558–1603) (Ch. 7).

encore When performers repeat a performance or a portion of the performance at the request of an audience determined by the level of applause and/or cheers the audience gives in response to the performance (Ch. 2).

English Restoration (see **Restoration**) (Ch. 8).

ensemble A group of actors and/or performers (Ch. 4).

Ensler, Eve (b. 1953) Contemporary playwright focusing on women's issues; best known for her work *The Vagina Monologues* (Ch. 11).

environmental stage Aims to eliminate the space and distinction between the actors onstage and the audience by using the total theatre space to create the environment for the production. As a result it is usually a small, nontraditional space or black box type of theater (Ch. 5).

epic Long, narrative poems celebrating the exploits of a hero or a people (Ch. 7).

episodic A plot connected by characters, an image or motif, a place, or the like, not by the usual cause and effect (Ch. 3).

ethnic American theatre Theatre forms combining histories of particular racial heritages with contemporary living conditions in the United States (Ch. 11).

Euripides (480–406 B.C.E.) The last of the great classical Greek tragedians; author of *Medea* and *The Bacchae* (Ch. 7).

Existentialism A post–World War II movement that views the world as a godless, senseless place where human beings live in a meaningless void (Ch. 10).

exposition In a play, information about prior events or offstage events, which is necessary for the understanding of the plot of the play. This information is usually given in the form of a narrative (Ch. 3).

expressionism A theatre style that attempts to expose life through the lens of the author or the protagonist as he experiences it, frequently through dream and nightmare imagery. It is especially anti-industrial, antimilitary, and antiurban (Ch. 10).

falling action An event that relaxes the tension or conflict of a play (Ch. 3).

feminist theatre A type of women's theatre with a political/social agenda and a desire to address and change gender dynamics (Ch. 11).

fight director Person who choreographs any fight sequences, balancing realistic violence with safety and theatricality (Ch. 6).

flat A frame made of wood usually covered by fabric to create a set, particularly a wall (Ch. 5).

fly space Area above the stage where sets and scenery may be hoisted out of sight by the use of counterweights or pulleys (the fly system) when not in use (Ch. 5).

focus The spot on the stage that attracts the audience's attention designated by the director (Ch. 5).

foreshadowing A structural device in the form of a warning of impending danger that is used to increase tension (Ch. 3).

forestage (see **apron**) (Ch. 5).

forum theatre Community problem-solving theatre developed by Augusto Boal in which a "joker" sets rules for audience/actor engagement in an issue (Ch. 11).

fourth wall A device of Realism created in the mid-nineteenth century in which an imaginary wall is placed between the actors and the audience (Ch. 2).

French Neoclassicism An influential seventeenth-century style of formal playwrighting that desired to emulate Aristotle and the Greek classical playwrights (Ch. 8).

Freud, Sigmund (1856–1939) Developer of theories of psychoanalysis and the unconscious mind whose theories heavily influenced the development of Realism in the theatre (Ch. 9).

Fugard, Athol (b. 1932) South African playwright, whose anti-apartheid plays got him in trouble with the authorities (Dramatic Interlude 4, Ch. 11).

fusion Blending theatrical forms from different cultures into a single performance (Ch. 11).

futurism A movement of art beginning in early twentieth-century Italy that glorifies the age of mechanization and the energy of the Industrial Age (Ch. 10).

García Márquez, Gabriel (b. 1928) Colombian fiction writer and Nobel Prize Laureate who was instrumental in introducing the techniques of Magic Realism to the international community (Ch. 9).

Gay Theatre Alliance The first organization uniting regional gay and lesbian theatres into a single force (Ch. 11).

Georg II, Duke of Saxe-Meiningen (1826–1914) German who is often referred to as the Father of Modern Directing; developed the role of the director as a single voice controlling all elements of production (Ch. 4).

Georgian Period referring to the second half of the eighteenth century and specifically to the reigns of King George II and III in England (Ch. 8).

Georgian Comedy Eighteenth-century English comedy that tended to the sentimental rather than the satirical (Ch. 8).

gesture Any physical movement used as a form of communication. It can be accompanied by verbal communication or it can stand alone. On stage, actors use gestures to enhance their communication and to help bring a sense of real life to a text. They can be planned or unplanned (Ch. 2).

geza Special effects music used in Kabuki theatre (Ch. 7).

Gidayu, Takemoto (1651–1714) Credited with founding the Bunraku puppet theatre in Japan in 1684. The term *gidayu* is now used to denote a singer-chanter in Kabuki and Bunraku performance (Ch. 7).

given circumstances The facts that create the world of a play (Ch. 3).

Glaser, Sherry (b. 1960) Prominent solo performer whose work *Family Secrets* has helped define the one-person show (Ch. 11).

Globe Theatre One of the theatre buildings used by Shakespeare's company for the public performance of plays (Ch. 7).

Goethe, Johann Wolfgang von (1749–1832) German playwright of the Romantic movement, author of *Faust* (Ch. 9).

"Golden Age" Any period of greatness, as testified to by later generations, such as the "Golden Age" of Greek tragedy or the "Golden Age" of the musical (Ch. 7, Ch. 8).

Goldsmith, Oliver (1730–1774) English playwright of Georgian comedy, such as *She Stoops to Conquer* (Ch. 8).

griot/griotte The singer, storyteller, and keeper of the community's collective memory/history in traditional African theatre (Ch. 2, Ch. 3).

Grotowski, Jerzy (b. 1933) European director who used the text as a springboard for conceptualized productions (Ch. 4).

hanamichi In the Japanese Kabuki theatre, a long, narrow pathway leading from behind the audience to the stage where actors make entrances and exits and express heightened dramatic text (Ch. 7).

Handspring Puppet Company South African puppetry performance and design company established in 1981 by Adrian Kohler and Basil Jones (Ch. 6).

Hansberry, Lorraine (1930–1965) African American playwright whose *Raisin in the Sun* was the first play by a female African American ever produced on Broadway (Ch. 11).

Harlem Renaissance Period centered in Harlem in the 1920s and 1930s in which African Americans expressed themselves through a collective arts and music movement (Ch. 11).

Hashigakari In the Japanese *Noh* theatre, the pathway from the dressing area to the stage (Ch. 7).

Hausa Known in the Hausa language as *K'ungiyar Yazi Dogo*, a Niger theatre troupe that creates devised works around a theme (Ch. 1).

Hellman, Lillian (1905–1984) American master of Realism; her plays include *The Children's Hour* and *The Little Foxes* (Ch. 9, Ch. 11).

hero The character or figure who symbolizes the culture's most valued traits and is the central figure in a heroic tragedy or play (Ch. 2).

Hinduism One of the world's oldest religions, which provided the spiritual/philosophical foundations for Sanskrit dance/drama (Ch. 7).

Homer A person (or persons) who first recorded the ancient stories of Greece in the eighth century B.C.E. including the *Iliad* and the *Odyssey* (Ch. 7).

house The seating area in a modern theatre (Ch. 6).

house holder An acting company member who retains a share of the theatre himself (Ch. 8).

house manager   The person charged with all audience issues from seating and program distribution to start time for the show to assisting patrons with physical impairments (Ch. 6).

Hroswitha   (935–975) German female playwright (and nun) who adapted ideas of Roman comedies into plays (Ch. 11).

Hugo, Victor   (1802–1885) French playwright of the Romantic movement; author of the Romanticism Manifesto and the play *Hernani* (Ch. 9).

Hwang, David Henry   (b. 1957) Asian American playwright; author of *M. Butterfly* (Dramatic Interlude 1, Ch. 11).

Ibsen, Henrik   (1828–1906) Norwegian playwright who is called by some the Father of Modern Realism; author of *A Doll's House* and *Ghosts* (Ch. 9).

image theatre   Form developed by Augusto Boal in which human sculptures and tableaus are used to alter power relationships (Ch. 11).

imagination   The power to form mental images of what is not present, as well as the power to create new ideas by combining previous experiences (Ch. 1).

improvisation   An acting technique or exercise that frees a performer's imagination and allows him to create and respond without a defined script or rehearsed behavior. It can be spontaneous dialogue (ad-lib) or stage business created by an actor in the moment of the performance (Ch. 11).

impulse   The incitement to action by a stimulus or a driving force or an impelling force (Ch. 1).

inciting incident   The event that sets the action of a play into motion (Ch. 3).

Innamorati   One of the stock character types of the *Commedia dell'arte*, meaning young lovers (Ch. 7).

intermission   A small pause in the action of a production where the audience is permitted to leave their seats for a short time that usually lasts for 10 to 15 minutes (Ch. 1).

invisible theatre   Augusto Boal's format in which scripted scenes are presented in public places to stimulate debate and discussion over social issues (Ch. 11).

Isms   A nickname commonly applied to the variety of styles that emerged during the twentieth century and that continue to impact theatre today. Examples include Futur*ism* and Expression*ism* (Ch. 10).

Izumo no Okuni   The young Japanese woman credited with the first "weird and flashy" entertainment that evolved into the Kabuki theatre (Ch. 7).

Jacobean   Referring to drama written during the reign of James I of England (1603–1642) (Ch. 7).

jidaimono   A type of Kabuki play focused on history; translation for "period things" (Ch. 7).

jing   In *xiqu*, the "painted faces" roles, often depicting gods, demons, or heroes (Ch. 8).

Jinguju   Another name for Beijing Opera, the most popular form of Chinese theatre in the world today (Ch. 8).

jorjuri   The chorus in a Kabuki play (Ch. 7).

jukebox musicals   Musical theatre productions using previously released popular songs, sharing a connection with a particular singer or group, rather than original scores (Ch. 10).

Kabuki   One of the classical theatres of Japan dating from the seventeenth century; a popular form in contrast with the elitist form of the *Noh* (Ch. 7).

Kabuki Juhachiban   The body of 18 classical Kabuki plays still performed today (Ch. 7).

Kalidasa   One of the three great playwrights of the classical Sanskrit tradition; author of *The Recognition of Shakuntala,* regarded by Sanskrit scholars as "the perfect play" (Ch. 7).

Kan'ami Kiyotsugu/Zeami Motokiyo   Japanese father/son team responsible for creation of the *Noh* drama and most of its extent texts (Ch. 7).

Kathakali   A popular form of Indian classical drama, meaning literally "story play"; an intense all-night outdoor theatre event designed to evoke mystery and fear (Ch. 8).

key grip   The supervisor of the crew in filmmaking charged with both camera work and lighting needs (Ch. 6).

Kunqu   A refined, elitist form of *xiqu* or Chinese opera, beginning in 1644 and still performed occasionally today (Ch. 8).

Kushner, Tony   (b. 1956) Prominent American playwright who is best known for his "gay fantasia on national themes," *Angels in America* (Ch. 11).

Laramie Project   Significant example, under the guidance of Moisés Kaufman, of devised, collaborative theatre creation (Ch. 11).

lazzi   Comic bits (singular is *lazzo*) found in the *Commedia dell'arte* style of performance (Ch. 7).

League of Resident Theatres   (LORT) Professional organization uniting and promoting regional non-profit theatres (Ch. 11).

light plot   The diagram that illustrates all the lighting instruments, how they are hung, and what areas of the stage they are focused to light (Ch. 5).

lighting design   The plan for lighting a production, created by the lighting designer, taking into account the needs of the production, communication with other members of the production team, and the *elements* of lighting design: *intensity, direction, spread, color, movement* (Ch. 5).

lighting designer   The artist who is responsible for creating the lighting vision of a production (Ch. 5).

Lim, Genny   (b. 1946) Asian American twentieth-century playwright (Dramatic Interlude 5).

literary manager   A dramaturg who works for theatre companies to read, research, and evaluate the plays that are performed (Ch. 6).

Ludlam, Charles   (1943–1987) Founder of the Ridiculous Theatrical Company and author of "drag" plays (Ch. 11).

lyrics   In a musical, the sung words of a song (Ch. 10).

magic realism   A theatrical genre in which the boundaries between the natural and the supernatural are blurred; particularly found in plays from non-Western traditions (Ch. 9).

Mahabharata   One of the two great epics of Indian tradition (Ch. 7).

managing director   A member of the producing team who is in charge of finances and budgetary concerns (Ch. 6).

Marlowe, Christopher   (c. 1564–1593) The most famous Tudor-era playwright; author of *Tamburlaine the Great, Doctor Faustus, The Jew of Malta,* and *Edward II* (Ch. 7).

Marx, Karl   (1818–1883) Political theorist, whose *The Communist Manifesto* influenced the development of Realism in the theatre (Ch. 9).

mask   Establishing a character by covering the face. Also, the piece used to cover the face. It may be full-face or cover only part of the face. It may be three-dimensional or include makeup. Used since the beginning of theatre including Greek, Roman, and *Commedia dell'arte*. Many non-Western theatre traditions have always included masks and continue to do so today (Ch. 5).

masking   Anything designed to block the audience's view of the backstage area.

master carpenter   Usually the senior carpenter, the most skilled of the team constructing scenery or props; answers to the shop foreman (Ch. 6).

master electrician   The person in charge of hanging, focusing, and wiring the lights for a production; answers to the lighting designer (Ch. 6).

medium   The raw material chosen by the artist as the starting place for creative activity. A painter may choose between oil and watercolor, while a playwright may choose between media and live theatre (Ch. 3).

mega musicals   A live theatre phenomenon similar to the Hollywood film blockbuster, involving a large production, usually with an element of flash or special effects, that aims to sell an extraordinary number of tickets and blow all the competition out of the water (Ch. 10).

Meisner, Stanford   (1905–1997) American acting teacher, disciple of Stanislavski, who developed a training system involving repetition exercises. He defined acting as "the ability to live truthfully under imaginary circumstances" (Ch. 4).

melodrama   A specific type of plot-oriented drama with clearly defined characters who articulate middle-class values (Ch. 8).

Method, The   A system of actor training developed by Lee Strasberg that focuses on the truth of emotional memory or recall (Ch. 4).

miko   Female storyteller, performer, and shaman in traditional Japanese oral theatre (Ch. 2).

Miller, Arthur   (1915–2005) American master of Realism; author of *All My Sons* and *Death of a Salesman* (Ch. 9).

minstrel show   A nineteenth-century racist style of performance in which white performers in blackface denigrated African American culture (Ch. 8).

Mnouchkine, Ariane   (b. 1939) Fusion artist and director of the Théâtre du Soleil (Ch. 11).

model   A three-dimensional representation of a design, created by the designer, most usually a scenic/properties designer (Ch. 5).

Molière (1622–1673) French comic playwright who transcended the rigors of neoclassic demands to create universally respected comedies of manners and satire; strongly influenced by *Commedia dell'arte* troupes (Ch. 8).

monologue Unbroken speech in a play usually directed to the audience (Ch. 2).

mood A play's predominant attitude, which is particularly comic or serious (Ch. 3).

morality plays Late medieval dramas intended to teach a moral lesson (Ch. 7).

motivation The conscious or subconscious reason a character chooses a behavior or action (Ch. 3).

multiculturalism The effort to achieve an inclusive society by giving equal voice and representation to underrepresented groups of people.

music director Person who guides the singers and orchestra through the score in a musical (Ch. 6).

musical A form of theatre that highlights song and dance integrated with spoken text (Ch. 10).

musical comedy A form of musical theatre that has a light-hearted, rapid moving comic story and is integrated with popular music (Ch. 10).

musical reviews Productions which, rather than tell a story of some kind, celebrate the work of a single composer, composing team, or a group of talented performers (Ch. 10).

myths Stories about heroes or supernatural beings, often explaining the origins of natural phenomena or aspects of human behavior; most focused on truth rather than fact (Ch. 2).

naturalism A movement in nineteenth-century Europe that represents Realism in its most radical form and shows that nature and the social environment control human behavior (Ch. 9).

Natya Shastra The Canons of Dance and Drama, first written by the sage Bharata as a guide to all elements of Sanskrit dance/drama (Ch. 2, Ch. 7).

Negro Ensemble Company Company founded in 1967 in New York City and associated with more than 200 landmark African American plays and productions (Ch. 11).

neoclassicism A seventeenth-century revival in the artistic and literary philosophies of Ancient Greece and Rome and the effort to express them in a more current fashion (Ch. 8).

New Comedy Comic dramas of Greece of the late fourth to second centuries B.C.E., tending toward domestic and romantic comedy (Ch. 7).

Noh Also spelled No; a classical dance drama created in fourteenth-century Japan that relies heavily on tradition. This style of drama predates Kabuki (Ch. 7).

Noh stage A very specific design for stage, theatre space, costumes, etc., in which *Noh* drama is performed (Ch. 5).

nonprofit theatre Designation allowing a company to employ other resources, such as grants and donations, rather than simply box office, to support a theatre (Ch. 11).

Nuyorican A blending of cultures for those of Puerto Rican origin living in the New York City area, evolving into a particular form of Hispanic theatre, music, and arts (Ch. 11).

off Broadway Small professional theatres in New York City located outside the Broadway district. Today, it is considered a scaled down version of Broadway. Originally it was a movement initiated in the 1940s inspired by Broadway commercialism as an outlet to provide a more experimental atmosphere for new and innovative works unhindered by commercial influences. Many American actors and directors jump-start their careers off Broadway (Ch. 11).

off-off Broadway Nontraditional, nonprofessional theatre in New York City that displays new talent in experimental, unconventional and original work productions. This movement was created in the 1960s as a result of the commercialism of Broadway and increasing commercialism of off Broadway (Ch. 11).

Old Comedy Greek comic plays written in the classical period that directly or indirectly comment on the social, political, and/or cultural issues of the times. It is usually filled with physical and obscene humor (Ch. 7).

O'Neill, Eugene (1888–1953) American master of Realism; author of *A Moon for the Misbegotten* and *Long Day's Journey into Night* (Ch. 9).

onnagata Male performer in traditional Japanese theatre who specialized in playing female roles (Ch. 4, Ch. 7).

Onwueme, Tess (b. 1955) Contemporary Nigerian playwright associated with the feminist movement in that country (Ch. 11).

opening night   During a run of a production, it is the first full-priced performance open to the public (Ch. 4).

opera   A style of music performance that is generally through song, meaning it has few or no spoken words. It is also generally grand and sweeping in scale (Ch. 8).

oral tradition   Theatre based in spoken word and communal memory rather than written text (Ch. 2).

orature   Term recently coined to describe rich, sophisticated oral traditions in the arts (Ch. 7).

orchestra   In ancient Greek theatre, the circular area in front of the stage that was the performance area for the chorus (Ch. 7).

original practice   Producing classical works for contemporary audiences, with as many as possible of the conventions (such as all-male actors in Shakespeare) that would have been employed when they were first presented long ago (Ch. 11).

pageant wagons   The movable stage/wagon on which medieval biblical plays were mounted (Ch. 7).

Pantalone   A stock character in the *Commedia dell'arte* tradition; the miser (Ch. 7).

performance   Live public execution of at least partially planned behavior or action.

performance art   An art form created in the mid-twentieth century that focuses on visual expression of personal truth and a state of being, more than literal expression and telling a story. There are usually one or more performers with a blend of music, painting, dance, theatre, poetry, and visual arts in performance art pieces (Ch. 11).

Plautus   Roman comic playwright who specialized in popular farcical comedy (Ch. 7).

playback theatre   An improvisational form in which actors recreate personal stories of audience members (Ch. 11).

playwright   The person who writes the script for a play (Ch. 3).

plot   In a play, the arranged set of events and the way those events unfold to tell a story while simultaneously creating maximum dramatic impact (Ch. 3).

point of attack   In a play, the beginning moment that starts the action of the play, chosen by the playwright out of the larger story of a character's life (Ch. 3).

polis   Greek city-state (Ch. 7).

present tense   The moment of here and now. All action in a play takes place in the *now* or current moment for the characters (Ch. 3).

preview   A free or discounted performance. It is usually scheduled after or during dress rehearsal and right before opening night (Ch. 4).

problematizing   Making a play into a project that addresses a concern of the director, turning a relatively minor concern of the playwright into the major focus of the production (Ch. 3).

producer   Any individual, group, or institution that controls the business side of a production (Ch. 6).

production concept   The thematic approach to a specific production (Ch. 4).

projection designer   The artist/technician responsible for incorporating media, such as film footage and photo stills, into a live theatre production (Ch. 5).

prop master   The staff member responsible for most objects handled by actors during performance (Ch. 5).

props   An abbreviation for properties, it includes set props, which are items like furniture that dress the set, and hand props, which are any items used by the actors on stage (Ch. 6).

proscenium arch   The arch that serves as a frame separating the stage space from the audience area (Ch. 2).

proscenium stage   An arrangement of a theatre area in which the audience faces the actor on only one side (Ch. 5).

protagonist   In Greek theatre, the main actor. Today it is known as the central character that drives the action onward; also known as the hero (Ch. 3).

public relations/promotion   The link between the production and the general public; department in charge of generating attendance through advertising and other means (Ch. 6).

Puig, Manuel   (1932–1990) Argentinean playwright and novelist whose work of Magic Realism, *Kiss of the Spider Woman*, achieved international acclaim, and was eventually made into a film and a Broadway musical (Ch. 9).

queer theory Movement that rejects sexual labels as insufficient and redefines "queer" as any behavior that does not fit within rules (Ch. 11).

Racine, Jean (1639–1699) Influential tragic playwright of French neoclassicism; considered the darling of seventeenth-century Paris and earned the respect of Louis XIV with plays like *Andromaque*, considered by some to be his masterpiece (Ch. 8).

Raffo, Heather Heather Raffo is a Lucille Lortel Award—winning Iraqi American playwright and actress, best known for writing and playing the leading role in the one-woman play *9 Parts of Desire*.

Ramayana One of the two great epics of Indian tradition (Ch. 7).

realism A form of theatre where the behavior on stage happens as it would in life (Ch. 2).

realism The cultural movement that supports theatrical realism and extended the belief that these plays could be a force for social and political change (Ch. 9).

regional theatre Professional, not-for-profit, non-touring theatre located outside New York City (see **League of Resident Theatres**) (Ch. 11).

Renaissance The "rebirth" or renewed excitement in learning that has occurred in many cultures at different times. In Europe, a renaissance of interest in the culture of ancient Greece and Rome began in Italy 1450–1650 and spread throughout Western Europe (Ch. 7).

renderings The work of designers that are frequently beautiful, detailed paintings or drawing of scenery, costumes, etc. (Ch. 5).

repertory A decided assortment of performance pieces done by a company, sometimes involving plays moving in and out of presentation at various times during a season (Ch. 11).

resolution The point of the play, usually the final scene, where the results of the climax are revealed and any loose ends are tied up (Ch. 3).

Restoration In England, a return to the theatre after the reestablishment of the monarchy in 1660; noted for clever and lustful comedies (Ch. 8).

reviewer A person employed by various media, charged with attending the opening performance of a play and articulating a response to it for the benefit of potential audiences (Ch. 12).

rising action The intensifying action of a play, occurring between the inciting incident and the climax (Ch. 3).

ritual A traditional, cultural, or individual practice involving well-defined and exact movements, music, or spoken text that serves to communicate with deities or to provide structure and comfort to the society or individual (Ch. 2).

Rivera, José (b. 1955) Twentieth-century Cuban American master playwright (Ch. 11).

rock musical A musical that encompasses rock and roll music (Ch. 10).

Rodgers (Richard) and Hammerstein (Oscar) Twentieth-century American musical composer/lyricist team whose works did much to define the "Golden Age" of the American musical (Ch. 10, Ch. 11).

romanticism A movement in nineteenth-century Europe from neoclassic formulism toward enormous passions, exotic and distorted stories, gaudy writing, and inclusive worldviews (Ch. 9).

run-throughs Rehearsals where the entire play is performed without stopping (Ch. 4).

running crew Those who assist behind the scenes in a production during performance, as opposed to those involved in construction (Ch. 6).

Sanchez-Scott, Milcha (b. 1955) American playwright exploring the experiences of Latinos through the styles of Magic Realism and Realism (Dramatic Interlude 3).

Sanskrit The classical language of India and South/Southwest Asia; currently one of 23 official languages of India used in Hindu and Buddhist ceremonies (Ch. 7).

Sanskrit drama Traditional theatre of India (Ch. 4).

scenario The blueprint for *Commedia dell'arte* performance, outlining the plot, some key lines, and where to put *lazzi* (Ch. 7).

scene design The act of shaping and defining the stage space (Ch. 5).

Schiller, Friedrich (1759–1805) German playwright of the Romanticist school; a major figure in the *Sturm und Drang* (Storm and Stress) movement (Ch. 9).

scrim A gauze curtain that seems opaque when lit from the front but becomes transparent when lit from behind (Ch. 5).

script The text of a play (Ch. 3).

Second City, The Chicago-based company considered one of the most influential sources in improvisational theatre (Ch. 11).

set   The physical scenery for a play or scene (Ch. 5).

sewamono   A style of Kabuki play focused on domestic issues; translation: "common things" (Ch. 7).

Shakespeare, William   (1564–1616) A major playwright of the Elizabethan era who is considered by some to be the best English playwright of all time (Dramatic Interludes 1 and 3, Ch. 7).

shamisen   A Japanese three-stringed musical instrument (Ch. 7).

Shanghai Opera   Traditional people's theatre centered in its namesake city that features all-female performers (Ch. 4).

Shaw, George Bernard   (1856–1950) English playwright of the Realist movement; author of *Mrs. Warren's Profession* and *Arms and the Man* (Dramatic Interlude 2, Ch. 9).

Sheridan, Richard Brinsley   (1751–1816) English playwright of Georgian comedy, such as *The Rivals* (Ch. 8).

shite   The protagonist or doer in *Noh* theatre (Ch. 7).

shop foreman   A person charged with particular responsibility of an area in the construction of a production; answers to shop supervisors (Ch. 6).

shop supervisors   Skilled technicians who oversee the entire workings of a construction shop, may be scenery, costumes, etc.; answers to the producer and designer (Ch. 6).

show and tell   Usually the first meeting of the full company and production team where designs are shared and often the first full reading of the script takes place (Ch. 4).

S´hudraka   One of the three great classical Sanskrit playwrights, author of *The Little Clay Cart* (Ch. 7).

Siddhartha Gautama   **(Buddha)** (563–483 B.C.E.) Hindu prince who achieved enlightenment, influential in the spread of Sanskrit dramatic conventions throughout Asia (Ch. 7).

sight lines   An audience's visual boundary. Sight lines extend horizontally as well as vertically and anything beyond the sight lines is out of the audience's sight (Ch. 5).

sing-through musicals   A form of musical theatre, similar to opera, where there is little or no actual spoken dialogue and there is music running through the entire event, with all lines sung (Ch. 10).

skene   In ancient Greek theatre, the building and façade behind the stage, used as a changing house and to indicate locations (Ch. 7).

sketches   The first design step for scenic and costume designers; a quick drawing meant to communicate an approach or idea to other members of the team (Ch. 5).

slice of life   Theatre that aims to depict natural everyday life; synonymous with pure naturalism, a term first used by Émile Zola. Slice of life plays usually follow a character's life for the duration of the realistic time the actual play lasts. For example, if the play lasts two hours, it highlights only two hours of the world of the play (Ch. 9).

soliloquy   A monologue in which the character speaks his or her thoughts aloud, not directed toward any other person (Ch. 2).

Sophocles   (496–406 B.C.E.) Greek tragedian of the fifth-century B.C.E., or "Golden Age" of Athens; considered by some to be the finest of the Greek tragic playwrights (Dramatic Interlude 4, Ch. 7).

sound design   Planning those aural elements, including sound effects and musical underscoring, that augment the spoken lines of the actors (Ch. 5).

Soyinka, Wole   (b. 1934) Nigerian playwright and Nobel Prize Laureate whose political plays got him into trouble with the authorities (Ch. 11).

space   A place transformed for a performance; one of the four elements of theatre (Ch. 1).

Spiderwoman Theater   Native American performance group, revitalizing the ancient stories and performance styles of their culture to address contemporary women's issues (Ch. 11).

stage makeup   That worn on the actor's face or body to indicate character. Types of makeup include *straight* (such as street makeup), *corrective* (generally used to "beautify" an actor), *age*, *character* (may include prosthetics and other artificial elements), and *stylization* (which can range from Kabuki to *Cats*) (Ch. 5).

stage manager   Person who overlooks the execution of a production. This person acts as the go-between for the director, the performers, and the entire production staff. The stage manager is vital to the production and works closely with the director from the beginning of a production until the end. In professional theatre, it is common for directors to leave a show before the end of a run, leaving the stage manager in charge of the production (Ch. 6).

Stanislavski, Konstantin (1863–1938) Called the Father of Modern Acting; developed the System, a highly influential method of actor training that encouraged realistic and detailed performances (Ch. 4).

star In a production, the actor who is usually well known enough that his presence brings in an audience. The star is usually paid more and may receive certain perks because of his status (Ch. 4).

star system Nineteenth-century touring technique in which the star or lead actor purchased the rights to a play and produced it to his or her own advantage (Ch. 4).

stock characters Stereotypical characters that are usually less than three-dimensional. Stock characters were first valued in Western theatre in the Roman comedies of Plautus. His stock characters were recreated during the Italian Renaissance in the *Commedia dell'arte*. These types of characters are still popular today (Ch. 7).

Stomp Percussion/dance theatre phenomenon employing common objects for sound and rough edged street choreography (Ch. 11).

story A tale told about the life of someone real or imaginary who has experienced or dreamed something worthy of attention; one of the four elements of theatre (Ch. 1).

Strasberg, Lee (1901–1982) American acting teacher and disciple of Konstantin Stanislavski who developed a school of acting based on emotional memory or recall, called The Method (Ch. 4).

Strindberg, August (1849–1912) Swedish playwright who was an early master of Naturalism (*Miss Julie, The Father*) but later rejected Naturalism as inadequate and pioneered Expressionism on stage (*Road to Damascus, Ghost Sonata*) (Ch. 9).

Stroman, Susan (b. 1954) Choreographer/director credited with creating the dance play with her production of *Contact* (Ch. 11).

structural elements Those pieces of the puzzle in the play that combine to communicate the author's meaning, including the inciting incident, rising actions, etc. (Ch. 3).

Sturm und Drang An influential German faction of nineteenth-century Romantic playwrights (particularly Goethe and Schiller) whose work tends to depict a highly emotional, stormy, heroic individual in conflict with conventional society (Ch. 9).

stylization The process of taking a play beyond reality through distortion, exaggeration, or some other stretch of convention (Ch. 2, Ch. 10).

superobjective A term used by Konstantin Stanislavski to denote a character's overarching objective that embodies the major intention or desire of a character and carries him or her through all or most of the play (Ch. 3, Ch. 4).

suspension of disbelief Willingness on the part of the audience to "give over" to a theatre performance; to "believe," allowing an empathetic response to the work (see **aesthetic distance**) (Ch. 1).

sutradhara Sanskrit term for the director and trainer of traditional Indian dance theatre (Ch. 3).

swatch A representative piece of fabric or material used to communicate the costume designer's plan to the rest of the production team (Ch. 5).

symbolism A theatre movement that attempts to capture the ineffable, mystical, and subconscious onstage through poetry, repeated imagery, and avoidance of plot and action-oriented structures (Ch. 10).

System, the A term commonly used to denote Konstantin Stanislavski's system of actor training (Ch. 4).

teatro buffo A Cuban vaudevillian blend of stock characters, farce, music, and dance (Ch. 11).

Teatro Campesino Politically active Hispanic American theatre company, founded by Luis Valdez in 1965 (Ch. 11).

technical director Head of the technical areas, including set construction, lighting and sound, and cost-effectiveness; involved in all stages of production, from planning to closing night and strike (Ch. 6).

technical rehearsal The practice of plays that incorporates the technical and design elements for the first time (Ch. 4).

text The play script (Ch. 3).

theatre A performing art comprised of a live actor, a live audience, a space, and a story or idea (Ch. 1).

thespian An actor. The term is borrowed from the semi-mythical man known as Thespis, who was identified by Aristotle as the first Greek actor (Ch. 2).

thrust stage A type of theatre space in which the spectators are placed on three sides of the stage (Ch. 5).

total theatre   From Asia, an absolute integration of all performance elements including acting, mime, music, dance, and text (Ch. 11).

traditional director   Director who attempts to stay true to the text for inspiration in production, to be contrasted with the conceptual director (Ch. 4).

tragedy   One of the most renowned of all dramatic genres; a serious play with an unhappy ending, in which the main character, or hero, elicits our sympathy through forces or events that were out of the characters' control (Ch. 1).

trilogy   In ancient Greece, three tragedies penned by the same playwright and presented on one day (Ch. 7).

Tudor   Referencing plays written during the reign of Henry VIII (1509–1547) (Ch. 7).

unified production concept   The idea, first practiced by Georg II, Duke of Saxe-Meiningen, that the production must be controlled through the single artistic vision of the director (Ch. 4).

Unities   Perceived requirements in French neoclassicism. Though only *preferred* by their historic mentor Aristotle, the Unities involve consistency of time, place, and action in a play (Ch. 8).

upstage   The part of the stage that is the farthest from the audience (Ch. 4).

Valdez, Luis   (b. 1940) Mexican American theatre artist who practices his art among the disenfranchised to promote social change and empowerment (Ch. 11).

values   In character analysis, what a character believes to be true and important (Ch. 3).

Vedas   Books outlining ethical behavior that form the spiritual/philosophical foundation of the Hindu religion (Ch. 7).

Wagato   In Kabuki theatre, a style of performance characterized as "soft" rather than aggressive or *aragato* (Ch. 7).

Warren, Mercy Otis   (1728–1814) American woman playwright whose works were considered major propaganda efforts supporting the American Revolution (Ch. 11).

Williams, Tennessee   (Thomas Lanier) (1911–1983) American master of Realism; author of *The Glass Menagerie* and *A Streetcar Named Desire* (Ch. 9).

Wilson, August   (1945–2005) Major American playwright and author of a 10-play cycle on the African American experience of the past century (Dramatic Interlude 6, Ch. 11).

Wolfe, George C.   (b. 1954) Writer of some of the most influential African American plays of the twentieth century, most notably *The Colored Museum* (Ch. 11).

women's theatre   Theatre focused specifically on the perspectives, interests, and voices of women (Ch. 11).

world of the play   The given circumstances of the environment, created by a playwright, in which characters will present the dramatic action of the play (Ch. 3).

Xiqu   "Tuneful theatre" in Chinese; the common term for all forms of traditional Chinese Theatre; also known as Chinese opera (Ch. 7).

Yoruba   An ancient and continuing West African culture/nation, particularly hard hit by the ravages of the Western slave trade (Ch. 7).

Zaju   The earliest form of *xiqu* or Chinese opera (c. 900–c. 1400); a comic form of popular theatre with songs, acrobatics, clowns, and puppets (Ch. 7).

zanni   Comic servants in *Commedia dell'arte* (Ch. 7).

zarzuela   A form of court entertainment from the Spanish Golden Age that includes brief stylized musical drama, founded on mythology with showy scenic effects and motivated by Italian opera and intermezzi (Ch. 11).

Zola, Émile   (1840–1902) French theorist and playwright of Naturalism; authored *Thérèse Raquin*, considered by many to be the first naturalistic play (Ch. 9).

Selected Bibliography

General References

Banham, Martin, Errol Hill, and George Woodyard, eds. *Cambridge Guide to African and Caribbean Theatre.* New York: Cambridge University Press, 1994.

Brandon, James R. *The Cambridge Guide to Asian Theatre.* Martin Banham, advisory ed. New York: Cambridge University Press, 1993.

Brockett, Oscar G., and Franklin J. Hildy. *History of the Theatre.* Boston: Allyn & Bacon, 2003.

Brown, John Russell. *The Oxford Illustrated History of Theatre.* New York: Oxford University Press, 1995.

Crow, Brian, with Chris Banfield. *An Introduction to Postcolonial Theatre.* New York: Cambridge University Press, 1996.

Meserve, Walter J. *Chronological Outline of World Theatre.* New York: Prospero Press, 1992.

Nagler, A. M., ed. *A Source Book in Theatrical History.* New York: Dover Publications, 1959.

Weiss, Judith A. *Latin American Popular Theatre: The First Five Centuries.* Albuquerque: University of New Mexico Press, 1993.

Wickham, Glynne. *A History of the Theater.* New York: Cambridge University Press, 1992.

Wilmeth, Don B., and Christopher Bigsby. *The Cambridge History of American Theatre.* 3 vols. New York: Cambridge University Press, 1998–2000.

Chapter 1

Barba, Eugenio and Nicola Savarese. *The Secret Life of the Performer.* New York: Routledge, 1991.

Barrault, Jean-Louis. *Reflections on the Theatre.* London: Salisbury, 1951.

Brook, Peter. *The Empty Space.* New York: Atheneum, 1986.

Brook, Peter. *Threads of Time.* Washington, DC: Counterpoint, 1998.

Cole, David. *The Theatrical Event.* Middletown, CT: Wesleyan University Press, 1975.

Craig, Edward Gordon. *On the Art of the Theatre.* Boston: Small, Maynard, 1924.

Fergusson, Francis. *The Idea of a Theater.* Princeton: Princeton University Press, 1968.

Goffman, Erving. *The Presentation of Self in Everyday Life.* New York: Doubleday, 1959.

Granville-Barker, Harley. *On Dramatic Method.* New York: Hill and Wang, 1956.

Hartnoll, Phyllis, ed. *The Oxford Companion to the Theatre.* New York: Oxford University Press, 1981.

Roach, Joseph. *The Player's Passion.* Newark: University of Delaware Press, 1963.

Vanden Heuvel, Michael. *Performing Drama/Dramatizing Performance.* Ann Arbor: University of Michigan Press, 1991.

Chapter 2

Aristotle. *Poetics.* Translated by Gerald F. Else. Ann Arbor: University of Michigan Press, 1967.

Bertrand, Diane Gonzalez. *Sweet Fifteen.* Houston: Piñata Books, 1995.

Bocking, Brian. *A Popular Dictionary of Shinto.* Lincolnwood, IL: NTC Publishing Group, 1995.

Campbell, Joseph. *Myths to Live By.* New York: Viking, 1972.

Campbell, Joseph. *Transformations of Myth Through Time.* New York: Harper & Row, 1990.

Campbell, Joseph, with Bill Moyers. *The Power of Myth.* New York: Doubleday, 1988.

Davalos, Karen Mary. "La Quinceañera: Making Gender and Ethnic Identities." *Frontiers: A Journal of Women Studies,* Vol. 16, No. 2/3, Gender, Nations, and Nationalisms (1996), pp. 101–127.

Jones, Robert Edmund. *The Dramatic Imagination: Reflections and Speculations on the Art of the Theatre.* 2nd ed. New York: Routledge, 2004.

King, Elizabeth. *Quinceañera: Celebrating Fifteen.* New York: Dutton's Children's Books, 1998.

Kitagawa, Joseph M. *Religion in Japanese History.* New York: Columbia University Press, 1966.

Kojiki. Translated by Donald L. Philippi. Tokyo: University of Tokyo Press, 1968.

Nihongi: Chronicles of Japan from the Earliest Times to A.D. 697. Translated by W. G. Aston. London: George Allen & Unwin, 1956.

Patton, Kimberley Christine, and John Stratton Hawley, eds. *Holy Tears*. Princeton: Princeton University Press, 2005.

Rangacharya, Adya. *The Natya Sastra: English Translation with Critical Notes*. New Delhi: Munshiram Manoharlal Publishers, 2003.

Tarlekar, G. H. *Studies in the Natyasastra: With Special Reference to the Sanskrit Drama in Performance*. New Delhi: Motilal Banarsidass Publishers, 1999.

Chapter 3

Ball, David. *Backwards & Forwards: A Technical Manual for Reading Plays*. Carbondale, IL: Southern University Press, 1983.

Barranger, Milly. *Understanding Plays as Texts for Performance*. 3rd ed. New York: Allyn & Bacon, 2003.

Cole, Toby, ed. *Playwrights on Playwrighting: The Meaning and Making of Modern Drama from Ibsen to Ionesco*. New York: Hill & Wang, 1960.

Grote, David. *Script Analysis: Reading and Understanding the Playscript for Production*. Belmont, CA: Wadsworth, 1985.

Hayman, Ronald. *How to Read a Play*. New York: Grove Press, 1999.

Longman, Stanley Vincent. *Page and Stage: An Approach to Script Analysis*. New York: Allyn & Bacon, 2004.

Smiley, Sam. *Playwriting: The Structure of Action*. New Haven, CT: Yale University Press, 2005.

Thomas, James Michael. *Script Analysis for Actors, Directors, and Designers*. Oxford: Focal Press, 1999.

Waxberg, Charles. *The Actor's Script: Script Analysis for Performers*. Portsmouth, NJ: Heinemann, 1998.

Chapter 4

Arnott, Peter D. *Public and Performance in the Greek Theatre*. New York: Routledge, 1989.

Baumer, Rachel Van M., and James R. Brandon, eds. *Sanskrit Drama in Performance*. Honolulu: University of Hawaii Press, 1981.

Benedetti, Jean (translator). *An Actor's Work*, by Konstantin Stanislavski. New York: Routledge, 2009.

Benedetti, Robert. *The Actor at Work*. 9th ed. New York: Allyn & Bacon, 2005.

Boleslavski, Richard. *Acting: The First Six Lessons*. New York: Theatre Arts Books, 1933.

Brook, Peter. *Between Two Silences*. Dallas: Southern Methodist University Press, 1999.

Cohen, Robert, and John Harrop. *Creative Play Direction*. 2nd ed. Englewood Cliffs, NJ: Prentice-Hall, 1984.

Cole, Toby, and Helen Krich Chinoy, eds. *Actors on Acting*. New York: Crown, 1970.

Cole, Toby, and Helen Krich Chinoy, eds. *Directors on Directing*. rev. ed. Indianapolis: Bobbs-Merrill, 1963.

Felner, Mira. *Free to Act: An Integrated Approach to Acting*. 2nd ed. New York: Allyn & Bacon, 2004.

Garfield, David. *A Player's Place: The Story of the Actor's Studio*. New York: Macmillan, 1980.

Grotowski, Jerzy. *Towards a Poor Theatre*. New York: Simon & Schuster, 1986.

Hodge, Francis. *Play Directing: Analysis, Communication, and Style*. Englewood, NJ: Prentice-Hall, 1982.

Kenny, Don. *On Stage in Japan*. Tokyo: Shufunotomo, 1974.

Kominiz, Laurence. *The Stars Who Created Kabuki*. Tokyo: Kodansha International, 1997.

Osinski, Zbigniew. *Grotowski and His Laboratory*. Translated and abridged by Lillian Vallee and Robert Finlay. New York: Performing Arts Journal Publications, 1986.

Pickard-Cambridge, A. W. *Dithyramb, Tragedy, and Comedy*. 2nd ed. Revised by John Gould and D. M. Lewis. Oxford: Clarendon Press, 1962.

Riley, Jo. *Chinese Theatre and the Actor in Performance*. New York: Cambridge University Press, 1997.

Stanislavski, Constantine. *An Actor Prepares*. Reprint ed. New York: Routledge, 1989.

Stanislavski, Constantine. *Building a Character*. Reprint ed. New York: Routledge, 1989.

Stanislavski, Constantine. *Creating a Role*. Reprint ed. New York: Routledge, 1989.

Strasberg, Lee. *A Dream of Passion*. Boston: Little, Brown & Company, 1987.

Suzuki, Tadashi. *The Way of Acting*. New York: Theatre Communications Group, 2000.

Chapter 5

Anderson, Barbara, and Cletus Anderson. *Costume Design*. New York: Holt, Rinehart, and Winston, 1984.

Aronson, Arnold. *American Set Design*. New York: Theatre Communications Group, 1985.

Barton, Lucy. *Historic Costume for the Stage*. Boston: Baker's Plays, 1935.

Bergman, Gosta M. *Lighting in the Theatre*. Totowa, NJ: Rowman & Littlefield, 1977.

Corson, Richard. *Stage Makeup*. 8th ed. Englewood Cliffs, NJ: Prentice Hall, 1989.

Ingham, Rosemary. *From Page to Stage: How Theatre Designers Make Connections Between Scripts and Images*. Portsmouth, NH: Heinemann, 1998.

Lebrecht, James, and Deena Kaye. *Sound and Music for the Theatre: The Art and Technique of Design*. 2nd ed. Oxford: Focal Press, 2000.

Mielziner, Jo. *Designing for the Theatre*. New York: Atheneum, 1965.

Oenslager, Donald. *Stage Design: Four Centuries of Scenic Design*. New York: Viking, 1975.

Pecktal, Lynn. *Costume Design*. New York: Back Stage Books, 1993.

Rosenthal, Jean, and Lael Wertenbaker. *The Magic of Light*. Boston: Little, Brown & Company, 1972.

Shaoshan, Shi. *Makeup Designs in Traditional Chinese Opera*. Beijing: Ke xue chu ban she, 1995.

Takeda, Sharon Sadako, ed. *Miracles and Mischief: Noh and Kyogen Theatre in Japan*. Los Angeles: Los Angeles County Museum of Art, 2002.

Xiafeng, Pan. *Stagecraft of Peking Opera: From Its Origins to the Present Day*. Beijing: New World Press, 1995.

Chapter 6

Bellman, Willard F. *Scenography and Stage Technology: An Introduction*. New York: Harper & Row, 1977.

Blau, Herbert. *The Audience*. Baltimore: Johns Hopkins University Press, 1990.

Cardullo, Bert, ed. *What Is Dramaturgy?* New York: Peter Lang, 1995.

Cohen, Edward M. *Working on a New Play*. New York: Limelight Editions, 1997.

Farber, Donald C. *From Option to Opening*. Waleboro, NH: Longwood, 1989.

Farber, Donald C. *Producing Theatre*. New York: Limelight Editions, 1997.

Gree, Joann. *The Small Theatre Handbook: A Guide to Management and Production*. Boston: Harvard Common Press, 1981.

Howard, John T. *A Bibliography of Theatre Technology: Acoustics and Sound, Lighting, Properties, and Scenery*. Westport, CT: Greenwood Press, 1982.

Ingham, Rosemary, and Liz Covey. *The Costume Designer's Handbook*. Portsmouth, NH: Heinemann, 1992.

Jonas, Susan and Geoffrey S. Proehl, eds. *Dramaturgy in American Theatre*. Orlando: Harcourt Brace, 1997.

Langley, Stephen. *Theatre Management in America*. New York: Drama Book Publishers, 1990.

Literary Managers and Dramaturgs of the Americas. http://www.lmda.org.

Motley. *Designing and Making Stage Costumes*. London: Studio Vista, 1964.

Motley. *Theatre Props*. New York: DBS Publications, 1976.

Newman, Danny. *Subscribe Now!: Building Arts Audiences*. New York: TCC, 1983.

Payne, Darwin Reid. *Computer Scenographics*. Carbondale, IL: Southern Illinois University Press, 1994.

Reid, Francis. *The Stage Lighting Handbook*. New York: Theatre Arts Books, 1996.

Reiss, Alvin. *The Arts Management Reader*. New York: Audience Arts, 1979.

Stage Manager's Association. http://www.stagemanagers.org.

Chapter 7

Benegal, Som. *A Panorama of Theatre in India*. Bombay: Popular Prakashan, 1968.

Butler, James A. *The Theatre and Drama of Greece and Rome*. San Francisco: Chandler, 1972.

Chambers, E. K. *The Elizabethan Stage*. 4 vols. London: Oxford University Press, 1923.

Chambers, E. K. *The Medieval Stage*. 2 vols. Oxford: Clarendon Press, 1903.

Conteh-Morgan, John. *African Drama and Performance*. Bloomington: Indiana University Press, 2004.

Earnst, Earle. *The Kabuki Theatre*. New York: Grove Press, 1956.

Immoos, Thomas. *The Japanese Theatre*. Translated by Hugh Young, photographs by Fred Mayer. London: Studio Vista, 1977.

Keene, Donald. *Noh and Bunraku*. New York: Columbia University Press, 1970.

Kott, Jan. *The Eating of the Gods: An Interpretation of Greek Tragedy*. Translated by Boleslaw Taborski and Edward J. Czerwinski. Reprint ed. Evanston, IL: Northwestern University Press, 1987.

Miettinen, Jukka O. *Classical Dance and Theatre in South-East Asia*. Oxford: Oxford University Press, 1992.

Nagler, A. M. *The Medieval Religious Stage: Shapes and Phantoms*. New Haven, CT: Yale University Press, 1976.

Thompson, George. *A Documentary History of African Theatre*. Evanston, IL: Northwestern University Press, 1998.

Varapande, M. L. *Ancient Indian and Indo-Greek Theatre*. New Delhi: Shakti Malik Abhinav Publications, 1981.

Wickham, Glynne. *The Medieval Theatre*. London: St. Martin's Press, 1974.

Chapter 8

Banham, Martin. *African Theatre in Development*. Oxford: J. Currey, 1999.

Banham, Martin. *African Theatre: Playwrights & Politics*. Oxford: J. Currey, 2001.

Bradby, David. *The Cambridge Companion to Molière*. London: Cambridge University Press, 2006.

Holland, Peter. *The Ornament of Action: Text and Performance in Restoration Comedy*. New York: Cambridge University Press, 1979.

Lancaster, H. C. *A History of French Dramatic Literature in the Seventeenth Century*. 5 vols. Baltimore: Johns Hopkins Press, 1929–1942.

Layiwola, Dele. *African Theatre in Performance: A Festschrift in Honour of Martin Banham*. London: Harwood Academic, 2000.

Loftis, John Clyde. *Sheridan and the Drama of Georgian England*. Oxford: Blackwell, 1976.

Nicoll, Allardyce. *History of English Drama, 1600–1900*. 6 vols. London: Cambridge University Press, 1955–1959.

Siu, Wang-Ngai, *Chinese Opera: Images and Stories*. Vancouver: University of British Columbia Press, 1997.

Styan, J. L. *The English Stage: A History of Drama and Performance*. London: Cambridge University Press, 1996.

Styan, J. L. *Restoration Comedy in Performance*. London: Cambridge University Press, 1986.

Tan Gudnason, Jessica. *Chinese Opera*. New York: Abbeville Press, 2001.

Zugang, Wu, Huang Zuolin, and Mei Shaowu. *Peking Opera and Mei Lanfang*. Beijing: New World Press, 1981.

Chapter 9

Berlin, Normand. *Eugene O'Neill*. New York: Grove Press, 1982.

Bloom, Harold. *Arthur Miller*. New York: Chelsea House, 1987.

Bloom, Harold. *Tennessee Williams*. New York: Chelsea House, 2000.

Boxill, Roger. *Tennessee Williams*. London: St. Martin's Press, 1987.

Boyer, Robert D. *Realism in European Theatre and Drama, 1870–1920: A Bibliography*. Westport, CT: Greenwood Press, 1979.

Burroughs, Catherine B. *Women in British Romantic Theatre: Drama, Performance, and Society, 1790–1840*. London: Cambridge University Press, 2000.

Cave, Richard Allen. *The Romantic Theatre: An International Symposium*. Buckinghamshire: Colin Smythe, 1986.

Daniels, Barry. *Revolution in the Theatre: French Romantic Theories of Drama*. Westport, CT: Greenwood Press, 1983.

Disher, Maurice Willson. *Melodrama: Plots that Thrilled*. London: Rockliff Press, 1954.

Hudston, Sara. *Victorian Theatricals: From Menageries to Melodrama*. London: Methuen, 2000.

Innes, C. D. *A Source Book on Naturalist Theatre*. New York: Routledge, 2000.

Kernan, Alvin B. *Classics of the Modern Theatre, Realism and After*. New York: Harcourt, Brace & World, 1965.

Kindelan, Nancy Anne. *Shadows of Realism: Dramaturgy and the Theories and Practices of Modernism*. Westport, CT: Greenwood Press, 1996.

Koon, Helene. *Eugène Scribe*. Woodbridge, CT: Twayne, 1980.

Lacey, Stephen. *British Realist Theatre: The New Wave in its Context 1956–1965*. New York: Routledge, 1995.

Lederer, Katherine. *Lillian Hellman*. Woodbridge, CT: Twayne, 1979.

Marker, Lise-Lone. *David Belasco: Naturalism in the American Theatre*. Princeton: Princeton University Press, 1974.

McConachie, Bruce A. *Melodramatic Formations: American Theatre and Society, 1820–1870*. Iowa City: University of Iowa Press, 1992.

Moody, Richard. *America Takes the Stage: Romanticism in American Drama and Theatre, 1750–1900*. Bloomington: Indiana University Press, 1969.

Porter, Laurence M. *Victor Hugo*. Woodbridge, CT: Twayne, 1999.

Schumacher, Claude. *Naturalism and Symbolism in European Theatre, 1850–1918*. London: Cambridge University Press, 1996.

Chapter 10

Artaud, Antonin. *The Theatre and Its Double*. Translated by Mary C. Richards. New York: Grove Press, 1958.

Berghaus, Günter. *Italian Futurist Theatre, 1909–1944*. Oxford: Clarendon Press, 1998.

Bordman, Gerald. *American Musical Theatre*. New York: Oxford University Press, 1978.

Brecht, Bertolt. *Brecht on Theatre*. Translated by John Willet. New York: Hill & Wang, 1965.

Brockett, Oscar G., and Robert Findlay. *Century of Innovation: A History of European and American Theatre and Drama Since 1870*. Englewood Cliffs, NJ: Prentice-Hall, 1973.

Demastes, William W. *Theatre of Chaos: Beyond Absurdism, into Orderly Disorder*. New York: Cambridge University Press, 1998.

Esslin, Martin. *The Theatre of the Absurd*. New York: Doubleday, 1969.

Ganzel, Kurt. *The Encyclopedia of Musical Theatre*. Oxford: Blackwell, 1994.

Gordon, Mel. *Dada Performance*. New York: PAJ Publications, 1987.

Harris, Andre B. *Broadway Theatre*. London: Routledge, 1994.

Hiroshima and Nagasaki: The Physical, Medical, and Social Effects of the Atomic Bombings. The Committee for the Compilation of Materials on Damage Caused by the Atomic Bombs in Hiroshima and Nagasaki. Translated by Eisei Ishikawa and David L. Swain. New York: Basic Books, 1981.

Johnson, Walter Gilbert. *August Strindberg*. Boston: Twayne, 1976.

Kitchen, Martin. *Europe Between the Wars*. 2nd ed. New York: Pearson Longman, 2006.

Kuhns, David F. *German Expressionist Theatre: The Actor and Stage*. New York: Cambridge University Press, 1997.

Lagercrantz, Olof Gustaf Hugo. *August Strindberg*. New York: Farrar, Straus, Giroux, 1984.

Mayberry, Bob. *Theatre of Discord: Dissonance in Beckett, Albee, and Pinter*. Rutherford, NJ: Fairleigh Dickinson University Press, 1989.

McGuinness, Patrick. *Maurice Maeterlinck and the Making of Modern Theatre*. New York: Oxford University Press, 2000.

Rose, Margaret. *The Symbolist Theatre Tradition from Maeterlinck and Yeats to Beckett and Pinter*. Milano: Edizioni Unicopli, 1989.

Samuel, R. H. *Expressionism in German Life, Literature, and the Theatre, 1910–1924*. Philadelphia: A. Saifer, 1971.

Walker, Julia A. *Expressionism and Modernism in the American Theatre: Bodies, Voices, Words*. New York: Cambridge University Press, 2005.

Woll, Allen. *Black Musical Theatre*. Baton Rouge: Louisiana State University Press, 1989.

Chapter 11

Bicât, Tina, and Chris Baldwin, eds. *Devised and Collaborative Theatre: A Practical Guide*. Marlborough: Crowood, 2002.

Boal, Augusto. *Rainbow of Desire*. Translated by Adrian Jackson. New York: Routledge, 1995.

Boal, Augusto. *Theatre of the Oppressed*. Translated by Charles A. & Maria-Odilia Leal McBride. New York: Theatre Communications Group, 1985.

Brandon, James R., ed. *No and Kyogen in the Contemporary World*. Honolulu: University of Hawaii Press, 1997.

D'Aponte, Mimi. *Seventh Generation: An Anthology of Native American Plays*. New York: Theatre Communications Group, 1999.

Darby, Jaye T., and Hanay Geiogamah. *American Indian Theatre in Performance: A Reader*. Los Angeles: UCLA American Indian Studies Center, 2000.

Hay, Samuel A. *African American Theatre: A Historical and Critical Analysis*. New York: Cambridge University Press, 1994.

Hill, Errol. *A History of African American Theatre*. New York: Cambridge University Press, 2003.

Kanellos, Nicolás. *A History of Hispanic Theatre in the United States: Origins to 1940*. Austin: University of Texas Press, 1990.

Koppett, Kat. *Training to Imagine: Practical Improvisation Theatre Techniques to Enhance Creativity, Teamwork, Leadership and Learning*. With a foreword by Sivasailam "Thiagi" Thiagarajan. Sterling, VA: Stylus, 2001.

Lee, Esther Kim. *A History of Asian American Theatre*. New York: Cambridge University Press, 2006.

Lee, Sang-Kyong. *East Asia and America: Encounters in Drama and Theatre*. Honolulu: University of Hawai'i Press, 2000.

Pronko, Leonard. *Theatre East and West: Perspectives Toward a Total Theatre*. Berkeley: University of California Press, 1967.

Ramírez, Elizabeth C. *Chicanas/Latinas in American Theatre: A History of Performance*. Bloomington: Indiana University Press, 2000.

Schotz, Amiel. *Theatre Games and Beyond: A Creative Approach for Performers*. Colorado Springs, CO: Meriwether, 1998.

Svich, Caridad. *Out of the Fringe: Contemporary Latina/Latino Theatre and Performance*. New York: Theatre Communications Group, 2000.

Um, Hae-Kyung. *Diasporas and Interculturalism in Asian Performing Arts: Translating Traditions*. New York: Routledge Curzon, 2005.

Wetmore, Kevin J. *Black Dionysus: Greek Tragedy and African American Theatre*. Jefferson, NC: McFarland & Co., 2003.

Chapter 12

Bradby, David, and John McCormick. *People's Theatre*. Tottowa, NJ: Rowman and Littlefield, 1978.

Carlson, Marvin. *Performance: A Critical Introduction*. New York: Routledge, 2003.

Dukore, Bernard F. ed. *Dramatic Theory and Criticism*. New York: Holt, Rinehart & Winston, 1974.

Harris, Andre B. *Broadway Theatre*. London: Routledge, 1994.

Hudson, Suzanne. *Writing about Theatre and Drama*. Belmont, CA: Thomson Wadsworth, 2006.

Kauffman, Stanley. *Theatre Criticisms*. New York: Performing Arts Journal Publications, 1984.

Kirby, Michael. ed. *The New Theatre*. New York: New York University Press, 1974.

Lewis, Robert. *Advice to the Players*. New York: Harper & Row, 1980.

Palmer, Richard H. *The Critic's Canon: Standards of Theatrical Reviewing in America*. Westport, CT: Greenwood, 1988.

Rigg, Diana. *No Turn Unstoned: The Worst Theatrical Reviews Ever*. London: Book Club Associates, 1982.

Stefanova-Penova, Kalina. *Who Calls the Shots on the New York Stages? The New York Drama Critics*. New York: Routledge, 1993.

Styan, J. L. *Drama, Stage and Audience*. New York: Cambridge University Press, 1975.

Index

A

absurdism
  characteristics of, 341–343
  defined, 341
  in film, 345
Abydos Passion Play, 34
Académie Française, 278–279
Access Theater Company, 12
Acting: Onstage and Off, 418
action. *See also* dramatic action
  character analysis and, 90–91
  in melodrama, 284
  in plays, 76
  rising and falling, 87–88
actors and acting
  absurdism, 342
  African theatre, 256–257
  Beijing opera, 271
  British *vs.* American performance
    style, 115–116
  Dadaist theatre, 338
  didacticism and role of, 345
  early history of, 102–104
  Eastern evolution of, 108–111
  Elizabethan theatre, 252
  English Restoration theatre, 276
  expressionism, 340
  futurist theatre, 336–337
  Georgian drama, 283
  Greek theatre, 238–239
  internal *vs.* external acting, 115–116
  Kabuki theatre, 229–231
  Kathakali theatre, 269–270
  Kunqu, 267
  modern actor, 117
  naturalist theater, 316
  Noh theatre, 227–228
  politicians as, 128–129
  production process for, 100–101
  production timetable for, 102
  realism and, 312
  romantic theatre, 309
  screen *vs.* stage acting, 126–128
  Stanislavski and character acting,
    111–114
  symbolist theatre, 335
  teachers of, 114–115

  as theatre element, 7–10
  Western evolution of, 104–106
Actors' Equity Association, 103, 191
act structure, 279
Act Without Words, 342
Adding Machine, The, 340
Adler, Stella, 114–115
Adulateur, The, 390
adventure, in melodrama, 285
Aeschylus, 32, 236–238, 299
aesthetic distance, 19
African American theatre
  historical evolution of, 384–387
  musicals, 355, 385–387
  reviews of, 446, 448
African diaspora, theatre of, 285–290,
  299
African Footprint, 358
African Grove, 384
African theatre
  decline and rebirth of, 258–259, 290
  drama in, 256–257
  early plays from, 34, 38–39
  European colonial influences in, 259,
    285–287
  global influence of, 377–379
  historical evolution of, 254–259
  imitation to ritual in, 41–43
  mask design in, 167–169
  sources for, 256
  stage space in, 257–258
  style and function of, 256–257
  worldview in, 254–255
age, makeup for, 166
AIDS crisis, gay theatre and, 392
Ain't Misbehavin', 355, 385
Ajib wa Gharib, 259
Albee, Edward, 24, 183, 342, 411
Aldridge, Ira, 384
allegory, 242
  in African theatre, 267
Alley Theatre, 143
All in the Family, 313
All My Sons, 318
Altar Boyz, 358
ambient sound, 174

American Dream, The, 342
American Dreamz, 278
American Pie, 124
American Sign Language (ASL),
  theatre and use of, 51
American theatre
  African diaspora in, 288–290
  ethnic theatre, 380–389
American Theatre Magazine, 407
amplification, sound design, 174
An Actor Prepares, 111
An Actor's Work, 113
Analects, 224
analysis, directing process, 122
Ananse (spider), 377
Anderson, Laurie, 399–400
Anderson, Maxwell, 435–436
Andreyev, Leonid, 335
Andromaque, 279
Angels in America, 392, 426
Animal House, 124
Anna in the Tropics, 183, 383
antagonist, dramatic structure and, 85
Antigone, 17, 82, 85, 89, 157, 237,
  293–295, 299
anti-realism theatrical style, 332
Antoine, André, 315–316, 316–317
Any Woman Can't, 320
apartheid, South African theatre
  depictions of, 377
Appia, Adolphe, 152, 334
apron (stage extension), English
  Restoration theatre and, 275–276
Aquarius Theatre, 384
arena stage, 147–148
arias, in *Kunqu,* 266
Aristophanes, 104, 236, 237–238, 240,
  241
Aristotle, 235–236, 278–279
  theory of theatre and, 43
Arms and the Man, 17, 132–135,
  139–141
Artaud, Antonin, 379, 389, 398
artistic director, 184–185
ARTSEARCH, 407
Ashtabula Grange Record, 420

485